T0257936

Computer Science:
Concepts and Applications

Edited by **Tom Halt**

New York

Published by Willford Press,
118-35 Queens Blvd., Suite 400,
Forest Hills, NY 11375, USA
www.willfordpress.com

Computer Science: Concepts and Applications
Edited by Tom Halt

© 2016 Willford Press

International Standard Book Number: 978-1-68285-247-7 (Hardback)

This book contains information obtained from authentic and highly regarded sources. Copyright for all individual chapters remain with the respective authors as indicated. All chapters are published with permission under the Creative Commons Attribution License or equivalent. A wide variety of references are listed. Permission and sources are indicated; for detailed attributions, please refer to the permissions page and list of contributors. Reasonable efforts have been made to publish reliable data and information, but the authors, editors and publisher cannot assume any responsibility for the validity of all materials or the consequences of their use.

The publisher's policy is to use permanent paper from mills that operate a sustainable forestry policy. Furthermore, the publisher ensures that the text paper and cover boards used have met acceptable environmental accreditation standards.

Trademark Notice: Registered trademark of products or corporate names are used only for explanation and identification without intent to infringe.

Printed in the United States of America.

Contents

Permissions

List of Contributors

Preface

This book has been a concerted effort by a group of academicians, researchers and scientists, who have contributed their research works for the realization of the book. This book has materialized in the wake of emerging advancements and innovations in this field. Therefore, the need of the hour was to compile all the required researches and disseminate the knowledge to a broad spectrum of people comprising of students, researchers and specialists of the field.

This book is aimed to provide a comprehensive insight into the field of computer science. Computer science is a multidisciplinary field that incorporates both theory and applications of computations. It includes both framework and designing of computers as well as the modeling and analyses of various algorithms and programs that support different computational operations. It incorporates principles and concepts from various scientific disciplines like electrical engineering, physics and mathematics. This book is an assimilation of the various concepts and applications of computer science. The important topics elucidated in this comprehensive book includes different computational methodologies and techniques for solving complex tasks in various disciplines, assessment of existing information systems, artificial intelligence, soft computing, etc. The researches and case studies collated in this book aim to provide a coherent overview of the diverse concepts and applications of computer science at present. It is an excellent reference book for the students, researchers and experts involved in the field of computer science.

At the end of the preface, I would like to thank the authors for their brilliant chapters and the publisher for guiding us all-through the making of the book till its final stage. Also, I would like to thank my family for providing the support and encouragement throughout my academic career and research projects.

Editor

The paraconsistent process order control method

Kazumi Nakamatsu · Jair M. Abe

Abstract We have already developed some kinds of para-consistent annotated logic programs. In this paper we propose the paraconsistent process order control method based on a paraconsistent annotated logic program called before–after extended vector annotated logic program with strong nega-tion (bf-EVALPSN) with a small example of pipeline process order verification. Bf-EVALPSN can deal with before–after relations between two processes (time intervals) in its annota-tions, and its reasoning system consists of two kinds of infer-ence rules called the basic bf-inference rule and the transitive bf-inference rule. We introduce how the bf-EVALPSN-based reasoning system can be applied to the safety verification for process order.

Keywords Paraconsistent annotated logic program · Before–after relation · Bf-EVALPSN · Process order control

1 Introduction

A family of paraconsistent logic called annotated logics PT was proposed by da Costa et al. [4]. They can deal with incon-sistency with many truth values called *annotations*, although the semantics of annotated logics is basically two valued. The paraconsistent annotated logic has been developed from the viewpoint of logic programming [3], aiming at application to computer science. Furthermore, we have developed the paraconsistent annotated logic program to deal with incon-sistency and some kinds of non-monotonic reasoning in a framework of annotated logic programming by using onto-logical (strong) negation and the stable model semantics [6], which is called annotated logic program with strong negation (ALPSN for short). Later, to deal with defeasible reasoning [14], we proposed a new version of ALPSN called vector annotated logic program with strong negation (VALPSN for short) and applied it to resolving conflicts [7]. Furthermore, we have extended VALPSN to deal with deontic notions (obligation, forbiddance, etc.) and named extended VALPSN (EVALPSN for short) [8,9]. We have shown that EVALPSN can deal with defeasible deontic reasoning and the safety verification for process control.

Considering the safety verification for process control, there are many cases in which the safety verification for process order is significant. For example, suppose a pipeline network in which two kinds of liquids, nitric acid and caus-tic soda, are used for cleaning the pipelines. If those liquids are processed continuously and mixed in the same pipeline by accident, explosion by neutralization would be caused. To avoid such a dangerous accident, the safety for process order should be strictly verified in a formal way. However, it seems to be a little difficult to utilize EVALPSN for the safety verification of process order control different from that of process control. Therefore, we have developed EVALPSN toward treating before–after relations between time intervals and applied it to process order control [11], which has been named before–after (bf)-EVALPSN. The before–after rela-tion reasoning system based on bf-EVALPSN consists of two groups of inference rules called the basic bf-inference rule and the transitive bf-inference rule.

K. Nakamatsu (✉)
School of Human Science and Environment, University of Hyogo,
Shinzaike, Himeji 670-0092, Japan
e-mail: nakamatu@shse.u-hyogo.ac.jp

J. M. Abe
ICET-Paulista University, São Paulo, SP, CEP 04026-022, Brazil

J. M. Abe
Institute of Advanced Studies, University of Sao Paulo,
Cidade Universitaria, São Paulo, SP, CEP 05508-970, Brazil
e-mail: jairabe@uol.com.br

The original ideas of treating such before–after relations in logic were proposed for developing practical planning and natural language understanding systems by Allen [1] and Allen and Ferguson [2]. In his logic, before–after relations between two time intervals are represented in some special predicates and treated in a framework of first-order temporal logic. On the other hands, in bf-EVALPSN, before–after relations between two time intervals are regarded as paraconsistency between before and after degrees, and they can be represented more minutely in vector annotations of a special literal $R(p_i, p_j, t)$ representing the before–after relation between two processes (time intervals) at time t. Bf-EVALPSN-based before–after relation reasoning system consists of two kinds of efficient inference rules called the basic bf-inference rule and the transitive bf-inference rule that can be implemented as a bf-EVALPSN.

This paper is organized as follows: in Sect. 2, EVALPSN is reviewed briefly; in Sect. 3, bf-EVALPSN is formally defined and its simple reasoning example is introduced; in Sect. 4, the bf-EVALPSN reasoning system consisting of two kinds of inference rules is defined and explained in detail with some examples; in Sect. 5, the paraconsistent process order control method based on bf-EVALPSN reasoning is introduced with a small example of pipeline process order control; lastly, we conclude this paper.

2 Annotated logic program EVALPSN

In this section, we review EVALPSN briefly [9]. Generally, a truth value called an *annotation* is explicitly attached to each literal in annotated logic programs [3]. For example, let p be a literal and μ an annotation, then $p : \mu$ is called an *annotated literal*. The set of annotations constitutes a complete lattice. An annotation in EVALPSN has a form of $[(i, j), \mu]$ called an *extended vector annotation*. The first component (i, j) is called a *vector annotation* and the set of vector annotations constitutes the complete lattice,

$$\mathcal{T}_v(n) = \{(x, y) \mid 0 \le x \le n, 0 \le y \le n, x, y, n \text{ are integers}\}$$

in Fig. 1. The ordering ($\preceq_v$) of $\mathcal{T}_v(n)$ is defined as: let $(x_1, y_1), (x_2, y_2) \in \mathcal{T}_v(n)$,

$$(x_1, y_1) \preceq_v (x_2, y_2) \text{ iff } x_1 \le x_2 \text{ and } y_1 \le y_2.$$

For each extended vector annotated literal $p : [(i, j), \mu]$, the integer i denotes the amount of positive information to support the literal p and the integer j denotes that of negative one. The second component μ is an index of fact and deontic notions such as obligation, and the set of the second components constitutes the complete lattice,

$$\mathcal{T}_d = \{\perp, \alpha, \beta, \gamma, *_1, *_2, *_3, \top\}.$$

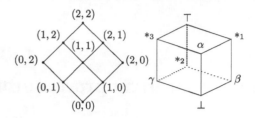

Fig. 1 Lattice $\mathcal{T}_v(2)$ and lattice $\mathcal{T}_d$

The ordering ($\preceq_d$) of $\mathcal{T}_d$ is described by the Hasse's diagram in Fig. 1. The intuitive meaning of each member of $\mathcal{T}_d$ is $\perp$(unknown), α(fact), β(obligation), γ(non-obligation), $*_1$(fact and obligation), $*_2$(obligation and non-obligation) and $*_3$(fact and non-obligation), $\top$(inconsistency).

Then, the complete lattice $\mathcal{T}_e(n)$ of extended vector annotations is defined as the product, $\mathcal{T}_v(n) \times \mathcal{T}_d$. The ordering ($\preceq_e$) of $\mathcal{T}_e(n)$ is defined: let $[(i_1, j_1), \mu_1], [(i_2, j_2), \mu_2] \in \mathcal{T}_e$,

$$[(i_1, j_1), \mu_1] \preceq_e [(i_2, j_2), \mu_2] \text{ iff } (i_1, j_1) \preceq_v (i_2, j_2)$$

and $\mu_1 \preceq_d \mu_2$.

There are two kinds of *epistemic negations* ($\neg_1$ and $\neg_2$) in EVALPSN, both of which are defined as mappings over $\mathcal{T}_v(n)$ and $\mathcal{T}_d$, respectively.

Definition 1 (*epistemic negations* $\neg_1$ *and* $\neg_2$ *in EVALPSN*)

$$\neg_1([(i, j), \mu]) = [(j, i), \mu], \quad \forall \mu \in \mathcal{T}_d,$$
$$\neg_2([(i, j), \perp]) = [(i, j), \perp], \quad \neg_2([(i, j), \alpha]) = [(i, j), \alpha],$$
$$\neg_2([(i, j), \beta]) = [(i, j), \gamma], \quad \neg_2([(i, j), \gamma]) = [(i, j), \beta],$$
$$\neg_2([(i, j), *_1]) = [(i, j), *_3], \quad \neg_2([(i, j), *_2]) = [(i, j), *_2],$$
$$\neg_2([(i, j), *_3]) = [(i, j), *_1], \quad \neg_2([(i, j), \top]) = [(i, j), \top].$$

If we regard the epistemic negations as syntactical operations, the epistemic negations followed by literals can be eliminated by the syntactical operations. For example, $\neg_1(p : [(2, 0), \alpha]) = p : [(0, 2), \alpha]$ and $\neg_2(q : [(1, 0), \beta]) = p : [(1, 0), \gamma]$. There is another negation called *strong negation* ($\sim$) in EVALPSN, and it is treated as well as classical negation [4].

Definition 2 (*strong negation* $\sim$) Let F be any formula and $\neg$ be $\neg_1$ or $\neg_2$.

$$\sim F =_{\text{def}} F \rightarrow ((F \rightarrow F) \wedge \neg(F \rightarrow F)).$$

Definition 3 (*well-extended vector annotated literal*) Let p be a literal.

$$p : [(i, 0), \mu] \quad \text{and} \quad p : [(0, j), \mu]$$

are called *well-extended vector annotated literals*, where i, j are non-negative integers and $\mu \in \{\alpha, \beta, \gamma\}$.

Definition 4 (*EVALPSN*) If $L_0, \ldots, L_n$ are weva-literals,

$$L_1 \wedge \ldots \wedge L_i \wedge \sim L_{i+1} \wedge \ldots \wedge \sim L_n \rightarrow L_0$$

Fig. 2 Before (be)/after (af) and disjoint before (db)/after (da)

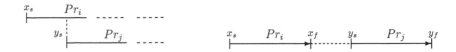

is called an *EVALPSN clause*. An EVALPSN is a finite set of EVALPSN clauses.

Here, we comment that if the annotations α and β represent fact and obligation, notions "fact", "obligation", "forbiddance" and "permission" can be represented by extended vector annotations, $[(m, 0), \alpha]$, $[(m, 0), \beta]$, $[(0, m), \beta]$, and $[(0, m), \gamma]$, respectively, in EVALPSN, where m is a non-negative integer.

3 Before–after EVALPSN

In this section, we review bf-EVALPSN. The details are found in [12,13].

In bf-EVALPSN, a special annotated literal $R(p_m, p_n, t)$: $[(i, j), \mu]$ called *bf-literal* whose non-negative integer vector annotation (i, j) represents the before–after relation between processes Pr_m and Pr_n at time t is introduced. The integer components i and j of the vector annotation (i, j) represent the after and before degrees between processes $Pr_m(p_m)$ and $Pr_n(p_n)$, respectively, and before–after relations are represented paraconsistently in vector annotations.

Definition 5 (*bf-EVALPSN*) An extended vector annotated literal,

$$R(p_i, p_j, t):[(i, j), \mu]$$

is called a *bf-EVALP literal* or a *bf-literal* for short, where (i, j) is a vector annotation and $\mu \in \{\alpha, \beta, \gamma\}$. If an EVALPSN clause contains bf-EVALP literals, it is called a *bf-EVALPSN clause* or just a *bf-EVALP clause* if it contains no strong negation. A *bf-EVALPSN* is a finite set of bf-EVALPSN clauses.

We provide a paraconsistent before–after interpretation for vector annotations representing bf-relations in bf-EVALPSN, and such a vector annotation is called a *bf-annotation*. Exactly speaking, there are 15 kinds of bf-relation according to before–after order between four start/finish times of two processes.

Before (be)/*after* (af) is defined according to the bf-relation between each start time of the two processes. If one process has started before/after another one starts, then the bf-relations between them are defined as "before/after", which are represented in the left in Fig. 2.

We introduce other kinds of bf-relations as well as before (be)/after (af).

Disjoint before (db)/*after* (da) is defined as having a time lag between the earlier process finish time and the later one's start time; this is described on the right in Fig. 2.

Immediate before (mb)/*after* (ma) is defined as having no time lag between the earlier process finish time and the later one's start time; it is described on the left in Fig. 3.

Joint before (jb)/*after* (ja) is defined as two processes that overlap, where the earlier process had finished before the later one finished; it is described on the right in Fig. 3.

S-included before (sb)/*S-included after* (sa) is defined as two processes, where one had started before the other started, but finished at the same time; it is described on the left in Fig. 4.

Included before (ib)/*after* (ia) is defined as two processes, where one had started/finished before/after another one started/finished; it is described on the right in Fig. 4.

F-included before (fb)/*after* (fa) is defined as two processes that started at the same time, but with one finishing before another one finished; it is described in the left in Fig. 5.

Paraconsistent before–after (pba) is defined as having two processes that started at the same time and also finished at the same time; it is described on the right in Fig. 5.

The epistemic negation over bf-annotations, be, af, db, da, mb, ma, jb, ja, ib, ia, sb, sa, fb, fa and pba is defined and the complete lattice of bf-annotations is shown in Fig. 6.

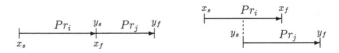

Fig. 3 Immediate before (mb)/after (ma) and joint before (jb)/after (ja)

Fig. 4 S-included before (sb)/after (sa) and included before (ib)/after (ia)

Fig. 5 F-included before (fb)/after (fa) and paraconsistent before–after (pba)

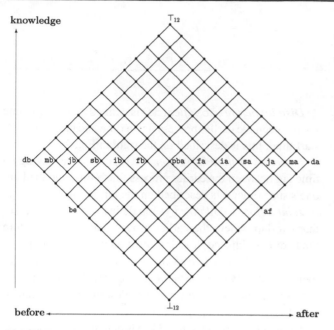

Fig. 6 The complete lattice $\mathcal{T}_v(12)_{\text{bf}}$ for bf-annotations

Definition 6 (*epistemic negation* $\neg_1$ *for bf-annotations*) The epistemic negation $\neg_1$ over the bf-annotations is obviously defined as the following mappings:

$$\neg_1(\text{af}) = \text{be}, \quad \neg_1(\text{be}) = \text{af}, \quad \neg_1(\text{da}) = \text{db},$$
$$\neg_1(\text{db}) = \text{da}, \quad \neg_1(\text{ma}) = \text{mb}, \quad \neg_1(\text{mb}) = \text{ma},$$
$$\neg_1(\text{ja}) = \text{jb}, \quad \neg_1(\text{jb}) = \text{ja}, \quad \neg_1(\text{sa}) = \text{sb},$$
$$\neg_1(\text{sb}) = \text{sa}, \quad \neg_1(\text{ia}) = \text{ib}, \quad \neg_1(\text{ib}) = \text{ia},$$
$$\neg_1(\text{fa}) = \text{fb}, \quad \neg_1(\text{fb}) = \text{fa}, \quad \neg_1(\text{pba}) = \text{pba}.$$

Therefore, each bf-annotation can be translated into vector annotations as $\text{bf} = (0, 8)$, $\text{db} = (0, 12)$, $\text{mb} = (1, 11)$, $\text{jb} = (2, 10)$, $\text{sb} = (3, 9)$, $\text{ib} = (4, 8)$, $\text{fb} = (5, 7)$ and $\text{pba} = (6, 6)$.

4 Reasoning system in bf-EVALPSN

To represent the *basic bf-inference rule* in bf-EVALPSN, we newly introduce two literals:

$\text{st}(p_i, t)$, which is interpreted as process Pr_i starts at time t, and

$\text{fi}(p_i, t)$, which is interpreted as process Pr_i finishes at time t.

Those literals are used for expressing process start/finish information and may have one of the vector annotations, $\{\perp(0, 0), \text{t}(1, 0), \text{f}(0, 1), \top(1, 1)\}$, where annotations $\text{t}(1, 0)$ and $\text{f}(0, 1)$ can be intuitively interpreted as "true" and "false", respectively.

First of all, we introduce a group of basic bf-inference rules to be applied at the initial stage (time t_0), which are named $(0, 0)$-*rules*.

(0,0)-rules Suppose that no process has started yet and the vector annotation of bf-literal $R(p_i, p_j, t)$ is $(0, 0)$, which shows that there is no knowledge in terms of the bf-relation between processes Pr_i and Pr_j, then the following two basic bf-inference rules are applied at the initial stage.

(0,0)-rule-1 If process Pr_i started before process Pr_j starts, then the vector annotation $(0, 0)$ of bf-literal $R(p_i, p_j, t)$ should turn to $\text{be}(0, 8)$, which is the greatest lower bound of the set, $\{\text{db}(0, 12), \quad \text{mb}(1, 11), \text{jb}(2, 10), \text{sb}(3, 9), \text{ib}(4, 8)\}$.

(0,0)-rule-2 If both processes Pr_i and Pr_j have started at the same time, then it is reasonably anticipated that the bf-relation between processes Pr_i and Pr_j will be one of the bf-annotations, $\{\text{fb}(5, 7), \quad \text{pba}(6, 6), \quad \text{fa}(7, 5)\}$ whose greatest lower bound is $(5, 5)$ (refer to Fig. 6). Therefore, the vector annotation $(0, 0)$ of bf-literal $R(p_i, p_j, t)$ should turn to $(5, 5)$.

$(0, 0)$-rule-1 and $(0, 0)$-rule-2 are translated into the bf-EVALPSN,

$$R(p_i, p_j, t) : [(0, 0), \alpha] \wedge \text{st}(p_i, t) : [\text{t}, \alpha]$$
$$\wedge \sim \text{st}(p_j, t) : [\text{t}, \alpha] \rightarrow R(p_i, p_j, t) : [(0, 8), \alpha] \quad (1)$$
$$R(p_i, p_j, t) : [(0, 0), \alpha] \wedge \text{st}(p_i, t) : [\text{t}, \alpha]$$
$$\wedge \text{st}(p_j, t) : [\text{t}, \alpha] \rightarrow R(p_i, p_j, t) : [(5, 5), \alpha] \quad (2)$$

Suppose that $(0, 0)$-rule-1 or 2 has been applied, then the vector annotation of bf-literal $R(p_i, p_j, t)$ should be one of $(0, 8)$ or $(5, 5)$. Therefore, we need to consider two groups of basic bf-inference rules to be applied for following $(0, 0)$-rule-1 and 2, which are named $(0,8)$-*rules* and $(5,5)$-*rules*, respectively.

(0,8)-rules Suppose that process Pr_i has started before process Pr_j starts, then the vector annotation of bf-literal $R(p_i, p_j, t)$ should be $(0, 8)$. We have the following inference rules to be applied for following $(0, 0)$-rule-1.

(0,8)-rule-1 If process Pr_i has finished before process Pr_j starts, and process Pr_j starts immediately after process Pr_i finished, then the vector annotation $(0, 8)$ of bf-literal $R(p_i, p_j, t)$ should turn to $\text{mb}(1, 11)$.

(0,8)-rule-2 If process Pr_i has finished before process Pr_j starts, and process Pr_j has not started immediately after process Pr_i finished, then the vector annotation $(0, 8)$ of bf-literal $R(p_i, p_j, t)$ should turn to $\text{db}(0, 12)$.

(0,8)-rule-3 If process Pr_j starts before process Pr_i finishes, then the vector annotation $(0, 8)$ of bf-literal $R(p_i, p_j, t)$ should turn to $(2, 8)$ that is the greatest lower bound of the set, $\{\text{jb}(2, 10), \quad \text{sb}(3, 9), \quad \text{ib}(4, 8)\}$.

$(0, 8)$-rule-1, 2 and 3 are translated into the bf-EVALPSN,

$$R(p_i, p_j, t):[(0, 8), \alpha] \wedge \text{fi}(p_i, t):[\text{t}, \alpha]$$
$$\wedge \text{st}(p_j, t):[\text{t}, \alpha] \to R(p_i, p_j, t):[(1, 11), \alpha] \quad (3)$$
$$R(p_i, p_j, t):[(0, 8), \alpha] \wedge \text{fi}(p_i, t):[\text{t}, \alpha]$$
$$\wedge \sim \text{st}(p_j, t):[\text{t}, \alpha] \to R(p_i, p_j, t):[(0, 12), \alpha] \quad (4)$$
$$R(p_i, p_j, t):[(0, 8), \alpha] \wedge \sim \text{fi}(p_i, t):[\text{t}, \alpha]$$
$$\wedge \text{st}(p_j, t):[\text{t}, \alpha] \to R(p_i, p_j, t):[(2, 8), \alpha] \quad (5)$$

(5,5)-rules Suppose that both processes Pr_i and Pr_j have already started at the same time then the vector annotation of bf-literal $R(p_i, p_j, t)$ should be $(5, 5)$. We have the following inference rules to be applied for following $(0, 0)$-rule-2.

(5,5)-rule-1 If process Pr_i has finished before process Pr_j finishes, then the vector annotation $(5, 5)$ of bf-literal $R(p_i, p_j, t)$ should turn to $\text{sb}(5, 7)$.

(5,5)-rule-2 If both processes Pr_i and Pr_j have finished at the same time, then the vector annotation $(5, 5)$ of bf-literal $R(p_i, p_j, t)$ should turn to $\text{pba}(6, 6)$.

(5,5)-rule-3 If process Pr_j has finished before process Pr_i finishes, then the vector annotation $(5, 5)$ of bf-literal $R(p_i, p_j, t)$ should turn to $\text{sa}(7, 5)$.

Basic bf-inference rules $(5, 5)$-rule-1, 2 and 3 are translated into the bf-EVALPSN,

$$R(p_i, p_j, t):[(5, 5), \alpha] \wedge \text{fi}(p_i, t):[\text{t}, \alpha]$$
$$\wedge \sim \text{fi}(p_j, t):[\text{t}, \alpha] \to R(p_i, p_j, t):[(5, 7), \alpha] \quad (6)$$
$$R(p_i, p_j, t):[(5, 5), \alpha] \wedge \text{fi}(p_i, t):[\text{t}, \alpha]$$
$$\wedge \text{fi}(p_j, t):[\text{t}, \alpha] \to R(p_i, p_j, t):[(6, 6), \alpha] \quad (7)$$
$$R(p_i, p_j, t):[(5, 5), \alpha] \wedge \sim \text{fi}(p_i, t):[\text{t}, \alpha]$$
$$\wedge \text{fi}(p_j, t):[\text{t}, \alpha] \to R(p_i, p_j, t):[(7, 5), \alpha] \quad (8)$$

If one of $(0, 8)$-rule-1,2, $(5, 5)$-rule-1,2 and 3 has been applied, a final bf-annotation such as $\text{jb}(2, 10)$ between two processes should be derived. However, even if $(0, 8)$-rule-3

has been applied, no bf-annotation could be derived. Therefore, a group of basic bf-inference rules named $(2, 8)$-rules should be considered for following $(0, 8)$-rule-3.

(2,8)-rules Suppose that process Pr_i has started before process Pr_j starts and process Pr_j has started before process Pr_i finishes, then the vector annotation of bf-literal $R(p_i, p_j, t)$ should be $(2, 8)$ and the following three rules should be considered.

(2,8)-rule-1 If process Pr_i finished before process Pr_j finishes, then the vector annotation $(2, 8)$ of bf-literal $R(p_i, p_j, t)$ should turn to $\text{jb}(2, 10)$.

(2,8)-rule-2 If both processes Pr_i and Pr_j have finished at the same time, then the vector annotation $(2, 8)$ of bf-literal $R(p_i, p_j, t)$ should turn to $\text{fb}(3, 9)$.

(2,8)-rule-3 If process Pr_j has finished before Pr_i finishes, then the vector annotation $(2, 8)$ of bf-literal $R(p_i, p_j, t)$ should turn to $\text{ib}(4, 8)$.

Basic bf-inference rules $(2, 8)$-rule-1, 2 and 3 are translated into the bf-EVALPSN,

$$R(p_i, p_j, t):[(2, 8), \alpha] \wedge \text{fi}(p_i, t):[\text{t}, \alpha]$$
$$\wedge \sim \text{fi}(p_j, t):[\text{t}, \alpha] \to R(p_i, p_j, t):[(2, 10), \alpha] \quad (9)$$
$$R(p_i, p_j, t):[(2, 8), \alpha] \wedge \text{fi}(p_i, t):[\text{t}, \alpha]$$
$$\wedge \text{fi}(p_j, t):[\text{t}, \alpha] \to R(p_i, p_j, t):[(3, 9), \alpha] \quad (10)$$
$$R(p_i, p_j, t):[(2, 8), \alpha] \wedge \sim \text{fi}(p_i, t):[\text{t}, \alpha]$$
$$\wedge \text{fi}(p_j, t):[\text{t}, \alpha] \to R(p_i, p_j, t):[(4, 8), \alpha] \quad (11)$$

The application orders of all basic bf-inference rules are summarized in Table 1.

Now, we introduce the *transitive bf-inference rule*, which can reason a vector annotation of bf-literal transitively.

Suppose that there are three processes Pr_i, Pr_j and Pr_k starting sequentially, then we consider deriving the vector annotation of bf-literal $R(p_i, p_k, t)$ from those of bf-literals $R(p_i, p_j, t)$ and $R(p_j, p_k, t)$ transitively. We describe only the variation of vector annotations in the following rules.

Table 1 Application orders of basic bf-inference rules

Vector annotation	Rule	Vector annotation	Rule	Vector annotation	Rule	Vector annotation
			Rule-1	$(0, 12)$		
			Rule-2	$(1, 11)$		
	Rule-1	$(0, 8)$			Rule-1	$(2, 10)$
$(0, 0)$			Rule-3	$(2, 8)$	Rule-2	$(3, 9)$
					Rule-3	$(4, 8)$
			Rule-1	$(5, 7)$		
	Rule-2	$(5, 5)$	Rule-2	$(6, 6)$		
			Rule-3	$(7, 5)$		

Transitive bf-inference rules

TR0 $(0, 0) \wedge (0, 0) \rightarrow (0, 0)$

TR1 $(0, 8) \wedge (0, 0) \rightarrow (0, 8)$

   TR1-1 $(0, 12) \wedge (0, 0) \rightarrow (0, 12)$

   TR1-2 $(1, 11) \wedge (0, 8) \rightarrow (0, 12)$

   TR1-3 $(1, 11) \wedge (5, 5) \rightarrow (1, 11)$

   TR1-4 $(2, 8) \wedge (0, 8) \rightarrow (0, 8)$

     TR1-4-1 $(2, 10) \wedge (0, 8) \rightarrow (0, 12)$

     TR1-4-2 $(4, 8) \wedge (0, 12) \rightarrow (0, 8)$ (12)

     TR1-4-3 $(2, 8) \wedge (2, 8) \rightarrow (2, 8)$

       TR1-4-3-1 $(2, 10) \wedge (2, 8) \rightarrow (2, 10)$

       TR1-4-3-2 $(4, 8) \wedge (2, 10) \rightarrow (2, 8)$ (13)

       TR1-4-3-3 $(2, 8) \wedge (4, 8) \rightarrow (4, 8)$

       TR1-4-3-4 $(3, 9) \wedge (2, 10) \rightarrow (2, 10)$

       TR1-4-3-5 $(2, 10) \wedge (4, 8) \rightarrow (3, 9)$

       TR1-4-3-6 $(4, 8) \wedge (3, 9) \rightarrow (4, 8)$ (14)

       TR1-4-3-7 $(3, 9) \wedge (3, 9) \rightarrow (3, 9)$

     TR1-4-4 $(3, 9) \wedge (0, 12) \rightarrow (0, 12)$

     TR1-4-5 $(2, 10) \wedge (2, 8) \rightarrow (1, 11)$

     TR1-4-6 $(4, 8) \wedge (1, 11) \rightarrow (2, 8)$

     TR1-4-7 $(3, 9) \wedge (1, 11) \rightarrow (1, 11)$

   TR1-5 $(2, 8) \wedge (5, 5) \rightarrow (2, 8)$

     TR1-5-1 $(4, 8) \wedge (5, 7) \rightarrow (2, 8)$ (15)

     TR1-5-2 $(2, 8) \wedge (7, 5) \rightarrow (4, 8)$

     TR1-5-3 $(3, 9) \wedge (5, 7) \rightarrow (2, 10)$

     TR1-5-4 $(2, 10) \wedge (7, 5) \rightarrow (3, 9)$

TR2 $(5, 5) \wedge (0, 8) \rightarrow (0, 8)$

   TR2-1 $(5, 7) \wedge (0, 8) \rightarrow (0, 12)$

   TR2-2 $(7, 5) \wedge (0, 12) \rightarrow (0, 8)$ (16)

   TR2-3 $(5, 5) \wedge (2, 8) \rightarrow (2, 8)$

     TR2-3-1 $(5, 7) \wedge (2, 8) \rightarrow (2, 10)$

     TR2-3-2 $(7, 5) \wedge (2, 10) \rightarrow (2, 8)$ (17)

     TR2-3-3 $(5, 5) \wedge (4, 8) \rightarrow (4, 8)$

     TR2-3-4 $(7, 5) \wedge (3, 9) \rightarrow (4, 8)$

   TR2-4 $(5, 7) \wedge (2, 8) \rightarrow (1, 11)$

   TR2-5 $(7, 5) \wedge (1, 11) \rightarrow (2, 8)$ (18)

TR3 $(5, 5) \wedge (5, 5) \rightarrow (5, 5)$

   TR3-1 $(7, 5) \wedge (5, 7) \rightarrow (5, 5)$ (19)

   TR3-2 $(5, 7) \wedge (7, 5) \rightarrow (6, 6)$

Note (I) The name of a transitive bf-inference rule such as **TR1-4-3** indicates the application sequence of transitive bf-inference rules until the transitive bf-inference rule has been applied. For example, if the rule **TR1** has been applied, one

of the rules **TR1-1**, **TR1-2**, ... or **TR1-5** should be applied at the following stage; and if the rule **TR1-4** has been applied after the rule **TR1**, one of the rules **TR1-4-1**, **TR1-4-2**, ... or **TR1-4-7** should be applied at the following stage; on the other hand, if one of the rules **TR1-1**, **TR1-2** or **TR1-3** has been applied after the rule **TR1**, there should be no transitive bf-inference rule to be applied at the following stage because one of bf-relations $\mathrm{db}(0, 12)$, $\mathrm{mb}(1, 11)$ has been derived.

Note (II) Transitive bf-inference rules,

TR1-4-2 (12),   **TR1-4-3-2** (13),   **TR1-4-6** (14),

TR1-5-1 (15),   **TR2-2**   (16),   **TR2-3-2** (17),

TR2-5   (18),   **TR3-1**   (19)

have no following rule to be applied, even though they cannot derive the final bf-relations between processes represented by bf-annotations such as $\mathrm{jb}(2, 10)$. For example, suppose that the rule **TR1-4-3-2** has been applied, then vector annotation $(2, 8)$ of bf-literal (p_i, p_k, t) just indicates that the final bf-relation between processes Pr_i and Pr_k is represented by one of three bf-annotations, $\mathrm{jb}(2, 10)$, $\mathrm{sb}(3, 9)$ or $\mathrm{ib}(4, 8)$ because vector annotation $(2, 8)$ is the greatest lower bound of those bf-annotations. Therefore, if one of transitive bf-inference rules (12),(13),(14),(15),(16), (17),(18) and (19), has been applied, one of $(0, 8)$-rule, $(2, 8)$-rule or $(5, 5)$-rule should be applied for deriving the final bf-annotation at the following stage. For example, if the rule **TR1-4-3-2** has been applied, $(2, 8)$-rule should be applied at the following stage.

5 The process order control method in bf-EVALPSN

In this section, we present the process order control method with a simple example for pipeline process order verification.

The process order control method has the following three steps:

Step 1 translate the safety properties of the process order control system into bf-EVALPSN;

Step 2 verify if permission for starting the process can be derived from the bf-EVALPSN in *step1* by the basic bf-inference rule and the transitive bf-inference rule or not.

The verification *step 2* can be carried out not only just before starting the process, but also at any time.

We assume a pipeline system consisting of two pipelines, PIPELINE-1 and 2, which deal with pipeline processes Pr_0, Pr_1, Pr_2 and Pr_3. The process schedule of those processes are shown in Fig. 7. Moreover, we assume that the pipeline system has four safety properties SPR-$i(i = 0, 1, 2, 3)$.

SPR-0 process Pr_0 must start before any other processes, and process Pr_0 must finish before process Pr_2 finishes,

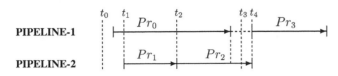

Fig. 7 Pipeline process schedule

SPR-1 process Pr_1 must start after process Pr_0 starts,
SPR-2 process Pr_2 must start immediately after process Pr_1 finishes,
SPR-3 process Pr_3 must start immediately after processes Pr_0 and Pr_2 finish.

Step 1 All safety properties SPR-i($i = 0, 1, 2, 3$) can be translated into the following bf-EVALPSN clauses.

$$\text{SPR-0} \sim R(p_0, p_1, t):[(0, 8), \alpha] \to \text{st}(p_1, t):[\texttt{f}, \beta], \tag{20}$$

$$\sim R(p_0, p_2, t):[(0, 8), \alpha] \to \text{st}(p_2, t):[\texttt{f}, \beta], \tag{21}$$

$$\sim R(p_0, p_3, t):[(0, 8), \alpha] \to \text{st}(p_3, t):[\texttt{f}, \beta], \tag{22}$$

$$\text{st}(p_1, t):[\texttt{f}, \beta] \wedge \text{st}(p_2, t):[\texttt{f}, \beta]$$
$$\wedge \text{st}(p_3, t):[\texttt{f}, \beta] \to \text{st}(p_0, t):[\texttt{f}, \gamma], \tag{23}$$

$$\sim \text{fi}(p_0, t):[\texttt{f}, \beta] \to \text{fi}(p_0, t):[\texttt{f}, \gamma], \tag{24}$$

where bf-EVALPSN clauses (20), (21) and (22) declare that if process Pr_0 has not started before other processes Pr_i($i = 1, 2, 3$) start, it should be forbidden from starting each process Pr_i($i = 1, 2, 3$); bf-EVALPSN clause (23) declares that if each process Pr_i($i = 1, 2, 3$) is forbidden from starting, it should be permitted to start process Pr_0; and bf-EVALPSN clause (24) declares that if there is no forbiddance from finishing process Pr_0, it should be permitted to finish process Pr_0.

$$\text{SPR-1} \sim \text{st}(p_1, t):[\texttt{f}, \beta] \to \text{st}(p_1, t):[\texttt{f}, \gamma], \tag{25}$$

$$\sim \text{fi}(p_1, t):[\texttt{f}, \beta] \to \text{fi}(p_1, t):[\texttt{f}, \gamma], \tag{26}$$

where bf-EVALPSN clause (25)/(26) declares that if there is no forbiddance from starting/finishing process Pr_1, it should be permitted to start/finish process Pr_1, respectively.

$$\text{SPR-2} \sim R(p_2, p_1, t):[(11, 0), \alpha] \to \text{st}(p_2, t):[\texttt{f}, \beta], \tag{27}$$

$$\sim \text{st}(p_2, t):[\texttt{f}, \beta] \to \text{st}(p_2, t):[\texttt{f}, \gamma], \tag{28}$$

$$\sim R(p_2, p_0, t):[(10, 2), \alpha] \to \text{fi}(p_2, t):[\texttt{f}, \beta], \tag{29}$$

$$\sim \text{fi}(p_2, t):[\texttt{f}, \beta] \to \text{fi}(p_2, t):[\texttt{f}, \gamma], \tag{30}$$

where bf-EVALPSN clause (27) declares that if process Pr_1 has not finished before process Pr_2 starts, it should be forbidden from starting process Pr_2; the vector annotation $(11, 0)$ of bf-literal $R(p_2, p_1, t)$ is the greatest lower bound of $\{\text{da}(12, 0), \text{ma}(11, 1)\}$, which implies that process Pr_1 has finished before process Pr_2 starts; bf-EVALPSN clauses (28)/(30) declare that if there is no forbiddance from starting/finishing process Pr_2, it should be permitted to start/finish process Pr_2, respectively; and bf-EVALPSN clauses (29) declare that if process Pr_0 has not finished before process Pr_2 finishes, it should be forbidden from finishing process Pr_2.

$$\text{SPR-3} \sim R(p_3, p_0, t):[(11, 0), \alpha] \to \text{st}(p_3, t):[\texttt{f}, \beta], \tag{31}$$

$$\sim R(p_3, p_1, t):[(11, 0), \alpha] \to \text{st}(p_3, t):[\texttt{f}, \beta], \tag{32}$$

$$\sim R(p_3, p_2, t):[(11, 0), \alpha] \to \text{st}(p_3, t):[\texttt{f}, \beta], \tag{33}$$

$$\sim \text{st}(p_3, t):[\texttt{f}, \beta] \to \text{st}(p_3, t):[\texttt{f}, \gamma], \tag{34}$$

$$\sim \text{fi}(p_3, t):[\texttt{f}, \beta] \to \text{fi}(p_3, t):[\texttt{f}, \gamma], \tag{35}$$

where bf-EVALPSN clauses (31), (32) and (33) declare that if one of processes Pr_i($i = 0, 1, 2$) has not finished yet, it should be forbidden from starting process Pr_3; and bf-EVALPSN clauses (34)/(35) declare that if there is no forbiddance from starting/finishing process Pr_3, it should be permitted to start/finish process Pr_3, respectively.

Step 2 Here, we show how the bf-EVALPSN process order safety verification is carried out at five time points, t_0, t_1, t_2, t_3 and t_4 in the process schedule (Fig. 7). We consider five bf-relations between processes Pr_0, Pr_1, Pr_2 and Pr_3, represented by the vector annotations of bf-literals,

$$R(p_0, p_1, t), \quad R(p_0, p_2, t), \quad R(p_0, p_3, t),$$
$$R(p_1, p_2, t), \quad R(p_2, p_3, t)$$

which should be verified based on safety properties SPR-0, 1, 2 and 3 in real time.

Initial stage (at time t_0) no process has started at time t_0, thus, the bf-EVALP clauses,

$$R(p_0, p_1, t_0):[(0, 0), \alpha], \tag{36}$$
$$R(p_1, p_2, t_0):[(0, 0), \alpha], \tag{37}$$
$$R(p_2, p_3, t_0):[(0, 0), \alpha] \tag{38}$$
$$R(p_0, p_2, t_0):[(0, 0), \alpha], \tag{39}$$
$$R(p_0, p_3, t_0):[(0, 0), \alpha] \tag{40}$$

are obtained by transitive bf-inference rule **TR0**; then, bf-EVALP clauses (36), (39) and (40) satisfy each body of bf-EVALPSN clauses (20), (21) and (22), respectively; therefore, the forbiddance,

$$\text{st}(p_1, t_0):[\texttt{f}, \beta], \tag{41}$$

$$\text{st}(p_2, t_0):[\texttt{f}, \beta], \tag{42}$$

$$\text{st}(p_3, t_0):[\texttt{f}, \beta] \tag{43}$$

from starting each process $\text{Pr}_i (i = 1, 2, 3)$ is derived. Moreover, since bf-EVALP clauses (41), (42) and (43) satisfy the body of bf-EVALPSN clause (23), the permission for starting process Pr_0,

$$\text{st}(p_0, t_0):[\texttt{f}, \gamma]$$

is derived; therefore, process Pr_0 is permitted to start at time t_0.

2nd Stage (at time t_1) process Pr_0 has already started but all other processes $\text{Pr}_i (i = 1, 2, 3)$ have not started yet; then the bf-EVALP clauses,

$$R(p_0, p_1, t_1):[(0, 8), \alpha], \tag{44}$$

$$R(p_1, p_2, t_1):[(0, 0), \alpha], \tag{45}$$

$$R(p_2, p_3, t_1):[(0, 0), \alpha] \tag{46}$$

are obtained, where the bf-EVALP clause (44) is derived by basic bf-inference rule $(0, 0)$-rule-1. Moreover, the bf-EVALP clauses,

$$R(p_0, p_2, t_1):[(0, 8), \alpha], \tag{47}$$

$$R(p_0, p_3, t_1):[(0, 8), \alpha] \tag{48}$$

are obtained by transitive bf-inference rule TR1; as bf-EVALP clause (44) does not satisfy the body of bf-EVALPSN clause (20), the forbiddance from starting process Pr_1,

$$\text{st}(p_1, t_1):[\texttt{f}, \beta] \tag{49}$$

cannot be derived. Then, since there is no forbiddance (49), the body of bf-EVALPSN clause (25) is satisfied and the permission for starting process Pr_1,

$$\text{st}(p_1, t_1):[\texttt{f}, \gamma]$$

is derived. On the other hand, since bf-EVALP clauses (47) and (48) satisfy the body of bf-EVALPSN clauses (27) and (31), respectively, the forbiddance from starting both processes Pr_2 and Pr_3,

$$\text{st}(p_2, t_1):[\texttt{f}, \beta], \quad \text{st}(p_3, t_1):[\texttt{f}, \beta]$$

are derived; therefore, process Pr_1 is permitted to start at time t_1.

3rd Stage (at time t_2) process Pr_1 has just finished and process Pr_0 has not finished yet; then, the bf-EVALP clauses,

$$R(p_0, p_1, t_2):[(4, 8), \alpha], \tag{50}$$

$$R(p_1, p_2, t_2):[(1, 11), \alpha], \tag{51}$$

$$R(p_2, p_3, t_2):[(0, 8), \alpha] \tag{52}$$

are derived by basic bf-inference rules $(2, 8)$-rule-3, $(0, 8)$-rule-2 and $(0, 0)$-rule-1, respectively. Moreover, the bf-EVALP clauses,

$$R(p_0, p_2, t_2):[(2, 8), \alpha],$$

$$R(p_0, p_3, t_2):[(0, 12), \alpha]$$

are obtained by transitive bf-inference rules **TR1-4-6** and **TR1-2**, respectively. Then, since bf-EVALP clause (51) does not satisfy the body of bf-EVALPSN clause (27), the forbiddance from starting process Pr_2,

$$\text{st}(p_2, t_2):[\texttt{f}, \beta] \tag{53}$$

cannot be derived. Since there is no forbiddance (53), it satisfies the body of bf-EVALPSN clause (28), and the permission for starting process Pr_2,

$$st(p_2, t_2):[\texttt{f}, \gamma]$$

is derived. On the other hand, since bf-EVALP clause (53) satisfies the body of bf-EVALPSN clause (31), the forbiddance from starting process Pr_3,

$$t(p_3, t_2):[\texttt{f}, \beta]$$

is derived; therefore, process Pr_2 is permitted to start. However, process Pr_3 is still forbidden from starting at time t_2.

4th Stage (at the t_3) process Pr_0 has finished, process Pr_2 has not finished yet, and process Pr_3 has not started yet; then, the bf-EVALP clauses,

$$R(p_0, p_1, t_3):[(4, 8), \alpha], \tag{54}$$

$$R(p_1, p_2, t_3):[(1, 11), \alpha], \tag{55}$$

$$R(p_2, p_3, t_3):[(0, 8), \alpha] \tag{56}$$

in which the vector annotations are the same as in the previous stage are obtained because bf-annotations of bf-EVALP clauses (54) and (55) have been already reasoned, and the before–after relation between processes Pr_2 and Pr_3 is the same as in the previous stage. Moreover, the bf-EVALP clauses,

$$R(p_0, p_2, t_3):[(2, 10), \alpha], \tag{57}$$

$$R(p_0, p_3, t_3):[(0, 12), \alpha] \tag{58}$$

are obtained, where bf-EVALP clause (57) is derived by basic bf-inference rule $(2, 8)$-rule-1. Then, bf-EVALP clause (57) satisfies the body of bf-EVALP clause (33), and the forbiddance from starting process Pr_3,

$$S(p_3, t_3):[\texttt{f}, \beta]$$

is derived. Therefore, process Pr_3 is still forbidden from starting because process Pr_2 has not finished yet at time t_3.

5th Stage (at time t_4) process Pr_2 has just finished and process Pr_3 has not started yet; then, the bf-EVALP clauses,

$$R(p_0, p_1, t_4) : [(4, 8), \alpha], \tag{59}$$

$$R(p_1, p_2, t_4) : [(1, 11), \alpha], \tag{60}$$

$$R(p_2, p_3, t_4) : [(1, 11), \alpha], \tag{61}$$

$$R(p_0, p_2, t_4) : [(2, 10), \alpha], \tag{62}$$

$$R(p_0, p_3, t_4) : [(0, 12), \alpha] \tag{63}$$

are obtained. bf-EVALP clause (61) is derived by basic bf-inference rule (0, 8)-rule-2. Moreover, since bf-EVALP clauses (59), (62) and (63) do not satisfy the bodies of bf-EVALP clauses (31), (32) and (33), the forbiddance from starting process Pr_3,

$$st(p_3, t_4) : [f, \beta] \tag{64}$$

cannot be derived. Therefore, the body of bf-EVALPSN clause (34) is satisfied, and the permission for starting process Pr_3,

$$st(p_3, t_4) : [f, \gamma]$$

is derived. Therefore, process Pr_3 is permitted to start because processes Pr_0, Pr_1 and Pr_2 have finished at time t_4.

6 Concluding remarks

In this paper, we have introduced the process order control method based on a paraconsistent annotated logic program bf-EVALPSN, which can deal with before–after relation between processes with a small pipeline process order safety verification control.

We would like to conclude this paper by describing the advantages and disadvantages of the process order control method based on bf-EVALPSN safety verification.

Advantages

– If a bf-EVALPSN is locally stratified [5], it can be easily implemented in Prolog, C language, Programmable Logic Controller (PLC) ladder program, etc. In practice, such control bf-EVALPSNs are locally stratified.
– It has been proved that EVALPSN can be implemented as electronic circuits on micro chips [10]. Therefore, if real-time processing is required in the system, the method might be very useful.
– The safety verification methods for both process control and process order control can be implemented under the same environment.

Disadvantages

– Since EVALPSN/bf-EVALPSN itself is basically not a specific tool of formal safety verification, it includes complicated and redundant expressions to construct safety verification systems. Therefore, it should be better to develop safety verification-oriented tool or programming language based on EVALPSN/bf-EVALPSN if EVALPSN/bf-EVALPSN can be applied to formal safety verification.

References

1. Allen, J.F.: Towards a general theory of action and time. Artif. Intell. **23**, 123–154 (1984)
2. Allen, J.F., Ferguson, G.: Actions and events in interval temporal logic. J. Log. Comput. **4**, 531–579 (1994)
3. Blair, H.A., Subrahmanian, V.S.: Paraconsistent logic programming. Theor. Comput. Sci. **68**, 135–154 (1989)
4. da Costa, N.C.A., et al.: The paraconsistent logics $P\mathcal{T}$. Zeitschrift für Mathematische Logic und Grundlangen der Mathematik **37**, 139–148 (1989)
5. Gelder, A.V., Ross, K.A., Schlipf, J.S.: The well-founded semantics for general logic programs. J. Assoc. Comput. Mach. ACM **38**, 620–650 (1991)
6. Nakamatsu, K., Suzuki, A.: Annotated semantics for default reasoning. In: Proceedings of the 3rd Pacific Rim International Conference of Artificial Intelligence (PRICAI94), pp. 180–186. International Academic Publishers (1994)
7. Nakamatsu, K.: On the relation between vector annotated logic programs and defeasible theories. Log. Log. Philos. **8**, 181–205 (2001)
8. Nakamatsu, K., et al.: A defeasible deontic reasoning system based on annotated logic programming. In: Proceedings of the 4th International Conference of Computing Anticipatory Systems (CASYS2000), AIP Conference Proceedings, vol. 573, pp. 609–620. American Institute of Physics (2001)
9. Nakamatsu, K., et al.: Annotated Semantics for Defeasible Deontic Reasoning. LNAI 2005, pp. 432–440. Springer, New York (2001)
10. Nakamatsu, K., Mita, Y., Shibata, T.: An intelligent action control system based on extended vector annotated logic program and its hardware implementation. J. Intell. Autom. Soft Comput. **13**, 222–237 (2007)
11. Nakamatsu, K.: The paraconsistent annotated logic program EVALPSN and its application. Comput. Intell. Compend. Stud. Comput Intell. **115**, 233–306 (2008). Springer
12. Nakamatsu, K., Abe, J.M.: The development of paraconsistent annotated logic program. Int. J. Reason.-Based Intell. Syst. **1**, 92–112 (2009)
13. Nakamatsu, K., Abe, J.M., Akama, S.: A logical reasoning system of process before–after relation based on a paraconsistent annotated logic program bf-EVALPSN. J. Knowl.-Based Intell. Eng. Syst. **15**, 145–163 (2011)
14. Nute, D.: Basic defeasible logics. In: del Cerro, L. F., Penttonen, M. (eds.) Intensional Logics for Programming, pp. 125–154. Oxford University Press, Oxford (1992)

2

WORL: a nonmonotonic rule language for the semantic web

Son Thanh Cao · Linh Anh Nguyen · Andrzej Szałas

Abstract We develop a new Web ontology rule language, called WORL, which combines a variant of OWL 2 RL with eDatalog⁻. We allow additional features like negation, the minimal number restriction and unary external checkable predicates to occur at the left-hand side of concept inclusion axioms. Some restrictions are adopted to guarantee a translation into eDatalog⁻. We also develop the well-founded semantics and the stable model semantics for WORL as well as the standard semantics for stratified WORL (SWORL) via translation into eDatalog⁻. Both WORL with respect to the well-founded semantics and SWORL with respect to the standard semantics have PTime data complexity. In contrast to the existing combined formalisms, in WORL and SWORL negation in concept inclusion axioms is interpreted using nonmonotonic semantics.

Keywords OWL 2 RL · Datalog with negation · Semantic Web · Rule languages

S. T. Cao
Faculty of Information Technology, Vinh University,
182 Le Duan, Vinh, Nghe An, Vietnam
e-mail: sonct@vinhuni.edu.vn

L. A. Nguyen (✉) · A. Szałas
Institute of Informatics, University of Warsaw,
Banacha 2, 02-097 Warsaw, Poland
e-mail: nguyen@mimuw.edu.pl

L. A. Nguyen
VNU University of Engineering and Technology,
144 Xuan Thuy, Hanoi, Vietnam

A. Szałas
Department of Computer and Information Science,
Linköping University, 581 83 Linköping, Sweden
e-mail: andsz@mimuw.edu.pl

1 Introduction

In recent years, the Semantic Web area has been rapidly developed and attracted lots of attention. A central idea of the Semantic Web is that ontologies are a proper bridge among users and search engines, ensuring more accurate search results. Therefore, Web Ontology Language (OWL), built on the top of XML and RDF, serves as an important tool for specifying ontologies and reasoning about them. Together with rule languages, it serves as a main knowledge representation formalism for the Semantic Web.

The main semantical and logical foundation of OWL are description logics (DLs). Such logics represent the domain of interest in terms of concepts, individuals, and roles. A concept is interpreted as a set of individuals, while a role is interpreted as a binary relation between individuals. A knowledge base in a DL consists of an RBox of role axioms, a TBox of terminological axioms and an ABox of facts about individuals.

The second version OWL 2 of OWL, recommended by the W3C consortium in 2009, is based on the DL $\mathcal{SROIQ}$. This logic is highly expressive but has intractable combined complexity (N2ExpTime-complete) and data complexity (NP-hard) for basic reasoning problems. Thus, W3C recommended also profiles OWL 2 EL, OWL 2 QL and OWL 2 RL, which are restricted sublanguages of OWL 2 Full and enjoy PTime data complexity. These profiles are based on the families of description logics $\mathcal{EL}$ [3,4], DL-Lite [5] and Description Logic Programs (DLP) [13], respectively. There are also more sophisticated fragments of DLs with PTime data complexity: Horn-$\mathcal{SHIQ}$ [15], Horn-$\mathcal{SROIQ}$ [21] and Horn-DL [20].

Rule languages provide very useful knowledge representation formalisms applicable to the Semantic Web. Some fragments of DLs like DLP [13] can be translated into rule languages. But most importantly, rule languages can be combined with DLs to develop more expressive formalisms. An early attempt to achieve such a combination was SWRL [14], a rule language using only concept names, role names and the equality predicate. However, without restrictions its combination with OWL DL is undecidable.

A knowledge base in other combined languages is usually specified as a pair $\langle \mathcal{O}, \mathcal{P} \rangle$, where $\mathcal{O}$ is an ontology in some DL and $\mathcal{P}$ is a set of rules, e.g., specified in Datalog or its suitable extension, which can use concept names and role names. Interaction between $\mathcal{O}$ and $\mathcal{P}$ is either one-way ($\mathcal{O}$ affects $\mathcal{P}$) or two-way (where $\mathcal{P}$ may also affect $\mathcal{O}$). The approach of defining a knowledge base as a pair $\langle \mathcal{O}, \mathcal{P} \rangle$ is adopted in a considerable number of works, including [8] (on $\mathcal{AL}$-log), [17] (on *CARIN*), [19] (on *DL-safe rules*), [24] (on $\mathcal{DL}$+log), [18,16] (on *hybrid MKNF*), [9] (on *hybrid programs*), [23] (on *OntoDLV*), [10] (on *dl-programs*). In these works, if negation is allowed in $\mathcal{P}$ then $\mathcal{P}$ and its interaction with $\mathcal{O}$ are interpreted using some nonmonotonic semantics (e.g., the stable model semantics, the MKNF semantics or the well-founded semantics). However, $\mathcal{O}$ is always interpreted using the usual (monotonic) semantics.

In the current paper we treat such a pair $\langle \mathcal{O}, \mathcal{P} \rangle$ just as a layer and study the case when $\mathcal{O}$ can be translated to an eDatalog$^\neg$ program and $\mathcal{P}$ is an eDatalog$^\neg$ program. eDatalog$^\neg$ extends Datalog$^\neg$ by allowing two basic types (for individuals and data constants), external checkable predicates and the equality predicate (between individuals). Concept names and role names are allowed both in heads and bodies of program clauses. Our approach is novel in the following aspects:

- Negation in $\mathcal{O}$ is interpreted using a nonmonotonic semantics (the well-founded semantics, the stable model semantics, or the standard semantics for stratified knowledge bases); this differs from all the above-mentioned works [8–10,16–19,23,24].
- We combine $\mathcal{O}$ and $\mathcal{P}$ into one set (called a layer, which is divided into a TBox consisting of concept inclusion axioms/program clauses and an ABox consisting of facts). This allows for a tighter integration between DLs and rules. It may seem similar to the approach of SWRL, but we also allow ordinary predicates, use a nonmonotonic semantics for negation, and design the language appropriately to get decidability and PTIME data complexity (w.r.t. the well-founded semantics, and the standard semantics for stratified knowledge bases).
- To reflect modularity of ontologies (e.g., the import feature of ontologies), we define a knowledge base to be a hierarchy of layers (a tree or a rooted directed acyclic graph of layers). Each layer in turn may be stratifiable and divided further into strata. The granulation is not substantial for the well-founded semantics, as the whole knowl-

edge base will be flattened to a set of program clauses and facts.
- However, it is substantial for the stable model semantics (see Example 8). Furthermore, when each layer of the considered knowledge base is stratifiable and the standard semantics is used for it, layers not only emphasize modularity but also affect the semantics (flattening the knowledge base may result in an unstratifiable layer).

The Web ontology rule language we define in this paper, WORL, combines a variant of OWL 2 RL with eDatalog$^\neg$. Similarly to our previous work on OWL 2 eRL$^+$ [6], we:

- disallow those features of OWL 2 RL that play the role of constraints (i.e., the ones that are translated to negative clauses of the form $\varphi \rightarrow \perp$);
- allow unary external checkable predicates;
- allow additional features like negation and the constructor $\geq n\, R.C$ to occur at the left-hand side of $\sqsubseteq$ in concept inclusion axioms.

Some restrictions are adopted for the additional features to guarantee a translation of WORL programs into eDatalog$^\neg$. We also define the rule language SWORL (stratified WORL) and develop the well-founded semantics and the stable model semantics for WORL as well as the standard semantics for SWORL via translation into eDatalog$^\neg$. Both WORL with respect to the well-founded semantics and SWORL with respect to the standard semantics have PTIME data complexity.

This paper is a revised and extended version of our conference paper [7]. Comparing to [7], in the current paper, we additionally provide the standard model semantics for WORL, a direct method for checking stratifiability of TBoxes, all the proofs and a number of illustrative examples. The three semantics for eDatalog$^\neg$ which we consider are now presented in a uniform manner.

The rest of this paper is structured as follows. In Sect. 2 we introduce eDatalog$^\neg$, stratified eDatalog$^\neg$, and their semantics. In Sect. 3 we present WORL, a translation of WORL into eDatalog$^\neg$, and its well-founded semantics and stable model semantics. Section 4 is devoted to SWORL and its standard semantics. Section 5 concludes "this work". In the Appendix, we present a direct method for checking stratifiability of TBoxes.

2 Preliminaries

We denote the set of *concept names* by CNames, and the set of *role names* by RNames.

From the point of view of OWL, there are two basic types: *individual* (i.e. *object*) and *literal* [22] (i.e. *data con-*

stant). We denote the *individual* type by *IType*, and the *literal* type by *LType*. Thus, a concept name is a unary predicate of type $P(IType)$, a *data type* is a unary predicate of type $P(LType)$, an *object role name* is a binary predicate of type $P(IType \times IType)$, and a *data role name* is a binary predicate of type $P(IType \times LType)$. For simplicity, we do not provide specific data types like integer, real or string. Apart from concept names and role names, we will also use a set OPreds of *ordinary predicates* (including data types) and a set ECPreds of *external checkable predicates*. We assume that the sets CNames, RNames, OPreds and ECPreds are finite and pairwise disjoint. By a set of *defined predicates* we mean:

$$DPreds = CNames \cup RNames \cup OPreds.$$

With each k-ary predicate from OPreds we associate its type $P(T_1 \times \cdots \times T_k)$, where each T_i is either *IType* or *LType*. A k-ary predicate from ECPreds has the type $P(LType^k)$. We assume that each predicate from ECPreds has a fixed meaning which is checkable in the following sense:

> if p is a k-ary predicate from ECPreds and $d_1, \ldots, d_k$ are constants of *LType*, then the truth value of $p(d_1, \ldots, d_k)$ is fixed and computable in polynomial time (in the number of bits used for $d_1, \ldots, d_k$).

For example, one may want to use the binary predicates $>$, $\geq$, $<$, $\leq$ on real numbers with the usual semantics.

We assume there is only one equality predicate '$=$', which belongs to OPreds and has the type $P(IType \times IType)$. For data constants, we assume the Unique Names Assumption instead.

A *term* is either an individual (of type *IType*) or a literal (of type *LType*) or a *variable* (of type *IType* or *LType*). If p is a predicate of type $P(T_1 \times \cdots \times T_k)$, and for $1 \leq i \leq k$, t_i is a term of type T_i, then $p(t_1, \ldots, t_k)$ is an *atomic formula* (also called an *atom*). An atom is *ground* if it contains no variables.

An *interpretation* $\mathcal{I} = \langle \Delta_o^{\mathcal{I}}, \Delta_d^{\mathcal{I}}, \cdot^{\mathcal{I}} \rangle$ consists of a non-empty set $\Delta_o^{\mathcal{I}}$ called the *object domain* of $\mathcal{I}$, a non-empty set $\Delta_d^{\mathcal{I}}$ disjoint with $\Delta_o^{\mathcal{I}}$ called the *data domain* of $\mathcal{I}$, and a function $\cdot^{\mathcal{I}}$ which maps:

- every individual a to an element $a^{\mathcal{I}} \in \Delta_o^{\mathcal{I}}$,
- every literal d to a unique[1] element $d^{\mathcal{I}} \in \Delta_d^{\mathcal{I}}$,
- every concept name A to a subset $A^{\mathcal{I}}$ of $\Delta_o^{\mathcal{I}}$,
- every data type DT to a subset $DT^{\mathcal{I}}$ of $\Delta_d^{\mathcal{I}}$,
- every predicate of type $P(T_1 \times \cdots \times T_k)$ in DPreds different from '$=$' to a subset of $\Delta_1 \times \cdots \times \Delta_k$, where $\Delta_i = \Delta_o^{\mathcal{I}}$ if $T_i = IType$, and $\Delta_i = \Delta_d^{\mathcal{I}}$ if $T_i = LType$,
- predicate '$=$' to a congruence of $\mathcal{I}$.[2]

---

[1] i.e., if $d_1 \neq d_2$ then $d_1^{\mathcal{I}} \neq d_2^{\mathcal{I}}$.

[2] Recall that a congruence is an equivalence relation preserving functions and relations occurring in the language.

A *Herbrand interpretation* is a set of ground atoms of predicates from DPreds. An *ABox* is a finite Herbrand interpretation.

The *size* of a ground atom is the number of bits used for its representation. The *size* of an ABox is the sum of the sizes of its atoms.

By *EqAxioms* we denote the following set of axioms:

$$x = x$$
$$x = y \rightarrow y = x$$
$$x = y \wedge y = z \rightarrow x = z$$
$$x_i = x_i' \wedge p(x_1, \ldots, x_i, \ldots, x_k) \rightarrow p(x_1, \ldots, x_i', \ldots, x_k),$$

where p is any k-ary predicate of DPreds different from '$=$' and i is any natural number between 1 and k such that the ith argument of p is of type *IType*.

A Herbrand interpretation $\mathcal{H}$ is *closed w.r.t. EqAxioms* if for every ground instance $\varphi_1 \wedge \cdots \wedge \varphi_k \rightarrow \psi$ (with $k \geq 0$) of an axiom in *EqAxioms* using the individuals and data constants occurring in $\mathcal{H}$, if $\{\varphi_1, \ldots, \varphi_k\} \subseteq \mathcal{H}$ then $\psi \in \mathcal{H}$.

Given a Herbrand interpretation $\mathcal{H}$ that is closed w.r.t. *EqAxioms*, let $\mathcal{I}$ be the interpretation specified as follows:

- $\Delta_o^{\mathcal{I}}$ is the set of all individuals occurring in $\mathcal{H}$,
- $\Delta_d^{\mathcal{I}}$ is the set of all data constants occurring in $\mathcal{H}$,
- for every k-ary predicate $p \in$ DPreds,

$$p^{\mathcal{I}} = \{\langle t_1, \ldots, t_k \rangle \mid p(t_1, \ldots, t_k) \in \mathcal{H}\}.$$

Observe that $=^{\mathcal{I}}$ is a congruence of $\mathcal{I}$. We call the quotient $\mathcal{I}/_=$ of $\mathcal{I}$ by the congruence $=^{\mathcal{I}}$ the *traditional interpretation corresponding to* $\mathcal{H}$.

2.1 The rule language eDatalog$^\neg$

In [6], we defined eDatalog as an extension of Datalog with the equality predicate, external checkable predicates, and a relaxed range-restrictedness condition. In this subsection, we define the rule language eDatalog$^\neg$ similarly as an extension of Datalog$^\neg$, but using the full range-restrictedness condition.

An *eDatalog$^\neg$ program clause* is a formula of the form

$$(\varphi_1 \wedge \cdots \wedge \varphi_h \wedge \neg\psi_1 \wedge \cdots \wedge \neg\psi_k$$
$$\wedge \, \xi_1 \wedge \cdots \wedge \xi_l \wedge \neg\zeta_1 \wedge \cdots \wedge \neg\zeta_m) \rightarrow \alpha \qquad (1)$$

where $h, k, l, m \geq 0$, $\varphi_1, \ldots, \varphi_h, \psi_1, \ldots, \psi_k, \alpha$ are atoms of predicates from DPreds, and $\xi_1, \ldots, \xi_l, \zeta_1, \ldots, \zeta_m$ are atoms of predicates from ECPreds, with the property that every variable occurring in α or some ψ_i, ξ_i or ζ_i occurs also in some atom φ_j (this is the *range-restrictedness condition*).

The atom α in (1) is called the *head* of the program clause. If p is the predicate of α then the clause is called a *program clause defining p.* The formula at the left-hand side of $\rightarrow$ in (1) is called the *body* of the program clause.

An *eDatalog$^\neg$ program* is a finite set of eDatalog$^\neg$ program clauses. An *eDatalog$^\neg$ knowledge base* is a pair $\langle \mathcal{P}, \mathcal{A} \rangle$ consisting of an eDatalog$^\neg$ program $\mathcal{P}$ and an ABox $\mathcal{A}$. A *query* is defined to be a formula that can be the body of an eDatalog$^\neg$ program clause.

Example 1 Let $\mathcal{P}$ be the following eDatalog$^\neg$ program:

$$[acceptable(X) \wedge hasPrice(X, Y)$$
$$\wedge\, acceptable(X') \wedge hasPrice(X', Y') \wedge Y < Y']$$
$$\rightarrow excluded(X')$$
$$acceptable(X) \wedge \neg excluded(X) \rightarrow preferable(X)$$

and let $\mathcal{A} = \{acceptable(a), acceptable(b), hasPrice(a, 100), hasPrice(b, 120)\}$. Then $KB = \langle \mathcal{P}, \mathcal{A} \rangle$ is an eDatalog$^\neg$ knowledge base. Here, '<' is an external checkable predicate with the usual semantics; X and X' are variables of type *IType*; Y and Y' are variables of type *LType*; a and b are objects (of type *IType*); 100 and 120 are data constants (of type *LType*).

2.2 Stratified eDatalog$^\neg$

A *stratification* of an eDatalog$^\neg$ program $\mathcal{P}$ is a sequence of eDatalog$^\neg$ programs $\mathcal{P}_1, \dots, \mathcal{P}_n$ such that:

- $\{\mathcal{P}_1, \dots, \mathcal{P}_n\}$ is a partition of $\mathcal{P} \cup EqAxioms$,
- for some mapping $f : \text{DPreds} \rightarrow \{1, \dots, n\}$, every predicate $p \in \text{DPreds}$ satisfies the following conditions:

  - the program clauses in $\mathcal{P} \cup EqAxioms$ defining p are in $\mathcal{P}_{f(p)}$,
  - if $\mathcal{P} \cup EqAxioms$ contains a program clause defining p in the form

    $$(\varphi_1 \wedge \cdots \wedge \varphi_h \wedge \neg\psi_1 \wedge \cdots \wedge \neg\psi_k \wedge \xi_1 \wedge \cdots \wedge \xi_l$$
    $$\wedge \neg\zeta_1 \wedge \cdots \wedge \neg\zeta_m) \rightarrow \alpha$$

    then for every $1 \leq i \leq h$ and $1 \leq j \leq k$:
    - if p'_i is the predicate of φ_i then $f(p'_i) \leq f(p)$,
    - if p''_j is the predicate of ψ_j then $f(p''_j) < f(p)$.

Given a stratification $\mathcal{P}_1, \dots, \mathcal{P}_n$ of $\mathcal{P}$, each $\mathcal{P}_i$ is called a *stratum* of the stratification, and f is called the *stratification mapping*. Let us emphasize that $f('=') \leq f(p)$ for all $p \in \text{DPreds}$.

An eDatalog$^\neg$ program $\mathcal{P}$ is called a *stratified eDatalog$^\neg$ program* if it has a stratification. It is called a *semipositive eDatalog$^\neg$ program* if it has a stratification with only one stratum.[3]

---

[3] Facts supplied to that only stratum are kept separately, e.g., in an ABox.

A pair $\langle \mathcal{P}, \mathcal{A} \rangle$ is called a *stratified eDatalog$^\neg$ knowledge base* if it is an eDatalog$^\neg$ knowledge base with $\mathcal{P}$ being a stratified eDatalog$^\neg$ program.

Example 2 The program $\mathcal{P}$ given in Example 1 is a stratified eDatalog$^\neg$ program with two strata. Each program clause of $\mathcal{P}$ forms a stratum.

2.3 Semantics of eDatalog$^\neg$

Let $\langle \mathcal{P}, \mathcal{A} \rangle$ be an eDatalog$^\neg$ knowledge base. By $\mathcal{P}^{gr}_{\mathcal{A}}$ we denote the set of all ground instances of the program clauses of $\mathcal{P} \cup EqAxioms$ that use only individuals and data constants occurring in $\mathcal{P}$ or $\mathcal{A}$.

By $\mathcal{P}_{\mathcal{A}}$ we denote the set of all clauses

$$(\varphi_1 \wedge \cdots \wedge \varphi_h \wedge \neg\psi_1 \wedge \cdots \wedge \neg\psi_k) \rightarrow \alpha$$

such that $\mathcal{P}^{gr}_{\mathcal{A}}$ contains a program clause

$$(\varphi_1 \wedge \cdots \wedge \varphi_h \wedge \neg\psi_1 \wedge \cdots \wedge \neg\psi_k$$
$$\wedge \xi_1 \wedge \cdots \wedge \xi_l \wedge \neg\zeta_1 \wedge \cdots \wedge \neg\zeta_m) \rightarrow \alpha \quad (2)$$

where all $\xi_1, \dots, \xi_l$ are true and all $\zeta_1, \dots, \zeta_m$ are false (by the fixed meaning of external checkable predicates).

Example 3 Consider the eDatalog$^\neg$ knowledge base $\langle \mathcal{P}, \mathcal{A} \rangle$ given in Example 1. Then $\mathcal{P}_{\mathcal{A}}$ consists of a number of ground instances of clauses of *EqAxioms* and the following clauses:

$$[acceptable(a) \wedge hasPrice(a, 100) \wedge$$
$$acceptable(a) \wedge hasPrice(a, 120)] \rightarrow excluded(a)$$
$$[acceptable(a) \wedge hasPrice(a, 100) \wedge$$
$$acceptable(b) \wedge hasPrice(b, 120)] \rightarrow excluded(b)$$
$$[acceptable(b) \wedge hasPrice(b, 100) \wedge$$
$$acceptable(a) \wedge hasPrice(a, 120)] \rightarrow excluded(a)$$
$$[acceptable(b) \wedge hasPrice(b, 100) \wedge$$
$$acceptable(b) \wedge hasPrice(b, 120)] \rightarrow excluded(b)$$
$$acceptable(a) \wedge \neg excluded(a) \rightarrow preferable(a)$$
$$acceptable(b) \wedge \neg excluded(b) \rightarrow preferable(b).$$

Note that the predicate '<' does no longer occur in $\mathcal{P}_{\mathcal{A}}$.

Note that $\mathcal{P}_{\mathcal{A}} \cup \mathcal{A}$ is a ground Datalog$^\neg$ program. Furthermore, if $\langle \mathcal{P}, \mathcal{A} \rangle$ is a stratified eDatalog$^\neg$ knowledge base then $\mathcal{P}_{\mathcal{A}} \cup \mathcal{A}$ is a ground stratified Datalog$^\neg$ program. We define:

- the well-founded model of an eDatalog$^\neg$ knowledge base $\langle \mathcal{P}, \mathcal{A} \rangle$ to be the well-founded model of the ground Datalog$^\neg$ program $\mathcal{P}_{\mathcal{A}} \cup \mathcal{A}$ [11],
- a stable model of an eDatalog$^\neg$ knowledge base $\langle \mathcal{P}, \mathcal{A} \rangle$ to be a stable model of the ground Datalog$^\neg$ program $\mathcal{P}_{\mathcal{A}} \cup \mathcal{A}$ [12],
- the standard model of a stratified eDatalog$^\neg$ knowledge base $\langle \mathcal{P}, \mathcal{A} \rangle$ to be the standard model of the stratified Datalog$^\neg$ program $\mathcal{P}_{\mathcal{A}} \cup \mathcal{A}$ [1].

Let φ be a query and θ be a ground substitution for all the variables of φ. We say that θ is an *answer* to φ w.r.t. $\langle \mathcal{P}, \mathcal{A} \rangle$ and the *well-founded semantics* if $\varphi\theta$ holds in the well-founded model of $\langle \mathcal{P}, \mathcal{A} \rangle$.[4] Similarly, θ is called an *answer* to φ w.r.t. $\langle \mathcal{P}, \mathcal{A} \rangle$ and the *stable model semantics* if $\varphi\theta$ holds in a stable model of $\langle \mathcal{P}, \mathcal{A} \rangle$. If $\langle \mathcal{P}, \mathcal{A} \rangle$ is stratifiable then θ is called an *answer* to φ w.r.t. $\langle \mathcal{P}, \mathcal{A} \rangle$ and the *standard semantics* if $\varphi\theta$ holds in the standard model of $\langle \mathcal{P}, \mathcal{A} \rangle$.

As a Datalog$^\neg$ program may have zero or more than one stable model, an eDatalog$^\neg$ knowledge base may also have zero or more than one stable model. Note that we adopt the answer set programming approach to deal with the case when an eDatalog$^\neg$ knowledge base has more than one stable model.

Proposition 1 *The data complexity of eDatalog$^\neg$ with respect to the well-founded semantics is in* PTIME.

Proof Let $\langle \mathcal{P}, \mathcal{A} \rangle$ be an eDatalog$^\neg$ knowledge base. The set $\mathcal{P}_{\mathcal{A}}^{gr}$ can be constructed in polynomial time and has polynomial size in the size of $\mathcal{A}$. As the truth values of the atoms of external checkable predicates that occur in $\mathcal{P}_{\mathcal{A}}^{gr}$ can be computed in polynomial time, $\mathcal{P}_{\mathcal{A}}$ can also be constructed in polynomial time and has polynomial size in the size of $\mathcal{A}$. It is well known that the well-founded model of the Datalog$^\neg$ program $\mathcal{P}_{\mathcal{A}} \cup \mathcal{A}$ can be constructed in polynomial time and has polynomial size in the size of $\mathcal{P}_{\mathcal{A}} \cup \mathcal{A}$ (see, e.g., [1]). Thus, the well-founded model of $\langle \mathcal{P}, \mathcal{A} \rangle$ can be constructed in polynomial time and has polynomial size in the size of $\mathcal{A}$. Consequently, answering queries to $\langle \mathcal{P}, \mathcal{A} \rangle$ w.r.t. the well-founded semantics can be done in polynomial time in the size of $\mathcal{A}$.   □

Lemma 1 *Given an eDatalog$^\neg$ knowledge base KB $= \langle \mathcal{P}, \mathcal{A} \rangle$ with $\mathcal{P}$ being a semipositive eDatalog$^\neg$ program, the standard Herbrand model of KB can be computed in polynomial time and has polynomial size in the size of $\mathcal{A}$.*

Proof Recall that $\mathcal{P}_{\mathcal{A}}^{gr}$ has polynomial size in the size of $\mathcal{A}$ (when $\mathcal{P}$ is fixed). Let $\mathcal{P}'_{\mathcal{A}}$ be the set of all the program clauses

$$\varphi_1 \wedge \cdots \wedge \varphi_h \rightarrow \alpha$$

such that $\mathcal{P}_{\mathcal{A}}^{gr}$ contains a program clause

$$(\varphi_1 \wedge \cdots \wedge \varphi_h \wedge \neg\psi_1 \wedge \cdots \wedge \neg\psi_k$$
$$\wedge \xi_1 \wedge \cdots \wedge \xi_l \wedge \neg\zeta_1 \wedge \cdots \wedge \neg\zeta_m) \rightarrow \alpha$$

where $\{\psi_1, \ldots, \psi_k\} \cap \mathcal{A} = \emptyset$, all $\xi_1, \ldots, \xi_l$ are true and all $\zeta_1, \ldots, \zeta_m$ are false (by the fixed meaning of external checkable predicates). The set $\mathcal{P}'_{\mathcal{A}}$ is a Datalog program, which can be computed in polynomial time and has polynomial size in

the size of $\mathcal{A}$. The least Herbrand model of $\mathcal{P}'_{\mathcal{A}}$ can be computed in polynomial time and has polynomial size in the size of $\mathcal{P}'_{\mathcal{A}}$ (see, e.g., [1]). Thus, it can be computed in polynomial time and has polynomial size in the size of $\mathcal{A}$. That model is the same as the standard Herbrand model of *KB*.   □

Corollary 1 *Given a stratified eDatalog$^\neg$ knowledge base KB $= \langle \mathcal{P}, \mathcal{A} \rangle$, the standard Herbrand model of KB can be computed in polynomial time and has polynomial size in the size of $\mathcal{A}$. As a consequence, the data complexity of stratified eDatalog$^\neg$ with respect to the standard semantics is in* PTIME.

3 The web ontology rule language WORL

3.1 Syntax and notation of WORL

We use:

- the truth symbol $\top$ to denote *owl:Thing* [22],
- a and b to denote *individuals* (i.e. *objects*),
- d to denote a *literal* (i.e. a data constant),
- A and B to denote concept names (i.e. *Class* elements [22]),
- C and D to denote *concepts* (i.e. *ClassExpression* elements [22]),
- $lC_{\pm}$ and lC to denote concepts like a *subClassExpression* of [22],
- rC to denote a concept like a *superClassExpression* of [22],
- eC to denote a concept like an *equivClassExpression* of [22],
- DT to denote a *data type* (i.e. a *Datatype* of [22]),
- DR to denote a *data range* (i.e. a *DataRange* of [22]),
- p_{uec} to denote a unary predicate from ECPreds,
- r and s to denote *object role names* (i.e. *ObjectProperty* elements [22]),
- R and S to denote *object roles* (i.e. *ObjectPropertyExpr.* elements [22]),
- σ and ϱ to denote *data role names* (i.e. *DataProperty* elements [22]).

The families of R, DR, $lC_{\pm}$, lC, rC, eC are defined by the following BNF grammar, where $n \geq 2$:

$$R := r \mid r^-$$
$$DR := DT \mid DT \sqcap DR$$
$$lC_{\pm} := A \mid \neg A \mid \{a\} \mid lC_{\pm} \sqcap lC_{\pm} \mid lC_{\pm} \sqcup lC_{\pm} \mid \exists R.lC_{\pm} \mid$$
$$\exists R.\top \mid \geq n\, R.lC_{\pm} \mid \exists\sigma.DR \mid \exists\sigma.p_{uec} \mid \exists\sigma.\{d\}$$
$$lC := A \mid \{a\} \mid lC \sqcap lC_{\pm} \mid lC_{\pm} \sqcap lC \mid lC \sqcup lC \mid \exists R.lC_{\pm} \mid$$
$$\exists R.\top \mid \geq n\, R.lC_{\pm} \mid \exists\sigma.DR \mid \exists\sigma.p_{uec} \mid \exists\sigma.\{d\}$$

---

[4] The well-founded model is treated as a three-valued interpretation.

$$rC := A \mid rC \sqcap rC \mid \forall R.rC \mid \exists R.\{a\} \mid \forall \sigma.DR \mid \exists \sigma.\{d\} \mid$$
$$\leq 1\ R.lC_\pm \mid\ \leq 1\ R.\top$$
$$eC := A \mid eC \sqcap eC \mid \exists R.\{a\} \mid \exists \sigma.\{d\}$$

Here, by r^- we denote the inverse of an object role r. Notice the occurrences of $lC_\pm$ in the definition of lC. They are accompanied by lC or R to guarantee the so called *safeness* (*range-restrictedness*) condition.

Comparing with [6], it can be seen that $\neg A$, $\geq n\ R.lC_\pm$ and $\exists \sigma. p_{uec}$ for $lC_\pm$ are additional features w.r.t. OWL 2 RL.

The class constructor *ObjectOneOf* [22] can be written as $\{a_1, \ldots, a_k\}$ and expressed as $\{a_1\} \sqcup \cdots \sqcup \{a_k\}$. We will use the following abbreviations: Func (Functional), InvFunc (InverseFunctional), Sym (Symmetric), Trans (Transitive), Key (HasKey).

A *DL TBox axiom*, like a *ClassAxiom* or a *Datatype Definition* or a *HasKey* axiom of OWL 2 RL [22], is an expression of one of the following forms, where $h, k \geq 0$ and $h + k \geq 1$:

$$lC \sqsubseteq rC, \ eC = eC', \tag{3}$$
$$DT = DR, \ \mathsf{Key}(lC_\pm, R_1, \ldots, R_h, \sigma_1, \ldots, \sigma_k).$$

An *RBox axiom*, like an *ObjectPropertyAxiom* or a *Data PropertyAxiom* of OWL 2 RL [22], is an expression of one of the following forms:

$$R_1 \circ \cdots \circ R_k \sqsubseteq S, \ R = S, \ R = S^-, \ \exists R.\top \sqsubseteq rC,$$
$$\top \sqsubseteq \forall R.rC, \mathsf{Func}(R), \ \mathsf{InvFunc}(R), \ \mathsf{Sym}(R), \mathsf{Trans}(R),$$
$$\sigma \sqsubseteq \varrho, \ \sigma = \varrho, \ \exists \sigma \sqsubseteq rC, \ \top \sqsubseteq \forall \sigma.DR. \tag{4}$$

Note that axioms of the form $R = S$, $R = S^-$, $\mathsf{Sym}(R)$ or $\mathsf{Trans}(R)$ are expressible by axioms of the form $R_1 \circ \cdots \circ R_k \sqsubseteq S$, and hence can be deleted from the above list.

An RBox axiom of the form $\exists R.\top \sqsubseteq rC$ (resp. $\top \sqsubseteq \forall R.rC$, $\exists \sigma \sqsubseteq rC$, $\top \sqsubseteq \forall \sigma.DR$) stands for an *ObjectPropertyDomain* (resp. *ObjectPropertyRange*, *Data PropertyDomain*, *DataPropertyRange*) axiom as in [22].

One can classify these latter axioms as DL TBox axioms instead of RBox axioms. Similarly, $\mathsf{Key}(\ldots)$ axioms can be classified as RBox axioms instead.

We accept the following definitions:

- A (WORL) *TBox axiom* is either a DL TBox axiom (as defined by (3)) or an RBox axiom (as defined by (4)) or an eDatalog$^\neg$ program clause.
- A (WORL) *TBox* is a finite set of TBox axioms.
- A *WORL knowledge layer* is a pair $\mathcal{L} = \langle \mathcal{T}, \mathcal{A} \rangle$ consisting of a TBox $\mathcal{T}$ and an ABox $\mathcal{A}$.

Note that we defined an ABox to be a finite set of ground atoms of predicates from DPreds. If one wants to add an assertion of the form $C(a)$ to a WORL knowledge layer $\langle \mathcal{T}, \mathcal{A} \rangle$,

where C is a complex concept belonging to the rC family, he or she can add the assertion $A(a)$ to $\mathcal{A}$ and add the axiom $A \sqsubseteq C$ to $\mathcal{T}$, where A is a fresh concept name.

WORL knowledge bases are defined inductively as follows:

- a WORL knowledge layer is a WORL knowledge base,
- if $\mathcal{L}$ is a WORL knowledge layer and $KB_1, \ldots, KB_k$ are WORL knowledge bases then $KB = \langle \mathcal{L}, \{KB_1, \ldots, KB_k\} \rangle$ is a WORL knowledge base.

A WORL knowledge base $\langle \mathcal{L}, \{KB_1, \ldots, KB_k\} \rangle$ can be thought of as an ontology with $\mathcal{L}$ being a set of direct statements, and $KB_1, \ldots, KB_k$ being subontologies.

Example 4 This example is based on the ones of [1,11,12]. It is about a two players game with states a, b, c, d, e, f, g. A player wins if the opponent has no moves. The allowed moves are illustrated below:

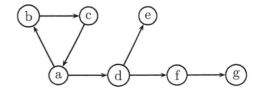

We use a concept name *winning* and a role name *move*. Let $\mathcal{T}$ be the TBox consisting of only the axiom

$$\exists move.\neg winning \sqsubseteq winning$$

and let $\mathcal{A}$ be the ABox consisting of the assertions $move(a, b)$, $\ldots, move(f, g)$ that correspond to the edges in the above graph. Then $KB = \langle \mathcal{T}, \mathcal{A} \rangle$ is a WORL knowledge base.

3.2 Translating WORL into eDatalog$^\neg$

We first define a translation π that translates a TBox axiom to a set of formulas of classical first-order logic. After that we will refine π to get a translation that converts a TBox to an eDatalog$^\neg$ program.

For an eDatalog$^\neg$ program clause φ, let $\pi(\varphi) = \{\varphi\}$.

For a DL TBox axiom or an RBox axiom φ, let $\pi(\varphi)$ be defined as in Fig. 1, where $\pi_{(x)}$ is an auxiliary translation that translates each concept or data range to a formula, where x denotes a variable.

For $\pi_{(x)}(\varphi)$ in the cases when φ is $\exists R.C$, $\exists R.\top$, $\geq n\ R.C$, $\exists \sigma.DR$ or $\exists \sigma.p_{uec}$, note that φ occurs in the left-hand side of $\rightarrow$ and the introduced variables are existentially quantified. Those quantifiers change to universal when taken out of the scope of $\rightarrow$.

The translation π is very intuitive and we use it also for specifying the meanings of TBox axioms. Given an interpretation $\mathcal{I}$ and a DL TBox axiom or an RBox axiom φ, we define that $\mathcal{I} \models \varphi$ iff $\mathcal{I} \models \pi(\varphi)$, where the latter satisfaction

Fig. 1 The translation π for DL TBox axioms and RBox axioms. All variables for $\pi(.)$ like x, y, z, u, v are fresh (new) variables. Variables y and z used for $\pi_{(x)}(.)$ are also fresh variables. For $\pi(\text{Key}(\ldots))$, note that no new objects will be "created" and x, y will only be instantiated by named individuals

$$
\begin{array}{ll}
\pi(\top \sqsubseteq C) & = \{\pi_{(x)}(C)\} \\
\pi(\exists \sigma \sqsubseteq C) & = \{\sigma(x,y) \rightarrow \pi_{(x)}(C)\} \\
\pi(C \sqsubseteq D) & = \{\pi_{(x)}(C) \rightarrow \pi_{(x)}(D)\} \\
\pi(C = D) & = \{\pi_{(x)}(C) \rightarrow \pi_{(x)}(D), \ \pi_{(x)}(D) \rightarrow \pi_{(x)}(C)\} \\
\pi(DT = DR) & = \{\pi_{(x)}(DT) \rightarrow \pi_{(x)}(DR), \ \pi_{(x)}(DR) \rightarrow \pi_{(x)}(DT)\} \\
\pi(R = S) & = \{R(x,y) \rightarrow S(x,y), \ S(x,y) \rightarrow R(x,y)\} \\
\pi(R = S^-) & = \{R(x,y) \rightarrow S(y,x), \ S(y,x) \rightarrow R(x,y)\} \\
\pi(R_1 \circ \ldots \circ R_k \sqsubseteq S) & = \{R_1(x_0,x_1) \wedge \ldots \wedge R_k(x_{k-1},x_k) \rightarrow S(x_0,x_k)\} \\
\pi(\sigma \sqsubseteq \varrho) & = \{\sigma(x,y) \rightarrow \varrho(x,y)\} \\
\pi(\sigma = \varrho) & = \{\sigma(x,y) \rightarrow \varrho(x,y), \ \varrho(x,y) \rightarrow \sigma(x,y)\} \\
\pi(\text{Func}(R)) & = \{R(x,y) \wedge R(x,z) \rightarrow y = z\} \\
\pi(\text{InvFunc}(R)) & = \{R(y,x) \wedge R(z,x) \rightarrow y = z\} \\
\pi(\text{Sym}(R)) & = \{R(x,y) \rightarrow R(y,x)\} \\
\pi(\text{Trans}(R)) & = \{R(x,y) \wedge R(y,z) \rightarrow R(x,z)\} \\
\pi(\text{Key}(C, R_1, \ldots, R_h, \sigma_1, \ldots, \sigma_k)) & = \{[\pi_{(x)}(C) \wedge \pi_{(y)}(C) \wedge \\
\multicolumn{2}{l}{\bigwedge_{1 \leq i \leq h}(R_i(x,u_i) \wedge R_i(y,u_i)) \wedge \bigwedge_{1 \leq i \leq k}(\sigma_i(x,v_i) \wedge \sigma_i(y,v_i))] \rightarrow x = y\}}
\end{array}
$$

$$
\begin{array}{ll}
\pi_{(x)}(DT) & = DT(x) \\
\pi_{(x)}(DT \sqcap DR) & = DT(x) \wedge \pi_{(x)}(DR) \\
\pi_{(x)}(A) & = A(x) \\
\pi_{(x)}(\neg A) & = \neg A(x) \\
\pi_{(x)}(\{a\}) & = (x = a) \\
\pi_{(x)}(C \sqcap D) & = \pi_{(x)}(C) \wedge \pi_{(x)}(D) \\
\pi_{(x)}(C \sqcup D) & = \pi_{(x)}(C) \vee \pi_{(x)}(D) \\
\pi_{(x)}(\forall R.C) & = R(x,y) \rightarrow \pi_{(y)}(C) \\
\pi_{(x)}(\exists R.C) & = R(x,y) \wedge \pi_{(y)}(C) \\
\pi_{(x)}(\exists R.\{a\}) & = R(x,a) \\
\pi_{(x)}(\exists R.\top) & = R(x,y) \\
\pi_{(x)}(\geq n\, R.C) & = \bigwedge_{1 \leq i \leq n}(R(x,y_i) \wedge \pi_{(y_i)}(C)) \wedge \bigwedge_{1 \leq i \neq j \leq n} \neg(y_i = y_j) \\
\pi_{(x)}(\forall \sigma.DR) & = \sigma(x,y) \rightarrow \pi_{(y)}(DR) \\
\pi_{(x)}(\exists \sigma.DR) & = \sigma(x,y) \wedge \pi_{(y)}(DR) \\
\pi_{(x)}(\exists \sigma.p_{uec}) & = \sigma(x,y) \wedge p_{uec}(y) \\
\pi_{(x)}(\exists \sigma.\{d\}) & = \sigma(x,d) \\
\pi_{(x)}(\leq 1\, R.C) & = R(x,y) \wedge R(x,z) \wedge \pi_{(y)}(C) \wedge \pi_{(z)}(C) \rightarrow y = z \\
\pi_{(x)}(\leq 1\, R.\top) & = R(x,y) \wedge R(x,z) \rightarrow y = z
\end{array}
$$

relation $\models$ is defined as usual. We say that $\mathcal{I}$ is a model of a TBox $\mathcal{T}$, denoted by $\mathcal{I} \models \mathcal{T}$, if $\mathcal{I} \models \varphi$ for all $\varphi \in \mathcal{T}$.

Example 5 Continuing Example 4, we have that:

$\pi(\exists move.\neg winning \sqsubseteq winning)$

$\quad = \{move(x,y) \wedge \neg winning(y) \rightarrow winning(x)\}$.

Example 6 For $\varphi = (\exists r.(A_1 \sqcup A_2) \sqsubseteq \forall r.B)$, we have

$\pi(\varphi) = \{r(x,y) \wedge (A_1(y) \vee A_2(y)) \rightarrow (r(x,z) \rightarrow B(z))\}$.

As for free variables, x, y and z are universally quantified. The only formula of $\pi(\varphi)$ is not an eDatalog$^\neg$ program clause. The intended translation of φ to a set of eDatalog$^\neg$ program clauses is

$\pi_3(\varphi) = \{r(x,y) \wedge A_1(y) \wedge r(x,z) \rightarrow B(z),$
$\qquad\qquad r(x,y) \wedge A_2(y) \wedge r(x,z) \rightarrow B(z)\}$.

To specify π_3, we use auxiliary translations $\pi_{2,l}$ and π_2 such that:

– when $\pi_{2,l}$ is applicable to a formula ψ of predicate logic, $\pi_{2,l}(\psi)$ is a set of conjunctions of atomic formulas such that, for any interpretation $\mathcal{I}$, $\mathcal{I} \models \bigvee \pi_{2,l}(\psi)$ iff $\mathcal{I} \models \psi$; for example,

$\pi_{2,l}(r(x,y) \wedge (A_1(y) \vee A_2(y)))$

$\quad = \{r(x,y) \wedge A_1(y), \ r(x,y) \wedge A_2(y)\};$

– when π_2 is applicable to a formula ψ of predicate logic, $\pi_2(\psi)$ is a set of eDatalog$^\neg$ program clauses such that, for any interpretation $\mathcal{I}$, $\mathcal{I} \models \bigwedge \pi_2(\psi)$ iff $\mathcal{I} \models \psi$.

We define:

$\pi_{2,l}(\xi) = \{\xi\}$ if ξ is not of any of the forms $\varphi \wedge \psi$,
$\qquad\qquad\qquad \varphi \vee \psi, r^-(x,y)$
$\pi_{2,l}(r^-(x,y)) = \{r(y,x)\}$
$\pi_{2,l}(\varphi \vee \psi) = \pi_{2,l}(\varphi) \cup \pi_{2,l}(\psi)$
$\pi_{2,l}(\varphi \wedge \psi) = \{\varphi' \wedge \psi' \mid \varphi' \in \pi_{2,l}(\varphi) \text{ and } \psi' \in \pi_{2,l}(\psi)\}$
$\pi_2(\xi) = \{\xi\}$ if ξ is not of any of the forms $\varphi \wedge \psi$,
$\qquad\qquad\qquad \varphi \rightarrow \psi, \ r^-(x,y)$
$\pi_2(r^-(x,y)) = \{r(y,x)\}$
$\pi_2(\varphi \rightarrow \psi) =$
$\quad \{\varphi' \wedge \xi' \rightarrow \zeta' \mid \varphi' \in \pi_{2,l}(\varphi) \text{ and } (\xi' \rightarrow \zeta') \in \pi_2(\psi)\} \cup$
$\quad\quad \{\varphi' \rightarrow \psi' \mid \varphi' \in \pi_{2,l}(\varphi), \ \psi' \in \pi_2(\psi) \text{ and } \psi' \text{ is not}$
$\quad\quad\quad \text{of the form } \xi' \rightarrow \zeta'\}$
$\pi_2(\varphi \wedge \psi) = \pi_2(\varphi) \cup \pi_2(\psi)$.

We also need the following definitions of π_3:

– if φ is an eDatalog$^\neg$ program clause then $\pi_3(\varphi) = \{\varphi\}$,
– if φ is a DL TBox axiom or an RBox axiom φ then

$$\pi_3(\varphi) = \bigcup_{\psi \in \pi(\varphi)} \pi_2(\psi),$$

– if φ is a TBox $\mathcal{T}$ then $\pi_3(\mathcal{T}) = \bigcup_{\varphi \in \mathcal{T}} \pi_3(\varphi)$.

Lemma 2 *For any (WORL) TBox $\mathcal{T}$, $\pi_3(\mathcal{T})$ is an eDatalog$^\neg$ program equivalent to $\mathcal{T}$ in the sense that, for any interpretation $\mathcal{I}$, $\mathcal{I} \models \pi_3(\mathcal{T})$ iff $\mathcal{I} \models \mathcal{T}$.*

Proof Let ψ denote a formula of classical first-order logic. It can be proved by induction on the structure of ψ that $\pi_{2,l}(\psi)$ and $\pi_2(\psi)$ are sets of formulas such that, for any interpretation $\mathcal{I}$,

– $\mathcal{I} \models \bigvee \pi_{2,l}(\psi)$ iff $\mathcal{I} \models \psi$,
– $\mathcal{I} \models \bigwedge \pi_2(\psi)$ iff $\mathcal{I} \models \psi$.

Consequently, for any interpretation $\mathcal{I}$ and any DL TBox axiom or RBox axiom φ, $\mathcal{I} \models \pi_3(\varphi)$ iff $\mathcal{I} \models \pi(\varphi)$. By definition, $\mathcal{I} \models \varphi$ iff $\mathcal{I} \models \pi(\varphi)$. Therefore, $\pi_3(\mathcal{T})$ is equivalent to $\mathcal{T}$.

It remains to show that $\pi_3(\mathcal{T})$ is an eDatalog$^\neg$ program.

In the following, let α denote an atomic formula. We define the families of $l\psi_\pm$, $l\psi$ and $r\psi$ as follows (by using BNF grammar for $l\psi_\pm$ and $r\psi$):

$l\psi_\pm := \alpha \mid \neg\alpha \mid r^-(t, t') \mid l\psi_\pm \wedge l\psi_\pm \mid l\psi_\pm \vee l\psi_\pm$

$l\psi := l\psi_\pm$ with the safeness condition

$r\psi := \alpha \mid r^-(t, t') \mid r\psi \wedge r\psi \mid l\psi \rightarrow r\psi$

where a formula ψ of the $l\psi_\pm$ family satisfies the safeness condition if translating ψ to the conjunctive normal form by using the distributive laws of $\wedge$ and $\vee$ results in $\psi_1 \vee \cdots \vee \psi_k$ (where each ψ_i does not contains $\vee$) such that every variable occurring in some ψ_i occurs (among others) in some positive atom of ψ_i.

It is straightforward to prove by induction on the structure of C that:

– if C is a concept of the lC family then $\pi_{(x)}(C)$ is a formula ψ of the $l\psi$ family such that translating ψ to the conjunctive normal form by using the distributive laws of $\wedge$ and $\vee$ results in $\psi_1 \vee \ldots \vee \psi_k$ (where each ψ_i does not contains $\vee$) such that variable x occurs in each ψ_i,
– if C is a concept of the rC family then $\pi_{(x)}(C)$ is a formula of the $r\psi$ family such that if a variable y different from x occurs in the formula then it occurs (among others) in the left-hand side of some $\rightarrow$ in the formula.

Next, it can be proved by induction on the structure of φ that:

– if ψ is a formula of the $l\psi$ family then $\pi_{2,l}(\psi)$ is a set of formulas of the $l\psi$ family without the connective $\vee$ and atoms of the form $r^-(t, t')$,
– if φ is a DL TBox axiom or an RBox axiom then $\pi(\varphi)$ is a set of formulas of the $r\psi$ family such that every variable occurring in a formula from $\pi(\varphi)$ occurs (among others) in some positive atom of the formula in the left-hand side of some $\rightarrow$,
– if φ is a DL TBox axiom or an RBox axiom and $\psi \in \pi(\varphi)$ then $\pi_2(\psi)$ is a set of eDatalog$^\neg$ program clauses.

Therefore, $\pi_3(\mathcal{T})$ is an eDatalog$^\neg$ program. $\square$

3.3 The well-founded semantics of WORL

The *flattened version* of a WORL knowledge base KB is the WORL knowledge layer denoted by *flatten(KB)* and defined as follows:

– if KB is a layer then *flatten(KB)* $= KB$,
– else if $KB = \langle \mathcal{L}, \{KB_1, \ldots, KB_k\}\rangle$, $\mathcal{L} = \langle \mathcal{T}, \mathcal{A}\rangle$ and *flatten(KB$_i$)* $= \langle \mathcal{T}_i, \mathcal{A}_i\rangle$ for $1 \leq i \leq k$, then

$$\textit{flatten(KB)} = \langle \mathcal{T} \cup \mathcal{T}_1 \cup \cdots \cup \mathcal{T}_k, \mathcal{A} \cup \mathcal{A}_1 \cup \cdots \cup \mathcal{A}_k\rangle.$$

Given a WORL knowledge base KB with *flatten(KB)* $= \langle \mathcal{T}, \mathcal{A}\rangle$, the *well-founded (Herbrand) model* of KB, denoted by WF_{KB}, is defined to be the well-founded model of the eDatalog$^\neg$ knowledge base $KB' = \langle \pi_3(\mathcal{T}), \mathcal{A}\rangle$.

An *answer* to a query φ w.r.t. that KB and the *well-founded semantics* is an answer to φ w.r.t. that KB' and the well-founded semantics of eDatalog$^\neg$.

The *data complexity* of WORL w.r.t. the well-founded semantics is the complexity of the problem of finding all answers to a query φ w.r.t. a WORL knowledge base KB and the well-founded semantics, measured w.r.t. the sum of the sizes of all ABoxes used in KB when assuming that DPreds, φ and all the TBoxes used in KB are fixed and checking whether a ground atom of an external checkable predicate is true or false can be done in polynomial time.

The following theorem immediately follows from Proposition 1.

Theorem 1 *The data complexity of WORL with respect to the well-founded semantics is in* PTIME.

Example 7 Let A, B, C, D be concept names and let $\mathcal{T}_1$, $\mathcal{T}_2$, $\mathcal{T}$ be the TBoxes and $\mathcal{A}_1$, $\mathcal{A}_2$, $\mathcal{A}$ be the ABoxes specified below:

$\mathcal{T}_1 = \{A \sqcap \neg B \sqsubseteq C\}$ $\mathcal{A}_1 = \{A(u), A(v), B(u)\}$
$\mathcal{T}_2 = \{A \sqcap \neg C \sqsubseteq B\}$ $\mathcal{A}_2 = \{A(u), A(v)\}$
$\mathcal{T} = \{B \sqcap C \sqsubseteq D\}$ $\mathcal{A} = \emptyset$

Then $KB_1 = \langle \mathcal{T}_1, \mathcal{A}_1 \rangle$, $KB_2 = \langle \mathcal{T}_2, \mathcal{A}_2 \rangle$ and $KB = \langle \langle \mathcal{T}, \mathcal{A} \rangle, \{KB_1, KB_2\} \rangle$ are WORL knowledge bases. The knowledge base KB consists of the main layer $\langle \mathcal{T}, \mathcal{A} \rangle$ and the additional layers KB_1 and KB_2. Flattening KB results in

$$KB' = \langle \mathcal{T}_1 \cup \mathcal{T}_2 \cup \mathcal{T}, \{A(u), A(v), B(u)\} \rangle.$$

The well-founded model of KB' is

$$\{A(u), A(v), B(u), \neg C(u), \neg D(u), u = u, v = v, u \neq v, v \neq u\}.$$

The remaining atoms $B(v)$, $C(v)$ and $D(v)$ have value "unknown". The query $D(x)$ w.r.t. KB and the well-founded semantics has no answers, while the query $\neg D(x)$ has one answer $\{x/u\}$.

3.4 The stable model semantics of WORL

An *answer set* of a WORL knowledge base is defined inductively as follows:

– An *answer set* of a WORL knowledge layer $\langle \mathcal{T}, \mathcal{A} \rangle$ is defined to be the set of all ground atoms of predicates from DPreds that hold in a stable model of $\langle \mathcal{T}, \mathcal{A} \rangle$ (Each stable model of $\langle \mathcal{T}, \mathcal{A} \rangle$ gives an answer set).
– An *answer set* of a WORL knowledge base KB of the form $\langle \mathcal{L}, \{KB_1, \ldots, KB_k\} \rangle$, where $\mathcal{L} = \langle \mathcal{T}, \mathcal{A} \rangle$, is defined to be an answer set of the WORL knowledge layer $\langle \mathcal{T}, \mathcal{A} \cup \mathcal{A}_1 \cup \cdots \cup \mathcal{A}_k \rangle$, where each $\mathcal{A}_i$ is an answer set of the WORL knowledge base KB_i.

Let φ be a query and θ be a ground substitution for all the variables of φ. We say that θ is an *answer* to φ w.r.t. a WORL knowledge base $\langle \mathcal{P}, \mathcal{A} \rangle$ and the *stable model semantics* if $\varphi\theta$ holds in the interpretation that corresponds to an answer set of $\langle \mathcal{P}, \mathcal{A} \rangle$ (Notice that the answer set programming approach is adopted here).

Example 8 Reconsider the WORL knowledge bases KB_1, KB_2 and KB given in Example 7. The knowledge base KB_1 has only one answer set

$$\{A(u), A(v), B(u), C(v), u = u, v = v\}.$$

The knowledge base KB_2 has only one answer set

$$\{A(u), A(v), B(u), B(v), u = u, v = v\}.$$

Consequently, the knowledge base KB has only one answer set

$$\{A(u), A(v), B(u), B(v), C(v), D(v), u = u, v = v\}.$$

The query $D(x)$ w.r.t. KB and the stable model semantics has the only answer $\{x/v\}$, and the query $\neg D(x)$ has the only answer $\{x/u\}$. Notice the difference between the stable model semantics and the well-founded semantics.

Also observe that the flattened version KB' of KB (given in Example 7) has two answer sets:

$$\{A(u), A(v), B(u), B(v), u = u, v = v\},$$
$$\{A(u), A(v), B(u), C(v), u = u, v = v\}.$$

4 Stratified WORL

A TBox $\mathcal{T}$ is said to be *stratifiable* if $\pi_3(\mathcal{T})$ is a stratified eDatalog$^\neg$ program. In the "Appendix" we present a direct method for checking stratifiability of a TBox without using translation.

A WORL knowledge layer $\langle \mathcal{T}, \mathcal{A} \rangle$ is called a *SWORL knowledge layer* if $\mathcal{T}$ is stratifiable. A WORL knowledge base is called a *SWORL knowledge base* if it is either a SWORL knowledge layer or a pair $\langle \mathcal{L}, \{KB_1, \ldots, KB_k\} \rangle$ where $\mathcal{L}$ is a SWORL knowledge layer and each KB_i is a SWORL knowledge base.

Note that flattening a SWORL knowledge base $\langle \mathcal{L}, \{KB_1, \ldots, KB_k\} \rangle$ may result in a WORL knowledge layer that is not stratifiable.

Let KB be a SWORL knowledge base. The *standard Herbrand model* of KB, denoted by $\mathcal{H}_{KB}$, is defined as follows:

– If KB is a SWORL knowledge layer $\langle \mathcal{T}, \mathcal{A} \rangle$ then $\mathcal{H}_{KB}$ is the standard Herbrand model of the stratified eDatalog$^\neg$ knowledge base $\langle \pi_3(\mathcal{T}), \mathcal{A} \rangle$.
– If $KB = \langle \mathcal{L}, \{KB_1, \ldots, KB_k\} \rangle$ and $\mathcal{L} = \langle \mathcal{T}, \mathcal{A} \rangle$ then $\mathcal{H}_{KB}$ is the standard Herbrand model of the stratified eDatalog$^\neg$ knowledge base $\langle \pi_3(\mathcal{T}), \mathcal{A} \cup \mathcal{H}_{KB_1} \cup \cdots \cup \mathcal{H}_{KB_k} \rangle$.

The *standard model* of a SWORL knowledge base KB is defined to be the traditional interpretation corresponding to $\mathcal{H}_{KB}$ and is denoted by $\mathcal{M}_{KB}$.

The notion of *answer* to a query w.r.t. a SWORL knowledge base and the data complexity of SWORL are defined as usual:

– Given a SWORL knowledge base KB and a query φ, a (correct) *answer* to φ w.r.t. KB and the *standard semantics* is a ground substitution θ for all the variables of φ such that $\mathcal{M}_{KB} \models \varphi\theta$, where $\models$ is the satisfaction relation defined in the usual way.
– The *data complexity* of SWORL w.r.t. the standard semantics is the complexity of the problem of finding all answers to a query φ w.r.t. a SWORL knowledge base KB and the standard semantics, measured w.r.t. the sum of the sizes of all ABoxes used in KB when assuming that DPreds, φ, the structure of KB and all the TBoxes used in KB are fixed and checking whether a ground atom of an external checkable predicate is true or false can be done in polynomial time.

Theorem 2 *The data complexity of SWORL with respect to the standard semantics is in* PTIME.

Proof Let *KB* be a SWORL knowledge base and n be the sum of the sizes of all ABoxes used in *KB*. We prove by induction on the structure of *KB* that the standard Herbrand model $\mathcal{H}_{KB}$ of *KB* can be computed in polynomial time and has polynomial size in n :

- If *KB* is a SWORL knowledge layer $\langle \mathcal{T}, \mathcal{A} \rangle$ then $\mathcal{H}_{KB}$ is the standard Herbrand model of the stratified eDatalog¬ knowledge base $\langle \pi_3(\mathcal{T}), \mathcal{A} \rangle$, and by Corollary 1, $\mathcal{H}_{KB}$ can be computed in polynomial time and has polynomial size in n.
- If $KB = \langle \langle \mathcal{T}, \mathcal{A} \rangle, \{KB_1, \ldots, KB_k\} \rangle$ then:
- By the inductive assumption, $\mathcal{H}_{KB_1}, \ldots, \mathcal{H}_{KB_k}$ can be computed in polynomial time and have polynomial size in n.
- $\mathcal{H}_{KB}$ is the standard Herbrand model of the stratified eDatalog¬ knowledge base $\langle \pi_3(\mathcal{T}), \mathcal{A} \cup \mathcal{H}_{KB_1} \cup \cdots \cup \mathcal{H}_{KB_k} \rangle$, and by Corollary 1, $\mathcal{H}_{KB}$ can be computed in polynomial time and has polynomial size in the size of $\mathcal{A} \cup \mathcal{H}_{KB_1} \cup \cdots \cup \mathcal{H}_{KB_k}$.
- Hence, $\mathcal{H}_{KB}$ can be computed in polynomial time and has polynomial size in n.

As a consequence, the data complexity of SWORL w.r.t. the standard semantics is in PTIME. □

The standard semantics of SWORL coincides with the well-founded semantics when restricting to SWORL knowledge bases that are single layers and to queries of the form $(\varphi_1 \wedge \cdots \wedge \varphi_h \wedge \xi_1 \wedge \cdots \wedge \xi_l \wedge \neg \zeta_1 \wedge \cdots \wedge \neg \zeta_m)$, where $\varphi_1, \ldots, \varphi_h$ are atoms of predicates from DPreds and $\xi_1, \ldots, \xi_l, \zeta_1, \ldots, \zeta_m$ are atoms of predicates from ECPreds.

4.1 Example: apartment renting

In this subsection we discuss apartment renting, a common activity that is often tedious and time-consuming. The example is based on the one of [2]. The difference is that we use SWORL instead of defeasible logic.

We begin by presenting the potential renter's requirements:

- Carlos is looking for an apartment of at least 45 m² with at least two bedrooms. If it is on the third floor or higher, the house must have an elevator. Also, pet animals must be allowed.
- Carlos is willing to pay \$300 for a centrally located 45 m² apartment, and \$250 for a similar flat in the suburbs. In addition, he is willing to pay an extra \$5 per m² for a larger apartment, and \$2 per m² for a garden.

- He is unable to pay more than \$400 in total. If given the choice, he would go for the cheapest option. His second priority is the presence of a garden; his lowest priority is additional space.

We use the following predicates to describe properties of apartments:

- $hasSize(X, Y)$: Y is the size of apartment X,
- $bedrooms(X, Y)$: apartment X has Y bedrooms,
- $hasPrice(X, Y)$: Y is the rent price of apartment X,
- $floor(X, Y)$: apartment X is on the Yth floor,
- $garden(X, Y)$: apartment X has a garden of size Y,
- $withLift(X)$: there is an elevator in the house of X,
- $allowsPets(X)$: pets are allowed in apartment X,
- $central(X)$: apartment X is centrally located.

The predicates $hasSize$, $bedrooms$, $hasPrice$, $floor$ and $garden$ are data role names, while the predicates $withLift$, $allowsPets$ and $central$ are concept names. These predicates are specified by ABox assertions.

We define a number of predicates. The first one is $withGarden$, specified by:

$$garden(X, Y) \rightarrow withGarden(X). \tag{5}$$

We use predicate $offers(X, N, Y, Z)$ defined as follows:

$$[hasSize(X, Y) \wedge central(X) \wedge \neg withGarden(X)]$$
$$\rightarrow offers(X, 1, Y, 0) \tag{6}$$
$$[hasSize(X, Y) \wedge central(X) \wedge garden(X, Z)]$$
$$\rightarrow offers(X, 2, Y, Z) \tag{7}$$
$$[hasSize(X, Y) \wedge \neg central(X) \wedge \neg withGarden(X)]$$
$$\rightarrow offers(X, 3, Y, 0) \tag{8}$$
$$[hasSize(X, Y) \wedge \neg central(X) \wedge garden(X, Z)]$$
$$\rightarrow offers(X, 4, Y, Z). \tag{9}$$

The predicate $offers(X, N, Y, Z)$ means Carlos is willing to pay $f(N, Y, Z)$ dollars for apartment X, where $f(N, Y, Z)$ is defined as

$$f(N, Y, Z) = \begin{cases} 300 + 5(Y - 45) & \text{if } N = 1 \\ 300 + 5(Y - 45) + 2.Z & \text{if } N = 2 \\ 250 + 5(Y - 45) & \text{if } N = 3 \\ 250 + 5(Y - 45) + 2.Z & \text{if } N = 4. \end{cases}$$

This function is used only to specify the external checkable predicate

$$tooExpensive(N, Y, Z, P) \equiv (f(N, Y, Z) < P),$$

which in turn is used in the following program clause:

$$[offers(X, N, Y, Z) \wedge hasPrice(X, P) \wedge$$
$$tooExpensive(N, Y, Z, P)] \rightarrow excluded_0(X). \tag{10}$$

Thus, $excluded_0(X)$ means apartment X is unacceptable.

Apartments acceptable to Carlos are defined by the following DL TBox axiom:

$[\exists hasSize.(\geq 45) \sqcap \exists bedrooms.(\geq 2) \sqcap (\exists floor.(\leq 2)$

$\sqcup withLift) \sqcap allowsPets \sqcap \neg excluded_0$

$\sqcap \exists hasPrice.(\leq 400)] \sqsubseteq acceptable.$ (11)

In the above axiom, (≥ 45), (≥ 2), (≤ 2) and (≤ 400) are unary external checkable predicates.

Among the acceptable apartments, the cheapest ones are preferable:

$[acceptable(X) \wedge hasPrice(X, Y) \wedge$

$acceptable(X') \wedge hasPrice(X', Y') \wedge Y < Y']$

$\rightarrow excluded_1(X')$ (12)

$acceptable(X) \wedge \neg excluded_1(X) \rightarrow preferable_1(X).$ (13)

Among the cheapest apartments that are acceptable, the ones with a garden are more preferable:

$[preferable_1(X) \wedge \neg withGarden(X) \wedge$

$preferable_1(X') \wedge withGarden(X')]$

$\rightarrow excluded_2(X)$ (14)

$preferable_1(X) \wedge \neg excluded_2(X) \rightarrow preferable_2(X).$ (15)

Among those apartments, Carlos will rent a largest one:

$[preferable_2(X) \wedge hasSize(X, Y) \wedge$

$preferable_2(X') \wedge hasSize(X', Y') \wedge Y < Y']$

$\rightarrow excluded_3(X)$ (16)

$preferable_2(X) \wedge \neg excluded_3(X) \rightarrow mayRent(X).$ (17)

In the program clauses (12) and (16), '<' is a binary external checkable predicate.

Let $\mathcal{T} = \{(5), ..., (17)\}$. It is a stratifiable TBox. Only (11) is a DL TBox axiom, while the other axioms are eDatalog$^\neg$ program clauses. The program clauses (5), (13), (15) and (17) can also be expressed as DL TBox axioms, treating $withGarden$, $acceptable$, $excluded_1$, $preferable_1$, $excluded_2$, $preferable_2$, $excluded_3$ and $mayRent$ as concept names.

Translating the TBox $\mathcal{T}$ to a stratified eDatalog$^\neg$ program $\mathcal{P} = \pi_3(\mathcal{T})$, the DL TBox axiom (11) is replaced by the following eDatalog$^\neg$ program clauses:

$[hasSize(X, Y_1) \wedge Y_1 \geq 45 \wedge bedrooms(X, Y_2) \wedge Y_2 \geq 2$

$\wedge floor(X, Y_3) \wedge Y_3 \leq 2 \wedge allowsPets(X) \wedge \neg excluded_0(X)$

$\wedge hasPrice(X, Y_4) \wedge Y_4 \leq 400] \rightarrow acceptable(X)$ (18)

$[hasSize(X, Y_1) \wedge Y_1 \geq 45 \wedge bedrooms(X, Y_2) \wedge Y_2 \geq 2$

$\wedge withLift(X) \wedge allowsPets(X) \wedge \neg excluded_0(X)$

$\wedge hasPrice(X, Y_4) \wedge Y_4 \leq 400] \rightarrow acceptable(X).$ (19)

A possible stratification of $\mathcal{P}$ is: $\{(5)\}$, $\{(6), (7), (8), (9), (10)\}$, $\{(18), (19), (12)\}$, $\{(13), (14)\}$, $\{(15), (16)\}$, $\{(17)\}$.

Let $\mathcal{A}$ be the ABox consisting of the ground atoms of predicates $bedrooms$, $hasSize$, $central$, $floor$, $withLift$, $allowsPets$, $garden$ and $hasPrice$ that reflect the information contained in the following table:

Flat	Bedrooms	Size	Central	Floor	Lift	Pets	Garden	Price
a1	1	50	Yes	1	No	Yes		300
a2	2	45	Yes	0	No	Yes		335
a3	2	65	No	2	No	Yes		350
a4	2	55	No	1	Yes	No	15	330
a5	3	55	Yes	0	No	Yes	15	350
a6	2	60	Yes	3	No	No		370
a7	3	65	Yes	1	No	Yes	12	375

For example, $bedrooms(a1, 1)$, $hasSize(a1, 50)$, $central(a1)$, $floor(a1, 1)$, $allowsPets(a1)$ and $hasPrice(a1, 300)$ are the atoms of $\mathcal{A}$ that involve apartment $a1$. As ABoxes contain only positive information, only atom $withLift(a4)$ of predicate $withLift$ occurs in $\mathcal{A}$.

The pair $KB = \langle \mathcal{T}, \mathcal{A} \rangle$ is a SWORL knowledge layer (and a SWORL knowledge base). The standard Herbrand model $\mathcal{H}_{KB}$ contains atoms $acceptable(X)$ only for $X \in \{a3, a5, a7\}$ and atoms $preferable_1(X)$ only for $X \in \{a3, a5\}$. Only atom $preferable_2(a5)$ of predicate $preferable_2$ and atom $mayRent(a5)$ of predicate $mayRent$ occur in $\mathcal{H}_{KB}$.

5 Conclusions

We have developed the Web ontology rule languages WORL and SWORL together with the well-founded semantics and the stable model semantics for WORL and the standard semantics for SWORL. Both WORL with respect to the well-founded semantics and SWORL with respect to the standard semantics have PTime data complexity.

As WORL can be translated into eDatalog$^\neg$ and SWORL can be translated into stratified eDatalog$^\neg$, the languages WORL and SWORL are not more expressive than eDatalog$^\neg$ and stratified eDatalog$^\neg$, respectively. However, WORL and SWORL allow using also syntax of description logic (and hence also OWL). This has the same benefits as in the case OWL 2 RL compared to eDatalog, and is very useful for applications of the Semantic Web. As Web ontology rule languages, WORL and SWORL have the advantage of using efficient computational methods of Datalog$^\neg$ (extended for eDatalog$^\neg$).

Using nonmonotonic semantics for negation in concept inclusion axioms is a novelty of our approach. Modularity of SWORL is also worth mentioning.

Acknowledgments This work was supported by the Polish National Science Center (NCN) under Grants No. 2011/01/B/ST6/02769 and 2011/01/B/ST6/02759. The first author would also like to thank the Warsaw Center of Mathematics and Computer Science for support.

6 Appendix: Checking stratifiability of TBoxes

We specify a dependency relation between the predicates occurring in a TBox for deciding whether the TBox is stratifiable.

For φ being either a concept of the lC family but not of the form $\geq n\,R.C$, or an expression of the form $R, R_1 \circ \cdots \circ R_k$, $\top$, σ or $\exists\sigma$, let $Preds_-(\varphi)$ be the set of the concept names that occur in φ under negation, and let $Preds_+(\varphi)$ be the set of the predicates from DPreds that occur in φ but do not belong to $Preds_-(\varphi)$.

For a concept C belonging to the rC family, define $LPreds_+(C)$, $LPreds_-(C)$ and $RPreds(C)$ as follows:[5]

- case $C = A$:
  $LPreds_+(C) = LPreds_-(C) = \emptyset, RPreds(C) = \{A\}$;
- case $C = D_1 \sqcap D_2$:
  $LPreds_+(C) = LPreds_+(D_1) \cup LPreds_+(D_2)$,
  $LPreds_-(C) = LPreds_-(D_1) \cup LPreds_-(D_2)$,
  $RPreds(C) = RPreds(D_1) \cup RPreds(D_2)$;
- case $C = \forall r.D$ or $C = \forall r^-.D$:
  $LPreds_+(C) = \{r\} \cup LPreds_+(D)$,
  $LPreds_-(C) = LPreds_-(D)$,
  $RPreds(C) = RPreds(D)$;
- case $C = \exists r.\{a\}$ or $C = \exists r^-.\{a\}$:
  $LPreds_+(C) = LPreds_-(C) = \emptyset, RPreds(C) = \{r\}$;
- case $C = \forall\sigma.DR$:
  $LPreds_+(C) = \{\sigma\}, LPreds_-(C) = \emptyset$,
  $RPreds(C)$ is the set of all data types occurring in DR;
- case $C = \exists\sigma.\{d\}$:
  $LPreds_+(C) = LPreds_-(C) = \emptyset, RPreds(C) = \{\sigma\}$;
- case $C = \leq 1\,r.D$ or $C = \leq 1\,r^-.D$:
  $LPreds_+(C) = \{r\} \cup Preds_+(D)$,
  $LPreds_-(C) = Preds_-(D)$,
  $RPreds(C) = \{'='\}$;
- case $C = \leq 1\,r.\top$ or $C = \leq 1\,r^-.\top$:
  $LPreds_+(C) = \{r\}, LPreds_-(C) = \emptyset, RPreds(C) = \{'='\}$.

Let $LPreds_+(R) = LPreds_-(R) = \emptyset$ and $RPreds(r) = RPreds(r^-) = \{r\}$. Let $LPreds_+(\sigma) = LPreds_-(\sigma) = \emptyset$ and $RPreds(\sigma) = \{\sigma\}$.

It can be proved that a TBox $\mathcal{T}$ is stratifiable if $\mathcal{T}$ does not use the concept constructor $\geq n\,R.C$ and there exists a function f from DPreds to positive natural numbers such that:

---
[5] Where L stands for "left of $\rightarrow$" and R stands for "right of $\rightarrow$".

- for every eDatalog$^\neg$ program clause φ in $\mathcal{T} \cup EqAxioms$, if q is the predicate of the head of φ and p is a predicate from DPreds that occurs in the body of φ then $f(p) \leq f(q)$, and additionally, if p occurs under negation in φ then $f(p) < f(q)$;
- for every axiom of the form $\varphi \sqsubseteq \psi$ in $\mathcal{T}$ and for every $q \in RPreds(\psi)$:

  - for every $p \in Preds_+(\varphi) \cup LPreds_+(\psi)$,
    $f(p) \leq f(q)$;
  - for every $p \in Preds_-(\varphi) \cup LPreds_-(\psi)$,
    $f(p) < f(q)$;

- for every axiom of the form $\varphi = \psi$ in $\mathcal{T}$, all the predicates occurring in $\varphi = \psi$ have the same f value;
- for every axiom $\mathsf{Key}(C, R_1, \ldots, R_h, \sigma_1, \ldots, \sigma_k)$ in $\mathcal{T}$: $Preds_-(C) = \emptyset$ and, for every predicate p belonging to $Preds_+(C)$ or $\{\sigma_1, \ldots, \sigma_k\}$ or occurring in $R_1, \ldots, R_h$, $f(p) = f('=')$;
- for every axiom of the form $\mathsf{Func}(R)$ or $\mathsf{InvFunc}(R)$ in $\mathcal{T}$, where $R = r$ or $R = r^-$, we have that $f(r) = f('=')$.

To check whether a TBox $\mathcal{T}$ is stratifiable one can construct a graph of dependencies between the predicates occurring in $\mathcal{T}$. The condition $f(p) \leq f(q)$ (resp. $f(p) < f(q)$) is expressed by an edge with mark $+$ (resp. $-$) from vertex p to vertex q. The TBox is stratifiable if that graph does not contain any cycle with an edge marked by $-$.

References

1. Abiteboul, S., Hull, R., Vianu, V.: Foundations of Databases. Addison and Wesley, Reading (1995)
2. Antoniou, G., van Harmelen, F.: A Semantic Web Primer. MIT Press, Cambridge (2004)
3. Baader, F., Brandt, S., Lutz, C.: Pushing the EL envelope. In: Proceedings of IJCAI'2005, pp. 364–369. Morgan-Kaufmann, San Franciso (2005).
4. Baader, F., Brandt, S., Lutz, C.: Pushing the EL envelope further. In: Proceedings of the OWLED 2008 DC Workshop on OWL: Experiences and Directions (2008)
5. Calvanese, D., De Giacomo, G., Lembo, D., Lenzerini, M., Rosati, R.: Tractable reasoning and efficient query answering in description logics: the DL-Lite family. J. Autom. Reason. **39**(3), 385–429 (2007)
6. Cao, S.T., Nguyen, L.A., Szałas, A.: On the Web ontology rule language OWL 2 RL. In: Proceedings of ICCCI 2011. LNCS, vol. 6922, pp. 254–264. Springer, Berlin (2011)
7. Cao, S.T., Nguyen, L.A., Szalas, A.: WORL: a Web ontology rule language. In Proceedings of KSE'2011, pp. 32–39. IEEE Computer Society (2011)
8. Donini, F.M., Lenzerini, M., Nardi, D., Schaerf, A.: AL-log: Integrating Datalog and description logics. J. Intell. Inf. Syst. **10**(3), 227–252 (1998)
9. Drabent, W., Maluszynski, J.: Well-founded semantics for hybrid rules. In: Proceedings of RR'2007. LNCS, vol. 4524, pp. 1–15. Springer, Berlin (2007)

10. Eiter, T., Ianni, G., Lukasiewicz, T., Schindlauer, R.: Well-founded semantics for description logic programs in the Semantic Web. ACM Trans. Comput. Log. **12**(2), 11 (2011)

11. Van Gelder, A., Ross, K.A., Schlipf, J.S.: The well-founded semantics for general logic programs. J. ACM **38**(3), 620–650 (1991)

12. Gelfond, M., Lifschitz, V.: The stable model semantics for logic programming. In Proceedings of ICLP/SLP'1988, pp. 1070–1080. MIT Press, Cambridge (1988)

13. Grosof, B.N., Horrocks, I., Volz, R., Decker, S.: Description logic programs: combining logic programs with description logic. In: Proceedings of WWW'2003, pp. 48–57 (2003)

14. Horrocks, I., Patel-Schneider, P.F., Bechhofer, S., Tsarkov, D.: OWL rules: A proposal and prototype implementation. J. Web Sem. **3**(1), 23–40 (2005)

15. Hustadt, U., Motik, B., Sattler, U.: Reasoning in description logics by a reduction to disjunctive Datalog. J. Autom. Reason. **39**(3), 351–384 (2007)

16. Knorr, M., Alferes, J.J., Hitzler, P.: A coherent well-founded model for hybrid MKNF knowledge bases. In: Proceedings of ECAI'2008. Frontiers in Artificial Intelligence and Applications, vol. 178, pp. 99–103. IOS Press, Amsterdam (2008)

17. Levy, A.Y., Rousset, M.-C.: Combining Horn rules and description logics in CARIN. Artif. Intell. **104**(1–2), 165–209 (1998)

18. Motik, B., Rosati, R.: Reconciling description logics and rules. J. ACM. **57**(5) (2010)

19. Motik, B., Sattler, U., Studer, R.: Query answering for OWL-DL with rules. J. Web Sem. **3**(1), 41–60 (2005)

20. Nguyen, L.A., Nguyen, T.-B.-L., Szałas, A.: Horn-DL: an expressive Horn description logic with PTime data complexity. In Proceedings of RR'2013. LNCS, vol. 7994, pp. 259–264. Springer, Berlin (2013)

21. Ortiz, M., Rudolph, S., Simkus, M.: Worst-case optimal reasoning for the Horn-DL fragments of OWL 1 and 2. In: Proceedings of KR'2010. AAAI Press, Cambridge (2010)

22. http://www.w3.org/TR/owl2-profiles/#OWL_2_RL (2009)

23. Ricca, F., Gallucci, L., Schindlauer, R., Dell'Armi, T., Grasso, G., Leone, N.: OntoDLV: an ASP-based system for enterprise ontologies. J. Log. Comput. **19**(4), 643–670 (2009)

24. Rosati, R.: DL+log: Tight integration of description logics and disjunctive Datalog. In: Proceedings of KR'2006, pp. 68–78. AAAI Press, Cambridge (2006)

3

Curve interpolation and shape modeling via probabilistic nodes combination

Dariusz Jacek Jakóbczak

Abstract The proposed method, called probabilistic nodes combination (PNC), is the method of 2D curve interpolation and modeling using the set of key points (knots or nodes). Nodes can be treated as characteristic points of the object for modeling. The model of each individual symbol or data can be built by choice of probability distribution function and nodes combination. PNC modeling via nodes combination and parameter γ as probability distribution function enables curve parameterization and interpolation for each specific data or handwritten symbol. Two-dimensional curve is modeled and interpolated via nodes combination and different functions as discrete or continuous probability distribution functions: polynomial, sine, cosine, tangent, cotangent, logarithm, exponent, arcsin, arccos, arctan, arccot or power function. The novelty of the paper consists of two generalizations: generalization of previous MHR method with various nodes combinations and generalization of linear interpolation with different (no basic) probability distribution functions and nodes combinations.

Keywords Curve interpolation · PNC method · Shape representation · Contour parameterization · Nodes combination · Probabilistic modeling

1 Introduction

Probabilistic modeling is still a developing branch of computer science: operational research (for example probabilistic model-based prognosis) [1], decision making techniques and

D. J. Jakóbczak (✉)
Department of Electronics and Computer Science,
Technical University of Koszalin, Sniadeckich 2,
75-453 Koszalin, Poland
e-mail: djakob@ie.tu.koszalin.pl; dariusz.jakobczak@tu.koszalin.pl

probabilistic modeling [2], artificial intelligence and machine learning. Different aspects of probabilistic methods are used: stochastic processes and stochastic model-based techniques, Markov processes [3], Poisson processes, Gamma processes, a Monte Carlo method, Bayes rule, conditional probability and many probability distributions. In this paper the goal of probability distribution function is to describe the position of unknown points between the given interpolation nodes. two-dimensional curve (opened or closed) is used to represent the data points.

The paper clarifies the significance and novelty of the proposed method compared to existing methods (for example, polynomial interpolations and Bézier curves in Sect. 2.1). Previous published papers of the author dealt with the method of Hurwitz–Radon matrices (MHR method). The novelty of this paper and the proposed method consists in the fact that calculations are free from the family of Hurwitz–Radon matrices. The problem statement of this paper is: *how to reconstruct (interpolate) missing points of 2D curve having a set of interpolation nodes (key points) and using the information about probabilistic distribution of unknown points.* For example, the simplest basic distribution leads to the easiest interpolation—linear interpolation. Apart from probability distribution, additionally there is the second factor of the proposed interpolation method: nodes combination. The simplest nodes combination is zero. Thus, the proposed curve modeling is based on two agents: probability distribution and nodes combination. The first trial of probabilistic modeling in the MHR version was described in [4]. The significance of this paper consists in generalization for the MHR method: the computations are done without matrices in curve fitting and shape modeling, with clear point interpolation formula based on probability distribution function (continuous or discrete) and nodes combination. The paper also consists of generalization for linear interpolation with different (no basic) probability distribution functions and nodes combinations. So this paper answers the question: "Why and when should we use PNC method?".

Curve interpolation [5] represents one of the most important problems in mathematics and computer science: how do we model the curve [6] via a discrete set of two-dimensional points [7]? Also the matter of shape representation (as closed curve—contour) and curve parameterization is still open [8]. For example, pattern recognition, signature verification or handwriting identification problems are based on curve modeling via the choice of key points. So interpolation is not only a pure mathematical problem, but important task in computer vision and artificial intelligence. The paper wants to approach a problem of curve modeling by characteristic points. The proposed method relies on nodes combination and functional modeling of curve points situated between the basic set of key points. The functions that are used in calculations represent a whole family of elementary functions with inverse functions: polynomials, trigonometric, cyclometric, logarithmic, exponential and power function. These functions are treated as probability distribution functions in the range [0; 1].

2 Shape representation and curve reconstruction

An important problem in machine vision and computer vision [9] is that of appropriate shape representation and reconstruction. Classical discussion about shape representation is based on the problem: contour versus skeleton. This paper votes for contour which forms the boundary of the object. The contour of the object, represented by contour points, consists of information which allows us to describe many important features of the object as shape coefficients [10]. In the paper, contour deals with a set of curves. Curve modeling and generation is a basic subject in many branches of industry and computer science, for example in the CAD/CAM software.

The representation of shape has a great impact on the accuracy and effectiveness of object recognition [11]. In the literature, shape has been represented by many options including curves [12], graph-based algorithms and medial axis [13] to enable shape-based object recognition. Digital curve (open or closed) can be represented by chain code (Freeman's code). Chain code depends on selection of the started point and transformations of the object. So Freeman's code is one of the methods to describe and find the contour of the object. An analog (continuous) version of Freeman's code is the curve $\alpha - s$. Another contour representation and reconstruction is based on Fourier coefficients calculated in discrete Fourier transformation (DFT). These coefficients are used to fix the similarity of the contours with different sizes or directions. If we assume that the contour is built from segments of a line and fragments of circles or ellipses, Hough transforma-tion is applied to detect the contour lines. Also, geometrical moments of the object are used during the process of object shape representation [14].

2.1 A comparative analysis with other interpolation methods (why only polynomials?)

All interpolation theory is based on polynomials. But why? Many kinds of polynomials are used for interpolation: classical polynomials, trigonometric polynomials, orthogonal polynomials (Tschebyscheff, Legendre, Laguerre), rational polynomials. But what about the exceptional situations with unexpected features of curve, data or nodes. Then polynomials are not the solution, for example when:

1. The curve is not a graph of function (no matter—open or closed curve).
2. The curve does not have to be smooth at the interpolation nodes: for example, curve representing symbols, signature, handwriting or other specific data.
3. Nodes are fixed and there is no possibility of choosing "better" nodes as for orthogonal polynomials.
4. The curve differs considerably from any interpolation polynomial.
5. The curve fails to be differentiable at some points.
6. between each pair of nodes we are not interested in linear interpolation (basic probability distribution and zero nodes combination), but there ought to be some generalization (even for two nodes only) with other probability distributions and nodes combinations.
7. Interpolated points depend on some chosen nodes (two nearest nodes or more) via nodes combination $h(p_1, p_2, \ldots, p_m)$ in (1).
8. We are not interested in the formula of interpolation function (for lower computational costs), but only calculated points of modeled curve are ready to be used in numerical computations.
9. The formula of curve or function is known, but for some reason (for example, high computational costs or hard polynomial interpolation), the curve has to be modeled or fitted in some way for numerical calculations—the examples for PNC interpolation (in MHR version) of functions $f(x) = 2/x$ and $f(x) = 1/(1 + 5x^2)$ with quantified measures and experimental comparison with classical polynomial interpolation in [15].
10. Extrapolation problem is also a big numerical challenge and PNC interpolation enables the extension into extrapolation [16] with α outside of [0; 1] and $\gamma = F(\alpha)$ still strictly monotonic, $F(0) = 0$, $F(1) = 1$. So for example $\gamma = \alpha^2$ is impossible for extrapolation if $\alpha \le 0$ [17]. Polynomial or other interpolations are sometimes useless for extrapolation.

11. Having only nodes the user may have "negative" information (from specific character of data): no polynomial interpolation.
12. All calculations are numerical (discrete)—even $\gamma = F(\alpha)$ is to be given in tabular (discrete) form. There is no need to build continuous function: polynomial or others.
13. The parametric version of the modeled curve is to be found.

The above 13 important and heavy individual and characteristic features of some curves and their interpolations show that there may exist situations with unexpected assumptions for interpolation.

Why not classical interpolation? Classical methods are useless to interpolate the function that fails to be differentiable at one point, for example the absolute value function $f(x) = |x|$ at $x = 0$. If point $(0; 0)$ is one of the interpolation nodes, then precise polynomial interpolation of the absolute value function is impossible. Also, when the graph of the interpolated function differs from the shape of the polynomial considerably, for example $f(x) = 1/x$, interpolation is very hard because of existing local extrema and the roots of the polynomial. We cannot forget about the Runge's phenomenon: when nodes are equidistance then high-order polynomial oscillates toward the end of the interval, for example close to -1 and 1 with function $f(x) = 1/(1 + 25x^2)$ [7]. These classical negative cases do not appear in the proposed PNC method. Experimental comparison for PNC with polynomial interpolation is to be found in [15,18].

Nowadays, methods apply mainly polynomial functions in different versions (trigonometric, orthogonal, rational) and for example Bernstein polynomials in Bézier curves, splines [19] and NURBS [20]. But Bézier curves do not represent the interpolation method (rather interpolation-approximation method) and cannot be used for example in handwriting modeling with key points (interpolation nodes). In comparison, the PNC method with Bézier curves, Hermite curves and B-curves (B-splines) or NURBS has one unpleasant feature: small change of one characteristic point can result in unwanted change of the whole reconstructed curve. Such a feature does not appear in the proposed PNC method which is more stable than Bézier curves. Only the first and last characteristic points are situated on the Bézier curve (interpolation), the rest of the characteristic points lay outside the Bézier curve (approximation). Numerical methods for data interpolation are based on polynomial or trigonometric functions, for example Lagrange, Newton, Aitken and Hermite methods. These methods have many weak sides [21] and are not sufficient for curve interpolation in the situations when the curve cannot be built by polynomials or trigonometric functions. Also, there exist several well-established methods of curve modeling, for example shape-preserving techniques

[22], subdivision algorithms [23] and others [24] to overcome the difficulties of polynomial interpolation, but probabilistic interpolation with nodes combination seems to be quite novel in the area of shape modeling. The proposed 2D curve interpolation is the functional modeling via any elementary functions and it helps us to fit the curve during the computations.

This paper presents novel probabilistic nodes combination (PNC) method of curve interpolation. This paper takes up the new PNC method of two-dimensional curve modeling via the examples using the family of Hurwitz–Radon matrices (MHR method) [25], but not only that (other nodes combinations). The method of PNC requires minimal assumptions: the only information about a curve is the set of at least two nodes. The proposed PNC method is applied to curve modeling via different coefficients: polynomial, sinusoidal, cosinusoidal, tangent, cotangent, logarithmic, exponential, arcsin, arccos, arctan, arccot or power. The function for PNC calculations is chosen individually at each interpolation and represents the probability distribution function of parameter $\alpha \in [0; 1]$ for every point situated between two interpolation knots. The PNC method uses two-dimensional vectors (x, y) for curve modeling—knots $p_i = (x_i, y_i) \in \boldsymbol{R}^2$ in the PNC method, $i = 1, 2, \ldots n$:

1. PNC needs two knots or more ($n \geq 2$).
2. If the first node and the last node are the same ($p_1 = p_n$), then the curve is closed (contour).
3. For more precise modeling, knots ought to be settled at key points of the curve, for example local minimum or maximum and at least one node between two successive local extrema.

Condition 3 means for example the highest point of the curve in a particular orientation, convexity changing or curvature extrema. So this paper wants to answer the question: how do we interpolate the curve by a set of knots [26]?

Nodes on Fig. 1 represent the characteristic points of the handwritten letter or symbol: if $n = 5$ then the curve is open and if $n = 6$ then the curve is closed (contour). The examples of PNC curve modeling for these nodes are described

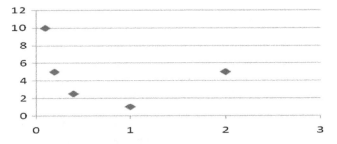

Fig. 1 Five knots of the curve before modeling

later in this paper (Sect. 3). The coefficients for PNC curve modeling are computed using nodes combinations and probability distribution functions: polynomials, power functions, sine, cosine, tangent, cotangent, logarithm, exponent or arcsin, arccos, arctan or arccot.

3 Novelty of probabilistic interpolation and modeling technique

The method of PNC enables computing points between two successive nodes of the curve: calculated points are interpolated and parameterized for real number $\alpha \in [0; 1]$ in the range of two successive nodes. The PNC method uses the combinations of nodes $p_1 = (x_1, y_1)$, $p_2 = (x_2, y_2), \ldots, p_n = (x_n, y_n)$ as $h(p_1, p_2, \ldots, p_m)$ and $m = 1, 2, \ldots n$. Nodes combination h is defined individually for each curve to interpolate points (x, y) with second coordinate $y = y(c)$ for any first coordinate $x = c$ situated between nodes (x_i, y_i) and (x_{i+1}, y_{i+1}):

$$c = \alpha \cdot x_i + (1 - \alpha) \cdot x_{i+1}, \quad i = 1, 2, \ldots n - 1,$$
$$y(c) = \gamma \cdot y_i + (1 - \gamma)y_{i+1} + \gamma(1 - \gamma) \cdot h(p_1, p_2, \ldots, p_m),$$
$$\alpha \in [0; 1], \quad \gamma = F(\alpha) \in [0; 1]. \tag{1}$$

So, c and α represent the same—coordinate x of any point (x, y) between two successive nodes (x_i, y_i) and (x_{i+1}, y_{i+1}): having c we can calculate α and vice versa. PNC curve modeling relies on two factors: function $\gamma = F(\alpha)$ and nodes combination $h(p_1, p_2, \ldots, p_m)$. Function F is a probabilistic distribution function for random variable $\alpha \in [0; 1]$ and parameter γ leads PNC interpolation into probabilistic modeling. The second factor, the combination of nodes h, is responsible for making dependent a reconstructed point on the coordinates of several nodes. The simplest case is for $h = 0$. Here are the examples of h computed for the MHR method [18]:

$$h(p_1, p_2) = \frac{y_1}{x_1}x_2 + \frac{y_2}{x_2}x_1$$

(only two neighboring nodes are taken for PNC calculations) or

$$h(p_1, p_2, p_3, p_4)$$
$$= \frac{1}{x_1^2 + x_3^2}(x_1 x_2 y_1 + x_2 x_3 y_3 + x_3 x_4 y_1 - x_1 x_4 y_3)$$
$$+ \frac{1}{x_2^2 + x_4^2}(x_1 x_2 y_2 + x_1 x_4 y_4 + x_3 x_4 y_2 - x_2 x_3 y_4)$$

(more than two neighboring nodes are used in PNC interpolation).

The examples of other nodes combinations are presented in Sect. 3. Formula (1) represents curve parameterization $(x(\alpha), y(\alpha))$ between two successive nodes (x_i, y_i) and

(x_{i+1}, y_{i+1}) as $\alpha \in [0; 1]$:

$$x(\alpha) = \alpha \cdot x_i + (1 - \alpha) \cdot x_{i+1}$$

and

$$y(\alpha) = F(\alpha) \cdot y_i + (1 - F(\alpha))y_{i+1}$$
$$+ F(\alpha)(1 - F(\alpha)) \cdot h(p_1, p_2, \ldots, p_m),$$
$$y(\alpha) = F(\alpha) \cdot (y_i - y_{i+1})$$
$$+ (1 - F(\alpha)) \cdot h(p_1, p_2, \ldots, p_m)) + y_{i+1}.$$

The proposed parameterization gives us an infinite number of possibilities for curve calculations (determined by choice of F and h) as there is an infinite number of human handwritten letters and symbols. Nodes combination is the individual feature of each modeled curve (for example a handwritten character). Coefficient $\gamma = F(\alpha)$ and nodes combination h are key factors in PNC curve interpolation and shape modeling.

3.1 Distribution functions in PNC interpolation and curve fitting

Points settled between the nodes are computed using the PNC method. Each real number $c \in [a; b]$ is calculated by a convex combination $c = \alpha \cdot a + (1 - \alpha) \cdot b$ for

$$\alpha = \frac{b - c}{b - a} \in [0; 1].$$

The key question is dealing with coefficient γ in (1). The simplest way of PNC calculation means $h = 0$ and $\gamma = \alpha$ (basic probability distribution). Then, PNC represents a linear interpolation. The MHR method [27] is not a linear interpolation. MHR [15] is an example of PNC modeling.

Each interpolation requires specific distribution of parameter α and γ (1) depending on parameter $\alpha \in [0; 1]$:

$$\gamma = F(\alpha), \quad F : [0; 1] \rightarrow [0; 1], F(0) = 0, F(1) = 1$$

and F is strictly monotonic.

Coefficient γ is calculated using different functions (polynomials, power functions, sine, cosine, tangent, cotangent, logarithm, exponent, arcsin, arccos, arctan or arccot, also inverse functions) and the choice of function is connected with initial requirements and curve specifications. Different values of coefficient γ are connected with applied functions $F(\alpha)$. The functions (2)–(34) represent the examples of probability distribution functions for random variable $\alpha \in [0; 1]$ and real number $s > 0$:

1. power function

$$\gamma = \alpha^s \quad \text{with } s > 0. \tag{2}$$

For $s = 1$: basic version of PNC and MHR [28] methods when $\gamma = \alpha$.

2. sine

$$\gamma = \sin(\alpha^s \cdot \pi/2), \quad s > 0 \tag{3}$$

or

$$\gamma = \sin^s(\alpha \cdot \pi/2), \quad s > 0. \tag{4}$$
$$\text{For } s = 1 : \gamma = \sin(\alpha \cdot \pi/2). \tag{5}$$

3. cosine

$$\gamma = 1 - \cos(\alpha^s \cdot \pi/2), \quad s > 0 \tag{6}$$

or

$$\gamma = 1 - \cos^s(\alpha \cdot \pi/2), \quad s > 0. \tag{7}$$
$$\text{For } s = 1 : \gamma = 1 - \cos(\alpha \cdot \pi/2). \tag{8}$$

4. tangent

$$\gamma = \tan(\alpha^s \cdot \pi/4), \quad s > 0 \tag{9}$$

or

$$\gamma = \tan^s(\alpha \cdot \pi/4), \quad s > 0. \tag{10}$$
$$\text{For } s = 1 : \gamma = \tan(\alpha \cdot \pi/4). \tag{11}$$

5. logarithm

$$\gamma = \log_2(\alpha^s + 1), \quad s > 0 \tag{12}$$

or

$$\gamma = \log_2^s(\alpha + 1), \quad s > 0. \tag{13}$$
$$\text{For } s = 1 : \gamma = \log_2(\alpha + 1). \tag{14}$$

6. exponent

$$\gamma = \left(\frac{a^\alpha - 1}{a - 1}\right)^s, \quad s > 0 \text{ and } a > 0 \text{ and } a \neq 1. \tag{15}$$
$$\text{For } s = 1 \text{ and } a = 2 : \gamma = 2^\alpha - 1. \tag{16}$$

7. arcsine

$$\gamma = 2/\pi \cdot \arcsin(\alpha^s), \quad s > 0 \tag{17}$$

or

$$\gamma = (2/\pi \cdot \arcsin\alpha)^s, \quad s > 0. \tag{18}$$
$$\text{For } s = 1 : \gamma = 2/\pi \cdot \arcsin(\alpha). \tag{19}$$

8. arccosine

$$\gamma = 1 - 2/\pi \cdot \arccos(\alpha^s), \quad s > 0 \tag{20}$$

or

$$\gamma = 1 - (2/\pi \cdot \arccos\alpha)^s, \quad s > 0. \tag{21}$$
$$\text{For } s = 1 : \gamma = 1 - 2/\pi \cdot \arccos(\alpha). \tag{22}$$

9. arctangent

$$\gamma = 4/\pi \cdot \arctan(\alpha^s), \quad s > 0 \tag{23}$$

or

$$\gamma = (4/\pi \cdot \arctan\alpha)^s, \quad s > 0. \tag{24}$$
$$\text{For } s = 1 : \gamma = 4/\pi \cdot \arctan(\alpha). \tag{25}$$

10. cotangent

$$\gamma = \text{ctg}(\pi/2 - \alpha^s \cdot \pi/4), \quad s > 0 \tag{26}$$

or

$$\gamma = \text{ctg}^s(\pi/2 - \alpha \cdot \pi/4), \quad s > 0. \tag{27}$$
$$\text{For } s = 1 : \gamma = \text{ctg}(\pi/2 - \alpha \cdot \pi/4). \tag{28}$$

11. arccotangent

$$\gamma = 2 - 4/\pi \cdot \text{arcctg}(\alpha^s), \quad s > 0 \tag{29}$$

or

$$\gamma = (2 - 4/\pi \cdot \text{arcctg}\alpha)^s, \quad s > 0. \tag{30}$$
$$\text{For } s = 1 : \gamma = 2 - 4/\pi \cdot \text{arcctg}(\alpha). \tag{31}$$

Functions used in γ calculations (2)–(31) are strictly monotonic for random variable $\alpha \in [0; 1]$ as $\gamma = F(\alpha)$ is a probability distribution function. Also, inverse function $F^{-1}(\alpha)$ is appropriate for γ calculations. The choice of function and value s depends on curve specifications and individual requirements.

The proposed (2)–(31) probability distributions are continuous, but of course parameter γ can represent discrete probability distributions, for example: $F(0.1) = 0.23$, $F(0.2) = 0.3$, $F(0.3) = 0.42$, $F(0.4) = 0.52$, $F(0.5) = 0.63$, $F(0.6) = 0.69$, $F(0.7) = 0.83$, $F(0.8) = 0.942$, $F(0.9) = 0.991$. What is very important in the PNC method is that two curves (for example a handwritten letter) may have the same set of nodes, but different h or γ results in different interpolations (Figs. 2, 3, 4, 5, 6, 7, 8, 9, 10, 11, 12, 13, 14, 15, 16, 17, 18).

The algorithm of PNC interpolation and modeling (1) is as follows:

Step 1: Choice of knots p_i at key points.

Step 2: Choice of nodes combination $h(p_1, p_2, \ldots, p_m)$.

Step 3: Choice of distribution $\gamma = F(\alpha)$: (2)–(31) or others (continuous or discrete).

Step 4: Determining values of α: $\alpha = 0.1, 0.2\ldots0.9$ (nine points) or $0.01, 0.02\ldots0.99$ (99 points) or others.

Step 5: The computations (1).

These five steps can be treated as the algorithm of PNC method of curve modeling and interpolation (1). Without knowledge about the formula of curve or function, PNC inter-

polation has to implement the coefficients γ (2)–(31), but PNC is not limited only to these coefficients. Each strictly monotonic function F between points $(0; 0)$ and $(1; 1)$ can be used in PNC modeling.

4 Handwritten symbol modeling and curve fitting

Curve knots $p_1 = (0.1; 10)$, $p_2 = (0.2; 5)$, $p_3 = (0.4; 2.5)$, $p_4 = (1; 1)$ and $p_5 = (2; 5)$ from Fig. 1 are used in some examples of PNC method in handwritten character modeling. Figures 2, 3, 4, 5, 6, 7, 8, 9 represent PNC as MHR interpolation [29] with different γ. The points of the curve are calculated with no matrices ($N = 1$) and $\gamma = \alpha$ in example 1 and with matrices of dimension $N = 2$ in Examples 2–8 for $\alpha = 0.1, 0.2, \ldots, 0.9$.

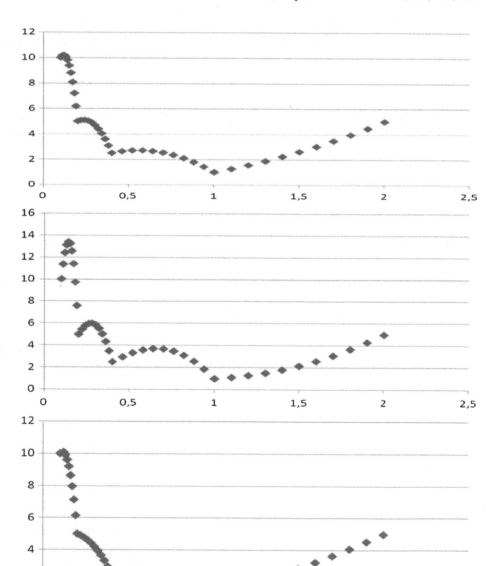

Fig. 2 PNC character modeling for nine reconstructed points between nodes

Fig. 3 Sinusoidal modeling with nine reconstructed curve points between nodes

Fig. 4 Tangent character modeling with nine interpolated points between nodes

Fig. 5 Tangent curve modeling with nine recovered points between nodes

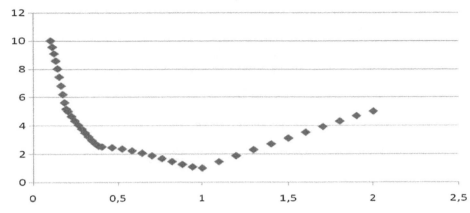

Fig. 6 Tangent symbol modeling with nine reconstructed points between nodes

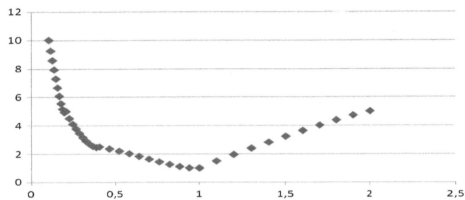

Fig. 7 Sinusoidal modeling with nine interpolated curve points between nodes

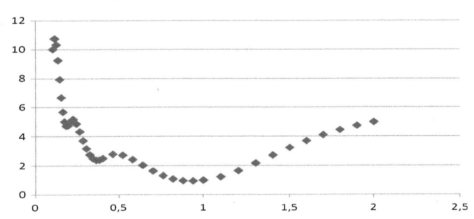

Example 1 PNC curve interpolation (1) for $\gamma = \alpha$ and

$$h(p_1, p_2) = \frac{y_1}{x_1} x_2 + \frac{y_2}{x_2} x_1 :$$

For $N = 2$ (Examples 2–8) MHR version [30] as PNC method gives us

$$h(p_1, p_2, p_3, p_4)$$
$$= \frac{1}{x_1^2 + x_3^2} (x_1 x_2 y_1 + x_2 x_3 y_3 + x_3 x_4 y_1 - x_1 x_4 y_3)$$
$$+ \frac{1}{x_2^2 + x_4^2} (x_1 x_2 y_2 + x_1 x_4 y_4 + x_3 x_4 y_2 - x_2 x_3 y_4).$$

Example 2 PNC sinusoidal interpolation with $\gamma = \sin(\alpha \cdot \pi/2)$.

Example 3 PNC tangent interpolation for $\gamma = \tan(\alpha \cdot \pi/4)$.

Example 4 PNC tangent interpolation with $\gamma = \tan(\alpha^s \cdot \pi/4)$ and $s = 1.5$.

Example 5 PNC tangent curve interpolation for $\gamma = \tan(\alpha^s \cdot \pi/4)$ and $s = 1.797$.

Example 6 PNC sinusoidal interpolation with $\gamma = \sin(\alpha^s \cdot \pi/2)$ and $s = 2.759$.

Example 7 PNC power function modeling for $\gamma = \alpha^s$ and $s = 2.1205$.

Example 8 PNC logarithmic curve modeling with $\gamma = \log_2(\alpha^s + 1)$ and $s = 2.533$.

Fig. 8 Power function curve modeling with nine recovered points between nodes

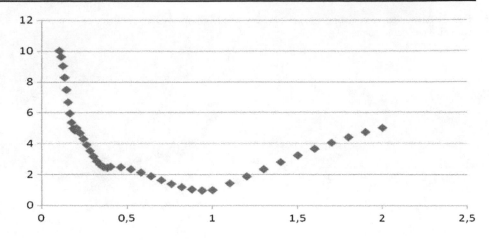

Fig. 9 Logarithmic character modeling with nine reconstructed points between nodes

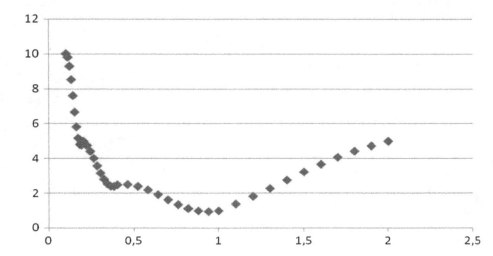

Fig. 10 Quadratic symbol modeling with nine reconstructed points between nodes

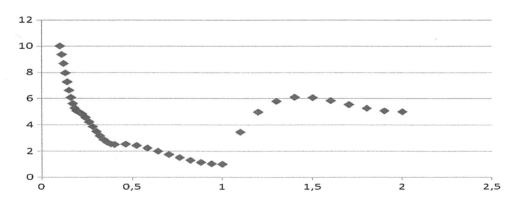

Fig. 11 Cubic character modeling with nine reconstructed points between nodes

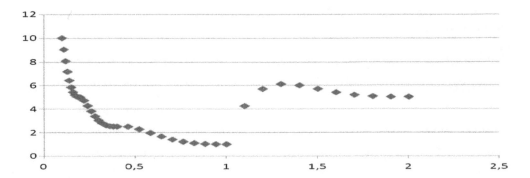

Fig. 12 Quadratic contour modeling with nine reconstructed points between nodes

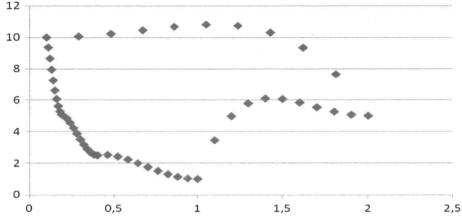

Fig. 13 Cubic shape modeling with nine reconstructed points between nodes

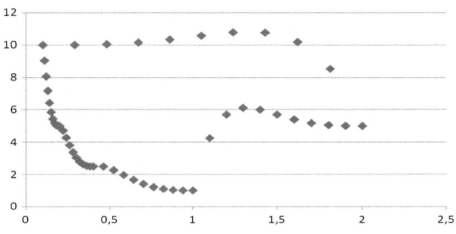

Fig. 14 Beta distribution in handwritten character modeling

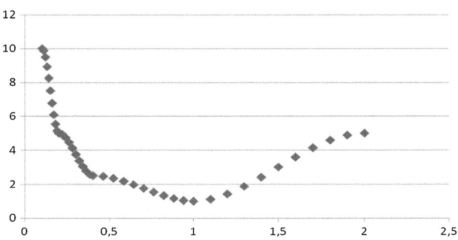

These eight examples demonstrate the possibilities of PNC curve interpolation and handwritten character modeling for key nodes in the MHR version. Here are other examples of PNC modeling (but not MHR):

Example 9 PNC for $\gamma = \alpha^2$ and $h(p_1, p_2) = x_1 y_1 + x_2 y_2$:

Example 10 PNC for $\gamma = \alpha^3$ and $h(p_1, p_2) = x_1 y_1 + x_2 y_2$:

If we consider Fig. 1 as closed curve (contour) with the node $p_6 = p_1 = (0.1; 10)$, then Examples 9 and 10 give the shapes:

Example 11 PNC for $\gamma = \alpha^2$ and $h(p_1, p_2) = x_1 y_1 + x_2 y_2$:

Example 12 PNC for $\gamma = \alpha^3$ and $h(p_1, p_2) = x_1 y_1 + x_2 y_2$:

Every man has an individual style of handwriting. Recognition of handwritten letter or symbol needs modeling, and the model of each individual symbol or character can be built

Fig. 15 Beta distribution in handwritten symbol modeling

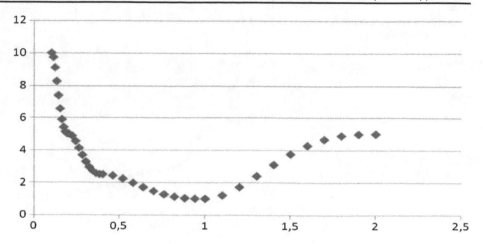

Fig. 16 Beta distribution in handwritten letter modeling

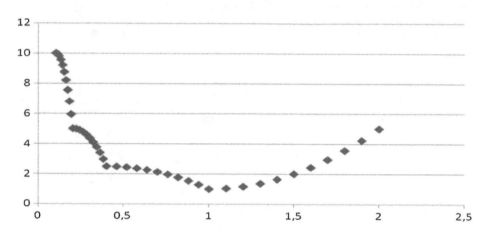

Fig. 17 Exponential distribution in handwritten character modeling

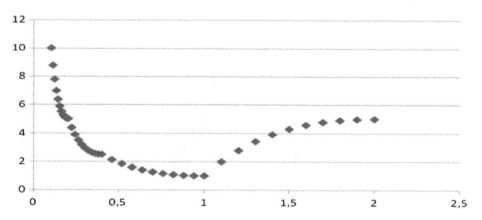

by choice of γ and h in (1). PNC modeling via nodes combinations h and parameter γ as probability distribution function enables curve interpolation for each specific letter or symbol.

The number of reconstructed points depends on a user by value α. If for example $\alpha = 0.01, 0.02, \ldots, 0.99$, then 99 points are interpolated for each pair of nodes. The reconstructed values and interpolated points, calculated by the PNC method, are applied in the process of curve modeling. Every curve can be interpolated by some distribution function as parameter γ and nodes combination h. Parameter γ is treated as the probability distribution function for each curve.

4.1 Beta distribution

Considering the probability distribution functions used nowadays for random variable $\alpha \in [0; 1]$—one distribution deals with the range $[0; 1]$, beta distribution. The probability density function f for random variable $\alpha \in [0; 1]$ is:

$$f(\alpha) = c \cdot \alpha^s \cdot (1 - \alpha)^r, \quad s \geq 0, r \geq 0. \tag{32}$$

When $r = 0$ probability density function (32) represents $f(\alpha) = c \cdot \alpha^s$ and then probability distribution function F is like (2), for example $f(\alpha) = 3\alpha^2$ and $\gamma = \alpha^3$. If s and r

Fig. 18 Exponential distribution in handwritten symbol modeling

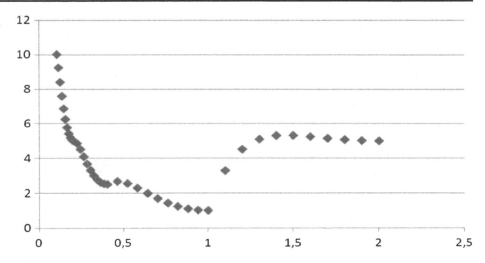

are positive integer numbers, then γ is the polynomial; for example $f(\alpha) = 6\alpha(1 - \alpha)$ and $\gamma = 3\alpha^2 - 2\alpha^3$. So, beta distribution gives us coefficient γ in (1) as the polynomial because of interdependence between probability density f and distribution F functions:

$$f(\alpha) = F'(\alpha), \quad F(\alpha) = \int_0^\alpha f(t)\,dt. \tag{33}$$

For example, (33):

$$f(\alpha) = \alpha \cdot e^\alpha \quad \text{and} \quad \gamma = F(\alpha) = 1 - (1 - \alpha)e^\alpha. \tag{34}$$

The basic distribution ($\gamma = \alpha$) with nodes combination $h = 0$ turns PNC interpolation (1) to linear interpolation. What about PNC in the case of yet another distribution in the range $[0; 1]$: beta distribution (32)? Power functions as γ used in Examples 1, 7 and 9–12 are also connected with beta distribution. Here are the examples of PNC modeling for beta distribution with nodes combination $h = 0$.

Example 13 PNC for $\gamma = 3\alpha^2 - 2\alpha^3$ and $h(p_1, p_2) = 0$:

Example 14 PNC for $\gamma = 4\alpha^3 - 3\alpha^4$ and $h(p_1, p_2) = 0$:

Example 15 PNC for $\gamma = 2\alpha - \alpha^2$ and $h(p_1, p_2) = 0$:

Examples 9–12 represent beta distribution with $h(p_1, p_2) = x_1 y_1 + x_2 y_2$.

4.2 Exponential distribution

Exponential distribution deals with random variable ≥ 0, but in the PNC interpolation random variable $\alpha \in [0; 1]$. Then exponential distribution is represented by distribution function (34):

$$\gamma = F(\alpha) = 1 - (1 - \alpha)e^\alpha.$$

Example 16 PNC for $\gamma = 1 - (1 - \alpha)e^\alpha$ and $h(p_1, p_2) = 0$:

Example 17 PNC for $\gamma = 1 - (1 - \alpha)e^\alpha$ and $h(p_1, p_2) = \frac{y_2}{y_1} + \frac{x_2}{x_1}$:

These examples show the variety of possibilities in curve modeling via the choice of nodes combination and probability distribution function for interpolated points.

5 Conclusions

Why and when should we use the PNC method? Interpolation methods and curve fitting represent huge problems that each individual interpolation is exceptional and requires specific solutions. The PNC method is a novel tool with all its pros and cons. The user has to decide which interpolation method is the best in a single situation. The choice is yours if you have any choice. The presented method is such a new possibility for curve fitting and interpolation when specific data (for example handwritten symbol or character) starts up with no rules for polynomial interpolation. This paper consists of two generalizations: of the previous MHR method with various nodes combinations and of linear interpolation with different (no basic) probability distribution functions and nodes combinations.

The method of probabilistic nodes combination (PNC) enables interpolation and modeling of two-dimensional curves using nodes combinations and different coefficients γ: polynomial, sinusoidal, cosinusoidal, tangent, cotangent, logarithmic, exponential, arcsin, arccos, arctan, arccot or power function, and also inverse functions. This probabilistic view is a novel approach for a problem of modeling and interpolation. Computer vision and pattern recognition are interested in appropriate methods of shape representation and curve modeling. The PNC method represents the possibilities of shape reconstruction and curve interpolation via the choice of nodes combination and probability distribution function for interpolated points. It seems to be quite new to look at the problem of contour representation and curve modeling in artificial intelligence and computer vision.

The function for γ calculations is chosen individually at each curve modeling and treated as a probability distribution function: γ depends on the initial requirements and curve specifications. The PNC method leads to curve interpolation as handwriting modeling via a discrete set of fixed knots. So, PNC makes a combination of two important problems possible: interpolation and modeling. The main features of the PNC method are:

a) the smaller the distance between the knots, it is better;
b) calculations for coordinates close to zero and near extremum require more attention because of the importance of these points;
c) PNC interpolation develops a linear interpolation into other functions as probability distribution functions;
d) PNC is a generalization of the MHR method via different nodes combinations;
e) interpolation of L points is connected with the computational cost of rank $O(L)$ as in the MHR method;
f) nodes combination and coefficient γ are crucial in the process of curve probabilistic parameterization and interpolation: they are computed individually for a single curve.

Future works include application of the PNC method in signature and handwriting recognition, choice and features of nodes combinations and coefficient γ, implementation of PNC in computer vision and artificial intelligence in shape geometry, contour modelling, object recognition and curve parameterization.

Open Access This article is distributed under the terms of the Creative Commons Attribution License which permits any use, distribution, and reproduction in any medium, provided the original author(s) and the source are credited.

References

1. Lorton, A., Fouladirad, M., Grall, A.: A methodology for probabilistic model-based prognosis. Eur. J. Oper. Res. **225**, 443–454 (2013)
2. Pergler, M., Freeman, A.: Probabilistic modeling as an exploratory decision-making tool. McKinsey Working Papers on Risk 6, pp. 1–18 (2008)
3. Cocozza-Thivent, C., Eymard, R., Mercier, S., Roussignol, M.: Characterization of the marginal distributions of Markov processes used in dynamic reliability. J. Appl. Math. Stoch. Anal. 1–18 (2006). Article ID 92156
4. Jakóbczak, D.: Probabilistic modeling of signature using the method of Hurwitz–Radon matrices. Glob. Perspect. Artif. Intell. **1**(1), 1–7 (January 2013)
5. Collins II, G.W.: Fundamental Numerical Methods and Data Analysis. Case Western Reserve University, Cleveland (2003)
6. Chapra, S.C.: Applied Numerical Methods. McGraw-Hill, New York (2012)
7. Ralston, A., Rabinowitz, P.: A First Course in Numerical Analysis, 2nd edn. Dover Publications, New York (2001)
8. Zhang, D., Lu, G.: Review of shape representation and description techniques. Pattern Recognit. **1**(37), 1–19 (2004)
9. Ballard, D.H.: Computer Vision. Prentice Hall, New York (1982)
10. Tadeusiewicz, R., Flasiński, M.: Image Recognition. PWN, Warsaw (1991)
11. Saber, E., Yaowu, X., Murat Tekalp, A.: Partial shape recognition by sub-matrix matching for partial matching guided image labeling. Pattern Recognit. **38**, 1560–1573 (2005)
12. Sebastian, T.B., Klein, P.N.: On aligning curves. IEEE Trans. Pattern Anal. Mach. Intell. **25**(1), 116–124 (2003)
13. Liu, T., Geiger, D.: Approximate tree matching and shape similarity. In: International Conference on Computer Vision, Corfu-Greece (1999)
14. Choraś, R.S.: Computer Vision. Exit, Warsaw (2005)
15. Jakóbczak, D.: Object modeling using method of Hurwitz-Radon matrices of rank k. In: Wolski, W., Borawski, M. (eds.) Computer Graphics: Selected Issues, pp. 79–90. University of Szczecin Press, Szczecin (2010)
16. Jakóbczak, D.: Data extrapolation and decision making via method of Hurwitz–Radon matrices. In: Jedrzejowicz, P., Nguyen, NT., Hoang, K. (eds.) Computational Collective Intelligence: Technologies and Applications (Proc. of ICCCI 2011, Part 1). Lecture Notes in Computer Science, vol. 6922, pp. 173–182. Springer, Berlin (2011)
17. Jakóbczak, D.: Curve extrapolation and data analysis using the method of Hurwitz–Radon matrices. Folia Oecon. Stetin. Szczec. Univ. **9**(17), 121–138 (2011)
18. Jakóbczak, D.: Curve interpolation using Hurwitz–Radon matrices. Pol. J. Environ. Stud. **3B**(18), 126–130 (2009)
19. Schumaker, L.L.: Spline Functions: Basic Theory. Cambridge Mathematical Library, Cambridge (2007)
20. Rogers, D.F.: An Introduction to NURBS with Historical Perspective. Morgan Kaufmann Publishers, Menlo Park (2001)
21. Dahlquist, G., Bjoerck, A.: Numerical Methods. Prentice Hall, New York (1974)
22. Dejdumrong, N.: A shape preserving verification techniques for parametric curves. Comput. Graph. Imaging Vis. **2007**, 163–168 (2007)
23. Dyn, N., Levin, D., Gregory, J.A.: A 4-point interpolatory subdivision scheme for curve design. Comput. Aided. Geom. Design **4**, 257–268 (1987)
24. Kozera, R.: Curve Modeling via Interpolation Based on Multidimensional Reduced Data. Silesian University of Technology Press, Gliwice (2004)
25. Jakóbczak, D.: 2D and 3D image modeling using Hurwitz–Radon matrices. Pol. J. Environ. Stud. **4A**(16), 104–107 (2007)
26. Jakóbczak, D.: Shape representation and shape coefficients via method of Hurwitz–Radon matrices. In: Computer Vision and Graphics: Proceedings of ICCVG: Part I. Lecture Notes in Computer Science, vol. 6374, pp. 411–419. Springer, Berlin (2010)
27. Jakóbczak, D.: Application of Hurwitz–Radon matrices in shape representation. In: Banaszak, Z., Świć, A. (eds.) Applied Computer Science: Modelling of Production Processes, vol. 1, no. 6, pp. 63–74. Lublin University of Technology Press, Lublin (2010)
28. Jakóbczak, D.: Implementation of Hurwitz–Radon matrices in shape representation. In: Choraś, R.S. (ed.) Image Processing and Communications: Challenges 2. Advances in Intelligent and Soft Computing, vol. 84, pp. 39–50. Springer, Berlin (2010)
29. Jakóbczak, D.: Object recognition via contour points reconstruction using Hurwitz–Radon matrices. In: Józefczyk, J., Orski, D.

(eds.) Knowledge-Based Intelligent System Advancements: Systemic and Cybernetic Approaches, pp. 87–107. IGI Global, Hershey (2011)

30. Jakóbczak, D.: Curve parameterization and curvature via method of Hurwitz–Radon matrices. Image Process. Commun. Int. J. 1–2(16), 49–56 (2011)

4

Feature selection and replacement by clustering attributes

**Tzung-Pei Hong · Yan-Liang Liou ·
Shyue-Liang Wang · Bay Vo**

Abstract Feature selection is to find useful and relevant features from an original feature space to effectively represent and index a given dataset. It is very important for classification and clustering problems, which may be quite difficult to solve when the amount of attributes in a given training data is very large. They usually need a very time-consuming search to get the features desired. In this paper, we will try to select features based on attribute clustering. A distance measure for a pair of attributes based on the relative dependency is proposed. An attribute clustering algorithm, called Most Neighbors First, is also presented to cluster the attributes into a fixed number of groups. The representative attributes found in the clusters can be used for classification such that the whole feature space can be greatly reduced. Besides, if the values of some representative attributes cannot be obtained from current environments for inference, some other possible attributes in the same clusters can be used to achieve approximate inference results.

Keywords Attribute clustering · Feature selection ·
Representative attribute · Relative dependency

This is an extended version of the paper presented in The Sixth
International Conference on Machine Learning and Cybernetics.

T.-P. Hong
Department of Computer Science and Information Engineering,
National University of Kaohsiung, Kaohsiung, Taiwan

Y.-L. Liou
Department of Electrical Engineering,
National University of Kaohsiung, Kaohsiung, Taiwan
e-mail: egghead221@gmail.com

S.-L. Wang
Department of Information Management,
National University of Kaohsiung, Kaohsiung, Taiwan
e-mail: slwang@nuk.edu.tw

T.-P. Hong (✉)
Department of Computer Science and Engineering,
National Sun Yat-sen University, Kaohsiung, Taiwan
e-mail: tphong@nuk.edu.tw

B. Vo
Ton Duc Thang University, Ho Chi Minh, Vietnam
e-mail: vdbay@it.tdt.edu.vn

1 Introduction

Although a wide variety of expert systems has been built, knowledge acquisition remains a development bottleneck [2,21]. Building a large-scale expert system involves creating and extending a large knowledge base over the course of many months or years. Shortening the development time is thus the most important factor for the success of an expert system. In the past, machine-learning techniques were successfully developed to ease the knowledge-acquisition bottleneck. Among the proposed approaches, deriving rules from training examples is the most common [9,14,15]. Given a set of examples, a learning program tries to induce rules that describe each class.

In some application domains, the amount of attributes (or features) of given training data is very large (e.g. decades to hundreds). In this case, much computational time is needed to derive classification rules from the data. Besides, derived rules may contain too many features and more rules than actually desired may be obtained due to over-specialization. In fact, not all the attributes are indispensable. Some redundant, similar or dependent attributes may exist in the given training data. This phenomenon mainly results from attribute dependency. Redundant and similar attributes can be thought of as two special cases of dependent attributes. If there exists some dependency relationship between attributes, the dimension of the training data may thus be reduced.

The concept of reduced attributes has been used in many places. For example, in the rough set theory [16–19], the reduced set of attributes is also called a "reduct". Many possible reducts may exist at the same time. Even only a reduced set of attributes is used for classification, the indiscernibility relations still preserve among the attributes [10]. A minimal reduct, just as its literal meaning shows, is a reduct which cannot be reduced any more. It may not be unique as well. The classification work for a high-dimensional dataset can be done faster if a minimal reduct instead of the original entire set of attributes is used. Finding a minimal reduct is an NP-hard problem [20,22]. Besides, there may be no minimal reduct due to noise in training examples.

Some researches about finding approximate reducts were thus proposed. An approximate reduct is a minimal reduct with acceptable tolerance. It can usually be found in much shorter time relative to an exact minimal reduct. Besides, it usually consists of less attributes than an exact one. It is thus a good trade-off among accuracy, practicability and execution time. Many approaches for finding approximate reducts were proposed [3,7,26,27]. For example, Wróblewski [25] used the genetic algorithm to find approximate minimal reducts. Sun and Xiong [23] proposed an approach compatible with incomplete information systems. Al-Radaideh et al. [1] used the discernibility matrix and a weighting strategy to find the minimal reduct in a greedy strategy. Gao et al. [4] proposed a feature ranking strategy (similar to attribute weighting) with a sampling process included. Recently, approaches based on soft sets for attribute selection has also been proposed to reduce the execution time [13,20].

All the approaches mentioned above focus on the issue of finding a minimal reduct as soon as possible. However, if there are training examples with missing or unknown values, the approach may not correctly work. Besides, if only the chosen reduct is used in a learning process, the rules cannot contain other attributes and are hard to use if some attribute values in the reduct cannot be obtained in current environments.

In this paper, we solve the above problems from another viewpoint–attribute clustering. Note that we are doing clustering for attributes rather than for objects. Like the conventional clustering approaches for objects, the attributes within the same cluster are expected to possess high similarity, but within different clusters possess low similarity. Here, the dependency degrees between attributes are used to represent the similarities. Since the attributes are grouped into several clusters according to their similarity degrees, an attribute selected from a cluster can thus represent the attributes within the same cluster. An approximate reduct could then be formed from the chosen attributes gathered together. Note that the obtained result in this way is usu-ally an approximate reduct. The proposed approach has the following three advantages.

1. Guessing a missing value of an attribute from the other attributes within the same cluster should be more accurate and faster than that from all attributes.
2. If an object has missing values, its class can also be decided by the other attributes within the same cluster.
3. The proposed approach is flexible for representing rules since each attribute in a rule can be displaced with other attributes in the same cluster.

Besides, the proposed algorithm for clustering attributes is also implemented to verify its effects. Experimental results show that the average similarity of each cluster is related to the cluster number. As the cluster number increases, the average similarity of a cluster will also increase.

The remainder of this paper is organized as follows: Some related concepts including reduct, relative dependency and clustering are reviewed in Sect. 2. The proposed dissimilarity between a pair of attributes is explained in Sect. 3. An attribute clustering algorithm is proposed in Sect. 4. An example is given in Sect. 5 to illustrate the proposed algorithm. The experimental results and some discussions are described in Sect. 6. Conclusions and future work are finally stated in Sect. 7.

2 Related work

In this section, some important concepts related to this paper are briefly reviewed. The concept of reducts is first introduced, followed by the concept of relative dependency. Next, two famous clustering approaches, k-means and k-medoids, are described and compared. The reasons for why they are not suitable for clustering attributes are also described. An attribute clustering approach is thus proposed due to these problems and limitations.

2.1 Reducts

Let $I = (U, A)$ be an information system, where $U = \{x_1, x_2, \ldots, x_N\}$ is a finite non-empty set of objects and A is a finite non-empty set of attributes called condition attributes [10]. A decision system is an information system of the form $I = (U, A \cup \{d\})$, where d is a special attribute called decision attribute and $d \notin A$ [10]. For any object $x_i \in U$, its value for a condition attribute $a \in A$, is denoted by $f_a(x_i)$. The indiscernibility relation for a subset of attributes B is defined as:

$$\text{IND}(B) = \{(x, y) \in U \times U \mid \forall a \in B, \ f_a(x) = f_a(y)\},$$

where B is any subset of the condition attribute set A (i.e. $B \subseteq A$) [11]. If the indiscernibility relations from both A and

B are the same [i.e. $\text{IND}(B) = \text{IND}(A)$], then B is called a reduct of A. That means the attributes used in the information system can be reduced to B, with the original indiscernibility information still kept. Furthermore, if an attribute subset B satisfies the following condition, then B is called a minimal reduct of A:

$$\text{IND}(B) = \text{IND}(A) \quad \text{and} \quad \forall B' \subseteq B \ \text{IND}(B') \neq \text{IND}(A).$$

Take the simple information system in Table 1 as an example. In Table 1, the attribute set A consists of three attributes {Age, Income, Children} and the object set U consists of five objects $\{x_1, x_2, x_3, x_4, x_5\}$. Since $\text{IND}(\{\text{Age, Children}\})$ $= \text{IND}(A) = \{(x_1, x_1), (x_2, x_2), (x_3, x_3), (x_4, x_4), (x_5, x_5)\}$, the attribute subset {Age, Children} is a reduct of the information system. Besides, since neither $\text{IND}(\{\text{Age}\})$ nor $\text{IND}(\{\text{Children}\})$ equals $\text{IND}(A)$, the attribute subset {Age, Children} is a minimal reduct.

When a decision system, instead of an information system, is considered, the definition of a reduct B ($B \subseteq A$) can be modified as follows [25]:

$$\forall x_i, x_j \in U, \text{ if } f_B(x_i) = f_B(x_j), \text{ then } d(x_i) = d(x_j),$$

where $d(x_i)$ denotes the value of the decision attribute of the object x_i, $f_B(x_i)$ denotes the attribute values of x_i for the attribute set B. Similarly, if no subset of B can satisfy the above condition, B is called a minimal reduct in the decision system. Take the simple decision system shown in Table 2 as an example. It is modified from Table 1.

In Table 2, a decision attribute, Buying computers, is added to the original information system (Table 1) to form a decision system. In this example, the attribute subset {Age, Income} is not a reduct since the two objects x_1 and x_4 have

Table 1 A simple information system

Object	Age	Income	Children
x_1	Young	Low	No
x_2	Middle	Middle	Yes
x_3	Senior	High	Yes
x_4	Young	Low	Yes
x_5	Senior	Middle	No

Table 2 A simple decision system

Object	Age	Income	Children	Buying computers
x_1	Young	Low	No	No
x_2	Middle	Middle	Yes	No
x_3	Senior	High	Yes	Yes
x_4	Young	Low	Yes	Yes
x_5	Senior	Middle	No	No

the same values for the two attributes but belong to different classes. On the contrary, the attribute subset {Age, Children} is a reduct for the decision system. Furthermore, it is a minimal reduct since neither {Age} nor {Children} is a reduct. Finding minimal reducts has been proven as an NP-Hard problem. Li et al. [11] proposed the concept of "approximate" reducts to speed up the searching process. An approximate reduct allows for some reasonable tolerance degrees, but can greatly reduce the computation complexity. Next, the concept of relative dependency is introduced.

2.2 Relative dependency

Han [5] and Li et al. [11] developed an approach based on the relative dependency to find approximate reducts. The relative dependency is motivated by the operation "projection", which is very important in the relational algebra. It can also be easily executed by SQL or other query languages. Given an attribute subset $B \subseteq A$ and a decision attribute d, the projection of the object set U on B is denoted by $\Pi_B(U)$ and can be computed by the following two steps: removing attributes in the different set $(A - B)$ and merging all the remaining rows which are indiscernible [11]. Thus, among the tuples with the same attribute values for B, only one is kept and the others are removed. For example, the projection of the data in Table 2 on the attribute {Age} is shown below:

$$\Pi_{\{\text{Age}\}}(U) = \{x_1, x_2, x_3\}.$$

In this example, x_4 and x_5 are removed since they have the same value of the attribute Age as x_1 and x_3 have. Similarly, the projection on the attribute Children and on the attribute subset {Age, Children} is shown below:

$$\Pi_{\{\text{Children}\}}(U) = \{x_1, x_2\}, \quad \text{and}$$
$$\Pi_{\{\text{Age, Children}\}}(U) = \{x_1, x_2, x_3, x_4, x_5\}.$$

Han et al. thus defined the relative dependency degree (δ_B^D) of the attribute subset B with regard to the set of decision attributes D as follows:

$$\delta_B^D = \frac{|\Pi_B(U)|}{|\Pi_{B \cup D}(U)|},$$

where $|\Pi_B(U)|$ and $|\Pi_{B \cup D}(U)|$ are the numbers of tuples after the projection operations are performed on U according to B and $B \cup D$, respectively. Take the decision system shown in Table 2 as an example. $|\Pi_{\{\text{Age}\}}(U)| = |\{x_1, x_2, x_3\}| = 3$ and $|\Pi_{\{\text{Age, Buying computers}\}}(U)| = |\{x_1, x_2, x_3, x_4, x_3\}| = 5$. The relative dependency degree of {Age} with regard to {Buying computers} is thus 3/5, which is 0.6.

The goal of the paper is to cluster attributes such that the process of finding approximate reducts can be improved. For achieving this goal, it is thus important to develop an evaluation method which can measure the similarity of attributes.

This paper extends the concept of the relative dependency to compute the similarity between any two attributes and proposes an attribute clustering method. The proposed approach will be described in Sect. 3.

2.3 The k-means and the k-medoids clustering approaches

The k-means and the k-medoids approaches are two well-known partitioning (or clustering) strategies. They are widely used to cluster data when the number of clusters is given in advance. The k-means clustering approach [12] consists of two major steps: (1) reassigning objects to clusters and (2) updating the centers of clusters. The first step calculates the distances between each object and the k centers and reassigns the object to the group with the nearest center. The second step then calculates the new means of the k groups just updated and uses them as the new centers. These two steps are then iteratively executed until the clusters no longer change.

The k-medoids approach [8] adopts a quite different way of finding the centers of clusters. Assume k centers have been found. The k-medoids approach selects another object at random and replaces one of the original centers with the new object if better clustering results can be obtained. The absolute-error criterion [6] shown below is used to decide whether the replacement is better or not:

$$E = \sum_{j=1}^{k} \sum_{p \in C_j} |p - o_j|,$$

where E is the sum of the absolute errors for all the objects in the data set, p is an object in cluster C_j, o_j is the current center of C_j, and the absolute value $|p - o_j|$ means the distance between the two objects p and o_j. For each randomly selected object $o_{j'}$, one of the original k centers, say o_j, will be replaced with it and its new sum E' of absolute errors will be calculated. E' will then be compared with the previous E. If E' is less than E, then $o_{j'}$ is more suitable as a center than o_j. $o_{j'}$ thus actually replaces o_j as a new cluster center; otherwise, the replacement is aborted. The same procedure is repeated until the cluster centers no longer change.

The complexity of the k-medoids approach is in general higher than the k-means approach, but the former can guarantee that all the centers of clusters obtained are objects themselves. This feature is important to the proposed attribute clustering here, since not only the attributes are clustered but also the representative attribute of each cluster has to be found. On the contrary, the k-means approach may use non-object points as cluster centers. Note that both the k-means and the k-medoids approaches are mainly designed to cluster objects, but not attributes. As mentioned above, the goal of the paper is to cluster attributes. An attribute clustering method based on k-medoids is thus proposed to achieve this purpose. It also uses a better search strategy to find centers

in a dense region, instead of random selection in k-medoids. Besides, a method to measure the distances (dissimilarities) among attributes is also needed.

3 Attribute dissimilarity

In this paper, we partition the attributes into k clusters according to the dependency between each pair of attributes. Each cluster can thus be represented by its representative attribute. The whole feature spaces can thus be greatly reduced.

For most clustering approaches, the distance between two objects is usually adopted as a measure for representing their dissimilarity, which is then used for deciding whether the objects belongs to the same cluster or not. In this paper, the attributes, instead of the objects, are to be clustered. The conventional distance measures such as Euclidean distance or Manhattan distance are thus not suitable since the attributes may have different formats of data, which are hard to compare. For example, assume there are two attributes, one of which is age and the other is gender. It is thus hard to compare the two attributes via the traditional distance measure. Below, a measure based on the concept of relative data dependency is proposed to achieve it. It was proposed by Han et al. [5] and can be thought of as a kind of similarity degrees.

Given two attributes A_i and A_j, the relative dependency degree of A_i with regard to A_j is denoted by $\text{Dep}(A_i, A_j)$ and is defined as:

$$\text{Dep}(A_i, A_j) = \frac{|\Pi_{A_i}(U)|}{|\Pi_{A_i, A_j}(U)|},$$

where $|\Pi_{A_i}(U)|$ is the projection of U on attribute A_i. Note that the original relative dependency degree only considers the relative dependency between a condition attribute set and a decision attribute set. Here we extend the above formula to estimate the relative data dependency between any pair of attributes. The dependency degree is not symmetric, such that the condition $\text{Dep}(A_i, A_j) = \text{Dep}(A_j, A_i)$ is not always valid. We thus use the average of $\text{Dep}(A_i, A_j)$ and $\text{Dep}(A_j, A_i)$ to represent the similarity of the two attributes A_i and A_j. This extended relative dependency is thought of as the similarity of the two attributes. The distance (dissimilarity) measure for the pair of attributes A_i and A_j is thus proposed as follows:

$$d(A_i, A_j) = \frac{1}{\text{Avg}(\text{Dep}(A_i, A_j), \text{Dep}(A_j, A_i))}.$$

Take the distance between the two attributes Age and Children in Table 2 as an example. Since $|\Pi_{\{Age\}}(U)| = 3$, $|\Pi_{\{Children\}}(U)| = 2$ and $|\Pi_{\{Age, Children\}}(U)| = 5$, the relative dependency degrees $\text{Dep}(Age, Children)$ and $\text{Dep}(Children, Age)$ are 0.6 and 0.4, respectively. The distance $d(Age, Children)$ is thus $1/\text{Avg}(0.6, 0.4)$, which is 2.

4 The proposed algorithm

In this section, an attribute clustering algorithm called Most Neighbors First (MNF) is proposed to cluster the attributes into a fixed number of groups. Assume the number k of desired clusters is known. Some preprocessing steps such as removal of inconsistent or incomplete tuples and discretization of numerical data are first done. After that, the proposed MNF attribute clustering algorithm is used to partition the feature space into k clusters and output the k representative attributes of the clusters.

The proposed clustering algorithm MNF is based on the k-medoids approach. Unlike the k-means approach, the proposed algorithm always updates the centers by some existing objects. Besides, it uses a better search strategy to find centers in a dense region, instead of random selection in k-medoids.

The proposed algorithm MNF consists of two major phases: (1) reassigning the attributes to the clusters and (2) updating the centers of the clusters. In the first phase, the proposed distance measure is used to find the nearest center of each attribute. The attribute is then assigned to the cluster with that center. In the second phase, each cluster C_i uses a searching radius r_i to decide the neighbors of each attribute in C_i. The attribute with the most neighbors in a cluster is then chosen as the new center. The proposed algorithm is described in details below.

The MNF attribute clustering algorithm:

Input: An information system $I = (U, A \cup \{d\})$ and the number k of desired clusters.

Output: k appropriate attribute clusters with their representative attributes.

Step 1 Randomly select k attributes $\{A_1^c, A_2^c, \ldots, A_k^c\}$ as the initial representative attributes (centers) in the k clusters, where A_t^c stands for the representative attribute (center) of the t-th cluster C_t, $A_t^c \in A$. Denote $A_c = \{A_1^c, A_2^c, \ldots, A_k^c\} \subseteq A$ as the initial representative attribute set.

Step 2 For each non-representative attribute $A_i \in A - A_c$, compute the dissimilarity (distance) $d(A_i, A_t^c)$ between attribute A_i and each representative attribute A_t^c as:

$$d(A_i, A_t^c) = \frac{1}{\text{Avg}(\text{Dep}(A_i, A_t^c), \text{Dep}(A_t^c, A_i))},$$

where $\text{Dep}(A_i, A_t^c)$ represents the relative dependency degree of A_i with regard to A_t^c and $\text{Dep}(A_t^c, A_i)$ represents the relative dependency degree of A_t^c with regard to A_i, $t \in \{1, 2, \ldots, k\}$.

Step 3 Allocate all non-center attributes to their nearest centers according to the distances found in Step 2. Collect a center attribute with its allocated attributes as a cluster.

Step 4 For each cluster C_t, calculate the distances between any two different attributes within C_t.

Step 5 Calculate the radius r_t of each cluster C_t as:

$$r_t = \frac{\sum_{i \neq j} d(A_{t,i}, A_{t,j})}{C_2^{n_t}},$$

where $d(A_{t,i}, A_{t,j})$ is the distance between any two attributes $A_{t,i}$ and $A_{t,j}$ within the cluster C_t, n_t is the number of attributes within C_t, and $C_2^{n_t}$ is the number of attribute pairs in the cluster, which is $\frac{n_t(n_t-1)}{2}$.

Step 6 For each attribute $A_{t,i}$ (including the center A_t^c) within a cluster C_t, find the set of attributes [(called Near$(A_{t,i})$] with their distances from $A_{t,i}$ within r_t. That is:

$$\text{Near}(A_{t,i}) = \{A_{t,j} \mid A_{t,j} \in C_t \text{ and } d(A_{t,i}, A_{t,j}) \leq r_t\}.$$

Step 7 For each cluster C_t, find the attribute $A_{t,l}$ with the most attributes in its Near set. Set $A_{t,l}$ as the new center A_t^c of C_t.

Step 8 Repeat Steps 2–7 until the clusters have converged.

Step 9 Output the final clusters and their centers as the representative attributes.

After Step 9, k clusters of attributes are formed and k representative attributes for the feature space are found.

5 An example

In this section, a simple example is given to show how the proposed algorithm can be used to cluster the attributes. Table 3 shows the scores of eight students. There are eight condition attributes $A = \{PR, CA, DM, C++, JAVA, DB, DS, AL\}$, respectively stands for the eight subjects: Probability, Calculus, Discrete Mathematics, C++, JAVA, Database, Data Structure and Algorithms. The values of the condition attributes are $\{A, B, C, D\}$, which stand for the grade levels of a subject. There is one decision attribute $\{ST\}$, which stands for $\{$Study for Master Degree$\}$ and has two possible classes $\{$Yes, No$\}$. In this example, the number of clusters is

Table 3 An example for attribute clustering

Object	PR	CA	DM	C++	JAVA	DB	DS	AL	ST
x_1	A	B	A	B	B	A	B	B	Yes
x_2	A	B	B	C	A	B	C	B	No
x_3	B	B	B	A	B	B	A	A	Yes
x_4	B	C	C	C	C	B	C	C	No
x_5	C	C	C	D	C	C	D	C	No
x_6	B	B	C	D	C	D	D	C	No
x_7	B	B	C	B	B	A	B	C	Yes
x_8	A	A	A	A	B	B	A	B	Yes

set at 2 (i.e. $k = 2$). For the set of data, the proposed algorithm proceeds as follows.

Step 1 k attributes are randomly selected as the initial centers of the clusters. In this example, k is set at 2. Assume that the two attributes DM and DS are selected as the initial centers of the two clusters C_1 and C_2, respectively.

Step 2 The distances (dissimilarities) between each non-center attribute and each center are calculated. Take the distance between PR and DM as an example. Since $|\Pi_{PR}| = 3$, $|\Pi_{DM}| = 3$ and $|\Pi_{PR,DM}| = 5$, the relative dependency degrees Dep(PR, DM) is calculated as 0.6 and Dep(DM, PR) is 0.6 as well. The distance between the two attributes is thus calculated as:

$$d(PR, DM) = \frac{1}{Avg(0.6, 0.6)} = 1.67.$$

All the distances between non-center attributes and representative centers are shown in Table 4.

Step 3 All non-center attributes are allocated to their nearest centers. Thus, cluster C_1 contains {PR, CA, AL, DM} and cluster C_2 contains {C++, JAVA, DB, DS}.

Step 4 The distances between any two different attributes in the same clusters are calculated. The results are shown in Table 5.

Step 5 The searching radius of each cluster is calculated. Take the cluster C_1 as an example. It includes four attributes {PR,

Table 4 The distances between non-center attributes and representative centers

Cluster C_1		Cluster C_2	
Attribute pair	Distance	Attribute pair	Distance
d(PR, DM)	1.67	d(PR, DS)	2.33
d(CA, DM)	1.67	d(CA, DS)	2.27
d(C++, DM)	2	d(C++, DS)	1
d(JAVA, DM)	1.67	d(JAVA, DS)	0.8
d(DB, DM)	2	d(DB, DS)	0.8
d(AL, DM)	1.33	d(AL, DS)	2

Table 5 The distances between any two attributes within the same clusters

Within cluster C_1		Within cluster C_2	
Attribute pair	Distance	Attribute pair	Distance
d(PR, DM)	1.67	d(C++, DS)	1
d(PR, AL)	1.33	d(C++, DB)	1.25
d(CA, AL)	1.67	d(JAVA, DB)	2
d(PR, CA)	1.67	d(C++, JAVA)	1.67
d(CA, DM)	1.67	d(JAVA, DS)	1.25
d(AL, DM)	1.33	d(DB, DS)	1.25

CA, AL, DM}. The distances between each pair of attributes in C_1 are {1.67, 1.67, 1.33, 1.67, 1.67, 1.33}. The radius r_1 is then calculated as:

$$r_1 = \frac{1.67 + 1.67 + 1.33 + 1.67 + 1.67 + 1.33}{6} = 1.56.$$

Step 6 The Near set of each attribute in a cluster is calculated. Take the attribute PR in cluster C_1 as an example. Its distance from the other three attributes CA, AL and DM in the same cluster are calculated as 1.67, 1.33 and 1.67. Near(PR) thus includes only the attribute AL since only AL is within the radius r_1 (1.56), which is found from Step 5. Similarly, the Near sets of the other three attributes in the cluster C_1 are found as follows:

Near(CA) $= \phi$,
Near(AL) $=$ {PR, DM}, and
Near(DM) $=$ {AL}.

Step 7 Since the attribute AL has the most attributes in its Near set for the cluster C_1, AL then replaces the attribute DM as the new center of C_1. Similarly, the original center DS for C_2 has the most attributes in its Near set. DS is thus still the center of C_2.

Step 8 Steps 2–7 are repeated until the two clusters no longer change. The final clusters can thus be found as follows:
$C_1 =$ {PR, CA, AL, DM}, with the center AL.
$C_2 =$ {C++, JAVA, DB, DS}, with the center DS.

Step 9 The final clusters and their centers as the representative attributes are then output. The attributes in the same cluster can thus be considered to possess similar characteristics in classification and can be used as alternative attributes of the representative one.

6 Experimental results

In this section, the implementation of the proposed algorithm for clustering attributes is described. The experiments were implemented in C++ on an AMD Athlon 64 X2 Dual Core 3800+ personal computer with 2.01 GHz and 1 GB RAM. The real-world dataset, the Wisconsin Database of Breast Cancers (WDBC) [24], was used to verify the approach. The characteristics of the dataset are shown in Table 6.

Each attribute in the dataset is numerical, so discretization should be first done. In this paper, the discretization is performed by two methods. The first one is equal width which

Table 6 The characteristics of the dataset of WDBC

Number of instances	569
Number of attributes	30
Number of classes	2
Number of missing attributes	0

discretizes the range of an attribute in equal intervals; the other one is equal frequency which considers the appearing frequency of each value of an attribute. The average intradistance (dissimilarity) in a cluster is used as a measure to evaluate the goodness of the results. It is defined as the average distance between an attribute and its representative attribute in the same cluster. Formally, it can be represented by the following formula:

$$\text{AvgIntraD} = \frac{1}{k} \sum_{i=1}^{k} \frac{1}{|C_i| - 1} \sum_{A_j \in C_i - A_i^c} d(A_j, \ A_i^c),$$

where C_i is the i-th attribute cluster. The results of AvgIntra D along with different cluster numbers by the two discretization methods are shown in Fig. 1.

As Fig. 1 showed, the average intradistances decreased along with the increase of the cluster number for both the two discretization methods. Besides, the discretization method by equal width performed better than that by equal frequency.

Another evaluation measure for the clustering results was by the average intrasimilarity in clusters, which was defined as follows:

$$\text{AvgIntraS} = \frac{1}{k} \sum_{i=1}^{k} \frac{1}{|C_i| - 1} \sum_{A_j \in C_i - A_i^c} \text{Sim}(A_j, \ A_i^c),$$

where $\text{Sim}(A_j, A_i^c)$ denotes the average dependency degree for a non-representative attribute A_j and its representative attribute in the same class. $\text{Sim}(A_j, A_i^c)$ was computed as follows:

$$\text{Sim}(A_j, \ A_i^c) = \frac{\text{Dep}(A_j, \ A_i^c) + \text{Dep}(A_i^c, \ A_j)}{2}.$$

The results of AvgIntra S along with different cluster numbers by the two discretization methods are shown in Fig. 2.

As Fig. 2 showed, the average intrasimilarity increased along with the increase of the cluster number for both the two discretization methods. The same as before, the discretization method by equal width performed better than that by equal frequency.

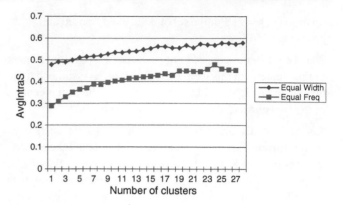

Fig. 2 The average intra similarities along with different cluster numbers by the two discretization methods

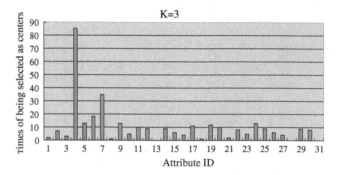

Fig. 3 The frequencies of being selected as centers for $k = 3$

The main purpose of attribute clustering was to select representative attributes to replace the whole set. Since the representative attributes selected by the algorithms were not always the same, the algorithm was thus run for 100 times and the frequency for each attribute being selected as a representative attribute was counted. For example, the selected frequencies of all the attributes when the cluster number k is 3 are shown in Fig. 3.

As Fig. 3 showed, attribute 4 and attribute 7 were the two most frequently chosen attributes in the experiments. Therefore, the two attributes could be chosen and another one might be selected from the set of attributes 5, 6, 9, 17, 19, 24, which had their frequencies more than 10 times and formed the third cluster. The results for $k = 6$ and $k = 9$ are also shown in Figs. 4, 5 for a comparison.

As Figs. 4 and 5 showed, the difference of the frequencies of the attributes being selected as centers was smaller and smaller when the cluster number k increased. This phenomenon resulted from the fact that the attributes in the same cluster would become more similar to each other when the cluster number increased. Attribute would thus be chosen as centers with a more uniform opportunity. In this case, some other criteria, such as attribute cost and ratio of missing values may be used to aid the selection of representative attributes.

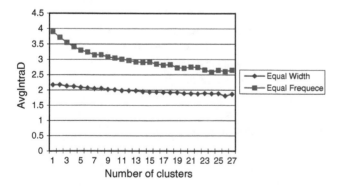

Fig. 1 The average intra distances along with different cluster numbers by the two discretization methods

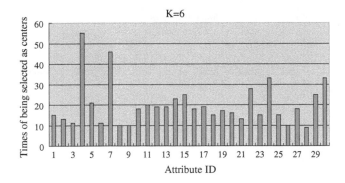

Fig. 4 The frequencies of being selected as centers for $k = 6$

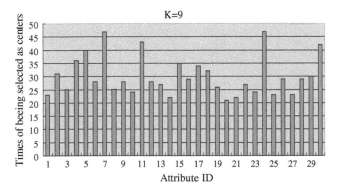

Fig. 5 The frequencies of being selected as centers for $k = 9$

7 Conclusions and future work

In this paper, we have attempted to use attribute clustering for feature selection. A measure of the attribute dissimilarity based on the relative dependency is proposed to calculate the distance between two attributes. An attribute clustering algorithm, called Most Neighbors First, has also been proposed to find centers in a dense region, instead of random selection in k-medoids. The proposed attribute clustering approach consists of two major phases: reassigning attributes to clusters and updating centers of clusters. After the attributes are organized into several clusters by their similarity degrees, the representative attributes in the clusters can be used for classification such that the whole feature space can be greatly reduced. Besides, if the values of some representative attributes cannot be obtained from current environments for inference, some other possible attributes in the same clusters can be used to achieve approximate inference results.

Experimental results show that the average similarity in the same cluster will increase along with the increase of cluster numbers. Besides, the discretization method is an important factor for the final results. The discretization method by equal width performs better than that by equal frequency.

At last, the proposed attribute clustering approach has to know the number of clusters in advance. This requirement results in the limitation of its applications. In the future, we will try to develop other new approaches for attribute clustering, while the number of clusters is unknown. We will also attempt to apply the proposed approach to some real application domains.

References

1. Al-Radaideh, Q.A., Sulaiman, M.N., Selamat, M.H., Ibrahim, H.: Approximate reduct computation by rough sets based attribute weighting. In: The IEEE International Conference on Granular, Computing, vol. 2, pp. 383–386 (2005)
2. Buchanan, B.G., Shortliffe, E.H.: Rule-based expert system: the MYCIN experiments of the Standford heuristic programming projects. Addison-Wesley, Massachusetts (1984)
3. Dong, J.Z., Zhong, N., Ohsuga, S.: Using rough sets with heuristics to feature selection, new directions in rough sets data mining, granular-soft computing. Springer, Berlin (1999)
4. Gao, K., Liu, M., Chen, K., Zhou, N., Chen, J.: Sampling-based tasks scheduling in dynamic grid environment. In: The Fifth WSEAS International Conference on Simulation, Modeling and Optimization, pp. 25–30 (2005)
5. Han, J.: Feature selection based on rough set and information entropy. In: The IEEE International Conference on Granular Computing, vol. 1, 153–158 (2005)
6. Han, J., Kamber, M.: Data mining: concepts and techniques. Morgan Kaufmann, San Francisco (2006)
7. Hong, T.P., Wang, T.T., Wang, S.L.: Knowledge acquisition from quantitative data using the rough-set theory. Intell Data Anal. **4**, 289–304 (2000)
8. Kaufman, L., Rousseeuw, P.J.: Finding groups in data: an introduction to cluster analysis. John Wiley & Sons, Toronto (1990)
9. Kodratoff, Y., Michalski, R.S.: Machine learning: an artificial intelligence artificial intelligence approach. Morgan Kaufmann Publishers, San Mateo (1983)
10. Komorowski, J., Polkowski, L., Skowron, A.: Rough sets: a tutorial.
11. Li, Y., Shiu, S.C.K., Pal, S.K.: Combining feature reduction and case selection in building CBR classifiers. IEEE Trans. Knowl. Data Eng. **18**(3), 415–429 (2006)
12. Lloyd, S.P.: Least square quantization in PCM. Bell Labs, USA (1957)
13. Mamat, R., Herawan, T., Deris, M.M.: MAR: maximum attribute relative of soft set for clustering attribute selection. Knowl. Based Syst. **52**, 11–20 (2012)
14. Michalski, R.S., Carbonell, J.G., Mitchell, T.M.: Machine learning: an artificial intelligence approach. Morgan Kaufmann Publishers, Los Altos (1983)
15. Michalski, R.S., Carbonell, J.G., Mitchell, T.M.: Machine learning: an artificial intelligence approach. Morgan Kaufmann Publishers, Los Altos (1983)
16. Parmar, D., Wu, T., Blackhurst, J.: MMR: an algorithm for clustering categorical data using rough set theory. Data Knowl. Discov. **63**(3), 879–893 (2007)
17. Pawlak, Z.: Rough set. Int J Comput Inf Sci **11**(5), 341–356 (1982)
18. Pawlak, Z.: Why rough sets? In: The Fifth IEEE International Conference on Fuzzy Systems, vol. 2, pp. 738–743 (1996)
19. Pawlak, Z., Skowron, A.: Rudiments of rough sets. Int. J. Comput. Inf. Sci. **177**(1), 3–27 (2007)
20. Qin, H., Ma, X., Zain, J.M., Herawan, T.: A novel soft set approach in selecting clustering attribute. Knowl. Based Syst. **36**, 139–145 (2012)
21. Riley, G.: Expert systems: principles and programming. PWS-Kent, Boston (1989)

22. Skowron, A., Rauszer, C.: The discernibility matrices and functions in information systems, Handbook of Application and Advances of the Rough Sets Theory, pp. 331–362. Kluwer Academic Publishers, Dordrecht (1992)

23. Sun, H.Q., Xiong, Z.: Finding minimal reducts from incomplete information systems. In: The Second International Conference on Machine Learning and Cybernetics, vol. 1, pp. 350–354 (2003)

24. Wolberg, W.H., Street W.N., Mangasarian O.L.: (1995), UCI machine learning repository,
    Irvine, CA: University of California, Department of Information and Computer Science

25. Wroblewski, J.: Finding minimal reducts using genetic algorithms. In: The Second Annual Join Conference on Information Sciences, pp. 186–189 (1995)

26. Zhang, J., Wang, J., Li, D., He, H., Sun, J.: A new heuristic reduct algorithm based on rough sets theory. Lecture Notes in Computer Science, pp. 247–253. Springer, New York (2003)

27. Zhang, M., Yao, J.T.: A rough sets based approach to feature selection. In: The IEEE Annual Meeting of Fuzzy, Information, pp. 434–439 (2004)

5

A robust fingerprint watermark-based authentication scheme in H.264/AVC video

Bac Le · Hung Nguyen · Dat Tran

Abstract In this paper, we propose a novel technique that uses fingerprint features with coordinates (x, y), angle and type of feature as watermark information for authentication in H.264/AVC video. We utilize some techniques such as Gabor algorithm, locally adaptive thresholding, and Hilditch's thinning together with heuristic rules and Hamming measurement to optimally extract minutiae vector $(x, y$, angle, type) from fingerprint as well as to improve accuracy of matching process. Furthermore, to make our scheme robust, the minutiae vector will be converted to binary stream which is increased three times and the lowest frequency of DCT blocks of transition images or frames in H.264 video is properly chosen to hold them. With our proposed technique, the authentication scheme can achieve high capacity and good quality. Experimental results show that our proposed technique is robust against to H.264 encoder, time stretching in video, Gaussian noise, adding blur, frame removal in video, and cutting some regions in the frame of video.

Keywords Video watermarking · H.264/AVC video · Biometric authentication

B. Le (✉)· H. Nguyen
Faculty of Information Technology, University of Science, VNU, Ho Chi Minh City, Vietnam
e-mail: lhbac@fit.hcmus.edu.vn

H. Nguyen
e-mail: kimhung12345@gmail.com

D. Tran
Faculty of Information Sciences and Engineering, University of Canberra, Canberra, ACT 2601, Australia
e-mail: Dat.Tran@canberra.edu.au

1 Introduction

The digital world has invaded many aspects of our lives and moved to all households rapidly in the past decade. More and more digital data are available through various channels such as Internet and media discs. One of the reasons behind the rise of digital data is that users can easily and quickly make a perfect copy of movie, music, or image at large scale with low cost and high quality. Consequently, this has raised concerns about copyright protection against unauthorized duplications and other illegal activities when both content providers and owners realized that the traditional protection methods are no longer efficient and sufficient security [1]. For instance, encryption will not work anymore after decryption since consumers can freely manipulate the decrypted digital content. Other protection methods based on specific header can also easily be broken by removing the header or converting file format. As a result, digital watermarking, the art of hiding copyright information in the robust and invisible manner, has been investigated widely as a perfect complementary technology for copyright protection. With this approach, the embedded data portion considered as evidence to prove copyright of host signal is named watermark. Whereas, the unmarked data portion that needs protected is called host object or unwatermarked object. The marked or watermarked object will be generated after embedding watermark in host object. The relationship among three objects can be demonstrated in Fig. 1a.

Capacity, invisibility and robustness are the most important criteria in a digital watermarking system. *Capacity* is the amount of information (the number of bits) which can be embedded in one unit of the host object (e.g. sample, pixel, scene and so on). *Invisibility* regards to the similarity between unmarked and marked objects. It is usually evaluated by peak signal-to-noise ratio (PSNR). The higher PSRN

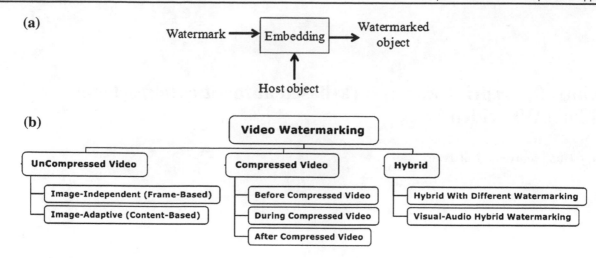

Fig. 1 **a** Digital watermarking system; **b** overview of different types of video watermarking approaches

value gives better invisibility. Finally, *robustness* is considered as the ability of extracting the hidden data from the watermarked signal as well as the survival of the watermark after manipulations or attacks. Because of various operations on digital signal, no watermarking scheme is robust perfectly. As usual, each approach can be robust against to some given and limited alterations. Even though there have been many studies with different approaches, none of the watermarking schemes is strongly enough to meet all requirements at the same time.

The embedded data is usually used to identify the original or copyright information about authors, legal owners, company logo, or signature [2,3]. Recently, biometric information such as iris, face and fingerprint have been utilized and employed as useful watermark [4,5] because it is unique, invariant, and cannot be changed even if stolen. In this paper, we make use important features of fingerprint consisting of the coordinates (x, y), angle and type of features (1 for bifurcation, 0 for ridge ending), namely major minutiae features, as a watermark to authenticate protected content. Hence, there will be about from 30 to 100 minutiae instead of whole fingerprint image embedded in host video [6]. In addition to high reliability of fingerprint, our approach meet the above-mentioned three prerequisites of watermarking problems.

Furthermore, there have been many methods and surveys on digital watermarking [7,8]; however, none of them focuses on video watermarking. Because video protection is not a simple extension of still image protection, more challenges have been encountered. Video watermarking approaches can be classified in Fig. 1b.

Uncompressed video watermarking methods: Most of existing video watermarking methods focus on raw video because of reusability and inheritability from existing image and audio methods. Raw video is simply considered as a sequence

of consecutive and equally time-spaced still images. In raw video watermarking algorithm, the inserted code can be casted directly into the video sequence and embedding process can be performed either in the spatial/temporal domain or transformed domain (e.g. DCT, DFT and SVD). Working with uncompressed video allows us to achieve the video-coding format independence and inherit the robustness of image and audio watermarking.

According to how a video is treated, there are two main sub-categories, namely, image-independent and image-adaptive. The first one considers a video as a set of independent still images, so any image watermarking method can be extended to video. Whereas, image-adaptive approaches are based on the video content, therefore, they can exploit more information from the host signal. Different from the first sub-category, content-based watermarking schemes have utilized the concept of Human Visual System (HVS) to adapt more efficiently to the local characteristics of the host signal. These schemes exploit more properties of the image so that they can maximize the watermark robustness while satisfying the transparency requirement.

Compressed video watermarking methods: A video is usually stored in a compression format, such as MPEG-2, MPEG-4 or H.264 to save in the storage space. Probably, raw video is not common because of its large size. Therefore, studies on video watermarking schemes focus on compressed video. The results have shown that inserting watermark into a compressed video allows real-time processing due to low computational complexity. However, it faces problems of video compression standard and payload.

So far, there have been three main approaches dealing with the compressed video watermarking problems shown in Fig. 1b. The first approach embeds watermark into raw video before compressing video such as the H.264/AVC video watermarking method of Profóck et al. [9] against lossy compression, the strong block selection method against lossy compression standards (e.g. H.264, XviD) of Polyák and Fehér [10] and the new watermarking method based on video 1-D DFT transform and Radon transform of Liu and Zhao [11]. The second approach is to embed watermark directly into the compressed bit stream by changing some parts such as replacing the value of some bytes in the compressed H.264/AVC bitstream [12] and replacing the bits in different blocks based on metadata generated during the pre-analysis [13] in the H.246/AVC compression standard. The third approach allows inserting embedded data into the host compressed video during the encoding such as the watermarking method based on the characteristics of the H.264 standard of Noorkami and Mersereau [14], the hybrid watermark method on the H.264 compression standard used for authentication and copyright protection Qiu et al. [15], the robust watermark method based on H.264/AVC video compression standard of Zhang et al. [16], the watermarking method for the authentication problem on the H.264 video of Su and Chen [7] and the robustness watermarking algorithm on Audio Video Coding Standard (AVS) video of Wanga et al. [17].

Hybrid watermarking methods: Pik-Wah [18] proposed a hybrid approach to improve the performance and robustness of the watermarking scheme. The scene-based watermarking scheme can be improved with two types of hybrid approaches: visual-audio hybrid watermarking and hybrid with different watermarking schemes. The visual-audio hybrid watermarking scheme applies the same watermark into both frames and audio. This approach takes the advantage of watermarking the audio channel, because it provides an independent means for embedding the error-correcting codes, which carry extra information for watermark extraction. Therefore, the scheme is more robust than other schemes which only use video channel alone. The hybrid approach with different watermarking schemes can further be divided into two classes: independent scheme and dependent scheme.

Even though there are many studies with different approaches, none of watermarking schemes is strongly enough capacity, invisibility and robustness at the same time. For instance, the method of Pröfrock et al. [9] against lossy compression H.264/AVC, robustness with regular video attacks and good video quality but not high capacity; the method of Polyák and Fehér [10] gives good results, lower complexity, faster execution, against H.264/AVC and XviD lossy compression process but not robustness with regular video attacks; the method of Liu and Zhao [11] only shows stable to H.264 compression standard, variable geometry and other attacks; and the method of Zou and Bloom [13] is done very quickly at low cost, good compression video quality but not robustness. However, our proposed scheme can achieve high capacity, good quality and robustness. That means our approach can solve three prerequisites of watermarking problems.

The paper is organized as follows: after the Introduction section, all related techniques imployed in this paper will be given in the Sect. 2. The proposed scheme will be demonstrated in Sect. 3. Section 4 will show experimental results and discussion. In final, conclusion as well as future research will be given in Sect. 5.

2 Related works

2.1 Pre-processing fingerprint image

The flowchart of pre-processing fingerprint image can be demonstrated in Fig. 2 with input is a fingerprint image and output is a high quality thinned fingerprint image.

Step 1: filtering

This step will give the high quality of fingerprint image. That means, it makes image clearer, improves the contrast between ridges and valleys, and connects the ridge breaks. There are many methods to enhance the quality of images from simple to complex, from space to frequency domain. However, the implementation of filters over entire image will not be effective. Instead, the filter will be applied on individual block with specific parameters will be more useful [19]. There are four popular context filters, namely, Gabor, Anisotropic, Watson, and STFT, whose parameters depend on the ridge direction and the ridge frequency. Corresponding to fingerprint image and based on experiments, Gabor filter is chosen in this scheme. It is a linear filter and described as follows:

$$G(x, y; \theta, f) = \exp\left\{-\frac{1}{2}\left[\frac{x_\theta^2}{\sigma_x^2} + \frac{y_\theta^2}{\sigma_y^2}\right]\right\} \cos(2\pi f x_\theta),$$

where θ is the orientation of the derived Gabor filter, f is the period of the sinusoidal plane wave, σ_x and σ_y which are standard deviations of the Gaussian envelope along x-axis and y-axis, respectively, and are definite as:

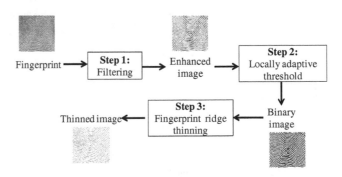

Fig. 2 Flowchart of pre-processing fingerprint

Fig. 3 Apply Gabor filter to
fingerprint

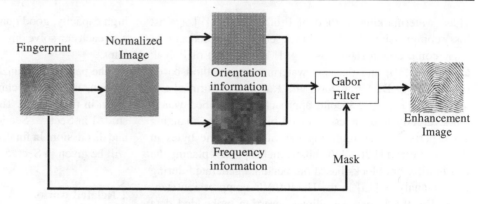

Fig. 4 Ridge ending and
bifurcation

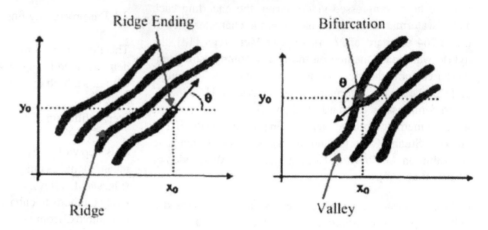

$x_\theta = x \cos\theta + y \sin\theta, \quad y_\theta = -x \sin\theta + y \cos\theta,$

$\sigma_x = k_x F(i, j), \quad \sigma_y = k_y F(i, j),$

To be enhanced by employing Gabor filter, the original finger-print image is first normalized and then extracts orientation and frequency information for the filtering. The filtering is performed in the spatial domain with a mask (usually sized 17×17). The whole process of enhancing fingerprint image through Gabor filter is described in Fig. 3.

Step 2: locally adaptive thresholding

This step transforms the 8-bit gray scale fingerprint image to 1-bit image with 0-value for ridges (black) and 1-value for valleys (white). It is also called image binarization. The simplest way to get the binary image is based on global threshold T:

$$I'(x, y) = \begin{cases} 1 & I(i, j) > T \\ 0 & I(i, j) \leq T \end{cases}.$$

However, this approach is not good in case of fingerprint image. Here, we use local threshold instead. That means the image is first divided into blocks. Within each block, a grayscale pixel will be transformed white if its value is larger than the mean intensity value of the current block.

Step 3: fingerprint ridge thinning

This step will eliminate the redundant pixels of ridges till these ridges are just one pixel wide. Amongst many thinning algorithms such as Holt and Stewart [20], Sten-tiford [21], Zhang–Suen [22], the experimental results show that Hilditch algorithm [23] is simple algorithm and gives better answer with the fingerprint image. The selected algorithm is described as following:

At point P1 on the ridge, consider the 8-neighbors of pixel P1. Then, calculate A(P1) and B(P1) where A(P1) is the number of pairs (0, 1) in the sequence P2, P3, P4, P5, P6, P7, P8, P9, P2 and B(P1) is the number of neighbor pixels whose values are not zero. Pixel P1 will be transformed from 1 (black) to 0 (white) if it satisfies the following four conditions: (1) $2 \leq B(P1) \leq 6$; (2) $A(P1) = 1$; (3) P2.P4.P8 = 0 or A(P2) != 1; (4) P2.P4.P6 = 0 or A(P4) != 1.

2.2 Extracting minutiae feature

There are two types of minutiae: ridge ending and ridge bifurcation are used for extracting and matching shown in Fig. 4. Note that a ridge ending is the point at which a ridge terminates, and a bifurcation is the point at which a single ridge splits into two ridges.

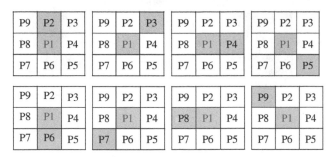

Fig. 5 Cases if P1 is ridge ending

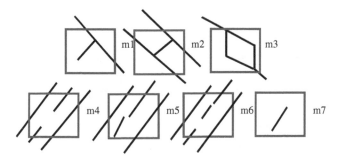

Fig. 6 Cases if P1 is bifurcation

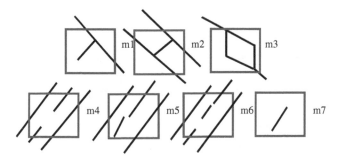

Fig. 7 False minutia structures

By dividing the image into overlapping blocks, sized 3 × 3, central point P1 is considered as ridge ending if it is the following cases (Fig. 5):

Point P1 is bifurcation if it is the following cases (Fig. 6):

The problems of ridge breaks due to lack of or over-ink or over-press will reduce the accuracy of minutiae extraction. There are 7 cases causing such problem considered as following (Fig. 7):

To remove false minutiae, we use heuristic rules as follows:

If the distance between one bifurcation and one termination is less than T ($T = 7$ by default) and the two minutiae are in the same ridge (m1 case). Remove both of them.

If the distance between two bifurcations is less than T and they are in the same ridge, remove the two bifurcations (m2, m3 cases).

If the distance between two ridge endings is less than T and their directions are coincident within a small angle variation. And they meet the condition that no termination is located between the two ridge endings. Then the two terminations are considered as false minutiae derived from a broken ridge and are removed (m4, m5, m6 cases).

If two terminations are located in a short ridge with length less than T, remove the two ridge endings (m7 case).

Where T is the average inter-ridge width representing the average distance between two parallel neighboring ridges. The following picture illustrates the minutiae extraction process (Fig. 8):

Notably, in the above figure, the red circles correspond to bifurcations (type = 1) and the blue circles correspond to the ridge endings (type = 0).

3 Proposed method

From all the research and general knowledge, this paper proposes a robust authentication in H.264 video based on the minutiae (x, y, angle, type) of fingerprint as follows (Fig. 9):

Our authentication scheme using fingerprint watermark consists of three phases as follows:

3.1 Embedding phase

The flowchart of embedding phase can be demonstrated in Fig. 10a.

First, the H.264 video is decoded into raw frames by the H.264 Decoder. Since the transition frames will loose the least data in the H.264 video encoding phase, they are selected from the raw frames. With each transition frame, it is divided into the 8 × 8 non-overlapping blocks. Discrete Cosine Transformation (DCT) will be applied to the set of blocks . In addition, the minutiae vector (x, y, angle, type) generated from fingerprint image after the pre-processing and extracting minutiae will be converted to binary stream (called S). Since binary sequence is much smaller than the transition frame size, we can increase S three times up to SSS. For instance, with minutiae vector (10, 12, 45, 1), we have $S = 00001010000011000010111011$ (with $10 = 00001010$, $12 = 00001100$, $45 = 00101101$, $1 = 1$) and $SSS = 00001010000011000010111011000010100000 11000010110110000101000001100001011011$. With the binary sequence SSS, we can embed one bit (S_k) of sequence S into one 8 × 8 block B_k by the following steps [24]:

Step 1: Choose two lowest frequencies from each block called $B1_k$ and $B2_k$. Select one parameter a such that

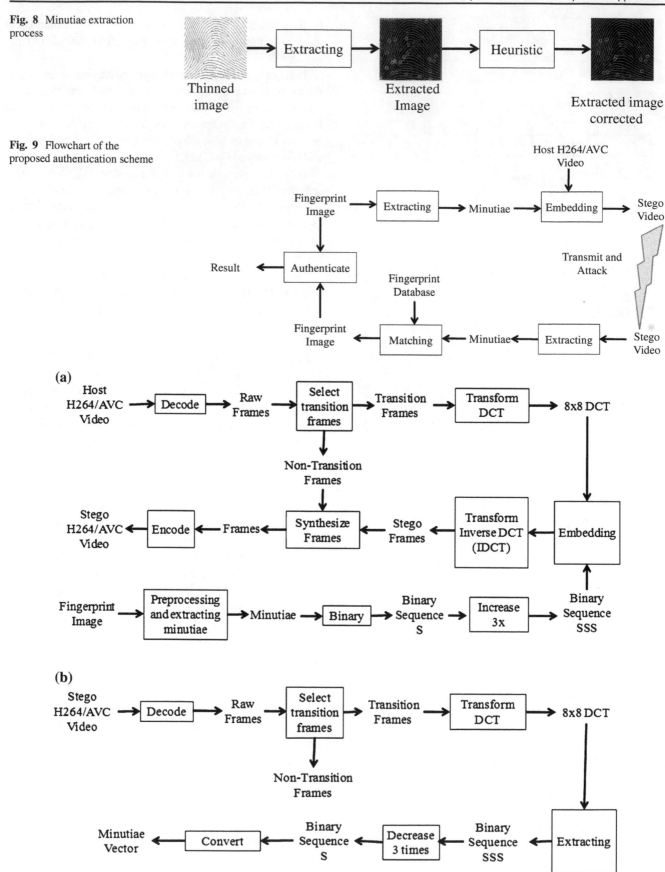

Fig. 8 Minutiae extraction process

Fig. 9 Flowchart of the proposed authentication scheme

Fig. 10 a Flowchart of embedding phase; **b** flowchart of extracting phase

Table 1 The PSNR values of
watermarked video

Authenticated Video kid.mp4 (800×480): 2MB					
Fingerprint Image	Fingerprint Image Size	Size of minutiae vector (bit)	PSNR (dB)	Size of minutia vector increase 3 times (bit)	PSNR (dB)
1.tif	64.2KB	1152	56.71262	3456	52.02355
1.jpg	13.9KB	1400	55.83754	4200	51.23702
2.jpg	9.41KB	1408	55.95424	4224	49.98475
2.tif	64.5KB	1120	56.68477	3360	50.88121
3.jpg	12.3KB	2208	54.37198	6624	51.31206
3.tif	64.5KB	960	57.42595	2880	51.51483
4.jpg	12.2KB	1856	54.77017	5568	51.68784
4.tif	64.5KB	1312	56.07391	3936	50.09165
6.tif	142KB	846	57.41139	2592	51.50177
10.tif	142KB	416	60.7918	1248	56.60345
Authenticated Video woman.mp4 (320×240): 6MB					
Fingerprint Image	Fingerprint Image Size	Size of minutiae vector (bit)	PSNR (dB)	Size of minutia vector increase 3 times (bit)	PSNR (dB)
1.tif	64.2KB	1152	49.66988	3456	44.9808
1.jpg	13.9KB	1400	48.71718	4200	44.1167
2.jpg	9.41KB	1408	50.29945	4224	44.33
2.tif	64.5KB	1120	49.91917	3360	44.1156
3.jpg	12.3KB	2208	45.10393	6624	42.044
3.tif	64.5KB	960	51.66206	2880	45.7509
4.jpg	12.2KB	1856	45.84466	5568	42.7623
4.tif	64.5KB	1312	50.62513	3936	44.6429
6.tif	142KB	846	52.09545	2592	46.1858
10.tif	142KB	416	54.59979	1248	50.4114

$a = 2(2t + 1)$ with t is a positive integer $(0 \leq t \leq 127)$ (t = 4, a = 18 by default).

Step 2: Calculate distance between the two frequencies, $d = |B1_k - B2_k| \pmod{a}$.

Step 3: Binary bit S_k will be embedded into frequencies $B1_k$ and $B2_k$ according to the following rules:

- If $S_k = $ '1' and $d \geq 2t+1$, we do not change anything. If $S_k = $ '1' and $d < 2t + 1$, either $B1_k$ or $B2_k$ will be changed such that $max(B1_k, B2_k) = max(B1_k, B2_k) + INT(0.75 \times a) - d$.
- If $S_k = $ '0' and $d < 2t + 1$, we do not change anything. If $S_k = $ '0' and $d \geq 2t + 1$, either $B1_k$ or $B2_k$ will be changed such that $max(B1_k, B2_k) = max(B1_k, B2_k) + INT(0.25 \times a) - -d$.

The three above steps will be repeated until the minutiae vector *SSS* is completely embedded in transition frames. To obtain the stego frames (the watermarked signal), Inverse Discrete Cosine Transformation (IDCT) will be applied to each block before combining all together. Afterwards the H.264/AVC encoder will be applied to the synthesized frames to obtain stego H.264/AVC video.

3.2 Extracting phase

The watermarked H.264 video may be attacked when it is transferred on a public channel. Therefore, the received H.264 video must be decoded into the raw frames by H.264 decoder. Similar to the embedding phase, the transition frames are selected from the raw frames then are divided into the 8×8 non-overlapping blocks. Discrete Cosine Transformation (DCT) will be applied to the set of blocks before extracting the minutiae vector. According to our approach, each minutia will be taken out based on selecting two lowest frequencies called $B1_k$ and $B2_k$ from each block. Then, based on the distance $d = |B1_k - B2_k| \pmod{a}$, minutia will be conducted as follows: If $d \geq 2t+1$ then $S_k = 1$ and if $d < 2t + 1$ then $S_k = 0$. After extracting, we get the binary sequence *SSS*. To obtain the minutiae vector, we decrease *SSS* three times down to *S*. The whole flowchart of this phase can be described in Fig. 10b.

Table 2 Authentication without attack when embedding into the randomly selected frames

Fingerprint Image Name	Fingerprint Image	Fingerprint Image Size (KB)	Embedded Minutiae Size (bit)	Extracted Minutiae Size (bit)	Bit Error	D	1 - D	Authentication
1.tif		64.2	1152	1152	435	0.377604	0.622396	True
1.jpg		13.9	1400	1400	558	0.396307	0.603693	False
2.jpg		8.89	1408	1408	540	0.383523	0.616477	True
2.tif		64.5	1120	1120	439	0.391964	0.608036	False
3.jpg		12.3	2208	2208	849	0.384511	0.615489	False
3.tif		64.5	960	960	391	0.407292	0.592708	False
4.jpg		12.2	1856	1856	689	0.371228	0.628772	True
4.tif		64.5	1312	1312	489	0.372713	0.627287	True
5.jpg		11.7	1984	1984	377	0.368164	0.631836	True
5.tif		64.5	1024	1024	734	0.36996	0.63004	True
6.jpg		13.6	1664	1664	601	0.361178	0.638822	True
6.tif		142	864	864	315	0.364583	0.635417	True
7.jpg		8.51	1408	1408	535	0.379972	0.620028	True

Table 2 continued

7.tif		64.5	1696	1696	635	0.37441	0.62559	True
8.jpg		11	2304	2304	908	0.394097	0.605903	False
8.tif		142	416	416	158	0.379808	0.620192	True
9.jpg		13.6	1984	1984	750	0.378024	0.621976	True
9.tif		142	512	512	199	0.388672	0.611328	False
10.jpg		9.41	1696	1696	628	0.370283	0.629717	True
10.tif		142	416	416	137	0.329327	0.670673	True
11.jpg		16.6	1504	1504	551	0.366356	0.633644	True
11.tif		64.5	992	992	377	0.38004	0.61996	True

3.3 Matching phase

This phase is to authenticate the legal of host H.264 video by matching the extracted minutiae vector with fingerprint database. Since minutiae vector is considered as a binary stream, Hamming distance is used to achieve good accuracy in authentication. The Hamming distance between two vectors $A = a_1a_2....a_n$ and $B = b_1b_2.....b_n$ is determined as $D = \frac{1}{n}\sum_{i=1}^{n}|a_i - b_i|$.

If D is less than a preset threshold $D_0(D_0 = 0.5$ by default) then 2 bit strings are matching. If there are several matching vectors, the smallest value of D is selected.

4 Results and discussion

Experiments were conducted on a PC with Intel(R) Core (TM)2 Duo CPU T5800 2.00GHz, RAM 4GB. The operating system is Windows 7 32-bit and our algorithms were programmed in Microsoft Visual C++ 6.0 and Microsoft Visual Studio 2008 with supporting of OpenCV and MediaNet Suite library. To illustrate our scheme, we used the fingerprint database consisting 1500 samples which were provided by Ministry of Public Security of Vietnam (Ho Chi Minh city branch). To demonstrate authentication ability, we used 11 fingerprint images each of which was saved in TIFF and JPEG formats. Details of these 22 files are listed in Table 1 below. The H.264 videos chosen in experiments are kid.mp4 and woman.mp4 sized 2 MB, 6 MB, respectively.

In our experiments, the peak signal-to-noise ratio (PSNR) is used to evaluate the quality of the watermarked frame. A higher PSNR means that the quality of the marked frame is better. The PSNR is defined as $PSNR = 10 \times \log_{10}\frac{255^2}{MSE}$ (dB), where MSE is the mean square error between the original frame and the watermarked one. For a host frame with size of $w \times h$, the formula for MSE is defined as

$$MSE = \frac{1}{w \times h}\sum_{x=1}^{h}\sum_{y=1}^{w}(G_{xy} - G'_{xy})^2 \qquad (1)$$

Table 3 Authentication without attack when embedding into the transition frames

Fingerprint Image Name	Fingerprint Image	Fingerprint Image Size (KB)	Embedded Minutiae Size (bit)	Extracted Minutiae Size (bit)	Bit Error	D	1 - D	Authentication
1.tif		64.2	1152	1152	311	0.269965	0.730035	True
1.jpg		13.9	1400	1400	407	0.289063	0.710937	True
2.jpg		8.89	1408	1408	389	0.276278	0.723722	True
2.tif		64.5	1120	1120	319	0.284821	0.715179	True
3.jpg		12.3	2208	2208	612	0.277174	0.722826	True
3.tif		64.5	960	960	288	0.3	0.7	True
4.jpg		12.2	1856	1856	490	0.264009	0.735991	True
4.tif		64.5	1312	1312	348	0.265244	0.734756	True
5.jpg		11.7	1984	1984	267	0.260742	0.739258	True
5.tif		64.5	1024	1024	521	0.262601	0.737399	True
6.jpg		13.6	1664	1664	422	0.253606	0.746394	True

where G_{xy} and G'_{xy} are the pixel values at position (x, y) of the host frame and the watermarked frame, respectively.

Our proposed scheme obtains good invisibility. Table 1 displays the quality of different videos which are embedded and evaluated by PSNR values.

A frame with $w \times h$ size can be embedded up to $(w \times h)/(8 \times 8)$ bits (each bit is embedded in to a 8×8 block) in the proposed method. If the number of bits to be embedded is bigger than the number of 8×8 blocks, we cannot embed each bit into each block. Instead, we will embed more than

Table 3 continued

6.tif		142	864	864	222	0.256944	0.743056	True
7.jpg		8.51	1408	1408	384	0.272727	0.727273	True
7.tif		64.5	1696	1696	453	0.267099	0.732901	True
8.jpg		11	2304	2304	660	0.286458	0.713542	True
8.tif		142	416	416	114	0.274038	0.725962	True
9.jpg		13.6	1984	1984	537	0.270665	0.729335	True
9.tif		142	512	512	144	0.28125	0.71875	True
10.jpg		9.41	1696	1696	446	0.262972	0.737028	True
10.tif		142	416	416	93	0.223558	0.776442	True
11.jpg		16.6	1504	1504	389	0.258644	0.741356	True
11.tif		64.5	992	992	270	0.272177	0.727823	True

one bit into the lowest coefficients of each block. For instance, after increasing three times, the minutiae of 3.jpg fingerprint image has 6,624 bits and the kid.mp4 video frame size is 800 × 480. So, we can embed up to (800 × 480)/(8 × 8) = 6,000 bits. In this case, we cannot embed each bit of the minutiae in to each 8 × 8 block. Therefore, we will embed two bits in the four lowest coefficients of each 8 × 8 block.

The PSNR in Table 1 is high (≥40 dB). Compared with the results of the PSNR in [11,14,25], the proposed watermarking method is high capacity.

Authentication was considered in the following cases:

Case 1: There is no attack over public channels. That means the images at both receiver and sender are the same.

Case 2: There are some attacks over public channels. In our scheme, we consider time stretching in video, Gaussian noise, adding blur, frame removal in video, cutting some regions in the frame of video, and converting H.264 video into another video format.

In the first case, the authentication results are recorded in Tables 2 and 3 with the protected video is kid.mp4.

After embedding the minutiae bits into the selected frames, these frames were attacked in the process of H.264/AVC compression such as image subtraction, image convolution, DCT transform, quantization, reconstruction and lossy entropy encoding. With a series of attacks, the experimental results in Tables 2 and 3 are relatively optimistic. Also through the Tables 2 and 3, the selection of

Table 4 Authentication with attack: stretching time, removing frame, Gaussian noise, adding blur, filtering median, cropping image in frame, converting into another video format

Fingerprint Image: 1.tif The embedded minutiae size : 1152 bits The extracted minutiae size: 1152 bits									
Attacks	**Attacked Video**	**D**	**1 - D**	**Auth**	**Attacks**	**Attacked Video**	**D**	**1 - D**	**Auth**
Stretch time (1s)		0.269965	0.730035	True	Gaussian noise		0.337543	0.662457	True
Stretch time (3s)		0.269965	0.730035	True	Adding blur		0.322691	0.677309	True
Stretch time (5s)		0.269965	0.730035	True	Filtering median		0.329029	0.670971	True
Remove frame (10%)		0.270833	0.729167	True	Crop image (1/4) in frame		0.357566	0.642434	True
Remove frame (25%)		0.270833	0.729167	True	Crop image (1/2) in frame		0.383162	0.616838	True
Remove frame (50%)		0.27691	0.72309	True	Crop image (3/4) in frame		0.426029	0.573971	False
Remove frame (75%)		0.27691	0.72309	True	Convert MP4 → AVI → MP4		0.391267	0.608733	False
Remove frame (90%)		0.27691	0.72309	True	Convert MP4 → WMA → MP4		0.397621	0.602379	False

"Auth" means Authentication

transition frames is better than the randomly selected frame. The transition frames are proceeded in the Intra prediction, the most content of the transition frame is retained and added in the picture reference list 0 and 1. The Inter prediction uses the picture reference list 0 and 1. Moreover, most of the video frames in the H.264 compression having high homology are in the Inter prediction.

In the second case, we considered some attacks including time stretching in video, Gaussian noise, adding blur, frame removal in video, cutting some regions in the frame of video, and converting H.264 video into another video format. The experimental results are presented in Table 4. The

protected video in this case is kid.mp4 and the fingerprint image is 1.tif. The experimental results show that vector extracted has the same size with the one embedded. Based on Hamming values D between the extracted minutiae and the matched sample, the matched sample is always found when threshold D_0 is set to 0.5. However those D values are ranged from 0.25 to 0.43, the authentication is still false in some cases. Moreover, from the results, we can see that our scheme is more robust to attacks. If attack occurs, two minutiae vectors are almost different; therefore, based on values of Hamming distance D, we can recognize if there was an attack.

	Mobile		Football		Table tennis		Foreman		Garden	
	Mark	No mark	Mark	No mark	Mark	No Mark	Mark	No Mark	Mark	No Mark
PSNR	40.7357	–	40.1152	–	40.1590	–	39.8379	–	40.9515	–
Translation	0.7443	0.0185	0.7142	0.0098	0.5769	–0.0084	0.8061	0.0025	0.6580	0.0189
Aspect to 4/3	0.6993	0.0075	0.7118	0.0110	0.6340	–0.0104	0.7314	–0.0029	0.6511	0.0095
to 11/9	–	–	0.7118	0.0110	0.6340	–0.0104	–	–	0.6511	0.0095
to 16/9	0.6993	0.0075	0.7118	0.0110	0.6340	–0.0104	0.7314	–0.0029	0.6511	0.0095
Swap	0.5567	–0.0648	0.5807	0.0472	0.5769	–0.0084	0.7788	–0.0161	0.3984	0.0413
Lost	0.7154	0.0399	0.6988	0.0200	0.6583	–0.0062	0.7772	0.0098	0.6388	0.0048
Gaussian LP	0.4109	–0.0124	0.3814	–0.0693	0.4001	–0.0136	0.4152	–0.0014	0.3750	–0.0692
Level	0.5894	–0.0097	0.6274	0.0176	0.6398	–0.0109	0.7200	–0.0036	0.5816	–0.0134
Rotation 0°	0.6993	–0.0036	0.7096	0.0074	0.6335	0.0013	0.7314	–0.0013	0.6528	–0.0054
1°	0.6923	–0.0072	0.6846	–0.0081	0.614	0.0003	0.7327	–0.0004	0.6551	–0.006
2°	0.6929	–0.0032	0.6872	–0.0015	0.6124	0.0011	0.7300	–0.0002	0.6270	–0.013
3°	0.6893	–0.0079	0.6928	0.0006	0.6132	0.0020	0.7306	0.0001	0.6334	–0.0109
4°	0.6949	–0.0029	0.6910	0.0020	0.6136	0.0012	0.7336	–0.0003	0.6280	–0.0029
5°	0.6937	–0.0021	0.6965	0.0045	0.6107	0.0010	0.7322	0.0004	0.6251	–0.0137
10°	0.6923	–0.0088	0.7060	0.0048	0.6237	0.0013	0.7311	0.0008	0.5961	–0.0026
15°	0.7136	0.0002	0.7217	0.0116	0.6231	0.0046	0.7383	0.0011	0.5899	–0.0202
20°	0.6961	–0.0027	0.7108	0.0056	0.6270	–0.0002	0.7261	0.0006	0.6494	–0.0079
25°	0.6943	–0.0048	0.7183	0.0139	0.6322	0.0012	0.7268	0.0019	0.6418	–0.0102
30°	0.7045	–0.0034	0.7236	0.0012	0.6481	0.0081	0.7139	0.0014	0.6404	–0.0081
35°	0.6837	–0.0054	0.7231	0.0043	0.6416	0.0050	0.7094	0.0013	0.6429	–0.0076
40°	0.6800	0.0042	0.7234	0.0129	0.6296	–0.0001	0.7130	0.0025	0.6417	–0.0096
45°	0.6773	–0.0012	0.7073	0.0026	0.6442	0.0052	0.6869	–0.0011	0.6425	–0.0006

Fig. 11 Extracting results in the paper [11]

Also through Table 4, we see that the authentication model is not affected by stretching time in video. Because this process only affects the time of frame displayed in the screen without changing the frame data, the removing process only affects the authentication model if and only if the transition frames are removed. Depending on the number of removed transition frames, the authentication result will be affected. For instances, there are three transition frames in kid.mp4 video. If we remove 10 % or 25 % frames of the video, it means one transition frame is removed. If we remove 50, 75 or 90 % frames of the video, it means two transition frames are removed. We have also found that the authentication model is robust with other attacks such as Gaussian noise, adding blur, filtering median, cropping image in the frame and not robust with the video format conversion.

Comparing with the experimental results in the papers [14] and [11], our results are also better (Fig. 11; Table 5).

5 Conclusion

In this article, we have proposed a video authentication scheme using fingerprint watermark. The experimental results show that our method has not only achieved high capacity together with good quality of watermarked video but also been robust against stretching time, removing frame,

Table 5 Extracting results in the paper [14]

Video sequence	Watermark bits	Re-encoding recovery rate (%)	Bit rate increase (%)
Carphone	44	58	0.80
Claire	22	83	0.44
Mobile	85	85	0.23
Mother	42	68	0.69
Table	38	62	0.31
Tempete	81	83	0.44

Gaussian noise, adding blur, filtering median, and cropping image in the frame attacks. The PSNR values are bigger than 40 dB in most cases. Otherwise, our scheme just embed about 30–100 minutiae, the proposed method is able to provide very high capacity. In the future, we will apply this authentication scheme in other common video standards such as MPEG-2, MPEG-4 and research another measure to replace Hamming distance for improving the accuracy of matching process.

Open Access This article is distributed under the terms of the Creative Commons Attribution License which permits any use, distribution, and reproduction in any medium, provided the original author(s) and the source are credited.

References

1. Ryoichi, S., Hiroshi, Y.: Consideration on copyright and illegal copy countermeasures under IT revolution. Joho Shori Gakkai Kenkyu Hokoku **2001**(52), 37–42 (2001)
2. Ramos, C., Reyes, R.R., Miyatake, M.N., Meana, H.P.: Image authentication scheme based on self-embedding watermarking. Lecture Notes Comput. Sci. **5856**, 1005–1012 (2009)
3. MeenakshiDevi, P., Venkatesan, M., Duraiswamy, K.: A fragile watermarking scheme for image authentication with tamper localization using integer wavelet transform. J. Comput. Sci. **5**(11), 831–837 (2009)
4. Hassanien, E.: Hiding Iris data for authentication of digital images using wavelet theory. Pattern Recognit. Image Anal. **16**, 637–643 (December 2006)
5. Allah, M.M.A.: Embedded biometric data for a secure authentication watermarking. In: IASTED International Conference: Signal Processing, Pattern Recognition, and Applications, pp. 191–196 (2007)
6. Federal Bureau of Investigation (FBI) John Edgar Hoover, The Science of Fingerprints: Classification and Uses, U.S. Government Printing Office, Washington D.C., (2006)
7. Su, P.C., Chen, I. F.: A digital watermarking scheme for authenticating H.264/AVC Compressed Video, 2008 ICS (2009)
8. Potdar, V.M., Han, S., Chang, E.: A Survey of Digital Image Watermarking Techniques. In: IEEE International Conference Industrial Informatics (INDIN), pp. 709–716 (2005)
9. Pröfrock, D., Richter, H., Schlauweg, M., Müller, E.: H.264/AVC video authentication using skipped macroblocks for an erasable watermark. In: Proc. SPIE Visual Communications and Image Processing, vol. 5960, pp. 1480–1489 (2005)
10. Polyák, T., Fehér, G.: Robust Block Selection for Watermarking Video Streams. In: Proceedings of the World Congress on Engineering 2008, WCE 2008, London, U.K., July 2–4, vol. I (2008)
11. Liu, Y., Zhao, J.: A new video watermarking algorithm based on 1D DFT and Radon transform. Signal Process. **90**(2) (2010)
12. Zou, D., Bloom, J.A.: H.264/AVC stream replacement technique for video watermarking. In: IEEE International Conference on Acoustics, Speech, and Signal Processing, ICASSP (2008)
13. Zou, D., Bloom, J.A.: H.264/AVC Substitution Watermarking: A CAVLC Example, Media Forensics and Security XI. In: Delp, E.J., Dittmann, J., Memon, N.D., Wong, P.W. (eds.) Proceedings of SPIE, vol. 7254 (2009)
14. Noorkami, M., Mersereau, R.M.: Compressed-domain video Watermarking for H.264. In: Proceedings of the International Conference on Image Processing, ICIP, vol. 2, pp. 890–893 (2005)
15. Qiu, G., Marziliano, P., Ho, A., He, D., Sun, Q.: A hybrid Watermarking scheme for H.264/AVC video. In: Proceedings of the 17th International Conference on Pattern Recognition, ICPR, vol. 4, pp. 865–868 (2004)
16. Zhang, J., Ho, A., Qiu, G., Marziliano, P.: Robust video watermarking of H.264/AVC. IEEE Trans. Circuits Syst. II Express Briefs **54**(2), 205–209 (2007)
17. Wanga, Y., Lua, Z., Fana, L., Zheng, Y.: Robust dual watermarking algorithm for AVS video. Signal Process. Image Commun. **24**(4), 333–344 (2009)
18. Chun-Shien, L., Jan-Ru, C., Kuo-Chin, F.: Real-time frame-dependent video Watermarking in VLC domain. Signal Process. **20**(7), 624–642 (2005)
19. Lee, J., Wang, S.D.: Fingerprint feature reduction by principal Gabor basis function. Pattern Recognit. **34**(11), 2245–2248 (2001)
20. Holt, M., Stewart, A.: A parallel thinning algorithm with fine grain subtasking. Parallel Comput. **10**, 329–334 (1989)
21. Stentiford, W.M.: Some new heuristics for thinning binary hand-printed characters for OCR. Trans. Syst. Man Cybern. **13**(1), 81–84 (1983)
22. Zhang, T.Y., Suen, C.Y.: A fast parallel algorithm for thinning digital patterns. Commun. ACM **27**(3), 236–239 (1986)
23. http://cgm.cs.mcgill.ca/~godfried/teaching/projects97/azar/skeleton.html
24. Nguyen, X.H., Tran Q.D.: An Image Watermarking Algorithm Using DCT Domain. In: Proceedings of the National Workshop: Selected Issues of Information Technology, pp. 146–151. Science and Technology Publisher, Ha Noi, Vietnam (2005)
25. Shahabuddin, S.; Iqbal, R.; Shirmohammadi, S.; Jiying Z.; Compressed-domain temporal adaptation-resilient watermarking for H.264 video authentication. In: IEEE International Conference on Multimedia and Expo, 2009. ICME 2009, New York (2009)

6

Cognitive information processing

Chi Tran

Abstract Today, under the "true or false" philosophy, we are confined within the 'syntactic' restrictions, in connection with the adoption of the counter-concepts/binary concepts presented by common words and Boolean numbers concerned with logical reasoning based on binary logic. In contrast, truth, according to Brouwer and Heyting (intuitive logic), *comes from the future*. It, according to Łukasiewicz (multi-valued logic), is *neither true nor false*. It should be a third option that transcends both, i.e., transcends the 'syntactic' restrictions to reach the 'semantic' and 'pragmatic' descriptions of available data. Truth, in this case, will be formulated in the new form of the meta-concept: *true-false* which is neither true nor false, likewise the 'affirmation and denial' idea of the Indian logic. It becomes a cognitive measure used to describe the human cognitive processing. It turned out that we need not only a new term that transcends limits of words and Boolean numbers to describe meta-concepts, but also a new approach based on new philosophy, logic and mathematics to process cognitive information using both physical and mental data. It refers, in this article, as denotation computing for determining the relative density of sand using CPT data. Instead of the counter-concept, "loose or consolidation or high consolidation" we use the meta-concept, "loose-consolidation-high consolidation" to represent the *objective–subjective* data. Their processing is developed for certain types of data structures designed for representing information content including cognitive measures depending on perception of engineers to exceed the syntax limits of binary concepts towards their semantic and pragmatic aspects. It is based on the integration of modern philosophy, epistemology, logic, and denotational mathematics.

Keywords Geotechnical engineering · Counter-concept · Meta-concept · Cognitive measure · Cognitive information processing · Denotational mathematics

1 Introduction

To identify what we consider the so-called objective reality through available data derived from the physical devices, we use traditionally logical reasoning within the 'syntactic' restrictions, which is based on the binary philosophy and two-valued logic. It we call the *information processing* in the 'syntactic' level—external *information processing* using the counter-concept/binary concept: 'true or false'—the first stage of our relationship with the real world. In contrast, when we experience what we feel a reality, which may extend beyond the boundary of syntax restrictions of language. For example, we have some objects/subjects which we do not know for sure of its existence or non-existence. However, we feel that it is neither existence nor non-existence, but a third option that transcends both. To describe what we have (feel) in our head, we may introduce a new concept originated from intuition and experiences depending on our perception derived from the so-called *true-false* philosophy according to monism rather than dualism. We cannot use common words with syntax restriction to describe this idea. We may use a new concept presented by *existence-nonexistence*, which represents both *existence* and *nonexistence*. It we call a meta-concept, which is derived from our intuition, commonsense and experiences. Hidden information containing in this *existence-nonexistence* concept, we call cognitive information, which represents the semantic and

C. Tran (✉)
Faculty of Technical Sciences, WM University, Olsztyn, Poland
e-mail: tran.chi@uwm.edu.pl

pragmatic aspects of observed object/subject. Thus, we have also a relationship with the real world—the second stage, which is strictly related to *cognitive processing* using cognitive measures. Then, we need a new technique that studies information as attributes of the real world, which shall be generally abstracted, quantitatively represented and mentally processed.

We propose in this paper, an *internal information processing* approach based on the integration of modern philosophy, epistemology, logic and denotational mathematics for certain types of data structures designed for representing information content including cognitive measures derived from intuition, commonsense and perception of engineers to exceed the syntax limits of binary concepts towards their semantic and pragmatic aspects. It refers as denotation computing using both physical and mental data to determine the relative density, I_D, of sands with cognitive measures determined by 'true-false' values. Instead of the counter-concept "loose or medium or high consolidation" according to dualism, we use rather the meta-concept, "loose-medium-high" consolidation, determined by both available data and mental data according to monism.

2 Philosophy of language

Linguists, in the nineteenth century, began to recognize the diversity of human language, and to question about the relationship between language and logic. Different concepts have been introduced, for example, syntactic, semantics, pragmatics, sense and denotation which are presented briefly as below.

Syntactic or syntax, is concerned with the way sentences are constructed from smaller parts, such as words and phrases. Two steps can be distinguished in the study of syntactic. The first step is to identify different types of units in the stream of speech and writing. The second step is to analyze how these units build up larger patterns, and in particular to find general rules that govern the construction of sentences. Syntactic is a branch of semiotics that deals with the formal relations between signs or expressions in abstraction from their signification and their interpreters.

Semantics is the subfield that is devoted to the study of meaning, as inherent at the levels of words, phrases, sentences, and larger units of discourse. A key concern is how meaning attaches to larger chunks of text, possibly as a result of the composition from smaller units of meaning. Traditionally, semantics has included the study of sense and denotation reference, truth conditions, argument structure and discourse analysis. The term *semantics* is applied to certain types of data structures, specifically designed and used for representing information content. Systems of categories are not

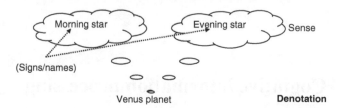

Fig. 1 Sense and denotation according to Frege's view

objectively "out there" in the world, but are rooted in people's experiences. Their meaning is not an objective truth, but a subjective construct, learned from experiences.

Pragmatics is the study of the relationships between the symbols of a language, their meaning, and the users of the language. It is a subfield of linguistics which studies the ways in which context contributes to meaning. *It studies how the transmission of meaning depends not only on the linguistic knowledge of the speaker and listener, but also on the context of the utterance, knowledge about the status of those involved, the inferred intent of the speaker, and so on.* In this respect, pragmatics explains how language users are able to overcome apparent ambiguity, since the meaning relies on the manner, place, time etc., of an utterance. Pragmatic awareness is regarded as one of the most challenging aspects of language learning, and comes only through experiences.

Sense and denotation Frege (1848–1925) [1,2] developed a theory of sense and denotation into a thoroughgoing philosophy of language. He gave a new and revised account of his logical calculus, and had evolved his now well-known theory of **sense** and **denotation**. By the **sense** of a statement or proposition, Frege understood its content, i.e., 'the meaning of words' in the syntactic level. While by denotation of a statement or proposition he understood the meaning, in the semantic and pragmatic levels, that transcends the language description. According to Frege, we can really learn that the statement "the morning star is identical to the morning star" is true by simply linguistic inspection, but, while, in fact both the statements "the morning star" and "the evening star" refer to is the planet namely Venus, we cannot learn the truth that "the morning star is identical to the evening star" simply by linguistic inspection. It is shown in the Fig. 1.

3 Counter-concepts/binary-concept

The *counter-concepts* such as *mind* **or** *brain*, *being* **or** *non-being*, *objectivity* **or** *subjectivity* and others are originated from *dualism*, which was originally created to denote co-eternal binary opposition, a meaning with syntactic restrictions that are preserved in metaphysical and philosophical duality discourse. For example, 'mind or brain' dualism claims that neither the mind nor brain can be reduced to each other in any way. This alternative idea, as well as

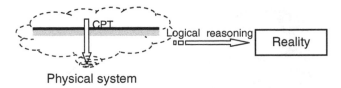

Physical system

Fig. 2 Objective reality derived from available data

"Discrimination-Non_discrimination-

Non_discrimination-Discrimination"

Fig. 3 Zhuang Zhou's "One" philosophy

counter-concepts such as *being or nonbeing* introduced later creates the so-called binary philosophy—Aristotle (344–322 BC, see Barnes, Jonathan). Here, "Being" and its opposition, "Nonbeing", are expressed in the law of the excluded middle, which states the necessity that either an assertion or its negation must be true or false.

Counter-concepts originating from 'being or nonbeing' philosophy are derived from observation, physical testing and logical reasoning based on two-valued logic, in which we have the so-called *material implication* presented logically in the form:

$$\forall_{p,q \in \{0,1\}} \; p \rightarrow q = 0 \text{ or } 1 \text{ (certainly)} \tag{1}$$

Meaning of these concepts can be determined by a common language in its syntactic aspects, without its semantic and pragmatic respects depending upon the individualized conscious or actual spiritual state of the observer. Consider, for example, behaviors of explored equipment such as the Cone Penetration Test, CPT, in the complex environments of soil. Available knowledge about soil properties can be obtained from observation of the behavior of the physical "CPT-soil" system and logical reasoning including traditional/deductive mathematics. It is seen as exploration strictly in the framework of the 'syntactic' restrictions, depending in no way upon the individual spiritual state of the controller, which is shown in the Fig. 2.

Study of the "CPT-soil" system must, in this case, resort to statistical descriptions and what has been determined is seen as 'objectivity'. Then, the laws of statistics enable us to understand the behavior of a multitude of disorganized complexities.

4 Meta-concept

Contrary to dualism, monism does not accept any fundamental divisions between physical and mental. It is a doctrine saying that *ultimate it reality is entirely of 'one' substance*. Monism [3] leads to other concepts named *meta-concepts*, which were originally created to denote a meaning beyond syntactic restrictions that are preserved in metaphysical, philosophical duality discourse. They are presented as follows.

'Affirmation-Denial' Concept: It was found in Indian logic (in the Rigveda 1000 B.C.) in which, we have the four-

cornered argumentation including: *affirmation X, denial of X, ¬X,* both *affirmation* and *denial, X ∧ ¬X, and neither of them ¬(X ∧ ¬X)*. Here, the joint *affirmation* and *denial X ∧ ¬X* represents a third option that transcends both *affirmation* and *denial*. It can be represented by a new meta-concept: 'affirmation-denial' in the form:

'affirmation-denial' is neither *affirmation* nor *denial*

It is impossible in two-valued logic, i.e., we cannot use it for logical reasoning based on binary logic. The efforts of Indian logic were concentrated on explaining the *unary underlying order* of Hindu philosophy. They want to come to adopt neutral monism, the view that *the possible reality*, which we could recognize by feeling originated from intuition, commonsense, is of one kind including *both affirmation and its denial*.

'Discrimination-Nondiscrimination' Concept: Fundamental undivided nature of reality is found in Zhuang Zhou's 'One' philosophy, (莊 周-Zhuang Zhou 369–286, in China [4]). It is shown in the Fig. 3.

The author claimed that the concept of true and the opposition of it, false, is seen as oneness and according to his dynamic thinking: "true becomes false and false becomes true ... we cannot know where is the starting point, where is the end ... as a *circle*, in which, we cannot distinguish big from small, good from evil, discrimination from non-discrimination and true from false". The original idea presented in brief in the form: "Discrimination-Nondiscrimination", is seen as the Zhuang Zhou's 'One' philosophy:

'Discrimination-Nondiscrimination' is neither *Discrimination* nor *Nondiscrimination*,

which, according to Suzuki [5] (鈴木 大拙 貞太郎 *Suzuki Daisetz Teitarō* 1962), is the most deep philosophical paradox. In fact, the author wanted to turn away from logical reasoning to recognize what originated directly from the observer's *perceptions*.

'Being-Nonbeing' Concept: The meta-concept: "sac-sac-khong-khong" i.e., *being-being-nonbeing-nonbeing* or briefly, *being-nonbeing* is found in the Vietnamese "one" philosophy. That is:

'being-nonbeing' is neither *being* nor *nonbeing*

but a third option that transcends both. In the framework of Indian logic, using box connective, ■ (affirmation), and diamond connective, ♦ (both ■ and ¬■), for the four-cornered argumentation: ■, ♦, ¬■ and ¬♦, we can represent 'Being' by four symbols, (■B, ♦B, ¬■B, ¬♦B), where we have certainty: ■B, ¬■B (negation), uncertainty: ♦B and ¬♦B (neither ■B nor ¬■B); similarly, 'Nonbeing' by (■N, ♦N, ¬■N, ¬♦N). Then, *being-nonbeing* reasoning based on Indian logic (four-valued logic) leads to 16 possibilities, which are presented in the form:

Is this "being-nonbeing"?

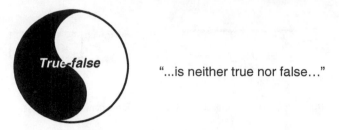

Fig. 4 Łukasiewicz's 'true-**false**' philosophy

"...is neither true nor false..."

ultimately the structures of thought and reality, subject and object, are identical. According to Hegel, people do not recognize that, *in truth, the identity is different*, that is to say, they are "one" —the *identity-different*.

Possible replies : {■B■N, ■B♦N, ■B¬■N, ■B¬♦N,

♦B■N, ♦B♦N, ♦B¬■N, ♦B¬♦N,

¬■B■N, ¬■B♦N, ¬■B¬■N, ¬■B¬♦N,

¬♦B■N, ¬♦B♦N, ¬♦B¬■N, ¬♦B¬♦N} = 2^4 possibilities

This is a consequence of both the observations that come from the eyes of the observer and his/her perceptions rooted from intuition, commonsense and experiences without logical reasoning, i.e., beyond the syntactic boundaries by a cognitive information processing.

While the *counter-concepts* 'being or nonbeing' are produced by the intercourse of the body senses with objects, the observer can quickly recognize being or non-being by his/her eyes. Consequently, four possibilities obtained from 'being **or** nonbeing' reasoning based on two-valued logic are presented in the form:

Is this "being or nonbeing"?
Possible replies: {BN, $B¬N$, $¬BN$, $¬B¬N$} = 2^2 possibilities

Thus, with the meta-concept: *being-nonbeing*, we can recognize many more possibilities, which we cannot obtain by logical reasoning based on two-valued logic. Many possibilities individually exist in the observer's spirit through actual information and his/her perceptions using 'to look inside' information processing—'true **and** false' reasoning rather than 'true **or** false' reasoning.

It is the conscious development [6], which defines the reality of semantic and pragmatic aspects using mental power of consciousness of the observer rather than a reality in terms of syntax derived from "being **or** non-being" reasoning.

'Subject-Object' concept: According to Hegel, the most important achievement of German idealism, starting with Kant and culminating in his own philosophy, was "the demonstration that reality is shaped through and through by mind and, when properly understood, is mind". Thus,

'True-false' Concept: The meta-concept *true-false* presented in Łukasiewicz's philosophy (1879–1956) as in [7]: "The truth about the future events is neither true nor false", i.e., it comes from intuition and commonsense or from the human cognitive processing depending on perceptions rather than 'true or false' reasoning in the syntactic framework. It is a cognizable value—'true-false' measure, τ, and the 'truth' of judgments or the *cognitive measures*, which is graphically presented in the form Fig. 4.

According to Łukasiewicz, for a cognitive measure, τ, $\tau = p$, $q \in [0, 1]$, instead of the *material implication*, we have a *strict implication* presented as:

$$\forall_{p,q \in [0,1]} p \to q = \min(1, \ 1 - p + q) \quad \text{(uncertainly)} \quad (2)$$

'Membership-nonmembership' concept: It is neither *membership* nor *nonmembership* [8], which is developed and leads to Zadeh's fuzzy logic.

Information Content of Meta-concepts: According to Frege, the denotation of statement, p, must be identified by truth values or an infinite number of thoughts (cognitive processing). That is:

p ⇒ p|Denotation = p|*thoughts*

Thought that comes to mind quickly without much personal reflection is a consequence derived from intuition, commonsense through perceptions, which is often roughly translated as 'feeling or to look inside'. It really describes a 'subjective evaluation'/'cognitive evaluation' in the semantic and pragmatic aspects—information content that exists in different ideas: 'Discrimination-Nondiscrimination' according to Zhuang Zhou' philosophy, 'being-nonbeing' according to Vietnamese philosophy, 'identity-different' according to Hegel's philosophy, 'membership-nonmembership' according to Zadeh's philosophy, 'true-false' according to Lukasiewicz's philosophy and 'truth comes from the future' according to intuitive logic of Brouwer and Heyting [9,10]. By this way, we can represent the meta-concept *affirmation-denial* as follows

affirmation-denial|thoughts = *affirmation-denial*| cognitive measures

The **True-false** measure, τ, referred as **cognitive** measure enables us to represent the semantic and pragmatic aspects of knowledge through the human pragmatic competences. Data with its *cognitive measure*, we call intelligent data and the knowledge derived from intelligent data we call the meta-knowledge. These can be estimated by how much it resonates with our being through an internal processing (feeling) of the human mind. We have, according to multi-valued logic, truer if fewer false and vice versa; that is:

$$True - false = True - false | \tau \, (true)$$
$$\wedge True - false | \tau \, (false) \qquad (3)$$

In the same way, we have:

Affirmation-denial = *Affirmation-denial*|τ (*affirmation*) $\wedge$ *Affirmation-denial*|τ(*denial*)
Being-Nonbeing = *Being-Nonbeing*|τ(*being*) $\wedge$ *Being-Nonbeing*|τ(*Nonbeing*)

These data structures are actually intended to represent the **information content** through cognitive measures, τ, determined under the epistemological aspect of engineers to expand the syntactic boundaries of available data into the semantic and pragmatic aspects. It is the result of quantity expressed by numbers through cognitive measures, quality expressed by words through meta-concepts and the human thought through cognitive information processing. Their integration held in relation to Frege's concept of sense and denotation of sentences and Lukasiewicz's multi-valued logic.

Let us return to geotechnical problems, it is seen as an exploration in the framework that transcends the 'syntactic' restrictions, depending on the individual spiritual state of the observer and scientist, which is shown in the Fig. 5.

5 Cognitive information processing using denotational mathematics

Note, that the symbol τ, in the framework of the fuzzy philosophy, is called a truth function that expresses the truth according to the degree of truth. In contrast, in the frame-

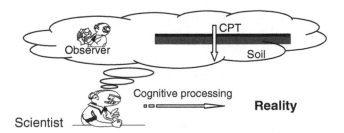

Fig. 5 Meta-knowledge that expresses *objective–subjective* reality

work of "being-nonbeing" of philosophy, it is called "true-false" function referred as the cognitive measures. Their processing—cognitive measure processing can be mathematically represented as follows.

Definition 1 *Borel* σ-*algebra*: let X be a non-empty set, $X \neq \varnothing$; the family $\mathbb{A}$ of subsets of the set X is called σ-*algebra* of subsets of X, if:

$$(X \in \mathbb{A}) \wedge (A \in \mathbb{A} \rightarrow (X - A) \in \mathbb{A})$$
$$\wedge \left(A_n \in \mathbb{A} \rightarrow \bigcup_{n=1}^{\infty} A_n \in \mathbb{A} \right) \qquad (4)$$

The σ-*algebra*, which is generated by all open intervals in $\mathfrak{R}^n$, is called Borel σ-*algebra* and denoted as ß. The elements of family ß are called Borel sets.

Definition 2 *Measure*: a function $\tau : \mathbb{A} \Rightarrow \overline{\mathfrak{R}}_+, \overline{\mathfrak{R}}_+ = \mathfrak{R} \cup \{+\infty\}$ is called a measure, if:

(a) $\forall (A \in \mathbb{A}) : \{(\tau(A) \geq 0) \wedge (\tau(\varnothing) = 0)\}$ (5)

(b) $\forall_{A_i \cap A_j = \varnothing; i \neq j} : \left\{ \tau \left(\overset{\infty}{\underset{i=1}{\cup}} A_i \right) = \sum_{i=1}^{\infty} \tau(A_i) \right\}$ (6)

Definition 3 *Measure of a set*: The function $\tau(A)$, $A \in \mathbb{A}$ is called a measure of set A; if $\tau(A) = 0$ then A is called a measurable-zero set, $\tau : \mathbb{A} \rightarrow [0, \infty]$ is called a *set function* determined on $\mathbb{A}$.

Definition 4 *Measurable set*: Assume, family $\mathfrak{I}$ composed of elements in the form of: $A = B \cup C$, $B \in \beta$, $\tau(C) = 0$; β is a Borel set; each element of set $\mathfrak{I}$ is called a measurable set (measurable in the sense defined by Lebesgue [11]), if:

$$\forall_{A \in \mathfrak{I}} : \tau(A) = \tau(B \cup C) = \tau(B) \qquad (7)$$

Definition 5 *Measurable function*: mathematically, let X be a non-empty set, let S be a σ-*field* of subsets of X, let f be a partial function from X to , $\overline{\mathfrak{R}}$, $\overline{\mathfrak{R}} = \mathfrak{R} \cup \{-\infty\} \cup \{+\infty\}$ and let A be an element of S. We say that f is measurable on A *iff*: for every real number r holds, as in [12].

$$A \cap LE - dom(f, \overline{\mathfrak{R}}(r)) \text{ is measurable on S} \qquad (8)$$

where , the functor LE-dom(f, a) yields a subset of X and is defined by:

$$x \in LE-dom(f, \ a) iff: x \in dom(f) \wedge \exists y\{y = f(x) \wedge y < a\}, \tag{9}$$

where y denotes an extended real number. In other way, let F be a class of all finite non-negative measurable functions defined on a measurable space, (X, $\mathbb{A}$). Moreover, let the set F_α be called an α-cut of f, $f \in$ F. Function $f : X \Rightarrow \overline{\mathfrak{R}}$ is called a *measurable function iff:* β is a Borel set and:

$$\forall_{B\in\beta} : \left\{ f^{-1}(B) = [x : f(x) \in B] \text{ belonging to } \sigma \right.$$
$$\left. -\text{algebra on } X \right\} \text{ albo} \tag{10}$$

$$\{\forall_{\alpha\in\mathfrak{R}} : F_\alpha = [x : f(x) > \alpha]\} \tag{11}$$

Definition 6 *Quantitative-qualitative* evaluation: Let X be a non-empty set; $\mathbb{A}$ be an σ-algebra on X; $\tau : \mathbb{A} \Rightarrow [0, \ 1]$ be a non-negative, real-valued *set function* defined on $\mathbb{A}$. τ is called a cognitive measure on (X, $\mathbb{A}$) *iff:*

a. τ is derived from available data with the respect of semantics and pragmatics.
b. $\tau(\varnothing) = 0$ when $\varnothing \in \mathbb{A}$.
c. $\{(E \in \mathbb{A}, \ F \in \mathbb{A}) \wedge (E \subset F)\}$ implies $\tau(E) \leq \tau(F)$.
d. $[(\{E_n\} \subset \mathbb{A}; \cup \{E_n\} \in \mathbb{A}) \wedge (\cap \{E_n\} \in \mathbb{A})]$ then

$$[\tau(\cup\{E_n\}) = \max \{\tau(E_n)\}] \wedge [\tau(\cap \{E_n\}) = \min\{\tau(E_n)\}]$$

This number is the *quantitative-qualitative* evaluation (a cognitive measure) corresponding to both quantity and quality factors in X. Hence, set $\varnothing$ has a minimum confidence: 0, i.e., $\tau(\varnothing) = 0$; total space X has a maximum confidence: 1, i.e., $\tau(X) = 1$ (boundary conditions); therefore, for every set of factors E i F, so that E $\subset$ F , the confidence of E cannot be greater than the confidence of F. This means that this measure fulfills the conditions: E $\in \mathbb{A}$, F $\in \mathbb{A}$ and E $\subset$ F implies $\tau(E) \leq \tau(F)$ (monotonicity conditions). Measure τ corresponding to above conditions is called a ***true-false measure– fuzzy measure*** in the measurable space (X, $\mathbb{A}$). Compared to a probabilistic measure, the additive condition $(\tau(E\cup F) = \tau(E) + \tau(F)$ for E $\cap$ F $= \varnothing$) has been replaced by condition (c); therefore, we call it (τ) a non-additive measure. τ is called a *lower or upper semi-continuous **true-false** measure* on $(X, \mathbb{A})$ *iff* it satisfies the above conditions [a, b and c (continuity from below)] or [a, b and d (continuity from above)], respectively. Both of them are simply called *semi-continuous **true-false measures***. Furthermore, we say that ***true-false*** measure or semi-continuous ***true-false*** measure, τ, is *regular iff* $X \in \mathbb{A}$ and $\tau(X) = 1$. A set function τ is called true-false *-additive measure iff* g: $\mathbb{A} \rightarrow [0, \ 1]$ on space $(X, \mathbb{A})$ such that $\tau(\cup_{t\in T} E_t) = sup_{t\in T} \tau(E_t)$ for any

subclass $\{E_t | t \in T\}$ of $\mathbb{A}$ whose union is in $\mathbb{A}$, where T is an arbitrary index set. For any E, $F \subseteq X$, a ***true-false measure*** is:

1. additive: $\forall_{E\cap F=\varnothing} \{\tau(E \cup F) = \tau(E) + \tau(F)\}$;
2. supermodular: $\tau(E \cup F) + \tau(E \cap F) \geq \tau(E) + \tau(F)$;
3. submodular: $\tau(E \cup F) + \tau(E \cap F) \leq \tau(E) + \tau(F)$;
4. superadditive: $\forall_{E\cap F=\varnothing} \{\tau(E\cup F)+\tau(E\cap F) \geq \tau(E)+ \tau(F)\}$;
5. subadditive: $\forall_{E\cap F=\varnothing}\{\tau(E \cup F) + \tau(E \cap F) \leq \tau(E)+ \tau(F)\}$;
6. symmetric: $|E| = |F| \rightarrow \tau(E) = \tau(F)$;
7. Boolean: $\tau(E) = 0 \vee 1$

It represents the human behavior that transcends the 'syntactic' boundaries of variable data with the respect of semantics and pragmatics.

The measure τ corresponding to above conditions is called *cognitive measure*—a *true-false measure* in the measurable space (X, $\mathbb{A}$), which we call a *non-additive* measure also. When it is used to define a function such as the Sugeno integral [13], these properties will be crucial in understanding the function's behavior. Let $\lambda \neq 0$ and $\{E_1, E_2, \ldots, E_n\}$ be a disjoint class of sets in $\mathbb{A}$; we have:

$$\tau \left(\overset{n}{\underset{i=1}{\cup}} E_i \right) = \frac{1}{\lambda} \left\{ \prod_{i=1}^{n} [1 + \lambda\tau(E_i)] - 1 \right\} \tag{12}$$

Definition A set function τ is called a λ *-fuzzy* measure on $\mathbb{A}$ *iff* it satisfies the $\sigma - \lambda$ -rule on $\mathbb{A}$, and there at least one set $E \in \mathbb{A}$ such that $\tau(E) < \infty$. A set function, τ, satisfies the λ-*rule* (on $\mathbb{A}$) *iff* there exists:

$$\lambda \in (-(1/\sup \tau), \ \infty) \cup \{0\}, \tag{13}$$

where, $\sup \tau = \sup_{E\in\mathbb{A}} \tau(E)$ such that:

$$\forall_{E,F\in\mathbb{A}, E\cup F\in\mathbb{A}, E\cap F = \varnothing}\{\tau(E \cup F)$$
$$= \tau(E) + \tau(F) + \lambda\tau(E)\tau(F)\} \tag{14}$$

τ satisfies the finite λ-rule (on $\mathbb{A}$) iff there exists the above-mentioned λ such that:

$$\forall_{E_i\in\mathbb{A}, i=1,2,\ldots,n, E_i\cap E_j=\varnothing, E_i\cup E_j\in\mathbb{A}, i\neq j} \tau \left(\overset{n}{\underset{i=1}{\cup}} E_i \right)$$
$$= \begin{cases} \frac{1}{\lambda} \left\{ \prod_{i=1}^{n} [1 + \lambda\tau(E_i)] - 1 \right\} & \text{as } \lambda \neq 0 \\ \sum_{i=1}^{n} \tau(E_i) & \text{as } \lambda = 0 \end{cases} \tag{15}$$

τ satisfies the finite $\sigma - \lambda$-rule (on A) *iff* there exists the above-mentioned λ such that:

$$\forall_{E_i \in \mathbb{A}, i=1,2,\dots,n, E_i \cap E_j = \varnothing, E_i \cup E_j \in \mathbb{A}, i \neq j} \tau \left(\bigcup_{i=1}^{\infty} E_i \right)$$

$$= \begin{cases} \frac{1}{\lambda} \left\{ \prod_{i=1}^{\infty} [1 + \lambda \tau(E_i)] - 1 \right\} & \text{as } \lambda \neq 0 \\ \sum_{i=1}^{\infty} \tau(E_i) & \text{as } \lambda = 0 \end{cases} \quad (16)$$

When $\lambda = 0$, the λ-rule, the finite λ-rule and $\sigma - \lambda$-rule is the additivity, the finite additivity and the σ-additivity, respectively. Note that if $\mathbb{A} = \mathfrak{R}$ is a non-empty class such that E, $F \in \mathfrak{R}$, $E \cup F \in \mathfrak{R}$ and $E - F \in \mathfrak{R}$ and g satisfies the λ-rule, then τ satisfies the finite λ-rule.

Sugeno λ-measure. The Sugeno λ-measure [13], is a special case of *fuzzy* measures defined iteratively. It has the following definition: let $X = \{x_1, x_2, \dots, x_n\}$ be a finite set and let $\lambda \in (-1, +\infty)$. A Sugeno λ-measure is a function τ from 2^X, (i.e., $\{0, 1\}^X$ is the set of all functions from X to $\{0, 1\}$) to $[0, 1]$ with properties:

$$\tau(X) = 1 \wedge (E, F \subseteq X \wedge E \cap F = \varnothing) \to \tau(E \cup F)$$
$$= \tau(E) + \tau(F) + \lambda \tau(E) \tau(F) \quad (17)$$

where λ is determined by:

$$1 + \lambda = \left\{ \prod_{i=1}^{n} [1 + \lambda \tau(E_i)] \right\}; \quad \lambda \in (-1, \infty) \wedge \lambda \neq 0 \quad (18)$$

An evaluation undertaken by a single expert is always influenced by his/her subjectivity. However, we can imagine that each quality factor x_i of a given object also has its inherent quality index $h(x_i) \in [0, 1]$, $i = 1, 2, \dots, n$. That is, we assume the existence of an objective evaluation function h: $X \to [0, 1]$. The most ideal evaluation, E^*, for the quality of the object is the fuzzy integral: $E^* = f h\, dg$ of this function h with respect to the importance measure g, which we call the *objective synthetic evaluation*. Wang (1984–1992) [14] introduced a generalization of the *fuzzy integral*. It is non-linear functional, where the integral is defined over measurable sets. Let $A \in \mathbb{A}$, $\mathbb{A}$ is a σ-algebra of sets in $\wp(X)$; $f \in \mathbf{F}$, $\mathbf{F}$ is the class of all finite non-negative measurable functions defined on measurable space $(X, \mathbb{A})$. For any given $f \in \mathbf{F}$, we write $F_\alpha = \{x | f(x) \geq \alpha\}$, $F_{\alpha+} = \{x | f(x) > \alpha\}$, where $\alpha \in [0, \infty]$. Let F_α and $F_{\alpha+}$ be called an α-cut and strict α-cut of f, respectively. Instead of the importance measure g, the *fuzzy integral* of f on A with respect to *true-false* measure, τ, is denoted by $f_A f\, d\tau$. To simplify the calculation of the fuzzy integral, for a given $(X, \mathbb{A}, \tau)$, $f \in \mathbf{F}$ and $A \in \mathbb{A}$,

we have:

$$\fint_A f\, d\tau = \sup_{\alpha \in \text{ALFA}} [\alpha \wedge \tau(A \cap F_\alpha)] \quad (19)$$

$$\text{ALFA} = \{\alpha | \alpha \in [0, \infty], \tau(A \cap F_\alpha) > \tau(A \cap F_\beta),$$
$$\text{for } - \text{any} : \beta > \alpha\} \quad (20)$$

The *True-false* measure referred as *fuzzy* measure enables us to represent the semantic and pragmatic aspects of knowledge through the human pragmatic competences. These can be estimated by how much it resonates with our being through an internal processing (feeling) of the human mind. It is the result of quantity expressed by numbers through cognitive measures, quality expressed by words through meta-concepts and the human thought through cognitive information processing together held in relation to Frege's concept of sense and denotation of sentences and Lukasiewicz's multi-valued logic.

6 Determining the relative density of sands, I_D, using CPT data

We can use I_D, for example, to indicate the state of denseness of sand soil. Current knowledge on the subject of sand consolidation is limited and qualitative. For example, soil consolidation states, s, are presented by loose (l—loose/Low consolidation) for $0 < I_D \leq 0.33$, moderately consolidated (m—medium consolidation) for $0.33 < I_D \leq 0.67$, or highly consolidated (h—high consolidation) for $I_D > 0.67$, which are shown in the Fig. 6.

The *counter-concept*, loose or medium or high consolidation, is represented logically in the form:

$$s \in \{l \vee m \vee h\} \quad (21)$$

where, $\vee$ denotes alternative operator (or) in two-valued logic. Then, we have loose consolidation for $I_D = 0.33$, medium consolidation for both $I_D = 0.34$ and $I_D = 0.67$. It, however, is hard to recognize, for both $I_D = 0.34$ and $I_D = 0.67$, the same conclusions—medium consolidation.

From engineering experiences, for $I_D = 0.34$, it really is neither loose nor medium consolidation, but a third option determined by cognitive evaluations formulated in the engineer's head that transcends both loose and medium consolidation depending on his/her intuition and experiences. That is to say, engineers have certainly in mind an infinite number of

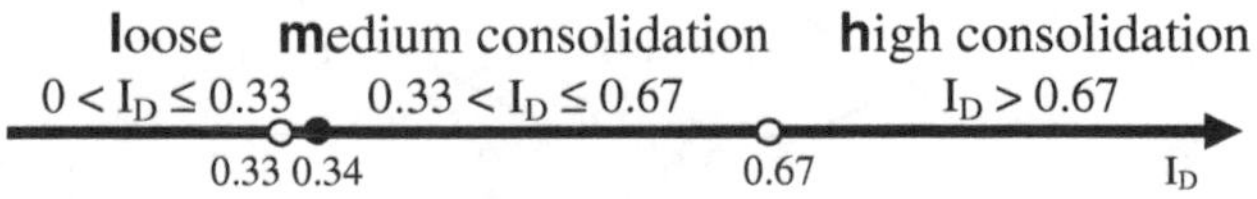

Fig. 6 Presentation of soil **consolidation states** based on 'true or false' philosophy

thoughts, which cannot be expressed by counter-concepts, in the framework of syntactic restriction of the common language, using words, *loose or medium* consolidation, and Boolean numbers. It we can represent rather by the meta-concept, *loose-medium*, with its denotation identified by an infinite number of *true-false* values referred as cognitive measures depending on perceptions originated from intuition and experiences of engineers. For example, for $I_D = 0.34$, according to Eq. (3) we have:

$$loose\text{-}medium|\tau(l) = 0.8 \wedge loose\text{-}medium|\tau(m) = 0.2.$$

It is concerned with a new approach to determine the relative density of soil, I_D, based on *true-false* philosophy that is presented below in the Sect. 6.2.

6.1 Determining relative density of sands using fuzzy philosophy

Traditionally, determining of the relative density of sands, I_D, using the Cone Penetration Test, CPT, is based on three **compressibility** qualifiers as low **or** medium **or** high. They are presented by interval numbers established depending on the current knowledge of the friction ratio, r, and the compressibility relationship. That are low, L, for $r = [0 \div 0.3]\%$, medium, M, for $r = [0.3 \div 0.7]\%$ and high, H, for $r= [0.7 \div 1.0]\%$, in which $r = f_s/q_c$ [%], where f_s denotes the sleeve friction, q_c denotes the cone-tip resistance. It refers as three base correlations, which is graphically presented in the Fig. 7.

According to the fuzzy approach, as in [15], three compressibility qualifiers: low (L), medium (M) and high (H) are represented by three fuzzy sets and expressed by three membership functions $\mu(L)$, $\mu(M)$ and $\mu(H)$, which are established on the base of engineering judgments. Those three fuzzy sets low, medium and high are shown in the Fig. 8.

To determine I_D, a weighted aggregation technique has been used to combine three base correlations, determined from the correlations, which are defined for sands of low, medium and high compressibility, respectively. The relative density I_D obtained from these base correlations, presented by Juang et. al. [15], is then aggregated as follows:

$$I_D = I_D^L w^L + I_D^M w^M + I_D^H w^H \tag{22}$$

where, I_D^k, $k = $ L, M, H are relative densities, determined from the correlations defined for sands of low, medium and high compressibility, respectively (they usually relate the cone-tip resistance (q_c) to I_D with consideration of effective overburden stress (σ'_v) and soil compressibility); w^k, denotes weights which are determined based on a "similarity" measure of three predefined levels of compressibility. The result based on fuzzy logic, obtained by Juang et al. is $I_D^J = 41\%$.

As the above aggregation, Eq. (22), is based on an implicit assumption that these effects of three compressibility levels (L, M, H) are viewed as additive. This assumption, however, is not always reasonable as indicated by Wang and Klir [14]. On the other hand, although the general idea of degrees of membership agrees well with the general idea of *true-false/one* philosophy, we have to see in this approach that the dividing compressibility of sands into three levels, which are described by three fuzzy sets low, medium and high separately or partly overlapped, does not agree with the "one" philosophy. In this case, saying as Hegel, *we are constantly using our one reality to subdivide and rearrange new sets of ones.*

6.2 Determining relative density of sands based on *True-False* philosophy

Let a set function, τ, be employed as a *true-false* measure/cognitive measure for available data, which is derived from the engineer's perceptions in the pragmatic and semantic respects depending on their intuition and experiences. It is a *qualitative–quantitative* evaluation used for the *meta-concept*, in which, three levels of compressibility, according to Hegel's philosophy, are undivided and expressed as 'one': Low–Medium–High, (L–M–H). It refers as appearance of the so-called *meta-state* of sand (three states, low, medium and high compressibility together, which is not loose and neither medium nor High). Three levels of compressibility are presented graphically for any value, r_i, in the Fig. 9.

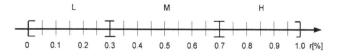

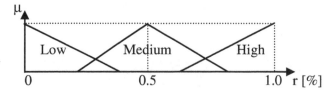

Fig. 7 Sand **compressibility** in the framework of *beingor nonbeing* philosophy

Fig. 8 Three levels of **compressibility** in the framework of *membership-non-membership* philosophy

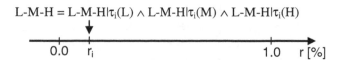

Fig. 9 Three levels of **compressibility** in the framework of *true-false* philosophy

This refers to the appearance of one state L–M–H presented in the form:

$$L - M - H = L \wedge M \wedge H \tag{23}$$

A set function, τ(L–M–H), is employed as a **true-false** measure (cognitive measure)—non-additive measure, i.e.,

$$\tau(\{L \cup M \cup H\}) \neq \tau(L) + \tau(M) + \tau(H).$$

We can distinguish different states depending on variable *true-false* measures, which is non-additive measure defined by:

$$\tau : R \rightarrow [0, 1] \tag{24}$$

It is a **qualitative–quantitative** evaluation of R, $R = \{r_i\}$, $i = 1, 2, \ldots, n$, for compressibility of sands in terms of multiple quality factors expressed by **true-false** measures, τ, As a result, the compressibility level of sands is low–medium–high, in which we can recognize low from medium, medium from high and vice versa through variable *true-false* measures $\tau(k)$, $k = L, M, H$ and *true-false* analysis, as in [16]. A **true-false** value of each predefined level of compressibility (low, medium, high) in respect of the given or actual compressibility, r_a, is determined on the base of "difference" of r_a and the numbers represented the low, medium, high levels of compressibility, respectively. For most NC sands, according to Robertson and Campanella (1985), the predefined value of r for medium compressibility $r^*(M)$ is about 0.5 %, but for sands of low compressibility $r^*(L) \approx 0\%$ and for sands of high compressibility it is $r^*(H) \approx 1\%$. Hence, the difference of k-level compressibility and number representing the given or actual compressibility, r_a, (diff$_{ra}(k)$) is defined as follows:

$$\mathrm{diff}_{ra}(k) = \left| r_a - r^*(k); \tau(r^*(k)) = \mathrm{maximum} \right|;$$
$$r^*(k) \in k \subset R \tag{25}$$

This is a distance between number, r_a, representing the actual compressibility and number $r^*(k)$, which represents the most probable value that reaches a maximum value for sand of low, medium and high compressibility. This distance is used as a means of measuring how close the actual compressibility is to each of the predefined levels of compressibility. For subjective evaluation: $\tau(r_1) = \tau(r_2) = \cdots = \tau(r_n)$, $(r_x \in k_j, x = 1, 2, \ldots, n)$ we have:

$$\mathrm{diff}_{ra}(k) = 0 \tag{26}$$

Smaller distance indicated a higher degree of similarity, and the level of compressibility corresponding to a higher is assigned a greater value of truth, which is represented as *true-false* function, τ:

$$\tau(k) = 1 - \mathrm{diff}_{ra}(k) \tag{27}$$

From that we can construct the λ-*true-false* measure for all the other subsets of set X, $X = \{L \cup M \cup H\}$ using Sugeno λ-measure. Then, we can calculate the λ-*true-false* measures, $\{\tau(L \cup M), \tau(L \cup H)$ and $\tau(M \cup H)\}$ by

$$\tau(R) = \tau(\{L \cup M \cup H\}) = 1$$
$$= \frac{1}{\lambda}\left\{ \prod_{i=1}^{n} \left[1 + \lambda\tau(\{k_j\}) \right] - 1 \right\} \tag{28}$$

From that, value λ can be found by:

$$\lambda = \left\{ \prod_{i=1}^{n} \left[1 + \lambda\tau(\{k_j\}) \right] \right\} - 1 \tag{29}$$

$$\tau(k_i \cup k_j) = \tau(k_i) + \tau(k_j) + \lambda\tau(k_i)\tau(k_j)$$
$$\text{for } k_i, k_j \in R, \ k_i \cap k_j = \varnothing \tag{30}$$

i.e., sand, having the compressibility level k is intuitively assigned to this *true-false* measure (cognitive measure) $\tau(k)$. From that, we can construct the λ-*true-false* measure for all the other subsets of set X, $X = \{L \cup M \cup H\}$. Then, we can calculate the λ-*true-false* measures, $\{\tau(L \cup M), \tau(L \cup H)$ and $\tau(M \cup H)\}$ by Eqs. (28, 29, 30) for different subsets $\{(L \cup M), (L \cup H)$ and $(M \cup H)\}$. In addition, we support here the given evaluations by three experts expressed by: $\tau_i^*(k), i = 1, 2, 3$. The relative densities, $I_D(k)$ are determined from the correlation defined for sands of low, medium and high compressibility, respectively. Scores of these may be regarded as a measurable function $f(k)$ defined on $(R, \wp(R))$ such that $f(k) \in [0, 1]$ for each $k \in R$. Then, relative density, I_D, by a cognitive processing with both physical and mental data using Sugeno type integral, as in [13], of a *measurable function* $f(k)$, $f(k) \in F_\alpha$ with respect to the *true-false* measure, τ, in the form:

$$I_D = \int f(k)\mathrm{d}\tau = \sup_{\alpha \in [0,\infty]} [\alpha \wedge \tau(R \cap F_\alpha)], \tag{31}$$

where,

$$F_\alpha = \{k \mid f(k) \geq \alpha\}, \quad k \subset R; \tag{32}$$

in which, $R = \{L, M, H\}$; L, M, H represent the loose, medium and high states of sands. The evaluations of three experts are shown in the following table.

Data and results:

1. Data from the Texas A&M University National Geotechnical Experimentation Site (Gibbens and Briaud 1994), four CPT sounding are obtained at this site. The data from four CPT sounding along with other pertinent data used for determining relative density are listed in Table 1.

Table 1 CPT data from Texas A&M University site (Gibbens and Briaud 1994)

CPT number	Depth (m)	σ'_v (kPa)	q_c (kPa)	f_s (kPa)	r_a (%)
1	3.0	46.5	6,260	38	0.61
2	3.0	46.5	6,590	35	0.53
5	3.0	46.5	6,590	43	0.65
6	3.0	46.5	6,190	37	0.60

Numerical data: $\sigma'_v = 46.5$ (kPa), $q_c = 6260$ (kPa), $f_s = 38$ (kPa) and the given friction ratio, $r_a = 0.61\%$, are used for determining relative density, I_D of sand and to illustrate the new approach.

According to Robertson and Campanella [15], the value, r, increases with increasing sand compressibility. For most NC sands, the r_m^* value for medium compressibility is about 0.5%, but the r_L^* value is almost 0 for sands of low compressibility and $r_H^* = 1\%$ (or more) for sands of high compressibility. For purpose of verifying the proposed model, the CPT data at the depth of 3 m are considered to be appropriate. Difference of low level compressibility (L) and the number represented the actual compressibility, r_a, $r_a = 0.61\%$, for example, is determined as follows:

$$\text{diff}(L)_{0.61} = 0.61 - 0.0 = 0.61$$

Then, from Eq. 27 we have:

$$\tau(L) = 1 - 0.61 = 0.39$$

Repeating this process for all other levels of compressibility, we obtain $\tau(M) = 0.89$, and $\tau(H) = 0.61$. From that we can construct the $\tau\lambda$-fuzzymodal measure for all other subsets of set R, $R = \{L, M, H\}$ as follows: firstly, λ parameter is determined using Eq. 29 as:

$$\lambda + 1 = (1 + 0.39\lambda)(1 + 0.89\lambda)(1 + 0.61\lambda)$$

The solution of this equation according to the unique root greater than -1 is -0.99. And the τ_λ-fuzzy measures for other subsets of set R are defined using Eq. 28, for example,

$$\tau(L \cup M) = 0.39 + 0.89 - 0.99(0.39)0.89 = 0.93$$

By similar ways, we can obtain $\tau(L \cup H) = 0.76$; $\tau(M \cup H) = 0.96$. Finally, value I_D is calculated by Eqs. (31), (32).

For example, for value $r_a = 0.61$ and various values of relative densities for separately states: loose, medium and high: $I_D^L = 0.526$, $I_D^M = 0.549$, $I_D^H = 0.575$, determined from the correlations defined for sand of low, medium, and high compressibility, respectively, we have:

$$I_D = \int f(k)d\tau = [0.526 \wedge \tau(L \cup M \cup H)]$$
$$\vee [0.549 \wedge \tau(M \cup H)]$$
$$\vee [0.575 \wedge \tau(H)]$$
$$= (0.526 \wedge 1) \vee (0.549 \wedge 0.96)$$
$$\vee (0.575 \wedge 0.61) = 0.575.$$

where '$\wedge$' and '$\vee$' denote 'min' and 'max' operations, respectively. The above process is repeated for data from other CPTs and the complete results are shown in Table 2.

In which, I_D values is determined by the proposed model using cognitive measures and fuzzy/true-false integral, I'_D values are the results obtained from Juang et al. (1996). Thus, I_D values determined by the proposed model in all four CPTs examined here agree well with the results obtained by Juang et al. [15].

2. Data from two sites, the **Hunter's point, California site** with their scores, for example, are given for available CPT data: $\sigma'_v = 81$ (kPa), $q_c = 5,030$ (kPa), $f_s = 3$ (kPa) and the given friction ratio, $r_a = 0.06\%$ are used for determining relative density, I_D of sand.

Details on the Hunter's point, California site are described in a Federal Highway Administration (FHwA) report by Dimillio et al. (1987) represented in Juang et al. [15], which documents the results of a pile prediction event. Although a thorough site investigation including several field tests was conducted, only those data required in the present study are summarized here. By the same way presented for Texas site, the predicted I_D^* values obtained from the proposed model using λ-true-false measures and fuzzy/true-false integral. To study the influence of subjective biases of the individual experts and to get a more reasonable evaluation, we can use an arithmetic average of scores given by a number of experts. We support, for this case, the given evaluations by three experts expressed by: $\tau_i^*(k)$, $i = 1, 2, 3$. From that we can construct the λ-**true-false** measure for all the other subsets of set

Table 2 Determination of relative density, I_D, by τ_λ-fuzzy measure and fuzzy integral and I'_D by Juang's et al. method (Texas A&M university site)

CPT nr.	$\tau(L)$ (−)	$\tau(M)$ (−)	$\tau(H)$ (−)	$\tau_{(L\cup M)}$ (−)	$\tau_{(L\cup H)}$ (−)	$\tau_{(M\cup H)}$ (−)	r_a (%)	I_D/I'_D (%)
1	0.39	0.89	0.61	0.93	0.76	0.96	0.61	57.5/55
2	0.57	0.97	0.53	0.99	0.80	0.98	0.53	56.2/56
5	0.35	0.85	0.65	0.92	0.78	0.97	0.65	58.9/57
6	0.40	0.90	0.60	0.96	0.77	0.98	0.60	57.1/55

Table 3 *Qualitative–quantitative* evaluations and numerical results, I_D^*

Expert	τ_i^*	τ_i^*	τ_i^*	$\tau(L\cup M)$	$\tau(L\cup H)$	$\tau(M\cup H)$	I_D^* (%)
1	0.80	0.30	0.10	0.95	0.85	0.38	41.0
2	0.80	0.50	0.10	0.98	0.84	0.56	42.8
3	0.80	0.30	0.20	0.93	0.88	0.46	42.8

X, $X = \{L\cup M\cup H\}$. Then, we can calculate the λ-***true-false*** measures for different subsets $\{(L\cup M), (L\cup H)$ and $(M\cup H)\}$ and the ***true-false*** measures of subsets $\{\tau(L\cup M), \tau(L\cup H)$ and $\tau(M\cup H)\}$ by Eqs. (28, 29, 30), and I_D^* by Eqs. (31, 32). Three given expert's evaluations and obtained results are shown in the following Table 3.

Obviously, the changes of results I_D^*, depending on changes of $\{\tau^*(L),\ \tau^*(M),\ \tau^*(H),\ \tau(L\cup M),\ \tau(L\cup H),\ \tau(M\cup H)\}$, confirm the requirement that the relative *true-false* measures, τ, of the compressibility are taken into account in the *true-false*-integral operator. To reduce the influence of qualitative biases of independent experts and to obtain a more reasonable evaluation of I_D^*, we can use an arithmetic average of the results obtained from the three experts. That is:

$$(0.41 + 0.428 + 0.428)/3 = 42.2\,\%.$$

Although those I_D^* values based on "one" philosophy agree well with the results based on fuzzy logic, as in [15], $I_D^J = 41\%$. These results of both methods are depended on the expert's *qualitative–quantitative* evaluations also, which we can improve by a process of inductive thinking.

7 Conclusions

To recognize the real world, we are confined by syntactic limits in the framework of binary philosophy. It is only a matter of habit, which we should change in the future from dualism with counter-concepts to a monism with new concepts named meta-concepts. It is really that, to describe the real systems like soil systems, a formulation of the counter-concept *loose* or *consolidation* based on available data resulted from physical experiments is insufficient. We need meta-concepts that transcend limitations of both common words and Boolean numbers. The meta-concept: *low–medium–high*, derived from perceptions of engineers rather than logical reasoning, represents a third option that transcends both *low*, *medium* and *high*.

These expressive needs require a theory of cognitive measures, a new field of mathematics for denotation computing and their integration with the achievements of modern information and communication technologies to create the so-called cognitive processing of information for various fields of science. These areas of research that require more intel-

ligence and contemplation for "the truth that comes from the future" should require being–nonbeing philosophy and multi-valued logic.

Generally we represent, in this paper, a new approach for cognitive information processing to expand the syntactic boundaries under the respects of semantics and pragmatics of the available data. It is applied to recognize the unknown reality of the real world rather than application of an approximation approach to improve the known reality through external information processing. It is based rather on the integration of modern philosophy, epistemology, logic, denotational mathematics and cognitive informatics using engineer's perceptions rooted from intuition, commonsense and experiences without logical reasoning based on binary logic.

Acknowledgments I would like to express many thanks for the support of the National Center of Sciences in Krakow and WM University of Olsztyn, Poland, grant nr. NN 506 215 440.

Open Access This article is distributed under the terms of the Creative Commons Attribution Noncommercial License which permits any noncommercial use, distribution, and reproduction in any medium, provided the original author(s) and source are credited.

References

1. Frege, F.L.G.: Über Sinn und Bedeutung. In: Zeitschrift für Philosophie und philosophische Kritik, vol. 100, pp. 25–50 (Translated as 'On Sense and Reference' by M. Black in Translations from the Philosophical Writings of Frege, G., Geach, P., Black, M. (eds. and trans.) 3rd edn. Blackwell, Oxford (1980))
2. Stanford Encyclopedia of Philosophy.
3. Thuc, N.D.: Lich su triet hoc dong Phuong (History of Eastern philosophy). Nha xuat ban van hoa, Hanoi, Viet Nam (1963)
4. Giang, T., Can. N.D.: Trang Tu (莊 周- Zhuang Zhou)-Nam Hoa Kinh t.1, 2; nha xuat ban Hanoi, Viet Nam (1992)
5. Suzuki, D.T.: C'est ici le paradoxe philosophique le plus profond; L'Essence du Bouddhisme, p. 88, Paris (1962)
6. Hunefeldt, T., Brunetti, R.: Artificial intelligence as "theoretical psychology" : Christopher Longguet-Higgins' contribution to cognitive science. Cognitive Processing International Quarterly of Cognitive Science, Marta Olivetti Belardinelli and Springer (2004)
7. Łukasiewicz, J.: O logice trójwartościowej (about three-valued logic). Ruch Filozoficzny (Philosophical movement), No. 5, pp. 169–170 (1920) (in Poland)
8. Zadeh, L.A.: Fuzzy sets. Inf. Contr. **8**(3), 338–353 (1965)
9. Heyting, A.: Intuitionism, An Introduction (Amsterdam, 1965) (1965)
10. Heyting, A. (ed.): L E J Brouwer, Collected Works 1. Philosophy and Foundations of Mathematics (Amsterdam, 1975) (1975)
11. Perrin, L.: Henri Lebesgue: Renewer of Modern Analysis. In: Le Lionnais, François. Great Currents of Mathematical Thought, vol. 1, 2nd edn. Courier Dover Publications. Plato J.V.: Creating Modern Probability, Its Mathematics. Physics and Philosophy in Historical Perspective. Cambridge Uni. Press 1994 (2004)
12. Kharazishvili, A.B.: On almost measurable real-valued functions. Studia Scientiarum Mathematicarum Hungarica **47**(2), 257–266 (2010) NULL

13. Sugeno, M.: Fuzzy Measures and Fuzzy Integrals: A Survey, pp. 89–102. North-Holland, Fuzzy Automata and Decision Processes. Amsterdam (1977)

14. Wang, Z., Klir, G.J.: Fuzzy Measure Theory. Plenum Press, N.Y. (1992)

15. Juang, C.H., Huang, X.H., Holtz, R.D., Chen, J.W.: Determining relative density of sands from CPT using fuzzy sets. J. Geol. Eng. **122**, 1–5 (1996)

16. Tran, C.: Dealing With Geotechnical Uncertainties by Being-Non-Being Philosophy and Multi-Valued Logic. (book) pub. WM Univ, Olsztyn, Poland (2012)

7

Alternating decision tree algorithm for assessing protein interaction reliability

Min Su Lee · Sangyoon Oh

Abstract This paper presents a machine learning approach for assessing the reliability of protein–protein interactions in a high-throughput dataset. We use an alternating decision tree algorithm to distinguish true interacting protein pairs from noisy high-throughput data using various biological attributes of interacting proteins. The alternating decision tree algorithm is used both for identifying discriminating biological features that could be used for assessing protein interaction reliability and for constructing a classifier to identify true positive interacting pairs. Experimental results show that the proposed approach has a good performance in distinguishing true interacting protein pairs from noisy protein–protein interaction data. Moreover, our alternating decision tree classifier supplemented with domain knowledge may be helpful to understand the biological conditions in connection with interacting protein pairs.

Keywords Alternating decision tree algorithm · Machine learning · Protein–protein interaction · Reliability

1 Introduction

Machine learning algorithms have been successfully applied to many bioinformatics problems. One of the key issues in bioinformatics is the analysis of protein–protein interactions (PPIs) [1], which is the fundamental basis of cellular oper-

ations. PPI knowledge is essential in predicting unknown functions of proteins [2–6], in clarifying biological pathways [7–10], and in understanding biological mechanisms in the disease [11]. Conventional studies on PPI have examined each interacting pair separately in terms of the physical and chemical properties of proteins. Thanks to advanced molecular-level technologies, large amounts of PPI data have been collected through high-throughput experiments by testing for physical interactions among multiple proteins. They include genome-scale Yeast Two-Hybrid assays (Y2H) [12–14] and protein complex identification methods through mass spectrometry [15, 16].

While vast amounts of data obtained from high-throughput experiments allow for efficient identification of different kinds of PPI information, they are prone to higher false positive rates than small-scale studies [17–22]. Some studies have reported that approximately half of the interactions obtained from high-throughput data may be false positives [17, 19]. This necessitates an additional experimental or computational method to estimate the reliability of each PPI precisely. To do this, selecting relevant properties of PPI as circumstantial evidences, and adopting efficient computational methodologies are important. Several circumstantial features have previously been used to identify true PPIs from high-throughput experimental data in yeast [17, 23–27].

The intersection of multiple high-throughput PPI datasets can be effective in obtaining more reliable PPIs. If an interaction is detected from two distinct experiments, the interaction can be regarded as more reliable. However, different experimental methods often generate different levels of information. For example, mass spectrometry detects which proteins are part of a stable complex, but does not necessarily indicate which proteins in the complex have a direct interaction. Mass spectrometry might also fail to uncover transient or weak interactions. Y2H might not detect interactions that are

M. S. Lee
Computational Omics Lab, School of Informatics and Computing, Indiana University, Bloomington, IN, USA

S. Oh (✉)
Department of Computer Engineering, Ajou University, Suwon, Republic of Korea
e-mail: syoh@ajou.ac.kr

dependent on post-translational modifications or that should be stabilized by the presence of another protein. Moreover, since PPI is very sensitive to experimental conditions, PPI data produced at different research groups are substantially different although the same technologies are used [12,13]. Due to these limitations in high-throughput technologies, the coverage of intersections is very small even with the immense amount of PPI datasets [17].

The conserved interactions between different species are named interlog [23]. If two proteins interact in one species, their ortholog proteins are more likely to interact with each other. This property has been used to enhance the confidence of prediction in high-throughput data [23,28].

Interaction network topology is another means of identifying true interactions. With the protein interaction network, the interaction generality measure (IG2) based on the topological properties [29], and statistical and topological correlation between the paired proteins [30] have been studied to assess the reliability of an interaction. Since proteins with more than one interaction partner are rare cases, these methods have a low sensitivity (i.e., a low true positive rate) although they have a high specificity (i.e., a low false positive rate).

Most of these methods use only one criterion at once and need an entire genome-scale PPI dataset to assess the reliability of each PPI pair. Each biological feature may also have false and missing values. Moreover, it is very difficult for biologists to define the proper cutoff values of confidence scores to distinguish between true positives and false positives. Since different biological features may cover different subsets of interacting pairs, a combination of various existing methods would be more effective.

Recently, computational methods for assessing the reliability of putative protein interaction have also been studied based on supervised machine learning techniques, such as Bayesian network [31,32], and maximum likelihood estimation [25]. Patil et al. [31] used a combination of three genomic features—Pfam domains, Gene Ontology annotations and sequence homology—to assign reliability to the protein–protein interaction. And Bayesian network approach was used to compute the likelihood ratio to be real interactions. Deng et al. [20] used another three attributes which are the distribution of gene expression correlation coefficients, the reliability based on gene expression correlation coefficient, and the accuracy of protein function predictions. And maximum likelihood method was used to estimate the reliability of protein interaction datasets based on the three attributes. Lin et al. [32] proposed a Bayesian network-based approach which assigns likelihood scores to individual protein pairs based on interlogs and their genomic features derived from microarray data and gene ontology.

In this paper, we present a new evaluation system for PPI datasets that can distinguish true interacting protein pairs from noisy datasets. This work is inspired by our previous

work that performs comparative study of classification methods for protein interaction verification system [33]. Through the empirical comparative study, K-nearest neighborhood and decision tree algorithm are the two top performance producers among other methods. We adopted a decision tree algorithm among those two methods since it can produce an interpretable output classifier with good performance. In this system, we use an alternating decision tree algorithm [27] that dynamically selects discriminating features among various attributes related with PPIs and trains an interpretable classifier that can distinguish true interacting protein pairs with confidence scores from noisy datasets. The system may help not only to identify relevant circumstantial evidences among various biological features for assessing reliability of PPIs, but also to understand the characteristics of true interacting protein pairs based on the alternating decision tree. The statistical evaluation of the system using tenfold cross-validation shows that the system performs well in terms of various performance measures. Specifically, the average rates of accuracy, sensitivity, precision, F-measure, and MCC (Matthew's correlation coefficient) are 97.13, 96.91, 97.33, 97.12, and 94.26 %, respectively.

The contributions of this study can be summarized as follows: Firstly, our proposed protein interaction evaluation system shows a good performance in distinguishing true interacting protein pairs from a noisy PPI dataset compared with similar approaches. Secondly, we use a novel negative example generation method for assessing protein interaction reliability. This helps to derive more reliable and high performance output model. Third, by applying ADTree algorithm, interpretable prediction model can be derived which shows the biological conditions of interacting protein pairs with confidence score. Also, missing values in query data can be more naturally handled by considering the reachable decision nodes in ADTree.

2 Materials and methods

In this section, we present a protein interaction evaluation system to assess the reliability of PPI data obtained from high-throughput experiments. To separate true positives and false positives from the putative PPI dataset, we have developed a classification model based on an alternating decision tree algorithm. Figure 1 shows the basic system architecture of the classification model. In Fig. 1, the solid arrows indicate the training process to construct a classifier, and the dotted arrows show the classifying process of querying high-throughput protein interaction data. Our evaluation system consists of a PPI database, a PPI annotation database, a computation module of circumstantial evidences for each PPI pair, an alternating decision tree algorithm for selecting relevant genomic features and training a classification model,

Fig. 1 System architecture for classifying high-throughput protein interaction pairs into positives and negatives

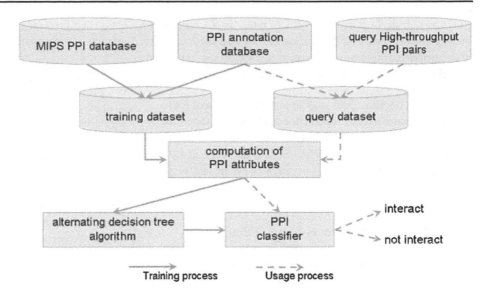

and a PPI classifier generated by the algorithm. The system first trains from a collection of protein pairs that consist of positive and negative PPI examples and their genomic features based on an alternating decision tree algorithm. The trained classifier can be used to distinguish true positive PPI pairs from the noisy query dataset based on the values of genomic evidences of each pair.

2.1 Training dataset

Genome-scale PPI data are currently available for *S. cerevisiae* [12,13,15,16], *H. pylori*, *C. elegans*, *D. melanogaster*, and *H. sapiens*. Since the number of protein–protein interaction pairs for yeast is larger than others, we evaluated our system using the yeast PPI data. The proposed system first trains with a set of reliable positive and negative protein interaction pairs. The quality of training dataset is a critical point to construct a reliable prediction model. An ideal training dataset should be independent from the discriminating features, sufficiently large for reliable statistics, and free of systematic biases [34,35]. Hence, the selection of a reliable training dataset is a definitely important procedure for constructing a robust PPI evaluation system.

Positive protein pairs were extracted from the MIPS database [36,37]. Manually collected MIPS database has been regarded as a trusted standard dataset. The MIPS database contains PPI pairs and protein complexes in yeast that provides annotations for experimental methods in PPIs. We used a protein complex dataset as a reliable positive protein pair by decomposing it into binary interactions [34]. The MIPS protein complex dataset consists of known protein complexes based on data collected from the literature, and most of these are derived from small-scale studies.

Unlike positive protein interaction pairs, negative protein interaction pairs are harder to define, because there is no experimentally verified set of non-interacting proteins. In fact, it is almost impossible to validate non-interacting protein pairs theoretically and empirically through rigorous wet lab experiments. Hence, we created negative datasets synthetically based on co-localization enrichment of interaction between two proteins. Interactions are strongly enriched between proteins that co-localize, but the degree of enrichment varies widely by compartment. Huh et al. [38] determined the subcellular localizations of each interacting protein pair and the fraction of the total number of interactions occurring for each localization pair. They compared the interaction between specific compartments to a randomized interaction set, showing that some compartments interact preferentially with others. We used this localization enrichment data among 22 subcellular locations to derive non-interacting proteins. To do this, we first generated random PPI pairs using proteins that appeared in positive datasets. Secondly, since proteins are located in several subcellular compartments by shuttling or transporting, we found all combinations of subcellular locations of two proteins among randomly generated PPI pairs. After that, we selected negative protein pairs whose minimum enrichment value for all possible co-localization cases was zero based on Huh et al.'s experimental results. Since previous researches have reported that approximately half of the interactions obtained from high-throughput data may be false positives [17,19], we finally adjusted the number of instances of negative protein pairs to that of corresponding positive protein pairs in order to conform the distribution of a sample to that of a population. As a result, our training dataset consisted of 8,250 positives and 8,250 negatives.

We think that this strategy of deriving negative datasets is more sophisticated than Jansen et al.'s [34] approach.

Jansen et al. derived negative protein pairs by selecting PPI pairs in different subcellular compartments based on localization attributes, including nucleus, mitochondria, cytoplasm, membrane, and secretory pathway [34,39].

This plot demonstrates overlapping proportion of each PPI attributes to positive and negative instances according to the type of attributes. 'pos' means overlap between each positive instances in a dataset and PPI attributes, and 'neg' means overlaps between each negative instances in a dataset and PPI attributes.

2.2 Biological attributes for evaluating PPIs

As we described in Sect. 1, each biological attribute, by itself, is only a weak predictor of protein interactions. Assessing the reliability of a protein interaction pair can be improved by integrating different biological attributes because the task depends on the existence of circumstantial evidence that supports it. When multiple distinct attributes all support a candidate interaction pair, the confidence of PPI increases. Different attributes may cover different subsets of interacting protein pairs, and in this case, attribute integration can increase the coverage.

Hence, we collected open biological features of two proteins and integrated seven biological attributes that can be used as indicators of putative interacting proteins. Table 1 gives some explanation of the biological attributes, which include the name of attribute, description, and the range of attribute value.

Interacting proteins whose transcripts are co-expressed are more likely to be credible [18,40,41]. Hence we computed Pearson's correlation of mRNA expression levels between two proteins (attribute 1 in Table 1) using publicly available time-series expression datasets (Rosetta compendium and yeast cell cycle). Since two interacting proteins should be present in a similar amount, the absolute expression lev-

els of two proteins (attribute 2 in Table 1) and the absolute amount of two proteins (attribute 3 in Table 1) were used [42].

Another important property of interacting proteins is that two proteins in the same biological process are more likely to interact. Attributes 4 and 5 in Table 1 are this functional similarity of two proteins in terms of biological ontology such as MIPS Functional catalog [43,44] and Gene Ontology about biological processes [45]. The similarity measure between two proteins was quantified by computing the frequencies of a set of functional terms that two proteins share based on semantic similarity measure [46]. In general, a lower frequency means a higher specificity of the functional term for the two proteins. Hence the semantic similarity of shared functional terms can be inferred by the frequency of the term.

Attributes 6 and 7 are related to the essentiality of two proteins in a cell. Attribute 6 computes a marginal essentiality of two proteins. Marginal essentiality is a measure of the importance of a non-essential gene in a cell that could be derived from topological characteristics of protein interaction networks [47]. Attribute 7 is based on the hypothesis that if two proteins are in the same protein complex or pathway, they are likely to share the essentiality in the cell because they should perform the same function together [36].

We considered some additional biological attributes for assessing PPIs such as co-regulation and interlog. However, we filtered them out since the training dataset rarely contains those attributes. Figure 2 shows the proportion of each attribute that appeared in the training dataset with respect to the positive and negative instances. Since these attributes can be computed only when both proteins have a corresponding annotation, the proportion of the attributes that appeared in the datasets was rather smaller.

Figure 3a shows an example of a decision tree in a graph, and Fig. 3b shows an alternating decision tree. Here, A and B are names of attributes, 1 and m are values of attributes, and Class +1 and Class −1 are

Table 1 Description of biological attributes

	Name	Description	Range
1	mRNA co-expression	Pearson correlation of mRNA expression levels between two proteins using microarray dataset	$-1 \leq x \leq 1$
2	Absolute mRNA expression	Similarity of expression levels of two proteins	$0 \leq x < 16$
3	Absolute protein abundance	Similarity of abundance levels of two proteins	$0 \leq x < 10$
4	MIPS functional similarity	Specificity of common MIPS functional category of two proteins	$0 \leq x < 7$
5	GO functional similarity	Specificity of common GO biological process category of two proteins	$0 \leq x < 7$
6	Marginal essentiality	Quantitative measure of a non-essential gene to a cell based on topological property within the interaction network	$-20 < x < 0$
7	Co-essentiality	Whether two proteins are both essential or not	0: lethal
			1: viable
			2: lethal/viable

Fig. 2 Overlaps between dataset and attributes

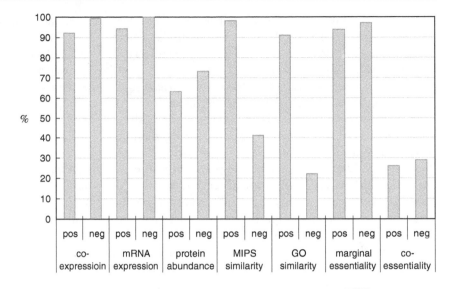

Fig. 3 Examples of Tree-based classifiers

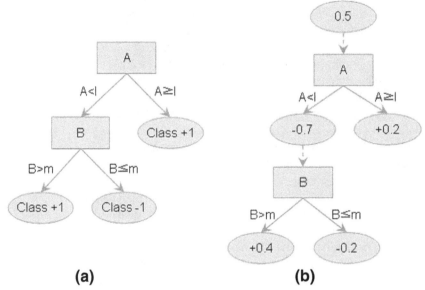

(a)   (b)

target classes of this classification task. In an alternating decision tree, unlike a decision tree, the classification result is the sign of the sum of the predictions along the path, instead of the label of the leaf.

2.3 Alternating decision tree algorithm

We applied a kind of decision tree algorithm to classify PPI pairs into positive and negative interactions. Decision tree algorithms have been successfully used to predict categorical class labels, such as positive and negative (Fig. 3a). A decision tree algorithm constructs a tree-like classification model which consists of nodes, branches and leaves. Each node in the tree specifies some attribute of the instance, and each branch descending from that node corresponds to one of the possible values for this attribute. Each leaf node represents one of the target classes. To build a decision tree, it basically

chooses an attribute that provides the maximum degree of discrimination for target classes. The information gain is a good measure to determine how well a given attribute separates the training instances according to their target class. The attribute with the highest information gain is chosen as the attribute for the current node, and the instances are partitioned accordingly. A resulting decision tree is composed of hierarchical if-then rules for values of attributes. Then, a decision tree algorithm classifies instances by evaluating their values of attributes from the root to some leaf node, and provides the classification results of the instance.

Decision tree algorithms have several advantages. Since decision trees use an intuitive white box model, it easily predicts the target class of query data using Boolean logic. Especially, decision trees are simple to understand and interpret. Moreover, decision tree algorithms are robust and scalable for large data and they can train a classification model in reasonable processing time. Hence the decision tree model is effective not only to filter noisy PPI pairs from high-throughput experimental PPI data, but also to gain important insights that describe circumstantial evidences of PPIs.

However, general decision tree algorithms also have some disadvantages. Sometimes, the number of nodes generated from a decision tree algorithm is too large to interpret. Moreover, the performance of general decision tree algorithms is not usually better than that of functional or statistical machine learning algorithms, such as neural networks, support vector machines, and Bayesian networks. Recently, decision tree-based algorithms have strictly improved and become sophisticated in combination with other methods such as boosting [27] or logistic regression [48].

An alternating decision tree [27] is a combination of a decision tree and boosting that generates classification rules often smaller in number of nodes and easier to interpret. Especially, an alternating decision tree gives a measure of confidence that is called classification margin.

An alternating decision tree algorithm can be defined as a sum of simple rules. It uses a generalized representation for classification rules that consists of alternating layers of prediction nodes (represented by ellipses in Fig. 3b) and splitter nodes (represented by rectangles in Fig. 3b). The values in a root node represent the initial probability for assigning the target class according to the training dataset. Alternating decision tree classifiers are then built according to a particular structure using boosting wherein simple rules are successively added to the alternating decision tree classifier until the unit classifier of the tree exhibits satisfactory performance. Since boosting iteration adds three nodes (one splitter node and two prediction nodes) to the tree, more boosting iterations will result in larger and potentially more accurate trees. Unlike original decision trees: an instance is mapped into a path along the tree from the root to one of the leaves and output is the label of the leaf, the classification result of an alternating decision tree became the sign of the sum of the predictions along the multi-path associated with the given instances. When some feature values are unknown, the alternating decision tree algorithm only considers the reachable decision nodes [27]. Since the algorithm can handle missing values in a dataset more naturally, the alternating decision tree algorithm can be applied to analyzing our PPI dataset which includes lots of missing values. Also, the alternating decision tree algorithm has shown competitive performances and has produced smaller and intuitive classification rules than general decision tree algorithms.

3 Experimental results and discussion

To learn a prediction model for assessing protein interaction reliability, we first prepared training interaction pairs

which are labeled with a target class, as described in Sect. 2.1. Then, seven biological attributes are integrated into the training pairs. Figure 2 demonstrates the proportion of each attribute appeared in the training dataset with respect to the positive and negative instances. We used the same number of positive and negative interactions for the training dataset of the alternating decision algorithm. We set the number of boosting interaction as 10 by considering both the accuracy and complexity of the system. The resulting alternating decision tree consisted of 10 splitter nodes and 21 prediction nodes. An exhaustive search method was used to build the alternating decision tree. Once an alternating decision tree is built, the system classifies any input PPI pairs into positives and negatives by searching possible paths along the tree and selecting the most confident prediction.

We computed the performances of the trained alternating decision tree classifier with tenfold cross-validation. Tenfold cross-validation means that the available examples are partitioned into ten disjoint subsets. The cross-validation procedure then runs ten times, and each time the procedure uses one of the ten subsets as the test set and the others for training sets. We used various performance criteria to evaluate the effectiveness of our system with the composition of training dataset. These criteria are calculated based on true positive (TP), true negative (TN), false positive (FP), and false negative (FN). The performance criteria that we used are as follows:

$$\text{Accuracy} = \frac{(TP + TN) \times 100}{TP + FP + FN + TN}$$

$$\text{Sensitivity} = \frac{TP \times 100}{TP + FN} = \text{Recall}$$

$$\text{Specificity} = \frac{TN \times 100}{FP + TN}$$

$$\text{Precision} = \frac{TP \times 100}{TP + FP}$$

$$F\text{-measure} = \frac{2 \times \text{Precision} \times \text{Recall}}{\text{Precision} + \text{Recall}} = \frac{2 \times TP \times 100}{2 \times TP + FP + FN}$$

$$\text{MCC} = \frac{TP \times TN - FN \times FP}{\sqrt{(TP + FN)(TP + FP)(TN + FN)(TN + FP)}}$$

The accuracy is the proportion of correctly classified examples among total examples. Sensitivity is the proportion of examples that were classified as positive class, among all examples that are truly positive class. It is equivalent to Recall. The specificity is the proportion of true negatives among all examples that are negative class. The precision is the proportion of the examples that are truly positive class among all those which were classified as positive class. The F-measure is a single measure that characterizes recall and precision. MCC is the Matthew's correlation coefficient. The Matthew's correlation coefficient ranges from -1 to 1. A value of MCC $= 1$ indicates the best prediction, and a

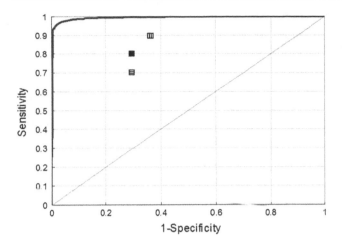

Fig. 4 Comparison of prediction power with similar studies using ROC *plot*

value of MCC = −1 indicates the worst possible prediction. A value of MCC = 0 would be expected for a random prediction scheme. The statistical evaluation of the system through tenfold cross validation shows that the proposed system performs well with average rates of 97.13 % of accuracy, 96.91 % of sensitivity, 97.35 % of specificity, 97.33 % of precision, 97.12 % of F-measure, and 94.26 % of MCC. These measures of discriminative power indicate that the model is not biased.

While traditional decision tree classifiers yield binary class labels, the alternating decision tree classifiers produce confidence measures representing the degree to which class the instance belongs to. Therefore, the result of alternating decision tree can be represented by ROC (receiver operating characteristic) curve as show in Fig. 4. ROC curve (Receiver operating characteristic curve) is a graphical plot of the sensitivity versus (1-specificity) for a binary classifier system as its discrimination threshold varies [48]. The ROC curve depicts relative trade-offs between sensitivity (benefits) and 1-specificity (costs). The ROC curve for a good classifier will be as close as possible to the upper-left corner of the chart.

We compared the performance of our system with other related studies using ROC plot (Fig. 4). The rectangle with horizontal stripe denotes the performance of Deng et al.'s [20] study, the rectangle with vertical stripe shows the performance of Patil et al.'s [31] study, and the black rectangle shows the performance of Lin et al.'s [32] study. Deng et al. used a maximum likelihood estimation method to assess protein interaction reliability using genomic features of gene expression correlation and protein function. Patil et al. proposed a Bayesian network based filtering method for high-throughput protein interaction data using biological features of protein domain, functional similarity, and homology. Lin et al. used Bayesian network-based integrative framework which assigns likelihood scores to each protein pairs based on genomic features of their interlogs. The genomic fea-

tures were derived from microarray data and gene ontology. Since each of studies uses different sets of training data and attributes, it is hard to compare their performance directly. Especially, the negative training datasets are very different among studies. Because there is no experimentally verified set of non-interacting pairs, negative datasets are usually generated synthetically. Our negative data generation method which utilizes co-localization enrichment information of interacting proteins may help to improve system performance. The result reflects that the relevancy and quality of training dataset determines the reliability and performance of output model. This ROC plot also shows robust performance of the alternating decision tree classifier compared with other similar studies which uses Bayesian network and maximum likelihood estimation.

The ROC curve shows the performance of alternating decision tree classifier. The rectangle with horizontal stripe denotes the performance of Deng et al.'s [20] study, the rectangle with vertical stripe shows the performance of Patil et al.'s [31] study, and the black rectangle shows the performance of Lin et al.'s [32] study.

The generated alternating decision tree shows the classification rules for assessing PPI reliability (Fig. 5). Since the alternating decision tree algorithm dynamically selects relevant attributes and disregards non-informative attributes, the output model can describe about the influence of combinatorial effects of attributes. The generated tree does not include any splitter node using 'absolute protein abundance' or 'co-essentiality' attribute which contains many missing entries. On the other hand, functional similarity measures (which are MIPS similarity and GO similarity) are highly used. And mRNA expression level and co-expression information was also used. In general, lower indices correspond to more influential nodes that were added earlier in the boosting process. From the alternating decision tree classifier, we can observe the following characteristics:

- Rule I: The most discriminative attribute was MIPS functional similarity. If the frequency of shared MIPS functional term between two proteins is less than 4.338, the interacting protein pair must be a positive pair.
- Rule II: If the Pearson's correlation coefficient of mRNA expression data of two interacting proteins is more than 0.326, the interacting protein pair must be a positive pair.
- Rules III, VII, and VIII: Like MIPS functional similarity, the smaller frequency of the shared GO functional term indicates the higher reliability of protein interactions.
- Rules IV and VI: Since marginal essentiality and absolute mRNA expression produce low confidential predictions, they could be regarded as relatively weak evidences for assessing protein–protein interaction reliability.

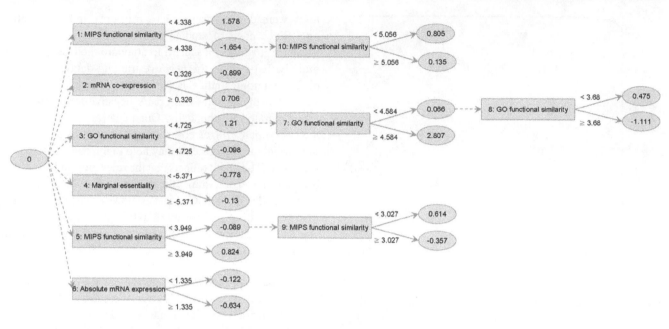

Fig. 5 An alternating decision tree classifier for assessing PPI reliability

Table 2 Reliability assessment of pure high-throughput PPI dataset

	Experimental method	# of detected interaction pairs	% of predicted positives
Ito et al. [13]	Yeast two hybrid assay	4,390	15.52
Garvin et al. [15]	Tandem-affinity purification and mass spectrometry	16,358	31.53

- Rule X: If the frequency of shared MIPS functional term is more than 5.056, the protein pair will be predicted as a negative interaction pair with high confidence. The confidence of prediction is calculated by summing the prediction values $[0 + (-1.654) + (+0.135) = -1.519]$ along the path. The sign of the resultant sum means the target class, and the absolute value represents the confidence of the prediction for the instance.

Since all types of the biological annotations in a protein are not always available, some feature values are frequently unknown. The proposed classification scheme based on alternating decision tree algorithm relieves this problem by considering only the reachable nodes whose associated predictions are large. As you can see from the above rule set, attributes that we used as the domain knowledge mutually make up for each other to cover the lack of information.

We investigated the alternating decision tree classifier with two sets of unlabeled high-throughput experimental datasets: The one was detected by Y2H assay by Ito et al. [13] and the other was obtained by mass spectrometry by Garvin et al. [15]. We filtered out some PPI pairs whose seven attributes are not annotated. The evaluation results are summarized in Table 2. The number of assessed positives in Ito et al.'s Y2H dataset and Garvin et al.'s mass spectrometry dataset

is relatively smaller than previous reports [18, 19], because our system predicts true interacting protein pair with high confidence. However, the percentile of reliable interacting pairs in Ito's dataset is very similar with Deng et al.'s [20] report which was 15 % sensitivity and specificity. As might have been expected, the percentile of predicted positives of Garvin et al.'s data is larger than that of Ito et al.'s data.

4 Conclusion

In this paper, we presented an assessment scheme for the reliability of candidate interacting proteins in a PPI dataset. This scheme is based on the alternating decision tree algorithm and utilizes the domain knowledge of PPIs. Since the quality of training data determines the reliability and robustness of classifiers, we carefully derived a negative dataset based on co-localization enrichment measure. As a result, we constructed an evaluation system for assessing protein interaction reliability using positive datasets obtained from known protein complex and negative datasets derived based on co-localization characteristics. The experimental results show that applying an alternating decision tree algorithm supplemented with various biological attributes provides excellent performance overall in distinguishing true interacting protein pairs from a noisy PPI dataset. Moreover, our alternating decision tree classifier is helpful to understand the biological conditions of interacting protein pairs with confidence score. The classifier may also be helpful in predicting new candidate interaction protein pairs.

Studies of biological networks should start with reliable interaction data. A number of reliable PPI datasets assessed by this system can be used as a valuable resource for proteomics research.

Open Access This article is distributed under the terms of the Creative Commons Attribution License which permits any use, distribution, and reproduction in any medium, provided the original author(s) and the source are credited.

References

1. Rivas, J., Fontanillo, C.: Protein–protein interactions essentials: Key concepts to building and analyzing interactome networks. PLOS Comput. Biol. **6**(6), e1000807 (2010)

2. Vazquez, A., Flammini, A., Maritan, A., Vespignani, A.: Global protein function prediction from protein–protein interaction networks. Nat. Biotechnol. (2003).

3. Letovsky, S., Kasif, S.: Predicting protein function from protein/protein interaction data: a probabilistic approach. Bioinformatics (2003).

4. Samanta, M.P., Liang, S.: Predicting protein functions from redundancies in large-scale protein interaction networks. PNAS (2003).

5. Spirin, V., Mirny, L.A.: Protein complexes and functional modules in molecular networks. PNAS **100**(21), 12123–12128 (2003).

6. Deng, M., Tu, Z., Sun, F., Chen, T.: Mapping gene ontology to proteins based on protein–protein interaction data. Bioinformatics (2004).

7. Steffen, M., Petti A., Aach J., D'haeseleer, P., Church, G: Automated modelling of signal transduction networks. BMC Bioinfo. **3**, 34 (2002)

8. Blow, N.: Systems biology: untangling the protein web. Nature **460**, 415–418 (2009)

9. Franceschini, A., Szklarczyk, D., Frankild, S., Kuhn, M., Simonovic, M., Roth, A., Lin, J., Minguez, P., Bork, P., Mering, C., Jensen, L.: STRING v9.1: protein–protein interaction networks, with increased coverage and integration. Nucl. Acids Res. **41**(D1), D808–D815 (2013)

10. Croft, D., O'Kelly, G., Wu, G., Haw, R., Gillespie, M., Matthews, L., Caudy, M., Garapati, P., Gopinath, G., Jassal, B., Jupe, S., Kalatskaya, I., Mahajan, S., May, B., Ndegwa, N., Schmidt, E., Shamovsky, V., Yung, C., Birney, E., Hermjakob, H., D'Eustachio, P., Stein, L.: Reactome: a database of reactions, pathways and biological processes. Nucl. Acids Res. **39**(suppl1), D691–D697 (2011)

11. Wu, G., Feng, X., Stein, L.: A human functional protein interaction network and its application to cancer data analysis. Gen Biol. **11**(5), R53 (2010)

12. Uetz, P., Giot, L., Cagney, G., Mansfield, T.A., Judson, R., Knight, J., Lockshon, D., Narayan, V., Srinivasan, M., Pochart, P., Qureshi-Emili, A., Li, Y., Godwin, B., Conover, D., Kalbfleish, T., Vijayadamodar, G., Yang, M., Johnston, M., Fields, S., Rothberg, J.: A comprehensive analysis of protein–protein interactions in Saccharomyces cerevisiae. Nature (2000).

13. Ito, T., Chiba, T., Ozawa, R., Yoshida, M., Hattori, M., Sakai, Y.: A comprehensive two-hybrid analysis to explore the yeast protein interactome. PNAS (2001).

14. Tong A.H., Drees B, Nardelli G, Bader G.D., Brannetti, B., Castagnoli, L., Evangelista, M., Ferracuti, S., Nelson, B., Paoluzi, S., Quondam, M., Zucconi, A., Hogue, C., Fields, S., Boone, C., Cesareni, C.: A combined experimental and computational strategy to define protein interaction networks for peptide recognition modules. Science (2002).

15. Gavin, A.C., Bosche, M., Krause, R., et al.: Functional organization of the yeast proteome by systematic analysis of protein complexes. Nature (2002).

16. Ho, Y., Gruhler, A., Heilbut, A., et al.: Systematic identification of protein complexes in Saccharomyces cerevisiae by mass spectrometry. Nature (2002).

17. von Mering, C., Krause, R., Snel, B., Cornell, M., et al.: Comparative assessment of large-scale data sets of protein–protein interactions. Nature (2002).

18. Deane, C.M., Salwinski, L., Xenarios, I., Eisenberg, D.: Protein interactions: two methods for assessment of the reliability of high throughput observations. Mol. Cell Proteomics **1**(5), 349–356 (2002)

19. Sprinzak, E., Sattath, S., Margalit, H. J.: How reliable are experimental protein–protein interaction data? J. Mol. Biol. **327**(5), 919–923

20. Deng, M., Sun, F., Chen, T.: Assessment of the reliability of protein–protein interactions and protein function prediction. Pac. Symp. Biocomput. 140–151 (2003)

21. Legrain, P., Wojcik, J., Gauthier, J.M.: Protein–protein interaction maps: a lead towards cellular functions. Trends Gen. (2001).

22. Mackay, J.P., Sunde, M., Lowry, J.A., Crossley, M., Matthews, J.M.: Protein interactions: is seeing believing? Trends Biochem. Sci. (2007).

23. Matthews, L.R., Vaglio, P., Reboul, J., Ge, H., et al.: Identification of potential interaction networks using sequence-based searches for conserved protein–protein interactions or "Interologs". Gen. Res. **11**(21):2120–2126 (2001)

24. Chatr-Aryamontri, A., Ceol, A., Licata, L., Cesareni, G.: Protein interactions: integration leads to belief. Trends Biochem. Sci. (2008)

25. Liu, Y., Liu, N., Zhao, H.: Inferring protein–protein interactions through high-throughput interaction data from diverse organisms. Bioinformatics (2005).

26. Ben-Hur, A., Noble, W.S.: Kernel methods for predicting protein–protein interactions. Bioinformatics (2005).

27. Freund, Y., Mason, L.: The alternating decision tree learning algorithm. In: Proceeding of the sixteenth international conference on data mining, pp. 124–133. (1999)

28. Sato, T., Yamanishi, Y., Kanehisa, M., Toh, H.: The inference of protein–protein interactions by co-evolutionary analysis is improved by excluding the information about the phylogenetic relationships. Bioinformatics (2005).

29. Saito, R., Suzuki, H., Hayashizaki, Y.: Construction of reliable protein–protein interaction networks with a new interaction generality measure. Bioinformatics (2003).

30. Bader, J.S., Chaudhuri, A., Rothberg, J.M., Chant, J.: Gaining confidence in high-throughput protein interaction networks. Nat. Biotech. (2004).

31. Patil, A., Nakamura, H.: Filtering high-throughput protein–protein interaction data using a combination of genomic features. BMC Bioinfo. (2005).

32. Lin, X., Liu, M., Chen, X.: Assessing reliability of protein–protein interactions by integrative analysis of data in model organisms. BMC Bioinfo. (2009).

33. Lee, M.S., Park, S.S.: Comparative analysis of classification methods for protein interaction verification system. Lecture Notes in Computer Science, vol. 4243, Advances in Information Systems, pp. 227–236 (2006)

34. Jansen, R., Yu, H., Greenbaum, D., Kluger, Y., et al.: A bayesian networks approach for predicting protein–protein interactions from genomic data. Science (2003).

35. Jasen, R., Greenbaum, D., Gerstein, M.: Relating whole-genome expression data with protein–protein interactions. Gen. Res. (2002).

36. Mewes, H.W., Ruepp, A., Theis, F., Rattei, T., Walter, M., Frishman, D., Suhre, K., Spannagl, M., Mayer, K. F. X., Stümpflen, V., Antonov, A.: MIPS: curated databases and comprehensive secondary data resources in 2010. Nucl. Acids Res. (2011)

37. Guldender, U., Munsterkotter, M., Oesterheld, M., Pagel, P., et al.: MPact: the MIPS protein interaction resource on yeast. Nucl. Acids Res. (2006).

38. Huh, W.K., Falvo, J.V., Gerke, L.C., et al.: Global analysis of protein localization in budding yeast. Nature (2003).

39. Lu, L.J., Xia, Y., Yu, H., Rives, A., et al.: Protein interaction prediction by integrating genomic features and protein interaction network analysis. In: Azuaje, F., Dopazo, J. (eds.) Data Analysis and Visualization in Genomics and Proteomics, pp. 61–81. John Wiley & Sons (2005)

40. Ge, H., Liu, Z., Church, G.M., Vidal, M.: Correlation between transcriptome and interactome mapping data from Saccharomyces cerevisiae. Nat. Genet. (2001).

41. Kemmeren, P., van Berkum, N.L., Vilo, J., Bijma, T., et al.: Protein interaction verification and functional annotation by integrated analysis of genome-scale data. Mol. Cell 9(5), 1133–1143 (2002)

42. Greenbaum, D., Jansen, R., Gerstein, M.: Analysis of mRNA expression and protein abundance data: an approach for the comparison of the enrichment of features in the cellular population of proteins and transcripts. Bioinformatics 18(4):585–596 (2002)

43. Tetko, I.V., Rodchenkov, I.V., Walter, M.C., Rattei, T., Mewes, H.W.: Beyond the "Best" Match: machine learning annotation of protein sequences by integration of different sources of information. Bioinformatics 24(5), 621–628 (2008)

44. Ashburner, M., et al.: The gene ontology consortium. Nat. Gen. 25, 25–29 (2000)

45. Lord, P.W., Stevens, R.D., Goble, C.A.: Investigating semantic similarity measures across the gene ontology: the relationship between sequence and annotation. Bioinformatics (2003).

46. Yu, H., Greenbaum, D., Xin Lu, H., Zhu, X., Gerstein, M.: Genomic analysis of essentiality within protein networks. Trends Gen. (2004).

47. Landwehr, N., Hall, M., Frank, E.: Logistic model trees. Mach. Learn. (2005).

48. Fawcett, T.: ROC Graphs: Notes and Practical Considerations for Researchers. HP Laboratories Technical report HPL-2003-4, Palo Alto (2004)

8

Hybrid intelligent diagnosis approach based on soft computing from signal and image knowledge representations for a biomedical application

Amine Chohra · **Nadia Kanaoui** ·
Véronique Amarger · **Kurosh Madani**

Abstract Fault diagnosis is a complex and fuzzy cognitive process, and soft computing methods as neural networks and fuzzy logic, have shown great potential in the development of decision support systems. Dealing with expert (human) knowledge consideration, Computer-Aided Diagnosis (CAD) dilemma is one of the most interesting, but also one of the most difficult problems. Among difficulties contributing to challenging nature of this problem, one can mention the need of fine classification and decision-making. In this paper, a brief survey on fault diagnosis systems is given first. Then, from a fault diagnosis system analysis of the classification and decision-making problem, a global diagnosis synopsis is deduced. Afterwards, a hybrid intelligent diagnosis approach, based on soft computing implying modular neural networks for classification and fuzzy logic for decision-making, is suggested from signal and image representations. The suggested approach is developed in biomedicine for a CAD, from Auditory Brainstem Response test, and the prototype design and experimental results are presented. In fact, a double classification is exploited in a primary fuzzy diagnosis, to ensure a satisfactory reliability. Then, this reliability is reinforced using a confidence parameter with the primary diagnosis result, exploited in a final fuzzy diagnosis giving the appropriate diagnosis with a confidence index. Indeed, experimental results demonstrate the efficiency and reliability of CAD for three classes: two auditory pathologies Retro-cochlear Class (RC) and Endo-cochlear Class (EC), and Normal auditory Class (NC). The generalization rate of NC is clearly higher for primary fuzzy diagnosis and final fuzzy diagnosis than that of the two classifications. The obtained rates for RC and EC are higher than obtained by image classification but quite similar than those obtained by signal classification. An important contribution of the final fuzzy diagnosis is the fact that a confidence index is associated with each fault diagnosis. Finally, a discussion is given with regard to the reliability and large application field of the suggested approach.

Keywords Decision support · Classification ·
Decision-making · Learning and adaptation ·
Neural networks · Fuzzy logic

A. Chohra (✉) · N. Kanaoui · V. Amarger · K. Madani
Images, Signals, and Intelligent Systems Laboratory (LISSI / EA 3956),
Senart Institute of Technology, Paris East University (UPEC),
Avenue Pierre Point, 77127 Lieusaint, France
e-mail: chohra@u-pec.fr

N. Kanaoui
e-mail: kanaoui@u-pec.fr

V. Amarger
e-mail: amarger@u-pec.fr

K. Madani
e-mail: madani@u-pec.fr

1 Introduction

A *diagnosis system* is basically one which is capable of identifying the nature of a problem by examining the observed symptoms. The output of such a system is a diagnosis (and possibly an explanation or justification) [1]. In many applications of interest, it is desirable for the system to not only identify the possible causes of the problem, but also to suggest suitable remedies (systems capable of advising) or to give a reliability rate of the identification of possible causes. Recently, several decision support systems and intelligent systems have been developed [2,3] and the diagnosis approaches based on such intelligent systems have been developed for industrial applications [1,4,5], and biomedicine applications [6–10]. Currently, one of the most used approaches to feature identification, classification, and decision-making problems inherent to fault detection and diagnosis, is soft computing implying mainly neural networks and fuzzy logic [1, 3–6, 9, 10].

Over the past decades, new approaches based on artificial neural networks have been developed aiming to solve real life problems related to optimization, modeling, decision-making, classification, data mining, and nonlinear functions (behavior) approximation. Inspired from biological nervous systems and brain structure, artificial neural networks could be seen as information processing systems, which allow elaboration of many original techniques covering a large application field based on their appealing properties such as learning and generalization capabilities [11–13].

Another aspect of increasing importance, and strongly linked to data processing and the amount of data available concerning processes or devices (due to the high level of sensors and monitoring), is the extraction of knowledge from data to discover the information structure hidden in it. Several approaches have been developed to analyze and classify biomedicine signals: electroencephalography signals [7], electrocardiogram signals [8], and particularly signals based on Auditory Brainstem Response (ABR) test, which is a test for hearing and brain (neurological) functioning, [6, 14–16]. Traditionally, biomedicine signals are processed using signal processing approaches, mainly based on peak and wave identification from pattern recognition approaches, such as in [6–8, 14–16]. The main problem is then to identify pertinent parameters. This task is not trivial, because the time (or frequency) is not always the variable that points up the studied phenomena's features leading then to a necessity of multiple knowledge representations (signal, image, …).

This paper deals with pattern recognition (classification) and decision-making based on Artificial Intelligence using soft computing implying neural networks and fuzzy logic applied to a biomedicine problem. The aim of this paper is absolutely not to replace specialized human but to suggest a decision support tool with a satisfactory reliability degree for Computer-Aided Diagnosis (CAD) systems. Thus, a global diagnosis synopsis is deduced from a fault diagnosis system analysis of the classification and decision-making problem,

given in Sect. 2. Afterwards, the decision-making problem from the results of two neural classifications is stated and a hybrid intelligent diagnosis approach is suggested in Sect. 3. In Sects. 4 and 5, the suggested approach is developed for a computer-aided auditory diagnosis, from signal and image representations, in order to achieve a diagnosis tool able to assert auditory pathologies based on ABR test which provides an effective measure of the integrity of the auditory pathway. Then, prototype design and experimental results are presented, and a discussion is given with regard to reliability and large application field.

2 Fault diagnosis system analysis

Globally, the main goals of fault diagnosis systems for CAD [5, 10] are: to detect if a fault is in progress as soon as possible, to classify the fault in progress, to be able to suggest suitable remedies (systems able of advising) or to give a reliability rate of the identified fault through a Confidence Index (*CI*).

CAD is an attractive area leading to future promising fault diagnosis applications. However, dealing with expert (human) knowledge consideration, the computer-aided diagnosis dilemma is one of most interesting, but also one of the most difficult problems. The fault diagnosis help is often related to the classification of several information sources implying different representations. Fault diagnosis can be obtained from the classification of only one kind of information (knowledge) representation. However, experts use several information to emit their diagnosis. Then, an interesting way to built efficient fault diagnosis system can be deduced from this concept in order to take advantage from several information. More, experts can use several information sources, in various forms; qualitative or quantitative data, signals, images, to emit their diagnosis. Thus, these information could be issued from different information sources and/or from different representations of a same test. For instance, in case of diagnosis of the same fault classes set, one can consider that these information are independently, in parallel, classified and after the decision-making of their

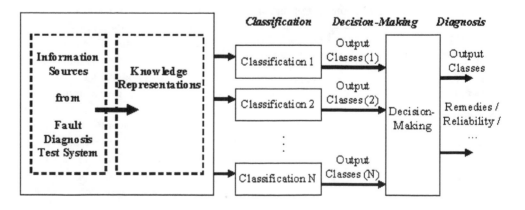

Fig. 1 Global diagnosis synopsis of the same fault classes set

results gives then final results as shown in Fig. 1. Final results give the fault classes set and suitable remedies or a reliability rate of the possible identified fault class.

3 Hybrid intelligent diagnosis approach

In order to study the decision-making phase of the global diagnosis synopsis suggested in Fig. 1, two different knowledge representations are considered from only one information source, as shown in Fig. 2. This configuration, in the case of diagnosis of the same fault classes set, leads to two different classifications. More, if such classifications are handled by neural networks, which are known to be appropriate for classification [11–13, 17] the decision-making appears to be difficult particularly in CAD. In such cases, CAD can be useful and efficient only if the results are given with a reliability parameter (e.g., a CI on each fault classes set result).

In fact, the classification stage consists of the signal classification which can be based on multilayer feedforward perceptron networks (MLP) or on radial basis function networks (RBF) networks as well as the image classification which can be based on the same networks. These networks are chosen from their theoretical and practical features particularly the fact that MLP are *neural global* approximators, whereas RBF are *neural local* approximators [11]. Practically, even if RBF classifiers usually converge faster than MLP in general during training, they are almost equivalent in terms of classification performance from a same knowledge representation of an information source. The interest here is to exploit these classifiers from two different knowledge representations of an information source. In this case, it is interesting, in a double classification, to choose (between MLP and RBF) the appropriate classifier to exploit the first knowledge representation and the appropriate one to exploit the second knowledge representation.

More, this choice is motivated by the fact that such networks can be used in a double classification in such a way to take advantage from their complementary classification performances (with a confidence parameter to enhance classification rates) as well as from their competitive classification performances (with the confidence parameter, this information will contribute to enhance, for instance, the *CI* in final decision-making in case of common classification, or inversely in case of contradictory classification) [3]. Indeed, in a double classification from signal and global image, it is appropriated to classify the signal (sampled amplitude of signal which is *more local than global*) using neural *local* approximators (RBF), while, it is appropriated to classify the global image (area mean grey level of global image which is *more global than local*) using neural *global* approximators (MLP).

By another way, the nature of neural classification results (neural outputs) of the neural architectures are, in general, not binary values. In fact, for instance, the typical MLP or RBF used for classification with sigmoïdal outputs give output class values between [0, 1] or outputs which are distances from RBF centers, respectively. This makes difficult the problem of the decision-making from two neural networks.

The analysis of neural classifier outputs shows that, in case of MLP, more the output is close to 1 and more this output will be close to be the identified fault class. Contrarily, more the output is close to 0 and more this output will be far to be the identified fault class. In case of RBF, the outputs are distances from RBF centers. In this case with a new scale of outputs it is easily to make output class values varying between [0, c], where c is a constant to be determined (e.g., see Sect. 5.1, Fig. 7a–c). Then, more the output which is a distance is close to c and more this output will be far to be identified as fault class. Contrarily, more the output is close to 0 and more this output will be close to be the identified fault class. From this purpose, one interesting way to built

Fig. 2 Decision-making from two neural classifications (diagnosis of the same fault classes set)

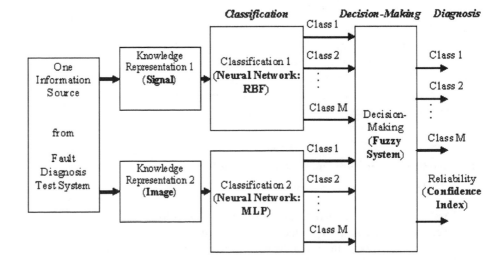

efficient decision-making from two neural classifiers is fuzzy logic [18, 19].

Elsewhere, such decision-making system should be useful and efficient giving a reliability parameter, e.g., a Confidence Index (CI) on each fault classes set result.

Then, a first way is to design a fuzzy system with seven (07) inputs (three inputs from first classifier, three inputs from second classifier, and one confidence parameter input) leading to a fuzzy rule base built of $3^7 = 2,187$ rules which is unfortunately a huge rule number difficult and hard to implement.

An interesting way is then to design two fuzzy classifiers for the decision-making:

- the first fuzzy system for the primary decision-making from two neural classifiers with (06) inputs (three inputs from first classifier and three inputs from second classifier) leading to a fuzzy rule base built of $3^6 = 729$ rules,
- the second fuzzy system for the final decision-making from the first fuzzy system and a confidence parameter, i.e., with four (04) inputs (three inputs from first fuzzy system and one confidence parameter input) leading to a fuzzy rule base built of $3^4 = 81$ rules.

Thus, two fuzzy decision-making systems are necessary, avoiding a decision system with a huge rule number and associating a confidence parameter to the decision, in order to decide from two neural classifiers and to give a reliability parameter (e.g., a Confidence Index CI) for a useful and efficient CAD.

Thus, the results of the two neural classifications, from knowledge representation 1 and knowledge representation 2, see Fig. 2, can be then efficiently exploited in a fuzzy system to ensure a satisfactory reliability. The fuzzy decision-making system based on a fuzzy inference can be exploited in order to capture the expert (human) knowledge [2, 20]. Then, the decision-making system allows to decide the fault classes diagnosis among: Class 1, Class 2, ..., and Class M, and its usefulness and efficiency are better traduced with the associated *CI* on its decision. Contrary to a time or frequency (signal) based representation, the image based one, taking benefit from it's 2-D nature, offers advantage a richer representation allowing to take into account more complex features (shapes, particular information, ...).

4 Biomedical application: computer-aided auditory diagnosis

The ABR test involves attaching electrodes to the head to record electrical activity from the auditory nerve (the hearing nerve) and other parts of the brain. This recorded electrical activity is known as Brainstem Auditory Evoked Potentials (BAEP).

4.1 Brainstem auditory evoked potentials (BAEP) clinical test

When a sense organ is stimulated, it generates a string of complex neurophysiology processes. BAEP are electrical response caused by the brief stimulation of a sense system. The stimulus gives rise to the start of a string of action's potentials that can be recorded on the nerve's course, or from a distance of the activated structures. BAEP are generated as follows (see Fig. 3a): the patient hears clicking noise or tone bursts through earphones. The use of auditory stimuli evokes an electrical response. In fact, the stimulus triggers a number of neurophysiology responses along the auditory pathway. An action potential is conducted along the eight nerve, the brainstem, and finally to the brain. A few times after the initial stimulation, the signal evokes a response in the area of brain where sounds are interpreted.

4.2 Extraction of the two knowledge representations (signal and image)

A technique of extraction [15] allows us, following 800 acquisitions such as described before, the visualization of the BAEP estimation on averages of 16 acquisitions. Thus, a surface of 50 estimations called Temporal Dynamic of the Cerebral trunk (TDC) can be visualized. The average signal, which corresponds to the average of the 800 acquisitions, and the TDC surface could then be obtained. Those are then processed into a signal representation as shown in Fig. 3b. In this figure, an example of TDC surface for a patient is shown. The average signal (named signal representation) is presented in front of TDC surface which is better shown in Fig. 3c.

Three patient classes are studied: Retro-cochlear auditory disorder patients (Retro-cochlear Class: RC), Endo-cochlear auditory disorder patients (Endo-cochlear Class: EC), healthy patients (Normal Class: NC). Figure 4a–c shows examples of signal representations for two patients: RC, EC, and NC, respectively.

The signal to image conversion (named image representation), shown in Fig. 5, is obtained after a TDC surface signal and image processing [9, 21]. Figure 5 presents image representations for the same six patients.

These figures (Figs. 4, 5) illustrate the fact that, signal or image representations could be very similar for patients belonging to different classes, and they could be very different for patients belonging to a same class, demonstrating the difficulty of their classification.

Fig. 3 **a** BAEP clinical test. **b** TDC surface. **c** Average signal processing

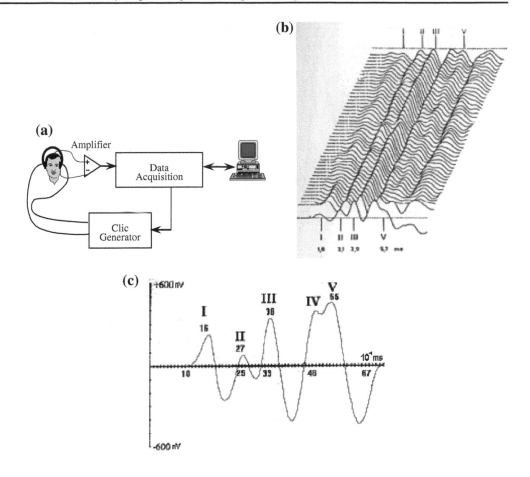

4.3 Suggested hybrid intelligent diagnosis system

The hybrid intelligent diagnosis system suggested in Fig. 6 is built of data processing stage, classification stage, primary fuzzy decision-making stage leading to a primary diagnosis, and final fuzzy decision-making stage leading to the final diagnosis. Note that this suggested diagnosis system is deduced from the synopsis of classification and decision-making presented in Fig. 2.

The data processing stage consists of extracting signal and image representations from data source (signals: TDC surface) and deducing the signal data and image data.

The classification stage consists of the signal classification which is based on RBF networks while the image classification is based on MLP networks. This choice is mainly based on the two facts (discussed in Sect. 3) that:

- MLP and RBF networks can be used in a double classification in such a way to take advantage from their complementary classification performances (with a confidence parameter to enhance classification rates) as well as from their competitive classification performances [3],
- MLP are *neural global* approximators, whereas RBF are *neural local* approximators [11].

The primary and final fuzzy decision-making stages consist of the Primary Fuzzy System (PFS) and Final Fuzzy System (FFS), respectively. These fuzzy decision-making systems are used to capture the decision-making behavior of a human expert while giving the appropriate diagnosis [2,17], i.e., it must mimic the input/output mapping of this human expert. Note that the two fuzzy inferences of PFS and FFS, based on Mamdani's fuzzy inference, are developed as detailed in the diagnosis approach using only image representation described in [9] with the simplification detailed in [22]. From this simplification, the fuzzy rule base of PFS which is built of $3^6 = 729$ rules will make in use only $2^6 = 64$ rules in each inference, while the fuzzy rule base of FFS which is built of $3^4 = 81$ rules will make in use only $2^4 = 16$ rules in each inference.

Thus, the double classification, from signal representation and image representation, is exploited in PFS to ensure a satisfactory reliability for a computer-aided auditory diagnosis. Input parameters, obtained from the two neural networks, of PFS are RC_S, EC_S, NC_S, RC_I, EC_I, and NC_I. Thus, for each input, PFS is able to decide of appropriate diagnosis among Primary Diagnosis outputs PD_{RC}, PD_{EC}, and PD_{NC}.

The diagnosis reliability obtained from the PFS is reinforced (enhanced) using the obtained diagnosis result associated with a confidence parameter, Auditory Threshold (AT) of

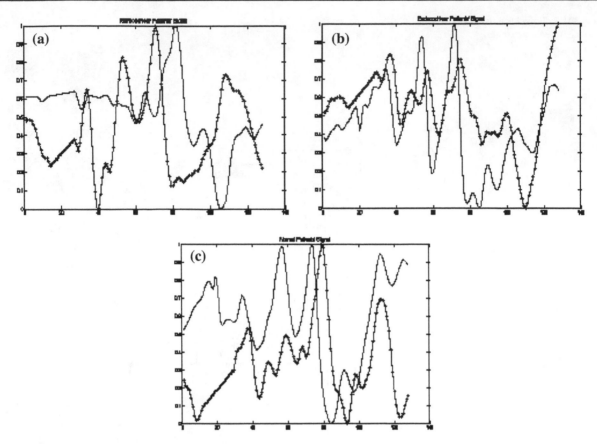

Fig. 4 Two examples of signal representations for patients. **a** RC. **b** EC. **c** NC

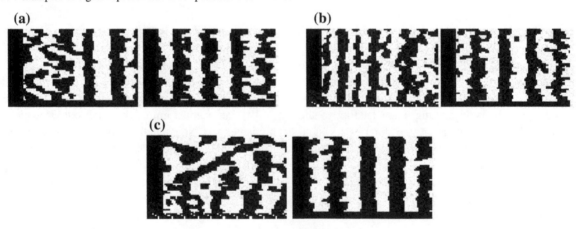

Fig. 5 Two examples of image representations for patients. **a** RC. **b** EC. **c** NC

patients, used as a confidence parameter, exploited in FFS in order to generate the final diagnosis result. Input parameters, issued from PFS, of FFS are AT, PD_{RC}, PD_{EC}, and PD_{NC}. Thus, for each input, FFS is able to decide of the appropriate diagnosis among Final Diagnosis outputs: FD_{RC}, FD_{EC}, and FD_{NC} with their Confidence Index (CI).

5 Prototype design and experimental results

For the validation of the suggested intelligent system, in the case of auditory diagnosis help, the used data base is issued from a specialized center in functional explorations in oto-neurology CEFON ("Centre d'Explorations Fonctionnelles Oto-Neurologiques, Paris, France.") [15]. This knowledge base is depicted for learning and for generalization in Table 1.

5.1 Prototype design

The neural classification results are presented in Table 2 for signal classification and in Table 3 for image classification. Learning database has successfully been learnt by the two classifications. The global correct classification rate is quite

Fig. 6 Hybrid intelligent diagnosis system synopsis for auditory diagnosis help. *RBF* radial basis function network, *RC* Retro-cochlear Class, *MLP* multilayer perceptron network, *EC* Endo-cochlear class, *S* signal, *I* image, *NC* normal-cochlear class, *AT* auditory threshold, *PD* primary diagnosis outputs, *FD* final diagnosis outputs, *CI* confidence index

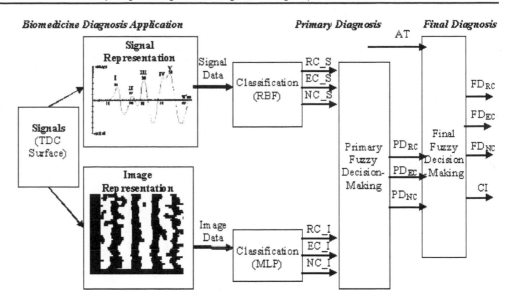

Table 1 Signal neural classification results (RBF)

Knowledge base	Learning base	Generalization base
Retro-cochlear	11	27
Endo-cochlear	6	71
Normal	7	84

Table 2 Signal neural classification results (RBF)

Signal results (RBF)	Learning rate (%)	Generalization rate (%)
Retro-cochlear	100	44.44
Endo-cochlear	100	52.11
Normal	100	58.33

Table 3 Image neural classification results (MLP)

Image results (MLP)	Learning rate (%)	Generalization rate (%)
Retro-cochlear	100	29.62
Endo-cochlear	100	35.21
Normal	100	70.23

similar for the two classifications, 51.62 % for signal one and 45.02 % for image one. However, correct classification rate is more homogeneous in case of signal classification. Image classification allows to obtain as far as 70.23 % of correct classification for NC. Obtained rates for RC and EC are then low and quite similar. With the two classifications, if EC are incorrectly classified by neural classifications, obtained class is NC (in majority). And, if NC are incorrectly clas-

sified by neural classifications, the obtained class is EC (in majority).

Primary Fuzzy System (PFS) The double classification, from signal representation and image representation is exploited in a Primary Fuzzy System (PFS) to ensure a satisfactory reliability of a Primary Diagnosis (PD). In order to exploit the expert (human) knowledge [2], the fuzzy decision-making system, developed in this Section, based on Mamdani's fuzzy inference must be able to decide of the appropriate PD among RC (PD_{RC}), EC (PD_{EC}), and Normal Class (PD_{NC}). The fuzzy decision-making system is suggested to the diagnosis decision-making help, i.e., to select the appropriate primary diagnosis for each patient among PD_{RC}, PD_{EC}, and PD_{NC}.

The input parameters are $RC\_S, EC\_S, NC\_S, RC\_I, EC\_I$, and NC_I. These inputs are obtained from neural networks, i.e., scaled from 0 to 1.

Then, the membership functions of RC_S, EC_S, and NC_S are defined as shown in Fig. 7a–c, where Near (N), Medium (M), and Far (F) are the fuzzy variables. The membership functions of RC_I, EC_I, and NC_I are defined as shown in Fig. 7d–f, where Far (F), Medium (M), and Near (N) are the fuzzy variables.

Thus, the input vector is then the vector $\mathbf{I} = [RC\_S, EC\_S, NC\_S, RC\_I, EC\_I, NC\_I]$. For each input, this *fuzzy decision-making system* must be able to select the appropriate primary diagnosis.

The *fuzzy decision-making system* is used to capture the decision-making behavior of a human expert while giving the appropriate diagnosis [17], i.e., it must mimic the input/output mapping of this human expert. Indeed, the latter has formulated his knowledge in a linguistic form which provides an explanation to give an appropriate primary diagnosis.

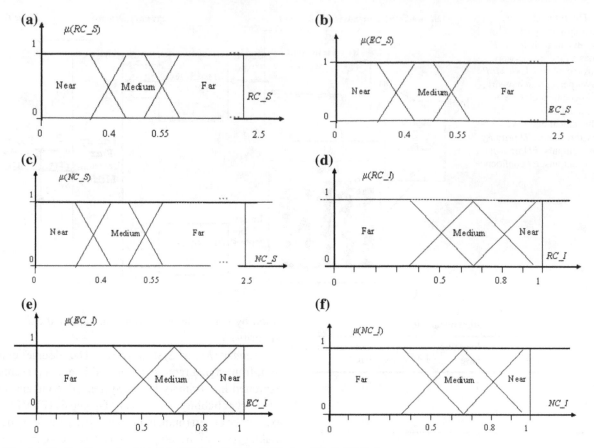

Fig. 7 Membership functions of: **a** *RC_S*. **b** *EC_S*. **c** *NC_S*. **d** *RC_I*. **e** *EC_I*. **f** *NC_I*

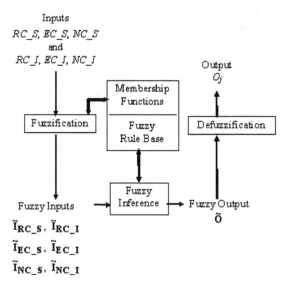

Fig. 8 Fuzzy decision-making system: Primary Fuzzy System (PFS)

To mimic this diagnosis, the fuzzy linguistic formulation is used and a set of fuzzy rules are then established. Thus, these fuzzy rules are used to incorporate this human expert knowledge in the suggested *fuzzy decision-making system*, illustrated in Fig. 8, where the vectors $\tilde{I}_{RC\_S}$, $\tilde{I}_{EC\_S}$, $\tilde{I}_{NC\_S}$, $\tilde{I}_{RC\_I}$,

$\tilde{I}_{EC\_I}$, and $\tilde{I}_{NC\_I}$ represent the fuzzy vectors of the input components *RC_S*, *EC_S*, *NC_S*, *RC_I*, *EC_I*, and *NC_I*, respectively; while $\tilde{O}$ represent the fuzzy vector of the output Oj which is a component of the vector $\mathbf{O} = [PD_{RC}, PD_{EC}, PD_{NC}]$ where PD_{RC}, PD_{EC}, PD_{NC} are Primary Diagnosis outputs RC, EC, and Normal Class, respectively.

The operation of the fuzzification calculates the degrees for each evaluated parameter (input) belonging to the three membership functions, e.g., for *RC_S* this operation calculates $\{\mu_N(RC\_S), \mu_M(RC\_S), \mu_F(RC\_S),\}$ with $\mu_N(RC\_S)$, $\mu_M(RC\_S)$ and $\mu_F(RC\_S)$ the membership degrees of fuzzy sets N, M, and F, respectively.

The fuzzy rule base is built of $3^6 = 729$ rules deduced from the six (06) inputs where each input has three (03) fuzzy variables. Thus, established fuzzy rules are:

If(*RC_S* is N and *EC_S* is N and *NC_S* is N and *RC_I* is F and *EC_I* is F and *NC_I* is F) Then
$\tilde{O} = [\mu(PD_{RC}), \mu(PD_{EC}), \mu(PD_{NC})]$,
If(*RC_S* is N and *EC_S* is N and *NC_S* is N and *RC_I* is F and *EC_I* is F and *NC_I* is M) Then
$\tilde{O} = [\mu(PD_{RC}), \mu(PD_{EC}), \mu(PD_{NC})]$,
...

If(*RC_S* is F and *EC_S* is F and *NC_S* is F and *RC_I* is N and *EC_I* is N and *NC_I* is M)Then

$\tilde{\mathbf{O}} = [\mu(PD_{RC}), \mu(PD_{EC}), \mu(PD_{NC})],$

If(RC_S is F and EC_S is F and NC_S is F and RC_I
is N and EC_I is N and NC_I is N) Then

$$\tilde{\mathbf{O}} = [\mu(PD_{RC}), \mu(PD_{EC}), \mu(PD_{NC})]. \qquad (1)$$

In this fuzzy rule base, the fuzzy decision-making vector $\tilde{\mathbf{O}}$ is expressed by:

$\tilde{\mathbf{O}}$

$$= [\mu_{(RC\_Sm, EC\_Sm, NC\_Sm, RC\_Im, EC\_Im, NC\_Im)}(PD_{RC}),$$

$$\mu_{(RC\_Sm, EC\_Sm, NC\_Sm, RC\_Im, EC\_Im, NC\_Im)}(PD_{EC}),$$

$$\mu_{(RC\_Sm, EC\_Sm, NC\_Sm, RC\_Im, EC\_Im, NC\_Im)}(PD_{NC})]$$
$$(2)$$

where $\mu_{(RC\_Sm, EC\_Sm, NC\_Sm, RC\_Im, EC\_Im, NC\_Im)}(O_j)$ represents the membership function degree of O_j with $m = 1$ or 2, see the simplification given below.

The fuzzy inference is achieved by the Min and Max operations. The particularity of the input parameters is that, for each given input, at least one membership function degree (among the three membership function degrees) is always equal to zero. Consequently, only two (02) membership function degrees are to be considered [22]. From this simplification, for each specific decision-making situation, the values of inputs are mapped to the discrete intervals to form the fuzzy sets:

$$\begin{aligned}
\tilde{\mathbf{I}}_{RC\_S} &= \{\mu_1(RC\_S), \mu_2(RC\_S)\}, \\
\tilde{\mathbf{I}}_{EC\_S} &= \{\mu_1(EC\_S), \mu_2(EC\_S)\}, \\
\tilde{\mathbf{I}}_{NC\_S} &= \{\mu_1(NC\_S), \mu_2(NC\_S)\}, \\
\tilde{\mathbf{I}}_{RC\_I} &= \{\mu_1(RC\_I), \mu_2(RC\_I)\}, \\
\tilde{\mathbf{I}}_{EC\_I} &= \{\mu_1(EC\_I), \mu_2(EC\_I)\}, \\
\tilde{\mathbf{I}}_{NC\_I} &= \{\mu_1(NC\_I), \mu_2(NC\_I)\},
\end{aligned} \qquad (3)$$

where for instance $\mu_m(RC\_S)$, with m = 1 or 2, are the membership function degrees of the input RC_S. With this description, one can have $2^6 = 64$ possible conditions corresponding to sixty four (64) fuzzy rules. Then, the level of certainty of each condition $\mu_1, \mu_2, \ldots, \mu_{64}$ can be found using the Min operation:

$$\mu_{cond}(RC\_S1, EC\_S1, NC\_S1, RC\_I1, EC\_I1, NC\_I1)$$
$$= MIN(\mu_1(RC\_S), \mu_1(EC\_S), \mu_1(NC\_S), \mu_1(RC\_I),$$
$$\mu_1(EC\_I), \mu_1(NC\_I)) = \mu_1,$$
$$\mu_{cond}(RC\_S1, EC\_S1, NC\_S1, RC\_I1, EC\_I1, NC\_I2)$$
$$= MIN(\mu_1(RC\_S), \mu_1(EC\_S), \mu_1(NC\_S), \mu_1(RC\_I),$$
$$\mu_1(EC\_I), \mu_2(NC\_I)) = \mu_2, \qquad (4)$$
$$\ldots$$
$$\mu_{cond}(RC\_S2, EC\_S2, NC\_S2, RC\_I2, EC\_I2, NC\_I2)$$
$$= MIN(\mu_2(RC\_S), \mu_2(EC\_S), \mu_2(NC\_S), \mu_2(RC\_I),$$
$$\mu_2(EC\_I), \mu_2(NC\_I)) = \mu_{64},$$

where cond represents the fuzzy set of conditions which is written as follows:

$$cond = \{\mu_1, \mu_2, \ldots, \mu_{64}\}. \qquad (5)$$

Each possible condition is associated with a decision-making situation O_j. Then, certainty of each situation is obtained by Max and Min operations as follows:

$$\mu_{PDRC} = MAX\{ MIN(\mu_1, \mu_{(RC\_S1, EC\_S1, NC\_S1,}$$
$$RC\_I1, EC\_I1, NC\_I1)(PD_{RC})),$$
$$MIN(\mu_2, \mu_{(RC\_S1, EC\_S1, NC\_S1, RC\_I1, EC\_I1, NC\_I2)}$$
$$(PD_{RC})),$$
$$\ldots$$
$$MIN(\mu_{64}, \mu_{(RC\_S2, EC\_S2, NC\_S2, RC\_I2, EC\_I2, NC\_I2)}$$
$$(PD_{RC}))\},$$
$$\mu_{PDEC} = MAX\{MIN(\mu_1, \mu_{(RC\_S1, EC\_S1, NC\_S1,}$$
$$RC\_I1, EC\_I1, NC\_I1)$$
$$(PD_{EC})),$$
$$MIN(\mu_2, \mu_{(RC\_S1, EC\_S1, NC\_S1, RC\_I1, EC\_I1, NC\_I2)} \quad (6)$$
$$(PD_{EC})),$$
$$\ldots$$
$$MIN(\mu_{64}, \mu_{(RC\_S2, EC\_S2, NC\_S2, RC\_I2, EC\_I2, NC\_I2)}$$
$$(PD_{EC}))\},$$
$$\mu_{PDNC} = MAX\{MIN(\mu_1, \mu_{(RC\_S1, EC\_S1, NC\_S1,}$$
$$RC\_I1, EC\_I1, NC\_I1)(PD_{NC})),$$
$$MIN(\mu_2, \mu_{(RC\_S1, EC\_S1, NC\_S1, RC\_I1, EC\_I1, NC\_I2)}$$
$$(PD_{NC})),$$
$$\ldots$$
$$MIN(\mu_{64}, \mu_{(RC\_S2, EC\_S2, NC\_S2, RC\_I2, EC\_I2, NC\_I2)}$$
$$(PD_{NC}))\}.$$

Collection of situations forms final fuzzy decision-making situation vector $\tilde{\mathbf{O}}$:

$$\tilde{\mathbf{O}} = \{\mu_{PDRC}(PD_{RC}), \mu_{PDEC}(PD_{EC}), \mu_{PDNC}(PD_{NC})\} \qquad (7)$$

The Max operation is used for the defuzzification process to give the final decision-making situation O_j:

$$O_j = Max\{\mu_{PDRC}, \mu_{PDEC}, \mu_{PDNC}\}. \qquad (8)$$

Final Fuzzy System (FFS) The diagnosis reliability obtained from the Primary Fuzzy System (PFS) is reinforced (enhanced) using the obtained diagnosis result with an auditory threshold parameter of patients exploited in a Final Fuzzy System (FFS) in order to generate the decision-making of the final diagnosis result. This FFS is designed and developed on the same methodology described before for the PFS, where the input parameters the Auditory Threshold (*AT*), PD_{RC}, PD_{EC}, and PD_{NC} and their related membership functions are illustrated in Fig. 9a–d, respectively. The outputs of this FFS are then the outputs FD_{RC}, FD_{EC}, and FD_{NC} giving the final diagnosis with a Confidence Index (*CI*) of this final diagnosis.

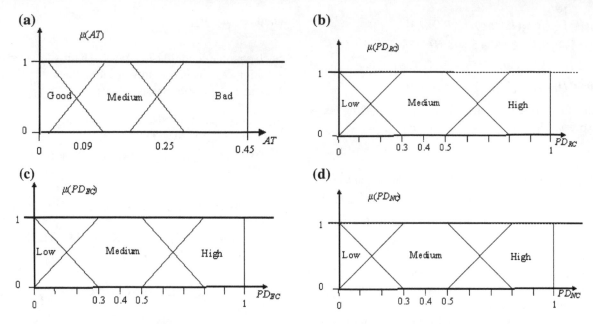

Fig. 9 Membership functions of: **a** auditory threshold (AT). **b** PD_{RC}. **c** PD_{EC}. **d** PD_{NC}

Table 4 Fuzzy decision-making system PFS results

Primary fuzzy system (PFS) results (%)	Learning rate (%)	Generalization rate (%)
Retro-cochlear	100	33.33 (37.03)
Endo-cochlear	100	29.57 (42.25)
Normal	100	63.09 (77.38)

Table 5 Fuzzy decision-making system FFS results

Final fuzzy system (FFS) results (%)	Learning rate (%)	Generalization rate (%)
Retro-cochlear	100	40.74 (51.85)
Endo-cochlear	100	49.29 (59.15)
Normal	100	84.52 (89.28)

5.2 Auditory diagnosis results

Tables 4 and 5 present the results obtained by fuzzy decision-making systems PFS and FFS, respectively. Rates written between brackets (x %) represent the generalization rates calculated taking into account the patients classified simultaneously in two classes. In majority of cases, these simultaneous classifications are obtained for EC and NC. For all the classes, the generalization rate of FFS is higher than this of PFS, showing the pertinent rule of the auditory threshold. The generalization rate of normal class is clearly higher for fuzzy decision-making system FFS than for the two classifications, achieving a value of 84.52 % (89.28 %). The obtained rates for RC and EC are higher than these obtained by the image classification but quite similar than those obtained by the signal classification.

An important contribution of FFS is that it gives each fault diagnosis associated with a *CI*. This is illustrated through the following result example with a high *CI*:

The fuzzy output $= \{\mu_{FDRC}, \mu_{FDEC}, \mu_{FDNC}, \mu_{CI}\}$
$= \{0.05, 0.94, 0.05, 0.96\}$.
Then, defuzzified output $= \mathrm{Max}\{\mu_{FDRC}, \mu_{FDEC}, \mu_{FDNC}\}$
$= \mathrm{Max}\{0.05, 0.94, 0.05\}$,
$= \mu_{FDEC} = 0.94$.

Then, the final result is, in this example, μ_{FDEC} and μ_{CI} equal to 0.94 and 0.96, respectively. This result means that the identified fault (pathology) diagnosis (0.94) is EC with a high *CI* (0.96).

6 Discussion and conclusion

In this paper, a hybrid intelligent diagnosis approach for computer-aided auditory diagnosis, based on neural classifications and fuzzy decision-making systems is suggested. In fact, the double classification is exploited in PFS, for a primary diagnosis, to ensure a satisfactory reliability. Second, this reliability is reinforced using a confidence parameter AT with the primary diagnosis result, exploited in FFS, in order to generate the final diagnosis giving the appropriate diagnosis with a *CI*. In effect, a first reliability degree of the suggested computer-aided diagnosis is obtained from the Primary Fuzzy System (PFS) exploiting the redundancy of the two neural classifiers. Then, this reliability degree is reinforced (enhanced) exploiting the obtained diagnosis result associated with a confidence parameter, Auditory Threshold (*AT*) of patients in the application at hand, in the Final Fuzzy System (FFS) in order to generate the final diagnosis result (the appropriate diagnosis with a confidence index *CI*). Note that such a confidence index is very desirable in decision support systems (decision help systems), and particularly in biomedicine (e.g., biomedical application at hand, see the example given at the end of Sect. 5).

In fact, the aim is then to achieve an efficient and reliable CAD system for three classes: two auditory pathologies RC and EC and normal auditory NC. A signal and an image, issued from ABR test, are used as the two initial data representations. Implementation and experimental results are presented and discussed. The generalization rate of NC is clearly higher for PFS and FFS than for the two classifications. The obtained rates for RC and EC are higher than obtained by image classification but quite similar than those obtained by signal classification. An important contribution of the final fuzzy system FFS is that it gives each fault diagnosis associated with a *CI*.

The original contribution of this paper relies on the following points:

- the fact to process the same information source (signal) in two different ways through two different knowledge representations (signal and image). A manner to give two results from two different points of view (a kind of multi-expert results, such redundancy is desirable, particularly in biomedicine). This idea emerged from the fact that some biomedical experts are able to make a diagnosis from the observation of a signal or image biomedical results. More, usually in such biomedical applications, the knowledge representation signal is only used. In fact, the image representation offers benefit of a richer information representation than the signal one. Then, such combination (signal and image) approach will also take advantage from features which are unreachable from one-dimensional signal. In effect, the interest from the image knowledge representation (of the signal) is that some pertinent features appear in such representation which are new, and interesting to exploit, with regard to the features which appear in the signal knowledge representation. Some of these signal and image pertinent features could be competitive, but also complementary. Then, both of them should be exploited to reinforce or in contrary decrease a certain diagnosis which will be traduced also in different degrees of the confidence index (*CI*) which will be given with the associated final diagnosis result.
- the hybrid intelligent nature of the suggested diagnosis approach using an appropriate neural classification for each knowledge representation (radial basis functions RBF for signal and multilayer perceptron MLP for image), and the fuzzy system for the decision-making process from the primary diagnosis results of the two neural networks (MLP and RBF) in order to give the

final diagnosis result associated with a confidence index (*CI*).

The choice of modular neural networks have been motivated from the theoretical and practical features such as their learning and generalization capabilities as classifiers, and particularly the fact that MLP are *neural global* approximators (sampled amplitude of signal which is *more local than global*), whereas RBF are *neural local* approximators (area mean grey level of global image which is *more global than local*). More, this choice is motivated by the fact that such networks can be used in a double classification in such a way to take advantage from their complementary classification performances (with a confidence parameter to enhance classification rates) as well as from their competitive classification performances (with the confidence parameter, this information will contribute to enhance, for instance, the *CI* in final decision-making in case of common classification, or inversely in case of contradictory classification). Due to the nature of the outputs of such neural networks (detailed in Sect. 3), one interesting way to built efficient decision-making from two neural networks is the choice of fuzzy logic.

Another important point motivating this choices (modular neural networks and fuzzy logic) is related to the number of fault classes used in each neural network outputs. In this paper, this number is related to the application at hand e.g., about three fault classes (Retro-cochlear Class RC, Endo-cochlear Class EC, and Normal auditory Class NC). Of course, for other applications of the suggested hybrid intelligent diagnosis this number could be more than three, in such case, the use of modular neural networks is judicious because one can always have more networks with always the number of their outputs which will be equal or less than three outputs, avoiding any combinatory explosion of the resulting number of fuzzy rules for the decision-making.

Thus, the suggested approach could be generalized to many output classes exploiting the concept of modular neural networks [3]. Such concept allows to avoid to deal with a huge number of fuzzy rules in case of a great number of output classes.

Of course, a number of current system's aspects could be investigated in order to enhance the final results. For this purpose, a fine tuning of fuzzy rules is necessary as well as a more detailed presentation of the results (the results presented are those only with a high *CI*).

An interesting alternative for future works, is also to investigate from rational analysis of fault diagnosis cognitive process other concepts besides fuzziness, such as causality,...

Finally, this approach could be applied to other diagnosis problem in biomedicine, where signal and image representation could be extracted from clinical tests. It is pertinent to notice that a large number of signal issued representations

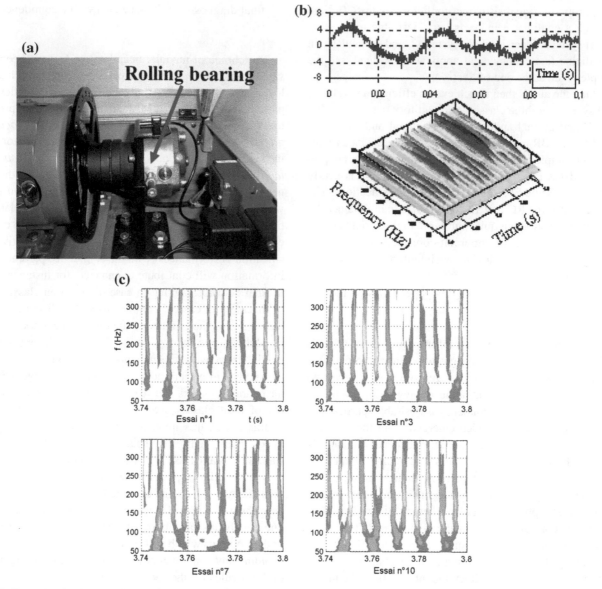

Fig. 10 Example of industrial diagnosis system and signal and image knowledge representations: **a** Revolving machine. **b** Signal knowledge representation and a wavelet transform representation. **c** Image knowledge representations (deduced from wavelet transform representation)

could be converted in image representations. Elsewhere, it could be used for industrial domain, e.g., mechatronic system as illustrated in Fig. 10, where a revolving machine is presented in Fig. 10a and two information (knowledge) representations are shown: a signal knowledge representation and a wavelet transform knowledge representation (time-frequency) [16] in Fig. 10b and image knowledge representations (deduced from wavelet transformation) in Fig. 10c. For industrial diagnosis problems, the suggested hybrid intelligent diagnosis approach can be used. In fact, the same classification and decision-making processing architecture of the approach can be used with corresponding specific pertinent parameters and mainly modifications will be in PFS and FFS rule bases from specific experimental data.

Open Access This article is distributed under the terms of the Creative Commons Attribution License which permits any use, distribution, and reproduction in any medium, provided the original author(s) and the source are credited.

References

1. Balakrishnan, K., Honavar, V.: Intelligent Diagnosis Systems, Technical Report, Iowa State University, Ames, Iowa 50011–1040, U.S.A. (1997)
2. Turban, E., Aronson, J.E.: Decision Support Systems and Intelligent Systems, Int edn, 6th edn. Prentice-Hall (2001)
3. Karray, F.O., De Silva, C.: Soft Computing and Intelligent Systems Design, Theory, Tools and Applications. Addison Wesley, ISBN 0-321-11617-8, Pearson Ed. Limited (2004)

4. Meneganti, M., Saviello, F.S., Tagliaferri, R.: Fuzzy neural networks for classification and detection of anomalies. IEEE Trans. Neural Netw. **9**(5), 848–861 (1998)

5. Palmero, G.I.S., Santamaria, J.J., de la Torre, E.J.M., Gonzalez, J.R.P.: Fault detection and fuzzy rule extraction in AC motors by a neuro-fuzzy ART-based system. Eng. Appl. Artif. Intell., **18**, 867–874 (2005) (Elsevier)

6. Piater, J.H., Stuchlik, F., von Specht, H., Mühler, R.: Fuzzy sets for feature identification in biomedical signals with self-assessment of reliability: an adaptable algorithm modeling human procedure in BAEP analysis. Comput. Biomed. Res. **28**, 335–353 (1995)

7. Vuckovic, A., Radivojevic, V., Chen, A.C.N., Popovic, D.: Automatic recognition of alertness and drowsiness from EEG by an artificial neural network. Med. Eng. Phys., **24**(5), 349–360 (2002)

8. Wolf, A., Barbosa, C.H., Monteiro, E.C., Vellasco, M.: Multiple MLP neural networks applied on the determination of segment limits in ECG signals. In: 7th International Work-Conference on Artificial and Natural NN, Proc. Part II, Menorca, Spain, June 2003, LNCS 2687, pp. 607–614. Springer, Berlin (2003)

9. Chohra, A., Kanaoui, N., Amarger, V.: A soft computing based approach using signal-to-image conversion for computer aided medical diagnosis (CAMD). In: Saeed, K., Pejas, J. (eds.) Information Processing and Security Systems, pp. 365–374. Springer, Berlin (2005)

10. Yan, H., Jiang, Y., Zheng, J., Peng, C., Li, Q.: A multilayer perceptron-based medical support system for heart disease diagnosis. Exp. Syst. Appl. (2005) (Elsevier)

11. Haykin, S.: Neural Networks: A Comprehensive Foundation, 2nd edn. Prentice-Hall (1999)

12. Zhang, G.P.: Neural networks for classification: a survey. IEEE Trans. Syst. Man Cybern. Part C Appl. Rev. **30**(4), 451–462 (2000)

13. Egmont-Petersen, M., De Ridder, D., Handels, H.: Image processing with neural networks-a review. Pattern Recognit. **35**, 2279–2301 (2002)

14. Don, M., Masuda, A., Nelson, R., Brackmann, D.: Successful detection of small acoustic tumors using the stacked derived-band auditory brain stem response amplitude. Am. J. Otol. **18**(5), 608–621 (1997)

15. Vannier, E., Adam, O., Motsch, J.F.: Objective detection of brainstem auditory evoked potentials with a priori information from higher presentation levels. Artif. Intell. Med. **25**, 283–301 (2002)

16. Bradley, A.P., Wilson, W.J.: On wavelet analysis of auditory evoked potentials. Clin. Neurophysiol. **115**, 1114–1128 (2004)

17. Azouaoui, O., Chohra, A.: Soft computing based pattern classifiers for the obstacle avoidance behavior of Intelligent Autonomous Vehicles (IAV). Int. J. Appl. Intell. **16**(3), 249–271 (2002) (Kluwer Academic Publishers)

18. Zadeh, L.A.: Fuzzy sets. Inf. Control **8**, 338–353 (1965)

19. Zadeh, L.A.: The calculus of fuzzy if / then rules. AI Expert, 23–27 (1992)

20. Lee, C.C.: Fuzzy logic in control systems: fuzzy logic controller-Part I & Part II. IEEE Trans. Syst. Man Cybern. **20**(2), 404–435 (1990)

21. Gonzalez, R.C., Woods, R.E.: Digital Image Processing, 2nd edn. Prentice-Hall (2002)

22. Farreny, H., Prade, H.: Tackling uncertainty and imprecision in robotics. In: 3rd International Symposium on Robotics Research, pp. 85–91 (1985)

9

Paraconsistent neurocomputing and brain signal analysis

Jair Minoro Abe · Helder F. S. Lopes ·
Kazumi Nakamatsu

Abstract In this work we summarize some of our studies on paraconsistent artificial neural networks (PANN) applied to electroencephalography. We give attention to the following applications: probable diagnosis of Alzheimer disease and attention-deficit/hyperactivity disorder (ADHD). PANNs are well suited to tackle problems that human beings are good at solving, like prediction and pattern recognition. PANNs have been applied within several branches and among them, the medical domain for clinical diagnosis, image analysis, and interpretation signal analysis, and interpretation, and drug development. For study of ADHD, we have a result of recognition electroencephalogram standards (delta, theta, alpha, and beta waves) with a median kappa index of 80 %. For study of the Alzheimer disease, we have a result of clinical diagnosis possible with 80 % of sensitivity, 73 % of specificity, and a kappa index of 76 %.

Keywords Artificial neural network · Paraconsistent logics · EEG analysis · Pattern recognition · Alzheimer disease · Dyslexia

J. M. Abe
Graduate Program in Production Engineering,
ICET-Paulista University, R. Dr. Bacelar, 1212,
São Paulo, SP CEP 04026-002, Brazil

J. M. Abe (✉) · H. F. S. Lopes
Institute For Advanced Studies, University of São Paulo,
São Paulo, Brazil
e-mail: jairabe@uol.com.br

H. F. S. Lopes
e-mail: helder.mobile@gmail.com

K. Nakamatsu
School of Human Science and Environment/H.S.E.,
University of Hyogo, Kobe, Japan
e-mail: nakamatu@shse.u-hyogo.ac.jp

1 Introduction

Generally speaking, artificial neural network (ANN) can be described as a computational system consisting of a set of highly interconnected processing elements, called artificial neurons, which process information as a response to external stimuli. An artificial neuron is a simplistic representation that emulates the signal integration and threshold firing behavior of biological neurons by means of mathematical structures. ANNs are well suited to tackle problems that human beings are good at solving, like prediction and pattern recognition. ANNs have been applied within several branches, among them, in the medical domain for clinical diagnosis, image analysis, and interpretation signal analysis and interpretation, and drug development.

So, ANN constitutes an interesting tool for electroencephalogram (EEG) qualitative analysis. On the other hand, in EEG analysis we are faced with imprecise, inconsistent and paracomplete data.

The EEG is a brain electric signal activity register, resultant of the space-time representation of synchronic postsynaptic potentials. The graphic registration of the sign of EEG can be interpreted as voltage flotation with mixture of rhythms, being frequently sinusoidal, ranging 1–70 Hz [1]. In the clinical-physiological practice, such frequencies are grouped in frequency bands as can see in Fig. 1.

EEG analysis, as well as any other measurements devices, is limited and subjected to the inherent imprecision of the several sources involved: equipment, movement of the patient, electric registers, and individual variability of physician visual analysis. Such imprecision can often include conflicting information or paracomplete data. The majority of theories and techniques available are based on classical logic and so they cannot handle adequately such set of information, at least directly.

Fig. 1 Frequency bands clinically established and usually found in EEG

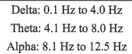

| Delta: 0.1 Hz to 4.0 Hz |
| Theta: 4.1 Hz to 8.0 Hz |
| Alpha: 8.1 Hz to 12.5 Hz |
| Beta: > 13 Hz |

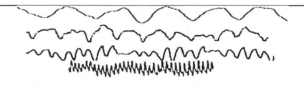

In this paper we employ a new kind of ANN based on paraconsistent annotated evidential logic $E\tau$, which is capable of manipulating imprecise, inconsistent, and paracomplete data to make a first study of the recognition of EEG standards.

The studies about recognition of EEG standards have application in two clinical areas: attention-deficit/hyperactivity disorder (ADHD) and Alzheimer disease (AD).

Recent researches reveal that 10 % of the world population in school age suffer of learning and/or behavioral disorders caused by neurological problems, such as ADHD, dyslexia, and dyscalculia, with predictable consequences in those students insufficient performance in the school [2–7]. EEG alterations seem to be associated those disturbances. Thus, some authors have proposed that there is an increase of the delta activity in EEG in those tasks that demand a larger attention to the internal processes.

Several studies on behavioral and cognitive neurology have been conducted to characterize dementias through biological and functional markers, for instance, the EEG activity, aimed at understanding the evolution of AD, following its progression, as well as leading toward better diagnostic criteria for early detection of cognitive impairment [8,9]. At present, there is no method able to determine a definitive diagnosis of dementia, where a combination of tests would be necessary to obtain a probable diagnosis [10].

Let us now make some considerations of how to apply paraconsistent artificial neural network (PANN) to analyze probable diagnosis for ADHD and AD.

2 Background

PANN is a new artificial neural network [11]. Its basis leans on paraconsistent annotated logic $E\tau$ [12]. Let us present it briefly.

The atomic formulas of the logic $E\tau$ are of the type $p_{(\mu,\lambda)}$, where $(\mu, \lambda) \in [0, 1]^2$ and $[0, 1]$ is the real unitary interval (p denotes a propositional variable). $p_{(\mu,\lambda)}$ can be intuitively read: "it is assumed that p's favorable evidence is μ and contrary evidence is λ". Thus

- $p_{(1.0,0.0)}$ can be read as a true proposition.
- $p_{(0.0,1.0)}$ can be read as a false proposition.
- $p_{(1.0,1.0)}$ can be read as an inconsistent proposition.
- $p_{(0.0,0.0)}$ can be read as a paracomplete (unknown) proposition.

Table 1 Extreme and non-extreme states

Extreme states	Symbol	Non-extreme states	Symbol
True	V	Quasi-true tending to inconsistent	QV → T
False	F	Quasi-true tending to paracomplete	QV → ⊥
Inconsistent	T	Quasi-false tending to inconsistent	QF → T
Paracomplete	⊥	Quasi-false tending to paracomplete	Qf → ⊥
		Quasi-inconsistent tending to true	QT → V
		Quasi-inconsistent tending to false	QT → F
		Quasi-paracomplete tending to true	Q⊥ → V
		Quasi-paracomplete tending to false	Q⊥ → F

- $p_{(0.5,0.5)}$ can be read as an indefinite proposition.

We introduce the following concepts (all considerations are taken with $0 \leq \mu, \lambda \leq 1$):

- Uncertainty degree : $G_{un}(\mu, \lambda) = \mu + \lambda - 1$ (2.1)
- Certainty degree : $G_{ce}(\mu, \lambda) = \mu - \lambda$ (2.2)

Intuitively, $G_{un}(\mu, \lambda)$ show us how close (or far) the annotation constant (μ, λ) is from inconsistent or paracomplete state. Similarly, $G_{ce}(\mu, \lambda)$ show us how close (or far) the annotation constant (μ, λ) is from true or false state. In this way we can manipulate the information given by the annotation constant (μ, λ). Note that such degrees are not metrical distance.

An order relation is defined on $[0, 1]^2$: $(\mu_1, \lambda_1) \leq (\mu_2, \lambda_2) \Leftrightarrow \mu_1 \leq \mu_2$, and $\lambda_2 \leq \lambda_1$, constituting a lattice that will be symbolized by τ.

With the uncertainty and certainty degrees we can get the following 12 output states (Table 1): *extreme states* and *non-extreme states*:

Some additional control values are:

- V_{scct} = maximum value of uncertainty control = Ft_{un}
- V_{scc} = maximum value of certainty control = Ft_{ce}
- V_{icct} = minimum value of uncertainty control = $-Ft_{un}$
- V_{icc} = minimum value of certainty control = $-Ft_{ce}$

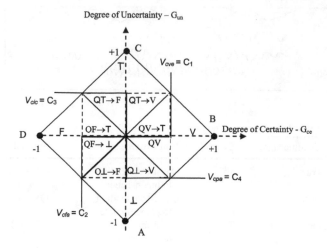

Fig. 2 Extreme and non-extreme states

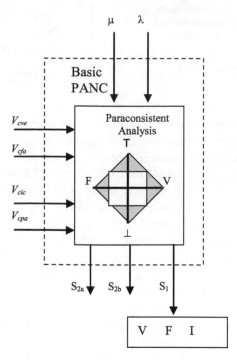

Fig. 3 Basic cell of PANN

Such values are determined by the knowledge engineer, depending on each application, finding the appropriate control values for each of them.

All states are represented in the next figure (Fig. 2).

3 The main artificial neural cells

In the PANN, the certainty degree G_{ce} indicates the 'measure' falsity or truth degree.

The uncertainty degree G_{un} indicates the 'measure' of the inconsistency or paracompleteness. If the certainty degree in module is low or the uncertainty degree in module is high, it generates a paracompleteness.

The resulting certainty degree G_{ce} is obtained as follows:

- If: $V_{cfa} = G_{ce} = V_{cve}$ or $-Ft_{ce} = G_{ce} = Ft_{ce} \Rightarrow G_{ce} =$ indefiniteness
- For: $V_{cpa} = G_{un} = V_{cic}$ or $-Ft_{un} = G_{un} = Ft_{un}$
- If: $G_{ce} = V_{cfa} = -Ft_{ce} \Rightarrow G_{ce} =$ false with degree G_{un}
- If: $Ft_{ce} = V_{cve} = G_{ce} \Rightarrow G_{ce} =$ true with degree G_{un}

A paraconsistent artificial neural cell (PANC) is called *basic* PANC (Fig. 3) when given a pair (μ, λ) is used as input and resulting as output:

- $S_{2a} = G_{un} =$ resulting uncertainty degree
- $S_{2b} = G_{ce} =$ resulting certainty degree
- $S_1 = X =$ constant of indefiniteness.

The uncertainty degree G_{un} indicates the 'measure' of the inconsistency or paracompleteness. If the certainty degree in module is low or the uncertainty degree in module is high, it generates an indefiniteness.

The resulting certainty degree G_{ce} is obtained as follows:

- If: $V_{cfa} = G_{ce} = V_{cve}$ or $-Ft_{ce} = G_{ce} = Ft_{ce} \Rightarrow G_{ce} =$ indefiniteness
- For: $V_{cpa} = G_{un} = V_{cic}$ or $-Ft_{un} = G_{un} = Ft_{un}$
- If: $G_{ce} = V_{cfa} = -Ft_{ce} \Rightarrow G_{ce} =$ false with degree G_{un}
- If: $Ft_{ce} = V_{cve} = G_{ce} \Rightarrow G_{ce} =$ true with degree G_{un}

A PANC is called *basic* PANC (Fig. 3) when given a pair (μ, λ) is used as input and resulting as output:

- $S_{2a} = G_{un} =$ resulting uncertainty degree
- $S_{2b} = G_{ce} =$ resulting certainty degree
- $S_1 = X =$ constant of Indefiniteness.

Using the concepts of *basic* PANC, we can obtain the family of PANC considered in this work: analytic connection (PANCac), maximization (PANCmax), and minimization (PANCmin) as described in Table 2 below:

To make easier the understanding on the implementation of the algorithms of PANC, we use a programming language Object Pascal, following logic of procedural programming in all samples.

3.1 Paraconsistent artificial neural cell of analytic connection (PANCac)

The PANCac is the principal cell of all PANN, obtaining the certainty degree (G_{ce}) and the uncertainty degree (G_{un}) from the inputs and the tolerance factors.

Table 2 Paraconsistent artificial neural cells

PANC	Inputs	Calculations	Output
Analytic connection: PANCac	μ	$\lambda_c = 1 - \lambda$	If $|G_{ce}| > Ft_{ce}$ then $S_1 = \mu_r$ and $S_2 = 0$
	λ	$G_{un}G_{ce}$,	If $|G_{un}| > Ft_{ct}$ and $|G_{un}| > |G_{ce}|$ then
	Ft_{un}	$\mu_r = (G_{ce} + 1)/2$	$S_1 = \mu_r$ and $S_2 = |G_{un}|$
	Ft_{un}		If not $S_1 = 1/2$ and $S_2 = 0$
Maximization: PANCmax	μ	G_{ce}	If $\mu_r > 0.5$, then $S_1 = \mu$
	λ	$\mu_r = (G_{ce} + 1)/2$	If not $S_1 = \lambda$
Minimization: PANCmin	μ	G_{ce}	If $\mu_r < 0.5$, then $S_1 = \mu$
	λ	$\mu_r = (G_{ce} + 1)/2$	If not $S_1 = \lambda$

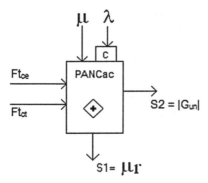

Fig. 4 Representation of PANCac

This cell is the link which allows different regions of PANN perform signal processing in distributed and through many parallel connections [11].

The different tolerance factors certainty (or contradiction) acts as inhibitors of signals, controlling the passage of signals to other regions of the PANN, according to the characteristics of the architecture developed (Fig. 4).

In Table 3, we have a sample of implementation made in Object Pascal.

3.2 Paraconsistent artificial neural cell of maximization (PANCmax)

The PANCmax allows selection of the maximum value among the entries.

Such cells operate as logical connectives OR between input signals. For this is made a simple analysis, through the equation of the degree of evidence (Table 4) which thus will tell which of the two input signals is of greater value, thus establishing the output signal [11] (Fig. 5).

In Table 4, we have a sample of implementation made in Object Pascal.

3.3 Paraconsistent artificial neural cell of minimization (PANCmin)

The PANCmin allows selection of the minimum value among the entries.

Table 3 PANCac implementation

```
function TFaPANN.PANCAC(mi, lambda, Ftce, Ftct: real; output:
integer): real;
var
  Gce: real;
  Gun: real;
  lambdacp: real;
  mir: real;
  S1, S2: real;

begin
  lambdacp := 1 - lambda;
  Gce := mi - lambdacp;
  Gun := mi + lambdacp - 1;
  mir := (Gce + 1) / 2;

  if (abs(Gce) > Ftce) then
  begin
    S1 := mir;
    S2 := 0;
  end
  else
  begin
    if (abs(Gun) > Ftct) and (abs(Gun) > abs(Gce)) then
    begin
      S1 := mir;
      S2 := abs(Gun);
    end
    else
    begin
      S1 := 0.5;
      S2 := 0;
    end;
  end;
  if output = 1 then result := S1 else result := S2;
end;
```

Table 4 PANCmax implementation

```
Function TFaPANN.PANCMAX(mi, lambda: real): real;
var
  mir: real;
begin
  mir := ((mi - lambda) + 1) / 2;
  if (mir > 0.5) then
    result := mi
  else
    result := lambda;
end;
```

Such cells operate as logical connectives AND between input signals. For this it is made a simple analysis, through the equation of the degree of evidence (Table 5) which thus will tell which of the two input signals is of smaller value, thus establishing the output signal [11].

In Table 5, we have a sample of implementation made in Object Pascal.

3.4 Paraconsistent artificial neural unit

A PANU is characterized by the association ordered PANC, targeting a goal, such as decision making, selection, learning, or some other type of processing.

Fig. 5 Representation of PANCmax

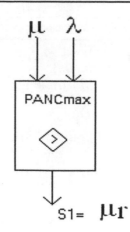

Table 5 PANCmin implementation

```
Function TFaPANN.PANCMIN(mi, lambda: real): real;
var
  mir: real;
begin
  mir := ((mi - lambda) + 1) / 2;
  if (mir < 0.5) then
      result := mi
  else
      result := lambda;
end;
```

When creating a PANU, one obtains a data processing component capable of simulating the operation of a biological neuron.

3.5 Paraconsistent artificial neural system

Classical systems based on binary logic are difficult to process data or information from uncertain knowledge. These data are captured or received information from multiple experts usually comes in the form of evidences.

Paraconsistent artificial neural system (PANS) modules are configured and built exclusively by PANU, whose function is to provide the signal processing 'similar' to processing that occurs in the human brain.

4 PANN for morphological analysis

The process of morphological analysis of a wave is performed by comparing with a certain set of wave patterns (stored in the control database). A wave is associated with a vector (finite sequence of natural numbers) through digital sampling. This vector characterizes a wave pattern and is registered by PANN. Thus, new waves are compared, allowing their recognition or otherwise.

Each wave of the survey examined the EEG corresponds to a portion of 1 s examination. Every second of the exam contains 256 positions.

The wave that has the highest favorable evidence and lowest contrary evidence is chosen as the more similar wave to the analyzed wave.

A control database is composed by waves presenting 256 positions with perfect sinusoidal morphology, with 0.5 Hz of variance, so taking into account delta, theta, alpha, and beta (of 0.5–30.0 Hz) wave groups.

In other words, morphological analysis checks the similarity of the passage of the examination of EEG in a reference database that represents a wave pattern.

4.1 Data preparation

The process of wave analysis by PANN consists previously of data capturing, adaptation of the values for screen examination, elimination of the negative cycle, and normalization of the values for PANN analysis.

As the actual EEG examination values can vary highly, in module, something 10–1,500 μV, we make a normalization of the values between 100 and −100 μV by a simple linear conversion, to facilitate the manipulation the data:

$$x = \frac{100 \cdot a}{m}, \qquad (4.1)$$

where m is the maximum value of the exam; a is the current value of the exam; x is the current normalized value.

The minimum value of the examination is taken as zero value and the remaining values are translated proportionally.

It is worth observing that the process above does not allow the loss of any wave essential characteristics for our analysis.

4.2 The PANN architecture

The architecture of the PANN used in decision making is based on the architecture of PANS for treatment of contradictions.

Such a system performs a treatment of the contradictions continuously if presented by the three information signal inputs, presenting as an output a resulting signal that represents a consensus among the three information. This is made by analyzing the contradiction between two signals, and by adding a third one; the output is chosen by dominant majority. The analysis is instantly carrying all processing in real time, similar to the functioning of biological neurons.

This method is used primarily for PANN (Fig. 8) to balance the data received from expert systems. After this the process uses a decision-making lattice to determine the soundness of the recognition (Table 6; Fig. 6).

A sample of morphological analysis implementation using Object Pascal is showed in Table 7.

The definition of regions of the lattice decision-making was done through double-blind trials, i.e., for each battery of tests, a validator checked the results and returned only the percentage of correct answers. After testing several different configurations, set the configuration of the lattice

Table 6 Lattice for decision-making used in the morphological analysis (Fig. 7)

Limits of areas of lattice			
True	Fe > 0.61	Ce < 0.40	G_{ce} > 0.22
False	Fe < 0.61	Ce > 0.40	G_{ce} ≤ 0.23

Ce contrary evidence, *Fe* favorable evidence, G_{ce} certainty degree

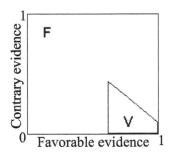

Fig. 6 Lattice for decision-making used in morphological analysis used after making PANN; *F* logical state false (it is interpreted as wave not similar); *V* logical state true (it is interpreted as wave similar)

Table 7 The architecture for morphological analysis implementation (Fig. 8)

```
function Tf_pann.Morphological_analysis(PA, PB, PC: real; tipo:
integer): real;
var
    C1, C2, C3, C4, C5, C6, C7: real;
begin
    C1 := FaPANN.PANCAC(PA, PB, 0, 0, 1);
    C2 := FaPANN.PANCAC(PC, PB, 0, 0, 1);
    C3 := FaPANN.PANCAC(PC, PA, 0, 0, 1);
    C4 := FaPANN.PANCMAX(C1, C2);
    C6 := FaPANN.PANCMAX(C4, C3);
    C5 := FaPANN.PANCMIN(C2, C3);
    C7 := FaPANN.PANCMIN(C1, C5);
    if tipo = 1 then
        result := FaPANN.CNAPCA(C6, C7, PC, PB, 1)
    else
        result := FaPANN.CNAPCA(C6, C7, PC, PB, 2);
end;
```

Fig. 7 Representation of PANCmin

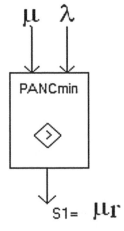

regions whose decision-making had a better percentage of success.

For an adequate PANN wave analysis, it is necessary that each input of PANN is properly calculated. These input vari-

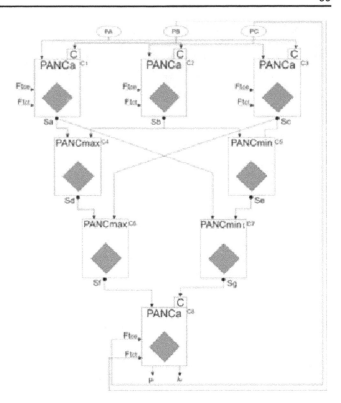

Fig. 8 The architecture for morphological analysis. Three expert systems operate: *PA* for check the number of wave peaks; *PB* for checking similar points, and *PC* for checking different points The 1st layer of the architecture: C1–PANC which processes input data of PA and PB; C2–PANC which processes input data of PB and PC; C3–PANC which processes input data of PC and PA. The 2nd layer of the architecture: C4–PANC which calculates the maximum evidence value between cells C1 and C2; C5–PANC which calculates the minimum evidence value between cells C2 and C3; The 3rd layer of the architecture: C6–PANC which calculates the maximum evidence value between cells C4 and C3; C7–PANC which calculates the minimum evidence value between cells C1 and C5. The 4th layer of the architecture: C8 analyzes the experts PA, PB, and PC and gives the resulting decision value. PANC A = paraconsistent artificial neural cell of analytic connection. PANCLs$_{Max}$ = paraconsistent artificial neural cell of simple logic connection of maximization. PANCLs$_{Min}$ = paraconsistent artificial neural cell of simple logic connection of minimization. Ft$_{ce}$ = certainty tolerance factor; Ft$_{un}$ = uncertainty tolerance factor. S_a = output of C1 cell; S_b = output of C2 cell; S_c = output of C3 cell; S_d = output of C4 cell; S_e = output of C5 cell; S_f = output of C6 cell; S_g = output of C7 cell. C = complemented value of input; μ_r = value of output of PANN; λ_r = value of output of PANN

ables are called expert systems as they are specific routines for extracting information.

In analyzing EEG signals, one important aspect to take into account is the morphological aspect. To perform such a task, it is convenient to consider an expert system which analyzes the signal behavior verifying which band it belongs to (delta, theta, alpha and beta).

The method of morphological analysis has three expert systems that are responsible for feeding the inputs of PANN with information relevant to the wave being analyzed: number of peaks, similar points, and different points.

Table 8 Checking the number of wave peaks function implementation

```
function Tf_pann.f_ EstimatedAveragePeak(vv: array of real;
total_elements: integer; Ftr: real): real;
  var
      last_larger_point, mean_peaks: real;
      peak_check: boolean;
      v_vector_aux_larger_value: real;
      a: integer;
      peaks: integer;

  begin
      last_larger_point := 0;
      peak_check := false;
      v_vector_aux_larger_value := 0;
      peaks := 0;
      mean_peaks := 0;

      for a := 1 to total_elements do
      begin
          if abs(vv[a - 1]) > v_vector_aux_larger_value then
              v_vector_aux_larger_value := vv[a - 1];

          if vv[a - 1] >= last_larger_point then
          begin
              last_larger_point := vv[a - 1];
              peak_check := false;
          end
          else
          begin
              if (peak_check = true) and
                 (vv[a - 1] > vv[a - 2]) then
              last_larger_point := vv[a - 1];
              if abs(last_larger_point - vv[a - 1]) >= ((Ftr /
100) * last_larger_point) then
              begin
                  if peak_check = false then
                  begin
                      peaks := peaks + 1;
                      mean_peaks := mean_peaks + last_larger_point;
                      peak_check := true;
                  end;
              end;
          end;

      end;

      result := mean_peaks / picos;

  end;
```

4.3 Expert system 1: checking the number of wave peaks

The aim of the *expert system 1* is to compare the waves and analyze their differences regarding the number of peaks.

In practical terms, one can say that when we analyzed the wave peaks, we are analyzing the resulting frequency of wave (so well rudimentary).

It is worth remembering that, because it is biological signal, we should not work with absolute quantification due to the variability characteristic of this type of signal. Therefore, one should always take into consideration a tolerance factor.

A sample of checking the number of wave peaks function implementation using Object Pascal is show in Table 8.

$$Se_1 = 1 - \left(\frac{(|bd - vt|)}{(bd + vt)} \right), \tag{4.2}$$

where vt is the number of peaks of the wave, bd is the number of peaks of the wave stored in the database, Se_1 is the value resulting from the calculation.

Table 9 Checking similar points function implementation

```
Function Tf_pann.f_SimilarPoints(vv, vb: array of real;
total_elements: integer; Ftr: real; max_value:real;
lager_field_value:real): real;
var
      a: integer;
      fieldx_bd: real;
      q: real;
begin
      q:=0;
      for a := 1 to total_elements do
      begin
          fieldx_bd := vb[a - 1];
          fieldx_bd := ((max_value * fieldx_bd) /
lager_field_value);
          if abs(fieldx_bd - vv[a - 1]) <= ((Ftr / 100) *
max_value) then
          begin
              q := q + 1;
          end;
      end;
      result := 1 - (strtofloat(floattostrf(((q /
total_elementos)), ffnumber, 18, 2)));
  end;
```

4.4 Expert system 2: checking similar points

The aim of the *expert system 2* is to compare the waves and analyze their differences regarding to similar points.

When we analyze the similar points, it means that we are analyzing how one approaches the other point.

It is worth remembering that, because it is biological signal, we should not work with absolute quantification due to the variability characteristic of this type of signal. Therefore, one should always take into consideration a tolerance factor.

A sample of checking similar points function implementation using Object Pascal is shown in Table 9.

$$Se_2 = \frac{\sum_{j=1}^{n} (x_j)}{n}, \tag{4.3}$$

where n is the total number of elements, x is the element of the current position, a j is the current position, Se_2 is the value resulting from the calculation.

4.5 Expert system 3: checking different points

The aim of the *expert system 3* is to compare the waves and analyze their differences regarding of different points.

When we analyze the different points, it means that we are analyzing how a point more distant from each other, so the factor of tolerance should also be considered.

A sample of checking different points function implementation using Object Pascal is shown in Table 10.

$$Se_3 = 1 - \left(\frac{\sum_{j=1}^{n} \left(\frac{|x_j - y_j|}{a} \right)}{n} \right), \tag{4.4}$$

where n is the total number of elements, a is the maximum amount allowed, j is the current position, x is the value of

Paraconsistent neurocomputing and brain signal analysis

Table 10 Checking different points function implementation

```
function Tf_pann.f_DifferentPoints(vv, vb: array of real;
total_elements:     integer;     Ftr,     max_value,
lager_field_value:real): real;
var
    a: integer;
    fieldx_bd, q: real;
begin
    q:=0;
    for a := 1 to total_elements do
    begin
        fieldx_bd := vb[a - 1];
        fieldx_bd  :=  ((max_value  *  fieldx_bd)  /
lager_field_value);
        if abs(fieldx_bd - vv[a - 1]) > ((Ftr / 100) *
max_value) then
        begin
            q := q + (abs(fieldx_bd - vv[a - 1]) / max_value);
        end;
    end;

    result  :=  1  -  (strtofloat(floattostrf(((q  /
total_elementos)), ffnumber, 18, 2)));

end;
```

Table 11 Contingency table

	Visual analysis					
	Delta	Theta	Alpha	Beta	Unrecognized	Total
PANN Analysis						
Delta	31	3	0	0	0	34
Theta	15	88	1	1	0	105
Alpha	0	5	22	0	0	27
Beta	0	0	1	3	0	4
N/D	7	2	1	0	0	10
Total	53	98	25	4	0	180

Index kappa = 0.80

wave 1, y is the value of wave 2, Se_3 is the value resulting from the calculation.

5 Experimental procedures: differentiating frequency bands

In our work we have studied two types of waves, specifically delta and theta waves band, where the size of frequency established clinically ranges (Fig. 1).

Seven examinations of different EEG were analyzed, being two examinations belonging to adults without any learning disturbance and five examinations belonging to children with learning disturbance [5,6,13].

Each analysis was divided into three rehearsals; each rehearsal consisted of 10 s of the analyzed, free from visual analysis of spikes and artifacts regarding the channels T3 and T4.

In the first battery of tests, a wave recognition filter belonging to the delta band was considered. In the second one, a wave recognition filter belonging to the theta band was considered. In the third one, none of the filters were considered for recognition (Tables 11, 12, 13, 14, 15, 16).

Table 12 Statistical results—sensitivity and specificity: delta waves

	Visual analysis		
	Delta	Not delta	Total
PANN			
True	31	124	155
False	22	3	25
Total	53	127	180

Sensitivity = 58 %; specificity = 97 %

Table 13 Statistical results—sensitivity and specificity: theta waves

	Visual analysis		
	Theta	Not theta	Total
PANN			
True	88	65	153
False	10	17	27
Total	98	82	180

Sensitivity = 89 %; specificity = 79 %

Table 14 Statistical results—sensitivity and specificity: alpha waves

	Visual analysis		
	Alpha	Not alpha	Total
PANN			
True	22	150	172
False	3	5	8
Total	25	155	180

Sensitivity = 88 %; specificity = 96 %

Table 15 Statistical results—sensitivity and specificity: beta waves

	Visual analysis		
	Beta	Not beta	Total
PANN			
True	3	175	178
False	1	1	2
Total	4	176	180

Sensitivity = 75 %; specificity = 99 %

Table 16 Statistical results—sensitivity and specificity: unrecognized waves

	Visual analysis		
	Unrecognized	Recognized	Total
PANN			
True	0	170	170
False	0	10	10
Total	0	180	180

Sensitivity = 100 %; specificity = 94 %

Table 17 Lattice for decision-making (Fig. 9) used in diagnostic analysis used after making PANN analysis (Fig. 10)

Characterization of the lattice	
Area 1	$G_{ce} \leq 0.1999$ and $G_{ce} \geq 0.5600$ and $|G_{un}| < 0.3999$ and $|G_{un}| \geq 0.4501$
Area 2	$0.2799 < G_{ce} < 0.5600$ and $0.3099 \leq |G_{un}| < 0.3999$ and $Fe < 0.5000$
Area 3	$0.1999 < G_{ce} < 0.5600$ and $0.3999 \leq |G_{un}| < 0.4501$ and $Fe > 0.5000$
Area 4	$G_{ce} > 0.7999$ and $|G_{un}| < 0.2000$

Ce contrary evidence, Fe favorable evidence, G_{ce} certainty degree, G_{un} uncertainty degree

6 Experimental procedures: applying in Alzheimer disease

It is known that the visual analysis of EEG patterns may be useful in aiding the diagnosis of AD and indicated in some clinical protocols for diagnosing the disease [14,15]. The most common findings on visual analysis of EEG patterns are slowing of brain electrical activity based on predominance of delta and theta rhythms and decrease or absence of alpha rhythm. However, these findings are more common and evident in patients in moderate or advanced stages of disease [8,16,17].

In this study we have 67 analyzed EEG records, 34 normal and 33 probable AD (p value $= 0.8496$) during the awake state at rest.

All tests were subjected to morphological analysis methodology for measuring the concentration of waves. Later this information is submitted to a PANN unit responsible for assessing the data and arriving at a classification of the examination in normal or probable AD (Table 17; Fig. 9).

6.1 Expert system 1: detecting the diminishing average frequency level

The aim of the *expert system 1* is to verify the average frequency level of alpha band waves and compare them with a fixed external parameter wave.

Such external parameter can be, for instance, the average frequency of a population or the average frequency of the last examination of the patient. This system also generates two outputs: favorable evidence μ normalized values ranging from 0 (corresponds to 100 %—or greater frequency loss) to 1 (which corresponds to 0 % of frequency loss) and contrary evidence λ (Eq. 6.1).

The average frequency of population pattern used in this work is 10 Hz.

$$\lambda = 1 - \mu \tag{6.1}$$

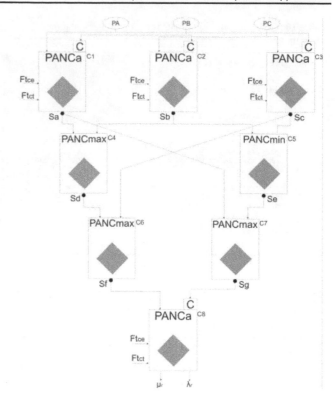

Fig. 9 The architecture for diagnosis analysis

6.2 Expert system 2: high-frequency band concentration

The role of the *expert system 2* is to analyze alpha band concentration. For this, we consider the quotient of the sum of fast alpha and beta waves over slow delta and theta waves (Eq. 6.2) as first output value. For the second output value (contrary evidence λ) is used Eq. 6.1.

$$\mu = \left(\frac{(A + B)}{(D + T)} \right), \tag{6.2}$$

where A is the alpha band concentration; B is the beta band concentration, D is the delta band concentration; T is the theta band concentration; and μ is the value resulting from the calculation.

6.3 Expert system 3: low frequency band concentration

The role of the *expert system 3* is to analyze theta band concentration. For this, we consider the quotient of the sum of slow delta and theta waves over fast alpha and beta waves (Eq. 6.3) as first output value. For the second output value (contrary evidence λ) is used Eq. 6.1.

$$\mu = \left(\frac{(D + T)}{(A + B)} \right) \tag{6.3}$$

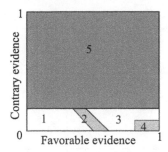

Fig. 10 Lattice for decision-making used in diagnostic analysis (Fig. 9). *Area 1* state logical false (AD likely below average population), *area 2* state logical Quasi-true (AD likely than average population); *area 3* state logical Quasi-false (normal below average population); *area 4* state logical true (normal above average population); *area 5* logical state of uncertainty (not used in the study area)

where A is the alpha band concentration; B is the beta band concentration. D is the delta band concentration; and T is the theta band concentration. μ is the value resulting from the calculation.

6.4 Results

See Table 18.

7 Experimental procedures: applying in attention-deficit/hyperactivity disorder (ADHD)

A similar architecture using PANN was built to study some cases in ADHD. Recent researches reveal that 10 % of the world population in school age suffer of learning and/or behavioral disorders caused by neurological problems, such as ADHD, dyslexia, and dyscalculia, with predictable consequences in those students' insufficient performance in the school [2–6,13].

Concisely, a child without intellectual lowering is characterized as bearer of ADHD when it presents signs of

- Inattention: difficulty in maintaining attention in tasks or games; the child seems not to hear what is spoken; difficulty in organizing tasks or activities; the child loses

things; the child becomes distracted with any incentive, etc.

- Hyperactivity: frequently the child leaves the class room; the child is always inconveniencing friends; the child runs and climbs in trees, pieces of furniture, etc; the child speaks a lot, etc.
- Impulsiveness: the child interrupts the activities of colleagues; the child does not wait his time; aggressiveness crises, etc.
- Dyslexia: the child begins to present difficulties to recognize letters or to read them and to write them although the child has not a disturbed intelligence, that is, a normal IQ;
- Dyscalculia: the child presents difficulties to recognize amounts or numbers and/or to figure out arithmetic calculations.

A child can present any combination among the disturbances above. All those disturbances have their origin in a cerebral dysfunction that can have multiple causes, many times showing a hereditary tendency.

Since from the first discoveries, those disturbances have been associated with cortical diffuse lesions and/or more specific, temporal-parietal areas lesions in the case of dyslexia and dyscalculia [2,5,13].

The disturbances of ADHD disorder seem to be associated with an alteration of the dopaminergic system, that is, it is involved with mechanisms of attention and they seem to involve a frontal-lobe dysfunction and basal ganglia areas [3,13].

EEG alterations seem to be associated with those disturbances. Thus, some authors have proposed that there is an increase of the delta activity in EEG in those tasks that demand a larger attention to the internal processes.

Other authors [1] have described alterations of the delta activity in dyslexia and dyscalculia children sufferers. Klimesch [18] has proposed that a phase of the EEG component would be associated with the action of the memory work. More recently, Kwak [19] has showed delta activity is reduced in occipital areas, but not in frontals, when dyslexic children were compared with normal ones.

In this way, the study of the delta and theta bands becomes important in the context of the analysis of learning disturbances.

So, in this paper we have studied two types of waves, specifically delta and theta wave bands, where the size of frequency established clinically ranges 1.0–3.5 and 4.0–7.5 Hz, respectively.

Seven exams of different EEG were analyzed, being two exams belonging to adults without any learning disturbance and five exams belonging to children with learning disturbances (exams and respective diagnoses given by

Table 18 Diagnosis: normal × probable AD patients

	Gold standard		
	AD patient (%)	Normal patient (%)	Total (%)
PANN			
AD patient	35.82	14.93	50.75
Normal patient	8.96	40.30	49.25
Total	44.78	55.22	100.00

Sensitivity = 80 %; specificity = 73 ; index of coincidence (kappa) 76 %

ENSCER—Teaching the Brain, EINA—Studies in Natural Intelligence and Artificial Ltda).

Each analysis was divided into three rehearsals, and each rehearsal consisted of 10 s of the analyzed, free from visual analysis of spikes and artifacts regarding the channels T3 and T4. In the first battery of tests, a delta recognition filter wave was considered. For second battery of tests, a theta recognition wave was considered. For the third battery of tests, none of the filters were considered for recognition, i.e., the system worked freely for any wave type recognition. The total number of exams is 180 (Tables 19, 20, 21, 22, 23, 24).

8 Conclusions

We believe that a process of the examination analysis using a PANN attached to EEG findings, such as relations between

Table 19 Contingency table

	Visual analysis					
	Delta	Theta	Alpha	Beta	Unrecognized	Total
PANN analysis						
Delta	31	3	0	0	0	34
Theta	15	88	1	1	0	105
Alpha	0	5	22	0	0	27
Beta	0	0	1	3	0	4
N/D	7	2	1	0	0	0
Total	53	98	25	4	0	180

Index kappa = 0.80

Table 20 Statistical results—sensitivity and specificity: delta waves

	Visual analysis		
	Delta	Not delta	Total
PANN analysis			
True	31	124	155
False	22	3	25
Total	53	127	180

Sensitivity = 58 %; specificity = 97 %

Table 21 Statistical results—sensitivity and specificity: theta waves

	Visual analysis		
	Theta	Not theta	Total
PANN analysis			
True	88	65	153
False	10	17	27
Total	98	82	180

Sensitivity = 89 %; specificity = 79 %

Table 22 Statistical results—sensitivity and specificity: alpha waves

	Visual analysis		
	Alpha	Not alpha	Total
PANN analysis			
True	22	150	172
False	3	5	8
Total	25	155	180

Sensitivity = 88 %; specificity = 96 %

Table 23 Statistical results—sensitivity and specificity: beta waves

	Visual analysis		
	Beta	Not beta	Total
PANN analysis			
True	3	175	178
False	1	1	2
Total	4	176	180

Sensitivity = 75 %; specificity = 99 %

Table 24 Statistical results—sensitivity and specificity: unrecognized waves

	Visual analysis		
	Unrecognized	Recognized	Total
PANN analysis			
True	0	180	180
False	0	0	0
Total	0	180	180

Sensitivity = 100 %; specificity = 100 %

frequency bandwidth and inter hemispheric coherences, can create computational methodologies that allow the automation of analysis and diagnosis.

These methodologies could be employed as tools to aid in the diagnosis of diseases such as dyslexia or Alzheimer, provided they have defined electroencephalographic findings.

In the case of Alzheimer's disease, for example, the studies carried out previously have shown satisfactory results [20] (but still far from being a tool to aid clinical) that demonstrated the computational efficiency of the methodology using a simple morphological analysis (only paraconsistent annotated logic $E\tau$). These results encouraged us to improve the morphological analysis of the waves and try to apply the method in other diseases besides Alzheimer's disease.

With the process of morphological analysis using the PANN, it becomes possible to quantify the frequency average of the individual without losing its temporal reference. This feature becomes a differential, compared to traditional analysis of quantification of frequencies, such as fast Fourier transform, aiming at a future application in real-time analysis, i.e., at the time of acquisition of the EEG exams.

Regarding the specificity, the method showed more reliable results. Taking into account an overall assessment in the sense we take the arithmetic mean of sensitivity (75.50 %) and specificity (92.75 %), we find reasonable results that encourage us to seek improvements in this study.

The consideration of morphological analysis of the main brain waves by employing PANN showed be effective, allowing interesting quantitative and qualitative examinations of EEG data. PANN has been applied in other branches: MICR automated recognition [16], computer-aided diagnosis (breast cancer) [17], and many other themes.

Open Access This article is distributed under the terms of the Creative Commons Attribution License which permits any use, distribution, and reproduction in any medium, provided the original author(s) and the source are credited.

References

1. Niedermeyer, E., da Silva, F.H.L.: Electroencephalography, 5th edn. Lippincott Williams & Wilkins, Philadelphia (2005)
2. Ansari, D., Karmiloff-Smith, A.: Atypical trajectories of number development: a neuroconstructivist perspective. Trends Cogn. Sci. **12**, 511–516 (2002)
3. Blonds, T.A.: Attention-deficit disorders and hyperactivity. In developmental disabilities in infancy and Ramus, F., developmental dyslexia: specific phonological deficit or general sensorimotor dysfunction? Curr. Opin. Neurobiol. **13**, 1–7 (2003)
4. Hynd, G.W., Hooper, R., Takahashi, T.: Dyslexia and language-based disabilities. In: Coffey, C.E., Brumbak, R.A. (eds.) Text Book of Pediatric Neuropsychiatry, pp. 691–718. American Psychiatric Press, Washington, DC (1985)
5. Lindsay, R.L.: Dyscalculia. In: Capute, A.J., Accardo, P.J. (eds.) Developmental Disabilities in Infancy and Childhood, pp. 405–415. Paul Brookes Publishing Co, Baltimore (1996)
6. Temple, E.: Brain mechanisms in normal and dyslexic readers. Curr. Opin. Neurobiol. **12**, 178–183 (2002)
7. Kwak, Y.T.: Quantitative EEG findings in different stages of Alzheimer's disease. J. Clin. Neurophysiol. **23**(5), 456–461 (2006)
8. Duffy, F.H., Albert, M.S., Mcnulty, G., Garvey, A.J.: Age differences in brain electrical activity of healthy subjects. Ann. Neural **16**, 430–438 (1984)
9. Nuwer, M.R., Comi, G., Emerson, R., Fuglsang-Frederiksen, J., GuériT, M., Hinrichs, H., Ikeda, A., Luccas, F.J.C., Rappelsberger, P.: IFCN standards for digital recording of clinical EEG. Electroencephalogr. Clin. Neurophysiol. **106**, 259–261 (1998)
10. Nitrini, R., Caramelli, P., Bottino, C.M., Damasceno, B.P., Brucki, S.M., Anghinah, R.: Academia Brasileira de Neurologia. Diagnosis of Alzheimer's disease in Brazil: diagnostic criteria and auxiliary tests. Recommendations of the Scientific Department of Cognitive Neurology and Aging of the Brazilian Academy of Neurology. Arq Neuropsiquiatr. **63**(3A), 9–713 (2005)
11. Da Silva Filho, J.I., Torres, G.L., Abe, J.M.: Uncertainty Treatment Using Paraconsistent Logic—Introducing Paraconsistent Artificial Neural Networks, vol. 211. IOS Press, Netherlands (2010). ISBN 978-1-60750-557-0.
12. Abe, J.M.: Foundations of annotated logics. PhD thesis (in Portuguese) USP, Brazil (1992)
13. Voeller, K.K.S.: Attention-deficit/hyperactivity: neurobiological and clinical aspects of attention and disorders of attention. In: Coffey, C.E., Brumbak, R.A. (eds.) Text Book of Pediatric Neuropsychiatry, pp. 691–718. American Psychiatric Press, Washington, D.C (1998)
14. Claus, J.J., Strijers, R.L.M., Jonkman, E.J., Ongerboer De Visser, B.W., Jonker, C., Walstra, G.J.M., Scheltens, P., Gool, W.A.: The diagnostic value of EEG in mild senile Alzheimer's disease. Clin. Neurophysiol. **18**, 15–23 (1999)
15. Crevel, H., Gool, W.A., Walstra, G.J.M.: Early diagnosis of dementia: which tests are indicated? What are their costs? J. Neurol. **246**, 73–78 (1999)
16. Souza, S., Abe, J.M., Nakamatsu, K.: MICR Automated Recognition Based on Paraconsistent Artificial Neural Networks, Procedia Computer Science, vol. 22, pp. 170–178. Elsevier, London (2013)
17. Amaral, F.V.: Paraconsistent mammography image attributes classifier in breast cancer diagnosis: based on paraconsistent artificial neural network. PhD thesis (in Portuguese) UNIP, Brazil (2013)
18. Klimeshc, W.: EEG alpha and theta oscillations reflect cognitive and memory performance: a review and analysis. Brain Res. Ver. **29**, 169–195 (1999)
19. Klimesch, W., Doppelmayr, H., Wimmer, J., Schwaiger, D., Rôhm, D., Bruber, W., Hutzler, F.: Theta band power changes in normal and dyslexic children. Clin. Neurophysiol. **113**, 1174–1185 (2001)
20. Lopes, H.F.S.: Aplicação de redes neurais artificiais paraconsistentes como método de auxílio no diagnóstico da doença de Alzheimer. MSc Dissertation (in Portuguese), Faculdade de Medicina-USP, São Paulo (2009)

10

Adaptive reversible data hiding with pyramidal structure

Yuh-Yih Lu · Hsiang-Cheh Huang

Abstract In this paper, we propose an adaptive algorithm for reversible data hiding by employing the characteristics and pyramidal relationships of original images. The major goal of reversible data hiding is to keep the reversibility of algorithm. By use of the pyramidal structure to explore the inherent characteristics of original images, regions with different smoothness levels can be determined, and then data hiding can be performed adaptively with the pre-determined threshold for balancing the output image quality and embedding capacity. On the one hand, larger capacity can be hidden into smoother regions with limited degradation of output image quality. On the other hand, the size of location map, which serves as the side information for keeping reversibility, can be reduced for embedding into smoother or less smooth regions of original image. By carefully manipulating difference values between layers in pyramidal structure, secret information can effectively be embedded. With our method, we observe better performances over relating methods with enhanced image quality, the more embedding capacity, and comparable amount of side information for decoding. More importantly, the reversibility of our method is guaranteed, meaning that original image and secret information can both be perfectly recovered at the decoder. Simulation results demonstrate that proposed method in this paper outperforms those in conventional algorithms.

Y.-Y. Lu
Minghsin University of Science and Technology, No.1,
Xinxing Rd., Xinfeng, Hsinchu 30401, Taiwan, R.O.C.
e-mail: yylu@must.edu.tw

H.-C. Huang (✉)
National University of Kaohsiung, No. 700 University Road,
Kaohsiung 811, Taiwan, R.O.C.
e-mail: huang.hc@gmail.com
URL: http://sites.google.com/site/hch888dr/

Keywords Reversible data hiding · Pyramidal structure · Histogram · Quad · Image quality · Capacity

1 Introduction

Information security is one of the popular research topics, and it is also an important issue for practical application. Among relating methods in information security and corresponding digital rights management (DRM) systems [1,2], cryptography and watermarking are two important categories. We focus on reversible data hiding algorithm in this paper, which belongs to a branch in watermarking researches and applications.

Watermarking researches have emerged for around 15 years, and reversible data hiding is a recently developed branch in watermarking researches [3,4]. For conventional watermarking, at the encoder, the secret information should be embedded into the original multimedia contents, digital images in most cases, by the use of algorithms developed by researchers. Then, the watermarked media can be transmitted to the receiver. Data loss or intentional attacks may be experienced during transmission. After reception of the delivered watermarked media, only the secret information needs to be extracted [1]. In contrast, for reversible data hiding, data embedding is similar to its counterpart with conventional watermarking applications. Different from watermarking, for reversible data hiding, after the reception of marked media, both the original content and embedded secret information need to be recovered and extracted perfectly with a reasonable amount of side information [5,6]. And this is the origin of the term "reversible" comes from. Besides the development of algorithms, reversible data hiding can be applicable to the protection of medical images [7,8], or the integration with encryption techniques [9]. Due to this kind of characteristics, during the transmission, the watermarked media need to be kept intact.

Suppose that there are lots of medical images in the database of some hospital. Due to the stressful environment, especially in ICU, doctors or nurses may unintentionally put Patient A's personal data and medical records into Patient B's images. With the aid of reversible data hiding, Patient A's medical records can be embedded into Patient A's images beforehand [7]. For the doctors and nurses, while retrieving patients' marked images, corresponding medical records can also be extracted to compare to the database. Also, original images can be perfectly recovered to meet the integrity. Should there be any mismatch, doctors or nurses are alarmed to prevent anything unexpected from happening. Thus, reversible data-hiding techniques can be applicable for practical use.

For evaluating performances of algorithms, and for making fair comparisons, parameters from different aspects should be considered. These parameters include the following.

- *Reversibility* it implies that marked image should be decomposed into original image and secret information perfectly at the decoder.
- *Output image quality, or imperceptibility* it denotes the resemblance between the original and output images, meaning that the error induced from data embedding should be as small as possible.
- *Capacity* it means the number of bits that can be embedded in the original image, which is expected to be larger than some reasonable amount. Larger capacity provides the flexibility for the selection of secret information, however, larger degradation may be expected correspondingly.
- *Side information, or the overhead for decoding* it should be as little as possible to make the proposed algorithm suitable for practical applications.

As far as we know, considering practical implementations, some tradeoffs among the parameters should be watched for the design of algorithm. For instance, embedding more capacity into original image introduces larger error, hence the degradation of quality of marked image. We suggest choosing the two criteria of obtaining at least 1.0 bit/pixel (bpp) of maximal embedding capacity, and reaching at least 30 dB in peak signal-to-noise ratio (PSNR) of output image quality. With our algorithm, reversible data hiding can be reached with adaptive embedding and pyramidal structure based on parameters listed above. Reversible data-hiding methods, which will be described in Sect. 2, have their inherent limitations and drawbacks even though lots of advantages can be observed. More importantly, few methods take the characteristics of original images into account in this field. Here,

we make use of pyramidal structure of original image for obtaining the larger number of secret bits for embedding, with similar quality of the output images. Simulation results reveal that the algorithm proposed in this paper outperforms conventional ones by use of eight test images.

This paper is organized as follows. In Sect. 2, we describe fundamental concepts of reversible data hiding algorithms, including the histogram-based and difference expansion (DE)-based schemes. The reason why reversibility can be guaranteed is also addressed. Then, in Sect. 3, by considering inherent characteristics of images, we can utilize the difference values, and present the better way to make use of the pyramidal structure for reversible data hiding. Simulation results are demonstrated in Sect. 4, which point out the guaranteed image quality, the more embedding capacity, and the less side information needed for the proposed algorithm. Finally, we conclude this paper in Sect. 5.

2 Implementations for reversible data hiding

The framework of reversible data hiding can be demonstrated in Fig. 1. On the one hand, in Fig. 1a, it depicts the encoder framework. Original image and secret information are integrated altogether with the devised algorithm to form the marked image. For keeping reversibility, the necessary amount of side information should also be provided to the

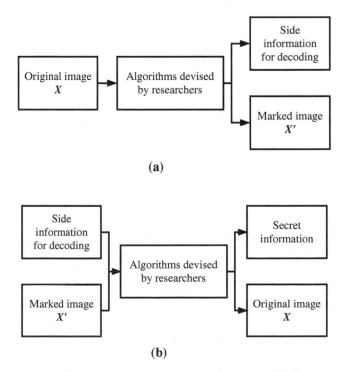

(a)

(b)

Fig. 1 Framework of reversible data hiding. **a** Encoder framework. **b** Decoder framework

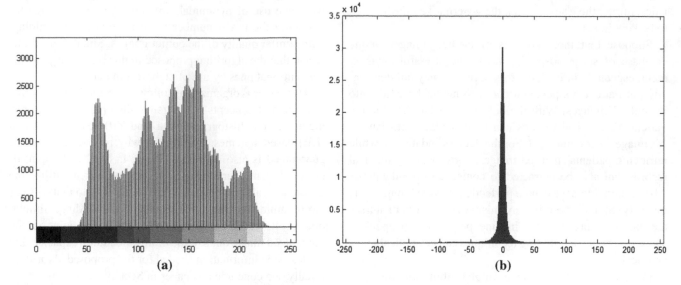

Fig. 2 Comparisons of histogram and difference histogram with Lena. **a** Histogram of Lena, H, with the peak occurrence of 2,966. **b** Difference histogram of Lena, D, with the peak occurrence of 30,150

decoder. On the other hand, in Fig. 1b, it displays the decoder framework. It is easily observed that blocks in Fig. 1b are placed in reverse order comparing to its counterpart in Fig. 1a. By doing so, both the original image and secret information can be perfectly separated from the marked image with the devised algorithm. And this is the major reason about the name of "reversible data hiding".

Practical implementations for making reversible data-hiding possible can roughly be categorized into two major branches. From global point of view, by carefully modifying the histogram, we can reversibly embed the secret information into original image with schemes in [10–12]. Schemes in this branch are referred to as the histogram-based schemes. On the other hand, considering local characteristics of original image, we can embed secret information by intentionally doubling the difference value between neighboring pixel pairs with schemes in [13–15]. Schemes in this branch are referred to as the DE-based schemes.

Here, we briefly address the advantages and drawbacks of both schemes. First, for the histogram-based schemes, it has the advantage of guaranteed output image quality because the mean square error (MSE) between the marked and original image is limited to be below 1, leading to the result of at least 48.13 dB in PSNR value [3]. The major drawback of histogram-based schemes is the limited number of capacity, which is constrained by the peak of the histogram.

Next, for the DE-based schemes, it utilizes the difference value between two neighboring pixels for embedding one secret bit, leading to the capacity of 0.5 bit/pixel (bpp). However, after modifying the difference values, it may cause the overflow for producing the marked image. By following [5] and [6], the side information is named 'location map' (LM),

which should be recorded in advance to keep the reversibility. There are some effective means for reducing the size of LM in [13] and [14]. Besides, unlike the histogram-based schemes, output image quality cannot be guaranteed.

It may be constructive to integrate the two schemes altogether and to acquire the advantages from both schemes. We take the histogram H in Fig. 2a, and difference histogram D in Fig. 2b of test image Lena with size of 512×512. With the 8-bit grey-level representation, the pixel values are integers between 0 and 255. Consequently, the range of difference values lies between -255 and 255. We observe that the peak values of Fig. 2a and b are 2,966 and 30,150, respectively, which results in 10.17 times difference. If we can borrow the concept in histogram-based schemes in Fig. 2a and integrate into DE-based scheme in Fig. 2b, larger capacity may be expected by utilizing the difference histogram. Output image quality can also be controlled when the limited amount of capacity is embedded.

Here is a simple illustration for reversible data hiding with difference histogram. The difference histogram can be produced from the difference between neighboring pixels. In Fig. 2b, we observe the difference histogram D is concentrated around 0. Here, D is an array, and we can denote the array by $D = [d[-255], d[-254], \ldots, d[-1], d[0], d[1], \ldots, d[254], d[255]]$, because the difference values lie between -255 and 255. Next, the predetermined threshold value δ, which is a positive integer, is selected for data embedding, and it also serves as the side information at the decoder. For embedding the secret information, the altered difference histogram D' should be formed first. By following the same manner, D' can be represented with the notation of $D' = [d'[-255], d'[-254], \ldots, d'[-1], d'[0], d'[1], \ldots,$

d' [254], d' [255]]. Next, data embedding should meet one of the following cases.

Case 1. For $d[i]$, $i \geq \delta + 1$,

$$d'[i + 1] = d[i]. \tag{1}$$

Case 2. For $d[i]$, $i \leq -\delta$,

$$d'[i - 1] = d[i]. \tag{2}$$

Case 3. For $d[i]$, $-\delta + 2 \leq i \leq \delta - 1$, the values are kept the same. That is,

$$d'[i] = d[i]. \tag{3}$$

Case 4. For $i = -\delta + 1$ and $i = \delta$, the values are intentionally set to 0. That is,

$$d'[-\delta + 1] = d'[\delta] = 0. \tag{4}$$

We observe that the value of δ plays the role of the secret key in reversible data hiding with only a few bits of overhead. It has another advantage of ease of implementation because only the moving of some portion of difference histogram is needed, and there is no need for calculation. Besides the advantages indicated above, there is one drawback for the proposed algorithm. Under the extreme cases when the index i reaches -255 or 255, the overflow problem would occur, which can be easily observed from Eqs. (1) and (2). Such locations, or LM, should be recorded and served as the side information for decoding.

From Case 1 to Case 4, histogram occurrences at two difference values of δ and $(-\delta + 1)$, or the two bins as described in Case 4, are intentionally set to zero for hiding bit '0' and bit '1'. For embedding secret bits, the difference histogram containing the secret, D'', should be produced correspondingly. Again, by following the same manner, D'' can be represented with the notation of $D'' = [d''[-255], d''[-254], \ldots, d''[-1], d''[0], d''[1], \ldots, d''[254], d''[255]]$. For clarity, four the difference values (or the index i) at $-\delta$, $(-\delta + 1)$, δ, and $(\delta + 1)$ are employed for data embedding. Other elements in D'' are identical to their corresponding counterparts in D'. Embedding meets one of following conditions at the encoder.

- For embedding bit '1': for positive difference,

$$d''[\delta] = d'[\delta + 1]. \tag{5a}$$

For negative difference,

$$d''[-\delta + 1] = d'[-\delta]. \tag{5b}$$

- For embedding bit '0', keep the difference values the same. That is,

$$d''[\delta + 1] = d'[\delta + 1]. \tag{6a}$$

$$d''[-\delta] = d'[-\delta]. \tag{6b}$$

The difference values for remaining elements in D'' are identical to their corresponding counterparts in D'.

If we look into more detail in Eqs. (5a) and (5b), addition or subtraction by 1 implies the embedding of one bit. It has the potential to add or subtract the value of $2^n - 1$, with n being the number of secret bits, for data embedding. For instance, if $n = 2$, addition or subtraction the difference values by 0–3 is able to hide two bits at the same time. Meanwhile, for the locations of difference values larger than 252 or smaller than -252, they should be recorded as LM. It corresponds to the observation that for smoother regions, they have the potential to hide more bits simultaneously. Larger value of n, or embedding more bits at the same time, might be impractical because the added or subtracted value grows exponentially, which implies the increased amount of LM. By doing so, adaptive embedding can be achieved by incorporating with secret size and smoothness of original image.

For the extraction of secret bits and the recovery of original image, they correspond to the reverse procedures to data embedding, as depicted in the framework in Fig. 1. They can be described with the following procedures.

1. The side information, which includes LM and δ value, along with the marked image, should be obtained at the decoder.
2. Then, difference histogram containing secret bits D'' can be produced from marked image.
3. With the δ value, secret bits of 0 and 1 can be extracted from D'' with Eqs. (5a) and (6a). Next, D' can be recovered after the extraction of secret bits.
4. In D', remove the empty bins at $d'[-\delta + 1]$ and $d'[\delta]$. By adding back the extremes of $d[-255]$ and $d[255]$ from LM, original difference histogram D can be formed.
5. Recover the original image by adding the difference value back to the seed pixel.

With the descriptions above, we can find that reversibility can be guaranteed by manipulating difference histogram for reversible data hiding.

3 Proposed algorithm

We propose our algorithm by considering the three-tier procedures with the concepts described in Sect. 2. The difference

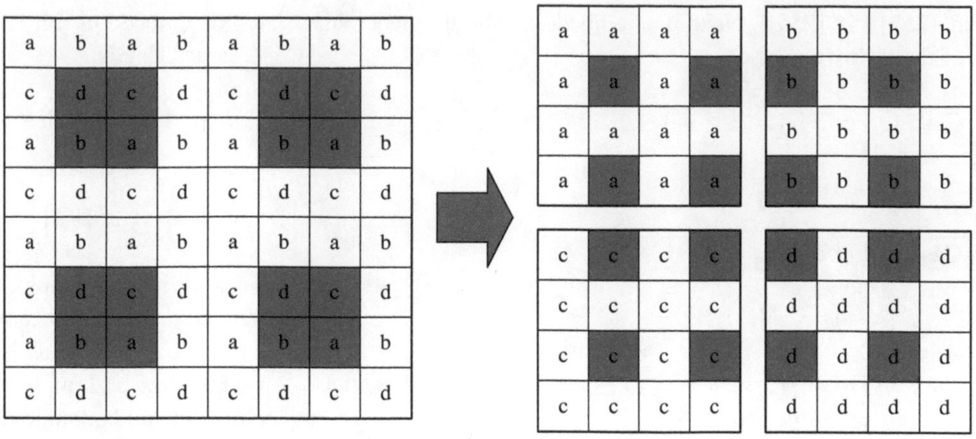

Fig. 3 The splitting of original image. Pixels in *red* in the *left image* are prepared for pyramidal structure. The image at the *right* side corresponds to the result after splitting

values between neighboring pixels, as well as the pyramidal structure, are utilized to look for better performances. As we mentioned in Sect. 1, for our algorithm, we suggest reaching the performances of at least 1.0 bpp of capacity, and at least 30 dB in PSNR of output image quality. After looking for major research databases, two relating papers [16,17] met the two criteria, and they are employed to make comparisons with proposed algorithm.

3.1 Tier #1: splitting of original image

By making good use of the characteristics of original image, we first divide the original image **X** into non-overlapping 2×2 blocks, and each block corresponds to one quad. In order to look for the reduction of side information to be provided to the receiver, and to make good use of difference values calculated from each quad, we choose regular pattern to serve as reference pixels for reversible data hiding.

For the ease of demonstration, we split the original image **X** into non-overlapping groups, and each group is composed of pixels from positions in 'a', 'b', 'c', and 'd', shown in the left part of Fig. 3. Next, we gather pixels in 'a', 'b', 'c', and 'd' together to form the sub-images of $\mathbf{X}_a$, $\mathbf{X}_b$, $\mathbf{X}_c$, and $\mathbf{X}_d$, respectively, depicted in the right part of Fig. 3. Each square block represents one pixel in the image.

Let the pixels in red serve as the reference points for data hiding. Because they are placed on regular positions, the side information for decoding may be reduced. We can use two bits to present the four types of positions of 'a', 'b', 'c', and 'd'. In addition, the arrangements of red pixel positions may associate with hierarchical coding, or layered coding, where the original image and the pixels in red may serve as the base layer and enhancement layer, respectively. For instance, we can gather pixels in red in the left part of Fig. 3 altogether to form a smaller image corresponding to the original image. We can carefully utilize the relationships between base and enhancement layers to look for better performances in reversible data hiding.

3.2 Tier #2: multi-level embedding of secret information

With the four split sub-images and the reference points, data embedding can be performed accordingly by following the concepts described in Sect. 2.

In each of the sub-images, we first divide the image into non-overlapping quads. We can observe the arrangement of one reference point (or the pixel in red) in one quad. We take the first quad in $\mathbf{X}_a$ as an instance in Fig. 3 for the better comprehension of our method. For other sub-images, by replacing the place of reference points, same steps can be performed subsequently. Pixels in this quad locate at $X_a(1, 1)$, $X_a(1, 2)$, $X_a(2, 1)$, and $X_a(2, 2)$, and the reference point, shown in red, is $X_a(2, 2)$. The luminance of the reference is kept unchanged, and three difference values can be calculated with the following equations:

$$d_1 = \text{lum}(X_a(1, 1)) - \text{lum}(X_a(2, 2)); \tag{7a}$$

$$d_2 = \text{lum}(X_a(1, 2)) - \text{lum}(X_a(2, 2)); \tag{7b}$$

$$d_3 = \text{lum}(X_a(2, 1)) - \text{lum}(X_a(2, 2)); \tag{7c}$$

Next, by following the methods in [16] and [17] with some modifications, based on the concept depicted in Eqs. (5a)–(6a), a predetermined threshold T, which relates to the embedding strength, should be compared with the difference values. Because the maximum of difference may be close to the threshold value T, overflow may occur, which would lead to the difficulty to keep reversibility of algorithm. Steps for performing data hiding can be executed as follows:

Step 1. If $\max(|d_1|, |d_2|, |d_3|) < \frac{1}{8}T$, two bits can be embedded, which are represented by b_1b_2, with $b_1, b_2 \in \{0, 1\}$. The difference value is modified by

$$d_i' = 4 \cdot d_i + b_1b_2, \quad i = 1, 2, 3. \tag{8}$$

Fig. 4 The pyramid structure. The reference points in Fig. 3 are denoted in the *left*, and gather them to become a quarter-sized image. By following this manner, pyramidal structure can be formed

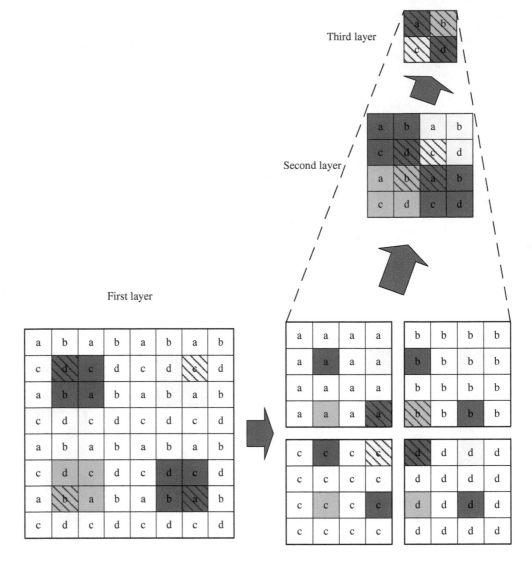

The two secret bits, $b_1 b_2 \in \{00,\ 01,\ 10,\ 11\}$, are concatenated together for embedding at the same time. Decimal forms of $b_1 b_2$ are expected for the modification of difference values as depicted in Eq. (8). Because the difference values are much smaller than T, a total of six bits can be embedded into a quad based on Eqs. (7a)–(7c), leading to the capacity of $\frac{6}{4} = 1.5$ bit/pixel (bpp).

Step 2. If $\frac{1}{8}T \leq \max(|d_1|,\ |d_2|,\ |d_3|) < \frac{1}{2}T$, one bit can be embedded, which is represented by b, with $b \in \{0,\ 1\}$. The difference value is modified by

$$d_i' = 2 \cdot d_i + b, \quad i = 1,\ 2,\ 3. \tag{9}$$

In Eq. (9), b denotes the secret bit. By doing so, three bits can be embedded into a quad, leading to the capacity of $\frac{3}{4} = 0.75$ bpp.

Step 3. If $\frac{1}{2}T \leq \max(|d_1|,\ |d_2|,\ |d_3|) < T$, one bit can be embedded. The difference value is modified by

$$d_i' = 2 \cdot \left\lfloor \frac{d_i}{2} \right\rfloor + b, \quad i = 1,\ 2,\ 3. \tag{10}$$

In Eq. (10), the new difference value d_i' is produced by changing the least significant bit of d_i, the symbol $\lfloor \bullet \rfloor$ means the floor function, b denotes the secret bit, and the capacity of 0.75 bpp can be reached.

Step 4. If $\max(|d_1|,\ |d_2|,\ |d_3|) \geq T$, no bit can be embedded because the difference becomes too large to become unsuitable for embedding. All the values in the quad are kept unchanged.

In order to avoid possible decoding errors, the four steps are recorded with the two-bit side information for correct decoding at the receiver. After performing one of the above four steps, the new difference value d_i' is added back with the luminance of the reference point, $X_a(2,\ 2)$. The new luminance values in the first quad of $\mathbf{X}_a$ can be calculated as

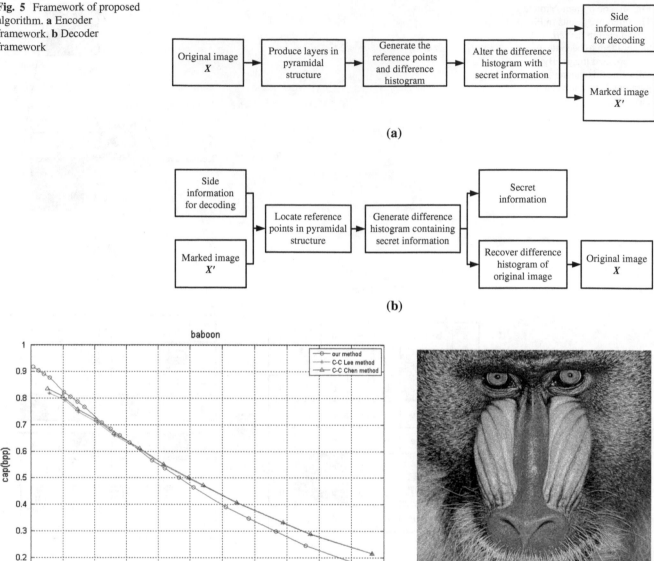

Fig. 5 Framework of proposed algorithm. **a** Encoder framework. **b** Decoder framework

(a)

(b)

Fig. 6 Results with baboon. **a** Performance evaluation and comparisons with [16] and [17]. **b** Subjective evaluation with the maximally allowable capacity when 260,679 bits (0.9944 bpp). Embedding strength is 48, and PSNR value is 30.1571 dB

follows.

$$X'_a(1, 1) = d'_1 + X_a(2, 2); \tag{11a}$$

$$X'_a(1, 2) = d'_2 + X_a(2, 2); \tag{11b}$$

$$X'_a(2, 1) = d'_3 + X_a(2, 2); \tag{11c}$$

$$X'_a(2, 2) = X_a(2, 2); \tag{11d}$$

With the operation in Eqs. (11a)–(11d), four sub-images containing hidden information, or $\mathbf{X}'_a$, $\mathbf{X}'_b$, $\mathbf{X}'_c$, and $\mathbf{X}'_d$, can be formed. Finally, by following the reverse operation to Fig. 3, the output image $\mathbf{X}'$ can be produced.

For the decoder, reverse steps can be performed accordingly, with the following steps. Steps for performing data extraction and recovery of original can be executed as follows:

Step 1. The image containing hidden secret, $\mathbf{X}'$, should be split using the method in Fig. 3.

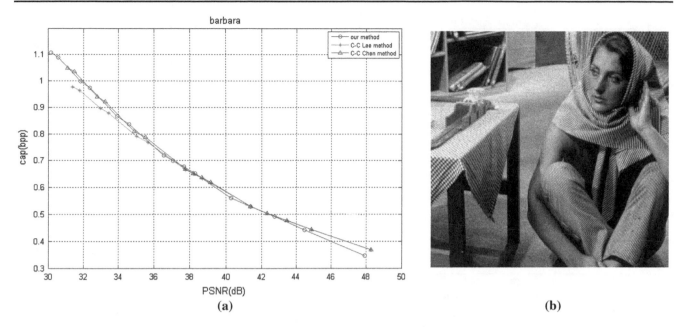

Fig. 7 Results with Barbara. **a** Performance evaluation and comparisons with [16] and [17]. **b** Subjective evaluation with the maximally allowable capacity when 310,653 bits (1.1850 bpp). Embedding strength is 48, and PSNR value is 30.1648 dB

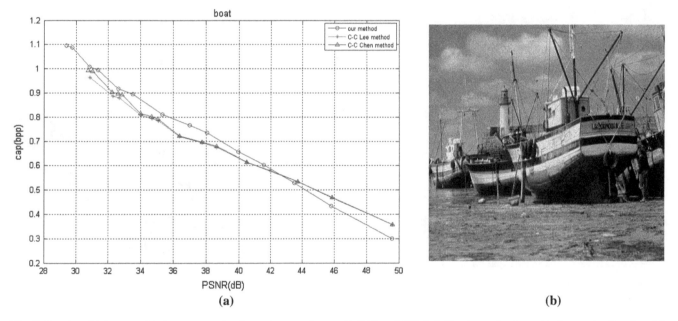

Fig. 8 Results with boat. **a** Performance evaluation and comparisons with [16] and [17]. **b** Subjective evaluation with the maximally allowable capacity when 307,743 bits (1.1739 bpp). Embedding strength is 48, and PSNR value is 29.3969 dB

Step 2. For every quad, the difference values are calculated with Eq. (7) based on the reference points.

$$d'_1 = X'_a(1, \ 1) - X_a(2, \ 2); \tag{12a}$$

$$d'_2 = X'_a(1, \ 2) - X_a(2, \ 2); \tag{12b}$$

$$d'_3 = X'_a(2, \ 1) - X_a(2, \ 2); \tag{12c}$$

Step 3. With the prespecified threshold value T, hidden secret can be extracted based on Eqs. (8), (9), or

(10). Original difference values can also be acquired simultaneously.

Step 4. Recover the original image $\mathbf{X}$ with the original difference values and the luminance of reference points.

3.3 Tier #3: employing the pyramidal structure

With the methods in Sect. 3.2, we can further perform data hiding with the pyramidal structure based on the reference points. From the depiction in Fig. 4, we take the three-layer

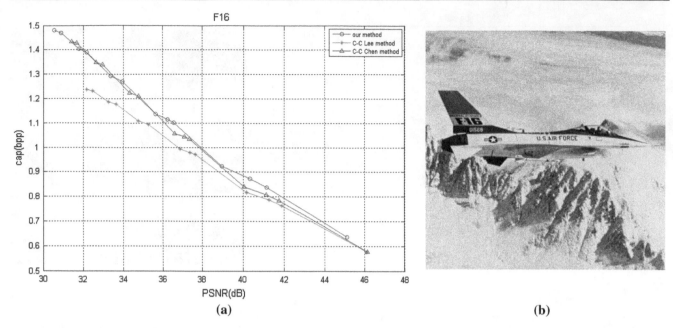

Fig. 9 Results with F16. **a** Performance evaluation and comparisons with [16] and [17]. **b** Subjective evaluation with the maximally allowable capacity when 408,414 bits (1.5580 bpp). Embedding strength is 48, and PSNR value is 30.5545 dB

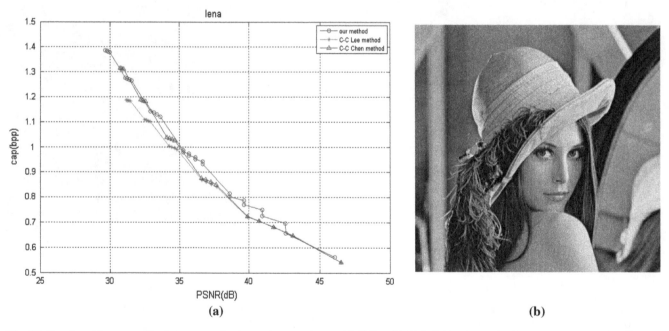

Fig. 10 Results with Lena. **a** Performance evaluation and comparisons with [16] and [17]. **b** Subjective evaluation with the maximally allowable capacity when 383,730 bits (1.4638 bpp). Embedding strength is 48, and PSNR value is 29.6477 dB

pyramidal structure as an example. The image in the lower part of Fig. 4 is the split image in the right part of Fig. 3, which denotes the first layer. By gathering all the reference points together, the second layer can be formed. With the same manner, the points with diagonal lines can form the third layer in the right part of Fig. 4. It implies the pyramidal structure at the right-hand side of Fig. 4. Each layer can be regarded as a new image relating to the original, and data

hiding can be performed accordingly with the predetermined embedding strength.

With the arrangements of pyramidal structure of the original image, for the use of the second layer, we may expect the increase of capacity by 25 %. Also, for the third layer, additional increase of $(25 \%)^2 = 6.25 \%$ in capacity may also be expected. For the upper layers, they may reside a much fewer capacity with the decreasing rate in a geometric man-

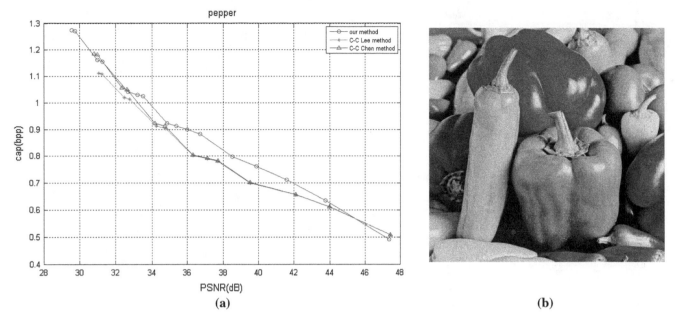

Fig. 11 Results with `pepper`. **a** Performance evaluation and comparisons with [16] and [17]. **b** Subjective evaluation with the maximally allowable capacity when 354,591 bits (1.3527 bpp). Embedding strength is 48, and PSNR value is 29.5643 dB

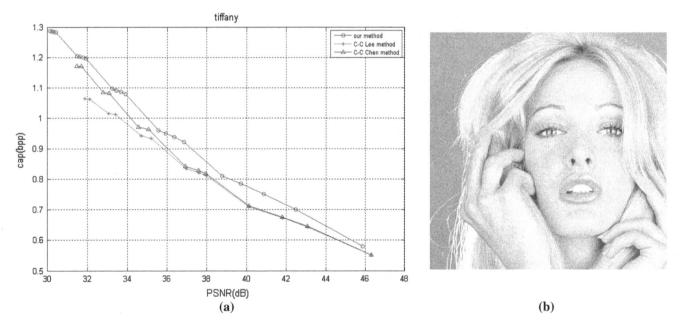

Fig. 12 Results with `Tiffany`. **a** Performance evaluation and comparisons with [16] and [17]. **b** Subjective evaluation with the maximally allowable capacity when 357,777 bits (1.3648 bpp). Embedding strength is 48, and PSNR value is 30.1508 dB

ner. Considering practical implementation, the use of three layers in pyramidal structure might be a feasible choice for images with sizes of 512×512.

Corresponding to the general framework of reversible data hiding in Fig. 1, we depict the framework of proposed algorithm in Fig. 5 for clarity. On the one hand, in Fig. 5a, at the encoder, pyramidal structure of original image is formed, and reference points are selected. Next, difference values are calculated, and then they are altered for embedding secret information. Finally, both the marked image and side information

for decoding are delivered to the decoder. On the other hand, at the decoder in Fig. 5b, procedures are in reverse order to the encoder counterpart. The frameworks in Fig. 5 correspond to the descriptions of proposed algorithm in Sect. 3.

4 Experimental results

In our simulations, we choose the eight test images `baboon`, `Barbara`, `boat`, `F16`, `Lena`, `pepper`,

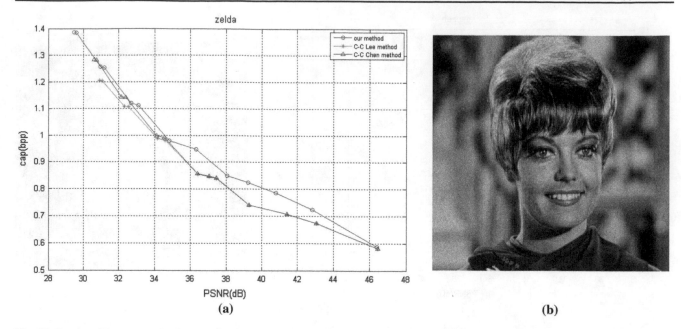

Fig. 13 Results with Zelda. **a** Performance evaluation and comparisons with [16] and [17]. **b** Subjective evaluation with the maximally allowable capacity when 383,658 bits (1.4635 bpp). Embedding strength is 48, and PSNR value is 29.4611 dB

Tiffany, and Zelda with the picture sizes of 512 × 512, for conducting simulations. The secret information to be hidden is the randomly generated bitstreams. Since the proposed method in this paper extends the concepts in [16] and [17], results from the two papers are also compared. Besides, performances with [12] exhibit inferior results than those in [16,17], and results in this paper, thus, we omit to make comparisons with the results in [12].

By properly adjusting the embedding strengths, performances with the eight test images in alphabetical order are depicted in Figs. 6, 7, 8, 9, 10, 11, 12, and 13. In each figure, taking Fig. 6 as an instance, Fig. 6a in the left presents performance comparisons with those in [16] and [17], and Fig. 6b in the right illustrates the subjective image quality for evaluations. For comparing the embedding capacity, we find that

with our algorithm, the more amount of secret can be embedded. Among them, the F16 image can hide at most 408,414 bits (or 1.5580 bpp) in Fig. 9a, and b is depicted for subjective comparisons, with the PSNR of 30.55 dB. We observe that except for the baboon image in Fig. 6, our algorithm outperforms that in [16] and [17]. It might be because the baboon image displays more active than others, which may lead to the large values in differences. However, for large embedding capacities in baboon, we embed more secret with better quality. For the remaining images in Figs. 7, 8, 9, 10, 11, 12 and 13, our algorithm performs better in general. Nevertheless, for low embedding capacities, it performs a bit inferior in Barbara in Fig. 7a and boat in Fig. 8a. It might be because pyramidal structure brings overhead into data embedding, and it causes degradation to output image

Table 1 Results for Lena with $T = 8$ for three-layer adaptive data hiding

Layers	PSNR (dB)	Increase in PSNR (dB)	Capacity (bpp)	Increase in capacity (%)
Layer 1	47.1431	–	0.49457	–
Layers 1 and 2	46.1763	−0.9668	0.61865	25.10
Layers 1, 2 and 3	46.0442	−1.0989	0.64005	29.43

Table 2 Results for Lena with $T = 16$ for three-layer adaptive data hiding

Layers	PSNR (dB)	Increase in PSNR (dB)	Capacity (bpp)	Increase in capacity (%)
Layer 1	39.7974	–	0.68904	–
Layers 1 and 2	38.8233	−0.9741	0.86127	25.00
Layers 1, 2 and 3	38.6599	−1.1375	0.89296	29.59

Table 3 Results for Lena with $T = 24$ for three-layer adaptive data hiding

Layers	PSNR (dB)	Increase in PSNR (dB)	Capacity (bpp)	Increase in capacity (%)
Layer 1	36.4280	–	0.81892	–
Layers 1 and 2	35.4465	−0.9815	1.02384	25.02
Layers 1, 2 and 3	35.2756	−1.1524	1.06433	29.97

Table 4 Results for Lena with $T = 32$ for three-layer adaptive data hiding

Layers	PSNR (dB)	Increase in PSNR (dB)	Capacity (bpp)	Increase in capacity (%)
Layer 1	34.0567	–	0.93922	–
Layers 1 and 2	33.0852	−0.9715	1.17380	24.98
Layers 1, 2 and 3	32.9010	−1.1557	1.22111	30.01

Table 5 Results for Lena with $T = 40$ for three-layer adaptive data hiding

Layers	PSNR (dB)	Increase in PSNR (dB)	Capacity (bpp)	Increase in capacity (%)
Layer 1	32.2541	–	1.04117	–
Layers 1 and 2	31.2833	−0.9708	1.30149	25.00
Layers 1, 2 and 3	31.0863	−1.1678	1.35452	30.10

Table 6 Results for Lena with $T = 48$ for three-layer adaptive data hiding

Layers	PSNR (dB)	Increase in PSNR (dB)	Capacity (bpp)	Increase in capacity (%)
Layer 1	30.8220	–	1.12453	–
Layers 1 and 2	29.8602	−0.9618	1.40555	24.99
Layers 1, 2 and 3	29.6477	−1.1743	1.46381	30.17

quality. We are revising our algorithm to conquer the extreme presentation for low capacity.

We also perform the detailed analysis of the results with Lena in Tables 1, 2, 3, 4, 5 and 6. We employ the three-layer pyramid for reversible data hiding. Under a variety of selections of predetermined threshold T, which is an integer with multiples of 8, we observe that if we use more layers for data embedding, then the output image quality gets degraded. We first observe that the increase in capacity is regular; if we use two or three layers for data embedding, the percentage of increase lies around 25 and 31.25 %, respectively. This comes from the observation that the area of the second layer is a quarter of the first later, while the area of the third layer is 1/16 of the first layer. Next, with additional layers for data embedding, the decrease in PSNR values can be expected, from 0.9618 to 0.9815 dB for using two layers, and from 1.0989 to 1.1743 dB for using three layers altogether. The decrease in PSNR comes from the selection of threshold T, and the different characteristics of original images in pyramidal structure. With our method, based on practical requirements, we can predict the necessary capacity with the adaptive embedding with pyramidal structure.

5 Conclusions

In this paper, we presented an adaptive algorithm of reversible data hiding, which employs pyramidal structure of original images for the better capability to hide more secret bits. Reversible data hiding with the alteration of difference values, obtained based on the characteristics of original images, has presented better performances compared to the conventional histogram-based schemes. For reversible data hiding, the reversibility must be retained at the decoder. Then, performances of algorithm, including the output image quality and capacity, can subsequently be examined.

Inspired by scalable coding of multimedia, we can carefully manipulate difference values in the original image between different layers of the pyramidal structure. Adaptive embedding can be applied to one of the four cases with the characteristics of original image. At the encoder, for adaptive embedding with pyramidal structure, performances with our algorithm present better in general for most test images. At the decoder, with the embedding strength, which implies the side information for decoding, the secret information can perfectly be retrieved. In addition, with the aid of location map, original image can perfectly be recovered. With our algorithm, we can embed more amount of secret with similar output quality. By use of the pyramidal structure, inherent characteristics can be utilized, and better performances can be obtained.

Acknowledgments This work is supported in part by the National Science Council of Taiwan, R.O.C., under Grants NSC102-2220-E-390-002. We would like to thank Mr. S. H. Li for part of the programming practices.

Open Access This article is distributed under the terms of the Creative Commons Attribution License which permits any use, distribution, and reproduction in any medium, provided the original author(s) and the source are credited.

References

1. Petitcolas, F.A.P., Anderson, R.J., Kuhn, M.G.: Information hiding—a survey. Proc. IEEE **87**(7), 1062–1078 (1999)
2. Huang, H.C., Fang, W.C.: Metadata-based image watermarking for copyright protection. Simul. Model. Pract. Theory **18**(4), 436–445 (2010)
3. Ni, Z., Shi, Y.-Q., Ansari, N., Su, W.: Reversible data hiding. IEEE Trans. Circuits Syst. Video Technol. **16**(3), 354–362 (2006)
4. Huang, H.C., Fang, W.C.: Techniques and applications of intelligent multimedia data hiding. Telecommun. Syst. **44**(3–4), 241–251 (2010)
5. Tian, J.: Reversible data embedding using a difference expansion. IEEE Trans. Circuits Syst. Video Technol. **13**(8), 890–896 (2003)
6. Alattar, A.M.: Reversible watermark using the difference expansion of a generalized integer transform. IEEE Trans. Image Process. **13**(8), 1147–1156 (2004)
7. Huang, H.C., Fang, W.C., Lai, W.H.: Secure medical information exchange with reversible data hiding. In: Proceedings of the IEEE International Symposium on Circuits and Systems, pp. 1424–1427 (2012)
8. Fallahpour, M., Megias, D., Ghanbari, M.: Reversible and high-capacity data hiding in medical images. IET Image Process. **5**(2), 190–197 (2011)
9. Zhang, X.: Separable reversible data hiding in encrypted image. IEEE Trans. Inf. Forensics Secur. **7**(2), 826–832 (2012)
10. Feng, G., Fan, L.: Reversible data hiding of high payload using local edge sensing prediction. J. Syst. Softw. **85**(2), 392–399 (2012)
11. Chung, K.L., Huang, Y.H., Yan, W.M., Teng, W.C.: Distortion reduction for histogram modification-based reversible data hiding. Appl. Math. Comput. **218**(9), 5819–5826 (2012)
12. Huang, H.C., Chang, F.C.: Hierarchy-based reversible data hiding. Expert Syst. Appl. **40**(1), 34–43 (2013)
13. Hu, Y., Lee, H.K., Li, J.: DE-based reversible data hiding with improved overflow location map. IEEE Trans. Circuits Syst. Video Technol. **19**(2), 250–260 (2009)
14. Liu, M., Seah, H.S., Zhu, C., Lin, W., Tian, F.: Reducing location map in prediction-based difference expansion for reversible image data embedding. Signal Process. **92**(3), 819–828 (2012)
15. Lee, C.F., Huang, Y.L.: An efficient image interpolation increasing payload in reversible data hiding. Expert Syst. Appl. **39**(8), 6712–6719 (2012)
16. Lee, C.C., Wu, H.C., Tsai, C.S., Chu, Y.P.: Adaptive lossless steganographic scheme with centralized difference expansion. Pattern Recognit. **41**(6), 2097–2106 (2008)
17. Chen, C.C., Tsai, Y.H.: Adaptive reversible image watermarking scheme. J. Syst. Softw. **84**(3), 428–434 (2011)

11

DC programming in communication systems: challenging problems and methods

Hoai An Le Thi · Tao Pham Dinh

Abstract Nonconvex optimization becomes an indispensable and powerful tool for the analysis and design of Communication Systems (CS) since the last decade. As an innovative approach to nonconvex programming, Difference of Convex functions (DC) programming and DC Algorithms (DCA) are increasingly used by researchers in this field. The objective of this paper is to show that many challenging problems in CS can be modeled as DC programs and solved by DCA-based algorithms. We offer the community of researchers in CS promising approaches in a unified DC programming framework to tackle various applications, such as routing, power control, congestion control of the Internet, resource allocation in networks, etc.

Keywords Communication systems · DC programming · DCA · Exact penalty · DC constraint · Mixed 0–1 DC programs

1 Introduction

Optimization plays a key role in communication systems since most of issues of this domain are related to optimization problems. Convex programming has been studied for about a century. It has provided both a powerful tool and an intriguing mentality for the analysis and design of communication systems over several years in the past. During the last decade, an increasing amount of effort has been put into nonconvex optimization to deal with challenge problems appeared in many applications of this filed (in fact, most real-life problems are of nonconvex nature). The absence of convexity creates a source of difficulties of all kinds, in particular, the distinction between the local and global minima, the nonexistence of verifiable characterizations of global solutions, etc., that causes all the computational complexity while passing from convex to nonconvex programming. In general, unlike the convex programming, there is no iterative algorithm converging directly to a global solution of a nonconvex program. Finding a global solution of a nonconvex program, especially in the large-scale setting, is the holy grail of optimizers.

The special context of practical problems in CS, along with the dramatic progress of novel technologies, requires well-adapted optimization techniques. For example, solution methods to network management in the context of mobile service should take into account the following questions:

- The topology of networks is dynamic and real-time data transmissions are needed. Hence, real-time algorithms are expected.
- Self-organization and self-configuration require all protocols in mobile networks to be distributive and collaborative. By the way, distributed algorithms are necessary.
- Location/tracking management, in addition to the handover management and routing. In the case of hybrid communication networks, the choice of the best access gateway among a number of available access technologies becomes one of the important considerations. Routing in hybrid networks should be handled by finding a suitable mathematical model and efficient algorithms.
- Multi-user communications service involves large scale setting optimization problems. Therefore, the algorithms should be able to solve large-size problems.

H. A. Le Thi (✉)
Laboratory of Theoretical and Applied Computer Science, UFR MIM, University of Lorraine, Ile du Saulcy, 57045 Metz, France
e-mail: hoai-an.le-thi@univ-lorraine.fr

T. Pham Dinh
Laboratory of Mathematics, LMI,
National Institute for Applied Sciences, Rouen, Avenue de l'Université, 76801 Saint-Etienne-du-Rouvray Cedex, France
e-mail: pham@insa-rouen.fr

Many challenging issues arise from nonconvex optimization in communication systems, especially how to design suitable models and develop efficient, fast, scalable and distributed algorithms to tackle large-scale practical problems in the areas of wireless networking, internet engineering, mobile services in self-organized hybrid networks.

A variety of nonconvex optimization techniques have been recently developed by researchers in optimization on one side and in communications systems on another side for studying communication theory as well as for solving practical problems in CS (see e.g, [1–9, 12, 14–21, 24–33, 38–54]. Generally, there are two different, but complementary approaches: global approaches such as Cutting Plane (CP), Branch and Bound (B&B), Branch and Cut (B&C) can guarantee the globality of the solutions but they are very expensive, and cannot handle problems of high dimensionality; and local approaches, on the contrary, are much faster while only local minima are available. Many current approaches are not generally effective for practical large-scale problems. Finding efficient algorithms that realize a compromise to overcome these drawbacks is a challenge of nonconvex programming. Such algorithms must exploit domain-specific structures of the problems being considered.

As an innovative approach to nonconvex programming, Difference of Convex functions (DC) programming and DC Algorithms (DCA) are increasingly used by researchers in CS (see e.g. [1, 2, 16, 22, 45, 54] and references therein). The objective of this paper is to show that many challenging problems in CS can be modeled as DC programs and solved by DCA-based algorithms. We offer the community of researchers in CS promising approaches in a unified DC programming framework to tackle various applications such as routing, power control, congestion control of the Internet, resource allocation in networks, etc.

1.1 Nonconvex optimization problems in CS

In terms of optimization, nonconvex problems appeared in CS can be divided into three classes:

- minimizing a nonconvex function on a convex set;
- minimizing a convex/nonconvex function on a nonconvex set;
- minimizing a convex/nonconvex function on a convex/nonconvex set with integer variables.

The reader will see that these classes of nonconvex programs in CS can be formulated or reformulated as DC programs and solved by DCA.

1.2 Why DC programming and DCA?

DC programming is an extension of convex programming which is sufficiently large to cover almost all nonconvex optimization problems, but not much to still allow using the arsenal of powerful tools in convex analysis and convex optimization. DC programming and DCA constitute the backbone of nonconvex programming and global optimization. The use of DCA for solving nonconvex optimization problems in CS is motivated by the following facts:

- DCA is a philosophy rather than an algorithm. For each problem, we can design a family of DCA-based algorithms. The flexibility of DCA on the choice of DC decomposition offers DCA schemes having the potential to outperform standard methods.
- By exploiting the nice effect of DC decomposition of the objective function we can build distributed algorithms. This issue is very important in communication networks that involve multi-users, in particular in the purpose of personalized mobile services.
- Convex analysis provides powerful tools to prove the convergence of DCA in a generic framework. Hence, any DCA-based algorithm enjoys (at least) general convergence properties of the generic DCA scheme that are already available.
- DCA is an efficient, fast and scalable method for smooth/nonsmooth nonconvex programming. To the best of our knowledge, DCA is actually one of the rare algorithms for nonsmooth nonconvex programming which allows to solve large-scale DC programs. DCA was successfully applied to a lot of different and various nonconvex optimization problems to which it quite often gave global solutions and proved to be more robust and more efficient than related standard methods. In particular, DCA has already efficiently solved large-scale DC programs in network optimization (see [1, 2, 24–27, 29–31, 45–51, 54] and the list of references in [22]).

We will show how to solve these three classes of problems in CS by DC programming and DCA. For beginning, let us give in Sect. 2, a brief introduction of DCA programming and DCA. The solution methods of each class of problem will be presented in Sects. 3, 4, and 5 where, in addition to development of generic models and algorithms, methods for typical applications in CS will be illustrated. In Sect. 6, we mention another issue in CS for which DCA can also be investigated. Section 7 concludes the paper.

2 DC programming and DCA

2.1 A brief introduction

We are working with the space $X = \mathbb{R}^n$ which is equipped with the canonical inner product $\langle \cdot, \cdot \rangle$ and the corresponding

Euclidean norm $\| \cdot \|$, thus the dual space Y of X can be identified with X itself. We follow [13,37], for definitions of usual tools in modern convex analysis, where functions could take the infinite values $+\infty$. A function $\theta : X \to \mathbb{R} \cup \{+\infty\}$ is said to be proper if it is not identically equal to $+\infty$. The effective domain of θ, denoted by $\mathrm{dom}\,\theta$, is

$$\mathrm{dom}\,\theta = \{x \in X : \theta(x) < +\infty\}.$$

The indicator function χ_C of a nonempty closed convex C set is defined by $\chi_C(x) = 0$ if $x \in C$, $+\infty$ otherwise. The set of all lower semicontinuous proper convex functions on X is denoted by $\Gamma_0(X)$. Let $\theta \in \Gamma_0(X)$, then the conjugate function of θ, denoted θ^*, is defined by

$$\theta^*(y) = \sup\{\langle x, y \rangle - \theta(x) : \ x \in X\}.$$

We have $\theta^* \in \Gamma_0(Y)$ and $\theta^{**} = \theta$.

Nonsmooth convex functions are handled using the concept of subdifferentials. For $\theta \in \Gamma_0(X)$ and $x_0 \in \mathrm{dom}\,\theta$, $\partial\theta(x_0)$ denotes the subdifferential of θ at x_0, and is defined by

$$\partial\theta(x_0) := \{y \in Y : \theta(x) \geq \theta(x_0) + \langle x - x_0, y \rangle, \ \forall x \in X\}. \tag{1}$$

Each $y \in \partial\theta(x_0)$ is called a subgradient of θ at x_0. The subdifferential $\partial\theta(x_0)$ is a closed convex set in Y. It generalizes the derivative in the sense that θ is differentiable at x_0 if and only if $\partial\theta(x_0) \equiv \{\nabla\theta(x_0)\}$. Recall the well-known properties related to subdifferential calculus of $\theta \in \Gamma_0(X)$:

$$y_0 \in \partial\theta(x_0) \Leftrightarrow x_0 \in \partial\theta^*(y_0) \Leftrightarrow \langle x_0, y_0 \rangle = \theta(x_0) + \theta^*(y_0); \tag{2}$$

$$\partial\theta^*(y_0) = \mathrm{argmin}\{\theta(x) - \langle x, y_0 \rangle : x \in X\}. \tag{3}$$

A function $\theta \in \Gamma_0(X)$ is said to be polyhedral convex if

$$\theta(x) = \max\{\langle a_i, x \rangle - \beta_i : i = 1, \ldots, m\} + \chi_C(x) \,\forall x \in X,$$

where C is a nonempty polyhedral convex set in X.

A DC program is of the form

$$(P_{dc})\,\alpha = \inf\{f(x) := g(x) - h(x) : \ x \in X\}, \tag{4}$$

with $g, h \in \Gamma_0(X)$. Such a function f is called a DC function, and $g - h$, a DC decomposition of f, while the convex functions g and h are DC components of f. In (P_{dc}) the nonconvexity comes from the concavity of the function— h (except the case h is affine since (P_{dc}) then is a convex program). It should be noted that a convex constrained DC program can be expressed in the form (4) by using the indicator function on C, that is

$$\inf\{f(x) := g(x) - h(x) : \ x \in C\}$$
$$= \inf\{\varphi(x) - h(x) : \ x \in X\}, \text{with } \varphi := g + \chi_C.$$

Hence, throughout this paper, DC program of the form (4) is referred to as "standard DC program".

Polyhedral DC programs (P_{dc}) (i.e., when g or h are polyhedral convex) play a key role in nonconvex programming (see [25,34,35] and references therein), and enjoy interesting properties related to local optimality and DCA's convergence.

The DC duality is based on the conjugate functions and the fundamental characterization of a convex function $\theta \in \Gamma_0(X)$ as *the pointwise supremum of a collection of affine minorants:*

$$\theta(x) = \sup\{\langle x, y \rangle - \theta^*(y) : y \in Y\}, \qquad \forall x \in X. \tag{5}$$

That associates the primal DC program (4) (P_{dc}) with its dual DC program (D_{dc}) defined by

$$(D_{dc}) \quad \alpha = \inf\{h^*(y) - g^*(y) : y \in Y\}, \tag{6}$$

and investigates their mutual relations. We observe the perfect symmetry between primal and dual DC programs: the dual to (D_{dc}) is exactly (P_{dc}).

It is worth noting the wealth of the vector space $DC(X) = \Gamma_0(X) - \Gamma_0(X)$ spanned by the "convex cone" $\Gamma_0(X)$ [34, 35]: it contains most realistic objective functions and is closed under operations usually considered in optimization.

The complexity of DC programs resides, of course, in the lack of verifiable globality conditions. Lets recall the general local optimality conditions in DC programming (subdifferential's inclusion): if x^* is a local solution of (P_{dc}) then

$$\emptyset \neq \partial h(x^*) \subset \partial g(x^*). \tag{7}$$

The condition (7) is also sufficient (for local optimality) in many important classes of DC programs (see [34,35]).

A point x^* is said to be *a critical point* of $g-h$ (or generalized KKT point for (P_{dc})) if

$$\partial h(x^*) \cap \partial g(x^*) \neq \emptyset. \tag{8}$$

Note that, by symmetry, the dual part of (7) and (8) are trivial.

DC Programming and DCA were introduced by Pham Dinh Tao in their preliminary form in 1985. These theoretical and algorithmic tools are extensively developed by Le Thi Hoai An and Pham Dinh Tao since 1994 to become now classic and increasingly popular. DCA is a continuous primal dual subgradient approach based on local optimality and duality in DC programming for solving standard DC programs (P_{dc}).

DCA's philosophy

The key idea behind DCA is to replace in (P_{dc}), at the current point x^k, the second component h with its affine minorant defined by

$$h_k(x) := h(x^k) + \langle x - x^k, y^k \rangle, \ y^k \in \partial h(x^k)$$

to give birth to the primal convex program of the form

(P_k) $\inf\{g(x) - h_k(x) : x \in X\}$
$\Longleftrightarrow \inf\{g(x) - \langle x, y^k \rangle : x \in X\}$

whose solution set is $\partial g^*(y^k)$. The next iterate x^{k+1} is taken in $\partial g^*(y^k)$.

Dually, a solution x^{k+1} of (P_k) is then used to define the dual convex program (D_{k+1}) obtained from (D_{dc}) by replacing g^* with its affine minorant

$(g^*)_k(y) := g^*(y^k) + \langle y - y^k x^{k+1} \rangle$

to obtain the convex program

(D_{k+1}) $\inf\{h^*(y) - [g^*(y^k) + \langle y - y^k, x^{k+1} \rangle] : y \in Y\}$
$\Leftrightarrow \inf\{h^*(y) - \langle y, x^{k+1} \rangle : y \in Y\}$

whose solution set is $\partial h(x^{k+1})$. The next iterate y^{k+1} is chosen in $\partial h(x^{k+1})$.

DCA scheme

Initialization: Let $x^0 \in \mathbb{R}^n$ be a guess, $k \leftarrow 0$.
Repeat

- Calculate $y^k \in \partial h(x^k)$
- Calculate $x^{k+1} \in \partial g^*(y^k)$, which is equivalent to

$$x^{k+1} \in \arg\min\{g(x) - \langle x, y^k \rangle : x \in \mathbb{R}^n\} \quad (P_k)$$

- $k \leftarrow k + 1$

Until convergence of $\{x^k\}$.

DCA's convergence properties:

Convergence properties of DCA and its theoretical basis can be found in [25,34,35]. For instance, it is important to mention that

i) DCA is a descent method without linesearch but with global convergence: the sequences $\{g(x^k) - h(x^k)\}$ and $\{h^*(y^k) - g^*(y^k)\}$ are decreasing.

ii) If the optimal value α of problem (P_{dc}) is finite and the infinite sequences $\{x^k\}$ and $\{y^k\}$ are bounded, then every limit point x^* (resp. y^*) of the sequence $\{x^k\}$ (resp. $\{y^k\}$) is a critical point of $g - h$ (resp. $h^* - g^*$), i.e. $\partial h(x^*) \cap \partial g(x^*) \neq \emptyset$ (resp. $\partial h^*(y^*) \cap \partial g^*(y^*) \neq \emptyset$).

iii) DCA has a *linear convergence* for DC programs.

iv) DCA has a finite convergence for polyhedral DC programs.

For a complete study of DC programming and DCA, the reader is referred to [25,34,35] and the references therein. Without going into details, let us mention the key properties of DCA.

2.2 Key properties of DCA

a. *Flexibility* the construction of DCA is based on g and h but not on f itself, and there are as many DCA as there are DC decompositions. This is a crucial fact in DC programming. It is important to study various equivalent DC forms of a DC program, because each DC function f *has infinitely many DC decompositions which have crucial implications for the qualities* (speed of convergence, robustness, efficiency, globality of computed solutions, etc.) of DCA.

b. DCA is a *descent method without linesearch*, with global convergence (i.e. DCA converges from an arbitrary initial point).

c. *Return from DC programming to convex programming* DCA consists in an iterative approximation of a DC program by a sequence of convex programs that will be solved by appropriate convex optimization algorithms. This property is called successive convex approximation (SCA) in some recent works in CS.

d. *Versatility* With suitable DC decompositions *DCA generates most standard algorithms in convex and nonconvex optimization*. Hence DCA offers a wide framework for solving convex/nonconvex optimization problems. In particular, DCA is a global approach to convex programming, i.e., it converges to optimal solutions of convex programs reformulated as DC programs. Consequently, it can be used to build efficient customized algorithms for solving convex programs generated by DCA.

2.3 How to apply DCA for solving practical problems

It would be wrong to think that using DCA for solving a practical problem is a simple procedure. Indeed, the generic DCA scheme is an overall philosophical idea rather than a single algorithm. There is not only one DCA but *a family* of DCAs for a considered problem. While DC decompositions exist for a very large class of functions, there are no general procedure for determining such DC decompositions. The design of an efficient DCA for a concrete problem is an art which should be based on theoretical tools and on its special structure. It consists of the five steps :

a. Find a DC formulation of the considered optimization problem: this can be done if the feasible domain C is a convex set and the objective function f is DC, otherwise we must use the approximation or reformulation technique based on relevant theoretical tools.

b. Design a DCA scheme for (P_{dc}). This consists of i) computing a subgradient of h and ii) solving the convex program of the form (P_k). In the ideal case (what is not always possible, especially for nondifferentiable DC programs) an optimal solution of (P_k) is explicitly determined, which corresponds to the explicit computation of a subgradient of g^*. Otherwise one should find efficient convex optimization algorithms suitably adapted to (P_k)'s specific structures in order to save computation time.

c. Search for "good" DC decompositions. If the computations in i) and ii) are not satisfactory (costly, computed solutions by DCA are not sufficiently good, ...) then one has to find more suitable DC decomposition. That is a difficult issue and should be done by exploiting distinctive features of the class of DC programs at hand. Here reformulation techniques play a key role to obtain suitable models. Reformulation techniques should be diversified and have recourse to good mathematical backgrounds in numerical analysis and optimization.

d. Search for "good" starting points. That can be done by combining with other approaches (heuristic or local search methods, solutions of convex relaxation problems in global optimization methods). Another efficient way in finding a convex minorant consists of the objective function on the feasible set C and solving the resulting convex program whose solution is used to initialize DCA. This strategy must be developed in depth and specifically, by exploiting the structure of the problem (P_{dc}).

e. Globalize DCA : to guarantee globality of sought solutions or to improve their quality it is advised to combine DCA with global optimization techniques.

It goes without saying that the two steps (c) and (d) and solution methods for convex programs (P_k) (if necessary) constitute *the key issues* for successful applications of DC programming and DCA.

We show below how to use DCA for solving the three classes of nonconvex problems in CS.

3 Minimizing a nonconvex function under a convex constraint set

The mathematical formulation of this class of problem is given by

(P) $\inf\{f(x) : x \in C\}$ (9)

where $C \subset \mathbb{R}^n$ is a closed nonempty convex set and f is a nonconvex function on $\mathbb{R}^n$. Many applications in CS can be formulated in the form of (P) whose typical examples are Network Utility Maximization (NUM) [9,30], power control problem [2,6,48,54]), dynamic spectrum management in DSL systems [27,53] MIMO relay optimization [15], sum-rate maximization, proportional-fairness and max–min optimization of SISO/MISO/MIMO ad hoc networks [14,17,43,44].

We will consider two examples of applications of DCA on NUM [30] and DSL [27]. Complete works on NUM and power control using DCA can be found in [24,48,31].

3.1 Can one get a DC formulation for any problem in this class?

The answer is "yes", one can always formulate (P) as a standard DC program of the form (P_{dc}). In fact, as indicated above, the vector space $\mathcal{DC}(X)$ contains most realistic objective functions. In the rare cases where f is not DC (for example, when f is a discontinuous function), one can approximate f by a DC function or use reformulation techniques to get an equivalent DC program.

3.2 Useful DC decompositions and corresponding DCA

To illustrate the way to construct DC decompositions and design the resulting DCA, let us show the two useful DC decompositions of the problem (P) in (9) and discuss on their effectiveness.

Assume that there exists a nonnegative number η (resp. ρ) such that the function $\frac{1}{2}\eta\|x\|^2 + f(x)$ (resp. $\frac{1}{2}\rho\|x\|^2 - f(x)$) is convex. We can now write (P) in the form of DC program (P_{dc}) with, for example, two following DC decompositions:

$$g(x) := \chi_C(x) + \frac{1}{2}\eta\|x\|^2 + f(x); \quad h(x) := \frac{1}{2}\eta\|x\|^2$$
(10)

and

$$g(x) := \chi_C(x) + \frac{1}{2}\rho\|x\|^2; \quad h(x) := \frac{1}{2}\rho\|x\|^2 - f(x).$$
(11)

The DCA applied to (P) with decomposition (10) and/or (11) can be described as follows.

Algorithm DCAP1 Let x^0 be given in $\mathbb{R}^n$. Set $k \leftarrow 0$.
Repeat

– Calculate x^{k+1} by solving the convex program

$$\min\left\{\frac{1}{2}\eta\|x\|^2 + f(x) - \langle x, \eta x^k\rangle : x \in C\right\},$$
(12)

– $k \leftarrow k + 1$

Until convergence of $\{x^k\}$.

Algorithm DCAP2: Let x^0 be given in $\mathbb{R}^n$. Set $k \leftarrow 0$.
Repeat

– Calculate $y^k \in \partial\left(\frac{1}{2}\rho\|.\|^2 - f(.)\right)(x^k)$

– Calculate x^{k+1} by solving the convex program

$$\min\left\{\frac{1}{2}\rho\|x\|^2 - \langle x, y^k\rangle : x \in C\right\},\tag{13}$$

i.e. $x^{k+1} = \text{Proj}_C(y^k/\rho)$.
– $k \leftarrow k + 1$

Until convergence of $\{x^k\}$.

Here, Proj_C stands for the orthogonal projection on C.

As indicated above, we are greatly interested in the choice of DC decompositions: what is "the best' among (10) and (11)? The answer depends on C and f. In fact, the performance of the DCA depends upon that of the algorithm for solving convex programs (12) and (13). For certain problems, for example, box constrained quadratic programming and ball constrained quadratic programming, Algorithm DCAP2 is greatly less expensive than Algorithm DCAP1, because the orthogonal projection onto C in these cases is given in explicit form (see for example [35]). In practice, when f is differentiable and the computation of its gradient is not difficult, and the projection on C can be inexpensively determined, the use of DCAP2 is very recommended.

For using the above DC decompositions the crucial question is how to determine a nonnegative number η (resp. ρ) such that the function $\frac{1}{2}\eta\|x\|^2 + f(x)$ (resp. $\frac{1}{2}\rho\|x\|^2 - f(x)$) is convex. In many practical problems such η and ρ exist and can be computed according to the properties of the function f. For example, when f is a *smooth function with Lipschitz continuous gradient* ρ is nothing but the Lipschitz constant of ∇f.

3.3 DCA for network utility maximization

Network utility maximization (NUM) has many applications in network rate allocation algorithms and Internet congestion control protocols. Consider a communication network with L links, each with a fixed capacity of c_l bps, and S sources (i.e., end users), each transmitting at a source rate of x_s bps. Each source s emits one flow, using a fixed set $L(s)$ of links in its path, and has a utility function $U_s(x_s)$. Each link l is shared by a set of sources denoted $S(l)$, (the set of users using link l). NUM, in its basic version, consists of maximizing the total utility of the network $\sum_s U_s(x_s)$ over the source rates x, subject to linear flow constraints for all links l:

maximize $$\sum_{s \in \mathcal{S}} U_s(x_s)$$

s.t $$\sum_{s \in S(l)} x_s \leq c_l \quad \forall l, \ x_s \geq 0 \ \ \forall s \in \mathcal{S},\tag{14}$$

where $\mathcal{S}$ denotes the set of users. Here the vector variable is $x = (x_s)_{s \in \mathcal{S}} \in \mathbb{R}^S$ and the constraint set is a well-defined

convex polytope. There are many nice properties of the basic NUM model due to several simplifying assumptions of the utility functions and flow constraints, which provide the mathematical tractability of problem (14) but also limit its applicability. In particular, the utility functions U_s are usually assumed to be concave increasing. In such a case, the optimization problem (14) is a convex program, and so far is easy to solve. In the past, maximization of concave utility functions and the resulting distributed rate allocation for elastic traffic have gained extensive attention. Based on the concavity and continuity assumptions on utility functions and the elasticity assumption on application traffic, rigorous mathematical frameworks for standard price-based distributed algorithms have been investigated.

However, it is known that for many multimedia applications, user satisfaction may assume nonconcave shape as a function of the allocated rate. Furthermore, in some other models of utility functions, the concavity assumption on $U_s(x_s)$ is also related to the elasticity assumption on rate demands by users. When demands for x_s are not perfectly elastic, $U_s(x_s)$ may not be concave. In this case, the resulting NUM becomes nonconvex and significantly harder to be analyzed and solved. Since inelastic flows with nonconcave utility functions represent important applications in practice, today solving the NUM problem with nonconcave utility function is a *challenge* of the analysis and design of communication systems by nonconvex optimization techniques.

As an illustrative example, we consider the NUM problem with Sigmoidal-like utility functions [30] that are used in many multimedia applications and Internet congestion control (for example, the utility for voice applications is modeled by a Sigmoidal function with a convex part at low rate and a concave part at high rate). Other useful utility functions can also be solved by DCA-based algorithms (see [24]).

Consider Sigmoidal utilities in a standard form:

$$U_s(x_s) = \frac{1}{1 + e^{-(a_s x_s + b_s)}},$$

where $a_s > 0$, $b_s < 0$ and a_s, b_s are integers. The Sigmoidal function is neither convex nor concave, but it is DC (difference of convex functions). Then the resulting NUM problem is a DC program. We are going to present a DC decomposition for the Sigmoidal function.

We have

$$U_s(x_s) = e^{(a_s x_s + b_s)} - \frac{e^{2(a_s x_s + b_s)}}{1 + e^{(a_s x_s + b_s)}}.$$

It is easy to verify that the functions

$$h_s(x_s) := e^{(a_s x_s + b_s)} \quad \text{and} \quad g_s(x_s) := \frac{e^{2(a_s x_s + b_s)}}{1 + e^{(a_s x_s + b_s)}}$$

are convex (their derivative is increasing). Therefore, U_s is a DC function, and so is $-U_s$.

Let K be the set defined by the constraints of Problem (14), say

$$K := \left\{ \sum_{s \in S(l)} x_s \leq c_l \quad \forall l \in \{1 \dots L\}, \; x_s \geq 0 \quad \forall s \in \mathcal{S} \right\}$$

and denote by χ_K the indicator function on K. Then the Sigmoidal NUM problem can be expressed as

$$\max_{x \in K} \left\{ U(x) := \sum_{s \in \mathcal{S}} U_s(x_s) \right\}$$

$$= -\min_{x \in K} \left\{ \sum_{s \in \mathcal{S}} \frac{e^{2(a_s x_s + b_s)}}{1 + e^{(a_s x_s + b_s)}} - e^{(a_s x_s + b_s)} \right\}$$

$$= -\min \{ g(x) - h(x) : x \in K \} \text{ where } g(x)$$

$$:= \sum_{s \in \mathcal{S}} g_s(x_s), \; h(x) := \sum_{s \in \mathcal{S}} h_s(x_s).$$

Since g_s and h_s are convex functions, the function g and h are convex too (note also that g and h are differentiable). Hence the Sigmoidal NUM problem is a DC program that can be written in the standard form as

$$\min \left\{ [\chi_K(x) + g(x)] - h(x) : x \in \mathbb{R}^S \right\}. \quad (15)$$

According to the general DCA scheme, applying DCA to (15) amounts to computing two sequences $\{y^k\}$ and $\{x^k\}$ in the way that

$$y^k = \nabla h(x^k),$$

$$x^{k+1} \in \operatorname{argmin} \left\{ [\chi_K(x) + g(x)] - \langle x, y^k \rangle : x \in \mathbb{R}^S \right\}.$$

Hence the algorithm can be described as follows.

Algorithm: DCA for Sigmoidal utility maximization:

1. Choose $x^0 \in \mathbb{R}^S$ as the initial point. Let $\epsilon > 0$ be sufficiently small, $k \leftarrow 0$.
2. **Repeat**
Set $y^k = (a_1 e^{a_1 x_1^k + b_1}, \dots, a_s e^{a_s x_1^k + b_1})$.
Set x^{k+1} as an optimal solution of the convex program

$$\min \left\{ \sum_{s \in \mathcal{S}} \frac{e^{2(a_s x_s + b_s)}}{1 + e^{(a_s x_s + b_s)}} - \langle x, y^k \rangle : x \in K \right\} \quad (16)$$

$k \leftarrow k + 1$
until $\|x^{k+1} - x^k\| \leq \epsilon(1 + \|x^k\|)$.

Note that the convex problem (16) can be distributedly implemented using the Lagrangian dual decomposition method as shown in [30].

3.4 Spectrum management problem (SMP)

Discrete multitone (DMT) [42] has been adopted as standard in various DSL applications such as asymmetric DSL (ADSL) and more recently for very-high-bit-rate digital subscriber line (VDSL) by International Telecommunication Union (ITU). For a sufficiently large number of sub-carriers, DMT transmission over a frequency-selective fading channel can be modeled as a set of K parallel independent flat-fading sub-carrier AWGN channels (Additive white Gaussian noise). Under this Gaussian assumption, the achievable bit-loading rate of user n on tone k is

$$r_k^n = \log_2 \left(1 + \frac{1}{\Gamma} \frac{|g_k^{n,n}|^2 p_k^n}{\sum_{m \neq n} |g_k^{n,m}|^2 p_k^m + \omega_k^n} \right)$$

$$= \log_2 \left(1 + \frac{1}{\Gamma} \frac{p_k^n}{\sum_{m \neq n} h_k^{n,m} p_k^m + \sigma_k^n} \right),$$

where p_k^n denotes user n's transmit power spectral density (PSD) on tone k; ω_k^n denotes user n's transmit noise power on tone k; $g_k^{n,m}$ is the channel path gain from user m to user n on tone k; $h_k^{n,m} = \frac{|g_k^{n,m}|^2}{|g_k^{n,n}|^2}$ is the normalized interference path power gain from user m to user n on tone k ; $\sigma_k^n = \frac{\omega_k^n}{|g_k^{n,n}|^2}$ is the noise variance of user n on tone k, and Γ is the SNR-gap to capacity. The data rate of user n is $R_n = f_s \sum_{k=1}^{K} r_k^n$, where f_s is the DMT symbol rate.

The goal of spectrum management problem is to achieve best possible user rates tradeoff among users in the network, i.e., to find the boundary of rate region. Assume that each user is subject to an individual total transmission power constraint. One way to define the SMP in the literature is consider the following optimization problem

$$\max_{p_1, p_2, \dots, p_K} \left\{ R_1 : R_n \geq T_n, \quad \forall n \geq 1; \; \sum_k p_k^n \leq P_n, \forall n, k; \right.$$

$$\left. p_k^n \leq p_k^{n,\text{mask}}, \quad \forall n, k \right\}, \quad (17)$$

where T_n is minimum target rates of user n and P_n is maximum total transmission power of user n. The SMP (17) aims to maximize the rate of user 1 while guarantees the achievable rates of other users higher than their required minimum target rates T_n. P_n denotes the maximum total transmission power of user n. Spectral mask constraints $p_k^{n,\text{mask}}$ may also be applied if needed.

Among various Dynamic Spectrum Management (DSM) techniques, centralized Optimal Spectrum Balancing (OSB) achieves the maximum data rates by computing the optimal PSDs (power spectral density) for all modems in DSL systems. The centralized algorithm based on dual decomposition for OSB, proposed in [3], decouples joint optimization across all tones to make the problem solvable per-tone basis. If the rate region is convex (the assumption that the rate region is convex is justified in [3] for two-user in DSL system, and the same logic for two-user can be applied to justify the convexity of rate region for multiple-user case), solving the problem (17) amounts to solving the following weighted sum rate optimization problem [5]:

$$\max_{p_1,\dots,p_K} \left\{ \sum_n \omega_n R_n : \sum_k p_k^n \le P_n \quad \forall n; \ 0 \le p_k^n \right.$$

$$\left. \le p_k^{n,\text{mask}} \quad \forall k, n \right\}, \tag{18}$$

where the weight for user 1, ω_1, is set to unity, resulting in the maximization of the rate of user 1; whereas $\omega_n \ge 0$, $n \ne 1$ can be adjusted to guarantee the target rate of user n. In [27], we have investigated DC programming and DCA for solving (18).

3.4.1 A nice DC formulation of SMP (18)

First, we write Problem (18) in the form of a minimization program

$$\min_{p=(p_1,\dots,p_K)} \left\{ f(p) := -\sum_{n=1}^N \omega_n R_n : \sum_{k=1}^K p_k^n \le P_n \ \forall n; \right.$$

$$\left. 0 \le p_k^n \le p_k^{n,\text{mask}} \ \forall k=1\dots K, n=1\dots N \right\}. \tag{19}$$

A natural DC decomposition of f (easily deduced from the definition of r_k^n) has been given in [27]. However, as indicated in [27], from numerical point of views, the DCA scheme corresponding to this DC decomposition is not interesting because it requires an iterative algorithm for solving a convex program at each iteration. In an elegant way we introduced in [27] a nice DC reformulation of the problem (19) (based on the second DC decomposition discussed in Sect. 2) for which the resulting DCA is explicitly determined via a very simple formula. Such a DC decomposition of f is inspired by the following result.

Theorem 1 *There exists $\rho > 0$ such that the function*

$$h(p) := \frac{1}{2}\rho\|p\|^2 - f(p) \tag{20}$$

is convex on C, the feasible set of (19), say $C := \{p \in \mathbb{R}^{K \times N} \mid \sum_{k=1}^K p_k^n \le P_n, 0 \le p_k^n \le p_k^{n,\text{mask}} \ \forall n = 1, 2, \dots, N; \ k = 1, 2, \dots, K\}$.

Proof See [27].   □

Using the theorem above, we get the next DC decomposition of f:

$$g(p) = \frac{1}{2}\rho\|p\|^2, \quad h(p) = \frac{1}{2}\rho\|p\|^2 - f(p), \tag{21}$$

and Problem (19) can be now written in the form

$$\min\{ f(p) := g(p) - h(p) \mid p \in C\}$$

or again, in the standard form of DC program:

$$\min\{\chi_C(x) + f(p)) \mid p \in \mathbf{R}^{N \times K}\}.$$

Then, DCA apply to Problem (19) is described as follows.

DCA-SMP

Initialization: Let $\epsilon > 0$ be given, $\mathbf{p}^{(0)} \in C$ be an initial point, set $r := 0$;

Repeat: set

$$\mathbf{q}^{(r)} = \nabla h(\mathbf{p}^{(r)}) = \rho \, \mathbf{p}^{(r)} - \nabla f(\mathbf{p}^{(r)})$$

and calculate $\mathbf{p}^{(r+1)} \in \partial(g+\chi_C)^*(\mathbf{q}^{(r)})$ by solving the linear constrained quadratic program

$$\min\left\{ \frac{1}{2}\rho\|p\|^2 - \langle p, \mathbf{q}^{(r)}\rangle \mid p \in C \right\} \tag{22}$$

Set $r + 1 \leftarrow r$

until either $\|\mathbf{p}^{(r+1)} - \mathbf{p}^{(r)}\| \le \epsilon(\|\mathbf{p}^{(r)}\|+1)$ or $|f(\mathbf{p}^{(r+1)}) - f(\mathbf{p}^{(r)})| \le \epsilon(|f(\mathbf{p}^{(r)})| + 1)$.

The advantage of the DC decomposition (21) is that the resulting DCA-SMP requires, at each iteration, the computation of the projection of a point on the set C (having very specific structure) for which efficient algorithms are available (see [27]).

4 Nonconvex constraint set

A typical application of this class of problems is *Internet routing* (see for example [5]). Mathematically, the nonconvex constraint set is expressed as

$$E := \{x \in C, \ f_i(x) := g_i(x) - h_i(x) \le 0, \ i = 1, \dots, m\}$$

where C is a closed nonempty convex set in $\mathbb{R}^n$, $g_i, h_i \in \Gamma_0(\mathbb{R}^n)$, $i = 0, \dots, m$, and $f_i(x) \le 0$ are called DC constraints. The generic formulation of this class of problems takes the form

$$\alpha = \inf \{ f_0(x) := g_0(x) - h_0(x) : x \in E \quad (P_{\text{dcg}}) \tag{23}$$

where E is assumed to be nonempty.

This class of nonconvex programs (called general DC programs) is the most general in DC Programming and, a fortiori, more difficult to treat than that of standard DC programs (P_{dc}) because of the nonconvexity of the constraints. It is not new and has been addressed in [34]. Its renewed interests is due to the fact that this class appears, increasingly, in many models of nonconvex variational approaches.

We can solve (P_{dcg}) by DCA via penalty techniques. First, we transform (P_{dcg})-(23) into (P_{dc}) via penalty techniques in DC programming.

Let the functions p and p^+ be defined by

$$p(x) := \max\{f_i(x) : i = 1, \ldots, m\};$$
$$I(x) := \{i \in \{1, \ldots, m\} : f_i(x) = p(x)\}$$
$$p^+(x) := \max\{0, p(x)\},$$

which are DC functions with the following DC decompositions (in case g_i, h_i are finite on C for $i = 1, \ldots, m$,(see, e.g., [34]), obtained directly from those of $f_i, i = 1, \ldots, m$.

$$p(x) = \max_{i=1,\ldots,m} \left\{ g_i(x) + \sum_{j=1,j\neq i}^{m} h_j(x) \right\} - \sum_{j=1}^{m} h_j(x) \tag{24}$$

$$p^+(x) = \max_{i=1,\ldots,m} \left\{ \sum_{j=1}^{m} h_j(x), g_i(x) + \sum_{j=1,j\neq i}^{m} h_j(x) \right\}$$
$$- \sum_{j=1}^{m} h_j(x). \tag{25}$$

The general DC program (P_{dcg})-(23) can then be formulated as

$$\alpha = \inf\{f_0(x) := g_0(x) - h_0(x) : x \in C, \; p^+(x) \le 0\} \tag{26}$$

and its penalized is a standard DC program

$$\alpha(\tau) = \inf\{\varphi_\tau(x) := f(x) + \tau p^+(x) : x \in C\}. \; (P_\tau) \tag{27}$$

Let DC decompositions of f_0 and p^+ be given by

$$f_0(x) = g_0(x) - h_0(x); \tag{28}$$
$$p^+(x) = p_1(x) - p_2(x), \tag{29}$$

where g_0, h_0, p_1, p_2 are convex functions defined on the whole space. Then, we have the following DC decomposition for φ_τ

$$\varphi_\tau(x) = g_\tau(x) - h_\tau(x), \tag{30}$$

where,

$$g_\tau(x):=g_0(x) + \tau p_1(x); \quad h_\tau(x):=h_0(x) + \tau p_2(x). \tag{31}$$

Exact penalty (relative the constraint $p^+(x) \le 0$) for (26) means that there is $\tau_0 \ge 0$ such that for all $\tau > \tau_0$ both DC programs (P_{dcg})-(23) and (P_τ)-(27) are equivalent in the sense that $\alpha(\tau) = \alpha$ and (P_{dcg})-(23) et (P_τ)-(27) have the same (global) solution set. In this case, the solution of (P_{dcg})-(23) can be achieved by applying DCA to a standard DC program (P_τ)-(27) with $\tau > \tau_0$.

Exact penalty techniques in DC programming have been widely investigated in our works [25,28,34]. However, from a computational point of view, an inconvenience of this exact penalty method is that the penalty parameter is generally unknown. Moreover, there are practical optimization problems for which the exact penalization is not satisfied. In [28], we proposed to develop the DCA for solving general DC program (P_{dcg})-(23) by using a penalty technique with updated parameter.

The generalized DCA can be deduced from DCA as follows: instead of fixing the penalty parameter τ, DCA is applied to the sequence of (P_{τ_k}) with an increasing sequence of penalty parameters $\{\tau_k\}$ given by a updating rule from the current iteration x^k such that x^{k+1} is the next iteration of DCA applied to (P_{τ_k}) from x^k. Our work consists in the statement of appropriate updating rules for the sequence $\{\tau_k\}$ and the refinement of constraint qualifications used, in order to ensure global convergence (to a critical point of (P_{dcg})-(23)) and efficiency of DCA1. It is also important that the sequence $\{\tau_k\}$ is constant after a certain rank. The penalty introduced uses l_∞- norm, but we can also consider the l_1-norm where $q(x) := \sum_{i=1}^{m} f_i^+(x)$ replaces $p^+(x)$.

Some other DCA-based algorithms for (P_{dcg})-(23) have been developed in [36].

5 Integer variables

Several applications in CS can be formulated as an optimization problem with (mixed) integer variables. Here we mention some classes of problems which have been successfully solved by DCA.

5.1 Cross-layer optimization in multi-hop time division multiple access (TDMA) networks

Efficient design of wireless networks is a challenging task due to the interference nature of shared wireless medium. Recently, the concept of cross-layer design has been investigated extensively. In [26,29] a cross-layer optimization framework, i.e., joint rate control, routing, link scheduling and power control for multi-hop TDMA networks, has been considered. Particularly, we studied a centralized controller that coordinates the routing process and transmissions of links such that the network lifetime is maximized [29] and the quality of-service (QoS) constraints on the minimum source rates are satisfied. Alternatively, the energy consumption is an important design criterion for a multi-hop wireless network. In [26], we considered the energy minimization-based cross-layer design problem. We will show below that the aforementioned problems can be formulated as mixed integer-linear programs (MILP) and then efficiently solved by DCA.

In the considered TDMA network, time is partitioned into fixed-length frames, and each frame is further divided into J time slots with unit duration. Since the resource allocation is the same in all frames, we concentrate our design on a single frame. A node may need to transmit in one or more slots for its own traffic and/or relay traffic from other nodes. If a node transmits in a slot, while its transmission power can be varied from $[0, P_{max}]$, its transmission rate is fixed at a unit rate. In the TDMA-based network, a channel is specified by two elements (j, l), $j \in \mathcal{J}$, $l \in \mathcal{L}$, where $\mathcal{J} = \{1, 2, \ldots, J\}$. For the channel, the resource allocation is denoted by (s_j^l, P_j^l), where $s_j^l = 1$ means link l is active at slot j while $s_j^l = 0$ otherwise, and $P_j^l > 0$ denotes the transmission power of link l at slot j if $s_j^l = 1$, $P_j^l = 0$ otherwise.

At each node, the difference of its outgoing traffic and its incoming traffic should be the traffic generated by itself, i.e.,

$$\sum_{l \in \mathcal{O}(n)} \sum_{j=1}^{J} s_j^l - \sum_{l \in \mathcal{I}(n)} \sum_{j=1}^{J} s_j^l = r_n, \quad n \in \mathcal{N} \tag{32}$$

where $\mathcal{O}(n)$ and $\mathcal{I}(n)$ are the set of outgoing links and incoming links at node n, respectively. The values of s_n for the non-source nodes are set to zero, or equivalently all the traffic entering such nodes must be routed.

The energy consumption at node $n \in \mathcal{N}$ can be written as

$$\mathcal{E}_n = \sum_{l \in \mathcal{O}(n)} \sum_{j=1}^{J} P_j^l + \sum_{l \in \mathcal{O}(n)} \sum_{j=1}^{J} \epsilon_l s_j^l$$
$$+ \sum_{l \in \mathcal{I}(n)} \sum_{j=1}^{J} \varepsilon_l s_j^l, \quad n \in \mathcal{N} \tag{33}$$

where ϵ_l and ε_l denote the energy needed to transmit and receive a unit of traffic over link l, respectively. Note that ϵ_l, ε_l include the energy consumed by the signal processing blocks at the link ends.

Interference Model

Wireless channel is a shared medium and interference-limited where links contend with each other for channel use. Moreover, interference relations among the nodes and/or links can be modeled in various ways, for example, by using the signal-to-interference-plus-noise-ratio (SINR)-based model [32,52]. Specifically, if the link $l \in \mathcal{L}$ is active at slot j (i.e., $s_j^l = 1$), the following inequality should hold so as to guarantee the transmission quality of the link

$$\text{SINR}_j^l = \frac{P_j^l h_{ll}}{\sum_{k \neq l} P_j^k h_{kl} + \eta_l} \geq \gamma^{\text{th}} \tag{34}$$

where SINR_j^l is the SINR for link l at slot j, h_{kl} is the path gain from the transmitter of link k to the receiver of link l, η_l is the noise power at receiver of link l, and γ th is the required SINR threshold for accurate information transmission.

We assume that all wireless nodes are low-mobility devices and/or the topology of the network is static or changes slowly allowing enough time for computing the new scheduler. An example of such networks is a wireless sensor network for environmental monitoring with fixed sensor loca-

tions. In this case, the need for distributed implementation is not necessary.

From the preceding discussions, the energy minimization-based cross-layer design, i.e., joint rate control, routing, link scheduling, and power allocation problem can be mathematically formulated as

$$\min_{r_n, P_j^l, s_j^l} \quad \sum_{n \in \mathcal{N}} \mathcal{E}_n \tag{35a}$$

subject to:

$$\sum_{l \in \mathcal{O}(n)} \sum_{j=1}^{J} s_j^l - \sum_{l \in \mathcal{I}(n)} \sum_{j=1}^{J} s_j^l = r_n, \quad n \in \mathcal{N} \tag{35b}$$

$$r_n \geq r_n^{\min}, \quad n \in \mathcal{N} \tag{35c}$$

$$\sum_{l \in \mathcal{I}(\hat{n})} \sum_{j=1}^{J} s_j^l = \sum_{n \in \mathcal{N}} r_n \tag{35d}$$

$$\sum_{l \in \mathcal{O}(n)} s_j^l + \sum_{l \in \mathcal{I}(n)} s_j^l \leq 1, \quad \forall n \in \{\mathcal{N} \cup \hat{n}\}, \; j=1, \ldots, J \tag{35e}$$

$$h_{ll} P_j^l \geq \gamma^{\text{th}} \sum_{k \neq l} P_j^k h_{kl} + \gamma^{\text{th}} \eta_l + D(s_j^l - 1),$$
$$\forall l \in \mathcal{L}, \; j = 1, \ldots, J \tag{35f}$$

$$0 \leq P_j^l \leq P_{\max} s_j^l, \quad \forall l \in \mathcal{L}, \; j = 1, \ldots, J \tag{35g}$$

$$s_j^l \in \{0, 1\}, \quad \forall l \in \mathcal{L}, \; j = 1, \ldots, J \tag{35h}$$

where $\hat{n}$ denotes the common sink node for all data generated in the network, D is a very large positive constant. The objective function is the energy consumption in the network.[1] Constraints (35b) ensure that the data generated by source nodes are routed properly. Constraints (35c) guarantee that the rate for each node is no less than a minimum rate. The minimum rates are possibly different for nodes and are usually determined by the network QoS. Nodes which do not generate traffic have $r_n = r_n^{\min} = 0$. Constraint (35d) is the flow conservation at the traffic destination for all the sources. Constraints (35e) state that a node can not receive and transmit simultaneously in one particular time slot. Constraints (35f) make sure the SINR requirement is met: if a link l is active in time slot j, then the SINR at receiver of link l must be larger than the given threshold γ^{th} which also depends on the system implementation. Constraint (35f) is automatically satisfied if link l is not scheduled in time slot j. Constraint (35g) states that if a link l is scheduled for time slot j, i.e., $s_j^l = 1$, then the corresponding power value P_j^l must be less than $P_{\max}$. Otherwise, P_j^l obviously equals to zero. We also impose binary integer constraints on s_j^l.

It can be seen that the cross-layer optimization problem (35a)–(35h) belongs to a class of well-known mixed-integer

---

[1] The traffic sink node consumes a fixed amount of energy within a frame for receiving data.

linear programs (MILPs). The combinatorial nature of the optimization (35a)–(35h) is not surprising and it has been shown in some previous works, albeit with different objective functions and formulations [7,32,52]. Theoretically, MILPs are NP-hard which is clearly inviable for practical scenarios when the dimension is large. It has been shown in [26] that, at optimality, the source rate constraints (35c) must be met with equalities for all sources.

Note that by considering (35a), one aims to minimize the total energy consumption, it may cause some particular nodes spending more energy than the other nodes, and thus, running out of energy quicker. Therefore, equal energy distribution among nodes is not optimal. Another design objective which may help to prevent such situation is as follows

$$\min_{r_n, P_j^l, s_j^l} \quad \max_{n \in \mathcal{N}} \mathcal{E}_n \qquad (36a)$$

subject to: The constraints (35b)–(35h). $\qquad$ (36b)

The optimization problem (36a)–(36b) aims at minimizing the maximum energy consumed at nodes(s). As a result, more nodes are likely to be involved in the routing algorithm, i.e., relaying information for other nodes. For simplicity, the optimization problem (35a)–(35h) is often considered in the literature.

The cross-layer optimization problem (35a)–(35h) has worst case exponential complexity when BnB methods are used to compute the solution. Moreover, when modeling practical networks and depending on the number of links, nodes and time slots, problem with large sizes may arise. As a result, it is extremely difficult to schedule links optimally. Most research in literature is based on heuristic at the cost of performance degradation, for example, see [7,8,52]. In [26], we investigated a DCA scheme to solve the mixed 0–1 linear program (35a)–(35h) efficiently.

The network lifetime maximization problem [29] is similar to (35a)–(35h) in which (35a) is replaced by network lifetime maximization.

5.2 Quality of service (QoS) routing problems

The Unicast (resp. Multicast) QoS routing emphasizes to find paths (resp. a set of paths) from a source node to a destination node (resp. a set of destination nodes) satisfying the QoS requirements. The Routing problems become more complex as far as we consider mobile networks or hybrid networks, because of dynamic topology and real time routing procedure. As an example, we consider a scenario in Multicast routing problem, such as we are staying in a car parking place. The mobile services are provided in each moving car, equipped with a mobile device, via a car service center likes in the car parking place. There are m cars sending their requests to a mobile car service center, they need help to find the route

to go to their destinations under the travel time constraint, the less latency traffic jam, the jitter time delay constraint, the travel cost (same sources, different destinations, considering local constraints to each mobile vehicle). Therefore, based on the temporary update data of the network state, the mobile car service system has to calculate the route and given the answer for each car in a few seconds. In this context, we need a centralized and efficient algorithm to calculate the routes.

The problem of finding a path in network with multiple constraints (the MCP problem) is NP-complete. We reformulated the MCP [46] and MCOP (multi-constrained optimal path problem) [47,51] problem as Binary Integer Linear Programs (BILP) and investigated DCA-based algorithms for solving them. The DCA is fast and furnished an optimal solution in almost all cases, and a near-optimal solution in the remaining cases. For large scale problems we investigated the proximal decomposition technique to solve convex subprograms at each iteration of DCA. Computational results show that this approach is efficient, especially for large-scale settings where the powerful CPLEX fails to be applicable.

5.3 The partitioning-hub location-routing problem

The Partitioning-Hub Location-Routing Problem (PHLRP) is a hub location problem involving graph partitioning and routing features. PHLRP consists of partitioning a given network into sub-networks, locating at least one hub in each sub-network and routing the traffic within the network at minimum cost. There are various important applications of PHLRP, such as the deployment of network routing protocol problems and the planning of freight distribution problems. In [50] we formulated this problem as an Binary Integer Linear Programming (BILP) and then investigate DCA for solving it. Preliminary numerical results are compared with the well-known commercial solver CPLEX, they show the efficiency and the superiority of DCA.

5.4 The car pooling problem

Car pooling is a well-known transport solution that consists of sharing a car between a driver and passengers sharing the same route, or part of it. The challenge is to minimize both the number of required cars and the additional cost in terms of time for the drivers. To solve the problem, several tasks should be performed: choosing drivers and passengers, allocating passengers to cars, computing an optimal route for the cars. As such, the car pooling transport problem may be described as some kind of fleet management problem. In [49], we formulated this problem as a Mixed Integer Linear Program for which DCA has been efficiently applied. In order to globally solve the problem, we combine DCA with classical Branch and Bound algorithm. DCA is used to calculate upper bound while lower bound is obtained from a linear relaxation problem. Preliminary numerical results are compared with CPLEX. They show the efficiency and the superiority of DCA-based algorithms.

5.5 The minimum m-dominating set problem

Let $G = (V, E)$ be a graph, where V is the set of nodes and E is the set of edges of G. A dominating set D of a graph $G = (V, E)$ is a subset of nodes $D \subseteq V$ such that every vertex not in D is joined to at least one member of D by some edge. The domination number $\gamma(G)$ is the number of vertices in a smallest dominating set for G. The dominating set problem is a classical NP-complete decision problem [10] and has various applications in CS. A classical network application for this problem would be to choose a set of locations to install relay antennas. In ad hoc networks, creating a dominating set is a way to organize the network and is generally used as a first step for generating a connected dominating set [11]. This problem is formulated as a BILP for which DCA is investigated in [39]. Numerical results show that the DCA is efficient even for very large instances of problem. Moreover, our algorithm obtained better solution in significantly less time than CPLEX.

In a general framework, we show below how to solve optimization problems with integer variables by DCA.

5.6 From combinatorial optimization to DC programming: reformulation

5.6.1 Mixed zero-one concave minimization programming problem

Let $D \neq \emptyset$ be a bounded polyhedral convex set in $\mathbb{R}^n$ and let $J \subset \{1, \ldots, n\}$.

$$\min\{f(x) : x \in D, \ x_i \in \{0, 1\}, \quad \forall i \in J\}, \qquad (37)$$

where f is a finite concave function on D.
Let $K := \{x \in D : 0 \leq x_i \leq 1, \quad \forall i \in J\}$ and define $p(x) = \sum_{i \in J} x_i(1 - x_i)$. Clearly, p is a concave function with nonnegative values on K and

$$\{x \in D, \ x_i \in \{0, 1\}\} = \{x \in K : p(x) = 0\}$$
$$= \{x \in K : p(x) \leq 0\}.$$

Hence (37) can be reformulated as (by Theorem below)

$$\min\{f(x) : x \in K, \ p(x) \leq 0\}$$

which is equivalent to, for any $t > t_o$

$$\min\{f(x) + tp(x) : x \in K\}. \qquad (38)$$

Theorem 2 *[23] Let K be a nonempty-bounded polyhedral convex set in $\mathbb{R}^n$ and f, p be finite concave on K. Assume the feasible set of (P) be nonempty and p be nonnegative on K. Then there exists $t_o \geq 0$ such that for every $t > t_o$ the following problems have the same solution sets:*

$$(P_t) \quad \alpha(t) = \inf\{f(x) + tp(x) : x \in K\},$$
$$(P) \quad \alpha = \inf\{f(x) : x \in K, \ p(x) \leq 0\}.$$

Furthermore

(i) *if the vertex set of K, denoted by $V(K)$, is contained in $\{x \in K : p(x) \leq 0\}$, then $t_o = 0$.*

(ii) *if $V(K)$ is not contained in $\{x \in K : p(x) \leq 0\}$, then $t_o \leq \frac{f(x^o) - \alpha(0)}{S}$ for every $x^o \in K$, $p(x^o) \leq 0$, where $S := \min\{p(x) : x \in V(K), \ p(x) > 0\}$.*

DCA for solving (P_t)

$$(P_t) \quad \alpha(t) = \inf_{x \in K}\{f(x) + tp(x)\}$$
$$= \inf_{x \in \mathbb{R}^n}\{F_t(x) := \chi_K(x) + f(x) + tp(x)\}.$$

Assuming that a subgradient of $-f$ is computable. One DC decomposition of F_t can be chosen as

$$F_t(x) := g(x) - h(x) \text{ with } g(x) := \chi_K(x),$$
$$h(x) := -f(x) - tp(x). \qquad (39)$$

In this case, (P_t) is a polyhedral DC program because χ_K is a polyhedral convex function, and the general DCA scheme becomes:

$$y^k \in \partial(-f(x^k) - tp(x^k));$$
$$x^{k+1} \in \text{argmin}\left\{-\langle x, y^k \rangle : x \in K\right\}. \qquad (40)$$

Besides the computation of subgradients of $-f$ and set $\nabla(-p)(x) = \sum_{i \in J}(2x_i - 1)$, the algorithm requires one linear program at each iteration The convergence properties can be stated as follows:

Theorem 3 i) *DCA generates a finite sequence $x^1, \ldots, x^{k_*}$ contained in $V(K)$ such that $f(x^{k+1}) + tp(x^{k+1}) \leq f(x^k) + tp(x^k)$, $p(x^{k+1}) \leq p(x^k)$ for each k, and x^{k_*} is a critical point of $g - h$.*

ii) *If, in addition, h is differentiable at x^{k_*}, then x^{k_*} is actually a local minimizer to (P_t).*

iii) *Let $t > t_1 := \max\left\{\frac{f(x) - \alpha(0)}{S} : x \in V(K) \cap \{x \in K : p(x) = 0\}\right\}$. If at an iteration q one has $p(x^q) = 0$, then $p(x^k) = 0$ and $f(x^{k+1}) \leq f(x^k) \forall k \geq q$.*

5.6.2 Extension cases

Based on new results related to exact penalty and error bounds in DC programming [28], the same reformulation technique via exact penalty can be used for

- Linear constrained mixed zero-one DC programming problems.
- Linear constrained mixed integer DC programming problems.

6 Another issue: solving convex programs by DCA

Another issue which is also important in CS but were not discussed in this paper is how to solve large-size convex programs. Although convex programming has been studied for about a century, an increasing amount of effort has been put recently into developing fast and scalable algorithms to deal with large scale problems. While some convex regularizations involve convex quadratic programs (QP) for which standard QP solvers can be certainly used, many first-order methods have been developed in the last years for large scale convex problems. Since DC programming and DCA encompass convex programming and convex programs can be recast as (infinitely many) DC programs to which DCAs become global, (i.e. providing optimal solutions), one can make use of these theoretical and algorithmic tools to better reformulate and solve convex programs.

7 Conclusion

We have presented DC programming and DCA for modeling and solving three challenging classes that cover most nonconvex programs in communication systems. These theoretical and algorithmic tools have been outlined in an appropriate way to make them understandable to the reader. They highlight the distinctive features (flexibility, versatility, inexpensiveness, scalability, efficiency and globality) of DC programming and DCA. It is desirable that our approaches will help researchers and practitioners tackle efficiently their nonconvex programs, especially in the large-scale setting.

References

1. Alvarado, A., Scutari, G., Pang, J.S.: A New Decomposition Method for Multiuser DC-Programming and its Applications, arXiv:1308.3521v2 [cs.IT] (2013).

2. Al-Shatri, H., Weber, T.: Achieving the maximum sum rate using D.C. programming in cellular networks. IEEE Trans. Signal Process. **60**(3), 1331–1341 (2012)

3. Cendrillon, R., Yu, W., Moonen, M., Verlinden, J., Bostoen, T.: Optimal multiuser spectrum management for digital subscriber lines. IEEE Trans. Comm. **54**, 922–933 (2006)

4. Chiang, M.: Geometric programming for communication systems. Found. Trends Commun. Inf. Theory **2**, 1–154 (2005)

5. Chiang, M.: Nonconvex optimization of communication systems. In: Gao, D., Sherali, H. (eds.) Advances in Mechanics and Mathematics, Special Volume on Strang's 70th Birthday, vol. 3, pp. 136–196. Springer, Berlin (2008)

6. Chiang, M., Hande, P., Lan, T., Tan, C.W.: Power control in wireless cellular networks. Found. Trends Netw. **2**, 1–156 (2008)

7. Commander, C.W., Pardalos, P.M.: A combinatorial algorithm for the TDMA message scheduling problem. Comput. Optim. Appl. **43**(3), 449–463 (2009)

8. ElBatt, T., Ephremides, A.: Joint scheduling and power control for wireless ad hoc networks. In: Proc. IEEE INFOCOM'02, pp. 976–984, New York, USA (2002)

9. Fazel, M., Chiang, M.: Nonconcave network utility maximization through sum of squares method. Proc. IEEE Control and Decision Conference, Seville, Spain (2005)

10. Garey, M.R., Johnson, D.S.: Computers and Intractability. A Guide to the Theory of NP-Completeness. W. H. Freeman Co, San Franciso (1990)

11. Guha, S., Khuller, S.: Approximation algorithms for connected dominating sets. Algorithmica Number **4**(20), 374–387 (1998)

12. Hande, P., Zhang, S., Chiang, M.: Distributed Rate Allocation for Inelastic Flows. IEEE/ACM Transactions on Networking, vol. 15, No 6 (2007)

13. Hiriart-Urruty, J.B., Lemaréchal, C.: Convex Analysis and Minimization Algorithms. Parts I&II. Springer, Berlin (1991)

14. Hong, M., Luo, Z.-Q.: Signal processing and optimal resource allocation for the interference channel. Elsevier e-Reference-Signal Processing (2013).

15. Khabbazibasmenj, A., Roemer, F., Vorobyov, S., Haardt, M.: Sumrate maximization in two-way AF MIMO relaying: polynomial time solutions to a class of DC programming problems. IEEE Trans. Signal Process. **60**(10), 5478–5493 (2012)

16. Kha, H.H., Tuan, H.D., Nguyen, H.H.: Fast global optimal power allocation in wireless networks by local D.C. programming. IEEE Trans. Wireless Commun. **11**(2), 510–512 (2012)

17. Kim, S.-J., Giannakis, G.B.: Optimal resource allocat ion for MIMO ad hoc cognitive radio networks. IEEE Trans. Inf. Theory **57**(5), 3117–3131 (2011)

18. Kelly, F.P., Maulloo, A., Tan, D.: Rate control for communication networks: shadow prices, proportional fairness and stability. J. Op. Res. Soc. **49**(3), 237–252 (1998)

19. Julian, D., Chiang, M., ONeill, D., Boyd, S.: QoS and fairness constrained convex optimization of resource allocation for wireless cellular and ad hoc networks. Proc. IEEE INFOCOM (2002)

20. La, R.J., Anantharam, V.: Utility-based rate control in the Internet for elastic trafic. IEEE/ACM Trans. Netw. **10**(2), 272–286 (2002)

21. Lee, J.W., Mazumdar, R.R., Shroff, N.: Non-convex optimization and rate control for multi-class services in the Internet. Proc. IEEE Infocom, Hong Kong, China (2004)

22. Le Thi, H.A., DC Programming and DCA.

23. Le Thi, H.A., Pham Dinh, T., Le, D.M.: Exact penalty in DC programming. Vietnam J. Math. **27**(2), 169–178 (1999)

24. Le Thi, H.A.: Network Utility Maximisation: a unified DC programming approach. Technical Report, LITA (2012)

25. Le Thi, H.A., Pham Dinh, T.: The DC (difference of convex functions) Programming and DCA revisited with DC models of real world nonconvex optimization problems. Ann. Oper. Res. **133**, 23–46 (2005)

26. Le Thi, H.A., Nguyen, T.K., Phan, T.K., Pham Dinh, T.: Energy minimization-based cross-layer design in wireless networks. In The

Proceedings of the 2008 High Performance Computing & Simulation Conference (HPCS 2008) Nicosia, Cyprus, June 3–6, pp 283–289 (2008)

27. Le Thi, H.A., Ta, A.S., Pham Dinh, T., Le, N.T.: Optimal Spectrum Balancing in Multi-User DSL Network by DC programming and DCA, Technical report, LITA-UPV-M (2009)

28. Le Thi, H.A.: Pham Dinh, T., Huynh, V.N.: Exact penalty and error bounds in DC programming. J. Global Optim. **52**(3), 509–535 (2012)

29. Le Thi, H.A., Nguyen, Q.T., Phan, T.K., Pham Dinh, T.: DC Programming and DCA Based Cross-layer Optimization in Multi-hop TDMA Networks. Intelligent Information and Database Systems. Lecture Notes in Artificial Intelligence LNCS/LNAI (2013, to appear)

30. Le Thi, H.A., Pham Dinh, T.: Network Utility Maximisation: a DC programming approach for Sigmoidal Utility function. Proceedings of IEEE conference Advance Techonogies for Communications ATC'13 Ho Chi Minh city october 16–18, 2013, 978–1–4799–1089–2/13/31.00. IEEE, pp. 50–54 (2013)

31. Le Thi, H.A., Ta, A.S., Pham Dinh, T.: DC programming and DCA for some resource allocation problems in Communication, Networks (2013, submitted)

32. Madan, R., Cui, S., Lall, S., Goldsmith, A.: Cross-layer design for lifetime maximization in interference-limited wireless sensor networks. IEEE Trans. Wireless Commun. **5**(11), 3142–3152 (2006)

33. Palomar, D.P., Chiang, M.: A tutorial on decomposition methods for network utility maximization. IEEE J. Select. Areas Commun. 24(8) (2006)

34. Pham Dinh, T., Le Thi, H.A.: Convex analysis approach to dc programming: theory, algorithms and applications. Acta Math. Vietnam. **22**(1), 289–357 (1997)

35. Pham Dinh, T., Le Thi, H.A.: DC optimization algorithms for solving the trust region subproblem. SIAM J. Optim. **8**, 476–505 (1998)

36. Pham Dinh, T., Le Thi, H.A.: Recent advances on DC programming and DCA. Transactions on Computational Collective Intelligence, Springer, Berlin (2013, to appear)

37. Rockafellar, R.T.: Convex Analysis. Princeton University Press, N.J. (1970)

38. Schleich, J., Bouvry, P., Le Thi, H.A.: Decentralized Fault-tolerant Connected Dominating Set Algorithm for Mobile Ad hoc Networks. Proceedings of the: International Conference on Wireless Networks, World Congress in Computer Science Computer Engineering, and Applied Computing, July 13–16, 2009. Las Vegas, USA, ICWN 2009, 354–360 (2009)

39. Schleich, J., Le Thi, H.A., Bouvry, P.: Solving the Minimum m-Dominating Set problem by a Continuous Optimization Approach based on DC Programming and DCA. J. Combin. Optim. **24**(4), 397–412 (2012)

40. Srikant, R.: The Mathematics of Internet Congestion Control. Birkhauser, Basel (2004)

41. Song, K.B., Cheung, S.T., Ginis, G., Cioffi, J.M.: Dynamic spectrum management for next-generation dsl systems. IEEE Commun. Mag. **40**, 101–109 (2002)

42. Starr, T., Cioffi, J.M., Silverman, P.: Understanding Digital Subscriber Line Technology. Prentice Hall, Upper Saddle River (1999)

43. Schmidt, D., Shi, C., Berry, R., Honig, M., Utschick, W.: Distributed resource allocation schemes: Pricing algorithms for power control and beamformer design in interference networks. IEEE Signal Process. Mag. **26**(5), 53–63 (2009)

44. Scutari, G., Facchinei, F., Song, P., Palomar, D., Pang, J.: Decomposition by partial linearization: Parallel optimization of multi-agent systems, IEEE Trans. Signal Process (2013, submitted).

45. Ta, A.S.: Contributions aux développements des nouvelles technologies de communication en transport multimodal par des techniques d'optimisation, thèse de doctorat soutenue au LMI-INSA de Rouen Juin (2012)

46. Ta, A.S., Le Thi, H.A., Khadraoui, D., Pham Dinh, T.: Solving QoS routing problems by DCA. In Intelligent Information and Database Systems. Lecture Notes in Artificial Intelligence (LNAI), vol. 5991, pp. 460–470. Springer, Berlin (2010)

47. Ta, A.S., Le Thi, H.A., Khadraoui, D., Pham Dinh, T.: Solving Multicast QoS Routing Problem in the context V2I Communication Services using DCA, 9th IEEE/ACIS ICIS: August 18–20, 2010, pp. 471–476. Yamagata, Japan (2010)

48. Ta, A.S., Le Thi, H.A., Pham Dinh, T.: Power control by DC programming and DCA. In: The proceedings of International Conference on Industrial Engineering and Systems Management IESM (2011)

49. Ta, A.S., Le Thi, H.A., Arnould, G., Khadraoui, D., Pham Dinh, T.: Solving car pooling problem using DCA. Proceedings of IEEE conference Global Information Infrastructure Symposium (GIIS 2011), Danang 4–6 (2011) (published by IEEE Xplore)

50. Ta, A.S., Le Thi, H.A., Khadraoui, D., Pham Dinh, T.: Solving Partitioning-Hub Location-Routing Problem using DCA. J. Ind. Manage. Optim. **8**(1), 87–102 (2012)

51. Ta, A.S., Le Thi, H.A., Pham Dinh, T., Khadraoui, D.: Solving many to many multicast QoS routing problem using dca and proximal decomposition technique, In Proc. IEEE International Conference on Computing, Networking and Communications, pages 809–814, Hawaii, American, 30 January-2 February (2012) (published by IEEEXplore)

52. Tang, J., Xue, G., Chandler, C., Zhang, W.: Link scheduling with power control for throughput enhancement in multihop wireless networks. IEEE Trans. Vehicular Tech. **55**(3), 733–742 (2006)

53. Tsiaflakis, P., Diehl, M., Moonen, M.: Distributed spectrum management algorithms for multiuser dsl networks **56**(10), 4825–4843 (2008)

54. Vucic, N., Shi, S., Schubert, M.: DC programming approach for resource allocation in wireless networks, pp. 380–386. In International Symposium on Modeling and Optimization in Mobile, Ad Hoc and Wireless Networks (WiOpt) (2010)

12

Analysis of a queue with two priority classes and feedback controls

Hung T. Tran · Tien V. Do · Laszlo Pap

Abstract In this paper, a queueing system with two priority classes of customers is investigated. In the queueing system, customers of high priority can preempt the service of customers of low priority. Customers can wait in buffers of finite size. A congestion control mechanism is proposed to model various practical problems. The steady-state probabilities are computed with the help of the framework of quasi-birth–death processes using the theory of generalized invariant subspace. Performance measures of interest are also derived and demonstrated by numerical results.

Keywords Priority · Feedback control · Queue · QBD

1 Introduction

The preemptive queue with two priority classes has been treated in earlier works [10,11,13] because it can be used for the performance evaluation of practical systems. Customers of two classes (high and low priority) arrive into the system. A server has a service capacity of multiple identical service units. Each high-priority customer requires a single service unit. The system works under the preemptive discipline, i.e. an admitted high-priority customer immediately gets service upon his arrival either by getting an idle service unit or by occupying service unit being used by low-priority customers. High-priority customers are served according to the first in first out (FIFO) and low-priority customers are

H. T. Tran · T. V. Do (✉) · L. Pap
Budapest University of Technology and Economics,
Budapest, Hungary
e-mail: do@hit.bme.hu

H. T. Tran · T. V. Do
Viet-Hung Industrial University, Hanoi City, Vietnam

served according to the processor sharing (PS) principle. Furthermore, the service capacity for low-priority customers depends on the number of high-priority customers in the system.

To take into account practical aspects, buffers of finite size for both two classes of customers are assumed in this paper. Furthermore, a proposed queue includes a congestion control mechanism. Once the number of low-priority customers in the system reaches the first control threshold, the arrival rate of low-priority customers is reduced to a guarantee arrival rate. If the number of low-priority customers is above the second control threshold, each arriving batch of low-priority customers will be discarded with a certain probability. Therefore, the proposed queue can be used to model Differentiated Service Architecture [14] in IP networks.

We show that this queue can be analyzed within the framework of Quasi Birth and Death (QBD) processes [4,5,7,8]. Closed-form expressions are given for the mean number of customers of each class, the batch and the customer loss probability of each class and the mean system time of customers.

The rest of the paper is organized as follows. In Sect. 2, a queue with two priority classes is discussed in details. Finally, numerical results illustrating the operation of the system are presented in Sect. 3. The paper ends with some conclusions in Sect. 4.

2 A system model and performance analysis

The system consists of a server and two finite queues. The service capacity of the server is assumed to be composed of N service units. There are two categories of customers: high priority (HP) and low priority (LP).

We assume that the interarrival times of batches of HP customers follow an exponential distributions with parameter

λ_{HP}. The size of the buffer for storing HP customers is K_{HP}. The batch size is upper-bounded by H (note that $K_{HP} \geq H$). A batch of b, $1 \leq b \leq H$, HP customers occurs with probability h_b, where $\sum_{b=1}^{H} h_b = 1$. Each HP customer requires a single service unit. The service time of a HP customer has an exponential distribution with rate μ_{HP}. High-priority customers are served according to the FIFO principle.

Let $I(t)$ denote the number of high-priority customers in the system at time t, $0 \leq I(t) \leq \mathcal{N} = N + K_{HP}$. Upon the arrival of a batch of b HP customers at time t,

- if all the N service units are occupied by high-priority customers, then the batch or a portion of the batch is put into the buffer of size K_{HP}, or the whole batch is rejected. A decision regarding the batch depends on the occupation level of the buffer and an applied admission rule.
- if the number i of service units occupied by other high-priority customers is less than N (i.e., $i < N$) and $b \leq N - i$, i HP customers is immediately served. Note that it is assumed that high-priority customers are allowed to push out low-priority customers being in service upon the arrival of high-priority customers.
- if the number i of service units occupied by other high-priority customers is less than N (i.e., $i < N$) and if $b > N - i$, the server is occupied by $N - i$ HP customers from the batch and $b - N + i$ HP customers will be tried to be placed in the buffer.

Two admission rules can be considered for the placement of customers into the buffer: whole batch acceptance (WBA) or partially batch acceptance (PBA). WBA means that the whole batch will be dropped if the system is not able to accept the whole batch. Under PBA only the part of batch is dropped, for which available room cannot be assured.

Batches of low-priority customers arrive according to a Poisson process. The batch size is upper-bounded by L. A batch of b, $1 \leq b \leq L$, LP customers occurs with probability l_b, where $\sum_{b=1}^{L} l_b = 1$. The service discipline of LP customers is processor sharing, a low-priority batch will get service immediately if there is service capacity not used by HP customers. Otherwise the batch is put into a buffer of size K_{LP}. Due to the preemptive nature of the system, low-priority customers under service may be pushed back into waiting room by high-priority customers. It is highly recommended that once a customer has been accepted into system, it will not be lost because of the aforementioned push-back mechanism. Therefore, at any time we require that no more than K_{LP} of low-priority customers (either being in service or waiting in queue) are in the system. Let $J(t)$ be the number of low-priority customers in the system, $0 \leq J(t) \leq K_{LP}$. If there are i high-priority and j low-priority customers in the system ($0 \leq i \leq N + K_{HP}$, $j \geq 1$), then each of the low-priority customers receives service at rate $\frac{\max(N-i,0)}{j} \mu_{LP}$.

Table 1 Parameters of the considered queue

λ_{HP}	Arrival rate of high-priority batches
λ_{LP}	Minimum arrival rate of low-priority batches
H	Upper bound of high-priority batches
L	Upper bound of low-priority batches
K_{HP}	Buffer size for the high-priority class
K_{LP}	Buffer size for the low-priority class
m_1	The first control level for low-priority class
m_2	The second control level $K_{LP} - m_2$
p_{dropp}	Dropping probability used for overload control

It is assumed that batches of low-priority customers arrive at rate $\lambda_{LP,j}$ for level j ($0 \leq j < m_1$). When the number of low-priority customers in the system reaches the level m_1, its (batch) arrival rate is forced to reduce from $\lambda_{L,j}$ to the guarantee value λ_{LP}. From the context of congestion control, it is natural to assume $\lambda_{LP,0} \geq \lambda_{LP,1} \geq \cdots \geq \lambda_{LP}$.

The second control level is set to $j = K_{LP} - m_2$. That means whenever the difference between the number of low-priority customers and the waiting room's capacity drops below m_2, each low-priority arrival batch will be discarded with the pre-defined probability p_{dropp}. The main parameters of the queue are summarized in Table 1.

The system is two-dimensional Markov process $(I(t), J(t)) = (i, j)$ with the state space $\{(i, j) : 0 \leq i \leq K_{HP} + N, 0 \leq j \leq K_{LP}\}$. Let $p_{i,j}$ denote the steady state probability of the state (i, j) as

$$p_{i,j} = \lim_{t \to \infty} \Pr(I(t) = i, J(t) = j), \quad (i = 0, \ldots, N$$
$$+ K_{HP}; \quad j = 0, 1, \ldots, K_{LP}).$$

We introduce the following vectors

$$\mathbf{v}_j = (p_{0,j}, p_{1,j}, \ldots, p_{\mathcal{N},j}) \quad \text{for} \quad j = 0, 1, \ldots K_{LP}.$$

In what follows, we provide an analysis for the WBA rule. Note that the analysis for the PBA rule can be performed in the same way. For the WBA rule, the generator matrix of this process will have the form shown in Fig. 1.

For $0 \leq j \leq K_{LP}$, we define the following matrix $\mathcal{A}_j = A_j - D^{A_j} - C_j - \sum_{s=1}^{L} B_{j-s,s}$, where D^{A_j} is matrix whose diagonal elements are the sum of the elements in the corresponding row of A_j.

The balance equations of the system are written as

$$\sum_{s=1}^{L} \mathbf{v}_{j-s} B_{j-s,s} + \mathbf{v}_j \mathcal{A}_j + \mathbf{v}_{j+1} C_j = 0, \tag{1}$$

and the normalization equation is

$$\sum_{j=0}^{K_{LP}} \mathbf{v}_j \mathbf{e} = 1.0, \tag{2}$$

where $\mathbf{e}$ is the unit vector.

Fig. 1 The block structure of the generator matrix of the queueing system $(m_1 = 3, m_2 = 4, L = 2)$

$$Q =$$

$$\begin{bmatrix}
\mathcal{A}_0 & B_{0,1} & B_{0,2} & & & & & & & & & \\
C_1 & \mathcal{A}_1 & B_{1,1} & B_{1,2} & & & & & & & & \\
 & C_1 & \mathcal{A}_2 & B_{2,1} & B_{2,2} & & & & & & & \\
 & & C_1 & \mathcal{A}_3 & B_1 & B_2 & & & & & & \\
 & & & C_1 & \mathcal{A}_4 & B_1 & B_2 & & & & & \\
 & & & & C_1 & \mathcal{A}_5 & B_1 & B_2 & & & & \\
 & & & & & C_1 & \mathcal{A}_6 & B_1 & B_2 & & & \\
 & & & & & & \ddots & & \ddots & & & \\
 & & & & & & C_1 & \mathcal{A}_{K_{LP}-4} & B_1 & & B_2 & \\
 & & & & & & & C_1 & \mathcal{A}_{K_{LP}-3} & B_{K_{LP}-3,1} & B_{K_{LP}-3,2} & \\
 & & & & & & & & C_1 & \mathcal{A}_{K_{LP}-2} & B_{K_{LP}-2,1} & B_{K_{LP}-2,2} \\
 & & & & & & & & & C_1 & \mathcal{A}_{K_{LP}-1} & B_{K_{LP}-1,1} \\
 & & & & & & & & & & C_1 & \mathcal{A}_{K_{LP}}
\end{bmatrix}$$

Fig. 2 Examples of transition matrices

$$A_j = A = \begin{bmatrix}
0 & h_1\lambda_{HP} & h_2\lambda_{HP} & \cdots & h_H\lambda_{HP} & & & & \\
\mu_{HP} & 0 & h_1\lambda_{HP} & \cdots & & \cdots & h_H\lambda_{HP} & & \\
 & \ddots & & \ddots & & \ddots & & & \\
 & & i\mu_{HP} & 0 & h_1\lambda_{HP} & \cdots & & h_H\lambda_{HP} & \\
 & & & \ddots & & \ddots & & \ddots & \\
 & & & N\mu_{HP} & 0 & & & h_{K_{HP}}\lambda_{K_{HP}} & \\
 & & & & \ddots & & \ddots & \vdots & \\
 & & & & & & & h_1\lambda_{HP} & \\
 & & & & & N\mu_{HP} & & 0 &
\end{bmatrix}\begin{matrix}0 \\ 1 \\ \vdots \\ i \\ \vdots \\ N \\ \vdots \\ \vdots \\ N+K_{HP}\end{matrix}$$

$$B_{j,s} = \begin{bmatrix}
l_s\lambda_{L,j} & & & & \\
 & l_s\lambda_{L,j} & & & \\
 & & \ddots & & \\
 & & & l_s\lambda_{L,j} &
\end{bmatrix} \quad \text{for } 0 \le j \le K_{LP}, 1 \le s \le L$$

$$C_{j,1} = C_1 = \begin{bmatrix}
N\mu_L & & & & \\
 & \ddots & & & \\
 & & 2\mu_L & & \\
 & & & \mu_L & \\
 & & & & 0 \\
 & & & & & \ddots \\
 & & & & & & 0
\end{bmatrix}\begin{matrix}0 \\ \vdots \\ N-2 \\ N-1 \\ N \\ \vdots \\ N+K_{HP}\end{matrix}$$

For $M_1 = m_1 + L \le j \le M_2 = \min(K_L - 1, K_L - m2)$, the Eq. (1) include only j-independent coefficient matrices and have a common form

$$\sum_{s=1}^{L} \mathbf{v}_{j-s} B_s + \mathbf{v}_j \mathcal{A} + \mathbf{v}_{j+1} C_1 = 0. \tag{3}$$

The examples of these matrices are shown in Fig. 2.

In the literature so far, attention is mainly focused on the steady-state analysis of infinite QBD-M processes [1,3,9] performed by a direct approach with spectral expansion method proposed in [3] or an indirect approach with reblocking technique applied in [12].

To cope with the numerical problem, we apply the theory of generalized invariant subspace [2]. Recall that with the theory of generalized invariant subspace, we are able to compute matrices $U = [\,U_1\ U_2\,]$ and $V = [\,V_1\ V_2\,]$, which makes the following decomposition possible

$$U^{-1}EV = \begin{bmatrix} E_{11} & 0 \\ 0 & E_{22} \end{bmatrix} \quad \text{and} \quad U^{-1}GV = \begin{bmatrix} G_{11} & 0 \\ 0 & G_{22} \end{bmatrix} \tag{4}$$

where matrices E and G are constructed from the QBD-M process as follows

$$G = \begin{bmatrix} 0 & 0 & \cdots & \cdots & -D_0 \\ I & 0 & \cdots & \cdots & -D_1 \\ 0 & I & \cdots & \cdots & -D_2 \\ \vdots & \vdots & \ddots & & \vdots \\ 0 & 0 & \cdots & I & -D_{y-1} \end{bmatrix}, \quad E = \begin{bmatrix} I & & & \\ & I & & \\ & & \ddots & \\ & & & I & \\ & & & & D_y \end{bmatrix} \tag{5}$$

matrix D_i ($i = 0, 1, \ldots, L+1$) is the coefficient matrix of $\mathbf{v}_{j-L+i}$ in the balance equations.

Let m_s and m_u denote the number of singularities of matrix pencil $\lambda E - G$, which lie inside and outside the open unit disk, respectively. Note that the singularities of the matrix pencil $\lambda E - G$, i.e. the roots of $det(\lambda E - G) = 0$ are exactly the roots of the equation $det(D(\lambda)) = 0$, where $D(\lambda) = D_0 + D_1\lambda + \ldots + D_{L+1}\lambda^{L+1}$. As a consequence, we have $m_s + m_u = m = (L+1) \times (\mathcal{N}+1)$. Matrices U_1, V_1 are of size $m \times m_u$, matrices U_2, V_2 are of size $m \times m_s$, matrices E_{11}, G_{11} are of size $m_u \times m_u$ and matrices E_{22}, G_{22} are of size $m_s \times m_s$, respectively.

Let define the following partition and matrices

$$U^{-1} = \begin{bmatrix} X_1 \\ X_2 \end{bmatrix}, \quad F_1 = E_{11}G_{11}^{-1}, \quad F_2 = G_{22}E_{22}^{-1},$$

$$T_n = (n\text{-th pos.}) \begin{bmatrix} 0 \\ \vdots \\ I \\ \vdots \\ 0 \end{bmatrix} \quad \text{for } 0 \le n \le L \tag{6}$$

matrices F_1 and F_2 are of size $m_u \times m_u$ and $m_s \times m_s$, respectively. Let define the grouping

$$\mathbf{w}_k = [\,\mathbf{v}_{M_1-L+k} \cdots \mathbf{v}_{M_1+k}\,] \tag{7}$$

for $0 \le k \le K = M_2 - M_1 + 1$ and

$$[\,\mathbf{p}_k\ \mathbf{q}_k\,] = \mathbf{w}_k[\,U_1\ U_2\,] \tag{8}$$

The vectors $\mathbf{p}_k$ and $\mathbf{q}_k$ ($0 \le k \le K$) are of size m_u and m_s, respectively. It can be easily checked that

$$\mathbf{w}_{k+1}E = \mathbf{w}_kG \quad 0 \le k \le K \tag{9}$$

By post-multiplying the Eq. (9) by matrix V and combining with Eq. (4), we obtain two un-couple generalized difference equations for $\mathbf{p}_k$ and $\mathbf{q}_k$

$$\mathbf{p}_{k+1}E_{11} = \mathbf{p}_kG_{11} \quad 0 \le k < K \tag{10}$$
$$\mathbf{q}_{k+1}E_{22} = \mathbf{q}_kG_{22} \quad 0 \le k < K \tag{11}$$

This follows that the next two expression hold

$$\mathbf{p}_k = \mathbf{p}_K F_1^{K-k} \quad \text{and} \quad \mathbf{q}_k = \mathbf{q}_0 F_2^k \tag{12}$$

We are now able to express the level probability vectors as

$$\begin{aligned} \mathbf{v}_{M_1-L+k} &= \mathbf{w}_k T_0 \\ &= \mathbf{p}_K F_1^{K-k} X_1 T_0 + \mathbf{q}_0 F_2^k X_2 T_0 \quad \text{for} \quad 0 \le k \le K \end{aligned} \tag{13}$$

and

$$\begin{aligned} \mathbf{v}_{M_1-L+K+n} &= \mathbf{w}_K T_n \\ &= \mathbf{p}_K X_1 T_n + \mathbf{q}_0 F_2^K X_2 T_n \quad \text{for} \quad 0 \le n \le L \end{aligned} \tag{14}$$

With the Eqs. (13) and (14), the unknown probability vectors we have to compute now are $\mathbf{v}_0, \ldots, \mathbf{v}_{M_1-L-1}$, $\mathbf{p}_K$, $\mathbf{q}_0$ and $\mathbf{v}_{M_2+2}, \ldots, \mathbf{v}_\mathcal{K}$, i.e. there are $(M_1 - L) + y + (\mathcal{K} - M_2 - 1) = M_1 + \mathcal{K} - M_2$ unknown vectors, each of size $\mathcal{N} + 1$. To get these unknown vectors, we have vector Eq. (1) for $j = 0, \ldots, M_1 - 1$ (the first M_1 equations) and for $j = M_2 + 1, \ldots, \mathcal{K}$ (the last $\mathcal{K} - M_2$ equations). However, only $M_1 + \mathcal{K} - M_2 - 1$ of these equations are linearly independent due to the fact that the generator matrix of the Markov process is singular. This means one equation must be replaced by the normalized Eq. (2). Using Eqs. (13) and (14), the equivalent form of (2) is

$$\begin{aligned} \sum_{j=0}^{M_1-L-1} \mathbf{v}_j\mathbf{e} &+ \sum_{j=M_2+2}^{\mathcal{K}} \mathbf{v}_j\mathbf{e} \\ &+ \mathbf{p}_K\left[\sum_{k=0}^{K} F_1^{K-k}X_1T_0 + \sum_{n=1}^{L} X_1T_n\right]\mathbf{e} \\ &+ \mathbf{q}_0\left[\sum_{k=0}^{K} F_2^kX_2T_0 + \sum_{n=1}^{L} F_2^KX_2T_n\right]\mathbf{e} = 1 \end{aligned} \tag{15}$$

What remains to be clarified is how to determine the values of m_u and m_s. For this aim, we take a corresponding infinite QBD-M process, which possesses the same balance equations (3) with the same level-independent coefficient matrices A, B_i ($1 \le i \le L$).

Using the interpretation of stability formulated in previous works (see [3,6]), stability condition of the corresponding infinite QBD-M process is checked by evaluating the inequality

$$\mathbf{v}\left(\sum_{s=1}^{L} s B_s\right)\mathbf{e} < \mathbf{v}(C_1)\mathbf{e} \qquad (16)$$

where $\mathbf{v}$ is a vector of size $\mathcal{N}+1$ and is the solution of the equations

$$\mathbf{v}\left(\mathcal{A} + \sum_{s=1}^{L} B_s + C_1\right) = 0; \quad \mathbf{v}.\mathbf{e} = 1 \qquad (17)$$

If the inequality (16) is fulfilled, then it is known from [3] that the $det(D(\lambda)) = 0$ equation has exactly $L*(\mathcal{N}+1)$ roots inside the unit disk. In this case, we have $m_u = (\mathcal{N}+1)$ and $m_s = L*(\mathcal{N}+1)$. Also from [3], the case in which the inequality does not hold implies that $m_u = (\mathcal{N}+1)+1$ and $m_s = L*(\mathcal{N}+1)-1$.

2.1 Average number of customers

Denote $\pi = \sum_{j=0}^{K_{LP}} \mathbf{v}_j$ and let π_i be the ith element of vector π.

For the high-priority class, the average number of customers in the queue is computed as

$$E_{\text{high}} = \sum_{i=N}^{N+K_{HP}} (i-N)\pi_i. \qquad (18)$$

The average number of low-priority customers in the system is calculated as

$$E_{\text{low}} = \sum_{j=0}^{K_{LP}} j\mathbf{v}_j\mathbf{e}. \qquad (19)$$

2.2 Batch loss probability

This parameter is defined as a probability that an arriving batch is rejected due to the lack of storage and/or due to the dropping control level. For the high-priority class, batch of size k is rejected only if the number of high-priority customers in the system is more than $(N+K_{HP})-k$ upon his arrival. Using PASTA (Poisson Arrivals See Time Average) property, the loss probability for high-priority batch of size k is

$$P(\text{HP batch of size } k \text{ loss}) = \sum_{i=(N+K_{HP}-k+1)^+}^{N+K_{HP}} \pi_i, \qquad (20)$$

where $(x)^+ = \max(x,0)$.

The batch loss priority for the high-priority class is

$$P(\text{HP batch loss}) = \sum_{k=1}^{H} h_k \left(\sum_{i=(N+K_{HP}-k+1)^+}^{N+K_{HP}} \pi_i\right). \qquad (21)$$

For the low-priority class, a batch of size k is always dropped with probability p_{dropp} if there are more than

$K_{LP} - m_2$ low-priority customers in the system. Moreover, this batch is also dropped if it observes more than $K_{LP} - k$ customers in the system. Therefore, two kinds of batch loss probability can be introduced. The first one, referred as the blocking probability, is caused merely by a finite buffer and is derived in the same way we have done for the high-priority class.

$$P^{(1)}(\text{LP batch of size } k \text{ loss}) = \sum_{j=(K_{LP}-k+1)^+}^{K_{LP}} \mathbf{v}_j.\mathbf{e}, \qquad (22)$$

$$P^{(1)}(\text{LP batch loss}) = \sum_{k=1}^{L} l_k \left(\sum_{j=(K_{LP}-k+1)^+}^{K_{LP}} \mathbf{v}_j.\mathbf{e}\right). \qquad (23)$$

The second kind of loss is caused by the interaction of the control feedback level and a finite buffer. This is referred to as the overall batch loss probability and is computed as

$$P^{(2)}(\text{LP batch of size } k \text{ loss}) = \sum_{j=(K_{LP}-k+1)^+}^{K_{LP}} \mathbf{v}_j.\mathbf{e}$$
$$+ \Omega_{(k \le m_2-1)} p_{\text{dropp}} \left(\sum_{j=K_{LP}-m_2+1}^{K_{LP}-k} \mathbf{v}_j\mathbf{e}\right), \qquad (24)$$

$$P^{(2)}(\text{LP batch loss})$$
$$= \sum_{k=1}^{L} l_k \cdot \left[\sum_{j=(K_{LP}-k+1)^+}^{K_{LP}} \mathbf{v}_j.\mathbf{e}\right.$$
$$\left. + \Omega_{(k \le m_2-1)} \cdot p_{\text{dropp}} \left(\sum_{j=K_{LP}-m_2+1}^{K_{LP}-k} \mathbf{v}_j\mathbf{e}\right)\right], \qquad (25)$$

where $\Omega_{\mathcal{X}}$ denotes the indication function, which is 0 if event $\mathcal{X}$ is false and 1 otherwise.

2.3 Customer loss probability

Let the average arrival batch size of the high-priority and the low-priority class be $\bar{h}$ and $\bar{l}$, respectively. It is clear that $\bar{h} = \sum_{i=1}^{H} i.h_i$ and $\bar{l} = \sum_{i=1}^{L} i.l_i$. The probability that a customer arrives in a batch with size k is equal to $k.h_k/\bar{h}$ (high-priority case) and $k.l_k/\bar{l}$ (low-priority case). When the WBA rule is applied, the probability that the customer in batch of size k is dropped is equal to the probability that the batch itself is dropped. Therefore, it follows that

$$P(\text{customer loss}) = \sum_{k=1}^{b_{\max}} \frac{k.r_k}{b}.P(\text{batch of size } k \text{ loss}). \qquad (26)$$

The expression above is valid for any class of customers. For the high-priority class, we have to make $b_{\max} = H$, $b = \bar{h}$, $r_k = h_k$ and use the Eq. (20). For the two kinds of low-priority loss, $b_{\max} = L$, $b = \bar{l}$, $r_k = l_k$ substitutions and Eqs. (22) or (24) are used.

2.4 Average queueing and system times

Applying Little's formula, the mean waiting time of a high-priority customer is written as

$$W_{\text{high}} = \frac{E_{\text{high}}}{\bar{h}\lambda_H(1 - P(\text{HP customer loss}))}. \tag{27}$$

For the low-priority customer, the mean system time is calculated again by Little's theorem

$$S_{\text{low}} = \frac{E_{\text{low}}}{\bar{l}\left(\sum_{j=0}^{K_{\text{LP}}} \lambda_{L,j}\mathbf{v}_j\mathbf{e}\right)(1 - P^{(2)}(\text{LP customer loss}))}. \tag{28}$$

2.5 System time distribution

For high-priority class, define the Laplace transform

$$S_i(s) = \begin{cases} \left(\frac{N\mu_H}{s+N\mu_H}\right)^{i-N}\left(\frac{\mu_H}{s+\mu_H}\right) & \text{for } N < i \leq N + K_H \\ \frac{\mu_H}{s+\mu_H} & \text{for } i \leq N \end{cases} \tag{29}$$

If a high-priority customer arrives in kth position of batch of size r and sees i other high-priority customers in the system (provided that a batch is accepted), then the Laplace transform of the system time distribution of that customer is given by $S_{i+k}(s)$. Since the probability of being in position k in batch of size r is $\xi_k = \frac{1}{r}$ and the distribution of batch size is known, the total probability rule yields

$$S_{HP}(s) = \sum_{i=0}^{N+K_H} \pi_i \left(\sum_{r=1}^{H} \Omega_{\{r+i \leq N+K_H\}} h_r \left(\sum_{k=1}^{r} \xi_k S_{i+k}(s)\right)\right) \tag{30}$$

The derivation of system time distribution for low-priority customer is done in two steps. First, for the sake of convenient interpretation, we renumber the states of the QBD-M process, i.e. each (i, j) state now corresponds to state with assigned index $j * (\mathcal{N} + 1) + i$. With this "transformation", each state of the process can be accessed not by a couple of index numbers, but by only one. Given a state having index k, an original couple of indexes are

$$j = \left[\frac{k}{\mathcal{N}+1}\right] \tag{31}$$
$$i = k - j * (\mathcal{N}+1) \tag{32}$$

where $[x]$ denotes the greatest integer, which is less than or equal to x. Let us denote the steady-state probability vector of the process by γ, which is in fact a rewritten version of all vectors $\mathbf{v}_j$ calculated in the previous section.

Second, the technique of Markov driven workload process is utilized to determine the system time distribution. Recall

that the service capacity for low-priority customers are evenly shared between them and it depends on the number of high-priority customers. In other words, one can consider a workload process controlled by our original Markov process. When a driving Markov process is in state k, the workload process accomplishes service at rate $r_k = \frac{\max(N-i,0)}{j}$ where i and j are determined from k as in the expression (31) and (32).

When a low-priority customer arrives, it brings its service requirement x. This customer will leaves the system when the workload process defined above accomplishes a work amount of x. The fact that the customer arrives alone or in batch with other ones does not matter at this point, because the essence here is upon an arrival a workload process changes its service rate due to the state change of a driving Markov process. That is the information of possible batch arrivals is indeed included in the generator matrix of the driving process.

Since the service requirement x is exponentially distributed with parameter μ_L, the Laplace transform of the density function of system time can be derived and appears to correspond to phase time distribution

$$S_{LP}(s) = \mathbf{p}_R[sI - (Q - \mu_L R)]^{-1} R\mu_L \mathbf{e} \tag{33}$$

where Q is the generator matrix of the driving Markov process, R is a diagonal matrix where the entry (k, k) gives the service rate in state k, and $\mathbf{p}_R = \frac{\gamma R}{\gamma R\mathbf{e}}$ is a row initial probability vector seen by the entering customer. The phase type distribution has the initial probability $\mathbf{p}_R$, transient matrix $Q - \mu_L R$ and vector $R\mu_L \mathbf{e}$ of rates to the absorbing state.

3 Numerical results

In what follows, unless otherwise stated, the parameter set $N = 10, \mu_{\text{LP}} = 1, \lambda_{\text{LP}} = 2, \mu_{\text{HP}} = 2, \lambda_{\text{HP}} = 4, K_{\text{LP}} = 50, H = L = 2$ is applied. The distribution of batch sizes is assumed to be uniform.

The impact of the dropping probability (p_{dropp}) on performance measures related to the low-priority class is shown in Figs. 3 and 4 for $m_1 = 3, K_{\text{HP}} = 10$. In Fig. 3, both the blocking and the overall loss probability are plotted as a function of the dropping probability. The first observation is that increasing the dropping probability of arriving batches increases slightly the overall and at the same time reduces significantly the blocking probability. The later performance measure is in connection with the mean queue length, which decreases with the dropping probability as shown in Fig. 4.

The second observation from the figures is that the smaller the control level $K_{\text{LP}} - m_2$ is chosen, the better performance is obtained from the aspect of the mean queue length and the blocking probability, at the same time, the worse the performance becomes from the aspect of overall loss probability. A

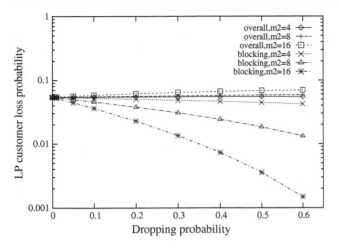

Fig. 3 LP customer loss probability versus the dropping probability

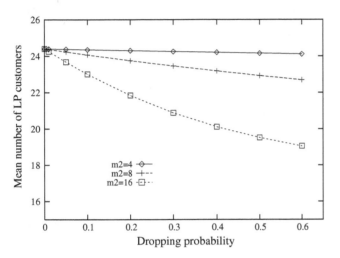

Fig. 4 Mean queue length of LP customers versus the dropping probability

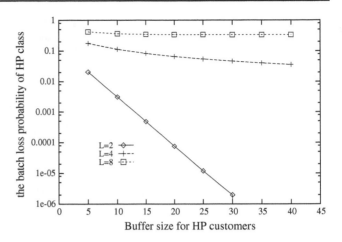

Fig. 5 HP batch loss probability versus buffer size

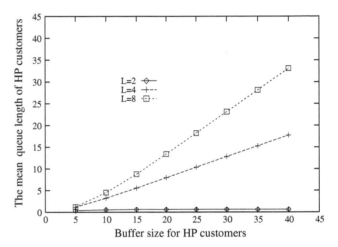

Fig. 6 Mean queue length of HP customer versus buffer size

trade-off between the increase of overall customer loss probability and the reduction of mean queue length (and through it, the mean system time) should be carefully considered when choosing an appropriate control level $K_{LP} - m_2$.

Figures 5 and 6 illustrate the effect of buffer size (K_{HP}) for customers of high priority on the queueing performance. The system parameters are $N = 5, m_1 = 5, m_2 = 8, p_{dropp} = 0.01$. The maximum size of arriving batches is chosen in sequence to be 2, 4 and 8. Obviously, increasing the buffer size reduces the batch loss probability as well as customer loss probability as Fig. 5 shows. The decreasing rate is quite fast when the maximum batch size is small (corresponding to small offered traffic) and seems to slow down when the maximum batch size (so as the offered traffic) becomes greater. Note that if reducing the batch (customer) loss probability is performed by increasing the storage requirement then it also implies the increasing of mean queue length and through it the mean queueing delay, especially in the case of heavy traffic load. This situation is depicted in Fig. 6.

Now we discuss the influence of offered traffic on the queueing performance with respect to interaction between two classes. The system parameters are $m_1 = 5, m_2 = 8$, $K_{HP} = 10, p_{dropp} = 0.01, \mu_{LP} = 1$. The offer traffic is increased by varying λ_{HP}/μ_{HP} meanwhile $r_{LP} = \lambda_{LP}/\mu_{LP}$ is fixed. Figures 7 and 8 clearly indicate the impact of the preemptive principle. As high-priority customers have the right to occupy service capacity over low-priority customers, the offered traffic of high priority first forces more customers of low priority to disclaim their service capacity and return to waiting condition. Until a certain value of λ_{HP}/μ_{HP}, there is no customer of the high-priority class in the queue and no high-priority customer loss at all. Further the increase of the offered traffic of high-priority customers causes the occupancy of buffers and initiates lost events relating to both two classes. However, due to the preemptive service discipline, the mean number of low-priority customers in the queue, as well as the customer loss probability of the low-priority class are increasing at a greater rate than the corresponding ones

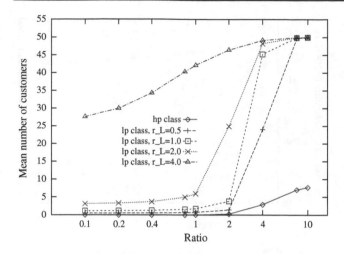

Fig. 7 Mean queue length versus offered traffic

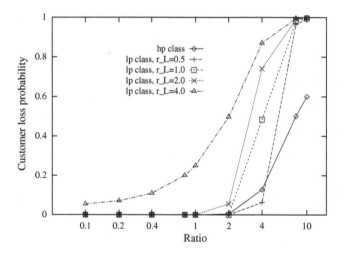

Fig. 8 Customers loss probability versus offered traffic

for the high-priority class. It is also worth emphasizing that the offered load of the low-priority class (expressed by parameter r_L) does not have any effect on the performance of the high-priority class. That is why for different values of r_L, the mean number and the loss probability of high-priority customers remains the same as plotted in Figs. 7 and 8.

4 Conclusion

In this paper, the steady-state analysis of a queue with two priority classes has been performed. To model some practical problems, additional extensions have been considered, such as finite capacity of buffers, batch arrival condition and level-dependent feedback control.

We have shown that the steady-state probabilities can be computed using the theory of generalized invariant subspace. Using the presented methodology, a performance trade-off can be achieved regarding the application of congestion control for networks.

Open Access This article is distributed under the terms of the Creative Commons Attribution License which permits any use, distribution, and reproduction in any medium, provided the original author(s) and the source are credited.

References

1. Tran, H.T., Do, T.V.: A new iterative method for systems with batch arrivals and batch departures. In: Proceedings of Communication Networks and Distributed Systems Modeling and Simulation Conference, CNDS'00, San Diego, USA (2000)
2. Akar, N., Sohraby, K.: Matrix-geometric Solutions in M/G/1 type Markov Chains with Multiple Boundaries: A Generalized State-space Approach. International Teletraffic Congress (1997)
3. Chakka, R.: Performance and Reliability Modelling of Computing System Using Spectral Expansion. PhD thesis, University of Newcastle upon Tyne (1995)
4. Chakka, R.: Spectral expansion method for QBD and QBD-M processes in performance modeling of computing and communication systems: a review. In: Krishna, P., Babu, M., Ariwa, E. (eds.) Global Trends in Information Systems and Software Applications, Communications in Computer and Information Science, vol. 270, pp. 794–810. Springer, Berlin (2012)
5. Chakka, R., Do, T.V.: Some new Markovian models for traffic and performance evaluation of telecommunication networks. In: Kouvatsos, D. (ed.) Network Performance Engineering, Lecture Notes in Computer Science, vol. 5233, pp. 642–664. Springer, Berlin (2011)
6. Ciardo, G., Smirni, E.: ETAQA: an efficient technique for the analysis of QBD-processes by aggregation. Perform. Eval. **36–37**, 71–93 (1999)
7. Do, T.V., Chakka, R.: Generalized QBD processes, spectral expansion and performance modeling applications. In: Kouvatsos, D. (ed.) Network Performance Engineering, Lecture Notes in Computer Science, vol. 5233, pp. 612–641. Springer, Berlin (2011)
8. Do, T.V., Chakka, R.: On the properties of generalised Markovian queues with heterogeneous servers. In: Nguyen, N.T., Do, T., Thi, H.A. (eds.) Advanced Computational Methods for Knowledge Engineering, Studies in Computational Intelligence, vol. 479, pp. 143–155. Springer, Berlin (2013)
9. Do, T.V., Chakka, R., Sztrik, J.: Spectral expansion solution methodology for QBD-M processes and applications in future internet engineering. In: Nguyen, N.T., Do, T., Thi, H.A. (eds.) Advanced Computational Methods for Knowledge Engineering, Studies in Computational Intelligence, vol. 479, pp. 131–142. Springer, Berlin (2013)
10. Falin, G., Khalil, Z., Stanford, D.A.: Performance analysis of a hybrid switching system where voice messages can be queued. Queue. Syst. **16**, 51–65 (1994)
11. Gail, H.R., Hantler, S.L., Taylor, B.A.: On a preemptive Markovian queue with multiple servers and two priority classes. Math. Oper. Res. **17**, 365–391 (1992)
12. Haverkort, B., Ost, A.: Steady state analysis of infinite stochastic petri nets: a comparing between the spectral expansion and the matrix geometric method. In: Proceedings of the 7th International Workshop on Petri Nets and Performance Models, pp. 335–346 (1997)
13. Stewart, W.J.: Probability, Markov Chains, Queues and Simulation: The Mathematical Basis of Performance Modeling. Princeton University Press, Cambridge (2009)
14. Xiao, X., Ni, L.M.: Internet QoS: the big picture. IEEE Netw. **13**, 1–13 (1999)

13

LICOD: A Leader-driven algorithm for community detection in complex networks

Zied Yakoubi · Rushed Kanawati

Abstract Leader-driven community detection algorithms (LdCD hereafter) constitute a new trend in devising algorithms for community detection in large-scale complex networks. The basic idea is to identify some particular nodes in the target network, called *leader nodes*, around which local communities can be computed. Being based on local computations, they are particularly attractive to handle large-scale networks. In this paper, we describe a framework for implementing LdCD algorithms, called LICOD. We propose also a new way for evaluating performances of community detection algorithms. This consists on transforming data clustering problems into a community detection problems. External criteria for evaluating obtained clusters can then be used for comparing performances of different community detection approaches. Results we obtain show that our approach outperforms top state of the art algorithms for community detection in complex networks.

Keywords Complex networks · Community detection · Leader-driven algorithms · Task-based evaluation

1 Introduction

Research in mining and analyzing large-scale complex networks has been boosted recently after discovering that much of complex networks extracted form natural and artificial systems share a set of non-trivial characteristics that distinguish them from pure random graphs. Basic topological characteristics of complex networks are: low separation degree (or what is better known as small-world feature [37]), power-law distribution of node's degrees [75], and high clustering

Z. Yakoubi · R. Kanawati (✉)
LIPN, CNRS UMR 7030, University Paris Nord, Villetaneuse, France
e-mail: rushed.kanawati@lipn.univ-paris13.fr

coefficient [46]. As a consequence of these basic topological features, almost all real-world complex networks exhibit a mesoscopic level of organization, called *communities* [58]. A community is loosely defined as a connected subgraph whose nodes are much linked with one each other than with nodes outside the subgraph. Nodes in a community are generally supposed to share common properties or play similar roles within the network. This suggests that we can gain much insight into complex networked systems by discovering and examining their underlaying communities. The semantic interpretation of a community depends on the type of the analyzed graph. In a metabolic network, a community would express a biological function in a cell [26]. In a network of transactions in an e-commerce site, this would express a set of similar customers [6]. Considering the web as a complex network, a community would be a set of pages dealing with a same topic [20].

More importantly, since the community-level structure is exhibited by almost all studied real-world complex networks, an efficient algorithm for detecting communities would be useful to implement a pre-treatment step for a number of general complex operations such as computation distribution, huge graph visualization and large-scale graph compression [25].

A quite big number of algorithms have been proposed for detecting communities in complex networks. Recent interesting survey tidies on this topic can be found in [21,66,83]. A quick review of the scientific literature allows to distinguish three different, but related problems:

- *Disjoint communities detection*: The goal here is to compute a partition of the graph node's set. One node can belong to only one community at once. Most of the work in the area of community detection deals with this problem [21].

- *Overlapping communities detection*: The goal is to compute soft clustering of the graph node's set where a node can belongs to several communities at once [61,64,77,87, 88].
- *Local community identification*: The goal here is to compute the community of a given node rather than partitioning the whole graph into communities. This can be useful in different settings, namely in the area of recommender systems [5,11,13,33].

Both problems, disjoint and overlapping community detection are NP-hard [10]. Different heuristics have been proposed to compute sub-optimal partitions. Most popular methods are based on applying greedy optimisation approaches of a graph partition quality measure [7,23,73]. The most applied graph partition criteria are the modularity initially introduced in [23]. However, some recent studies has pointed out some serious limitations of modularity optimization-based approaches [24,40]. These limitations have boosted the research for alternative approaches for community detection. Emergent approaches include label propagation approaches [71] and seed-centric ones [34]. The basic idea of seed-centric approaches is to select a set of nodes (i.e. seeds) around which communities are constructed. Being based on local computations, these approaches are very attractive to deal with large-scale and/or dynamic networks. One special case of seeds is to select nodes that are likely to act as leaders of their communities [36,76]. In this work, we propose a general framework for implementing Leader-driven community detection algorithms (LdCD hereafter) called LICOD. The approach we develop here is an extension of the work presented in [32]. Major enhancements are about transforming LICOD into a framework for implementing LdCD algorithms as described in Sect. 4. Another major new contribution concerns the evaluation process. Actually, since LdCD algorithms are not based on maximizing an objective function (i.e. the modularity), it is unfair to use the later criteria to compare these algorithms with popular modularity-guided approaches. One idea to provide fair evaluation criteria for different community detection algorithms is *task-oriented evaluation*. This can be conducted by evaluating how good are computed communities for realizing a given dependent task. In this paper, we propose using data clustering task for that purpose. The idea is to transform classical clustering benchmarks into a community detection problem. Algorithms can then be evaluated using classical extrinsic clustering evaluation metrics [52].

To sum up, main contributions of this paper are the following:

- Proposing LICOD, a general framework form implementing LdCD algorithms.
- Introducing task-oriented evaluation of community detection algorithms and providing an approach for evaluating

different community detection algorithms on data clustering tasks.

The remainder of this paper is organized as follows. Next in Sect. 2, we provide basic notations used in this paper. In Sect. 3, we review briefly major approaches for community detection algorithms as well as evaluation approaches. The LICOD approach is detailed in Sect. 4. Next, in Sect. 5, experimentation on both small benchmark networks and applying the proposed task-oriented evaluation approach are described. The clustering-oriented evaluation approach is described in Sect. 5.2. Obtained results are provided and commented. Finally, we conclude in Sect. 6.

2 Definitions and notations

In this study, we only consider simple unweighted, undirected graphs. A graph G is defined by a couple: $G = \langle V, E \rangle$ where $V = \{v_1 \ldots, v_n\}$ is a set of nodes (a.k.a actors, sites, vertices) and $E \subseteq V \times V$ is a set of links (a.k.a ties, arcs, or relationships). We denote by $n_G = |V|$ (reps. $m_G = |E|$) the number of nodes (reps. links) of graph G. The set of direct neighbors of a node $v \in V$ is given by the function $\Gamma(v)$. The number of direct neighbors of a node is the node's degree and is denoted by $d_v = |\Gamma(v)|$. The density of a graph G is given by the ratio of the number of existing links to the number of potential links. This is given by: $d(G) = \frac{2 \times m_g}{n_g \times (n_g - 1)}$. We denote by A the adjacency matrix of graph G. We have $A_{ij} = 1$ (resp. $A_{ij} = 0$) if nodes $v_i, v_j \in V$ are linked (resp. unlinked).

3 Related work

In this section, we provide a brief survey on both following topics related to the contributions of this paper: community detection algorithms and community evaluation approaches.

3.1 Community detection approaches

We focus in this study on approaches that aim to compute a partition, or disjoint communities of a complex network. A wide variety of different approaches have been proposed so far. Some comprehensive survey studies are provided in [21,66,83]. Here, we propose to classify existing approaches into four classes: Group-based approaches, network-based approaches, propagation-based approaches and seed-centric ones. Next we briefly review each of these identified classes.

3.1.1 Group-based approaches

These are approaches based on identifying groups of nodes that are highly connected or share some strong connection patterns. Some relevant connection patterns are the following:

- *High mutual connectivity*: a community can be assimilated to a maximal *clique* or to a γ-quasi-clique. A subgraph G is said to be γ-quasi-clique if $d(G) \leq \gamma$. Finding maximal cliques in a graph is known to be a NP-hard problem. Generally, cliques of reduced size are used as seeds to find larger communities. An example is the clique percolation algorithm [1,82]. Such approaches are relevant for networks that are rather dense.

- *High internal reachability*: One way to relax the constraint of having cliques or quasi-cliques is to consider the internal reachability of nodes within a community. Following this, a community core can be approximated by a maximal k-clique, k-club or k-core subgraph. A k-clique (resp. k-club) is a maximal subgraph in which the longest shortest path between any nodes (resp. the diameter) is $\leq k$. A k-core is a maximal *connected* subgraph in which each node has a degree $\geq k$. In [86], authors introduce the concept of k-*community* which is defined as a connected subgraph $G' = \langle V' \subset V, E' \subset E \rangle$ of a graph G in which for every couple of nodes $u, v \in V'$ the following constraint holds: $|\Gamma_G(v) \cap \Gamma_G(u)| \geq k$. The computational complexity of k-cores and k-communities is polynomial. However, these structures do not correspond to all the community, but are rather used as seeds for computing communities. An additional step for adding non-clustered nodes should be provided. In [67], authors propose to compute k-cores as mean to accelerate computation of communities using standard algorithms, but on size-reduced graphs.

3.1.2 Network-based approaches

These approaches consider the whole connection patterns in the network. Historical approaches include classical clustering algorithms. The adjacency matrix can be used as a similarity one, or topological similarity between each couple of nodes can also be computed. Spectral clustering approaches [59] and hierarchical clustering approaches can then be used [70]. Usually the number of clusters to be found should be provided as an input for the algorithm. Another drawback of spectral clustering is its high computation complexity which might be cubic on the size of the input dataset. Some distributed implementations of these approaches are proposed to provide efficient implementations [85]. More popular network-based approaches are those based on optimizing a quality metric of graph partition. Different partition quality metrics have been proposed in the scientific literature. The *modularity* is the most widely used one [58]. This is defined as follows. Let $\mathcal{P} = \{C_1, \ldots, C_k\}$ a partition of the node's set V of a graph. The modularity of the partition $\mathcal{P}$ is given by:

$$Q(\mathcal{P}) = \sum_{c \in \mathcal{P}} e(\mathcal{C}) - a(\mathcal{C})^2 \qquad (1)$$

where $e(\mathcal{C}) = \frac{\sum_{i \in \mathcal{C}} \sum_{j \in \mathcal{C}} A_{ij}}{2 \times m_G}$ is the fraction of links inside the community $\mathcal{C}$, and $a(\mathcal{C}) = \frac{\sum_{i \in \mathcal{C}} \sum_{j \in V} A_{ij}}{2.m_G}$ is the fraction of links incident to a node in $\mathcal{C}$. The computing complexity of Q is $(O)(m_G)$ [23]. Some recent work has extended the definition to bipartite and multipartite graphs [18,48,56] and even for multiplex and dynamic graphs [39,55]. Different heuristic approaches have been proposed for computing partitions that maximize the modularity. These can be classified into three main classes:

- *Agglomerative approaches*: These implement a bottom-up approach where an algorithm starts by considering each single node as a community. Then, it iterates by merging some communities guided by some quality criteria. The *louvain* algorithm [7] is one very known example of such approaches. The algorithm is composed of two phases. First, it looks for small communities by optimizing modularity in a local way. Second, it aggregates nodes of the same community and builds a new network whose nodes are the communities. Two adjacent communities merge if the overall modularity of the obtained partition can be enhanced. These steps are repeated iteratively until a maximum of modularity is reached. The computing complexity of the approach is empirically evaluated to be $\mathcal{O}(n \log(n))$.

- *Separative approaches*: These implement a top-down approach, where an algorithm starts by considering the whole network as a community. It iterates to select ties to remove to split the network into communities. Different criteria can be applied for tie selection. The Newman–Girvan algorithm is the most known representative of this class of approaches [58]. The algorithm is based on the simple idea that a tie linking two communities should have a high betweenness centrality. This is naturally true since an inter-community tie would be traversed by a high fraction of shortest paths between nodes belonging to these different communities. Considering the whole graph G, the algorithm iterates for m_G times, cutting at each iteration the tie with the highest betweenness centrality. This allows to build a hierarchy of communities, the root of which is the whole graph and leafs are communities composed of isolated nodes. Partition of highest modularity is returned as an output. The algorithm is simple to implement and has the advantage to discover automatically the best number of communities to identify. However, the computation complexity is rather high: $\mathcal{O}(n^2 \cdot m + (n)^3 \log(n))$. This is prohibitive to apply to large-scale networks.

- *Other optimization approach*: Other classical optimization approaches can also be used for modularity optimization such as applying genetic algorithms [31,47,68], evolutionary algorithms [29] or multi-objective optimization approaches [69].

All modularity optimization approaches make implicitly the following assumptions:

- The best partition of a graph is the one that maximize the modularity.
- If a network has a community structure, then it is possible to find a precise partition with maximal modularity.
- If a network has a community structure, then partitions inducing high modularity values are structurally similar.

Recent studies have showed that all three above-mentioned assumptions do not hold. In [24], authors show that the modularity function exhibits extreme degeneracies: it namely accepts an exponential number of distinct high scoring solutions and typically lacks for a clear global maximum. In [40], it has been shown that communities detected by modularity maximization have a resolution limit. These serious drawbacks of modularity-guided algorithms have boosted the research for alternative approaches. Some interesting emerging approaches are label propagation approaches [71] and seed-centric ones [34].

3.1.3 Propagation-based approaches

Even the top fast algorithm, the *louvain* approach, has a computation complexity that becomes costly for very large-scale networks that can be composed of millions of nodes as it is frequently the case when considering online social networks today. In addition, studied complex networks are very dynamic. A low complexity incremental approaches for community detection are then needed. Label propagation approaches constitute a first step in that direction [71,89]. The underlaying idea is simple: each node $v \in V$ in the network is assigned a specific label l_v. All nodes update in a synchronous way their labels by selecting the most frequent label in the direct neighborhood. In a formal way, we have:

$$l_v = \arg \max_l |\Gamma^l(v)|$$

where $\Gamma^l(v) \subseteq \Gamma(v)$ is the set of neighbors of v that have the label l. Ties situations are broken randomly. The algorithm iterates until reaching a stable state where no more nodes change their labels. Nodes having the same label are returned as a detected community. The complexity of each iteration is $\mathcal{O}(m)$. Hence, the overall computation complexity is $\mathcal{O}(km)$ where k is the number of iterations before convergence. Study reported in [45] shows that the number of iterations grows

in a logarithmic way with the growth of n; the size of the target network. In addition to its low computation complexity, the label propagation algorithm can readily be distributed allowing hence handling very large-scale networks [62,78, 92]. While the algorithm is very fast, it suffers from two serious drawbacks:

- First, there is no formal guarantee of the convergence to a stable state.
- Lastly, it lacks for robustness, since different runs produce different partitions due to random tie breaking.

Different approaches have been proposed in the literature to cope with these two problems. Asynchronous, and semi-synchronous label updating have been proposed to hinder the problem of oscillation and improve convergence conditions [14,71]. However, these approaches harden the parallelization of the algorithm by creating dependencies among nodes and they increase the randomness in the algorithm making the robustness even worse. Different other approaches have been developed to handle the problem of label propagation robustness. These include *balanced label propagation* [81], *label hop attenuation* [44] and *propagation preference*-based approaches [49]. Another interesting way to handle the instability of label propagation approaches consists simply on executing the algorithm k times and apply an ensemble clustering approach on the obtained partitions [33,41,63,74].

3.1.4 Seed-centric approaches

The basic idea underlaying seed-centric approaches is to identify some particular nodes in the target network, called *seed nodes*, around which local communities can be computed [32,65,76]. Algorithm 1 presents the general outlines of a typical seed-centric community detection algorithm. We recognize three principal steps:

1. Seed computation.
2. Seed local community computation.
3. Community computation out from the set of local communities computed in the previous step.

Algorithm 1 General seed-centric community detection algorithm

Require: $G = <V, E>$ a connected graph,
1: $\mathcal{C} \leftarrow \emptyset$
2: $S \leftarrow$ **compute_seeds(G)**
3: **for** $s \in S$ **do**
4:    $C_s \leftarrow$ **compute_local_com(s,G)**
5:    $\mathcal{C} \leftarrow \mathcal{C} + C_s$
6: **end for**
7: **return** **compute_community($\mathcal{C}$)**

Leader-driven algorithms constitute a special case of seed-centric approaches. Nodes of a network are *classified* into two (eventually overlapping) categories: leaders and followers. Leaders represent communities. An assignment step is applied to assign *followers* nodes to most relevant communities. Different algorithms apply different node classification approaches and different node assignment strategies. Three different LdCD algorithms have been proposed almost simultaneously in three different works [32,36]. Next, we present briefly the first two cited algorithms.

In [36] authors propose an approach directly inspired from the *K-means* clustering algorithm [27]. The algorithm requires as input the number k of communities to identify. This is clearly a major disadvantage of the approach that authors of the approach admit. k nodes are selected randomly. Unselected nodes are labeled as followers. Leaders and followers form hence exclusive sets. Each leader node represents a community. Each follower nodes is assigned to the most nearby leader node. Different levels of neighborhood are allowed. If no nearby leader is found the follower node is labeled as *outlier*. When all flowers nodes are handled. The algorithm computes a new set of k leaders. For each community, the most *central* node is selected as a leader. The process is iterated with the new set of k leaders until stabilization of the computed communities. The convergence speed depends on the quality of initially selected k leaders. Different heuristics are proposed to improve the selection of the initial set of leaders. The best approach according to experimentation is to select the top k nodes that have the top degree centrality and that share little common neighbors.

The algorithm proposed in [76] is much similar to our approach. It starts by computing the *closeness* centrality of all nodes. The closeness centrality of a node v is given by the inverse of the average distance to all other nodes in the network. Leaders will be any node whose closeness centrality is less than at least one of its neighbors. This heuristics results in a huge set of leaders. The list of leaders is sorted in decreasing order of closeness centrality. The list is then parsed assigning to each leader direct followers that are not already assigned to another leader. At the end, leaders that are not followed by any node are assigned to the community to which belong the majority of its direct neighbors.

3.2 Community evaluation approaches

The problem of performances evaluation of community detection algorithms still to be an open problem in spite of the huge amount of work in this area. Existing approaches can be divided into three main types:

1. Evaluation on networks for which a ground-truth decomposition into communities is known.

2. Evaluation in function of the topological features of computed communities.
3. Task-driven evaluation.

Next, we detail these different approaches.

3.2.1 Ground-truth comparison approaches

Networks with ground-truth partitions can be obtained by one of the following ways:

- *Annotation by experts*: For some networks representing real systems, experts in the system field have been able to define the community structure. Examples of such networks are given in Sect. 5.1. In general, these networks are rather very small (allowing hence to be handled by experts) and the defined community structure is usually given by a partition of the studied graph with no overlapping among defined communities.

- *Network generators use*: The idea here is to generate artificial networks with predefined community structure. Some early work in this area is the Girvan–Newman benchmark graph [23]. A more sophisticated generator is proposed in [42] where the user can control different parameters of the network including the size, the density, the degree distribution law, the clustering coefficient, the distribution of communities size as well as the separability of the obtained communities. While the approach is interesting, generated networks are not guaranteed to be similar enough to real complex networks observed in real-world applications.

- *Implicit community definition* : This approach is based on inferring the community structure in a graph applying simple rules taking usually the semantic of ties into account. For example in [90] authors define a community in the *Live journal* social network as groups of fans of a given artist. Communities in a co-authorship of scientific publications are taken to be authors participating in a same venue! The relevance of proposed rules seems to be questionable.

When a ground-truth community structure is available, classical external clustering evaluation indices can be used to evaluate and compare community detection algorithms. Different clustering comparison or similarities functions have been proposed in the literature [2]. In this work, we apply two widely used indices: the Adjusted Rand Index (ARI) [30] and the Normalized Mutual Information (NMI) [79].

The ARI index is based on counting the number of pairs of elements that are clustered in the same clusters in both compared partitions. Let $P_i = \{P_i^1, \ldots, P_i^l\}$, $P_j = \{P_j^1, \ldots, P_j^k\}$ be two partitions of a set of nodes V. The set of all (unordered) pairs of nodes of V can be partitioned into the following four disjoint sets:

- $S_{11} = \{$pairs that are in the same cluster under P_i and $P_j\}$
- $S_{00} = \{$pairs that are in different clusters under P_i and $P_j\}$
- $S_{10} = \{$pairs that are in the same cluster under P_i but in different ones under $P_j\}$
- $S_{01} = \{$pairs that are in different clusters under P_i but in the same under $P_j\}$

Let $n_{ab} = |S_{ab}|$, $a, b \in \{0, 1\}$, be the respective sizes of the above defined sets. The rand index initially defined in [72] is simply given by:

$$\mathcal{R}(P_i, P_j) = \frac{2 \times (n_{11} + n_{00})}{n \times (n - 1)}$$

In [30], authors show that the expected value of the Rand Index of two random partitions does not take a constant value (e.g. zero). They proposed an adjusted version which assumes a generalized hypergeometric distribution as null hypothesis: the two clusterings are drawn randomly with a fixed number of clusters and a fixed number of elements in each cluster (the number of clusters in the two clusterings need not be the same). Then the ARI is the normalized difference of the Rand Index and its expected value under the null hypothesis. It is defined as follows:

$$\text{ARI}(P_i, P_j) = \frac{\sum_{x=1}^{l} \sum_{y=1}^{k} \binom{|P_i^x \cap P_j^y|}{2} - t_3}{\frac{1}{2}(t_1 + t_2) - t_3} \qquad (2)$$

where:

$$t_1 = \sum_{x=1}^{l} \binom{|P_i^x|}{2}, \quad t_2 = \sum_{y=1}^{k} \binom{|P_j^y|}{2}, \quad t_3 = \frac{2t_1 t_2}{n(n-1)}$$

This index has expected value zero for independent clusterings and maximum value 1 for identical clusterings.

Another family of partitions comparisons functions is the one based on the notion of mutual information. A partition P is assimilated to a random variable. We seek to quantify how much we reduce the uncertainty of the clustering of randomly picked element from V in a partition P_j if we know P_i. The Shannon's entropy of a partition P_i is given by:

$$H(P_i) = -\sum_{x=1}^{l} \frac{|P_i^x|}{n} \log_2 \left(\frac{|P_i^x|}{n} \right)$$

Notice that $\frac{|P_i^x|}{n}$ is the probability that a randomly picked element from V be clustered in P_i^x. The mutual information between two random variables X, Y is given by the general formula:

$$\text{MI}(X, Y) = H(X) + H(Y) - H(X, Y) \qquad (3)$$

This can then be applied to measure the mutual information between two partitions P_i, P_j. The mutual information

defines a metric on the space of all clusterings and is bounded by the entropies of involved partitions. In [79], authors propose a normalized version given by:

$$\text{NMI}(X, Y) = \frac{\text{MI}(X, Y)}{\sqrt{H(X)H(Y)}} \qquad (4)$$

Another normalized version is also proposed in [22]. Other similar information-based indices are also proposed [52,60].

3.2.2 Topological measures for community evaluation

Two types of topological measures can be used to evaluate the *quality* of a computed community structure:

- Global measures that evaluate the quality of the computed partition as a whole. The modularity Q defined in [57] (see formula 1) is the most applied measure. Other modularity measures have also been proposed [51,54]. However, the different modularity limitations discussed earlier (see Sect. 3.1.2) hinder the utility of using it as an evaluation metric.
- Local topological measures. A number of local topological measures have been proposed to evaluate the quality of a given community. Most are used in the context of identifying ego-centered communities [4,11]. In [90], authors present an interesting survey on these measures. Let $f(c)$ be a community evaluation measure. The quality of a partition is then simply given by:

$$Q(\mathcal{C}) = \frac{\sum_i f(S_i)}{|\mathcal{C}|} \qquad (5)$$

3.2.3 Task-driven evaluation

The principle of task-driven evaluation is the following: Let T be a task where community detection can be applied. Let $per(T, Algo_{com}^x)$ be a performance measure for T execution applying the community detection algorithm $Algo_{com}^x$. We can then compare performances of different community detection algorithms by comparing induced $per(T, Algo_{com}^x)$ values. In [66], authors propose to use the recommendation task for evaluating purposes. In this work, we propose using the data clustering as an evaluation task.

4 The LICOD approach

4.1 Informal presentation

The basic idea underlaying the proposed algorithm is that a community is composed of two types of nodes: *Leaders* and

Followers. Algorithm 2 sketches the general outlines of the proposed approach. The algorithm functions as follows:

1. First, it searches for nodes in the network that are likely to be leaders in a community. Different node ranking metrics can be used to estimate the role of a node. These include the classical centrality metrics. Let $\mathcal{L}$ be the set of identified leaders. In Algorithm 2, this step is achieved by the function *isLeader*() (line 3).

2. The list $\mathcal{L}$ is then reduced by grouping leaders that are estimated to be in the same community. This is the task of the function *computeCommunitiesLeader*(), line 7 in Algorithm 2. Let $\mathcal{C}$ be the set of identified communities.

3. Each node in the network (a leader or a follower) computes its membership degree to each community in $\mathcal{C}$. A ranked list of communities can then be obtained, for each node, where communities with highest membership degree are ranked first (lines 9–13 in Algorithm 2).

4. Next, each node will adjust its community membership preference list by merging this with preference lists of its direct neighbors in the network. Different strategies borrowed form the social choice theory can applied here to merge the different preference lists. This step is iterated until stabilization of obtained ranked lists at each node. The convergence towards a stable sate is function of the applied voting scheme.

5. Lastly, each node will be assigned to top-ranked communities in its final obtained membership preference list.

The local voting process intends to ensure local homogeneity in nodes membership to different communities. Notice that the algorithm is designed as a general framework that allows testing different working hypothesis: How to select leader? How to compute community membership? And how to merge preferences of linked nodes? Next we describe possible choices for implementing each step.

4.2 Implementation issues

The LICOD algorithm is implemented using the *igraph* graph analysis toolkit [15]. We give next some details about the implementation of each of the main steps of the proposed algorithm.

4.2.1 Function *isLeader*()

One simple idea to distinguish leaders from follower nodes is to compare nodes centralities. Actually, leader nodes are expected to have higher centrality (whatever the centrality is) than ordinary nodes. Different centrality measures can be used. In our experiments, we have tested the following two basic centralities:

Algorithm 2 LICOD algorithm

Require: $G = <V, E>$ a connected graph
1: $\mathcal{L} \leftarrow \emptyset$ {set of leaders}
2: **for** $v \in V$ **do**
3:   **if** $isLeader(v)$ **then**
4:     $\mathcal{L} \leftarrow \mathcal{L} \cup \{v\}$
5:   **end if**
6: **end for**
7: $\mathcal{C} \leftarrow computeComumunitiesLeader(\mathcal{L})$
8: **for** $v \in V$ **do**
9:   **for** $c \in \mathcal{C}$ **do**
10:     $M[v, c] \leftarrow membership(v, c)$ {see equation 6}
11:   **end for**
12:   $P[v] = \textbf{sortAndRank}(M[v])$
13: **end for**
14: **repeat**
15:   **for** $v \in V$ **do**
16:     $P^*[v] \leftarrow \textbf{rankAggregate}_{x \in \{v\} \cap \Gamma_G(v)} P[x]$
17:     $P[v] \leftarrow P^*[v]$
18:   **end for**
19: **until** Stabilization of $P^*[v] \forall v$
20: **for** $v \in V$ **do**
21:   /* *assigning v to communities* */
22:   **for** $c \in P[v]$ **do**
23:     **if** $|M[v, c] - M[v, P[0]]| \leq \epsilon$ **then**
24:       $COM(c) \leftarrow COM(c) \cup \{v\}$
25:     **end if**
26:   **end for**
27: **end for**
28: **return** $\mathcal{C}$

Degree centrality (denoted dc): This is given by the proportion of nodes directly connected to the target node. Formally, the degree centrality of a node v is given by: $dc(v) = \frac{d_G(v)}{n_G - 1}$. The computation complexity is $\mathcal{O}(n_G)$.
Betweenness centrality $BC(v)$: The is given by the fraction of all-pairs shortest paths that pass through the target node. Formally, the betweenness centrality of a node v is given by $BC(v) = \sum_{s,t \in V} \frac{\sigma(s,t|v)}{\sigma(s,t)}$ where $\sigma(s,t)$ is the number of shortest paths linking s to t, and $\sigma(s,t|v)$ is the number of paths passing through node v other than s and t. The best known algorithm for computing this centrality has a computation complexity $\mathcal{O}(n_G . m_G + (n_G)^2 \log(n_G))$ [9].

The first centrality is local-computed metric while the later captures global proprieties of the network. A node is identified as a leader if its centrality is greater or equal to $\sigma \in [0, 1]$ percent of its neighbors centralities. The rational behind introducing the σ parameter is to be able to recover leaders connected to other leaders. Notice that the number of leaders will depend on the value of the threshold σ. More σ is high fewer are the leaders.

4.2.2 Function *computecommunitiesleaders*

Two leaders are grouped in the same community if the ratio of common neighbors to the total number of neighbors is above a given threshold $\delta \in [0, 1]$. The couple σ, δ determines in somehow, the number of communities detected by the algorithm.

4.2.3 Function memebership(v, c)

We propose to measure the membership degree of a node v to a community c by the inverse of the minimal shortest path that links v to one of the leaders of c.

$$membership(v, c) = \frac{1}{(min_{x \in COM(c)} SPath(v, x)) + 1}$$
(6)

It is easy to see that the previous function takes values in the range $\left[\frac{1}{Diameter(G)}, 1 \right]$. The diameter of a graph is the maximum of the shortest path between any pair of nodes. Notice also that for a community c, the membership of all its leaders is equal to 1.

4.2.4 Rank aggregation approaches

Let S be a set of elements to be ranked by a set of m rankers. We denote by S^{r_i} the ranking provided by ranker r_i. $\{S^{r_1}, \ldots, S^{r_m}\}$ is a set of all ranks provided by the m rankers. Notice that each list S^{r_i} represents a permutation of elements of S. An optimal ensemble ranking approach seeks for a permutation σ that has the minimum number of pairwise disagreements with all input ranks S^{r_i} [3,12,19,80]. The *Kendall Tau* distance computes the pairwise disagreement between two ranks defined over the same set of elements S. This is formally defined as follows:

$$\mathcal{K}(\pi, \sigma) = \sum_{x, y \in S} d_{\pi, \sigma}(x, y)$$
(7)

where:

$$d_{\pi, \sigma}(x, y) = \begin{cases} 0 & \text{if } \pi \text{ and } \sigma \text{ rank } x \text{ and } y \text{ in the same order} \\ 1 & \text{otherwise} \end{cases}$$

This problem has been extensively studied in the context of social choice algorithms [3]. Early work tackling this problem goes back the French revolution epoch with the work of Borda [8] and Marquis de Condorcet [16] striving to define a fair election rule. Rank aggregation approaches can be classified into two classes: position-based approaches and order-based ones [12].

One well-known position-based method is Borda's method [8]: A Borda score is computed for each element in the lists. For a set of complete ranked lists $L = [L_1, L_2, L_3, \ldots, L_k]$, the Borda's score of an element i and a list L_k is given by: $B_{L_k}(i) = \{count(j)|L_k(j) < L_k(i) \& j \in L_k\}$. The total Borda's score for an element is then: $B(i) = \sum_{t=1}^{k} B_{L_t}(i)$.

Elements are sorted in function of their total Borda score with random selection in case of ties.

Kemeny approaches are well-known order-based approaches. A Kemeny optimal aggregation [35] is an aggregation that has the minimum number of <div> pairwise disagreement as computed by the *Kendall tau* distance [43]. Computing an optimal Kemeny aggregation is NP-hard starting from a list of four candidates. Different approximate Kemeny aggregation approaches have been proposed in the literature. The basic idea of all proposed approximate Kemeny aggregation is to sort the candidate list, using standard sorting algorithms, but using a non-transitive comparison relationship between candidates. This relation is the following: s_i is preferred to s_j, noted $s_i \succ s_j$, if the majority of rankers ranks s_i before s_j. Since the $\succ$ relation is not transitive, different sorting algorithms will provide different rank aggregations with different proprieties. In [19] authors propose a *local Kemeny* aggregation applying a bubble sort algorithm. In [53] authors propose an *approximate Kemeny* aggregation applying quick sort algorithm .

4.2.5 Community assignment

A node v is assigned to top-ranked communities in the final community preference list P_v^*. As showed in lines 22–26 of Algorithm 2, a node is assigned simultaneously to communities for which its membership is ϵ-far from the membership degree to the top-ranked community. The ϵ threshold controls the degree of desired overlapping in identified communities. However, putting ϵ to 0 may still results in having overlapping communities since for a given node different communities may have the same membership degree.

5 Experimentation

5.1 Evaluation on benchmark networks

In a first experiment, we evaluate the proposed approach on a set of four widely used benchmark networks for which a ground-truth decomposition into communities is known. These networks are the following:

Zachary's karate club This network is a social network of friendships between 34 members of a karate club at a US university in 1970 [91]. Following a dispute, the network was divided into two groups between the club's administrator and the club's instructor. The dispute ended in the instructor creating his own club and taking about half of the initial club with him. The network can hence be divided into two main communities.

Dolphins social network This network is an undirected social network resulting from observations of a community of 62 dolphins over a period of 7 years [50]. Nodes represent dolphins and edges represent frequent associations between dolphin pairs occurring more often than expected by chance. Analysis of the data revealed two main groups.

American college football dataset This dataset contains the network of American football games [23]. The 115 nodes represent teams and the edges represent games between 2 teams. The teams are divided into 12 groups containing around 8–12 teams each and games are more frequent between members of the same group. Also teams that are geographically close but belong to different groups are more likely to play one another than teams separated by a large distance. Therefore, in this dataset groups can be considered as known communities.

American political books This is a political books co-purchasing network. Nodes represent books about US politics sold by the online bookseller *Amazon.com*. Edges represent frequent co-purchasing of books by the same buyers, as indicated by the "customers who bought this book also

Table 1 Basic topological characteristics of selected benchmark networks

Dataset	# Nodes	# Edges	# Real communities
Zachary	34	78	2
Football	115	616	11
US Politics	100	411	2
Dolphin	62	159	2

bought these other books" feature on Amazon. Books are classified into three disjoint classes: liberal, neutral or conservative. The classification was made separately by Mark Newman based on a reading of the descriptions and reviews of the books posted on Amazon.

Figure 1 shows the structure of the selected networks with real communities indicated by the color code. Table 1 gives the basic characteristics of these networks.

For each network we have applied the proposed algorithm by changing the configuration parameters as follows:

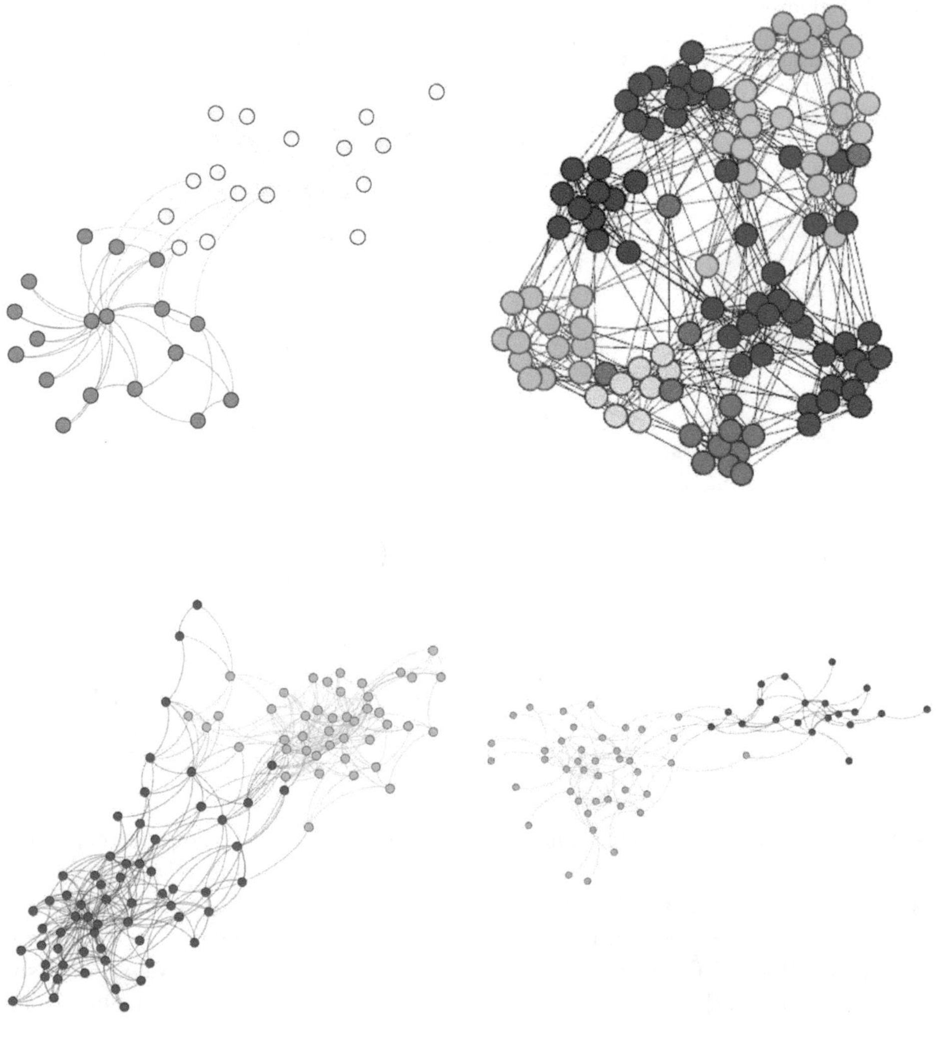

Fig. 1 Real community structure of the four selected benchmark networks. Zachary Karate Club Network [91], Collegae football network [23], US Politics books network [38], Dolphins social network [50]

Fig. 2 Performance of applying LICOD to Zachary Karate club network in function of σ in terms of NMI, ARI and the modularity Q

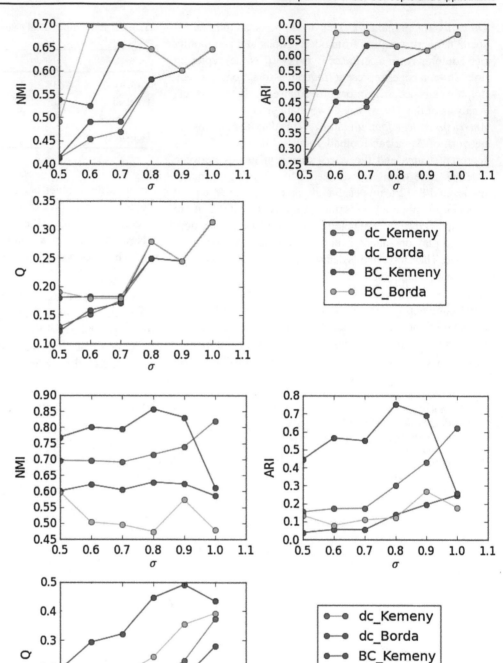

Fig. 3 Performance of applying LICOD to American college football network in function of σ in terms of NMI, ARI and the modularity Q

- Centrality metrics = [Degree centrality (dc), Betweenness centrality (BC)]
- Voting method = [Borda, Local Kemeny]
- $\sigma \in [0.5, 0.6, 0.7, 0.8, 0.9, 1.0]$
- $\delta \in [0.5, 0.6, 0.7, 0.8, 0.9, 1.0]$
- $\epsilon \in [0.0, 0.1, 0.2]$

For each configuration, we compute the NMI, ARI and the modularity Q. Figures 2, 3, 4 and 5 show the variations of these metrics, for each dataset, with the variation of σ. We have omitted to show the results with different values of δ since on these datasets the δ value has showed negligible impact on obtained results. The same

Fig. 4 Performance of applying LICOD to American political books networks in function of σ in terms of NMI, ARI and the modularity Q

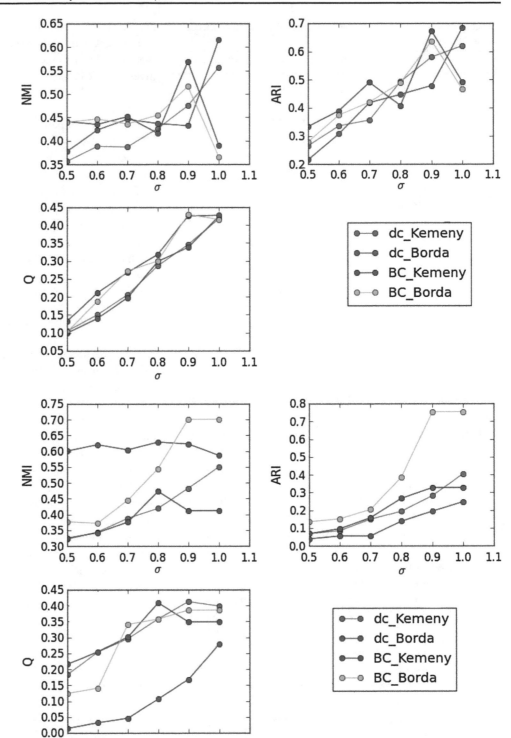

Fig. 5 Performance of applying LICOD to dolphins social network in function of σ in terms of NMI, ARI and the modularity Q

effect was observed for the ϵ parameter. On each figure, we plot four graphics showing the variation of NMI, ARI and Q, for each of the possible four configurations depending on the choice of the used centrality and the voting method.

These results show that the use of the betweenness centrality accelerate slightly the convergence for the right value to obtain. Local Kemeny voting methods out performs that Borda in the case of the football network only and gives comparable results for the US Politics network. Borda gives

Table 2 Comparison of performances of different community detection algorithms

Dataset	Algorithm	NMI	ARI	Q	# Communities
Zachary	Newman	0.57	0.46	0.40	5
	Louvain	0.58	0.46	0.41	4
	Walktrap	0.50	0.33	0.35	5
	LICOD	**0.60**	**0.62**	0.24	3
Football	Newman	0.87	0.77	0.59	10
	Louvain	0.89	0.80	0.60	10
	Walktrap	0.88	0.81	0.60	10
	LICOD	0.83	0.69	0.49	16
US Politics	Newman	0.55	0.68	0.51	5
	Louvain	0.57	0.55	0.52	4
	Walktrap	0.53	0.65	0.50	4
	LICOD	**0.68**	0.67	0.42	6
Dolphins	Newman	0.55	0.39	0.51	5
	Louvain	0.51	0.32	0.51	5
	Walktrap	0.53	0.41	0.48	4
	LICOD	0.41	0.32	0.35	**2**

Bold values indicate the best score by LICOD

good results only for the Dolphins network using also the betweenness centrality.

Increasing ϵ results in diminishing the NMI and ARI. This can be explained by the fact that high value of ϵ increases the overlapping degree of obtained communities while real communities we have here are all disjoint.

The best results are obtained for σ around 0.8, 0.9. This argues for the validity the idea of introducing the σ threshold and not to consider extreme cases where a node is qualified as a leader if it has the highest centrality in its direct neighborhood. We notice that the dynamic curves differ from one network to another, and this is closely related to the specificities of each network. The choice of a configuration of the proposed algorithm in function of the properties of the target network constitutes one interesting topic to cope with.

We also compared the results of our algorithm with results obtained by well-known algorithms: The Newman–Girvan algorithm [58], the WalkTrap algorithm [70] and the *Louvain*

algorithm [7]. The configuration adopted for LICOD is the following: Centrality metric is betweenness centrality, Voting method is local Kemeny, $\sigma = \delta = 0.9$, and $\epsilon = 0$. Table 2 gives obtained results on the four datasets.

These results show that LICOD performs better than the other algorithms for both Zachary and US Politics networks. It also gives competitive results in the other two networks. This could be explained by the absence of leaders in these two networks, which makes the communities detection task more difficult.

These results show also that the modularity metric does not correspond to the best decomposition into communities as measured by both NMI and ARI. For instance, the *Louvain* method obtains always the best modularity (even better than the modularity of the ground-truth decomposition), however, it is ranked not first according to NMI . Best results are obtained by our approach for high values of σ.

5.2 Data clustering-driven evaluation

We propose here to use the task of data clustering to apply a task-driven evaluation of community detection algorithms. The basic idea is to transform a data clustering problem into a community detection one. Some earlier work has already applied community detection algorithms to the clustering task [17]. Figure 6 illustrates the overall approach. First, a relative neighborhood graph (RNG), as defined in [84], is constructed over the set of items to cluster. The choice of RNG graph is motivated by the topological characteristics of these graphs that are connexe and sparse. To build an RNG graph, we first compute a similarity matrix between couple of items in the dataset (Fig. 7). This results in a symmetric square matrix of size $n \times n$ where n is the number of items in the dataset. A RNG graph is defined by the following simple construction rule: two points x_i and x_j are connected by an edge if they satisfy the following property:

$$d(x_i, x_j) \leq \max_l \{d(x_i, x_l), d(x_j, x_l)\}, \quad \forall l \neq i, j \quad (8)$$

where $d(x_i, x_j)$ is the distance function. A community detection algorithm is applied on the obtained graph to cluster the

Fig. 6 Applying community detection to data clustering

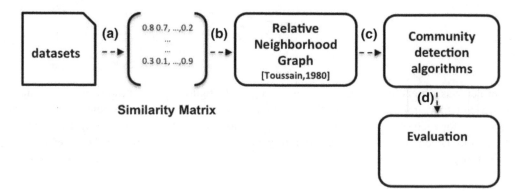

Fig. 7 Example of the generation of a RNG from a cloud of data: α and β are two relatifs neighbors because there is no other node in the intersection of the two circles centered, respectively, in α and β and with radius $d(\alpha, \beta)$

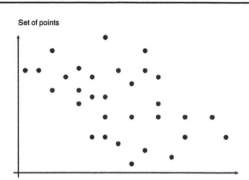

Set of points

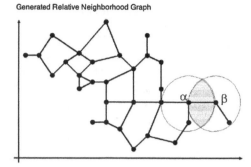

Generated Relative Neighborhood Graph

Table 3 Characteristics of used datasets

Dataset	Glass	Iris	Wine	Vehicle	Abalone
#Instances	214	150	178	846	772
#Attributes	10	4	13	18	8
#Classes	7	3	3	4	29

Table 4 Applied basic distance functions

Distance	Formula
Euclidean distance	$dist_{euc}(x, y) = \sqrt{\sum_{i=1}^{n} |x_i - y_i|^2}$
Cosine similarity	$dist_{cos}(x, y) = 1 - \frac{x.y}{|x||y|}$
Chebyshev distance	$d_{cheb}(x, y) = \max_i(x_i - y_i)$

Table 5 Topological characteristics of obtained RNG graphs

Dataset	Feature	Euclidean	Chebyshev	Cosine
Iris	#Edges	382	2,468	426
	Diameter	33	14	25
	Average degree	5.09	32.9	5.68
	Density	0.034	0.220	0.038
	Transitivity	0.055	0.340	0.011
Glass	#Edges	558	7,786	552
	Diameter	21	8	24
	Average degree	5.21	72.76	5.15
	Density	0.024	0.341	0.024
	Transitivity	0.0139	0.252	0.011
Wine	#Edges	380	514	438
	Diameter	102	84	59
	Average degree	4.26	5.77	4.92
	Density	0.024	0.032	0.027
	Transitivity	0	0.178	0
Vehicle	#Edges	2,598	4,072	2,764
	Diameter	63	54	45
	Average degree	6.14	9.62	6.53
	Density	0.007	0.011	0.007
	Transitivity	0.002	0.091	0
Abalone	#Edges	2,542	89,338	2,158
	Diameter	38	22	50
	Average degree	6.58	231.44	5.59
	Density	0.008	0.30	0.007
	Transitivity	0	0.49	0

given examples. Clustering evaluation criteria a-can then be used to compare different algorithms.

We have tested our approach on five classical datasets publicly available from UCI website.[1] The selected datasets are briefly described in Table 3.

We have constructed the different RNG graphs on these datasets using the following classical distance cited in Table 4.

Table 5 shows basic topological characteristics of obtained graphs. We can see that these graphs have some characteristics of real networks such as the small diameter and low density. However, the Chebyshev distance induces dense graphs though the obtained clustering coefficient is also high. We have also obtained graphs with a relatively high transitivity.

Based on these results, we have applied the community detection algorithms on RNG graphs defined by the Cosine distance function. We apply on the above generated graphs four different community detection algorithms: Louvain [7], the Newman–Girvan algorithm, the Walktrap algorithm and LICOD. Results are evaluated in terms of *NMI*, and *ARI* computed in function of the real classes defined in each dataset. We compute also the modularity Q to show that it does not always reflect the true quality of the community. Results

given in the Table 6 show that LICOD is ranked first for the two datasets: wine and abalone. It gives competitive results for the other datasets.

6 Conclusion

In this work, we contribute to the state of the art on community detection in complex networks by:

- Providing a new efficient algorithm for computing (eventually overlapping) communities.

---

[1] http://archive.ics.uci.edu/ml/datasets.html.

Table 6 Performance of LICOD vs Louvain, Walktrap, Newman–Girvan algorithms

Dataset	Algorithm	NMI	ARI	Q	#Communities
Iris	Newman	0.66	0.44	0.72	9
	Louvain	0.59	0.40	0.72	8
	Walktrap	0.64	0.47	0.68	12
	LICOD	0.59	0.42	0.64	8
Glass	Newman	0.45	0.21	0.76	11
	Louvain	0.47	0.21	0.75	12
	Walktrap	0.49	0.15	0.73	22
	LICOD	0.46	0.17	0.70	18
Wine	Newman	0.32	0.14	0.79	11
	Louvain	0.31	0.13	0.79	12
	Walktrap	0.32	0.11	0.77	15
	LICOD	**0.34**	**0.21**	0.72	14
Vehicle	Newman	0.23	0.10	0.79	17
	Louvain	0.25	0.11	0.78	14
	Walktrap	0.23	0.06	0.75	32
	LICOD	0.21	0.05	0.65	41
Abalone	Newman	0.34	0.10	0.83	15
	Louvain	0.35	0.10	0.83	19
	Walktrap	0.33	0.08	0.82	21
	LICOD	**0.44**	0.08	0.70	68

- Proposing a new approach for qualitative community evaluation using classical data clustering tasks.

Results obtained on both small benchmark social network and on clustering problems argue for the capacity of the approach to detect real communities. Future developments we are working include: testing the algorithm on large-scale networks, develop a full distributed self-stabilizing version exploiting the fact that major part of computations are made in a local manner and finally adapt the approach for K-partite and for multiplex networks [28].

Open Access This article is distributed under the terms of the Creative Commons Attribution License which permits any use, distribution, and reproduction in any medium, provided the original author(s) and the source are credited.

References

1. Adamcsek, B., Palla, G., Farkas, I.J., Derényi, I., Vicsek, T.: Cfinder: locating cliques and overlapping modules in biological networks. Bioinformatics **22**(8), 1021–1023 (2006)
2. Aggarwal, C.C., Reddy, C.K. (eds.) Data clustering: algorithms and applications. CRC Press, Boca Raton (2014)
3. Arrow, K.: Social choice and individual values, 2nd edn. Cowles Foundation, New Haven (1963)
4. Bagrow, J.P.: Evaluating local community methods in networks. J. Stat. Mech. **2008**(5), P05001 (2008)

5. Bagrow, J.P., Bollt, E.M.: A local method for detecting communities. Phys. Rev. E **72**, 046108 (2005)
6. Benchettara, N., Kanawati, R., Rouveirol, C.: Supervised machine learning applied to link prediction in bipartite social networks. In: International Conference on Advances in Social Network Analysis and Mining, ASONAM, pp. 326–330 (2010)
7. Blondel, V.D., Guillaume, J.-L., Lefebvre, E.: Fast unfolding of communities in large networks. J. Stat. Mech. Theory Exp. **2008**, P10008 (2008)
8. Borda, J.C.: Mémoire sur les élections au scrutin. Comptes rendus de l'Académie des sciences, traduit par Alfred de Grazia comme Mathematical Derivation of a election system, Isis, vol. 44, pp. 42–51 (1781)
9. Brandes, U.: A faster algorithm for betweenness centrality. J. Math. Sociol. **25**(2), 163–177 (2001)
10. Brandes, U., Delling, D., Gaertler, M., Görke, R., Hoefer, M., Nikoloski, Z., Wagner, D.: On modularity clustering. IEEE Trans. Knowl. Data Eng. **20**(2), 172–188 (2008)
11. Chen, J., Zaïane, O.R., Goebel, R.: ASONAM. In: Memon, N., Alhajj, R. (eds.) Local community identification in social networks, pp. 237–242. IEEE Computer Society, Athens (2009)
12. Chevaleyre, Y., Endriss, U., Lang, J., Maudet, N.: A short introduction to computational social choice. SOFSEM 2007: Theory and Practice of Computer Science, pp. 51–69 (2007)
13. Clauset, A.: Finding local community structure in networks. Phys. Rev. E. **72**, 026132 (2005)
14. Cordasco, G., Gargano, L.: Label propagation algorithm: a semi-synchronous approach. IJSNM **1**(1), 3–26 (2012)
15. Csardi, G., Nepusz, T.: The igraph software package for complex network research. Int. J. Complex Syst. 1695 (2006)
16. de Condorcet, M.: Essai sur l'application de l'analyse à la probabilité des décisions rendues à la pluralité des voix (1785)
17. de Oliveira, T.B.S., Zhao, L., Faceli, K., de Carvalho, A.C.P.L.F.: Data clustering based on complex network community detection. In: IEEE Congress on Evolutionary Computation, 2008 (CEC 2008), 1-6 June 2008, Hong Kong, pp. 2121–2126 (2008)
18. Du, N., Wang, B., Wu, B., Wang, Y.: Overlapping community detection in bipartite networks. In: IEEE WIC/ACM International Conference on Web Intelligence and Intelligent Agent Technology, 2008 (WI-IAT '08), vol 1, 9-12 Dec 2008, pp. 176–179 (2008)
19. Dwork, C., Kumar, R., Naor, M., Sivakumar, D.: Rank aggregation methods for the Web. In: Proceedings of the 10th international conference on World Wide Web (WWW '01). ACM, New York, NY, USA, pp. 613–622 (2001)
20. Flake, G.W., Lawrence, S., Giles, C.L., Coetzee, F.: Self-organization and identification of web communities. IEEE Comput. **35**(3), 66–71 (2002)
21. Fortunato, S.: Community detection in graphs. Phys. Rep. **486**(3–5), 75–174 (2010)
22. Fred, A.L.N., Jain, A.K.: Robust data clustering. In: CVPR. Proceedings of IEEE Computer Society(2), pp. 128–136 (2003)
23. Girvan, M., Newman, M.E.J.: Community structure in social and biological networks. PNAS **99**(12), 7821–7826 (2002)
24. Good, B.H., de Montjoye, Y.A., Clauset, A.: The performance of modularity maximization in practical contexts. Phys. Rev. **E(81)**, 046106 (2010)
25. Grabowski, S., Bieniecki, W.: Tight and simple web graph compression. CoRR, abs/1006.0 (2010)
26. Guimerà, R., Sales-Pardo, M., Amaral, L.A.N.: A network-based method for target selection in metabolic networks. Bioinformatics **23**(13), 1616–1622 (2007)
27. Hartigan, J.A., Wong, M.A.: Appl. Stat. **28**, 100–108 (1979)
28. Hmimida, M., Kanawati, R.: A seed-centric algorithm for community detection in multiplex networks. In: First European Conference on Social Network Analysis, Barcelona (2014)

29. Huang, Q., White, T., Jia, G., Musolesi, M., Turan, N., Tang, K., He, S., Heath, J.K., Yao, X.: PPSN (2). In: Coello, C.A.C., Cutello, V., Deb, K., Forrest, S., Nicosia, G., Pavone, M. (eds.) Community detection using cooperative co-evolutionary differential evolution. Lecture Notes in Computer Science, pp. 235–244. Springer, Berlin (2012)

30. Hubert, L., Arabie, P.: Comparing partitions. J. Classif. **2**(1), 192–218 (1985)

31. Jin, D., He, D., Liu, D., Baquero, C.: Genetic algorithm with local search for community mining in complex networks. In: ICTAI (1), pp. 105–112. IEEE Computer Society (2010)

32. Kanawati, R.: LICOD: Leaders identification for community detection in complex networks. In: SocialCom/PASSAT, pp. 577–582 (2011)

33. Kanawati, R.: On applying ensemble ranking to local community identication in complex networks. In: Perner, P. (ed.) Proceedings of the 10th International Conference on Machine Learning and Data Mining (MLDM). Springer, New York (2014)

34. Kanawati, R.. Seed-centric approaches for community detection in complex networks. In: Meiselwitz, G., (ed.) 6th International Conference on Social Computing and Social Media, volume LNCS 8531, pp. 197–208, Crete, Greece. Springer, New York (2014)

35. Kemeny, J.G.: Mathematics without numbers. Daedalus **88**, 571–591 (1959)

36. Khorasgani, R.R., Chen, J., Zaiane, O.R.: Top leaders community detection approach in information networks. In: 4th SNA-KDD Workshop on Social Network Mining and Analysis, Washington D.C. (2010)

37. Kleinberg, J.M.: NIPS. In: Dietterich, T.G., Becker, S., Ghahramani, Z. (eds.) Small-world phenomena and the dynamics of information, pp. 431–438. MIT Press, Cambridge (2001)

38. Krebs, V. Political books network.

39. Lambiotte, R.. Multi-scale modularity in complex networks. In: WiOpt, pp. 546–553. IEEE (2010)

40. Lancichinetti, A., Fortunato, S.: Limits of modularity maximization in community detection. Phys. Rev. E. **84**, 066122 (2011)

41. Lancichinetti, A., Fortunato, S.: Consensus clustering in complex networks. Sci. Rep. **2** (2012)

42. Lancichinetti, A., Radicchi, F.: Benchmark graphs for testing community detection algorithms. Phys. Rev. E **4**, 046110 (2008)

43. Lapata, M.: Automatic evaluation of information ordering: Kendall's Tau. Comput. Linguist. **32**(4), 471–484 (2006)

44. Leung, I.X., Hui, P., Lio, P., Crowcroft, J.: Towards real-time community detection in large networks. Phys. Rev. E. **79**(6), 066107 (2009a)

45. Leung, I.X.Y., Hui, P., Lio, P., Crowcroft, J.: Towards real-time community detection in large networks. Phys. Rev. E **79**(6), 1–10 (2009b)

46. Li, L., Alderson, D., Tanaka, R., Doyle, J. C., Willinger, W.: Towards a theory of scale-free graphs: definition, properties, and implications. Internet Math. **2**(4):431–523 (2005)

47. Li, S., Chen, Y., Du, H., Feldman, M.W.: A genetic algorithm with local search strategy for improved detection of community structure. Complexity **15**(4), 53–60 (2010)

48. Liu, X., Murata, T.: Community detection in large-scale bipartite networks. In: Web intelligence, pp. 50–57. IEEE (2009)

49. Lou, H., Li, S., Zhao, Y.: Detecting community structure using label propagation with weighted coherent neighborhood propinquity. Phys. A Stat. Mech. Appl. **392**(14), 3095–3105 (2013)

50. Lusseau, D., Schneider, K., Boisseau, O.J., Haase, P., Slooten, E., Dawson, S.M.: The bottlenose dolphin community of doubtful sound features a large proportion of long-lasting associations. Behav. Ecol. Sociobiol. **54**, 396–405 (2003)

51. Mancoridis, S., Mitchell, B.S., Rorres, C., Chen, Y.-F., Gansner, E.R.: Using automatic clustering to produce high-level system organizations of source code. In: IWPC, pp. 45–53 (1998)

52. Meila, M.: COLT. In: Schölkopf, B., Warmuth, M.K. (eds.) Comparing clusterings by the variation of information. Lecture Notes in Computer Science, pp. 173–187. Springer, New York (2003)

53. Melville, P., Subbian, K., Meliksetian, E., Perlich, C.: A predictive perspective on measures of influence in networks. In: 5th Annual Machine Learning Symposium, pp. 1–5 (2010)

54. Mirshahvalad, A., Lindholm, J., Derlen, M., Rosvall, M.: Significant communities in large sparse networks. PLoS ONE **7**(3): e33721 (2012).

55. Mucha, P.J., Richardson, T., Macon, K., Porter, M.A., Onnela, J.-P.: Community structure in time-dependent, multiscale, and multiplex networks. Science **328**(5980), 876–878 (2010)

56. Murata, T.: Detecting communities from tripartite networks. In: Rappa, M., Jones, P., Freire, J., Chakrabarti, S. (eds.) WWW, pp. 1159–1160. ACM (2010)

57. Newman, M.E.J.: Fast algorithm for detecting community structure in networks. Phys. Rev. E **69**(6), 066133 (2004)

58. Newman, M.J., Girvan, M.: Finding and evaluating community structure in networks. Phys. Rev. E **69**, 02613:1–022613:15 (2004)

59. Ng, A., Jordan, M., Weiss, Y.: On spectral clustering: analysis and an algorithm. In: Advances in neural information processing systems (NIPS), pp. 849–856, Vancouver, Canada (2001)

60. Nguyen, X.V., Epps, J., Bailey, J.: Information theoretic measures for clusterings comparison: is a correction for chance necessary? In: Danyluk, A.P., Bottou, L., Littman, M.L. (eds.) ICML, volume 382 of ACM International Conference Proceeding Series, p. 135. ACM (2009)

61. Orgaz, G.B., Menéndez, H.D., Camacho, D.: Adaptive k-means algorithm for overlapped graph clustering. Int. J. Neural Syst. **22**(5), 9 (2012)

62. Ovelgönne, M.: ASONAM. In: Rokne, J.G., Faloutsos, C. (eds.) Distributed community detection in web-scale networks, pp. 66–73. ACM, New York (2013)

63. Ovelgönne, M., Geyer-Schulz, A.: Cluster cores and modularity maximization. In: ICDM Workshops, pp. 1204–1213 (2010)

64. Palla, G., Derônyi, I., Farkas, I., Vicsek, T.: Uncovering the overlapping modular structure of protein interaction networks. FEBS J. **272**, 434 (2005)

65. Papadopoulos, S., Kompatsiaris, Y., Vakali, A.: A graph-based clustering scheme for identifying related tags in folksonomies. In: DaWak, pp. 65–76 (2010)

66. Papadopoulos, S., Kompatsiaris, Y., Vakali, A., Spyridonos, P.: Community detection in social media—performance and application considerations. Data Min. Knowl. Discov. **24**(3), 515–554 (2012)

67. Peng, C., Kolda, T. G., Pinar, A.: Accelerating community detection by using k-core subgraphs. CoRR, abs/1403.2226 (2014)

68. Pizzuti, C.: Boosting the detection of modular community structure with genetic algorithms and local search. In: Ossowski, S., Lecca, P., (eds.) SAC, pp. 226–231. ACM (2012)

69. Pizzuti, C.: A multiobjective genetic algorithm to find communities in complex networks. IEEE Trans. Evol. Comput. **16**(3), 418–430 (2012b)

70. Pons, P., Latapy, M.: Computing communities in large networks using random walks. J. Graph Algorithms Appl. **10**(2), 191–218 (2006)

71. Raghavan, U.N., Albert, R., Kumara, S.: Near linear time algorithm to detect community structures in large-scale networks. Phys. Rev. E **76**, 1–12 (2007)

72. Rand, W.M.: Objective criteria for the evaluation of clustering methods. J. Am. Stat. Assoc. **66**, 846–850 (1971)

73. Rosvall, M., Axelsson, D., Bergstrom, C.T.: The map equation. Eur. Phys. J. Spec. Top. **13**, 178 (2009)

74. Seifi, M., Guillaume, J.L.: WWW (Companion Volume). In: Mille, A., Gandon, F.L., Misselis, J., Rabinovich, M., Staab, S. (eds.)

Community cores in evolving networks, pp. 1173–1180. ACM, New York (2012)

75. Seshadri, M., Machiraju, S., Sridharan, A., Bolot, J., Faloutsos, C., Leskove, J.: Mobile call graphs: beyond power-law and log-normal distributions. In: Proceedings of the 14th ACM SIGKDD international conference on Knowledge discovery and data mining (KDD '08). ACM, New York, NY, USA, pp. 596–604 (2008)

76. Shah, D., Zaman, T.: Community detection in networks: The leader-follower algorithm. In: Workshop on Networks Across Disciplines in Theory and Applications, NIPS (2010)

77. Shi, C., Cai, Y., Fu, D., Dong, Y., Wu, B.: A link clustering based overlapping community detection algorithm. Data Knowl. Eng. **87**, 394–404 (2013)

78. Staudt, C., Meyerhenke, H.: Engineering high-performance community detection heuristics for massive graphs. In: ICPP, pp. 180–189. IEEE (2013)

79. Strehl, A., Ghosh, J.: Cluster ensembles: a knowledge reuse framework for combining multiple partitions. J. Mach. Learn. Res. **3**, 583–617 (2003)

80. Subbian, K., Melville, P.: Supervised rank aggregation for predicting influencers in twitter. In: SocialCom/PASSAT, pp. 661–665. IEEE (2011)

81. Subelj, L., Bajec, M.: Robust network community detection using balanced propagation. Eur. Phys. J. B **81**(3), 353–362 (2011)

82. Sun, P.-G., Gao, L.: A fast iterative-clique percolation method for identifying functional modules in protein interaction networks. Front. Comput. Sci. China **3**(3), 405–411 (2009)

83. Tang, L., Liu, H.: Community detection and mining in social media. Synthesis Lectures on Data Mining and Knowledge Discovery. Morgan & Claypool Publishers, San Rafael (2010)

84. Toussaint, G., Bhattacharya, B.K.: Optimal algorithms for computing the minimum distance between two finite planar sets. Pattern Recognit. Lett. **2**, 79–82 (1983)

85. Tsironis, S., Sozio, M., Vazirgiannis, M.: Accurate spectral clustering for community detection in mapreduce. In: Airoldi, E., Choi, D., Clauset, A., El-Arini, K., Leskovec, J. (eds.) Frontiers of network analysis: methods, models, and applications. Lake Tahoe, NIPS workshop (2013)

86. Verma, A., Butenko, S.: Graph partitioning and graph clustering. In: Bader, D.A., Meyerhenke, H., Sanders, P., Wagner, D. (eds.) Network clustering via clique relaxations: a community based approach. Contemporary Mathematics, pp. 129–140. American Mathematical Society, Providence (2012)

87. Whang, J.J., Gleich, D.F., Dhillon, I.S.: CIKM. In: He, Q., Iyengar, A., Nejdl, W., Pei, J., Rastogi, R. (eds.) Overlapping community detection using seed set expansion, pp. 2099–2108. ACM, New York (2013)

88. Xie, J., Kelley, S., Szymanski, B.K.: Overlapping community detection in networks: the state-of-the-art and comparative study. ACM Comput. Surv. **45**(4), 43 (2013)

89. Xie, J., Szymanski, B.K.: Community detection using a neighborhood strength driven label propagation algorithm. In: Proceedings of IEEE Network Science Workshop (2011)

90. Yang, J., Leskovec, J.: Defining and evaluating network communities based on ground-truth. In: Zaki, M.J., Siebes, A., Yu, J.X., Goethals, B., Webb, G.I., Wu, X. (eds.) ICDM, pp 745–754. IEEE Computer Society (2012)

91. Zachary, W.W.: An information flow model for conflict and fission in small groups. J. Anthropol. Res. **33**, 452–473 (1977)

92. Zhang, Y., Wang, J., Wang, Y., Zhou, L.: KDD. In: Iv, J.F.E., Fogelman-Soulié, F., Flach, P.A., Zaki, M.J. (eds.) Parallel community detection on large networks with propinquity dynamics, pp. 997–1006. ACM, New York (2009)

14

A simple distributed reasoning system for the connection calculus

Adam Meissner

Abstract We present a simple, distributed reasoning system for the first order logic, which applies a connection calculus as an inference method. The calculus has been proposed by Bibel as a generalization of some other popular approaches, like the tableau calculus or the resolution-based inference. The system is constructed in a lean deduction style and it has been inspired to some extent by a sequential reasoner leanCoP, implemented in Prolog. Our reasoner has a form of a relational program in the Oz language. In this programming model, a computational strategy is a parameter of a program having a form of a special object called a search engine. Therefore, the same program can be run in various ways, particularly in parallel on distributed machines. For this purpose, we use a parallel search engine available on the Mozart platform, which is a programming environment for Oz. We also describe results of experiments for estimating a speedup obtained by the distributed processing.

Keywords Distributed reasoning system · Connection calculus · Lean deduction · Oz language

1 Introduction

The term *reasoning system* or, synonymously, an *inference system* or a *reasoner* denotes a computer program intended for processing knowledge, which is expressed in a formal calculus, e.g. the first order logic (FOL). Programs of this type are successfully used in various fields, e.g. in expert systems, control in manufacturing, action planning in robotics,

predictive analytics or natural language processing. Nowadays, one can observe a growing popularity of "intelligent" tools, which apply miscellaneous forms of reasoning. This, in turn, increases a demand for efficient reasoning systems that can be easily adopted to different tasks and relocated among various computational environments. Unfortunately, the efficiency of reasoners is usually obtained by implementing complex optimization techniques. In consequence, the majority of reasoning systems are complicated constructions, difficult to modify and to transfer from one environment to another. Moreover, the complex system architecture often causes scalability problems and increases the probability of error occurrence.

The exception are so-called *lean reasoning systems*, i.e. relatively small programs containing only basic mechanisms, essential for soundness and completeness of an inference process. Well-known, precursory examples of lean reasoners are: PTTP [11], SATCHMO [6] or leanT^AP [2]. Programs of this type obviously can not solve hard inference problems. Nevertheless, this approach yields various benefits. In contrast to complex systems, lean reasoners are not hard to verify. Moreover, they can be easily modified and adapted to particular applications [1]. They are also remarkably efficient in solving less difficult problems. It follows from a lower overhead for handling their internal parts than it happens for advanced systems. Furthermore, lean reasoners can act as convenient test-beds for comparison of various inference techniques, where the absolute efficiency is not as important as the relative one.

We consider that the computational power of lean reasoning systems can be enhanced by introducing parallel and distributed computations to them. Therefore, we propose a distributed lean reasoner for FOL, as the main contribution of this paper. The key difficulty in designing a program of this type is to preserve its simplicity. In our approach, the rea-

---

A. Meissner (✉)
Institute of Control and Information Engineering, Poznań University of Technology, pl. M. Skłodowskiej-Curie 5, 60-965 Poznan, Poland
e-mail: Adam.Meissner@put.poznan.pl

soner is constructed in a declarative programming paradigm, which separates a program from a computational strategy. Hence, the reasoning system can keep its small size since it comprises only a description of basic inference instruments, while the operational semantics is defined outside.

Putting this idea into practice, we decided to use the *relational programming* model available in the Oz language [9], where a computational strategy is a parameter of the program execution. Some details of this conception are given in Sect. 4. Furthermore, we chose the *connection calculus* [3] as a reasoning formalism. It was proposed by Bibel as a generalization of some other popular approaches, like the tableau calculus or the resolution-based inference. The idea of parallel reasoning in the connection calculus is not new—it was considered e.g. by the authors of the paper [7] who defined a variant of the calculus suggesting how some inference steps can be parallelized. The authors also implemented their ideas as a short Prolog program, which can be regarded as a lean reasoning system. However, it is not clear if any attempts were made to run this program in parallel. Another successful example of a sequential lean reasoner for the connection calculus, also implemented in the Prolog language, is the system leanCoP [8]. This system is the inspiration for the solution presented here.

The rest of the paper is organized as follows: In Sect. 2 we present the principles of the connection calculus. Section 3 contains a description of the general reasoning algorithm. In Sect. 4 we describe crucial elements of the reasoning system. The description is preceded by the sketch of the relational programming model and distributed computing in the Oz language. Section 5 provides the results of experiments intended for estimating the speedup obtained by distributed computations. Section 6 concludes the paper with some final remarks.

2 Principles of the connection calculus

We briefly present the fundamentals of the connection calculus. In this description we use a standard FOL syntax and semantics as well as some elements of logic programming theory [5]. In particular, the alphabet encompasses constants a, b, c, variables x, y, z, functors f, g, h and predicates p, q, r. The symbol L denotes a *literal*, namely an atomic formula (i.e. a *positive* literal) or a negated atomic formula, i.e. a *negative* literal. An atomic formula is called in short an *atom*. All mentioned symbols can possibly be subscripted. The symbol θ stands for a *substitution* $\{x_1/t_1, \ldots, x_n/t_n\}$, where x_i is a variable and t_i is a term for $i = 1, n$. An *application of the substitution* θ to the expression E (namely, to a term or to a formula) results in the expression $E\theta$, which is obtained from E by replacing every occurrence of the variable x_i by the term t_i. The expression $E\theta$ is called an *instance* of the expression E. Moreover, a *copy* of the expression E is an instance of E with all variables renamed to new, unique identifiers. If the given expression does not contain variables then it is called *ground*. Two expressions E and E' are *unifiable* if there exists a *unifier* for them, that is to say, a substitution θ, such that $E\theta = E'\theta$.

The semantics of FOL is given by means of an interpretation $\mathcal{I}$, which is a pair $(\Delta^{\mathcal{I}}, \cdot^{\mathcal{I}})$ consisting of an interpretation domain and an interpretation function, respectively. The formulas F and G are called *equisatisfiable* if the formula F is satisfiable whenever the formula G is satisfiable too and *vice versa*. However, the formulas F and G can have different models. Every FOL formula can be transformed to an equisatisfiable formula of the form $(Qx_1) \ldots (Qx_n)F$, where Q is a quantifier (either existential or universal) and the formula F contains no quantifiers; $x_1, \ldots, x_n$ are all the variables occurring in F. Furthermore, every formula can also be transformed to the *disjunctive normal form* (DNF) or to the *conjunctive normal form* (CNF). In the first case the resulting formula is a disjunction $F_1 \vee \cdots \vee F_m$ where every F_i for $i = 1, m$ is a conjunction of literals. In the latter case, the result is a conjunction $G_1 \wedge \cdots \wedge G_n$ where every G_i is a disjunction of literals for $i = 1, n$. Details of these transformations can be found e.g. in [3].

In our context the *reasoning* consists in proving the validity of a given hypothesis by showing that it has some particular syntactic properties. For example, the formula F is valid, namely is a tautology, if it can be transformed to the form $F' \vee \sim F'$. The proof can also be given indirectly, that is to say, by demonstrating that the negation of the formula is unsatisfiable. One of possible reasoning methods is the connection calculus [3]. A characteristic feature of this approach is that hypotheses are represented as matrices of literals. In particular, one can distinguish two forms of the representation, namely a positive and a negative one.

In the first case, a hypothesis corresponding to the given matrix is regarded as a tautology, which is to be proven directly. Every column of the matrix is considered as a conjunction of its literals and the matrix represents a disjunction of columns. All the variables are existentially quantified by assumption. In other words, the matrix stands for the formula $(\exists)H$, where the subformula H is in DNF and contains no quantifiers. The formula is said to be *positively represented* by the matrix. For example, let G denote the following formula: $\exists x \exists y (\sim p_1(x, y) \wedge p_4(a, x) \wedge \sim p_6 \vee p_2(x) \wedge \sim p_5(b) \vee \sim p_3(y))$. The matrix, which represents it positively is given on the left-hand side of Fig. 1.

In case of the negative representation one assumes that a formula corresponding to a matrix is unsatisfiable and proofs constructed for this representation are indirect. Every row of the matrix is regarded as a disjunction of its literals while the matrix corresponds to a conjunction of rows. Variables in literals are implicitly universally quantified. Summing up,

$$\begin{bmatrix} \sim p_1(x, y) & p_2(x) & \sim p_3(y) \\ p_4(a, x) & \sim p_5(b) \\ \sim p_6 \end{bmatrix} \begin{bmatrix} p_3(y) \\ \sim p_2(x) & p_5(b) \\ p_1(x, y) & \sim p_4(a, x) & p_6 \end{bmatrix}$$

Fig. 1 Positive and negative representation of exemplary formulas

Fig. 2 Negative representation of the exemplary formula G_1

$$\begin{bmatrix} q \\ p(a, y) & \sim q \\ \sim p(x, b) & \sim p(x, c) \end{bmatrix}$$

the matrix stands for the formula $(\forall) H$, where the quantifier-free subformula H is in CNF.

Moreover, a positive representation of any formula F can by transformed to a negative representation of the formula $\sim F$ by making an anti-clockwise quarter rotation of the corresponding matrix and negating all the literals contained in it. For example, the transformation of the matrix on the left-hand side of Fig. 1 results in the matrix on the right-hand side of the same figure. One can observe, that it negatively represents the formula $\forall x \forall y ((p_1(x, y) \vee \sim p_4(a, x) \vee p_6) \wedge (\sim p_2(x) \vee p_5(b)) \wedge p_3(y))$, which is a negation of the exemplary formula G.

An easy transition between these two representations yields various advantages, which are not available in the majority of the other reasoning methods. One of them, pointed out in [3], is the possibility of a dual interpretation of a proof, i.e. either as a direct proof or as an indirect one. Another benefit of the connection calculus is the independence of a truth value of a formula, represented by a matrix, from some operations performed on matrices, which in particular correspond to commutativity of conjunction and disjunction symbols. More precisely, the following operations preserve the validity of a hypothesis given in the positive representation:

- changing order of columns in the matrix
- changing order of literals in a column
- adding a column $C\theta$ to the matrix containing the column C.

The symbol θ denotes any substitution being applied to all literals of the column C. In case of the negative representation, the unsatisfiability of the formula is an invariant of the following operations:

- changing order of rows in the matrix
- changing order of literals in the row
- adding a row $R\theta$ to the matrix containing the row R.

Let M be a matrix consisting of columns $C_1, \ldots, C_n$, which positively represents a formula F. A *path* in the matrix M is any sequence $L_1, \ldots, L_n$ of elements of M, such that the literal L_i is an element of the column C_i for $i = 1, n$. Let L be a positive literal; moreover let $neg(L) = \sim L$ and let $neg(\sim L) = L$. Two literals L and L' belonging to the

same path form a *connection* if there exists a unifier θ of $neg(L)$ and L'. It should be remarked that the unifier θ has to be applied to both the columns where the literals L and L' come from. For this reason, the columns are initially copied in order to save them for future instantiations, unless they are ground.

A set of connections in the matrix M is called a *mating* for M. A mating, in turn, is called *spanning* if every possible path in M contains at least one connection included in this mating. Furthermore, a matrix is *complementary* if there exists a spanning mating for it. One of fundamental results for the connection calculus states that the formula F is a tautology if and only if M is a complementary matrix [3]. Furthermore, a necessary condition for the existence of a spanning mating for M is that M contains at least one *positive column*, i.e. a column consisting of positive literals only.

For example, one has to prove that the following formula $\forall x \forall y (q \wedge (p(a, y) \vee \sim q) \wedge (\sim p(x, b) \vee \sim p(x, c)))$, denoted by G_1, is false. The negative representation of this formula is given in Fig. 2. A transition to the positive representation of the formula $\sim G_1$, having the form $\exists x \exists y (\sim q \vee \sim p(a, y) \wedge q \vee p(x, b) \wedge p(x, c))$, results in the matrix M, which is depicted in Fig. 3.

The process of the creation of a spanning mating for M follows in four steps and results in the complementary matrix M' presented in Fig. 4. In every step one connection is built, which is indicated by a dot-ended line.

Let the symbol $L_{i,j}$ denote an element of a matrix, which is located at the i-th row and j-th column. The first step consists

$$\begin{bmatrix} p(x, b) & \sim p(a, y) & \sim q \\ p(x, c) & q \end{bmatrix}$$

Fig. 3 Positive representation of the exemplary formula $\sim G_1$

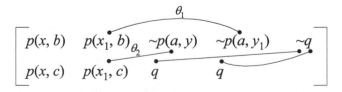

Fig. 4 A complementary matrix for the exemplary formula $\sim G_1$

in forming a connection between literals $L_{1,1}$ and $L_{1,2}$ from the matrix M. For this purpose, the columns C_1 and C_2 from M are copied into the columns C_2 and C_4 in the matrix M', respectively. In the next step, a unifier $\theta_1 = \{x_1/a, y_1/b\}$ is applied to them and the connection is formed. Subsequently, the literal $L_{2,2}$ is connected to the literal $L_{1,3}$ in the matrix M' using the substitution $\theta_2 = \{y/c\}$. It should be noticed that the column C_2 is not copied since it becomes ground in the former step. Also, for the sake of simplicity, a copy of the column C_3 is neglected as unnecessary for the creation of a spanning mating. In two final steps, the literals $L_{2,3}$ and $L_{2,4}$ are respectively connected to the literal $L_{1,5}$.

3 Reasoning method

The main goal of the reasoning algorithm is the creation of the spanning mating for the given matrix M. To do this, one has to check if every possible path in the matrix contains at least one connection. Let P denote a path being currently under construction. In other words, the matrix contains some columns, which the path P has not been conducted through. Hence, one has to select a column C of this type and then select a literal L from it. If P contains a literal L', which forms a connection with the literal L, then the creation of the path going through L can stop since every path starting from it contains a connection. Otherwise, the literal L should be added to P. The act of connecting a literal L to some element of the path P is called a *reduction step*, while adding a new literal to the path is an *extension step* [8].

As said in Sect. 2, a copy of every nonground column participating in a reduction step is added to the matrix M. Due to undecidability of FOL, this can result in an unlimited growth of a number of columns, which in turn prevents from finding a suitable mating for M. However, in some of such cases the spanning mating could be found if columns and literals were selected in a different order. This problem can be overcome by means of the *depth-first iterative deepening* (DFID) search strategy. Roughly speaking, the process of constructing a spanning mating for a given input matrix starts with a limited length of a path. Therefore, all possible paths are tried, whose length does not exceed the limit. If no spanning mating is found, the process starts again with a length limit increased. The initial limit, as well as its increment in every iteration are parameters of the DFID search. This method is proven to be asymptotically optimal among brute-force strategies in terms of proof length, space and time [4]. Hence, it is widely used in lean reasoners for undecidable logics.

Below, we present a reasoning algorithm for the connection calculus, whose general description is to be found in [3]. The algorithm is given in pseudocode since we try to keep as close as possible to the realization presented in the next section. Furthermore, the algorithm has a form of two subprograms, namely the function $Prove1$ and the procedure $Prove2$. The subprograms, in turn, consist of sequences of steps or statements, which are executed one by one. Each of them can either terminate (implicitly) successfully or with a failure. In the latter case, the whole subprogram terminates with a failure. Otherwise, namely if all elements of the subprogram terminate successfully then the subprogram terminates successfully, as well.

The pseudocode contains some boldfaced statements. In their description, we use the following metasymbols: $Expr$ (an expression), $Cond$ (a boolean expression), $Stat$ (a statement or a sequence of statements), Set (a set or a sequence). Moreover, the metasymbol $Elem$ stands for the specification of an element, which is to be selected from a given set. The specification comprises an identifier of the element. It may also contain some conditions and constraints, which have to be satisfied for a successful selection. All the mentioned symbols can possibly be subscripted. Additionally, the symbol $[Expr]$ denotes an optional expression $Expr$.

The statement **if** $Cond_1$ **then** $Stat_1$ [**elseif** $Cond_2$ **then** $Stat_2$] [**else** $Stat_3$] represents a decision. It has an intuitive semantics, whose definition is to be found e.g. in [9].

The statement **select** $Elem$ **from** Set declares a nondeterministic choice of the element $Elem$ from the set Set. In other words, any element can be selected, which satisfies the $Elem$ description. This issue is discussed in the sequel. After a successful selection of the element $Elem$, it is assumed to be removed from Set for further processing. On the other hand, the statement results in failure if the selection of an element is impossible, because for example Set is empty or it contains no element specified by $Elem$.

The statement **for** $Elem$ **in** Set **do** $Stat$ represents an iterative selection of the element $Elem$ from the set Set. Unlike the former statement, it always assumes an order of the given set. After a subsequent element is selected, it is considered to be removed from Set for the current iteration, which consists in the execution of the statement (or a sequence of statements) $Stat$. Furthermore, if $Stat$ executes the statement **continue** then the current iteration is interrupted and the control is passed to the next one.

The statement **exit** causes a successful termination of a procedure. The statement **return** $Expr$ acts similarly when used in a function, except it returns the value of $Expr$ to the function call. On the other hand, the statement **fail** makes a subprogram stop with a failure.

A top-level part of the algorithm is the function $Prove1$. It takes the matrix M, represented as a set of columns, and tries to build a spanning mating for it with respect to the limit Lim. One should observe, that the function returns the value $true$ only in case of a successful termination of the step 3.

Function $Prove1(M, Lim)$

Input: M – a matrix, Lim – a limit of a path length.

Output: the answer *true* if M is complementary; the answer *false* if M is not complementary; a *failure* if no spanning mating can be constructed for M with respect to Lim.

Step 1: **if** M contains no positive column **then return** *false*.

Step 2: **select** a positive column C **from** M.

Step 3: execute $Prove2(C, M, \varnothing, Lim)$.

Step 4: **return** *true*.

End Function.

The procedure $Prove2$ initially checks if the current column C, regarded as a set of literals, is empty. Such a column corresponds to a true formula (as an empty conjunction) and thus the matrix containing it is a tautology, as well. Otherwise, for every element L of the column C the reduction step (i.e. step 3) is tried. If the reduction is not possible, the extension step is undertaken, which is represented in the procedure by steps 3–8.

In particular, step 5 consists in the creation of a copy C'' of the column C'. However, making a copy of a column and reusing it in subsequent computations is pointless if the column is ground. In such a case, the column C' is not considered for further processing (see step 8). Moreover, the symbol $L|P$ denotes a path constructed from the path P by adding L to it as the first element; the value of the expression $length(P)$, in turn, is a number of elements of the sequence P. The function *unify*, given in step 7, realizes a unification algorithm. It results in failure if the arguments are not unifiable.

Procedure $Prove2(C, M, P, Lim)$

Input: C – a current column, M – a set of columns that the current path is to be conducted through, P – a current path, Lim – a limit of a path length.

Output: *success* if each path starting from P and leading through every element of C, and then through all columns in M, contains a connection; a *failure* otherwise.

Step 1: **if** $C = \varnothing$ **then exit.**

Step 2: **for** every literal L **in** C **do** execute the steps 3–8.

Step 3: **if** there exists a literal L' in P and a unifier θ of $neg(L)$ and L' **then** $P := P\theta$, $C := C\theta$, **continue.**

Step 4: **select** a column C' **from** M.

Step 5: $C'' := copy(C')$.

Step 6: **select** a literal L' **from** C''.

Step 7: $\sigma := unify(L', neg(L))$.

Step 8: **if** C' is ground **then** execute $Prove2(C''\sigma, M, (L|P)\sigma, Lim)$ **elseif** $lenght(P) < Lim$ **then** execute $Prove2(C''\sigma, M \cup \{C'\}, (L|P)\sigma, Lim)$ **else fail**.

End Procedure.

4 System description

Every reasoning system contains two basic elements. One of them is a realization of inference rules defining conclusions that can be obtained from premises. The other element is a strategy of searching for a proof, which determines a way the premises are selected in a reasoning process. Both the elements are naturally present in logic programming languages, e.g. in Prolog. Hence, reasoning systems are often implemented as logic programs. Unfortunately, the majority of the considered languages handle only one search strategy being fixed in the execution environment.

One of the exceptions is Oz—an experimental, multiparadigm programming language [9], whose execution environment is the Mozart platform [13]. The work on the language, as well as on its software platform began in nineties by a group of European laboratories, whose significant participants were German Research Centre for Artificial Intelligence (DFKI), Swedish Institute of Computer Science, Universite catholiqué de Louvain (Belguim) and Universität des Saarlandes (Germany). The Oz language enables the usage of many well-known programming models together in the same program, e.g. imperative and declarative programming, distributed programming, etc. Every model, called a *programming paradigm*, is represented by a characteristic set of Oz instructions. The paradigm corresponding to logic programming is named a *relational paradigm*. A declarative semantics of a relational program is similar to the Prolog one. However, a search strategy is not fixed like in the case of Prolog, but it is specified as a parameter of the program execution. Therefore, the same program can be run according to various search strategies. This possibility is very convenient, especially in the prototyping and testing phase. A realization of a search strategy has a form of a special object called a *search engine* (in short: an engine). A number of engines are available in libraries of the Mozart platform. They are implemented in the Oz language at an abstract level. In consequence, definitions of engines are relatively short, so they can be modified and extended with no particular effort. All these reasons decided that the system presented in the paper is realized as a relational program in the Oz language.

An operational semantics of a relational program is described using a *search tree*, whose nodes correspond to *computation spaces* (in short: spaces) [10]. The main use of spaces is to encapsulate computations. In other words, computations running in spaces are separated one from another and thus they can be performed independently. Going into some details, an execution of a program starts in the root space. Let us assume that the program contains a statement, which introduces a nondeterministic choice with n alternatives. In such a case, the respective node of the search tree has n child nodes. Each of them is a clone of the parent one, except it contains the information, which alternative it represents. Moreover, the execution of subsequent "nondeterministic statements" results in the further branching of the tree. Every dangling node corresponds to one possible result of computations, which can either be a success or a failure. Summing up, a relational program fully determines the shape of its search tree. The tree, however, is not built by the program but by a search engine. In this way the declarative semantics of a program, corresponding to the structure of the tree, is separated from its operational semantics. It should be underlined that computations performed in every branch are independent from the other branches. More precisely, they compete among one another for finding a solution. In consequence, a search tree can be easily constructed in parallel on distributed machines.

An appropriate, distributed search engine is an instances of the library class `Search.parallel`. It can be regarded as a team of concurrent autonomous agents comprising a *manager* and a group of *workers*. The manager controls the computations by finding a work for idle workers and collecting the results whereas the workers construct fragments of the search tree. Members of the team communicate by exchanging messages. A command, which creates a new engine specifies a computational environment, namely a set of machines connected in a network. The command also indicates a number of workers to be run on each of the machines. The engine starts on behalf of the manager, which sends a root of the search tree to a selected worker and puts the worker on a list of possibly busy workers. On the other hand, every idle worker sends a request for a job to the manager. In response, the manager tries to find a busy worker (registered on the list), which is ready to share its job. If such a worker is found, it sends a root of an unexplored subtree to the manager, which conveys it to the idle worker and puts this worker on the list. A worker can also inform the manager about finding a solution. After receiving such a message, the manager may tell all the workers to stop their jobs and close the engine. The detailed description of the engine architecture, including the communication protocol, is to be found in [10].

The reasoning system processes matrices, which are represented by Oz data structures. In particular, a matrix is a list of columns, while a column is a list of literals. We use the symbol O in the superscript to denote the Oz representation of the given expression. A negative literal has a general form of Oz *record* ([9]) $neg(L^O)$, whose *label* is a reserved symbol neg standing for the negation and the *field* L^O is an Oz counterpart of the positive literal L. In other words, L is an atom, namely a predicate possibly followed by a tuple of terms. Predicates, functors and constants are denoted by alphanumeric strings start-

ing from a lowercase letter, whereas variable names start from an uppercase one. A tuple of terms $(t_1, \ldots, t_n)$ is represented by the expression $(t_1^O \ t_2^O \ \ldots \ t_n^O)$ with a space character as a separator. Summing up, the exemplary matrix given in Fig. 1 has the following representation in Oz: `[[neg(p1(X Y)) p4(a X) neg(p6)] [p2(X) neg(p5(b))] [neg(p3(Y))]]`.

The key part of the system is the function `Prove1` and the procedure `Prove2`, which are defined below. They are a straightforward realization of the reasoning method described in Sect. 3. A crucial element of this realization is the selection mechanism, which corresponds to the statement **select** *Elem* **from** *Set*. It is used for choosing both a column from the matrix and a literal from the column. The mechanism has a form of the statement `{SelectNth Lst {Space.choose {Length Lst}} Elem Lst1}`. The procedure `SelectNth` selects the n-th element `Elem` from the list `Lst`, where n is a number specified by the second argument. The argument `Lst1` is a list obtained by removing the element `Elem` from `Lst`. The function call `{Length Lst}` returns a number of elements of the list `Lst`. The statement `{Space.choose N}` is executed in a computation space and it informs a search engine about a nondeterministic choice with `N` alternatives. The engine in the response clones the space `N` times and sends to each copy a numerical identifier ranging from 1 to `N`. The identifier becomes a value of the expression `{Space.choose N}`. In consequence, each element of the list `Lst` is to be processed further in a separate space.

The first argument (`Mat`) of the function `Prove1` is an input matrix, while the latter one (`Lim`) is a current limit of the path length. Generally, the call of this function may yield three different results. In particular, the value `true` is returned if one can construct a spanning mating for the matrix `Mat` and thus the formula represented by `Mat` is a tautology. On the other hand, i.e. when it can be proven that the spanning mating for `Mat` does not exist, the value `false` is returned. The function can also terminate by failure, which means that no spanning mating can be constructed for `Mat` with respect to the current limit of the path length. In such case, the computations can be repeated in a DFID manner, namely with an increased value of the argument `Lim`, as it is explained in Sect. 3.

The function initially checks if the matrix `Mat` is empty (line 2). If so, it returns `false` (line 7). Otherwise, a separate clone of the current space is created for each column `C` of the matrix `Mat` (line 3). If the column is not positive, i.e. it contains at least one negative literal, the further computations cease in failure (line 4); the function call `{Record.label L}` returns a label of the record `L`. In other case, that is to say, if the column `C` is positive, the procedure `Prove2` is executed for it (line 5).

```
1  fun {Prove1 Mat Lim}
2     if Mat \= nil then C Cs in
3        {SelectNth Mat {Space.choose {Length Mat}} C Cs}
4        if {Some C fun {$ L} {Record.label L} == neg end} then fail else
5           {Prove2 ['!'] (neg('!')|C)|Cs nil Lim}
6              true end
7     else fail end
8  end
```

The execution of the procedure `Prove2` results in failure if no spanning mating can be constructed for the input matrix with respect to `Lim`. In consequence, it causes a failure of the function `Prove1` (in line 5). On the other hand, namely when the mating is constructed, the procedure `Prove2` terminates successfully and the function `Prove1` returns the value `true`.

The first argument of the procedure `Prove2` (i.e. `Col`) is a list of literals corresponding to the current column. The argument `Mat`, in turn, is a list of remaining columns, which the current path is to be conducted through. The path, having

formula. In other case, namely when the current column is not empty, it is split to the current literal `L` and the remaining literals `Ls` (line 3). Then, the negated literal `NegL` is constructed for `L` (line 4) and the reduction step is tried for it (line 5). More precisely, the literal `L` forms a connection if `NegL` is successfully unified with some element of the current path. This ends the path led through the current literal. In consequence, the process of creation a spanning mating is continued for remaining literals of the current column (line 6). Otherwise, to wit when no reduction can be performed for `L`, the extension step is applied in lines 8–21.

```
1  proc {Prove2 Col Mat Path Lim}
2     if Col \= nil then Col1 Col2 L Ls NegL in
3        L = Col.1 Ls = Col.2
4        if {Record.label L} == neg then NegL = L.1 else NegL = neg(L) end
5        if {UnifiableMember NegL Path} then
6           {Prove2 Ls Mat Path Lim}
7        else
8           if Mat \= nil then Mat1 in
9              {SelectNth Mat {Space.choose {Length Mat}} Col1 Mat1}
10             if Col1 \= nil then L1 Ls1 in
11                {CopyTerm Col1 Col2}
12                {SelectNth Col2 {Space.choose {Length Col2}} L1 Ls1}
13                if {Not {OccurUnify L1 NegL}} then fail end
14                if {Not {NotGround Col1}} then
15                   {Prove2 Ls1 Mat1 L|Path Lim}
16                elseif Lim > {Length Path} then
17                   {Prove2 Ls1 Mat L|Path Lim}
18                else fail end
19             else fail end
20          else fail end
21          {Prove2 Ls Mat Path Lim} end
22     else skip end
23  end
```

a form of a list of literals, is represented by the argument `Path`. The last argument (`Lim`) is a number limiting the `Path` length. The initial call of the procedure (line 5 of the definition of the function `Prove1`) contains a technical trick, used at first in the system leanCoP. It consists in building an artificial current column `['!']`, which encompasses a reserved predicate `'!'`. This symbol must not occur in the input matrix. Furthermore, the original current column `C` is extended by the negation of the predicate `'!'` and added to the list of remaining columns, which is represented by the expression `(neg('!')|C)|Cs`. The aim of this artifice is to cause the initial current column `C` to be copied (line 11 of the definition of the procedure `Prove2`). Otherwise, the reasoning system is incomplete, namely it may not be able to prove some formulas, which are tautologies.

Initially, the procedure `Prove2` checks if the current column `Col` is empty (line 2). If so, the computations cease successfully (line 22) since the input matrix represents a true

It starts from checking if the list of remaining columns (i.e. `Mat`) is empty (line 8). In such case, any extension is impossible and thus the procedure terminates by failure (line 20). Otherwise, a column `Col1` is selected from `Mat` (line 9). If the column is empty (line 10) then it can not be used for an extension step and therefore the computations result in failure for it (line 19). In other case, the procedure creates a copy of `Col1` (line 11). It should be reminded that all variables appearing in `Col1` are replaced in the copy `Col2` by new, unique ones. The next step consists in the selection of a literal `L1` from the column `Col2`. If the literal does not form a connection with the current literal `L` then the computations terminate by failure for it (line 13). Otherwise, the current path can possibly be extended by the literal `L`, nevertheless, with regard to some other conditions. In particular, when the column `Col1` is ground (line 14), that is to say, it contains no variables, then it can be removed from the list of remaining columns for further processing. Such a list is indicated by `Mat1`. At last, the literal `L` is added to `Path` and the computations are continued for the other literals `Ls1` in the column `Col1` and for the list `Mat1` (Line 15). It should be remarked, that in the considered case the column `Col1` is identical to its copy `Col2`. On the other hand, when the column `Col1` is not ground, it can not be neglected in further processing. Therefore, the computations are continued for literals `Ls1` and for remaining columns `Mat` with `Col1` included (line 17). However, in this case the length of the current path must not exceed the limit `Lim` (line 16). Otherwise, the computations result in failure. Finally, after successful processing of the current literal `L`, the computations are continued for the rest of the current column, i.e. for the remaining literals represented by the symbol `Ls` (line 21).

Table 1 The computational time [s] for selected TPTP problems

Problem	1 Worker	2 Workers	3 Workers	4 Workers	5 Workers
SYN212-1	101.88	77.37	56.86	46.01	40.12
SET052-6	109.56	26.03	9.63	7.18	6.71
PUZ037-2	151.08	80.64	56.16	37.2	33.67
PLA010-1	190.41	167.78	146.44	112.19	61.55
MGT030-1	214.29	80.83	61.59	52.41	50.88
LCL009-1	59.68	56.8	56.23	5.79	5.18
GEO026-3	252.73	148.9	112.15	78.07	63.21
BOO012-1	33.34	33.11	5.28	5.29	5.28
ANA029-2	240.6	19.91	17.29	11.34	7.07

5 Experimental results

The experiments discussed in this section were aimed at estimating the speedup obtained by running the reasoning system in parallel on distributed machines with the increasing number of workers. The computational environment consisted of identical machines equipped with the processor Pentium P4D 3.4 GHz, 1 GB RAM, 1GBit Ethernet and Linux 2.6.32. All the computers were powered by the Mozart system 1.3.2. One of the machines was designated for running the manager while each of the other computers processed one worker.

All the testing hypotheses are tautologies coming from the TPTP library [12]. The formulas were chosen under the general criterion that the time of computations performed by one worker should be in the range from 30 to 300 s. Tests were run with the initial input depth equals 1 which was successively increased by 1. The results of the tests are collected in Table 1. The subsequent header row contains a problem name and a number of workers appearing in the given variant of the environment. Every entry in the table represents a computational time taken from the system clock as an arithmetic mean of 5 runs.

A speedup of computations is depicted in the bar chart given in Fig. 5. All bars are grouped in clusters corresponding to testing problems. Let T_i denote the time of computations performed in the environment consisting of the manager and i workers. Every bar represents a speedup $S_i = T_1/T_i$ obtained for the given problem and for $i = 2, 5$. The value of i is indicated by a shading of a bar, as it is given in the legend on the right side of the chart.

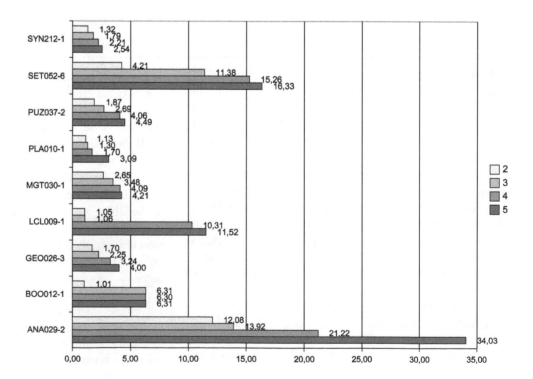

Fig. 5 Speedup for testing problems

Distinct speedup characteristics obtained for the input problems confirm rather an expected effect that the speedup depends on the structure of the constructed search tree. An increment of the speedup is nearly always positive except one case, i.e. the problem BOO012-1. However, the speedup fluctuates with the increasing number of workers. In some cases one can observe a surge in speedup, e.g. for problems SET052-6 (from S_2 to S_3), LCL009-1 (from S_3 to S_4), BOO012-1 (from S_1 to S_2) or ANA029-2 (from S_3 to S_4). It can be explained by the fact that the engine constructs the search tree until the first successful branch is found. Thus, the results of experiments strongly depend on the way the search tree is partitioned among the workers. In particular, the computational time reduces drastically if the failed branch appears as the first one in the subtree given to some worker. Another observation is the computational time nearly stops to decrease after reaching a value of around 5 s., e.g. for problems LCL009-1 or BOO012-1. This limitation may follow from the time overhead imposed by communication mechanisms of the network environment.

6 Final remarks

In this paper we describe a simple, distributed reasoning system for the first order logic. The system fits the lean deduction style and it uses a connection calculus as a reasoning method. The system is actually independent from the computational strategy thanks to implementing it in the relational model in the Oz language. We use the parallel search engine from the Mozart programming environment to run the system on distributed machines. Experiments show a reasonable speedup achieved by distributing the computations for some exemplary problems. However, the comprehensive analysis of the system efficiency requires more tests. The tests have to consider a greater number of workers and also a greater number of problems selected with regard to the structure of the search tree. These tests are planned for the future.

Open Access This article is distributed under the terms of the Creative Commons Attribution License which permits any use, distribution, and reproduction in any medium, provided the original author(s) and the source are credited.

References

1. Amir, E., Maynard-Zhang, P.: Logic-based subsumption architecture. Artif. Intell. **153**, 167–237 (2004)
2. Beckert, B., Possega, J.: leanT^AP: Lean, Tableau-based deduction. J. Autom. Reason. **15**(3), 339–358 (1995)
3. Bibel, W.: Automated Theorem Proving. Vieweg Verlag, Braunschweig (1987)
4. Korf, R.E.: Depth-first iterative-deepening: an optimal admissible tree search. Artif. Intell. **27**, 97–109 (1985)
5. Lloyd, W.L.: Foundations of Logic Programming, 2nd edn. Springer, Berlin (1987)
6. Manthey, R., Bry, F.: SATCHMO: A Theorem Prover Implemented in Prolog. LNCS, vol. 310, pp. 415–434. Springer, Berlin (1988)
7. Neugebauer, G., Schaub, T.: A Pool-Based Connection Calculus. Technical Report AIDA-91-02, TH Darmstadt (1991)
8. Otten, J., Bibel, W.: leanCoP: lean connection-based theorem proving. J. Symb. Comput. **36**(1–2), 139–161 (2003)
9. Van Roy, P., Haridi, S.: Concepts, Techniques, and Models of Computer Programming. The MIT Press, Cambridge (2004)
10. Schulte, Ch.: Programming Constraint Services. LNCS, vol. 2302. Springer, Berlin (2002)
11. Stickel, M.: A Prolog Technology Theorem Prover: A New Exposition and Implementation in Prolog. Technical Note No. 464, SRI Int., Manlo Park (1989)
12. Sutcliffe, G., Suttner, C.B., Yemenis, T.: The TPTP Problem Library. LNCS, vol. 814, pp. 252–266. Springer, Berlin (1994)
13. The Mozart Programming System. Accessed 29 Nov 2013

15

Loglog fault-detection rate and testing coverage software reliability models subject to random environments

Hoang Pham

Abstract Many software reliability growth models (SRGMs) have developed in the past three decades to quantify several reliability measures including the expected number of remaining faults and software reliability. The underlying common assumption of many existing models is that the operating environment and the developing environment are the same. In reality, this is often not the case because the operating environments are unknown due to the uncertainty of environments in the field. In this paper, we present two new software reliability models with considerations of the fault-detection rate based on a Loglog distribution and the testing coverage subject to the uncertainty of operating environments. Examples are included to illustrate the goodness-of-fit test of proposed models and several existing non-homogeneous Poisson process (NHPP) models based on a set of failure data collected from software applications. Three goodness-of-fit test criteria, such as, mean square error, predictive-ratio risk, and predictive power, are used as an example to illustrate the model comparisons. The results show that the proposed models fit significantly better than other existing NHPP models based on the studied criteria. As we know different criteria have different impacts in measuring the software reliability and that no software reliability model is optimal for all contributing criteria. In this paper, we also discuss a method, called normalized criteria distance, to show ways to rank and select the best model from among SRGMs based on a set of criteria taken all together. Examples show that the proposed method offers a promising technique for selecting the best model based on a set of contributing criteria.

H. Pham (✉)
Department of Industrial and Systems Engineering,
Rutgers University, Piscataway, NJ 08854, USA
e-mail: hopham@rci.rutgers.edu

Keywords Non-homogeneous Poisson process (NHPP) · Software reliability growth models · Loglog distribution · Normalized criteria distance · Operating environments

Abbreviations

$m(t)$	Expected number of software failures detected by time t, also known as mean value function
N	Number of faults that exist in the software before testing
$h(t)$	Time-dependent fault detection rate per unit of time

1 Introduction

Among all software reliability growth models (SRGMs), a large family of stochastic reliability models based on a non-homogeneous Poisson process (NHPP), known as NHPP reliability models, has been widely used to track reliability improvement during software testing. Many existing NHPP software reliability models [1–26] have been carried out through the fault intensity rate function and the mean value functions $m(t)$ within a controlled testing environment to estimate reliability metrics such as the number of residual faults, failure rate, and reliability of software. Generally, these models are applied to the software testing data and then used to make predictions on the software failures and reliability in the field. In other words, the underlying common assumption of such models is that the operating environments and the developing environment are about the same. The operating environments in the field for the software, in reality, are quite different. The randomness of the operating environments will affect the software failure and software reliability in an unpredictable way.

Estimating software reliability in the field is important, yet a difficult task. Usually, software reliability models are applied to system test data with the hope of estimating the failure rate of the software in user environments. Teng and Pham [3] have discussed a generalized model that captures the uncertainty of the environments and its effects upon the software failure rate. Other researchers [8, 19–21, 24, 27] have also developed reliability and cost models incorporating both testing phase and operating phase in the software development cycle for estimating the reliability of software systems in the field. Software development is a very complex process and there are still issues that have not yet been addressed. Testing coverage is one of these issues. Testing coverage [27] is a measure that enables software developers to evaluate the quality of the tested software and determine how much additional effort is needed to improve the reliability of the software. Testing coverage can provide customers with a quantitative confidence criterion when they plan to buy or use the software products.

In this paper, we present two new software reliability models. The first model is, called Loglog fault-detection rate, an NHPP model where the fault-detection rate is based on a loglog distribution function. The second is, called testing coverage model with uncertainty environments, also an NHPP with considerations of the uncertainty of operating environments where the testing coverage function follows the Loglog distribution. The explicit solution of the mean value functions for these new models are derived in Sect. 2. Criteria for model comparisons and a new method called normalized criteria distance (NCD), for selecting the best model is discussed in Sect. 3. Model analysis and results are discussed in Sect. 4 to illustrate the goodness-of-fit criteria of proposed models and compare them with several existing NHPP models based on three common criteria such as mean square error, predictive-ratio risk, and predictive power from a set of software failure data. Section 5 concludes the paper with remarks.

2 Software reliability modeling

2.1 An NHPP loglog fault-detection rate model

Many existing NHPP models assume that failure intensity is proportional to the residual fault content. A general NHPP mean value function $m(t)$ with time-dependent fault detection rate is given by [2]:

$$m(t) = N \left[1 - e^{-\int_0^t h(x)dx} \right] \tag{1}$$

In this paper, we consider that the software fault-detection rate per unit of time, $h(t)$, has a Vtub-shaped based on a

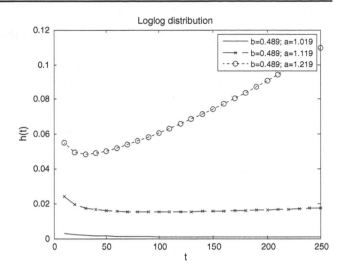

Fig. 1 Fault-detection rate function $h(t)$ for various values of a and $b = 0.489$

loglog distribution function and is given by [2]:

$$h(t) = b \ln(a) t^{b-1} a^{t^b} \qquad \text{for } a > 1,\ b > 0 \tag{2}$$

It should be noted that the loglog distribution has a unique Vtub-shaped curve while the Weibull distribution has a bathtub-shaped curve. They, however, are not the same. As for the Vtub-shaped from the Loglog distribution, after the infant mortality period, the system starts to experience at a relatively low increasing rate, but not at a constant rate, and then increases with failures due to aging. For the bathtub-shaped, after the infant mortality period, the useful life of the system begins. During its useful life, the system fails as a constant rate. This period is then followed by a wear out period during which the system starts slowly and increases with the onset of wear out. Figure 1 describes the Vtub-shaped function $h(t)$ for various values of parameter a where $b = 0.489$.

From Eq. (2), we can obtain the expected number of software failures detected by time t using Eq. (1):

$$m(t) = N \left(1 - e^{-\left(a^{t^b} - 1\right)} \right) \tag{3}$$

2.2 An NHPP testing coverage model with random environments

Testing coverage is important information for both software developers and customers of software products. Such information can be used by managers in order to determine how much additional effort is needed to improve the quality of the software products.

A generalized mean value function $m(t)$ based on the testing coverage function subject to the uncertainty of operating environments can be obtained by solving the following defined differential equation:

$$\frac{dm(t)}{dt} = \eta \frac{\frac{\partial c(t)}{\partial t}}{(1-c(t))}[N - m(t)] \tag{4}$$

where $c(t)$ represents the testing coverage and η is a random variable that represents the uncertainty of system detection rate in the operating environments with a probability density function g. The closed-form solution for function $m(t)$ in term of random variable η with an initial condition $m(0) = 0$ is given by:

$$m(t) = N\left[1 - e^{-\eta \int_0^t \frac{c'(x)}{(1-c(x))}dx}\right] \tag{5}$$

If we assume that the random variable η has a gamma distribution with parameters α and β where the pdf of η is given by

$$g(x) = \frac{\beta^\alpha x^{\alpha-1}e^{-\beta x}}{\Gamma(\alpha)} \qquad \text{for } \alpha,\ \beta > 0;\ x \geq 0 \tag{6}$$

then from Eq. (5), we can obtain [21]:

$$m(t) = N\left[1 - \left(\frac{\beta}{\beta + \int_0^t \frac{c'(s)}{1-c(s)}ds}\right)^\alpha\right] \tag{7}$$

In this paper, we assume that the testing coverage function has a loglog distribution [2] as follows:

$$c(t) = 1 - e^{1-a^{t^b}} \qquad \text{for } a > 1,\ b > 0 \tag{8}$$

Figures 2 and 3 describe the testing coverage function $c(t)$ and testing coverage rate $c'(t)$ for various values of parameter a where $b = 0.196$. We observe that for a given value b, as parameter a increases the testing coverage function increases but the testing coverage rate decreases.

Substitute the function $c(t)$ into Eq. (7), we can easily obtain the expected number of software failures detected by

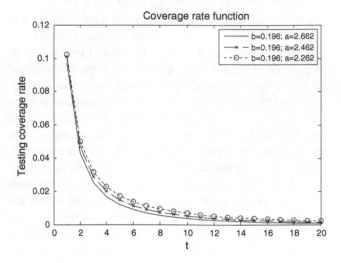

Fig. 3 Testing coverage rate function $c'(t)$ for various values of a and $b = 0.196$

time t with random environments:

$$m(t) = N\left(1 - \left(\frac{\beta}{\beta + a^{t^b} - 1}\right)^\alpha\right) \tag{9}$$

Table 1 summarizes the two proposed models and several existing well-known NHPP models with different mean value functions.

3 Normalized criteria distance method

Once the analytical expression for the mean value function $m(t)$ is derived, the model parameters to be estimated in the mean value function can be obtained with a help of developed Matlab programs that based on the least square estimate (LSE) method.

There are more than a dozen of existing goodness-of-fit test criteria. Obviously different criteria have different impact in measuring the software reliability due to the selection among the existing models and, however, that no software reliability model is optimal for all contributing criteria. This makes the job of developers and practitioners much more difficult when they need to select an appropriate model, if not the best, to use from among existing SRGMs for any given application based on a set of criteria.

In this section, we discuss a new method called, NCD, for ranking and selecting the best model from among SRGMs based on a set of criteria taken all together with considerations of criteria weight $w_1, w_2, \ldots, w_d$. Let s denotes the number of software reliability models with d criteria, and C_{ij} represents the criteria value of ith model of jth criteria where $i = 1, 2, \ldots, s$ and $j = 1, 2, \ldots, d$.

The NCD value, D_k, measures the distance of the normalized criteria from the origin for kth model and can be defined

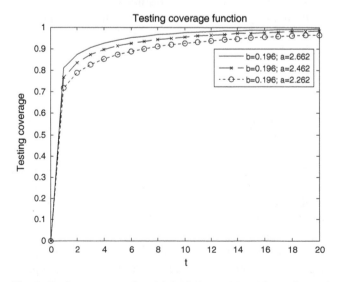

Fig. 2 Testing coverage function $c(t)$ for various values of a and $b = 0.196$

as follows [21]:

$$D_k = \sqrt{\left(\sum_{j=1}^{d} \left(\left(\frac{C_{kj}}{\sum_{i=1}^{s} C_{ij}} \right)^2 w_j \right) \right)} \quad k = 1, 2, \ldots, s \tag{10}$$

where s and d are the total number of models and total number of criteria, respectively, and w_j denotes the weight of the criterion j for $j = 1, 2, \ldots, d$.

Thus, the smaller the NCD value, D_k, it represents the better rank as compare to higher NCD value. In Sect. 4, we use three common criteria such as the mean square error, the predictive-ratio risk, and the predictive power, to illustrate the proposed NCD method.

4 Model analysis and results

4.1 Some existing criteria

As mentioned in Sect. 3, there are more than a dozen of existing goodness-of-fit criteria. In this study, we discuss briefly three common criteria in this section and use them to compare those models as listed in Table 1. They are: the mean square error, the predictive-ratio risk, and the predictive power.

The mean square error (MSE) measures the deviation between the predicted values with the actual observation and is defined as:

$$\text{MSE} = \frac{\sum_{i=1}^{n} (\hat{m}(t_i) - y_i)^2}{n - k} \tag{11}$$

where n and k are the number of observations and number of parameters in the model, respectively.

The predictive-ratio risk (PRR) measures the distance of model estimates from the actual data against the model estimate, and is defined as [17]:

$$\text{PRR} = \sum_{i=1}^{n} \left(\frac{\hat{m}(t_i) - y_i}{\hat{m}(t_i)} \right)^2 \tag{12}$$

where y_i is total number of failures observed at time t_i according to the actual data and $\hat{m}(t_i)$ is the estimated cumulative number of failures at time t_i for $i = 1, 2, \ldots, n$.

The predictive power (PP) measures the distance of model estimates from the actual data against the actual data, is as follows:

$$\text{PP} = \sum_{i=1}^{n} \left(\frac{\hat{m}(t_i) - y_i}{y_i} \right)^2 \tag{13}$$

For all these three criteria—MSE, PRR, and PP—the smaller the value, the better the model fits, relative to other models run on the same data set.

4.2 Software failure data

A set of system test data was provided in [2, p. 149] which is referred to as Phase 2 data set and is given in Table 2. In this data set the number of faults detected in each week of testing is found and the cumulative number of faults since the start of testing is recorded for each week. This data set provides the cumulative number of faults by each week up to 21 weeks. We perform the calculations for LSE estimates and other measures using Matlab programs.

Table 1 Software reliability models

Model	$m(t)$
Goel–Okumoto (G–O)	$m(t) = a(1 - e^{-bt})$
Delayed S-shaped	$m(t) = a(1 - (1 + bt)e^{-bt})$
Inflection S-shaped	$m(t) = \frac{a(1 - e^{-bt})}{1 + \beta e^{-bt}}$
Yamada imperfect debugging 1	$m(t) = a[1 - e^{-bt}]\left[1 - \frac{\alpha}{b}\right] + \alpha a t$
PNZ model	$m(t) = \frac{a}{1 + \beta e^{-bt}}\left([1 - e^{-bt}]\left[1 - \frac{\alpha}{b}\right] + \alpha t\right)$
Pham–Zhang model	$m(t) = \frac{1}{1 + \beta e^{-bt}}\left((c + a)(1 - e^{-bt}) - \frac{a}{b - \alpha}(e^{-\alpha t} - e^{-bt})\right)$
Dependent-parameter model	$m(t) = \alpha(1 + \gamma t)(\gamma t + e^{-\gamma t} - 1)$
Dependent-parameter model with $m(t_0) \neq 0$	$m(t) = m_0 \left(\frac{\gamma t + 1}{\gamma t_0 + 1}\right) e^{-\gamma(t - t_0)}$ $+ \alpha(\gamma t + 1)[\gamma t - 1 + (1 - \gamma t_0)e^{-\gamma(t - t_0)}]$
Loglog fault-detection rate model	$m(t) = N\left(1 - e^{-(a^{t^b} - 1)}\right)$
Testing coverage model with uncertainty	$c(t) = 1 - e^{1 - a^{t^b}}$ $m(t) = N\left(1 - \left(\frac{\beta}{\beta + a^{t^b} - 1}\right)^\alpha\right)$

Table 2 Phase 2 system test data [2]

Week index	Exposure time (cumulative system test hours)	Fault	Cumulative fault
1	416	3	3
2	832	1	4
3	1,248	0	4
4	1,664	3	7
5	2,080	2	9
6	2,496	0	9
7	2,912	1	10
8	3,328	3	13
9	3,744	4	17
10	4,160	2	19
11	4,576	4	23
12	4,992	2	25
13	5,408	5	30
14	5,824	2	32
15	6,240	4	36
16	6,656	1	37
17	7,072	2	39
18	7,488	0	39
19	7,904	0	39
20	8,320	3	42
21	8,736	1	43

Table 3 Model parameter estimation and comparison criteria

Model name	LSEs	MSE	PRR	PP
G–O model (model 1)	$\hat{a} = 98,295$ $\hat{b} = 5.2 \times 10^{-8}$	6.61	0.69	1.10
Delayed S-shaped (model 2)	$\hat{a} = 62.3$ $\hat{b} = 2.85 \times 10^{-4}$	3.27	44.27	1.43
Inflection S-shaped (model 3)	$\hat{a} = 46.6$ $\hat{b} = 5.78 \times 10^{-4}$ $\hat{\beta} = 12.20$	1.87	5.94	0.90
Yamada imperfect debugging (model 4)	$\hat{a} = 1.5$ $\hat{b} = 1.1 \times 10^{-3}$ $\hat{\alpha} = 3.8 \times 10^{-3}$	4.98	4.30	0.81
PNZ model (model 5)	$\hat{a} = 45.99$ $\hat{b} = 6.0 \times 10^{-4}$ $\hat{\alpha} = 0$ $\hat{\beta} = 13.24$	1.99	6.83	0.96
Pham–Zhang model (model 6)	$\hat{a} = 0.06$ $\hat{b} = 6.0 \times 10^{-4}$ $\hat{\alpha} = 1.0 \times 10^{-4}$ $\hat{\beta} = 13.2$ $\hat{c} = 45.9$	2.12	6.79	0.95
Dependent parameter model (model 7)	$\hat{a} = 3.0 \times 10^{-6}$ $\hat{\gamma} = 0.49$	43.69	601.34	4.53
Dependent parameter model with $m(t_0) \neq 0$, $t_0 \neq 0$ (model 8)	$\hat{a} = 890,996$ $\hat{\gamma} = 1.2 \times 10^{-6}$ $t_0 = 832$ $m_0 = 4$	24.79	1.14	0.73
Loglog fault-detection rate model (model 9)	$\hat{N} = 231.92$ $\hat{a} = 1.019$ $\hat{b} = 0.489$	7.03	0.05	1.21
Testing coverage model with uncertainty (model 10)	$\hat{N} = 43.25$ $\hat{a} = 2.662$ $\hat{b} = 0.196$ $\hat{\alpha} = 4.040$ $\hat{\beta} = 35.090$	1.80	2.06	0.77

4.3 Model results and comparison

Table 3 summarizes the results of the estimated parameters for all ten models as shown in Table 1 using the least square estimation (LSE) method and its criteria (MSE, PRR, and PP) values. The coordinates X, Y and Z in Fig. 4 illustrate the MSE, PRR, and PP criteria values, respectively, of the models. From Table 3, we observe that model 10 has the smallest MSE value, while model 9 has the smallest PRR value, and model 8 has the smallest PP value.

It is worthwhile noting that although both the PRR and PP values for the proposed testing coverage model with uncertainty (model 10) are slightly larger than the dependent parameter model (model 8), the MSE value for model 10 is significantly smaller than the dependent parameter model 8. Similarly, to compare all the models based on the PRR criterion, we find that the proposed loglog fault-detection rate (model 9) provides the best fit with the smallest PRR value.

As we can see from Table 3, the selection of the best model will then depend upon the modeling criteria. We now illustrate the proposed NCD method (in Sect. 3) to obtain the ranking results of all the ten models from Table 3 based on all three goodness-of-fit criteria such as MSE, PRR, and PP.

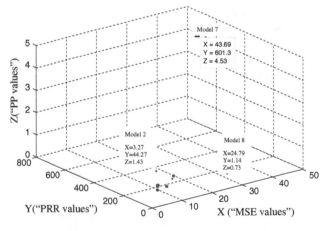

Fig. 4 A three-dimension plot (X, Y, Z) represents (MSE, PRR, PP) values when $w_1 = 0.3$, $w_2 = 100$, $w_3 = 0.1$

The modeling comparison and results for the case when all the criteria weight are the same (i.e., $w_1 = w_2 = w_3 = 1$) and when all are not the same ($w_1 = 0.3$, $w_2 = 100$, $w_3 = 0.1$) are presented in Tables 4 and 5, respectively. In other words, using Eq. (10) and the criteria values and results given in

Table 3, we obtain the NCD values and their corresponding ranking as shown in Table 4 for all $w_j = 1$ for $j = 1, 2,$ and 3. Table 5 shows the NCDs and their corresponding ranking when $w_1 = 0.3$, $w_2 = 100$, and $w_3 = 0.1$. In Fig. 4, the coordinates X, Y and Z represent the corresponding of the MSE, PRR, and PP values of each model for criteria weight $w_1 = 0.3$, $w_2 = 100$, and $w_3 = 0.1$. The delayed s-shaped (model 2) for example, $X = 3.27$, $Y = 44.27$, and $Z = 1.43$, indicates the MSE, PRR, and PP values of model 2. Figure 5 illustrates the model ranking based on the NCD values given in Table 5 for criteria weight $w_1 = 0.3$, $w_2 = 100$, and $w_3 = 0.1$. For example, a set of coordinates $(X = 10, Y = 1,$ and $Z = 0.03698)$ indicates that (shown in Table 5) model 10 is ranked the best (1st) where the NCD value is 0.03698.

Based on this study we can draw a conclusion that the proposed testing coverage model (model 10) and the loglog fault detection rate (model 9) can provide the best fit based on the MSE and PRR criteria, respectively. The NCD method in general is a simple and useful tool for modeling selection. Obviously, further work in broader validation of this conclusion is needed using other data sets as well as other comparison criteria.

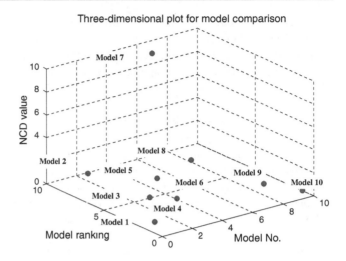

Fig. 5 A three-dimension plot with the model ranking and NCD values for $w_1 = 0.3$, $w_2 = 100$, $w_3 = 0.1$

5 Conclusion

We present two new software reliability models by considering a loglog fault-detection rate function and the testing

Table 4 Parameter estimation and model comparison when $w_j = 1$ for $j = 1, 2, 3$

Model/criteria	MSE (rank)	PRR (rank)	PP (rank)	NCD value (D_k)	Model rank
1. G–O model	6.61 (7)	0.69 (2)	1.10 (7)	0.106232216	6
2. Delayed S-shaped	3.27 (5)	44.27 (9)	1.43 (9)	0.129758016	8
3. Inflection S-shaped	1.87 (2)	5.94 (6)	0.90 (4)	0.070417115	2
4. Yamada imperfect debugging model	4.98 (6)	4.30 (5)	0.81 (3)	0.079212229	5
5. PNZ model	1.99 (3)	6.83 (8)	0.96 (6)	0.075194169	4
6. Pham–Zhang model	2.12 (4)	6.79 (7)	0.95 (5)	0.074845806	3
7. Dependent-parameter model	43.69 (10)	601.34 (10)	4.53 (10)	1.053569725	10
8. Dependent-parameter model with $m(t_0) \neq 0$, $t_0 \neq 0$	24.79 (9)	1.14 (3)	0.73 (1)	0.258395095	9
9. Loglog fault-detection rate model	7.03 (8)	0.05 (1)	1.21 (8)	0.115308973	7
10. Testing coverage model with uncertainty	1.80 (1)	2.06 (4)	0.77 (2)	0.060436587	1

Table 5 Parameter estimation and model comparison when $w_1 = 0.3$, $w_2 = 100$, $w_3 = 0.1$

Model/criteria	MSE (rank)	PRR (rank)	PP (rank)	NCD value (D_k)	Model rank
1. G–O model	6.61 (7)	0.69 (2)	1.10 (7)	0.046265595	2
2. Delayed S-shaped	3.27 (5)	44.27 (9)	1.43 (9)	0.65852017	9
3. Inflection S-shaped	1.87 (2)	5.94 (6)	0.90 (4)	0.091330651	5
4. Yamada imperfect debugging model	4.98 (6)	4.30 (5)	0.81 (3)	0.072219186	4
5. PNZ model	1.99 (3)	6.83 (8)	0.96 (6)	0.104518861	7
6. Pham–Zhang model	2.12 (4)	6.79 (7)	0.95 (5)	0.103971347	6
7. Dependent-parameter model	43.69 (10)	601.34 (10)	4.53 (10)	8.933743693	10
8. Dependent-parameter model with $m(t_0) \neq 0$, $t_0 \neq 0$	24.79 (9)	1.14 (3)	0.73 (1)	0.140433906	8
9. Loglog fault-detection rate model	7.03 (8)	0.05 (1)	1.21 (8)	0.04854067	3
10. Testing coverage model with uncertainty	1.80 (1)	2.06 (4)	0.77 (2)	0.036977987	1

coverage subject to the uncertainty of the operating environments. The explicit mean value function solutions for the proposed models are presented. The results of the estimated parameters of proposed models and other NHPP models and their MSE, PRR, and PP are also discussed. We also discuss an NCD method for obtaining the model ranking and selecting the best model from among SRGMs based on a set of criteria taken all together. Example results show that the presented new models can provide the best fit based on the NCD method as well as some studied criteria. Obviously, further work in broader validation of this conclusion is needed using other data sets as well as considering other comparison criteria.

Acknowledgments This paper was made possible by the support of NPRP 4-631-2-233 grant from Qatar National Research Fund (QNRF). The statements made herein are solely the responsibility of the author.

References

1. Goel, A.L., Okumoto, K.: Time-dependent fault-detection rate model for software and other performance measures. IEEE Trans. Reliab. **28**, 206–211 (1979)
2. Pham, H.: System Software Reliability. Springer, London (2006)
3. Teng, X., Pham, H.: A new methodology for predicting software reliability in the random field environments. IEEE Trans. Reliab. **55**(3), 458–468 (2006)
4. Ohba, M.: Inflexion S-shaped software reliability growth models. In: Osaki, s., Hatoyama, Y. (eds.) Stochastic Models in Reliability Theory, pp. 144–162. Springer-Verlag, Berlin, Germany (1984)
5. Pham, H.: Software reliability assessment: imperfect debugging and multiple failure types in software development. In: EG&G-RAAM-10737. Idaho National Engineering Laboratory (1993)
6. Pham, H.: A software cost model with imperfect debugging, random life cycle and penalty cost. Int. J. Syst. Sci. **27**(5), 455–463 (1996)
7. Ohba, M., Yamada, S.: S-shaped software reliability growth models. In: Proceeding of the 4th international conference on reliability and maintainability, pp. 430–436 (1984)
8. Teng, X., Pham, H.: A software cost model for quantifying the gain with considerations of random field environments. IEEE Trans. Comput. **53**(3) (2004)
9. Zhang, X., Teng, X., Pham, H.: Considering fault removal efficiency in software reliability assessment. IEEE Trans. Syst. Man Cybern. Part A **33**(1), 114–120 (2003)
10. Pham, H., Zhang, X.: NHPP software reliability and cost models with testing coverage. Eur. J. Oper. Res. **145**, 443–454 (2003)
11. Pham, H., Nordmann, L., Zhang, X.: A general imperfect software debugging model with s-shaped fault detection rate. IEEE Trans. Reliab. **48**(2), 169–175 (1999)
12. Pham, H., Zhang, X.: An NHPP software reliability model and its comparison. Int. J. Reliab. Qual. Saf. Eng. **4**(3), 269–282 (1997)
13. Pham, L., Pham, H.: Software reliability models with time-dependent hazard function based on Bayesian approach. IEEE Trans. Syst. Man Cybern. Part A **30**(1), 25–35 (2000)
14. Yamada, S., Ohba, M., Osaki, S.: S-shaped reliability growth modeling for software fault detection. IEEE Trans. Reliab. **12**, 475–484 (1983)
15. Yamada, S., Osaki, S.: Software reliability growth modeling: models and applications. IEEE Trans. Softw. Eng. **11**, 1431–1437 (1985)
16. Yamada, S., Tokuno, K., Osaki, S.: Imperfect debugging models with fault introduction rate for software reliability assessment. Int. J. Syst. Sci. **23**(12) (1992)
17. Pham, H., Deng, C.: Predictive-ratio risk criterion for selecting software reliability models. In: Proceeding of the 9th international conference on reliability and quality in design (2003)
18. Pham, H.: An imperfect-debugging fault-detection dependent-parameter software. Int. J. Autom. Comput. **4**(4), 325–328 (2007)
19. Zhang, X., Pham, H.: Software field failure rate prediction before software deployment. J. Syst. Softw. **79**, 291–300 (2006)
20. Sgarbossa, F., Pham, H.: A cost analysis of systems subject to random field environments and reliability. IEEE Trans. Syst. Man Cybern. Part C **40**(4), 429–437 (2010)
21. Pham, H.: A software reliability model with vtub-shaped fault-detection rate subject to operating environments. In: Proceeding of the 19th ISSAT international conference on reliability and quality in design, Hawaii (2013)
22. Kapur, P.K., Pham, H., Aggarwal, A.G., Kaur, G.: Two dimensional multi-release software reliability modeling and optimal release planning. IEEE Trans. Reliab. **61**(3), 758–768 (2012)
23. Kapur, P.K., Pham, H., Anand, S., Yadav, K.: A unified approach for developing software reliability growth models in the presence of imperfect debugging and error generation. IEEE Trans. Reliab. **60**(1), 331–340 (2011)
24. Persona, A., Pham, H., Sgarbossa, F.: Age replacement policy in random environment using systemability. Int. J. Syst. Sci. **41**(11), 1383–1397 (2010)
25. Xiao, X., Dohi, T.: Wavelet shrinkage estimation for non-homogeneous Poisson process based software reliability models. IEEE Trans. Reliab. **60**(1), 211–225 (2011)
26. Kapur, P.K., Pham, H., Chanda, U., Kumar, V.: Optimal allocation of testing effort during testing and debugging phases: a control theoretic approach. Int. J. Syst. Sci. **44**(9), 1639–1650 (2013)
27. Pham, H., Zhang, X.: NHPP software reliability and cost models with testing coverage. Eur. J. Oper. Res. **145**, 443–454 (2003)

Locality oriented feature extraction for small training datasets using non-negative matrix factorization

Khoa Dang Dang · Thai Hoang Le

Abstract This paper proposes a simple and effective method to construct descriptive features for partially occluded face image recognition. This method is aimed for any small dataset which contains only one or two training images per subject, namely Locality oriented feature extraction for small training datasets (LOFESS). In this method, gallery images are first partitioned into sub-regions excluding obstructed parts to generate a collection of initial basis vectors. Then these vectors are trained with Non-negative matrix factorization algorithm to find part-based bases. These bases finally build up a local occlusion-free feature space. The main contribution in this paper is the incorporation of locality information into LOFESS bases to preserve spatial facial structure. The presented method is applied to recognize disguised faces wearing sunglasses or scarf in a control environment without any alignment required. Experimental results on the Aleix-Robert database show the effectiveness of the LOFESS method.

Keywords Disguided face recognition · Partial occluded face recognition · Non-negative matrix factorization · Alignment free face recognition

1 Introduction

Human face recognition has been long studied in the research community with many achievements [1,2]. It plays an important role in security, supervision, human–machine interaction and more. Face images offer an advantage over other biometric features that it is far more easy to be captured with the help of digital cameras increasingly popular nowadays. For human, it is not so difficult to recognize people in many conditions. But for computers, there are many challenges still troubling researchers.

One problem that draws much of attention is recognizing a partially occluded face. The occlusion is caused by a facial accessory such as sunglasses or scarf [3]. This is also called disguised face recognition. A common solution is to focus on the feature representation so that discriminative information is effectively extracted. In addition, it is not always possible to acquire many photos of each person easily. In practice, some applications requiring this feature space is efficiently built based on a small training dataset, which means only one or two subject's images are available. This is also one of the main concerns in this paper.

The disguised face recognition has different approaches. Many of the state of the art methods, such as SRC [4] and RSC [5], utilize the redundant information based on the availability of large scale image galleries. This condition is unfeasible in some applications when only a very few number (one or two) of training images are available. In another approach, non-negative matrix factorization (NMF) based methods [9,10] show promising results when applying to small training datasets [14] due to their ability to learn part-based features naturally. However, these methods just focus to control the sparseness of NMF features, while spatial relationship information among bases is not exploited sufficiently. This paper concentrates on the problem of building an occlusion-excluded feature space for recognizing partial occluded faces, such as by wearing eyeglasses or scarves, based on a small gallery set, namely Locality oriented feature extraction for small training datasets (LOFESS). Each subject in the dataset has one or two images

K. D. Dang · T. H. Le (✉)
Department of Information Technology, University of Science,
227 Nguyen Van Cu Street, District 5, Ho Chi Minh City, Vietnam
e-mail: lhthai@fit.hcmus.edu.vn

K. D. Dang
e-mail: ddkhoa@fit.hcmus.edu.vn

captured in a controlled environment (straight faces with neutral expression and balanced light condition), without any alignment needed. Moreover, spatial information is explicitly employed to enhance the robustness to occlusion. Noted that this method can be extended for other types of disguises.

LOFESS first requires the disguise condition to be identified manually or automatically. It is assumed the occlusion detection step, which is out of the scope of this paper, has been done by another algorithm or by a user. Then, gallery images are split into suitable regions to construct an initial basis set. These bases are designed so that none of any pixel in the detected occluded area is involved. It is important and reasonable to remove these pixels because they certainly degrade the recognition performance. The next step is training these bases into localized facial components by Nonnegative matrix factorization. Basically, these components are matrices with all the entries are greater or equal to zero. This enable them to mutually combine together to reconstruct original faces. As a contribution, a splitting strategy is designed to incorporate spatial relationship into these components. Finally, occlusion-free bases are matched to identify the target.

Figure 1 summarizes the mentioned steps in this paper. To show the effectiveness of the proposed LOFESS method, we use a subset of the Aleix-Robert database [11] which is standard in many related research. This dataset offers a large amount of face images of 100 people wearing sunglasses or scarves which is a standard for experiments and comparison. The remainder of this paper is organized as follows. In Sect. 2, we highlight the main studies in this problem. Section 3 describes in detail our feature space construction LOFESS method following by the comparison with state of the art algorithms. Experimental methodology and results are presented in Sect. 4. Finally, we make a conclusion and propose future works in Sect. 5.

2 Backgrounds

This section mainly reviews the recent literature of feature representation for disguised face recognition. Features could be extracted at various scale from a whole face to small pixel blocks over the image and represented by code-based or subspace-based methods.

Intuitively, partial face occlusion significantly degrades the recognition performance. A possible approach is to recover these parts before recognizing who they are. Chiang and Chen's solution [6] automatically detects occlusion and recovers the occluded parts. At the end, the whole face is matched with faces recovered from person-specific PCA [12] eigenspaces after a gradual illumination adjustment process. As authors' discussion, this model depends heavily on manually fitting active appearance model (AAM) [13] landmarks on each input faces which is not reliable when eye region is covered.

Instead of recovering, most of recent arts choose to remove occluded parts and extract local features from the rest of the image. Code-based approaches have been widely investigated in the literature due to their high recognition performance. The main idea is to approximate original data through linear combination of only a few (sparse) coding basis, or atoms, chosen from an over complete dictionary. Wright et al. [4] recently proposed the sparse representation based classification (SRC) scheme for face recognition which achieved impressive performance. Images are split into a grid of smaller regions and applying SRC separately. Each block is treated as an atom without any projection into a subspace or feature extraction. Their method shows high robustness to face occlusion. Starting from this success, many variants of SRC make further improvements. Nguyen et al. [7] built a multi-scale dictionary. In their work, each image is scaled by 2 four times and split into 16, 8, 4 and 2 blocks, respectively, at each level. SRC is then performed on separated group of blocks. Yang and Zhang [15] integrated an additional occlusion dictionary. The built-in atoms are extracted from image local Gabor features [16] to enhance the compactness and reduce the computational cost of sparse coding. A separated block will be removed if it is classified as occluded or taken into account if it is non-occluded. These methods use simple voting strategies to fuse the recognition result from separated blocks so the spatial relationship among these blocks are not considered properly.

In the approach of combining sparse coding with global representation, Yang et al. [5] based on the maximum likelihood estimation principle to code an input signal by sparse regression coefficients. This method utilizes an iterative process to create a map weighting occluded and non-occluded pixels differently. The weighted input image is then

Fig. 1 An overview of face recognition based on our LOFESS method

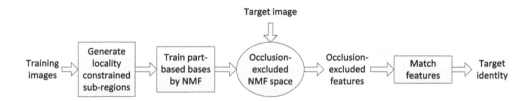

matched with template images in the dictionary. Zhou et al. [17] included the Markov Random Field model to identify and exclude corrupted regions from the sparse representation. This method can even iteratively reconstructed an input face from un-occluded part. Liao and Jain [18] proposed an alignment-free approach based on a large scale dictionary of SIFT descriptors. The disadvantage of all sparse-based methods in this problem context is a large number of gallery images must be obtained in advance to build dictionaries.

Non-negative matrix factorization (NMF) [9,10,19] is another approach which has been proven a useful tool for decomposing data into part-based components. These components are non-negative meaning all elements in factorized matrices are greater than or equal to zero. This idea comes from biological modeling research aiming to simulate receptive fields of human visual system where input signals are mutually added (not canceled each one out). One important property of NMF is it naturally results in sparse features which are highlighted salient local structures from the input data. This property is valuable when dealing with occlusion and dimension reduction. Showing that spareness of NMF bases is somehow a side effect, Hoyer [20] introduced a constraint term to explicitly control the degree of spareness of learned bases.

With the same purpose, Hoyer and Shastri [21,22] imposed non-negativity as a constraint in sparse coding model called Non-negative sparse coding (NNSC). This method pursuit sparseness and part-based representation at the same time. However, as we observed, the constraint is not enough to guarantee both properties simultaneously. Hoyer [20] has the same conclusion about the trade-off between sparsity, localization and data representation sufficiency. In these methods, learned bases converge randomly because there is no constraint on each facial part position. This shortcoming results in a waste of features and ineffectiveness when recognizing disguised faces not only because these features have nothing to deal with occluded regions but also degrade the recognition performance. To tackle this problem, Oh et al. [14] divided input images into non-overlapped patches to detect occlusion. Then, the matching is performed in the Local non-negative matrix factorization (LNMF) space [23] constructed by the selected occlusion-free bases.

Apart from the above discussed methods, there are various approaches base on face sub-images such as Martinez's probabilistic approach [25] which is able to compensate for partially occlusion, Ekenel and Stiefelhagen's alignment-based approach [24] resulted from Rentzeperis et al. [26] that registration errors have dominant impact on recognition performance over the lacking of discriminative information.

3 LOFESS: an effective and efficient feature representation for small training datasets

3.1 Face sub-regions with spatial relationship preserving constraints

This section proposes a new face sub-region representation to construct inputs for training by NMF in the next step, which are incorporated with spatial constraints at the same time.

This paper mainly deals with faces wearing sunglasses or scarves, but note that the same strategy could apply for other type of partial disguise.

The main point is to build a feature representation without taking any pixels in the eyes and mouth regions. However, these two regions are thought to carry most of identifying features of human face. Our aim is to exclude them but not affect or even boost the recognition performance. This could be achieved by employing spatial relationship to complement for the loss of information.

Input:

– A dataset consisting of m images at the same size of $p \times q$
– n is the number of basis vectors we wish to receive after training
– Information about occlusion (i.e. which part need removing) R

Loop for k from 1 to n
Choose one image I from the dataset randomly
Construct a new image

$$I'_{ij} = \begin{cases} I_{ij}, & r_1 \leqslant i \leqslant r_2, 1 \leqslant j \leqslant q \\ 0 \end{cases}$$

Choose $1 \leqslant r_1 < r_2 \leqslant p$ so that the image I' will not contain any pixel in the occluded regions R.
Transform I' into the column vector $w_k \in \mathbb{R}^{d \times 1}$, with $d = p \times q$
End loop
Output:

– The matrix $W_0 \in \mathbb{R}^{d \times n}$ including column vectors w_i.

In this data preparation step, information about occlusion could be supplied by a user or a result from an occlusion detection algorithm. This step acts as a guidance for features to converge into regions outside the occlusion, eyes or mouth, and just focus to extract information from other parts. Figures 2 and 3 show some sample bases before and after training. The top row (a) depicts original images I. The second row (b) is initial basis images I' with regions split from (a). The bottom row (c) are bases learned from (b), i.e. W^* (will be

Fig. 2 For recognizing subjects wearing sunglasses: from original images (**a**), initial basis images (**b**) are constructed, and final LOFESS bases (**c**) are learned with eye regions removed

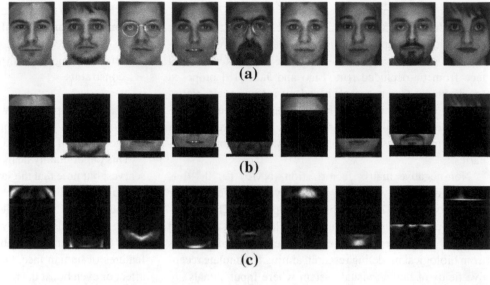

Fig. 3 For recognizing subjects wearing scarves: from original images (**a**), initial basis images (**b**) are constructed with mouth regions removed to learn final LOFESS bases (**c**)

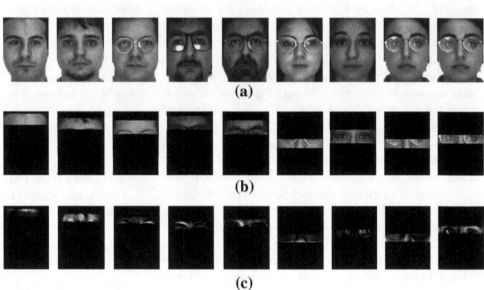

presented in the next section). These regions depend on the choice of r_1 and r_2 so that their combination could cover an entire face excluding occluded areas. Note that these figures were chosen randomly for illustration purpose, there is no correspondence between them.

The use of occluded regions could result in performance degradation. State of the art methods have employed different approaches to remove or avoid occlusion. LOFESS improves this idea by both zeroing out any pixel in occluded areas and preserving the facial structure at the same time. It means each LOFESS basis carries robust, complementary information (which person and which corresponding facial part) for recognition. Also note that only this step requires occlusion forms to be identified in advance. When matching, a testing image will be represented just based on available trained bases, none of which corresponds to occluded areas.

So occlusion is removed naturally without any additional computation.

If there is no or minor occlusion that could be neglected, all facial regions are taken in to account. The problem then becomes recognizing faces without occlusion and the algorithm is still applied properly.

3.2 Training occlusion-free part-based features with NMF

The NMF aims to learn part-based representation of faces. Let V is a column vector matrix, each column represents an image in the training dataset. This method tries to find basis vectors W and coefficients H that best approximate V, i.e. minimize the error:

$$\varepsilon = \|V - WH\| \tag{1}$$

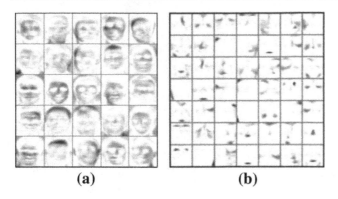

(a) **(b)**

Fig. 4 Example basis vectors learned by the original NMF

with the constraint of non-negative on W and H (all negative values will be assigned by zeros during computation). The optimal solution for W and H is given by iterating the following Multiplicative Update Rule algorithm [9]. The iteration stops when ε lower than a predefined threshold or after a certain number of update times.

$$H_{au} = H_{au} \frac{\left(W^T V\right)_{au}}{\left(W^T W H\right)_{au}} \quad (2)$$

$$W_{ia} = W_{ia} \frac{\left(V H^T\right)_{ia}}{\left(W^T H H^T\right)_{ia}} \quad (3)$$

with a, u, i are row and column indexes.

Originally, H and W are randomly generated. However, in practice, it doesn't guarantees bases will converge to local parts as expected and usually results in global representation [20,27] (Fig. 4a).

LOFESS initializes W from W_0 in Sect. 3.1. This method differs from Hoyer's [20], called Non-negative sparse coding (NNSC), which tried to control the localization of W and spareness of H at the same time. NNSC is not able to decide which local part on a face to focus on. In Fig. 4b from Hoyer's paper, these features converged randomly to any part. For instance, a region around one's eyes is useless when recognizing a person wearing sunglasses.

3.3 Face recognition with locality constrained features

We improved the model from Shastri and Levine [22] by adding spatial constraint in the feature extraction phase (Fig. 5).

3.3.1 Training

From the initial dataset $D \in \mathbb{R}^{p \times q \times m}$ consisting of m images at the same size $p \times q$, we construct the matrix $V \in \mathbb{R}^{d \times m}$, $W_0 \in \mathbb{R}^{d \times n}$ and initialize a matrix $H_0 \in \mathbb{R}^{n \times m}$ with random values, $d = p \times q$.

NMF takes V, W_0 and H_0 as the inputs. After the training, we will receive the optimal bases W^* and coefficients H^*. Together, $W^* H^*$ best approximates the training set V. Figures 2c and 3c depict some samples of W^*, note that none of them relates to occluded areas.

The feature space W^+ is constructed and each column vector v_k in V is projected on this space to obtain a feature vector h_i

$$W^+ = \left(W^{*\top} W^*\right)^{-1} W^{*\top} \quad (4)$$

$$h_i = W^+ v_i, \quad i = 1 \dots m \quad (5)$$

In some practical situations, a person may wear sunglasses, a scarf, both or anything else. Depend on occlusion types, several corresponding W^+ could be constructed in advanced.

3.3.2 Matching

Let $y \in R^{d \times 1}$ represents an image of an unidentified subject wearing disguise. Base on the form of disguise, identified by a user or an algorithm, e.g. sunglasses or a scarf, the corresponding W^+ is chosen. Project y onto the feature space W^+ to receive vector h_y

$$h_y = W^+ y \quad (6)$$

The subject is assigned to the nearest neighbor class based on the Euclidean distance from h_y to all h_i of training images. It means find

$$k = \min_i \mathrm{d}(h_y, h_i) = \min_i L_2(h_y, h_i), \quad \text{with } i = 1 \dots m \quad (7)$$

In conclusion, y belongs to the same class of v_k.

The matching process is illustrated in Figs. 6 and 7. Training (a) and testing (e) images are projected on W^+ (b and f are the same) to produce feature vectors h_i and h_y (c and g). The feature vectors impose representation (d and h) of input images based on non-occluded bases.

3.4 Merits of LOFESS

The proposed method LOFESS has the following merits in the small training dataset context. Firstly, LOFESS is robust to various types of partial occlusion. It transforms a disguised face into the occlusion-excluded LOFESS space and perform the matching only on visible parts. The strength of LOFESS is spatial relationship is preserved to complement for losing information in occluded parts. Secondly, LOFESS achieves high recognition performance on small training datasets because it exploits both global and local information from limited resources. Each basis corresponds

Fig. 5 Training and matching process

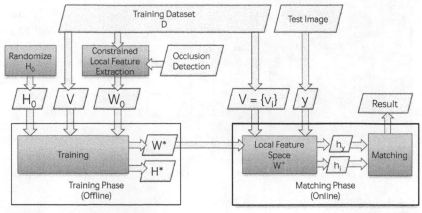

Fig. 6 Matching between training and testing samples in the sunglasses dataset

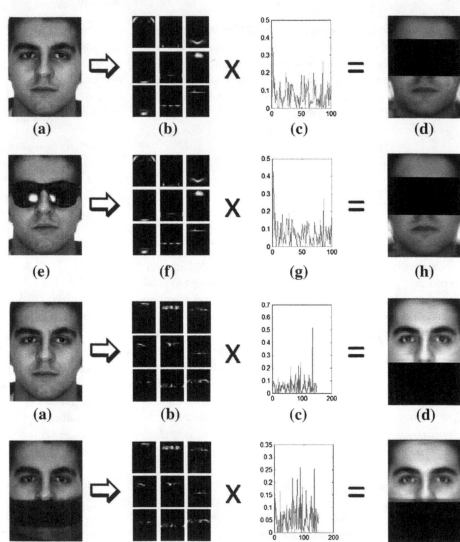

Fig. 7 Matching between training and testing samples in the scarf dataset

to a facial part and its relative position to the whole face structure implies spatial relationship. Indeed, within a single basis, the meaningful information (nonzero pixels) concentrates in a small region. In this paper, we keep the whole image for easy visualization and interpretation. When implementing, a suitable data structure could be employed to reduce the number of dimensions by dismissing or compressing blank (black) regions. Thirdly, LOFESS is easily incorporated with prior knowledge from occlusion detection algorithms or from a user in semi-supervised applications. Automatic detection

Table 1 Comparison between LOFESS and other methods

	Sparseness	Locality	Minimum number of training images
SRC	On coefficients	Block partitioning sparse error term	8 images/person
RSC	On coefficients	Sparse error term	4 images/person
NMF	On bases	Spatially localized	1 images/person
SLNMF	On bases	Spatially localized	1 images/person
LOFESS	On bases	Spatially localized + structure constraint preserving images/person	1 images/person

are not readily applied in practice and cost more computation. Meanwhile, supervising applications are usually monitored by users. LOFESS only requires a user to mark occluded region in a template image in the beginning. The template is then applied to all images and no need any user interaction afterward. This way of manipulation is easy and fast for users as well as support the system reliability.

3.5 Comparison with existing methods

LOFESS can be considered as a method for learning sparse features with locality constraints to construct an occlusion-free feature space. At first, constraints are applied on original data regarding to occlusion types. After that, this data becomes input to an iterative training process to learn part-based bases. These bases form a subspace on which an input face is projected to find a occlusion-excluded representation suitable for small training datasets. In this section, LOFESS is compared with two representative approaches based on the same sparseness property as summarized in Table 1.

SRC and variants (e.g. RSC) seek for sparse combination of bases, which means choosing a set of coefficients with very few elements greater than zero. In return, bases are dense to produce enough information for recognition. To achieve robustness to occlusion, these bases are split into a grid or selective regions. Each region is treated separately and results are fused by voting. This doesn't take into account the spatial relationship between regions. Additional sparse error term is integrated to overcome this drawback but consumes more time and computation. As reported in authors' paper [4], it took more than 20 s to process one image. Moreover, the number of gallery images needed to reach the optimal performance is more than the assumption in this problem, which is one or two training images per person.

NMF-based methods, on the other hand, try to learn sparse bases and combination of these bases to represent input faces. The spatially localized bases enhance the ability to handle occlusion better and faster. One drawback is the algorithms

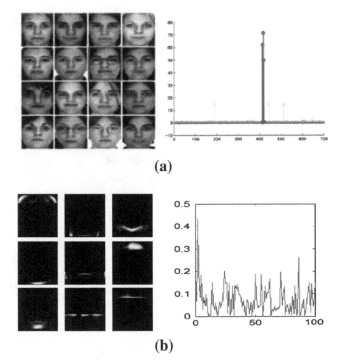

(a)

(b)

Fig. 8 A sample of bases and coefficients of SRC and LOFESS

might correspond to occluded regions and degrade the recognition performance.

explicitly. The constraint acts as a guidance for features training to concentrate on non-occluded facial parts. Figure 8 illustrates some bases and coefficient vectors of SRC (adopted from author's paper) and LOFESS (NMF-based) methods.

4 Experiments

4.1 Aleix-Roberts datasets

We evaluated the performance of LOFESS on the Aleix-Robert database [11] collected by Aleix Martine and Robert Benavente in Barcelona, 1999. There are 100 subjects, 50

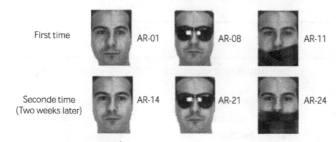

First time · AR-01 · AR-08 · AR-11

Seconde time (Two weeks later) · AR-14 · AR-21 · AR-24

Fig. 9 AR subset examples

men and 50 women, in the AR database. Each person has 2 images captured in 2 weeks apart for one facial status, there are 13 statuses in total.

This paper focuses on the disguised faces, so only AR-01 and AR-14 were chosen for training, AR-14, AR-08, AR-11, AR-21 and AR-24 for testing (Fig. 9). Each subset contains 100 images of 100 subjects captured in two week time apart in different conditions.

- AR-01, AR-14: neutral faces
- AR-08, AR-21: faces wearing sunglasses
- AR-11, AR-24: faces wearing scarves

Images are converted to 165 × 120 gray-scale in the preprocessing step.

4.2 Evaluation criteria

We performed extensive tests to evaluate the proposed method based on three criteria as summarized in Table 2.

4.2.1 Precision

This is the most popular criterion to evaluate the recognition rate, given by

$$P = \frac{\text{\# correctly classified images}}{\text{\# total classified images}}$$

AR-01 and AR-14 are used for training. AR-08, AR-11, AR-21 and AR-24 are for testing. Then results are compared with SLNMF [14] because both of them having the same experiment configuration.

4.2.2 Two week time recognition

Is LOFESS robust for recognizing a face two weeks later? In this test, only one image per subject in the subset AR-01 (Neu-1) was used for training and AR-08 (Sg-1), AR-11 (Sc-1), AR-13 (Neu-2), AR-21 (Sg-2), AR-24 (Sc-2) for testing. LOFESS was compared with SLNMF and RSC [5] based on the same testing configuration.

Table 2 Experiment summary

	Precision	2-week time	ROC
LOFESS	✓	✓	✓
SLNMF	✓	✓	
SRC		✓	

4.2.3 ROC curve

This curve reflects the correspondence between the true acceptance rate and false acceptance rate (plotted as the y and x axes, respectively) when recognition threshold is increased from 0 to 1. To our knowledge, there hasn't been any method addressing this problem has plotted the ROC curve for these AR datasets. We hope to provide another benchmark for later research.

4.3 Experimental results

4.3.1 Precision

Table 3 shows the recognition results on faces wearing sunglasses (a) and scarves (b). The main tables summarize recognition rates based on various local region sizes (in rows) and number of basis vectors n (in columns). Two sub-tables on the right and the bottom calculate the min, max and mean for each value of n and region size.

In detail, when the number of basis vectors varies from 10 to 300, the average precision increases from 68.8 to 91.17 % for the sunglasses subset and from 58.83 to 87.75 % for the scarf subset. But the rate is not stable if we look at the sub-table for region size, it goes up and down unpredictably. The wider the local region is, the smaller size of the basis is needed to achieve high recognition rate. This implies the optimal precision achieved with the appropriate choice of sufficient number of basis vectors and suitable regions size.

Tables 4 and 5 compared LOFESS and SLNMF under various number of bases. In case of recognizing targets with sunglasses, LOFESS outperforms SLNMF in all tests. But with scarf disguises, LOFESS is comparative with SLNMF in situations when only a few number of bases are allowed.

4.3.2 Two week time recognition

Optimal LOFESS recognition rate in each test is compared with SLNMF and RSC methods in this experiment as illustrated in Table 6. LOFESS and SLNMF used only one training image per subject in the subset AR-01, while RSC used up to 4 images in AR-01, AR-05, AR-06 and AR-07. Comparing with SLNMF, LOFESS outperformed in all tests. The main reason is LOFESS removes all occluded bases totally from

Table 3 Recognition precision on AR-08 and AR-21 (a), AR-11 and AR-24 (b)

n	Local Region Height / Image Height (%)						Min	Mean	Max
	3%	6%	9%	12%	15%	18%			
10	67	63	70.5	65	77	66	63	68.08	77
20	65.5	84	77.5	78.5	83	85.5	65.5	79	85.5
30	83	87	85.5	82.5	85	86.5	82.5	84.92	87
40	83.5	86	85	86.5	84	86	83.5	85.17	86.5
50	85.5	86.5	84.5	83.5	85.5	89.5	83.5	85.83	89.5
60	86.5	87.5	89.5	83.5	86.5	90.5	83.5	87.33	90.5
70	87.5	89	88.5	89.5	85.5	87.5	85.5	87.92	89.5
80	85.5	88.5	90.5	91	89.5	90	85.5	89.17	91
90	87.5	85.5	90	90	88	90	85.5	88.5	90
100	88.5	91.5	89.5	88.5	91.5	92.5	88.5	90.33	92.5
150	89.5	89	89.5	90.5	92.5	89.5	89	90.08	92.5
200	88	89.5	90.5	91.5	89.5	91	88	90	91.5
300	92	92	91	88.5	92	91.5	88.5	91.17	92
Min	65.5	63	70.5	65	77	66			
Mean	83.81	86.08	86.31	85.31	86.88	87.38			
Max	92	92	91	91.5	92.5	92.5			

(a)

n	Local Region Height / Image Height (%)						Min	Mean	Max
	3%	6%	9%	12%	15%	18%			
10	46.5	40.5	70	75	63	58	40.5	58.83	75
20	53.5	74.5	71.5	72	71	63	53.5	67.58	74.5
30	77	76	84	67.5	79.5	71	67.5	75.83	84
40	80	85.5	83.5	80.5	85.5	86.5	80	83.58	86.5
50	67	86.5	85	74	83	74	67	78.25	86.5
60	78.5	85	87	80	86	87.5	78.5	84	87.5
70	85.5	83	83.5	83	85.5	87	83	84.58	87
80	84.5	80.5	88.5	82	87	84.5	80.5	84.5	88.5
90	87	89	86.5	90	86	85.5	85.5	87.33	90
100	81	89	87.5	83	90	90	81	86.75	90
150	89	86.5	87.5	90.5	86.5	87.5	86.5	87.92	90.5
200	87.5	88	87	88	86	86	86	87.08	88
300	89.5	90	89.5	86.5	85	86	85	87.75	90
Min	46.5	40.5	70	67.5	63	58			
Mean	77.42	81.08	83.92	80.92	82.62	80.5			
Max	89.5	90	89.5	90.5	90	90			

(b)

Table 4 Recognition rate on the sunglasses dataset with various numbers of basis

Methods	Number of basic vectors			
	50	100	200	300
LOFESS	89.5	92.5	91.5	92
IS-LNMF	84	88	90	90

Table 5 Recognition rate on the scarf dataset with various numbers of basis

Methods	Number of basic vectors			
	50	100	200	300
LOFESS	86.5	90	88	90
S-LNMF	86	90	92	92

recognition. Meanwhile, SLNMF still tries to exploit bases partially corresponding to occluded area. In testing against

Table 6 Two week time period recognition rate (%) between LOFESS and SLNMF

Methods	Neu-2	Sg-1	Sg-2	Sc-1	Sc-2	# galery images
LOFESS	80	91	67	91	61	1 image/person
S-LNMF	77	84	49	87	55	1 image/person

Table 7 Two week time period recognition rate (%) between LOFESS and RSC

Methods	Sg-1	Sg-2	Sc-1	Sc-2	# galery images
LOFESS	91	67	91	61	1 image/person
RSC	94.7	91	80.3	72.7	4 images/person

RSC, the subset AR-11 (Sg-1) noticeably showed LOFESS reached a higher rate (91 %) even with one training image while RSC needed 4 images (80.3 %). The significant difference in performance between sunglasses and scarf datasets could be attributed to imprecise localization errors [24,25] (Table 7).

4.3.3 ROC curves

In Fig. 10, two ROC curves, which shows ratios between TAR and FAR, were plotted. Parameter values of $n = 300$ and region size = 3 % of image height were choice because this configuration gave the optimal performance among the experiments. In both subsets, the curves were above average line (the diagonal). However, when TAR = 1, the FAR was also quite high about 0.55 and 0.45, respectively. This is reasoned fusing just two images for training.

4.4 Parameter configuration and effects

4.4.1 Local region size r_1, r_2 and the number of bases

In NMF-based methods, the number of bases could be infinite. LOFESS offers additional region size parameter. This allows more flexibility by tunning up both parameters for optimal solution. Here arises a question of how to find the best pairs of these values. Shatri and Levine [22] had a detailed survey on various number of basis vectors n from 10 to 200 with arbitrary region sizes. We performed experiments with the same bases number and varied the range of $[r_1, r_2]$ to occupy 3, 6, 9, 12, 15 and 18 percent of the image height. As presented in Table 3, region size tends to decrease while number of bases increases for the model to reach an saturated point. This implied the optimal recognition performance is reached when sufficient information is provided. A shortage or redundancy could downgrade the system.

Fig. 10 ROC curves for sunglasses (**a**) and scarf (**b**)

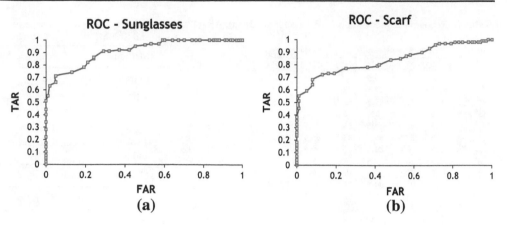

(a)

(b)

Table 8 Training time (min) for the sunglasses dataset

% image height	Number of bases								
	10	30	50	70	90	100	150	200	300
3	0.39	1.73	2.53	3.53	4.69	5.27	8.56	12.1	21.3
6	0.68	1.63	2.59	3.67	4.82	5.38	8.75	12.7	21.3
9	0.64	1.55	2.5	3.6	4.77	5.75	8.92	2.5	21.4
12	0.71	1.72	2.52	3.56	4.73	5.28	8.57	2.1	21.4
15	0.69	1.67	2.68	3.75	4.89	5.36	8.86	2.7	21.4
18	0.68	1.63	2.52	3.61	5.02	5.58	8.97	12.5	20.3

Table 9 Training time (min) for the scarf dataset

% image height	Number of bases								
	10	30	50	70	90	100	150	200	300
3	0.46	1.06	1.46	2.05	2.81	4.38	4.97	8.87	15.22
6	0.39	1.02	1.33	2.36	2.78	2.93	4.96	6.92	12.34
9	0.38	0.95	1.35	2.12	2.75	3	4.86	7.3	12.78
12	0.4	1	1.39	2.12	2.84	3.18	6.72	7.4	13.19
15	0.41	0.97	1.51	2.13	2.73	3.11	5.02	6.9	11.84
18	0.62	1.45	2.37	3.15	4.23	5.21	5.6	12.03	14.17

4.4.2 Training and matching time

In term of computation time, LOFESS converged after 200–500 iterations during training, which means the error function was almost stable. Detailed tables about training time (in min) corresponding to region size (in rows) and number of bases (in columns) are given in Tables 8 and 9. In return, the time for projecting a test image onto the LOFESS space and matching based on Euclidean distance is less than one second, which is ideal for real-time applications.

4.4.3 Occlusion form

Various occlusion forms should be handled differently due to their nature. For instance, a region occluded by scarf is wider than that by sunglasses. This loss in information some how accounts for different results between types of occlusion. Basically, this is the common fact encountered in almost appearance-based approaches [14]. LOFESS allows a user to input a parameter telling which region should be discarded prior to the training phase. Then, the method automatically learns bases form non-occluded parts. In testing phase, all images are projected on these bases so occlusion is removed naturally.

5 Conclusions and future works

This paper presented the method Locality constrained feature representation for the disguised face recognition based on a small training set (LOFESS), which contains only one or two images per subject. By introducing spatially localized facial structure constraints, LOFESS effectively and efficiently captures prominent part-based features from non-occluded parts. Experiments showed this method is competitive with state of the art methods on AR datasets and can be extended to deal with other types of disguise, not just sunglasses or scarf. LOFESS is especially suitable for human supervising applications in which a suspect has his or her photos captured once or twice, such as identification (ID) or passport photos. Due to the constraint, features trained by NMF algorithm become more spatially localized and converge faster into expected facial regions. As a result, it obtains high recognition results even with very few training images.

Instead of prior knowledge from a user, LOFESS can be integrated with automatic occlusion detection algorithms. This is considered as our future work. After detecting occluded part, it is easily to exclude these regions and then follows the same process as presented in this paper. Alignment algorithms could be considered to enhance LOFESS robustness against time elapse. Moreover, how relationship between the optimal number of basis and the size of the extracted regions (the value r_1 and r_2) affects recognition performance also needs to be studied further.

Acknowledgments This research is funded by Vietnam National University HoChiMinh City (VNU-HCMC) under the project "Feature descriptor under variation condition for real-time face recognition application", 2014.

Open Access This article is distributed under the terms of the Creative Commons Attribution License which permits any use, distribution, and reproduction in any medium, provided the original author(s) and the source are credited.

References

1. Sinha, P.: Face recognition by humans: nineteen results all computer vision researchers should know about. Proc. IEEE **94**(11), 1948–1962 (2006)
2. Zhao, W., Chellapa, R., Phillips, P.J., Rosenfeld, A.: Face recognition: a literature survey. J. ACM Comput. Surv. **35**(4), 399–458 (2003)
3. Azeem, A., Sharif, M., Raza, M., Murtaza, M.: A survey: face recognition techniques under partial occlusion. Int Arab J Inform Technol **11**(1), 1–10 (2011)
4. Wright, J., Yang, A.Y., Ganesh, A., Sastry, S.S., Ma, Y.: Robust face recognition via sparse representation. IEEE Trans. Partern Anal. Mach. Intell. **31**(2), 210–227 (2008)
5. Yang, M., Zhang, D., Yang, J., Zhang, D.: Robust sparse coding for face recognition. IEEE Conference on Computer Vision and Pattern Recognition, pp. 625–632 (2011)
6. Chiang, C.C., Chen, Z.W.: Recognizing partially occluded faces by recovering normalized facial appearance. Int. J. Innovative Comput. Inform. Control **7**(11), 6210–6234 (2011)
7. Nguyen, M., Le, Q., Pham, V., Tran, T., Le, B.: Multi-scale sparse representation for Robust Face Recognition. IEEE Third International Conference on Knowledge and Systems Engineering, KSE 2011, Hanoi, Vietnam, October 14–17, pp. 195–199 (2011). ISBN 978-1-4577-1848-9
8. Rui, M., Hadid, A., Dugelay, J.: Improving the recognition of faces occluded by facial accessories. IEEE International Conference on Automatic Face and Gesture Recognition and Workshops, pp. 442–447 (2011)
9. Lee, D.D, Seung, H.S.: Algorithms for non-negative matrix factorization. In: NIPS, pp. 556–562 (2000)
10. Lee, D.D., Seung, H.S.: Learning the parts of objects by non-negative matrix factorization. Nature **401**(6755), 788–791 (1999)
11. Martine, A., Benavente, R.: The AR face database. (2011)
12. Turk, M., Pentland, A.: Eigenfaces for recognition. J. Cognitive Neurosci. **3**(1), 71–86 (1991)
13. Matthews, I., Baker, S.: Active apprearance models revisited. Int. J. Comput. Vis. **60**(2), 135–164 (2004)
14. Hyun, J.O., Lee, K.M., Lee, S.U.: Occlusion invariant face recognition using selective local non-negative matrix factorization basis images. Image Vis. Comput. **26**(11), 1515–1523 (2008)
15. Yang, M., Zhang, L.: Gabor feature based sparse representation for face recognition with gabor occlusion dictionary. European Conference on Computer Vision, pp. 448–461 (2010)
16. Shen, L., Bai, L.: A review on gabor wavelets for face recognition. Pattern Anal. Appl. **9**, 273–292 (2006)
17. Zhou, Z., Wagner, A., Mobahi, H., Wright, J., Ma, Y.: Face recognition with contiguous occlusion using markov random fields. International Conference on Computer Vision, pp. 1050–1057 (2009)
18. Liao, S., Jain, A.K.: Partial face recognition: an alignment free approach. International Joint Conference on Biometrics Compendium Biometrics, pp. 1–8 (2011)
19. Lin, C.J.: On the convergence of multiplicative update algorithms for nonnegative matrix factorization. IEEE Trans. Neural Netw. **18**(6), 1589–1596 (2007)
20. Hoyer, P.O.: Non-negative matrix factorization with sparseness constraints. Machine Learning, pp. 1457–1469 (2004)
21. Hoyer, P.O.: Non-negative sparse coding. Neutral Networks for Signal Processing, pp. 557–565 (2002)
22. Shastri, B.J., Levine, M.D.: Face recognition using localized features based on non-negative sparse coding. Mach. Vis. Appl. **18**(2), 107–122 (2007)
23. Li, S.Z., Hou, X.W., Zhang, H.J., Cheng, Q.S.: Learning spatially localized part-based representation. IEEE Conference on Computer Vision Pattern Recognition, pp. 207–212 (2001)
24. Ekenel, H.K., Stiefelhagen, R.: Why is facial occlusion a challenging problem. In: International Conference on Biometrics (2009)
25. Martinez, A.M.: Recognizing imprecisely localized, partially occluded, and expression variant faces from a single sample per class. IEEE Trans. Patern Anal. Mach. Intell. **24**(6), 748–763 (2002)
26. Rentzeperis E., Stergiou A., Pnevmatikakis A., Polymenakos L.: Impact of face registration errors on recognition. In: Articial Intelligence Applications and Innovations, pp. 187–194 (2006)
27. Chen, Y., Bao, H., He, X.: Non-negative local coordinate factorization for image representation. IEEE Conference on Computer Vision and Pattern Recognition, pp. 569–574 (2011)

17

Parallel multiclass stochastic gradient descent algorithms for classifying million images with very-high-dimensional signatures into thousands classes

Thanh-Nghi Do

Abstract The new parallel multiclass stochastic gradient descent algorithms aim at classifying million images with very-high-dimensional signatures into thousands of classes. We extend the stochastic gradient descent (SGD) for support vector machines (SVM-SGD) in several ways to develop the new multiclass SVM-SGD for efficiently classifying large image datasets into many classes. We propose (1) a balanced training algorithm for learning binary SVM-SGD classifiers, and (2) a parallel training process of classifiers with several multi-core computers/grid. The evaluation on 1000 classes of ImageNet, ILSVRC 2010 shows that our algorithm is 270 times faster than the state-of-the-art linear classifier LIBLINEAR.

Keywords Support vector machine · Stochastic gradient descent · Multiclass · Parallel algorithm · Large-scale image classification

1 Introduction

Visual classification is one of the important research topics in computer vision and machine learning. Low-level local features and bag-of-words model (BoW) are the core of state-of-the-art visual classification systems. The usual pipeline for visual classification task involves three steps: (1) extracting features, (2) building codebook and encoding features, and (3) training classifiers. Most of the methods based on this pipeline have been only evaluated on small datasets, e.g. Caltech 101 [1], Caltech 256 [2], and PASCAL VOC [3] that can fit into desktop memory. In step 3, most researchers may choose either linear or non-linear support vector machines (SVM) classifiers that can be trained in a few minutes.

However, the emergence of ImageNet dataset [4] poses more challenges for training classifiers. ImageNet is much larger in scale and diversity than the other benchmark datasets. The current release ImageNet has grown a big step in terms of the number of images and the number of classes, as shown in Fig. 1—it has more than 14 million images for 21,841 classes (more than 1,000 images for each class on average).

With millions of images, training an accurate classifier may take weeks or even years [5,6]. Therefore, the recent works in large-scale learning classifiers have focused on building linear classifiers for large-scale visual classification tasks. In many test cases, linear SVM classifier is a trade-off between training time and classification accuracy [7]. Shalev-Shwartz et al. [8] and [9] propose stochastic gradient descent algorithms for SVM (denoted by SVM-SGD) that shows the promising results for large-scale binary classification problems. An extension of SVM-SGD [10] uses the one-versus-all strategy for dealing with large-scale images in very-high-dimensional signatures and thousands classes. However, the current version of SVM-SGD does not take into account the benefits of high-performance computing (HPC). On ILSVRC 2010, it takes very long time to train 1000 binary classifiers. Therefore, it motivates us to study how to speed-up SVM-SGD for large-scale visual classification tasks. In this paper, we extend the binary SVM-SGD in several ways to develop the new parallel multiclass SVM-SGD algorithms for efficiently classifying large image datasets into many classes. The idea is to build

1. A balanced training algorithm for binary SVM-SGD classifiers,

T.-N. Do (✉)
College of Information Technology, Can Tho University,
Can Tho, Vietnam
e-mail: dtnghi@cit.ctu.edu.vn

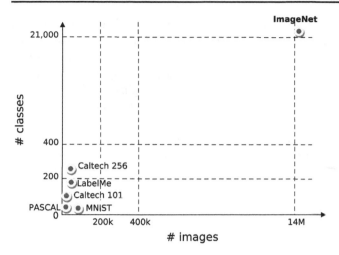

Fig. 1 A comparison of ImageNet with other benchmark datasets

2. A parallel training process of classifiers with several multi-core computers/grid.

The remainder of this paper is organized as follows: Sect. 2 briefly reviews the related work on large-scale visual classification. Section 3 introduces stochastic gradient descents for SVM. In Sect. 4, we present its improvement for large number of classes and describe how to speed-up the training process of SVM-SGD by using our balanced training algorithm and take into account the benefits of HPC. Section 5 presents numerical results before the conclusion and future work.

2 Related work

Many previous works on visual classification have relied on bag-of-words model, BoW [11], local feature quantization and SVM. These models may be enhanced by multi-scale spatial pyramids [12] on BoWs or histogram of oriented gradient [13] features. Some recent works consider exploiting the hierarchical structure of dataset for image recognition and achieve impressive improvements in accuracy and efficiency [14]. Related to classification is the problem of detection, often treated as repeated one-versus-all classification in sliding windows [3,15]. In many cases, such localization of objects might be useful for improving classification accuracy performance. However, in the context of large-scale visual classification with hundreds or thousands of classes, these common approaches become computationally intractable.

To address this problem, [16] study semi-supervised learning on 126 hand-labeled Tiny Images categories, [17] show classification experiments on a maximum of 315 categories. [18] do research with landmark classification on a collec-tion of 500 landmarks and 2 million images. On a small subset of ten classes, they have improved BoW classification by increasing the visual vocabulary up to 80 K visual words. Furthermore, the current released ImageNet makes the complexity of large-scale visual classification become a big challenge. To tackle this challenge, many researchers are beginning to study strategies on how to improve the accuracy performance and avoid using high-cost nonlinear kernel SVMs for training classifiers. The recent prominent works for these strategies are proposed in [5,6,19,20] where the data are first transformed by a nonlinear mapping induced by a particular kernel and then efficient linear classifiers are trained in the resulting space. They argue that the classification accuracy of linear classifiers with high-dimensional image representations is similar to low-dimensional BoW with non-linear kernel classifiers. Therefore, many previous works in large-scale visual classification have converged on building linear classifiers using the state-of-the-art linear classifier LIBLINEAR [21]. However, the recent works in [8] and [9] show empirically that SVM-SGD is faster than LIBLINEAR on many benchmark datasets. The recent work [20] and [10] study the impact of high-dimensional Fisher vectors on large-datasets. They show that the larger the training dataset, the higher the impact of the dimensionality on the classification accuracy. To get the state-of-the-art results on ILSVRC 2010, they make use of the spatial pyramids to increase the dimensionality of Fisher vector and then exploit Product Quantizer [22] to compress the data before training classifiers. With this method, the training data can fit into the main memory of a single computer (48 GB). To training classifiers, they employ Stochastic Gradient Descent [9] with early stopping, reweighting data, regularization, step size and the computation of dot product is parallelized on 16 cores of their computer. Our approach is quite different with this work in which we train classifiers with a sampling strategy and a smooth hinge loss function and parallelize the training task of binary classifiers on several multi-core computers.

A grid with several multi-core computers bring to us many advantages. Advanced technologies designed for the systems where several processes have access to shared or distributed memory space are becoming popular choice for high-performance computing algorithms. Therefore, it motivates us to investigate parallel solutions and demonstrate how SVM-SGD can benefit from modern platforms. Furthermore, in the case of large number of classes, we propose the balanced training algorithm that can be applied to speed-up the training process of classifiers without compromising classification accuracy. Our experiments show very good results and confirm that the balanced training algorithm and parallel solutions are very essential for large-scale visual classification in terms of training time and classification accuracy.

3 Support vector machines and stochastic gradient descent

3.1 Support vector machines (SVM)

Let us consider a linear binary classification task, as depicted in Fig. 2, with m datapoints x_i ($i = 1, \ldots, m$) in the n-dimensional input space R^n, having corresponding labels $y_i = \pm 1$. For this problem, the SVM algorithms [23] try to find the best separating plane (denoted by the normal vector $w \in R^n$ and the scalar $b \in R$), i.e. furthest from both class $+1$ and class -1. It can simply maximize the distance or margin between the supporting planes for each class ($x.w - b = +1$ for class $+1$, $x.w - b = -1$ for class -1). The margin between these supporting planes is $2/\|w\|$ (where $\|w\|$ is the 2-norm of the vector w). Any point x_i falling on the wrong side of its supporting plane is considered to be an error, denoted by z_i ($z_i \geq 0$). Therefore, the SVM has to simultaneously maximize the margin and minimize the error. The standard SVMs pursue these goals with the quadratic programming of (1).

$$\min \ \Psi(w, b, z) = \frac{1}{2}\|w\|^2 + C \sum_{i=1}^{m} z_i$$

$$s.t. : y_i(w.x_i - b) + z_i \geq 1 \tag{1}$$

$$z_i \geq 0,$$

where the positive constant C is used to tune errors and margin size.

The plane (w, b) is obtained by solving the quadratic programming (1). Then, the classification function of a new datapoint x based on the plane is

$$\text{predict}(x) = \text{sign}(w.x - b) \tag{2}$$

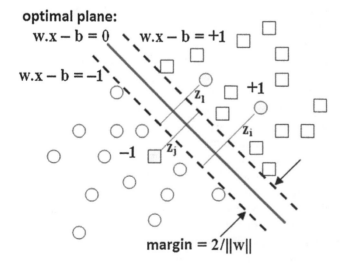

optimal plane:

margin = 2/‖w‖

Fig. 2 Linear separation of the datapoints into two classes

SVM can use some other classification functions, for example a polynomial function of degree d, a RBF (Radial Basis Function) or a sigmoid function. To change from a linear to non-linear classifier, one must only substitute a kernel evaluation in (1) instead of the original dot product. More details about SVM and other kernel-based learning methods can be found in [24].

Unfortunately, the computational cost requirements of the SVM solutions in (1) are at least $O(m^2)$, where m is the number of training datapoints, making classical SVM intractable for large datasets.

3.2 SVM with stochastic gradient descent (SGD)

We can reformulate the SVM problem in quadratic programming (1) in an unconstraint problem. We can ignore the bias b without generality loss. The constraints $y_i(w.x_i) + z_i \geq 1$ in (1) are rewritten as follows:

$$z_i \geq 1 - y_i(w.x_i) \tag{3}$$

The constraints (3) and $z_i \geq 0$ are rewritten by the hinge loss function:

$$z_i = max\{0, 1 - y_i(w.x_i)\} \tag{4}$$

Substituting for z from the constraint in terms of w into the objective function Ψ of the quadratic programming (1) yields an unconstrained problem (5):

$$\min \ \Psi(w, [x, y]) = \frac{\lambda}{2}\|w\|^2 + \frac{1}{m} \sum_{i=1}^{m} max\{0, 1 - y_i(w.x_i)\} \tag{5}$$

And then, [8,9] proposed the stochastic gradient descent method to solve the unconstrained problem (5). The stochastic gradient descent for SVM (denoted by SVM-SGD) updates w on T epochs with a learning rate η. For each epoch t, the SVM-SGD uses a single randomly received datapoint (x_i, y_i) to compute the sub-gradient $\nabla_t \Psi(w, [x_i, y_i])$ and update w_{t+1}.

As mentioned in [8,9], the SVM-SGD algorithm quickly converges to the optimal solution due to the fact that the unconstrained problem (5) is convex games on very large datasets. The algorithmic complexity of SVM-SGD is linear with the number of datapoints. An example of its effectiveness is given with the classification into two classes of 780,000 datapoints in 47,000-dimensional input space in 2 s on a PC and the test accuracy is similar to standard SVM.

4 Extentions of SVM-SGD to large number of classes

Most SVM algorithms are only able to deal with a two-class problem. There are several extensions of a binary classification SVM solver to multi-class (k classes, $k \geq 3$) classification tasks. The state-of-the-art multi-class SVMs are categorized into two types of approaches. The first one is considering the multi-class case in one optimization problem [25–27]. The second one is decomposing multi-class into a series of binary SVMs, including one-versus-all [23], one-versus-one [28] and Decision Directed Acyclic Graph [29].

In practice, one-versus-all, one-versus-one are the most popular methods due to their simplicity. Let us consider k classes ($k > 2$). The one-versus-all strategy builds k different classifiers where the ith classifier separates the ith class from the rest. The one-versus-one strategy constructs $k(k-1)/2$ classifiers, using all the binary pairwise combinations of the k classes. The class is then predicted with a majority vote.

When dealing with very large number of classes, e.g. thousands classes, the one-versus-one strategy is too expensive because it needs to train millions binary classifiers. Therefore, the one-versus-all strategy becomes popular in this case. However, the multiclass SVM-SGD algorithm using one-versus-all leads to the two problems:

1. the SVM-SGD algorithm deals with the imbalanced datasets for building binary classifiers,
2. the SVM-SGD algorithms also takes very long time to train very large number of binary classifiers in sequential mode using a single processor.

A recent multiclass SVM-SGD algorithm proposed by [10] uses the one-versus-all strategy for classifying large-scale images in very-high-dimensional signatures and thousands classes. The recommendations for this algorithm include early stopping, reweighting used to adjust the sample data, regularization, step size.

And then, our multiclass SVM-SGD algorithm also uses the one-versus-all approach to train independently k binary classifiers. We propose two ways for creating the new multiclass SVM-SGD algorithm being able to handle very large number of classes in high speed. The first one is to build balanced training of binary classifiers with a sampling strategy and a smooth hinge loss function. The second one is to parallelize the training task of all classifiers with several multi-core machines/grids.

4.1 Balanced training SVM-SGD

In the one-versus-all approach, the learning task of SVM-SGD tries to separate the ith class (positive class) from the $k-1$ others classes (negative class). For very large number of classes, e.g. 1,000 classes, this leads to the extreme imbalance between the positive and the negative class. The problem is well known as the class imbalance. The problem of the SVM-SGD algorithm comes from the update rule using a random received datapoint. The probability for a positive datapoint sampled is very small (about 0.001) compared with the large chance for a negative datapoint sampled (e.g. 0.999). And then, the SVM-SGD concentrates mostly on the errors produced by the nagative datapoints. Therefore, the SVM-SGD has difficulty to separate the positive class from the rest.

As summarized by the review papers of [30–32], and the very comprehensive papers of [33,34], solutions to the class imbalance problems were proposed both at the data and algorithmic level. At the data level, these algorithms change the class distribution, including over-sampling the minority class [35] or under-sampling the majority class [36,37]. At the algorithmic level, the solution is to re-balance the error rate by weighting each type of error with the corresponding cost.

Our balanced training SVM-SGD simultaneously uses the two approaches. Furthermore, the class prior probabilities in this context are highly unequal (e.g. the distribution of the positive class is 0.1 % in the 1,000 classes classification problem), and over-sampling the minority class is very expensive. Therefore, our balanced training SVM-SGD uses under-sampling the majority class (negative class). The balanced training SVM-SGD also modifies the updating rule using the skewed misclassification costs.

Although the SVM-SGD algorithm has impressive convergence properties due to the fact that the unconstrained problem (5) is convex games on very large datasets. The hinge loss function $L(w, [x_i, y_i]) = \max\{0, 1 - y_i(w.x_i)\}$ in the unconstrained problem (5) is discontinuously in the derivative at $y_i(w.x_i) = 1$, and then the SGD's convergence rate still cannot be faster than $O(\ln(T)/T)$ as mentioned in [38]. One way to resolve this issue is to use a surrogate smooth loss function of the hinge loss function in the unconstrained problem (5), this leads to achieve the optimal rate $O(1/T)$, illustrated in [39,40]. Then, we propose to substitute the hinge loss $L(w, [x_i, y_i]) = max\{0, 1 - y_i(w.x_i)\}$ in the unconstrained problem (5) by the smooth hinge loss [41], as follows:

$$L^s(w, [x_i, y_i]) = \begin{cases} \frac{1}{2} - y_i(w.x_i) & y_i(w.x_i) \leq 0 \\ \frac{1}{2}[1 - y_i(w.x_i)]^2 & 0 < y_i(w.x_i) < 1 \\ 0 & 1 \leq y_i(w.x_i) \end{cases}$$

$$(6)$$

And then our balanced training SVM-SGD for binary classification tasks (described in 1) updates w on T epochs. For each epoch t, the reduced dataset D' is created by the full set of positive class D_+ and under-sampling the negative class D'_-, the SVM-SGD randomly picks a datapoint (x_i, y_i) from the reduced dataset D' to compute the sub-gradient $\nabla_t \Psi(w, [x_i, y_i])$ (according to the smooth hinge loss (6) and update w_{t+1} (using the skewed misclassification costs) as follows:

$$w_{t+1} = w_t - \eta_t \nabla_t \Psi(w, [x_i, y_i]) = w_t - \eta_t(\lambda w_t$$
$$+ \nabla_t L^s(w, [x_i, y_i])) \qquad (7)$$

with $\nabla_t L^s(w, [x_i, y_i])$

$$= \begin{cases} -\frac{1}{|D_c|} y_i x_i & y_i(w_t.x_i) \le 0 \\ -\frac{1}{|D_c|} y_i x_i [1 - y_i(w_t.x_i)] & 0 < y_i(w_t.x_i) < 1 \quad (8) \\ 0 & 1 \le y_i(w_t.x_i) \end{cases}$$

where $|D_c|$ is the cardinality of the class $c \in \pm 1$.

Algorithm 1: Balanced training SVM-SGD for binary classification tasks

   input :

        training data of the positive class D_+
        training data of the negative class D_-
        positive constant $\lambda > 0$
        number of epochs T

   output:

        SVM-SGD model w

1   init $w_1 = 0$
2   **for** $t \leftarrow 1$ **to** T **do**
3   creating the reduced dataset D' from the full set of positive class D_+ and sampling without replacement D'_- from dataset D_- (with $|D'_-| = \sqrt{|D_-| \times |D_+|}$)
4   setting $\eta_t = \frac{1}{\lambda t}$
5   **for** $i \leftarrow 1$ **to** $|D_+|$ **do**
6   randomly pick a datapoint $[x_i, y_i]$ from reduced set D'
7   **if** $(y_i(w_t.x_i) \le 0)$ **then**
8            $w_{t+1} = w_t - \eta_t(\lambda w_t - \frac{1}{|D_{y_i}|} y_i x_i)$
9   **else if** $(y_i(w_t.x_i) < 1)$ **then**
10        $w_{t+1} = w_t - \eta_t\{\lambda w_t - \frac{1}{|D_{y_i}|} y_i x_i [1 - y_i(w_t.x_i)]\}$
11   **else**
12            $w_{t+1} = w_t - \eta_t \lambda w_t$
13   **end**
14   **end**
15 **end**
16 return w_{t+1}

We remark that the margin can be seen as the minimum distance between two convex hulls, H_+ of the positive class and H_- of the negative class (the farthest distance between the two classes). Under-sampling the negative class (D'_-) done by balanced training SVM-SGD provides the reduced convex hull of H_-, called H'_-. And then, the minimum distance between H_+ and H'_- is larger than H_+ and H_- (full dataset). It is easier to achieve the separating boundary than learning on the full dataset. Therefore, the training task of balanced SVM-SGD is fast to converge to the solution.

4.2 Parallel multiclass SVM-SGD training

For k classes problems, the multiclass SVM-SGD algorithm trains independently k binary classifiers. Although balanced training SVM-SGD deals with binary classification tasks with high speed, the multiclass SVM-SGD algorithm does not take the benefits of high-performance computing.

Our investigation aims at speedup training tasks of multiclass SVM-SGD with several multi-processor computers. The idea is to learn k binary classifiers in parallel.

The parallel programming is currently based on two major models, Message Passing Interface, MPI [42] and Open Multiprocessing, OpenMP [43]. MPI is a standardized and portable message-passing mechanism for distributed memory systems. MPI remains the dominant model (high performance, scalability, and portability) used in high-performance computing today. However, MPI process loads the whole dataset into memory during learning tasks, making it wasteful. The simplest development of parallel multiclass SVM-SGD algorithms is based on the shared memory multiprocessing programming model OpenMP. However, OpenMP is not guaranteed to make the most efficient computing. Finally, we present a hybrid approach that combines the benefits from both OpenMP and MPI models. The parallel learning for multiclass SVM-SGD is described in Algorithm 2. The number of MPI processes depends on the memory capacity of the HPC system used.

Algorithm 2: Hybrid MPI/OpenMP parallel multiclass SVM-SGD algorithm

   input :

        D the training dataset with k classes
        P the number of MPI processes

   output:

        SVM-SGD model

1   **Learning:**
2   $MPI - PROC_1$
3   *#pragma omp parallel for*
4   **for** $c_1 \leftarrow 1$ **to** k_1 **do**   /* class c_1 */
5   training SVM-SGD($c_1 - vs - all$)
6   **end**
7   $\vdots$
8   $MPI - PROC_P$
9   *#pragma omp parallel for*
10 **for** $c_P \leftarrow 1$ **to** k_P **do**   /* class c_P */
11   training SVM-SGD($c_P - vs - all$)
12 **end**

---

5 Experiments

We have implemented two parallel versions of SVM-SGD:

1. OpenMP version of balanced training SVM-SGD (Par-MC-SGD)
2. Hybrid MPI/OpenMP version of balanced training SVM-SGD (mpi-Par-MC-SGD)

Franc and Sonnenburg [44] have shown in their experiments that OCAS even in the early optimization steps shows often faster convergence than that seen so far in this domain prevailing approximative methods. Therefore, in this section we compare parallel algorithms of SVM-SGD with both OCAS and LIBLINEAR in terms of training time and classification accuracy.

OCAS. This is an optimized cutting plane algorithm for SVM [45] with the default parameter value $C = 1$.

LIBLINEAR. This is the linear SVM from [21] with default parameter value $C = 1$.

Par-MC-SGD, mpi-Par-MC-SGD. These are parallel balanced training SVM-SGD using $T = 20$ epochs and regularization term $\lambda = 0.0001$.

Our experiments are run on machine Linux 2.6.39-bpo.2-amd64, Intel(R) Xeon(R), CPU X5560, 2.8 GHz, 16 cores, and 96 GB main memory.

5.1 Dataset

The Par-MC-SGD, mpi-Par-MC-SGD algorithms are designed for large-scale datasets, so we have evaluated the performance of our approach on the three following datasets.

ImageNet 10. This dataset contains the 10 largest classes from ImageNet (24,807 images with size 2.4 GB). In each class, we sample 90 % images for training and 10 % images for testing (with random guess 10 %). First, we construct BoW of every image using dense SIFT descriptor (extracting SIFT on a dense grid of locations at a fixed scale and orientation) and 5,000 codewords. Then, we use feature mapping from [46] to get the high-dimensional image representation in 15,000 dimensions. This feature mapping has been proven to give a good image classification performance with linear classifiers [46]. We end up with 2.6 GB of training data.

ImageNet 100. This dataset contains the 100 largest classes from ImageNet (183,116 images with size 23.6 GB). In each class, we sample 50 % images for training and 50 % images for testing (with random guess 1 %). We also construct BoW of every image using dense SIFT descriptor and 5,000 codewords. For feature mapping, we use the same method as we do with ImageNet 10. The final size of training data is 8 GB.

ILSVRC 2010. This dataset contains 1,000 classes from ImageNet with 1.2M images (126 GB) for training, 50 K images (5.3 GB) for validation and 150 K images (16 GB) for testing. We use BoW feature set provided by [47] and the method reported in [48] to encode every image as a vector in 21,000 dimensions. We take ≤900 images per class for

training dataset, so the total training images is 887,816 and the training data size is 12.5 GB. All testing samples are used to test SVM models. Note that the random guess performance of this dataset is 0.1 %.

5.2 Training time

We have only evaluated the training time of SVM classifiers excluding the time needed to load data from disk. As shown in Figs. 3 and 4, on small and medium datasets as ImageNet 10, ImageNet 100, our parallel versions show a very good speed-up in training process, compared with OCAS and LIBLINEAR (Tables 1, 2).

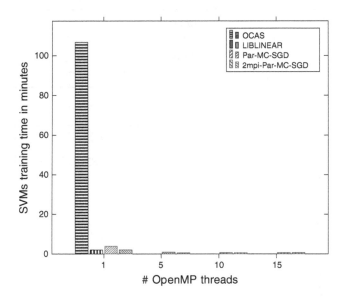

Fig. 3 SVMs training time with respect to the number of threads on ImageNet 10

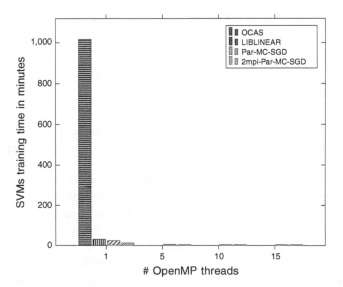

Fig. 4 SVMs training time with respect to the number of threads on ImageNet 100

Table 1 SVMs training time (minutes) on ImageNet 10

Method	# OpenMP threads			
	1	5	10	15
OCAS	106.67			
LIBLINEAR	2.02			
Par-MC-SGD	3.80	0.89	0.57	0.55
2mpi-Par-MC-SGD	1.99	0.54	0.54	**0.62**

Bold value indicates the best result

Table 2 SVMs training time (minutes) on ImageNet 100

Method	# OpenMP threads			
	1	5	10	15
OCAS	1016.35			
LIBLINEAR	30.41			
Par-MC-SGD	23.00	5.17	3.55	3.12
2mpi-Par-MC-SGD	12.15	3.11	2.78	**2.84**

Bold value indicates the best result

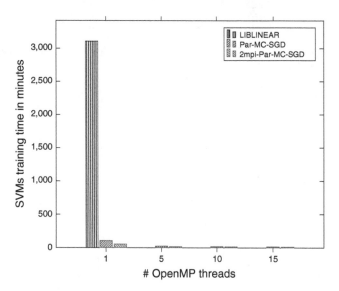

Fig. 5 SVMs training time with respect to the number of threads on ILSVRC 2010

ILSVRC 2010. Our implementations achieve a significant speed-up in training process when performing on large dataset ILSVRC 2010.

Balanced training SVM-SGD. As shown in Fig. 5, the balanced training version of SVM-SGD (Par-MC-SGD running with 1 thread) has a very fast convergence speed in training process: it is 30 times faster than LIBLINEAR (Table 3).

OpenMP balanced training SVM-SGD. On a multi-core machine, OpenMP version of balanced training SVM-SGD (Par-MC-SGD) achieves a significant speed-up in training process with 15 OpenMP threads. As shown in Fig. 5, our implementation is 249 times faster than LIBLINEAR

Table 3 SVMs training time (minutes) on ILSVRC 2010

Method	# OpenMP threads			
	1	5	10	15
OCAS	–			
LIBLINEAR	3106.48			
Par-MC-SGD	103.62	22.01	15.33	12.48
2mpi-Par-MC-SGD	51.97	14.11	11.69	**11.50**

Bold value indicates the best result

(Table 3). Due to the restriction of our computer (16 cores), we set the maximum number of OpenMP threads to 15. We can set more than 15 OpenMP threads, but according to our observation there is very few significant speed-up in training process because there is no more available core.

Hybrid MPI/OpenMP balanced training SVM-SGD. Although OpenMP balanced training SVM-SGD shows a significant speedup in training process, it does not ensure that the program achieves the most efficient high-performance computing on multi-core computer. Therefore, we explore this challenge using a combination of MPI and OpenMP models. With this approach, our implementation (mpi-Par-MC-SGD) achieves the impressive parallelization performance results on our computer. The program first loads the whole training data into computer memory and each MPI process can work with its local data independently. However, we cannot increase the number of MPI processes exceed the memory capacity of computer, because each MPI process occupies the main memory during its computation process, resulting in an increase in the overall memory requirement. OpenMP has been proven to work effectively on shared memory systems. It is used for fine-grained parallelization within each MPI process. Consequently, in each MPI process we can increase the number of OpenMP threads without demanding more extra memory. As shown in Fig. 5, our implementation achieves a significant performance in training process with 2 MPI processes and 15 OpenMP threads. It is 270 times faster than LIBLINEAR. On ILSVRC 2010, we need only 12 min to train 1000 binary classifiers, compared with LIB-LINEAR (~2 days and 4 h), as shown in Table 3. This result confirms that our approach has a great ability to scaleup to full ImageNet dataset with more than 21,000 classes.

5.3 Classification accuracy

As shown in Fig. 6, on the small datasets ImageNet 10 and medium dataset ImageNet 100, Par-MC-SGD provides very competitive performances when compared with LIBLIN-EAR.

We achieve a very good classification result on ILSVRC 2010. This is a large dataset with a large number of classes (1,000 classes) and a huge number of samples (more than 1

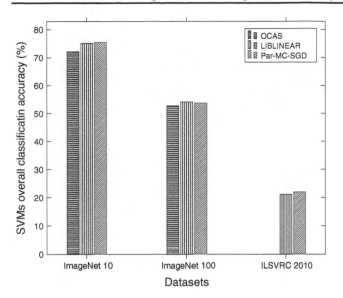

Fig. 6 Overall accuracy of SVM classifiers

Table 4 SVMs overall classification accuracy (%)

Dataset	ImageNet 10	ImageNet 100	ILSVRC 1000
OCAS	72.07	52.75	–
LIBLINEAR	75.09	54.07	21.11
Par-MC-SGD	**75.33**	53.60	**21.90**

Bold value indicates the best result

million samples), and the density of dataset is about 6 % (the proportion of non-zero elements of dataset in percent). Thus, it is very difficult for many state-of-the-art SVM solvers to obtain a high rate in classification performance. In particular, with the feature set provided by ILSVRC 2010 competition the state-of-the-art system [5] reports an accuracy of approximately 19 %, but it is far above random guess (0.1 %). And now our approach provides a significantly higher accuracy rate than [5] with the same feature set (21.90 vs. 19 %), as shown in Table 4. The relative improvement is more than 15 %. Moreover, we also compare our implementation with the current state-of-the-art of linear SVM classifiers LIB-LINEAR to validate our approach. As shown in Table 4, Par-MC-SGD outperforms LIBLINEAR (+ 0.79 %, the relative improvement is more than 3.7 %).

Note that Par-MC-SGD runs much faster than LIBLIN-EAR while yielding higher rate in classification accuracy.

6 Conclusion and future work

We have developed the extended versions of SVM-SGD in several ways to efficiently deal with large-scale datasets with very large number of classes like ImageNet. The primary idea is to build the balanced classifiers with a sampling strategy

and a smooth hinge loss function and then parallelize the training process of these classifiers with several multi-core computers.

Our approach has been evaluated on the 10, 100 largest classes of ImageNet and ILSVRC 2010. On ILSVRC 2010, our implementation is 270 times faster than LIBLINEAR. Therefore, we can achieve higher performances using more resources (CPU cores, computer, etc.). Furthermore, with our sampling strategy we significantly speed-up the training process of the classifiers while yielding a high performance in classification accuracy. We need only 12 min, to train 1,000 binary classifiers. Obviously, this is a roadmap towards full dataset with 21,000 classes of ImageNet. However, when the training data are larger, SVM-SGD requires a large amount of main memory due to loading the whole training data into main memory. This issue will be addressed in the next step. We may study the approach as reported in [49] and another possibility is to compress the training data and handle it on the fly [20]. In the near future we intend to provide more empirical test on full dataset with 21,000 classes of ImageNet and comparisons with parallel versions of LIBLINEAR.

Open Access This article is distributed under the terms of the Creative Commons Attribution License which permits any use, distribution, and reproduction in any medium, provided the original author(s) and the source are credited.

References

1. Li, F.F., Fergus, R., Perona, P.: Learning generative visual models from few training examples: an incremental bayesian approach tested on 101 object categories. Comput. Vis. Image Underst. **106**(1), 59–70 (2007)
2. Griffin, G., Holub, A., Perona, P.: Caltech-256 object category dataset. In: Technical Report CNS-TR-2007-001, California Institute of Technology (2007)
3. Everingham, M., Van Gool, L., Williams, C.K.I., Winn, J., Zisserman, A.: The pascal visual object classes (voc) challenge. Intern. J. Comput. Vis. **88**(2), 303–338 (2010)
4. Deng, J., Dong, W., Socher, R., Li, L.J., Li, K., Li, F.F.: Imagenet: a large-scale hierarchical image database. In: IEEE Computer Society Conference on Computer Vision and Pattern Recognition. pp. 248–255. (2009)
5. Deng, J., Berg, A.C., Li, K., Li, F.F.: What does classifying more than 10, 000 image categories tell us? In: European Conference on Computer Vision. pp. 71–84. (2010)
6. Lin, Y., Lv, F., Zhu, S., Yang, M., Cour, T., Yu, K., Cao, L., Huang, T.S.: Large-scale image classification: fast feature extraction and svm training. In: IEEE Computer Society Conference on Computer Vision and Pattern Recognition. pp. 1689–1696. (2011)
7. Dalal, N., Triggs, B.: Histograms of oriented gradients for human detection. In: IEEE Computer Society Conference on Computer Vision and Pattern Recognition. pp. 886–893. (2005)
8. Shalev-Shwartz, S., Singer, Y., Srebro, N.: Pegasos: Primal estimated sub-gradient solver for svm. In: Proceedings of the Twenty-

Fourth International Conference Machine Learning, pp. 807–814. ACM (2007)

9. Bottou, L., Bousquet, O.: The tradeoffs of large scale learning. In Platt, J., Koller, D., Singer, Y., Roweis, S. (eds.) Advances in Neural Information Processing Systems. NIPS Foundation, vol. 20, pp. 161–168. (2008)

10. Perronnin, F., Akata, Z., Harchaoui, Z., Schmid, C.: Towards good practice in large-scale learning for image classification. In: CVPR. pp. 3482–3489. (2012)

11. Csurka, G., Dance, C.R., Fan, L., Willamowski, J., Bray, C.: Visual categorization with bags of keypoints. In: In Workshop on Statistical Learning in Computer Vision. ECCV, pp. 1–22. (2004)

12. Lazebnik, S., Schmid, C., Ponce, J.: Beyond bags of features: spatial pyramid matching for recognizing natural scene categories. In: IEEE Computer Society Conference on Computer Vision and Pattern Recognition. pp. 2169–2178. (2006)

13. Dalal, N., Triggs, B.: Histograms of oriented gradients for human detection. In: IEEE Computer Society Conference on Computer Vision and Pattern Recognition. IEEE Computer Society pp. 886–893. (2005)

14. Griffin, G., Perona, D.: Learning and using taxonomies for fast visual categorization. In: IEEE Computer Society Conference on Computer Vision and Pattern Recognition. IEEE Computer Society (2008)

15. Vedaldi, A., Gulshan, V., Varma, M., Zisserman, A.: Multiple kernels for object detection. In: IEEE 12th International Conference on Computer Vision. IEEE, pp. 606–613. (2009)

16. Fergus, R., Weiss, Y., Torralba, A.: Semi-supervised learning in gigantic image collections. In: Advances in Neural Information Processing Systems. pp. 522–530. (2009)

17. Wang, C., Yan, S., Zhang, H.J.: Large scale natural image classification by sparsity exploration. In: Proceedings of the IEEE International Conference on Acoustics, Speech, and Signal Processing. IEEE, pp. 3709–3712. (2009)

18. Li, Y., Crandall, D.J., Huttenlocher, D.P.: Landmark classification in large-scale image collections. In: IEEE 12th International Conference on Computer Vision. IEEE, pp. 1957–1964. (2009)

19. Perronnin, F., Sánchez, J., Liu, Y.: Large-scale image categorization with explicit data embedding. In: CVPR. pp. 2297–2304. (2010)

20. Sánchez, J., Perronnin, F.: High-dimensional signature compression for large-scale image classification. In: IEEE Computer Society Conference on Computer Vision and Pattern Recognition. pp. 1665–1672. (2011)

21. Fan, R., Chang, K., Hsieh, C., Wang, X., Lin, C.: LIBLINEAR: a library for large linear classification. J. Mach. Learn. Res. 9(4), 1871–1874 (2008)

22. Jégou, H., Douze, M., Schmid, C.: Product quantization for nearest neighbor search. IEEE Trans. Pattern Anal. Mach. Intell. 33(1), 117–128 (2011)

23. Vapnik, V.: The Nature of Statistical Learning Theory. Springer, New York (1995)

24. Cristianini, N., Shawe-Taylor, J.: An Introduction to Support Vector Machines and Other Kernel-based Learning Methods. Cambridge University Press (2000)

25. Weston, J., Watkins, C.: Support vector machines for multi-class pattern recognition. In: Proceedings of the Seventh European Symposium on Artificial Neural Networks. pp. 219–224. (1999)

26. Guermeur, Y.: Svm multiclasses, théorie et applications (2007)

27. Crammer, K., Singer, Y.: On the algorithmic implementation of multiclass kernel-based vector machines. J. Mach. Learn. Res. 2, 265–292 (2001)

28. Krebel, U.: Pairwise classification and support vector machines. In: Support Vector Learning, Advances in Kernel Methods. pp. 255–268. (1999)

29. Platt, J., Cristianini, N., Shawe-Taylor, J.: Large margin dags for multiclass classification. Adv. Neural. Inf. Process. Syst. 12, 547–553 (2000)

30. Japkowicz, N. (ed.): AAAI'Workshop on Learning from Imbalanced Data Sets. Number WS-00-05 in AAAI Tech Report (2000)

31. Weiss, G.M., Provost, F.: Learning when training data are costly: the effect of class distribution on tree induction. J. Artif. Intell. Res. 19, 315–354 (2003)

32. Visa, S., Ralescu, A.: Issues in mining imbalanced data sets—a review paper. In: Midwest Artificial Intelligence and Cognitive Science Conf., Dayton, USA, pp. 67–73. (2005)

33. Lenca, P. anf Lallich, S., Do, T.N., Pham, N.K.: A comparison of different off-centered entropies to deal with class imbalance for decision trees. In: The Pacific-Asia Conference on Knowledge Discovery and Data Mining, LNAI 5012, pp. 634–643. Springer (2008)

34. Pham, N.K., Do, T.N., Lenca, P., Lallich, S.: Using local node information in decision trees: coupling a local decision rule with an off-centered. In: International Conference on Data Mining, Las Vegas, Nevada, USA, pp. 117–123. CSREA Press (2008)

35. Chawla, N.V., Lazarevic, A., Hall, L.O., Bowyer, K.W.: Smoteboost: improving prediction of the minority class in boosting. In: In Proceedings of the Principles of Knowledge Discovery in Databases, PKDD-2003. pp. 107–119. (2003)

36. Liu, X.Y., Wu, J., Zhou, Z.H.: Exploratory undersampling for class-imbalance learning. IEEE Trans. Syst. Man Cybern. Part B 39(2), 539–550 (2009)

37. Ricamato, M.T., Marrocco, C., Tortorella, F.: Mcs-based balancing techniques for skewed classes: an empirical comparison. In: ICPR. pp. 1–4. (2008)

38. Shamir, O.: Making gradient descent optimal for strongly convex stochastic optimization. CoRR abs/1109.5647 (2011)

39. Ben-David, S., Loker, D., Srebro, N., Sridharan, K.: Minimizing the misclassification error rate using a surrogate convex loss. In: ICML. (2012)

40. Ouyang, H., Gray, A.G.: Stochastic smoothing for nonsmooth minimizations: accelerating sgd by exploiting structure. CoRR abs/1205.4481 (2012)

41. Rennie, J.D.M.: Derivation of the f-measure. Accessed Feb 2004

42. MPI-Forum.: MPI: a message-passing interface standard

43. Board, OpenMP Architecture Review: OpenMP application program interface version 3 (2008)

44. Franc, V., Sonnenburg, S.: Optimized cutting plane algorithm for support vector machines. In: International Conference on Machine Learning. pp. 320–327. (2008)

45. Franc, V., Sonnenburg, S.: Optimized cutting plane algorithm for large-scale risk minimization. J. Mach. Learn. Res. 10, 2157–2192 (2009)

46. Vedaldi, A., Zisserman, A.: Efficient additive kernels via explicit feature maps. IEEE Trans. Pattern Anal. Mach. Intell. 34(3), 480–492 (2012)

47. Berg, A., Deng, J., Li, F.F.: Large scale visual recognition challenge 2010. In: Technical Report (2010)

48. Wu, J.: Power mean svm for large scale visual classification. In: IEEE Computer Society Conference on Computer Vision and Pattern Recognition. pp. 2344–2351. (2012)

49. Do, T.N., Nguyen, V.H., Poulet, F.: Gpu-based parallel svm algorithm. J. Front. Comput. Sci. Technol. 3(4), 368–377 (2009)

18

Applying authentication and network security to in-cloud enterprise resource planning system

Bao Rong Chang · Hsiu-Fen Tsai · Yun-Che Tsai · Yi-Sheng Chang

Abstract The service-oriented hosts in enterprises like enterprise resources planning (ERP) system have always encountered the crucial problem of unexpected down-time or system failure that will cause data loss and system termination. Failover is a challenge issue that cannot be done successfully between physical hosts. Traditional information security using demilitarized zone approach costs a lot. Therefore, this paper introduces in-cloud enterprise resources planning (in-cloud ERP) deployed in the virtual machine cluster together with access control authentication and network security which can resolve the three problems mentioned above. Access control authentication and network security have been implemented in the cloud computing system to prevent the service-oriented hosts form external fraud, intrusion, or malicious attacks. As a result of the experiments the number of accessing in-cloud ERP is 5.2 times as many as in-house ERP. The total expenditure of in-cloud ERP has decreased significantly to 48.4 % the cost of in-house ERP. In terms of operational speed, the approach proposed in this paper outperforms two well-known benchmark ERP systems, in-house ECC 6.0 and in-cloud ByDesign.

B. R. Chang (✉) · Y.-C. Tsai · Y.-S. Chang
Department of Computer Science and Information Engineering,
National University of Kaohsiung, Kaohsiung, Taiwan
e-mail: brchang@nuk.edu.tw

Y.-C. Tsai
e-mail: m1015507@mail.nuk.edu.tw

Y.-S. Chang
e-mail: m1025512@mail.nuk.edu.tw

H.-F. Tsai
Department of Marketing Management,
Shu Te University, Kaohsiung, Taiwan
e-mail: soenfen@stu.edu.tw

Keywords In-cloud enterprise resources planning · Access control authentication · Biometrics · Network security · Virtual network

1 Introduction

Nowadays the service-oriented hosts (e.g. ERP system, websites, databases, AP Server, file servers) in enterprises have often encountered the crucial problem of unexpected downtime or system failure that will cause data error, the termination of production lines, the pause of operating procedures, and even the loss of a huge of important data. Traditionally, a real host is difficult to transfer everything to another host timely and then resume its task as usual, and further data cannot be updated to the latest ones. Apparently software, hardware, and data are the most challenging problems for the failover problem. In this paper, we introduce in-cloud service solutions to the above-mentioned crucial problem to avoid data loss and system termination, as well as make good use of virtual machine (VM) cluster [1–3] to resolve the failover problem. As for information security, both access control authentication and network security have been implemented in the cloud computing system to prevent the service-oriented hosts form external fraud, intrusion, or malicious attacks. Advantages of in-cloud services include significant decrease of hardware cost, centralized monitoring, rapid and convenient management, dynamic optimization, highly efficient backup, and faster operational speed.

This paper introduces in-cloud enterprise resources planning (ERP) [4,5] in virtual environment and mobile device users can easily access the in-cloud services via wired or wireless network, as shown in Figs. 1 and 2, with access control authentication and network security [6]. As shown in Fig. 3, a open source ERP, OpenERP [7], has deployed

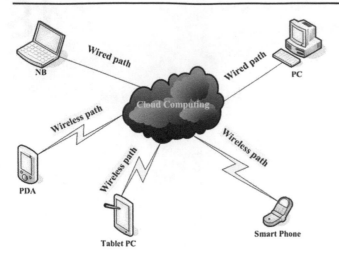

Fig. 1 Cloud-mobile computing services via WiFi/3G or Ethernet

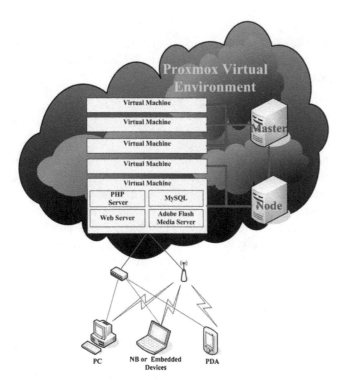

Fig. 2 Cloud-based proxmox virtual environment

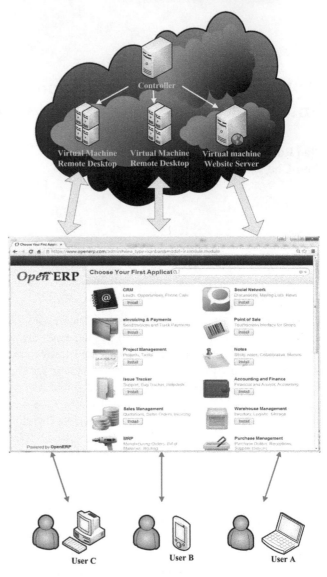

Fig. 3 OpenERP deployment (http://v6.openerp.com/node/910)

2 Related works

Virtual machine clustering system in cloud is an integration of virtualization, VMs, and virtual services so that it can make existing resources be fully applied, such as VMware ESX/ESXi Server [12], Microsoft Hyper-V R2 [13], or Proxmox Virtual Environment [14]. This system can let users run many operating systems in a single physical computer simultaneously which largely decreases the expense of purchasing PCs. Most important of all, it has the following major functions, including VM live migration, virtual storage live migration, distributed resource scheduling, high availability, fault tolerance, backup and disaster recovery, the transfer from physical machines to VMs, direct hardware accessing, virtual network switching, and so forth. For commercial purpose, it can promote energy efficiency,

successfully. In addition, its access control authentication [8,9] has brought into the VM to achieve identity verification, safe sign-in, and attendance audit, as shown in Figs. 4 and 5. Besides, the VMs are also used to establish the firewall and gateway to isolate the virtual (internal) network from Internet where this scheme has secured the OpenERP and its related database enough. This scheme is not similar to traditional intrusion prevention system (IPS) to prevent the system from potential BotNet [10] and malicious attacks [11] using a demilitarized zone (DMZ) between internet and intranet because the latter costs a lot.

Fig. 4 Access control in a firm

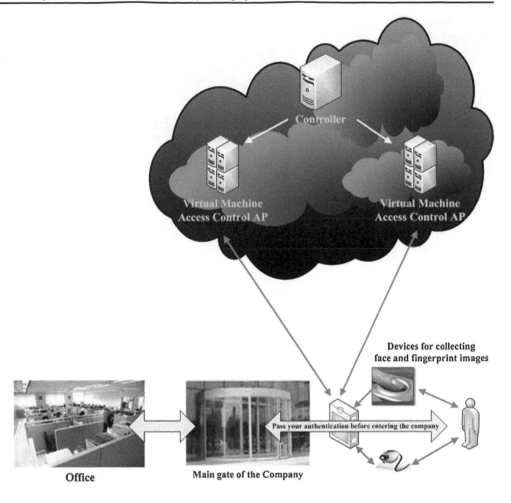

lower the demand for hardware, and increase the ratio of servers to operators to have a cost reduction. Besides, users can just use so-called low-cost thin client or PDA to link to the cloud platform to complete the routines rather than PCs. Furthermore, thin client has its own simple device architecture, extremely low possibility of malfunction, shutdown by overheating, and attacked by viruses. That mentioned above indeed saves not only cost but also power consumption.

Enterprise resources planning (ERP) is an enterprise resource management system that is a combination of enterprise management concepts, business processes, basic data, human and material resources, and computer hardware and software. ERP is an advanced business management model, that is also able to elevate business benefits. Having an overall balance, coordinating every management department, developing market-oriented activities, improving core competitiveness, and even attaining the best business benefits are the key functions. Cloud computing is highly beneficial for ERP. It is not necessary to modify or redesign the old system for transferring the original ERP to the cloud

platform, but all we need to do is simple transformation. The system will lessen the cost of redevelopment of programs, as well as there is no necessity for staffs to be retrained or to get accustomed to a new environment. In other words, we can create a similar system-dependent environment based on the virtualization technology, but it will actually become a more efficiently brand-new architecture. Staffs in enterprises operate at the same ERP as usual, and they conduct Web remote connection operation via the end-user devices like smart phones and tablets. With excellent flexibility and mobility, it broaden the working range from only offices to almost everywhere. This study introduces the open software, Proxmox Virtual Environment [14] hypervisor, as the cloud computing and service platform with the virtual environment. The kernel-based virtual machine (KVM) acts as the main core of VM, and it has installed the kernel of Linux-based operating system. OpenERP [7] is adopted in this study as an ERP application which provides many solutions for open-source softwares in the future, having it more expandable, making a great progress on cost deduction.

Fig. 5 Access control
authentication in cloud

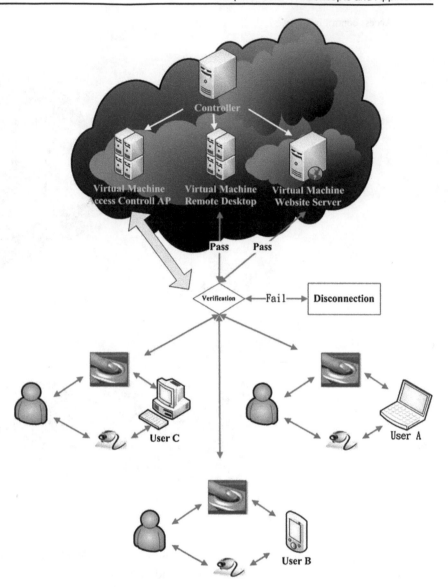

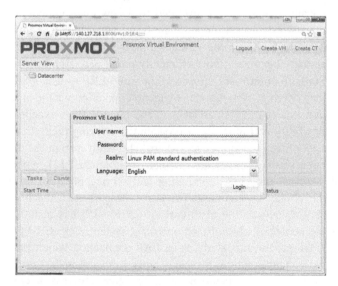

Fig. 6 Login to Proxmox VE virtual machine clustering server

3 Method and procedure

3.1 Virtual machine management and OpenERP in the cloud

The following procedure will give us an insight to under-stand how to set up a private cloud using the Proxmox VE hypervisor as well as to install OpenERP in the cloud.

(1) Build Proxmox VE virtual machine cluster, and through WebPages manage the VM. The webpages of login and management are shown individually in Figs. 6 and 7.
(2) Create a VM and set up its guest operating system in Proxmox VE virtual machine cluster.
(3) Set up OpenERP in VM, inclusive of OpenERP AP, Post-greSQL database, and web interface for end-user. Instal-

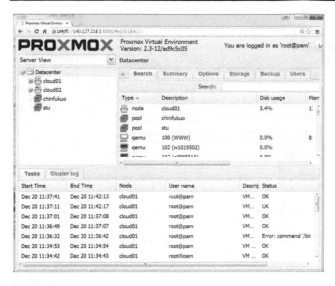

Fig. 7 Management webpage of Proxmox VE virtual machine clustering server

lation process is shown in Fig. 8 and the installation has completed as shown in Fig. 9.

(4) Sign in at http://localhost:8096 or http://IP:8096 with the browser on VM, pop up a login page of OpenERP as shown in Fig. 10, and then login to administrator to install the necessary modules as a result of an interface of user management as shown in Fig. 11.

(5) Set up AP server for biometric measures security [15]. When users sign in, it will collect users' biometric features with capturing devices at client side as the evidence of legal or illegal sign-in [16].

3.2 Enhancement of network security

Traditional information technology (IT) network management is a kind of the rather complicated work, which has concerned the difficulty of management increased by not only numerous servers, but also a large number of network cables. At this moment the benefits of virtualization will be immediately apparent because the layout or configuration of original complex network is sneaked and the original complex network becomes part of a virtual network, as well as the original servers can be consolidated into the virtual machines. Therefore, IT manager only needs to consider the inside and outside of the network configuration and security issues. The use of VMs to build firewall and gateway receives multiple benefits, that is, easy management, high scalability and low cost. For example, a VM equipped with pfSense [17] or Zentyal [18] system is all quite easy to manage a network system as shown in Fig. 12.

IT manager has to establish an external network interface because the web interface for an OpenERP [7] system needs to provide all kind of users from different domains. However, ERP databases containing sensitive information are not allowed to access its data directly from the external network, instead to set up an intranet one for data access. According to a variety of different VM managements, there are many different approaches to virtual network layout or configuration. For example, if virtual machine management has its own built-in NAT function, IT manager may install an OpenERP [7] into a VM with two network interface cards: one connected to the external network via the bridge mode for internet, whereas the other connected internally via NAT mode

Fig. 8 Installation for OpenERP system

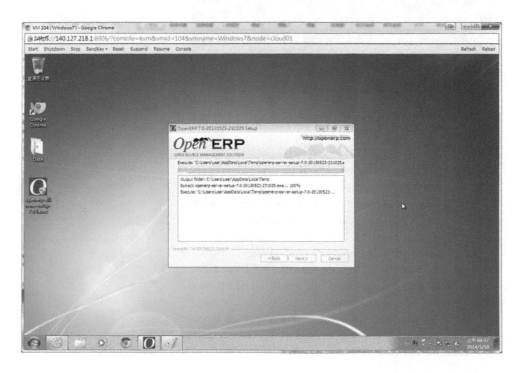

Fig. 9 OpenERP installation success

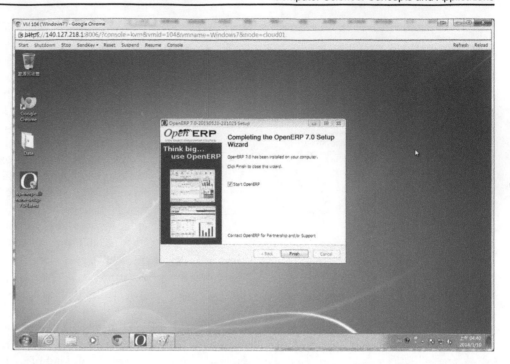

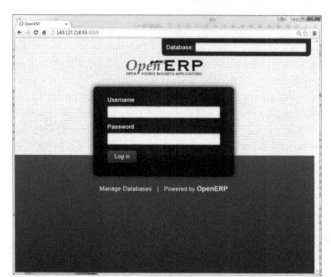

Fig. 10 Remote login to OpenERP system

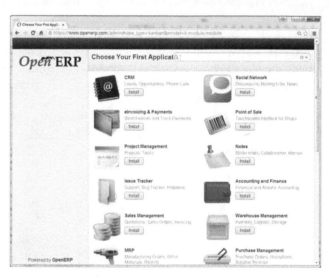

Fig. 11 An interface of user management in OpenERP

for intranet. Without software firewall for protection, the network does not come up with a hardware firewall, apparently leading to less secure environment in which even common network attacks may also cause system crash as shown in Fig. 13.

In addition to the scenario mentioned above, IT manager does not consider the use of the built-in NAT function in virtualization management, and in contrast takes alternative scheme into account employing pfSense [17] or Zentyal [18] to build a software firewall server. This way goes through port forwarding service to redirect http port packets to OpenERP. External network cannot access the interior one where

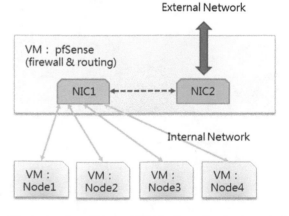

Fig. 12 Application pfSense establishing firewall and gateway in cloud

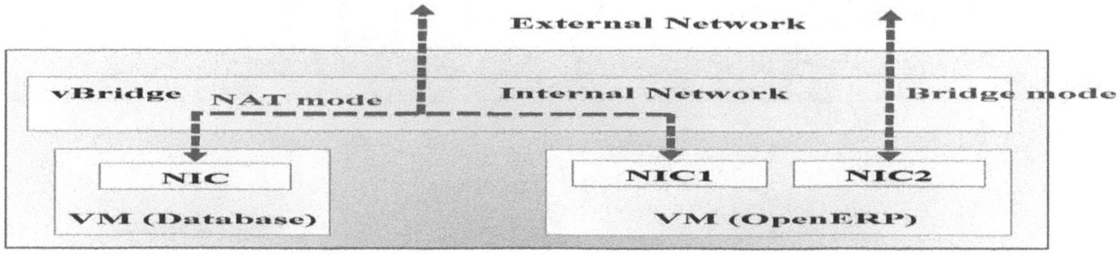

Fig. 13 A built-in NAT
function in virtualization
management establishing
network architecture

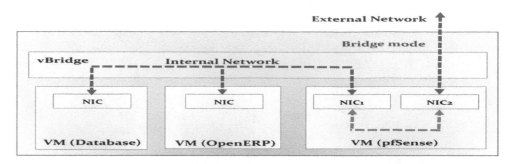

Fig. 14 Application pfSense
establishing network
architecture

Fig. 15 Access control authentication via face and fingerprint identification at a smart phone

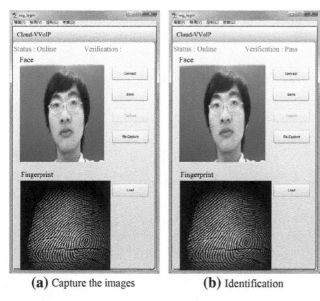

(**a**) Capture the images   (**b**) Identification

(**a**) List of products   (**b**) Sales order

Fig. 16 Sign-in to in-cloud OpenERP system on a smart phone

port forwarding service is not allowed or set. Besides protection against the common network attacks, it can also ensure
that the user interface gains both the security and stability as
shown in Fig. 14.

fingerprint at mobile device, deliver them to back-end server
for identification, and then return the result back to mobile
device. It takes about 2 s for identity verification as shown in
Fig. 15. After that we begin to test ERP routines as shown in
Fig. 16.

4 Experimental results and discussion

4.1 Smart phone remote login testing and access control authentication

Users sign in at http://IP:8096 with the browser on an Android
smart phone to sign in in-cloud ERP remotely via 3G/WiFi.
Next based on biometric measures the process of access control authentication is activated to capture human face and

4.2 Personal computer remote login testing and test of network security on ERP database

Users sign in http://IP:8096 with browser on a personal computer to sign in in-cloud ERP remotely via 3G/WiFi and then
go for access control authentication at PC. After that we begin
to test ERP routines as shown in Fig. 17. In terms of network

(a) List of products

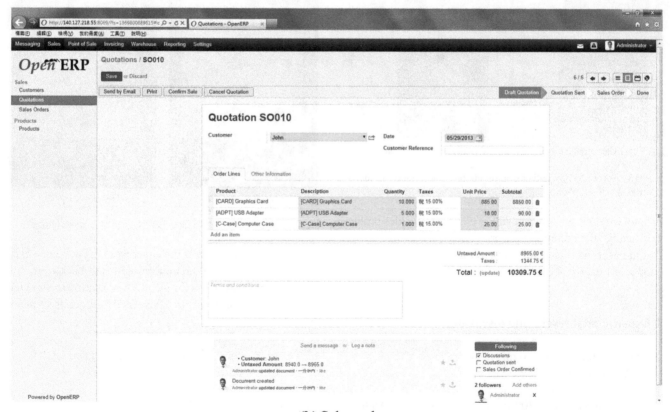

(b) Sales order

Fig. 17 Sign-in to in-cloud OpenERP system on a personal computer

Fig. 18 Simulation of SQL
Injection attack using jSQL
Injection v0.4

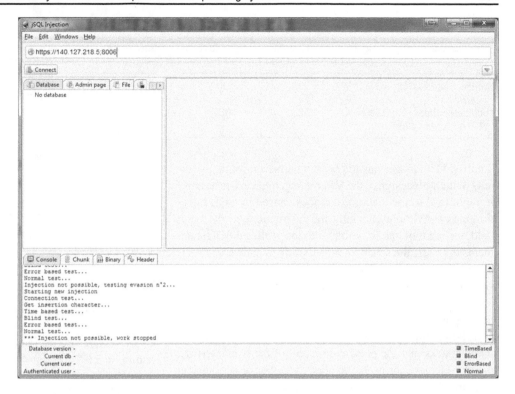

Fig. 19 Simulation of SQL
Injection attack using SQL
Power Injector 1.2

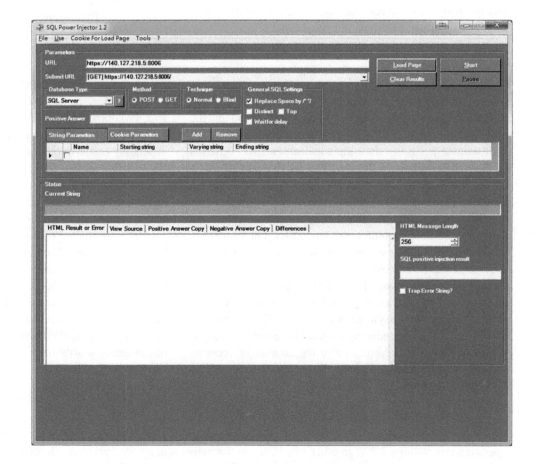

Table 1 A comparison of the number of accesses and total expenditure

ERP assessment	Case A: in-house ERP	Case B: in-cloud ERP	Ratio (B/A) (%)
Number of access (times/day)	63	328	520.6
Total expenditure (US dollars/month)	103.6	50.1	48.4

Table 2 Mobile phone power consumption estimation

Electricity	Theoretical power consumption	Measured power consumption
Battery capacity (mAh)	1,460	1,460
Voltage (V)	3.7 V	3.76–3.88 V
Watt hour	1.46 A $\times$ 3.7 V = 5.402 Wh (battery enclosure marked 5.5 Wh)	1.46 A $\times$ 3.82 V = 5.577 Wh

Table 3 Measured data in average for CPU

Electricity	Measured data
Voltage	1.09 V
Current	1.66 A
Power	1.66 A $\times$ 10 % $\times$ 1.09 V $\times$ 3,600 = 651.384 W

security, IT manager has to check whether or not the weakness of the web design of the VM management exists because it might lead to the malicious attacks caused by SQL Injection attack. Without checking the instructions in the input field, testing tool has been forced to insert illegal SQL statements to access the sensitive information in database. This is a scenario for the simulation of malicious attacks into a sensitive database. Therefore, two Open Source SQL Injection checking softwares are used as the testing tool: Java-based development jSQL Injection and .NET-based development SQL Power Injector. With this tool to launch a series of automatic attacks into the presentation part of the web interface, thereby IT manager is able to check whether or not outsider can directly access the database content. As a result, there is no SQL Injection vulnerability displayed in the testing tool and the following figures also show that no database was found in the target, as shown in Figs. 18 and 19.

4.3 Assessment and discussion

According to the experiments of online testing in the daily use of ERP in enterprise within a week, it was found that the growth rate of the use of in-cloud ERP increased dramatically approximate 5.2 times than the stand-alone ERP. In terms of the hardware cost in Taiwan, it costs the user $1,002.5 on the hardware equipment for a stand-alone ERP, i.e. in-house ERP, in which the additional cost will be paid for air conditioning monthly fee of $18.4, space rent of $26.7, and hardware equipment maintenance fee of $16.7. In regard with the amortization expensive per month for a period of 2 years, the total expenditure costs $2,486.3. In other words, it costs an average monthly usage fee of $103.6. In contrast, renting an in-cloud ERP service in virtual environment only needs about $50.1 monthly payment and it saves 1.07 times the cost of in-house ERP, i.e., reducing the total expenditure a lot. As shown in Table 1, a comparison of the number of accesses and the total expenditure for ERP, the proposed in-cloud ERP is exclusively superior to in-house ERP.

According to the electricity specification indicated on the casing of mobile phone battery, for example Sony Ericsson Xperia Ray, battery capacity has marked 1,460 mAh with operating rate voltage 3.7 V; in other words, it can theoretically deliver the power operational rate about 5.402 Wh, as listed in Table 2, when it works continuously and exhaus-

tively. As a result, the measured highest rating of power consumption 5.6721 Wh at Android mobile phone tested by software ZDbox [19] is a little bit higher than the theoretical one as indicated in Table 2.

The necessary data about CPU electricity as mentioned above, while ERP appliction is running in a PC, will be summarized herein in Table 3. As a result, ERP in cloud, the power consumption is about 681.264 W while ERP application is running in a PC.

When there are ten clients connected to a VM in Proxmox VE hypervisor, we can collect and organize the VM workload with Proxmox VE management tools at the master site to look at the information about CPU, memory, and bandwidth, depending on the number of simultaneous calls, as shown in Fig. 20 and listed in Table 4.

Two remarkable benchmark ERP platforms, ECC 6.0 [20] and ByDesign [21], are included in a comparative study for ERP performance evaluation where the most concerned measure in term of ERP operational speed is the response time for four operations: Create New Customer Master Data, Create New Material Master, Create Sales Order, and Search Function. As listed in Table 5, the comparison of performance with three different ERP systems, in-House ECC 6.0, in-cloud ByDesign, and in-cloud OpenERP, is consequently shown that the method we proposed here outperforms the others due to shorter response time in ERP operation.

However, the response time to several operational functions is measured individually as listed in Table 5, and the rating of three different ERP systems is the most concerned issue for the enterprise and its summary is listed in Table 6.

According to the assessment of several ERP systems as mentioned above, the in-cloud OpenERP system can perform very well with Proxmox VE hypervisor to show the following advantages: (a) reduction of the total expenditure on hard-

Fig. 20 Monitoring the VM workload in Proxmox VE

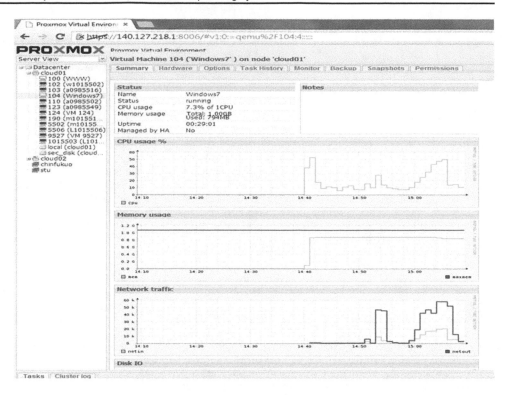

Table 4 Stress test of VM workload

Option	Quantity
Clients number	10
Bandwidth	20 Kbps
CPU usage	30 % of 1CPU
Memory usage	802 MB

Table 5 Performance comparison of ERP systems according to the operational speed

Operational speed	ECC 6.0 (in-house ERP)	ByDesign (in-cloud ERP)	OpenERP (in-cloud ERP)
Create new customer master data (mins)	7:10	4:40	3
Create new material master (mins)	12:40	10	8:30
Create sales order (mins)	5:20	2	1:30
Search function	2:10 mins	5 s	2 s

Table 6 The rating of three different ERP systems

Rating	ECC 6.0 (in-house ERP)	ByDesign (in-cloud ERP)	OpenERP (in-cloud ERP)
Total expenditure	High	Medium	Low
Response time	Long	Medium	Short
User interface	Average	Good	Excellent
Security	Medium	Low	High
Scalability	Small	Medium	Large

ware/software, IT equipment, and manpower for IT maintenance, (b) high elasticity for supporting mobile computing to fast response to the requests from clients so as to elevate the business competition, and (c) both distributed storage and centralized computation to increase data backup for achieving system reliability as well as enhancing data security.

5 Conclusions

This paper introduces in-cloud ERP deployed in the VM cluster together with access control authentication and network security. This scheme can resolve three problems: (a) unexpected down-time or system failure that will cause data loss and system termination, (b) failover cannot be done successfully between physical hosts, and (c) traditional information security using DMZ approach costs a lot. It turns out for easing data management, quickly responding to users' demands, making the products to be relatively outstanding among many enterprises, and obtaining the maximum benefit. Access control authentication and network security have been designed in the cloud computing system to prevent the service-oriented hosts form external fraud, intrusion, or malicious attacks. As a result, according to the experiments the proposed approach in this paper outperforms two well-known benchmark ERP systems, in-house ECC 6.0, and in-cloud ByDesign.

Acknowledgments This work is supported by the National Science Council, Taiwan, Republic of China, under Grant Number **NSC 100-2221-E-390 -011 -MY3**.

Open Access   This article is distributed under the terms of the Creative Commons Attribution License which permits any use, distribution, and reproduction in any medium, provided the original author(s) and the source are credited.

References

1. Beloglazov, A., Buyya, R.: Energy efficient allocation of virtual machines in cloud data centers. In: Proceedings 10th IEEE/ACM international conference on cluster, cloud and grid, computing, pp. 577–578 (2010)

2. Laurikainen, R., Laitinen, J., Lehtovuori, P., Nurminen, J.K.: Improving the efficiency of deploying virtual machines in a cloud environment. In: Proceedings 2012 international conference on cloud and service, computing, pp. 232–239 (2012)

3. Sotiriadis, S., Bessis, N., Xhafa, F., Antonopoulos, N.: Cloud virtual machine scheduling: modelling the cloud virtual machine instantiation. In: Proceedings sixth international conference on complex, intelligent and software intensive systems, pp. 233–240 (2012)

4. Yang, T.-S., Choi, J., Zheng, X., Sun, Y.-H., Ouyang, C.-S., Huang, Y.-X.: Research of enterprise resource planning in a specific enterprise. In: Proceedings 2006 IEEE international conference on systems, man, and cybernetics, pp. 418–422 (2006)

5. de Carvalho, R.A., Monnerat, R.M., Sun, Y.-H., Ouyang, C.-S., Huang, Y.-X.: Development support tools for enterprise resource planning. IT Prof. Mag. **10**(5), 39–45 (2008)

6. Wu, H.-Q., Ding, Y., Winer, C., Yao, L.: Network security for virtual machine in cloud computing. In: Proceedings 5th international conference on computer sciences and convergence information technology, pp. 18–21 (2010)

7. OpenERP, open source business applications: (2013)

8. Zhao, J.-G., Liu, J.-C., Fan, J.-J., Di, J.-X.: The security research of network access control system. In: Proceedings first ACIS international symposium on cryptography and network security, data mining and knowledge discovery, E-commerce & its applications and embedded systems, pp. 283–288 (2010)

9. Metz, C.: AAA protocols: authentication, authorization, and accounting for the Internet. IEEE Internet Comput. **3**(6), 75–79 (1999)

10. Zhang, L.-F., Persaud, A.G., Johnson, A., Yong, G.: Detection of stepping stone attack under delay and chaff perturbations. In: Proceedings 25th annual international performance, computing, and communications conference, p. 256 (2006)

11. Yang, H.-Y., Xie, L.-X., Xie, F.: A new approach to network anomaly attack detection. In: Proceedings fifth international conference on fuzzy systems and knowledge, discovery, pp. 317–321 (2008)

12. Chan, B.R., Tsai, H.-F., Chen, C.-M.: Evaluation of virtual machine performance and virtual consolidation ratio in cloud computing system. J. Inf. Hiding Multimed. Signal Process. **4**(3), 192–200 (2013)

13. Chang, B.R., Tsai, H.-F., Chen, C.-M., Lin, Z.-Y., Huang, C.-F.: Assessment of hypervisor and shared storage for cloud computing server. In: Proceedings the 3rd international conference on innovations in bio-inspired computing and applications, pp. 67–72 (2012)

14. Chang, B.R., Tsai, H.-F., Lin, Z.-Y., Chen, C.-M., Huang, C.-F.: Adaptive performance for VVoIP implementation in cloud computing environment. Lecture Notes Artif. Intell. **7198**(3), 356–365 (2012)

15. Wayman, J.L.: Biometrics in identity management systems. IEEE Secur. Priv. **6**(2), 30–37 (2008)

16. Chang, B.R., Huang, C.-F., Tsai, H.-F., Lin, Z.-Y.: Rapid access control on Ubuntu cloud computing with facial recognition and fingerprint identification. J. Inf. Hiding Multimed. Signal Process. **3**(2), 176–190 (2012)

17. pfSense.: (2013)

18. Zentyal.: (2013)

19. ZDbox, version: 3.5.222.:https://play.google.com/store/apps/details?id=com.zdworks.android.toolbox&feature=search _result#?t=W251bGwsMSwxLDEsImNvbS56ZHdvcmtzLm FuZHJvaWQudG9vbGJveCJd (2013)

20. Doedt, M., Steffen, B.,: Requirement-driven evaluation of remote ERP-system solutions: a service-oriented perspective. In: Proceedings 2011 34th IEEE software engineering, workshop, pp. 57–66 (2011)

21. Elragal, A., Kommos, M.E.: In-house versus in-cloud ERP systems: a comparative study. J. Enterp. Res. Plan. Stud. **2012**, (13). Article ID 659957 (2012)

19

An image segmentation approach for fruit defect detection using k-means clustering and graph-based algorithm

Van Huy Pham · Byung Ryong Lee

Abstract Machine vision has been introduced in variety of industrial applications for fruit processing, allowing the automation of tasks performed so far by human operators. Such an important task is the detection of defects present on fruit peel which helps to grade or to classify fruit quality. Image segmentation is usually the first step in detecting flaws in fruits and its result mainly affects the accuracy of the system. A diversity of methods of automatic segmentation for fruit images has been developed. In this paper, a hybrid algorithm, which is based on split and merge approach, is proposed for an image segmentation that can be used in fruit defect detection. The algorithm firstly uses k-means algorithm to split the original image into regions based on Euclidean color distance in $L^*a^*b^*$ space to produce an over-segmentation result. Then, based on a graph representation, a merge procedure using minimum spanning tree is then taken into account to iteratively merge similar regions into new homogenous ones. This combination is an efficient approach to employ the local and global characteristic of intensities in the image. The experiment showed good results in the terms of human observation and in processing time.

Keywords Image segmentation · Defect detection · K-means and graph

1 Introduction

Automatic inspection of fruits is the subject of many grading and sorting systems to decrease production costs and increase the quality of the production in the agro-industry. In the packing lines, where most external quality attributes are currently inspected visually, machine vision systems are powerful tools for performing this task automatically. These systems not only substitute human inspection but also improve its capabilities that go beyond the limited human capacity to evaluate long-term processes objectively or to appreciate the events that take place outside the visible electromagnetic spectrum that the human eye unable to see [1]. Such a system was developed in [2] for automatic grading of date fruits with the use of digital reflective near-infrared imaging.

The goal of many fruits' inspection systems based on computer vision is to extract features of the fruits of interest and relate them with the quality which is normally associated with the absence of defects on fruit peel. This makes the task of detection of defects present on fruit peel the target of many researches such as automatic citrus skin defect detection in [3] using a multivariate image analysis; detection of blemish in potatoes in [4], or in-line detection of apple defects in [5]. The core technique in this task is always related to image analysis and processing which is largely dependent on the segmentation procedure.

Image segmentation is usually the first step in detecting the flaws in fruits and its result mainly affects the successive stages in the process. It is a process of partitioning an image into some regions such that each region is homogeneous and none of the union of two adjacent regions is homogeneous [6]. In general, the automated segmentation is one of the most difficult tasks in the image analysis, because a false segmentation will cause degradation of the measurement process and therefore the interpretation may fail [7]. Variety approaches of segmentation for fruit defects detection have been developed in the literature. The existing techniques can be categorized into four classes ([6]): edge-based approaches, clustering-based approaches,

V. H. Pham (✉) · B. R. Lee
Department of Mechanical and Automotive Engineering,
University of Ulsan, Ulsan, South Korea
e-mail: pvhuy@ctu.edu.vn

B. R. Lee
e-mail: brlee@ulsan.ac.kr

region-based approaches, and split and merge approaches. However, as stated in [8], histogram-based thresholding is still the most referenced among segmentation methods.

Thresholding method is based on a threshold value to turn a gray-scale image into a binary image. The key of this method is to select a single threshold value or multiple-levels of thresholds. Riquelme et al. [8] and Liming and Yanchao [9] used simple Otsu's method to separate fruit area from background. Mery and Pedreschi [7] proposed an estimation for a global threshold using statistical approach and morphological operation to segment food images. Blasco et al. [10] used different thresholds for color channels in RGB color space to separate different categories of objects of interest and the background.

Most edge-based approaches use a differentiation filter to approximate the first-order image gradient or the image Laplacian to detect image edges and then, candidate edges are extracted by thresholding the gradient or Laplacian magnitude. Lopez [11] used a boundary detection method to segment defect areas in citrus based on Sobel gradient mask, and then boundaries of objects of interest were identified using neighborhood and gradient thresholds. A threshold for the Sobel operator was used in [2] to adjust the sensitivity of skin delamination detection. The main advantage of this approach is short computation time. However, these approaches suffer from serious difficulties in setting appropriate thresholds and producing continuous, one-pixel-wide contours [6].

In clustering-based approaches, image pixels are clustered according to their intensities or colors based on a pre-defined number of clusters. The number of obtained regions is usually greater than the cluster number because the location of pixels in the same cluster may not be adjacent. Several clustering-based approaches have been proposed, such as k-means or fuzzy-c-means (FCM). The main advantage of these approaches is that the difficult threshold setting problem could be avoided using iterative processes though it depends much on the number of clusters and the initial clusters. Moreover, the segmented contours are always continuous and one-pixel wide [6]. Because of the lack of using local properties of pixels, it may occur an over-segmentation problem. Usually, a merge process is further applied for solving this problem.

Region-based approaches are available because the segmented contours are always continuous and one-pixel wide. The goal in region-based approaches is detection of regions that satisfy certain pre-defined homogeneity criteria [6]. A region-oriented segmentation in [12] was proposed for detecting most common peel defects of citrus fruits and was able to correctly detect 95 % of the defects. The difficulty of the region-growing approach is to set a threshold which is sensitive in measuring the similarity. A similar watersheds' method such as flood algorithm was employed in [5] and

[13] for apple defect detection. However, different similarity threshold settings may lead to different segmentation results and may cause the over-segmentation problem.

In split and merge approaches, the input image is first sub-divided into a set of homogeneous primitive regions. Then, similar neighboring regions are merged according to certain decision rules. Several split approaches are available, such as pyramidal segmentation, watershed ([14]), FCM, and k-means, which usually produce over-segmentation results. Region adjacent graph (RAG) and nearest neighbor graph (NNG) are both available structures for merge process ([15]). RAG and NNG are usually applied with a greedy process for merging adjacent regions, until a pre-defined stop condition is satisfied.

The increase in computer power at affordable prices and the introduction of multiple core processors allow to process complex images in a short time and to use more complex algorithm. In this paper, based on split and merge approach, we proposed a new hybrid algorithm that uses k-means clustering and Graph-based technique for splitting and merging image regions to segment fruit images. This combination is an efficient approach to employ the local and global characteristic of the image intensities as shown in the experimental results.

The objective of this work is to develop a general algorithm to effectively segment objects in images to facilitate fruit defect detection. For splitting an image, a segmentation scheme using k-means clustering is used to over-segment the original image because it is known to give a good segmentation result and time efficiency. Region Adjacency Graph (RAG) is then used to represent region structure to facilitate the merge procedure where similar regions are iteratively merged into new homogeneous ones based on minimum spanning tree algorithm. The approach does not aim at all kinds of fruits. We just want to contribute one more choice among a variety of algorithms for the segmentation task. The selection of suitable algorithm is application dependent. The difficulties for fruit defect segmentation are not only kinds of fruits but also defect types of each kind of fruits. Some kinds of defects cannot be detected by nondestructive or appearance-based methods. To have agricultural expert knowledge is essential for algorithm design for a specific application. For academic research in the field of computer vision, our approach just limits at proposing a new hybrid algorithm for the segmentation task that hopefully can be applied successfully for some kinds of specific fruits and the fruits used in our experiments are just for illustration.

The rest of the paper is organized as follows: The proposed hybrid method is detailed in Sect. 2. In Sect. 3, system setup to acquire fruit images and experimental results are described. The conclusion is in Sect. 4.

2 Segmentation method

There exist several image analysis methods for defect detection, including global gray-level or gradient thresholding, simple background subtraction, statistical classification and color classification [16]. Blemish segmentation is a difficult problem, because various types of blemishes with different size and extent of damage may occur on fruit surfaces [13]. In general, thresholding method may be failed in case of a slightly discolored blemish on a light colored surface.

For image segmentation, split and merge approach is an efficient approach to employ local and global characteristics of color intensities of an image. The method subdivides an image initially into a set of arbitrary and disjoint regions by a fast over-segmentation algorithm which produces regions as parts of objects of interest. Then, those regions are iteratively merged until satisfying the homogeneous condition or when no further merging is possible. An important characteristic of graph-based method as stated in [17] is its ability to preserve detail in low-variability image regions while ignoring detail in high-variability regions.

Because of noise and high variation in the original image, the obtained image after applying the k-means algorithm may include many small regions that should be merged to nearby regions to speed-up the merge procedure. So we can filter out these small regions using a threshold of region size. In our algorithm, small regions or regions with size smaller than a pre-defined constant will be merged to the biggest nearby region.

The overall process is shown in the flowchart in Fig. 1.

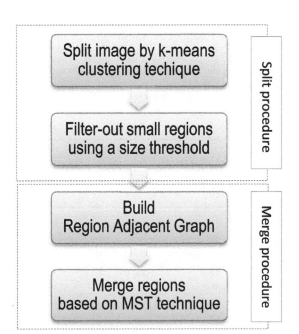

Fig. 1 Flowchart of the proposed algorithm

2.1 Split procedure

k-means is used in split procedure to produce initial regions. k-means is one of the simplest algorithms that solve the clustering problem. The k-means algorithm involves grouping pixels together whose feature vectors are close together. Here, it is used to group pixels in an image into a specified number of clusters which are then separated into various small regions based on adjacency relation.

The dimension of feature vectors depends on the number of color channels used. Lee [6] and Riquelme et al. [18] used gray-level based k-means for segmenting images. However, different color spaces such as RGB or Lab can be used to get more accurate result. In this paper, $L^*a^*b^*$ or CIE-Lab color space is used for k-means clustering. $L^*a^*b^*$ color space has an advantage of more perceptual uniformity than other spaces like RGB. Uniform changes of components in the $L^*a^*b^*$ color space aim to correspond to uniform changes in perceived color, so the relative perceptual differences between any two colors in $L^*a^*b^*$ can be approximated by treating each color as a point in a three-dimensional space (with three components: L^*, a^*, b^*). The distance between two colors can be measured by Euclidean distance.

The split algorithm is composed of the following steps:

Step 1: Place K points into the space represented by the objects (pixels) that should be clustered (according to K cluster). These points represent initial group centroids Z_k.

Step 2: Assign each object (pixel) to the group that has the closest centroid

$$x \in C_i \qquad \text{if dist}(x, Z_i) \leq \text{dist}\left(x, Z_j\right),$$
$$\text{for } j = 1, 2, \ldots, K (i \neq j)$$

where C_i is the ith cluster with the centroid Z_i.

Step 3: When all objects have been assigned, recalculate the cluster center Z_k- for all cluster C_k using the equation:

$$Z_k = \frac{1}{|C_k|} \sum_{s \in C_k} X_s, \quad k = 1, \ldots, K$$

where s is a member of C_k, X_s is the feature vector of s, and $|C_k|$ is the number of members in C_k.

Step 4: Repeat Steps 2 and 3 until the centroids no longer move (Z_k remains unchanged).

The selection of initial cluster centers is very important, and different sets of initial centers cause different results. In this paper, we divide the channel color range into $K + 1$ sections, and the end point of each section is chosen to be a component of the center. The initial cluster centers $Z_i = (Z_i^L, Z_i^a, Z_i^b)$ are determined as follow:

(a)   **(b)**

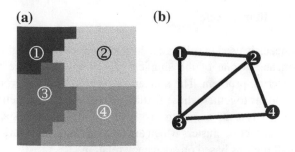

Fig. 2 Region adjacent graph. **a** Image regions, **b** corresponding RAG

Fig. 3 Experimental setup for mage acquisition.

$$Z_i^C = C_{\min} + i\frac{C_{\max} - C_{\min}}{K + 1} \quad \text{for } i = 1, 2, .. K$$

where C is a color channel (L^*, a^*, or b^*), K is the preferred number of clusters. $C_{\max}$ and $C_{\min}$ are, respectively, the maximum and minimum value of the color channel C.

The behavior of k-means algorithm is influenced by the specified cluster number K. Experiments in [19] showed that the proper number of clusters for most images is $K = 4$. After splitting, the number of segmented regions may be larger than the cluster number K because pixels in a cluster may not be adjacent.

The result after applying the k-means algorithm can include many small regions that are out of interest. So we can filter out these small regions using a threshold of region size. Small regions or regions with size smaller than a pre-defined constant will be merged to the biggest nearby region.

One limitation of k-means algorithm is that during the space partitioning process the algorithm does not take into consideration the local connections between the data points (color components of each pixel) and its neighbor. This fact will restrict the application of clustering algorithms to complex color-textured images since the segmented output will be over-segmented. Then, a merge procedure is taken into account to obtain the final segmentation.

2.2 Merge procedure

2.2.1 Build region adjacent graph (RAG) of regions

To merge over-segmented regions into better ones, a graph called Region Adjacent Graph is built. RAG is a usual data structure used to represent region neighborhood relations in a segmented image. It is a weighted unidirectional graph $G = \{V, E, W\}$, where each node in V represents a region of the over-segmented image and each edge in E is a symmetric dissimilarity function between adjacent regions. The weight set W of edges is defined by taking into account the mean value of brightness.

Figure 2a, b shows an example of a synthetic image and its corresponding RAG.

Table 1 Comparison of three segmentation methods

Image	Size	Graph-based segmentation	K-means segmentation		Proposed method			
		Time (s)	Time (s)	Number of regions	Min-size	T	Time (s)	Number of regions
3096.jpg	481×321	5	2.5	469	50	20	3.5	11
42049.jpg	481×321	3.7	1.2	1349	20	50	3	34
118035.jpg	481×321	4	1.7	702	10	20	3	66
skype.jpg	481×321	6.6	2.1	231	10	50	3.5	5
tree.jpg	321×481	4.8	3	3412	10	20	3	168
fruits.jpg	512×480	9.5	4.5	2179	10	50	6.4	59
airplane.jpg	512×512	20.5	3.8	2130	50	50	6.5	38
lena.jpg	512×512	12	2.6	2224	20	20	4.7	177

Fig. 4 Segmentation results for common images: the tested images (*left*), segmented results by k-means algorithm (*middle*) and segmented results by the proposed method (*right*).

RAG-based methods only consider local information for the region-merging task. As stated in [17], the image partitioning task is inherently hierarchical and it would be appropriate to develop a top-down segmentation strategy which returns a hierarchical partition of the image instead of a flat partition. The proposed method shares this perspective with a tree-based image bipartition using minimum spanning tree (MST).

2.2.2 Merge regions

Regions with similar intensity are desired to be merged. One of the issues in merging regions is the order of regions to be merged. In graph-based segmentation, this order is determined through the technique used in MST.

The use of Kruskal's algorithm to build minimum spanning trees for segmentation reflects the local properties of

Fig. 5 Segmentation results for
fruit images. fruit images (*left*),
results by k-means (*middle*), and
results by the proposed
algorithm (*right*)

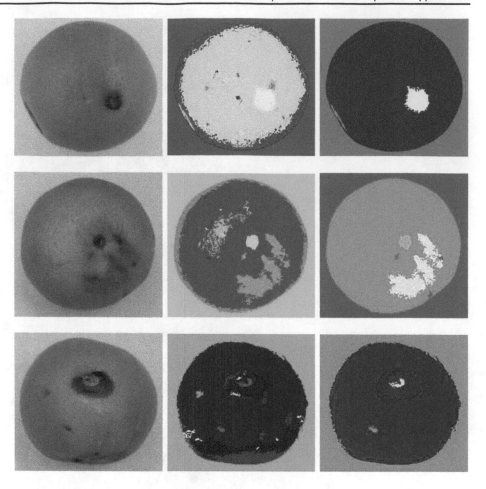

the image. A predicate is defined for measuring the merging
criteria and the algorithm makes greedy decisions to produce
the final segmentation.

After RAG is built, regions are merged when the following
simple condition is satisfied:

$$\left| \frac{1}{|R_i|} \sum_{p \in R_i} I_p - \frac{1}{|R_j|} \sum_{p \in R_j} I_p \right| < T$$

where threshold T is a global threshold parameter for dissimilarity between regions, p is an pixel in region R_i or R_j
and I_p is the intensity value of p.

For fruit defect detection, the defects usually appear in
darker color compared with the normal skin of fruits. The
selection of threshold T depends on the contrast of the defects
and the skin of fruits. Then image intensities are taken into
account in merge procedure to deal with the image contrast
and overcome the lighting effect on fruit peel.

Two neighboring regions should be merged if the new
combined region is homogeneous. Consequently, each region
is anticipated to be as large as possible under the merge condition. Then, the total number of regions is reduced as shown
in experimental results.

3 Experimental results

The system setup to acquire fruit images for the experiments
is shown in Fig. 3. The fruit to be taken was placed in the
center of a box whose inner surface is flat white to provide a
diffuse and uniform light. To provide uniform lighting, four
fluorescent tubes were used as the light source. A Canon CCD
camera (from Japan), with a lens of 2.8–4 focal length, was
mounted 25 cm above from the fruit. Tubes were positioned
to provide uniform and good illumination, from which the
shadow of fruit can be removed. To obtain images showing
entire fruit surface the fruit was manually rotated, by which
we can check whether the defects exist or not. The pixel
resolution was set at 2,353 × 1,568, and then the acquired
images were resized at the width of 256 pixels to be the input
for the experimental program.

For k-means algorithm, $k = 4$ was used as it is known to
yield good results in segmentation. Other parameters including minimum size of the regions and the threshold value used
in merge process were also set in each test.

The final results were evaluated by human inspection on
objects in the images. The number of regions and better segmentation in the terms of human observation were considered
for evaluation.

Fig. 5 (continued)

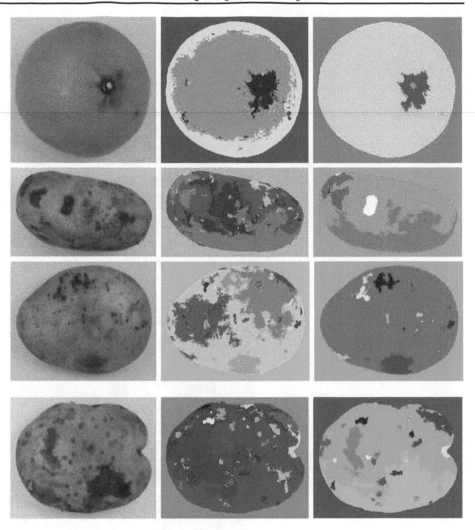

For experiment, we employed some images that are commonly used in segmentation test and also some fruit images. The segmented regions in result images are re-colored randomly to aid the observation.

Table 1 compares the result of three related segmentation algorithms: Graph-based segmentation, k-means segmentation and the proposed method. Because k-means segmentation creates an over-segmentation, the dramatically decrease in the number of regions in the proposed method together with good results in observation shows that it can improve the k-means segmentation, even though it is a little more time consuming. Figures 4 and 5 show some very good results in the terms of vision assessment on common images and fruit images.

In comparison with graph-based segmentation, the proposed method is more efficient in processing time as shown in Table 1. This is because the merging process in the proposed method starts with the regions obtained from split procedure instead of individual pixels used in graph-based technique. In addition, the processing time of the graph-based method

seriously depends on the number of pixels in the image. Hence, the graph-based segmentation showed the most time-consuming result in the experiment, especially on large-sized images.

To illustrate the efficiency of using $L^*a^*b^*$ color space on the method, two illustrations for the k-means algorithm were carried out: k-means using gray image and k-means using $L^*a^*b^*$ color image. The merge process is the same for the two illustrations. Figure 6 shows some results of the illustrations for different color spaces. The results in using $L^*a^*b^*$ color space are more accurate than those in using gray levels. However, the case of using gray levels has an advantage in computational time.

The proposed method has some advantages in comparison with Otsu's method. The result from Otsu's method is a binary image with scattered pixels which belongs to defects, while the proposed method gives continuous contour regions. One illustration for the better quality of the proposed method is shown in Fig. 7. Moreover, to find the defects by Otsu's method, the background in fruit

Fig. 6 Comparison of the method for gray-scale images and for $L*a*b*$ *color images*. The fruit images are on the first column, results of gray-level image are in the second column, and results in using $L*a*b*$ *color space* are in the last column. (Fruit images were from [9])

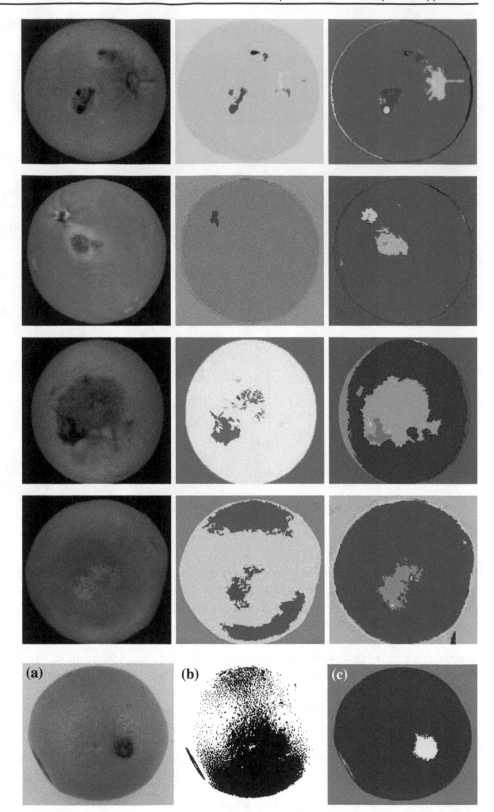

Fig. 7 A comparison with Otsu's method. **a** Fruit image, **b** segmented result by Otsu's method, **c** segmented result by the proposed method

image should be previously removed. For not too complex background, the proposed method can be used to detect background and defects once the result image was obtained.

4 Conclusion

This paper has introduced a split and merge approach for image segmentation that aims to detect defects on fruit peel.

The method firstly over-segmented the original image with k-means clustering technique in $L^*a^*b^*$ color space. Small regions then were filtered out by merging to the regions nearby. Next, RAG was built based on regions obtained from previous stage to serve the merging process. Regions are iteratively merged based on minimum spanning tree technique. The experiments showed that the proposed method is faster than graph-based algorithm because of using regions resulted from split procedure as the initial universe instead of pixels and higher quality than k-means only method. For a general image segmentation that aims to the quality of the segmentation, the method used $L^*a^*b^*$ color space in k-means algorithm implementation to obtain more accurate results as shown in the experiments. Moreover, the proposed method is superior to Otsu's method in the terms of continuous contour and better quality. The method can be improved to apply to different kinds of fruits by selecting more suitable starting centroids for k-means or the stop condition of merging. Fully automated segmentation has an important meaning in real applications. We propose as a future work the improvement of merging condition without parameters.

Open Access This article is distributed under the terms of the Creative Commons Attribution License which permits any use, distribution, and reproduction in any medium, provided the original author(s) and the source are credited.

References

1. Cubero, S., et al.: Advances in machine vision applications for automatic inspection and quality evaluation of fruits and vegetables. Food Bioprocess Technol. **4**(4), 487–504 (2011)
2. Lee, D.-J., et al.: Development of a machine vision system for automatic date grading using digital reflective near-infrared imaging. J. Food Eng. **86**(3), 388–398 (2008)
3. López-García, F., et al.: Automatic detection of skin defects in citrus fruits using a multivariate image analysis approach. Comput. Electron. Agric. **71**(2), 189–197 (2010)
4. Barnes, M., et al.: Visual detection of blemishes in potatoes using minimalist boosted classifiers. J. Food Eng. **98**(3), 339–346 (2010)
5. Xiao-bo, Z., et al.: In-line detection of apple defects using three color cameras system. Comput. Electron. Agric. **70**(1), 129–134 (2010)
6. Ho, S.-Y., Lee, K.-Z.: Design and analysis of an efficient evolutionary image segmentation Algorithm. J. VLSI Signal Process. Syst. Signal Image Video Technol. 35, 29–42 (2003)
7. Mery, D., Pedreschi, F.: Segmentation of color food images using a robust algorithm. J. Food Eng. **66**(3), 353–360 (2005)
8. Riquelme, M.T., et al.: Olive classification according to external damage using image analysis. J. Food Eng. **87**(3), 371–379 (2008)
9. Liming, X., Yanchao, Z.: Automated strawberry grading system based on image processing. Comput. Electron. Agric. **71**(Supplement 1), S32–S39 (2010)
10. Blasco, J., et al.: Automatic sorting of satsuma (Citrus unshiu) segments using computer vision and morphological features. Comput. Electron. Agric. **66**(1), 1–8 (2009)
11. Lopez, J., Aguilera, E., Cobos, M.: Defect detection and classification in citrus using computer vision. In: Neural information processing. Springer, Berlin, Heidelberg, pp. 11–18 (2009)
12. Blasco, J., Aleixos, N., Moltó, E.: Computer vision detection of peel defects in citrus by means of a region oriented segmentation algorithm. J. Food Eng. **81**(3), 535–543 (2007)
13. Yang, Q., Marchant, J.A.: Accurate blemish detection with active contour models. Comput. Electron. Agric. **14**(1), 77–89 (1996)
14. Navon, E., Miller, O., Averbuch, A.: Color image segmentation based on adaptive local thresholds. Image Vis. Comput. **23**(1), 69–85 (2005)
15. Pichel, J.C., Singh, D.E., Rivera, F.F.: Image segmentation based on merging of sub-optimal segmentations. Pattern Recognit. Lett. **27**(10), 1105–1116 (2006)
16. Yang, Q.: An approach to apple surface feature detection by machine vision. Comput. Electron. Agric. **11**(2–3), 249–264 (1994)
17. Felzenszwalb, P.F., Huttenlocher, D.P.: Efficient graph-based image segmentation. Int. J. Comput. Vis. **59**(2), 167–181 (2004)
18. Ilea, D.E.A.W., Paul, F.: Color image segmentation using a spatial k-means clustering algorithm. IMVIP 2006—10th International Machine Vision and Image Processing Conference (2006)
19. Pappas, T.N., Jayant, N.S.: An adaptive clustering algorithm for image segmentation. In: acoustics, speech, and signal processing, 1989. ICASSP-89, 1989 International Conference on (1989)

20

A survey on software fault detection based on different prediction approaches

Golnoush Abaei · Ali Selamat

Abstract One of the software engineering interests is quality assurance activities such as testing, verification and validation, fault tolerance and fault prediction. When any company does not have sufficient budget and time for testing the entire application, a project manager can use some fault prediction algorithms to identify the parts of the system that are more defect prone. There are so many prediction approaches in the field of software engineering such as test effort, security and cost prediction. Since most of them do not have a stable model, software fault prediction has been studied in this paper based on different machine learning techniques such as decision trees, decision tables, random forest, neural network, Naïve Bayes and distinctive classifiers of artificial immune systems (AISs) such as artificial immune recognition system, CLONALG and Immunos. We use four public NASA datasets to perform our experiment. These datasets are different in size and number of defective data. Distinct parameters such as method-level metrics and two feature selection approaches which are principal component analysis and correlation based feature selection are used to evaluate the finest performance among the others. According to this study, random forest provides the best prediction performance for large data sets and Naïve Bayes is a trustable algorithm for small data sets even when one of the feature selection techniques is applied. Immunos99 performs well among AIS classifiers when feature selection technique is applied, and AIRSParallel performs better without any feature selection techniques. The performance evaluation has been done based on three different metrics such as area under receiver operating characteristic curve, probability of detection and probability of false alarm. These three evaluation metrics could give the reliable prediction criteria together.

Keywords Software fault prediction · Artificial immune system · Machine learning · AISParallel · CSCA · Random forest

1 Introduction

As today's software grows rapidly in size and complexity, the prediction of software reliability plays a crucial role in software development process [1]. Software fault is an error situation of the software system that is caused by explicit and potential violation of security policies at runtime because of wrong specification and inappropriate development of configuration [2]. According to [3], analyzing and predicting defects[1] are needed for three main purposes, firstly, for assessing project progress and plan defect detection activities for the project manager. Secondly, for evaluating product quality and finally for improving capability and assessing process performance for process management. In fault prediction, previous reported faulty data with the help of distinct metrics identify the fault-prone modules. Important information about location, number of faults and distribution of defects are extracted to improve test efficiency and software quality of the next version of the software. Two benefits of software fault prediction are improvement of the test process by focusing on fault-prone modules and by identification the refactoring candidates that are predicted as fault-prone [4]. Numbers of different methods were used for software fault prediction such as genetic programming, decision

G. Abaei · A. Selamat (✉)
Faculty of Computing, University Technology Malaysia, Johor Baharu, 81310 Johor, Malaysia
e-mail: aselamat@utm.my

G. Abaei
e-mail: golnoosh.abaee@gmail.com

---

[1] Defects and faults have the same meaning in this paper.

trees, neural network, distinctive Naïve Bayes approaches, fuzzy logic and artificial immune system (AIS) algorithms. Almost all software fault prediction studies use metrics and faulty data of previous software release to build fault prediction models, which is called *supervised learning* approaches. Supervised machine learning classifiers consist of two phases: training and test phase; the result of training phase is a model that is applied to the testing data to do some prediction [5]. There are some other methods like clustering, which could be used when there are no previous available data; these methods are known as *unsupervised learning* approaches. It should be mentioned that some researchers like Koksal et al. [6] used another classification for data mining methods, which are famous as descriptive and predicative.

One of the main challenges in this area is how to get the data. In some works like in [7], a specific company provides the data, so the results are not fully trustable. Before 2005, more than half of the researches have used non-public datasets; however after that, with the help of PROMISE repository, the usage of public datasets reached to half [8], because the results are more reliable and not specific to a particular company. According to [8], software fault predictions are categorized based on several criteria such as metrics, datasets and methods. According to the literatures, software fault prediction models are built based on different set of metrics; method-level and class-level are two of the most important ones. Method-level metrics are suitable for both procedural and object-oriented programming style whereas class-level metrics are extracted based on object-oriented notation. It should be mentioned that compared to the other metrics, the method-level metrics is still the most dominant metrics prediction, followed by class-level metrics in fault prediction research area and machine-learning algorithms. It has been for many years that researchers work on different types of algorithms based on machine learning, statistical methods and sometimes the combination of them. In this paper, the experiments have been done on four NASA datasets with different population size using two distinct feature selection techniques that are principal component analysis (PCA) and correlation-based feature selection (CFS). We have changed the defect rates to identify what will be the effects on the predicting results. The predictability accuracy has been investigated in this paper based on two different method-level metrics, which are 21 and 37 static code attributes. The algorithms in this study are decision tree (C4.5), random forest, Naïve Bayes, back propagation neural network, decision table and various types of AIS such as AIRS1, AIRS2, AIRSParallel, Immunos1, Immunos2, Immunos99, CLONALG and clonal selection classification algorithm (CSCA). Three different performance evaluation metrics were used, area under receiver operating characteristic curve (AUC), probability of detection (PD) and probability of false alarm (PF), to give more reliable prediction analysis. Although we calculated accuracy along with above metrics, it does not have any impact on the evaluation process. Figure 1 shows the research done in this study.

We conducted four different types of experiment to answer six research questions in this paper. Research questions are listed as follows:

RQ1: which of the machine learning algorithms performs best on small and large datasets when 21-method-level metrics is used?

RQ2: which of the AIS algorithms performs best on small and large datasets when 21-method-level metrics is used?

Fig. 1 The studies done in this paper

```
1: M = 10
2: All = 37        # 37 method-level
3: Partial = 21    # 21 method-level
4: DATAS = (CM1, KC1, JM1, PC3)
5: FST = (PCA or CFS)   # feature selection techniques
6: LEARNERS = (J48, RF, NB, NN (back propagation), Decision Table, AIRS1, AIRS2,
               AIRSParallel, Immunos1, Immunos2, Immunos99, CLONALG, CSCA)


7: for data in DATAS
8:     for fst in FST
9:         data' = fst(data)
10: for i in 1 to M
11:     tests = bin[i]
12:     trainingdata = data' - tests
13: for learners in LEARNERS
14:     METHOD = (cfs learner)
15:     Predictor = learner (trainingdata)
16:     RESULT (METHOD) = apply predictors to test
```

RQ3: which of the machine learning algorithms performs best on small and large datasets when 37-method-level metrics is used?

RQ4: which of the machine learning algorithms performs best on small and large datasets when PCA and CFS applied on 21-method-level metrics?

RQ5: which of the AIS algorithms performs best on small and large datasets when PCA and CFS applied on 21-method-level metrics?

RQ6: which of the machine learning algorithms performs best and worst on CM1 public dataset when the rate on defected data is doubled manually?

The experiment 1 answered research question 1 (RQ1) and research question 2 (RQ2). Experiment 2 responded to research question 3 (RQ3). Experiment 3 shows the difference between the results obtained when no feature selection techniques were used. This experiment answered the research question 4 and 5. Finally, in experiment 4, to answer the last question, we doubled the defect rate of CM1 dataset to see whether it has any effect on the prediction model performances or not. This paper is organized as follows: the following section presents the related work. Section 3 explains different classifiers in AIS with its advantages and drawbacks. The feature selection and some of its methods are reviewed in Sect. 4. Experimental description and study analysis are described in Sects. 5 and 6, respectively, and finally Sect. 7 would be the results.

2 Related works

According to Catal [9], software fault prediction became one of the noteworthy research topics since 1990, and the number of research papers is almost doubled until year 2009. Many different techniques were used for software fault prediction such as genetic programming [10], decision trees [11] neural network [12], Naïve Bayes [13], case-based reasoning [14], fuzzy logic [15] and the artificial immune recognition system algorithms in [16–18]. Menzies et al. [13] have conducted an experiment based on public NASA datasets using several data mining algorithms and evaluated the results using probability of detection, probability of false alarm and balance parameter. They used log-transformation with Info-Gain filters before applying the algorithms and they claimed that fault prediction using Naïve Bayes performed better than the J48 algorithm. They also argued that since some models with low precision performed well, using it as a reliable parameter for performance evaluation is not recommended. Although Zhang et al. [19] criticized the paper but Menzies et al. defended their claim in [20]. Koru and Liu [21] have applied the J48, K-Star and random forest algorithms on public NASA datasets to construct fault prediction model based on 21 method-level. They used F-measures as an evaluation

performance metrics. Shafi et al. [22] used two other datasets from PROMISE repository, JEditData and AR3; they applied 30 different techniques on them, and showed that classification via regression and locally weighted learning (LWL) are better than the other techniques; they chose precision, recall and accuracy as an evaluation performance metrics. Catal and Diri [4] have used some machine learning techniques like random forest; they also applied artificial immune recognition on five NASA datasets and used accuracy and area under receiver operating characteristic curves as evaluation metrics. Turhan and Bener have used probability of detection, probability of false alarm and balance parameter [9,23]; the results indicate that independence assumption in Naïve Bayes algorithm is not detrimental with principal component analysis (PCA) pre-processing. Alsmadi and Najadat [24] have developed the prediction algorithm based on studying statistics of the whole dataset and each attributes; they proposed a technique to evaluate the correlation between numerical values and categorical variables of fault prone dataset to automatically predict faulty modules based on software metrics. Parvinder et al. [25] claimed that, the prediction of different level of severity or impact of faults in object oriented software systems with noise can be done satisfactory using density-based spatial clustering; they used KC1 from NASA public dataset. Burak et al. [26] analyzed 25 projects of the largest GSM operator in Turkey, Turkcell to predict defect before the testing phase, they used a defect prediction model that is based on static code attributes like lines of code, Halstead and McCabe. They suggested that at least 70 % of the defects can be detected by inspecting only 6 % of the code using a Naïve Bayes model and 3 % of the code using call graph-based ranking (CGBR) framework.

3 Artificial immune system

In late 1990, a new artificial intelligence branch that was called AIS was introduced. AIS is a technique to the scene of biological inspired computation and artificial intelligence based on the metaphor and abstraction from theoretical and empirical knowledge of the mammalian immune system. The immune system is known to be distributed in terms of control, parallel in terms of operation, and adaptive in terms of functions, all the features of which are desirable for solving complex or intractable problems faced in the field of artificial intelligence [27].

AISs embody the principles and advantages of vertebrate immune system. The AIS has been used in intrusion detection, classification, optimization, clustering and search problems [4].

In the AIS, the components are artificial cells or agents which flow through a computer network and process several

Fig. 2 The activity diagram of AIRS algorithm

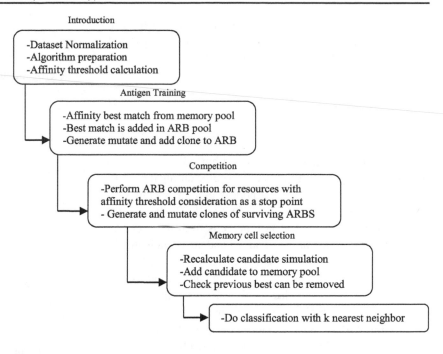

Fig. 2 The activity diagram of AIRS algorithm

tasks to identify and prevent attacks from intrusions. Therefore, the artificial cells are equipped with the same attributes as the human immune system. The artificial cells try to model the behavior of the immune-cells of the human immune system. Network security, optimization problems and distributed computing are some of the AIS's applications.

There are several classifiers available based on AIS paradigm, some of them are as follows: AIRS, CLONALG, and IMMUNOS81, each one of them is reviewed in the following subsections.

3.1 Artificial intelligence recognition system (AIRS)

Artificial intelligence recognition system is one of the first AIS techniques designed specifically and applied to classification problems. It is a novel immune inspired supervised learning algorithm [28,29].

AIRS has five steps: *initialization, antigen training, competition for limited resources, memory cell selection and classification* [4,27]. These five steps are summarized in Fig. 2.

First, the dataset is normalized, and then based on the Euclidian formula distances between antigens, which is called affinity, are calculated. Affinity threshold that is the user-defined value is calculated. Antibodies that are present in the memory pool are stimulated with a specific infected antigen, and the stimulated value is assigned to each cell. The cell, which has the highest stimulation value, is chosen as the finest memory cell. Afterwards, the best match from the memory pool is selected and added to the artificial recognition ball (ARB) pool. This pool contains both antigen and antibodies with their stimulation value along with some other information related to them. Next, the numbers of clones are

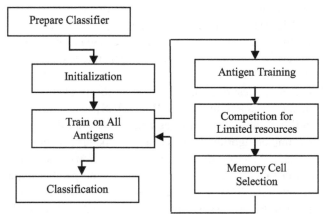

Fig. 3 The activity diagram of AIRS algorithm based on [27]

calculated and cloning starts. These clones are also added to the ARB pool. After that, competition for the finite resources begins. Again, ARB pool is stimulated with the antigens, and limited resources are assigned to them based on derived stimulation values. This is a recursive task until the stopping condition happens that is, if the stimulation level between ARB and antigen is less than the affinity threshold, it stops; otherwise, it goes on. After that, the ARB with the highest stimulation value is selected as a candidate to be a memory cell. The stimulation value is compared to the best previous matching value, if it is better; it is going to be replaced by the old one. Another explanation of the AIRS is shown in Fig. 3 and is described completely in [27].

In a simple word, each input vector is a representative of an antigen, and all attributes of this vector are the epitope of the antigens, which is recognizable by the antibodies. So each antigen with M epitope is like $Ag = [ep_1, ep_2, ep_3, \ldots]$.

For each epitope, one antibody is considered (Ab). The affinity between each pair of epitope of each antigen and antibody is calculated in Eqs. 1 and 2 as follows:

$$dist = \sqrt{\sum_{i=1}^{n} (v_{1i} - v_{2i})^2} \qquad (1)$$

$$Affinity = 1 - dist\ (Ab_k,\ ep_k) \qquad (2)$$

AIRSv1 is the first version of this algorithm. AIRSv1 (AIRS1) treats the ARB pool as a persistent resource during the entire training process whereas ARB pool is used as a temporary resource for each antigen in AIRSv2 (AIRS2). In another word, ARB's leftovers for past antigens from the previous ARB refinement step are maintained and are participated in a competition for limited resources. According to [28] this cause more time spending in rewarding and refining ARBs that belong to the same class of the antigen in question. In order to solve this problem, a user defined stimulation value is raised in AIRS2 and only clones of the same class as the antigen are considered in ARB pool. The other difference between these two algorithms is how mutation is done. In AIRS1, the mutate rate is a user defined parameter and shows the mutate degree for producing a clone; mutate rate is simply replaced with normalized randomly generated value. Mutate rate in AIRS2 is identified as proportional to its affinity to antigen in question. This approach performs a better search when there is a tight affinity. Both AIRS1 and AIRS2 show similar accuracy performance behavior except that, AIRS2 is a simpler algorithm and is also show better generalization capability in terms of improved data reduction of the training dataset [4,27]. Watkins [29] introduced the parallel implementation in 2005. The model shows the distributed nature and parallel processing attributes exhibited in mammalian immune system. The approach is simple and we have to add the following step to the standard AIRS training schema. If the dataset is not partitioned too widely, then the training speed is observable. AIRS Parallel have the following steps [4,27,29]:

- Divide the training dataset into np^2 partitions.
- Allocate training partitions to processes.
- Combine np number of memory pools.
- Use a merging approach to create the combined memory pool.

Acceptance of continuous and nominal variables, capacity to learn and recall large numbers of patterns, experienced-based learning, supervised learning, classification accuracy, user parameter and the ability to predict the training times are some of the design goals that could be noted for an AIRS-like supervised learning system.

---

^{2} np is the number of partitions.

3.2 CLONALG

The theory specifies that the organism has a pre-existing pool of heterogeneous antibodies that can recognize all antigens with some level of specificity [30].

As you may see in Fig. 4, when matching occurs, the candidate cell undergoes mitosis and produces B lymphoblast that could be one of the following:

- Plasma cell that produces antibody as an effector of the immune response.
- Long-lived memory cell, in case a similar antigen appears.

CLONal selection ALGorithm is inspired by the clonal selection theory of acquired immunity, previously known as CSA. A new clonal selection inspired classification algorithm is called CSCA.

CLONALG inspires some features from clonal selection theory, which is mentioned above. The goal here is to develop a memory pool containing best antigen matching antibodies that represent a solution to engineering problems.

The algorithm provides two searching mechanism for the desired final pool of memory antibodies. These two are noted in [30] as follows:

- Local search, provided via affinity maturation of cloned antibodies. More clones are produced for better-matched antibodies.
- A search that provides a global scope and involves the insertion of randomly generated antibodies to be inserted into the population to further increase the diversity and provide a means for potentially escaping local optima.

Figure 5 shows an algorithm based on GLONALG Theory. A CLONALG technique has a lower complexity and smaller number of user parameters compared to other AIS systems such as AIRS [31]. CLONALG algorithm is mainly used in three engineering problem domains: pattern recognition, function optimization and combinatorial optimization [30].

Parallel CLONALG works like a distributed system. The problem is divided into number of processes. The task of each one is preparation of themselves as antigen pools. After completion, all results will be sent to the root and the memory pool forms based on the combination of them.

There are some other classifications based on clonal selection algorithms such as CLONCLAS (CLONal selection algorithm for CLASsification) which is mostly used in character recognition. Here, there is a concept called class that contains an antibody and the antigen exposed to a class of specific antibody.

To improve and maximize the accuracy of the classification and also minimize the wrong classification, CSCA came to the picture. CSCA or clonal selection classifier algorithm

Fig. 4 The simple overview of the clonal selection process, image taken from [32]

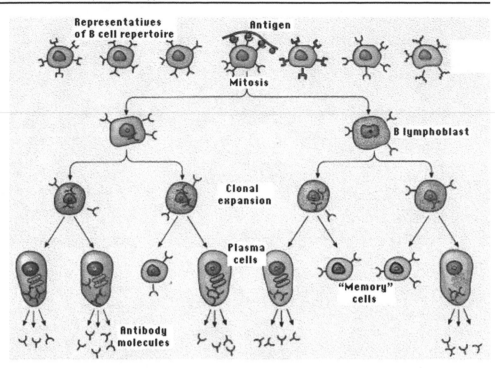

Fig. 5 Overview of the CLONALG algorithm

1: Prepare an antibody pool of size *N*; call it *AB*, which consist of two different areas, representatives of the solution section (*m*), and introducing additional diversity into the system section (*r*).

2: For (i = 1 to i <= *G* (user defined variable))

3:     Ag_i← a random antigen is selected from antigen pool

4:     $Ag_i$is shownto *AB*

5:         For (j = 1 to j <= *N*)

6:         AFF_{ij}← calculate affinity (based on Hamming Distance)

7:     Select *n* antibodies from *AFF* that has the highest affinity with Ag_i

8:     *CLset*← cloning takes place based on step (7) AFF_{ij} selections for each antibody

9:     *CLset*← mutate CLset affinity maturation based on their parent's affinity

10:    *CLset* members are exposed to Ag_i

11:        For (k = 1 to k <= *CLset*.length)

12:        Aff_{ik}← calculate affinity

13:    *CAN*← the *d* number of Antibodies (Ab) with the highest affinity in *CLset*

14:    If CAN_i–affinity > stimulated Antigen in *m* then swap (*m*, CAN_i)

15:    Swap (*d* number of remaining *Abs* in section *r* of the *AB*, new random antibodies

16: Finish, the memory *m* component of the antigen pool is taken as the algorithm solution

has four distinct steps, which is started with Initialization like every other AIS algorithm followed by repetition (loop) of Selection and Pruning, Cloning and Mutation and Insertion until the stopping point, and at the end it has Final Pruning and Classification.

In Initialization step, an antibody pool is created based on randomly selected antigen which has size *S*. In loop phase, there is a Selection and Pruning step that shows and scoring the antibody pool to each antigen set, which could be either correct classification score or misclassification score. After that selection rules are applied, antibodies with a misclassification score of zero are eliminated or antibodies with the fitness scoring of less than epsilon are removed from the chosen set and from the original antibody set as well. After that, all remaining antibodies in the selected set are cloned, mutated, and inserted to the main antibody set. When the loop condition is fulfilled, the Final Pruning step starts which exposes the final antibodies set to each antigen and calculates fitness scoring exactly like the loop step. Finally, the set of exemplar is ready in antibody set, so in case of any unclassified data instances that are exposed to the antibodies set, the affinities between each matches are calculated and selected and according to this result, unclassified data set could be classified. Figure 6 shows the CSCA steps.

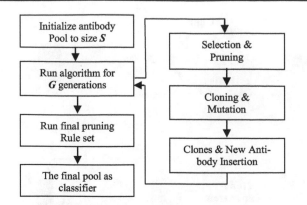

Fig. 6 Overview of the CSCA algorithm taken from [30]

3.3 Immunos81

Most of the issues that described in AIS are close to biological metaphor but the goal for Immunos81 is to reduce this part and focus on the practical application. Some of the terminologies are listed as below:

- T-Cell, both partitioning learned information and decisions about how new information is exposed to the system are

the duty of this cell, each specific antigen has a T-Cell, and it has one or more groups of B-Cells.

- B-Cell, there is an instance of a group of antigens.
- Antigen, this is a defect; it has a data vector of attributes where the nature of each attribute like name and data type is known.
- Antigen-Type, depends on the domain, antigens are identified by their names and series of attributes, which is a duty of T-Cell.
- Antigen group/clone based on the antigen's type or a specific classification label forms a group that is called clone of B-Cell and as mentioned above, are controlled by a T-Cell.
- The recognition part of the antibody is called paratope, which is bound to the specific part of the antigen, epitopes (attributes of the antigen).

This algorithm has three main steps: initialization, training and classification [33]; the general idea behind the Immunos81 is shown in Fig. 7.

To calculate the affinity values for each paratope across all B-Cells, Eq. 3 is used, p_i is the paratope affinity for the ith paratope, k is a scale factor and S is total number of B-Cell,

Fig. 7 Generalized version of the Immunos81 training scheme

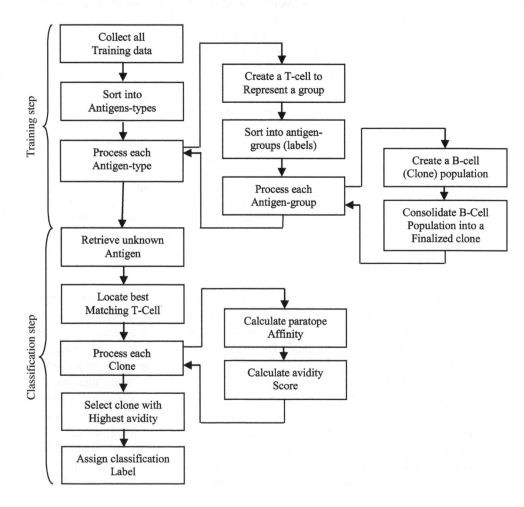

jth B-Cell affinity in a clone set is shown by a_i.

$$pa_i = k \cdot \sum_{S}^{j=1} a_j \tag{3}$$

There is another concept called Avidity, which is sum of affinity values scaled both by the size of the clone population and additional scale parameter, according to Eq. 4, ca is a clone avidity for the ith, k_{2i} defines by user, N is the total paratopes and total number of B-Cells in the ith clone set is shown by S_i.

$$ca_i = k_{2i} \cdot \left(\sum_{N}^{j=1} pa_j \right) \cdot S_i \tag{4}$$

There are two basic implementations for Immunos8 that are known as naïve immunos algorithms; they are called, Immunos1 and Immunos2. There is no data reduction in Immunos1, and it is similar to the k-nearest neighbors. The primary difference is obviously that the training population is partitioned and k is set to one for each partition; multiple-problem support can be provided with simpler mechanism that uses classifier for each problem, and each classifier has its own management mechanism. The Immunos2 implementation is the same as Immunos1 only seeks to provide some form of primary generalization via data reduction, so the closer representation to basic Immunos [33].

Immunos99 could be identified as a combination of Immunos81 and CSCA which some user-defined parameters are either fixed or removed from the CSCA. Immunos99 is very different from the AIR classifiers such as AIRS and CLONALG; they all do competition in a training phase so the size of the group set has some affection on affinity and avidity calculation. There is another distinguishing point also; there is a single exposure to the training set (only in CLONALG).

As mentioned before, there is a classification called antigen-group and antigen-type. If the algorithm could identify some groups of B-Cell that are able to identify a specific type of antigens which these antigens might be also in different forms, then we can conclude that, how well any B-Cells could respond to its designed class of antigens compared to any other classes. The training step is composed of four basic levels; first data is divided into antigen-groups, and then the B-Cell population is set for each antigen-group (same as the immunos). For user, defined number of times, the B-Cell is shown to the antigens from all groups and fitness value is calculated; population pruning is done after that, two affinity maturations based on cloning and mutations are performed and some random selected antigens from the same group are inserted to the set. The loop is finished here when it is fulfilled the stopping condition. After last pruning for each B-Cell population, the final B-Cell population is introduced as a classifier. The usefulness or fitness formula for each B-Cell is shown in Eq. 5.

$$\text{Fitness} = \frac{\text{Correct}}{\text{Incorrect}} \tag{5}$$

Correct means, sum of antigen ranked based score of the same group and incorrect means, sum of them in different groups of B-Cell. Here, all B-Cells have correct and incorrect scores, and also the antigen-group could not be changed; this is different from CSCA method.

4 Feature selection

Feature selection identifies and extracts the most useful features of the dataset for learning, and these features are very valuable for analysis and future prediction. So by removing less important and redundant data, the performance of learning algorithm could be improved. The nature of the training data plays the major role in classification and prediction. If the data fail to exhibit the statistical regularity that machine learning algorithms exploit, then learning will fail, so one of the important tasks here is removing the redundant data from the training set; it will, afterwards make the process of discovering regularity much easier, faster and more accurate.

According to [34], Feature selection has four different characteristics which are *starting point, search organization, evaluation strategy, and stopping criterion*. Starting point means from where the research should begin, it could be either begin with no feature and add a feature as you proceed forward, or it could be a backward process; you start with all attributes, and as you proceed, you do the feature elimination, or it could start from somewhere in the middle on the training set. In search organization step, suppose the dataset has N number of features, so there will be 2 N number of subsets. So the search could be either exhausted or heuristic.

Evaluation strategy is divided into two main categories, which are *wrapper*, and *filters*. Wrapper evaluated the importance of the features based on the learning algorithm, which could be applied on data later. It uses the search algorithm to search the entire feature's population, run the model on them, and evaluate each subset based on that model. This technique could be computationally expensive; it has been seen that it may have suffered from over fitting to the model. Cross validation is being used to estimate the final accuracy of the feature subset. The goal of cross-validation is to estimate the expected level of fit of a model to a data set that is independent of the data, which were used to train the model. In filters, the evaluation is being done based on heuristic's data and general characteristics of the data come to the picture. Searching algorithm in both techniques are similar but filter is faster and more practical when the populations of the features are high because the approach is based on general characteristic of heuristic data rather than a method with a learning algorithm to evaluate the merit of a feature subset.

Feature selection algorithms typically fall into two categories; it could be *either feature ranking* or *subset ranking*. If the ranking is done based on metric and all features that do not achieve a sufficient score are removed, it is called feature ranking but subset selection searches the set of possible features for the optimal subset, which includes wrapper and filter.

4.1 Principal component analysis

Principal component analysis is a mathematical procedure, the aim of which is reducing the dimensionality of the dataset. It is also called an orthogonal linear transformation that transforms the data to a new coordinate system. In fact, PCA is a feature extraction technique rather than a feature selection method. The new attributes are obtained by a linear combination of the original attributes. Here, the features with the highest variance are kept to do the reduction. Some papers like [35] used PCA for improving their experiments' performance. According to [36], the PCA technique transforms n vector $\{x_1, x_2, \ldots, x_n\}$ from the d-dimensional space to n vectors $\{x_1', x_2', \ldots, x_n'\}$ in a new d' dimensional space.

$$x_i' = \sum_{k=1}^{d'} a_{k,i} e_k, \quad d' \leq d, \tag{6}$$

where e_k are eigenvectors corresponding to d' largest eigen vectors for the scatter matrix S and $a_{k,i}$ are the projections (principal components original data sets) of the original vectors x_i on the eigenvectors e_k.

4.2 Correlation-based feature selection

Correlation-based feature selection is an automatic algorithm, which does not need user-defined parameters like the number of features that need to be selected. CFS is categorized aa filter.

According to [37], feature V_i is said to be relevant, If there exists some v_i and c for which $p(V_i = v_i) > 0$ such that in Eq. 7.

$$p(C = c | V_i = v_i) \neq p(C = c) \tag{7}$$

According to research on feature selection experiments, irrelevant features should be removed along with redundant information. A feature is said to be redundant if one or more of the other features are highly correlated with it [38]. As it was mentioned before, all redundant attributes should be eliminated, so if any features' prediction ability could be covered

by another, then it can be removed. CFS computes a heuristic measure of the "merit" of a feature subset from pair-wise feature correlations and a formula adapted from test theory. Heuristic search is used to traverse the space of feature subsets in reasonable time; the subset with the highest merit found during the search is reported. This method also needs discretizing the continuous features.

5 Experiment description

5.1 Dataset selection

Here, four datasets from REPOSITORY of NASA [39,40] are selected. These datasets are different in number of rows and rate of defects. The largest dataset is JM1 with 10,885 rows, which belongs to *real time predictive ground system project*; 19 % of these data are defected. The smallest dataset, CM1, belongs to *NASA spacecraft instrument project* and it has 498 modules and 10 % of the data are defected. KC1 is another dataset which belongs to *storage management project for receiving and processing ground data* with 2,109 modules. 15 % of the KC1 modules are defected. PC3 is the last dataset that has 1,563 modules; 10 % of the data are defected and it belongs to *flight software for earth orbiting satellite* [39]. It should mention that PC3 is used only in first two experiments.

5.2 Variable selection

Predictability performance is calculated based on two distinct method-level metrics 21 and 37. In this work, experiments that have not been performed in [4] are studied. All 21 metrics which are the combination of McCabe's and Halstead's attributes are listed in Table 1. McCabe's and Halstead's metrics are called module or method level metrics and the faulty or non-faulty label is assigned to each one of the modules. These set of metrics are also called static code attributes and according to [13] they are useful, easy to use and widely used. Most of these static codes could be collected easily, cheaply and automatically. Many researchers and verification and validation text books such as [13,41] suggest using complexity metrics to decide about which module is worthy of manual inspection. NASA researchers like Menzies et al. [13] with lots of experience about large governmental software have declared that they will not review software modules unless tools like McCabe predict that they are fault prone. Nevertheless, some researchers such as Shepperd and Ince [42] and Fenton and Pfleeger [43] argued that static codes such as McCabe are useless metrics, but Menzies et al. in [13,20] proved that prediction based on the selected dataset with static code metrics performed very well and based on their studies they built prediction model with higher proba-

Table 1 Attributes present in 21 method-level metrics [39,40]

Attributes names	Information
loc	McCabe's line count of code
v(g)	McCabe "cyclomatic complexity"
ev(g)	McCabe "essential complexity"
iv(g)	McCabe "design complexity"
n	Halstead total operators + operands
v	Halstead "volume"
l	Halstead "program length"
d	Halstead "difficulty"
i	Halstead "intelligence"
e	Halstead "effort"
b	Halstead "delivered bugs"
t	Halstead's time estimator
lOCode	Halstead's line count
lOComment	Halstead's count of lines of comments
lOBlank	Halstead's count of blank lines
lOCodeAndlOComment	Lines of code and comments
uniq_op	Unique operators
uniq_opnd	Unique operands
total_op	Total operators
total_opnd	Total operand
branchCount	Branch count of the flow graph

Table 2 Confusion matrix

	No (predicted)	Yes (predicted)
No (actual)	TN	FP
Yes (actual)	FN	TP

with 10 % faulty data, even if it predicts that all defective modules are defect free. Hence in this study, area under receiver operating characteristic curve values were used for benchmarking especially when the dataset is unbalanced. Other performance evaluation metrics that were used are: PD which is the number of fault-prone modules that are classified correctly and PF that is the number of not fault-prone modules that are classified incorrectly as defected, Table 2, Eqs. 8, 9 and 10 show all details about calculation of performance evaluation metrics. As a brief explanation, true negative (TN) means that the module is predicted as non-faulty correctly, whereas false negative (FN) means that the module is predicted as non-faulty wrongly. On the other hand, false positive (FP) means that the module is estimated as faulty incorrectly and true positive (TP) denotes that the module is predicted as faulty correctly.

$$\text{Accuracy} = \frac{TP + TN}{TP + FN + FP + TN} \tag{8}$$

$$\text{Recall(PD)} = \frac{TP}{TP + FN} \tag{9}$$

$$PF = \frac{FP}{FP + TN} \tag{10}$$

6 Analysis of the experiment

6.1 Experiment 1

Twenty-one method-level metrics were used for this experiment. All 13 machine-learning techniques were applied on four different NASA datasets, and the results were compared. Table 3 shows accuracy and AUC value of algorithms and Table 4 presents PD and PF values for this experiment. This experiment has been done to answer research question 1 and 2. Notable values obtained after applying each algorithm are specified in bold.

As mentioned earlier and according to Menzies et al. [13,20], a good prediction should have high AUC and PD values as well as low PF value, so with this consideration, we have evaluated the results. Figure 8 presents the performance comparison in terms of AUC among four different NASA projects. According to the figure, both random forest and decision table performed best compared to other algorithms for JM1. For KC1, Naïve Bayes also performed well along with random forest and decision table. Random forest performed best when it comes to CM1 as well. Figures 9, 10

bility of detection and lower probability of false alarm which was in contrast with Shepherd and Ince [42] and Fenton and Pfleeger [43] beliefs.

As it is shown in Table 1, the attributes mainly consist of two different types, McCabe and Halstead. McCabe argued that codes with complicated pathways are more error-prone. His metrics, therefore, reflects the pathways within a code module but Halstead argued that, code that is hard to read, is more likely to be fault prone.

5.3 Simulator selection

All the experiments have been done in WEKA, which is open-source software and implemented in JAVA; it is developed in the University of Waikato and it is used for machine learning studies [44].

5.4 Performance measurements criteria

We used tenfold cross validations and all experiments were repeated five times. According to Menzies et al. [13,20] since some models with low precision performed well, using it as a reliable parameter for performance evaluation is not good. They also mentioned that if the target class (faulty/non-faulty) is in the minority, accuracy is a poor measure as for example, a classifier could score 90 % accuracy on a dataset

Table 3 Accuracy and AUC values for different algorithms in experiment 1

Algorithms	JM1	KC1	CM1	PC3
Decision tree, J48				
Accuracy	79.50	84.54	87.95	88.36
AUC	0.653	0.689	0.558	0.599
Random forest				
Accuracy	81.14	85.44	87.95	89.89
AUC	**0.717**	**0.789**	**0.723**	**0.795**
Naïve Bayes				
Accuracy	80.42	82.36	85.34	48.69
AUC	0.679	**0.790**	0.658	0.756
NN, Back Propagation	.			
Accuracy	80.65	84.54	89.96	89.76
AUC	0.500	0.500	0.499	0.500
Decision Table				
Accuracy	80.91	84.87	89.16	89.51
AUC	**0.703**	**0.785**	0.626	0.657
AIRS1				
Accuracy	71.67	74.63	80.92	85.16
AUC	0.551	0.563	**0.549**	**0.577**
AIRS2				
Accuracy	68.53	68.90	84.94	88.10
AUC	0.542	0.529	0.516	0.549
AIRSParallel				
Accuracy	71.93	82.02	84.74	86.95
AUC	**0.558**	**0.605**	**0.543**	0.540
Immunosl				
Accuracy	56.37	50.55	32.93	17.98
AUC	0.610	0.681	0.610	0.529
Immunos2				
Accuracy	**80.65**	75.25	89.16	89.51
AUC	0.500	0.511	0.494	0.499
Immunos99				
Accuracy	74.10	53.39	36.75	39.21
AUC	0.515	0.691	0.613	0.584
CLONALG				
Accuracy	73.01	82.50	87.95	87.20
AUC	0.509	0.532	0.506	0.491
CSCA				
Accuracy	80.17	83.97	88.15	89.00
AUC	**0.549**	0.593	0.489	0.515

Table 4 PD and PF values for different algorithms in experiment 1

Algorithms	JM1	KC1	CM1	PC3
Decision tree, J48				
PD	0.232	0.331	0.061	**0.206**
PF	0.070	0.061	0.031	**0.039**
Random forest				
PD	**0.242**	0.313	0.061	0.181
PF	**0.052**	0.047	0.031	**0.019**
Naïve Bayes				
PD	0.201	0.377	**0.286**	0.085
PF	0.051	0.095	**0.089**	0.555
NN, Back Propagation				
PD	0.000	0.000	0.000	0.000
PF	0.000	0.000	0.002	0.000
Decision Table				
PD	**0.129**	0.166	0.000	0.000
PF	**0.028**	0.026	0.011	0.003
AIRS1				
PD	0.282	0.298	**0.224**	**0.231**
PF	0.179	0.172	**0.127**	**0.078**
AIRS2				
PD	0.309	0.298	0.102	0.131
PF	0.225	0.239	0.069	0.033
AIRSParallel				
PD	0.300	**0.294**	**0.163**	0.125
PF	0.183	**0.084**	**0.078**	0.046
Immunosl				
PD	0.685	0.936	0.969	0.969
PF	0.465	0.573	0.732	0.910
Immunos2				
PD	0.000	0.163	0.000	0.000
PF	0.000	0.140	0.001	0.003
Immunos99				
PD	0.155	0.917	0.918	0.925
PF	0.118	0.536	0.693	0.758
CLONALG				
PD	0.149	0.107	0.041	0.013
PF	0.130	0.044	0.029	0.030
CSCA				
PD	**0.138**	0.236	0.000	0.044
PF	**0.039**	0.050	0.022	0.014

and 11 have been drawn to show different evaluation values based on PF, PD and AUC for easier comparison between prediction models.

According to Fig. 9, both random forest and decision table have high AUC value but when we consider PF and PD values, random forest has better combination of low PF and high PD. Among AIS classifiers, although Immunos1 has higher AUC and PD compared to the others but PF value is high and not acceptable. Here AIRSParallel performed better. Figure 10 shows the comparison results for KC1, here also random forest, Naïve Bayes and decision tree have higher AUC values, but if we consider PF and PD values, decision tree will be eliminated. In AIS algorithms, both AIRSParallel and CSCA classifiers performed better than the oth-

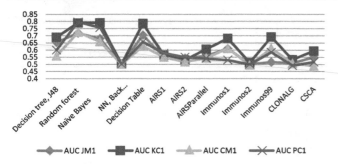

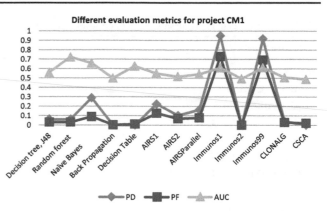

Fig. 8 Comparison between different AUC values in all four distinct NASA projects. The AUC values are represented on the *x* axis and different selected algorithms are shown in *y* axis

Fig. 11 Comparison between different evaluation metrics for project CM1. The percentage values for AUC, PF and PD are represented on the *x* axis and different selected algorithms are shown in *y* axis

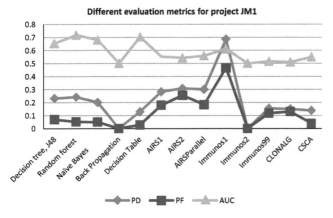

Fig. 9 Comparison between different evaluation metrics for project JM1. The percentage values for AUC, PF and PD are represented on the *x* axis and different selected algorithms are shown in *y* axis

From Tables 3 and 4, we could conclude that, random forest and decision table are the best classifiers when the size of the dataset is not that much small; of course Naïve Bayes is an acceptable algorithm as it performs well among the others for all four datasets. AIRSParallel is better than the others when the size of dataset is not so large, and CSCA performs well when the size of dataset is not small. It seems that if the algorithms execute best in big datasets, there is a high chance that they perform well with smaller datasets as well.

6.2 Experiment 2

As only for PC3, 37 method-level metrics was available; we applied 13 algorithms on PC3 dataset. The attributes and the results are shown in Tables 5 and 6, respectively.

To have a reliable results, this experiment has been repeated ten times but no significant changes are observed compared to the results obtained from 21 method-level metrics in experiment 2. There is only a slight change in accuracy, PD and PF values when AIRSParallel [27] classifier is used, so it seems that other 37 variables except common variables with 21 method-level do not have major effect on building a prediction model and it only increases the training time.

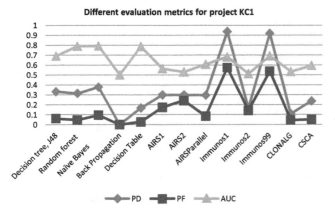

Fig. 10 Comparison between different evaluation metrics for project KC1. The percentage values for AUC, PF and PD are represented on the *x* axis and different selected algorithms are shown in *y* axis

6.3 Experiment 3

In this part, different feature selection techniques were applied on datasets to see their probable effects on the results and evaluation metrics. As it has been explained before, by eliminating the redundant attributes, performance of the model could be improved. Here two feature selection techniques, PCA and CFS, were used. When PCA applied on the 21 method-level metrics, the number of attributes is reduced to 7, 8 and 8 for CM1, PC1 and JM1, respectively. The results

ers. Results based on PC3 dataset are also similar to KC1 as they have similarities in number of modules and defect rate. According to Fig. 11, random forest followed by Naïve Bayes has highest AUC value for CM1, but Naïve Bayes performed better when PD and PF values are also considered. AIRS1 and AIRSParallel have better results compared to the other AIS algorithms.

Table 5 Attributes in PC3 datasets, 37 method-level metrics [45]

Attributes names
LOC_BLANK
BRANCH_COUNT
CALL_PAIRS
LOC_CODE_AND_COMMENT
LOC_COMMENTS
CONDITION_COUNT
CYCLOMATIC_COMPLEXITY
CYCLOMATIC_DENSITY
DECISION_COUNT
DECISION_DENSITY
DESIGN_COMPLEXITY
DESIGN_DENSITY
EDGE_COUNT
ESSENTIAL_COMPLEXITY
ESSENTIAL_DENSITY
LOC_EXECUTABLE
PARAMETER_COUNT
HALSTEAD_CONTENT
HALSTEAD_DIFFICULTY
HALSTEAD_EFFORT
HALSTEAD_ERROR_EST
HALSTEAD_LENGTH
HALSTEAD_LEVEL
HALSTEAD_PROG_TIME
HALSTEAD_VOLUME
MAINTENANCE_SEVERITY
MODIFIED_CONDITION_COUNT
MULTIPLE_CONDITION_COUNT
NODE_COUNT
NORMALIZED_CYLOMATIC_COMPLEXITY
NUM_OPERANDS
NUM_OPERATORS
NUM_UNIQUE_OPERANDS
NUM_UNIQUE_OPERATORS
NUMBER_OF_LINES
PERCENT_COMMENTS
LOC_TOTAL

Table 6 Comparision between PC3, 37 and 21 method-level metrics for experiment 2

Algorithms	PC3 (37)	PC3 (21)
AIRSParallel		
Accuracy	87.46	86.95
AUC	0.554	0.540
PD	0.150	0.125
PF	0.043	0.046

Table 7 Accuracy and AUC values for different algorithms using PCA in experiment 3

Algorithms	JM1	KC1	CM1
Decision tree, J48			
Accuracy	81.04	85.78	90.16
AUC	0.661	0.744	0.616
Random forest			
Accuracy	80.85	84.93	88.15
AUC	**0.706**	**0.782**	**0.736**
Naïve Bayes			
Accuracy	80.02	82.98	85.94
AUC	0.635	**0.756**	**0.669**
NN, Back Propagation			
Accuracy	79.78	81.18	89.56
AUC	0.583	0.665	0.515
Decision Table			
Accuracy	80.71	85.54	89.56
AUC	**0.701**	**0.765**	0.532
AIRS1			
Accuracy	67.02	73.88	84.14
AUC	0.555	0.580	0.530
AIRS2			
Accuracy	71.66	75.77	82.93
AUC	0.555	0.576	0.514
AIRSParallel			
Accuracy	71.62	80.65	85.95
AUC	0.568	0.609	0.549
Immunosl			
Accuracy	69.85	73.49	69.88
AUC	**0.638**	0.705	**0.660**
Immunos2			
Accuracy	80.65	84.54	**90.16**
AUC	0.500	0.500	0.500
Immunos99			
Accuracy	70.35	75.53	71.29
AUC	**0.632**	0.709	**0.650**
CLONALG			
Accuracy	73.27	80.75	87.15
AUC	0.517	0.505	0.505
CSCA			
Accuracy	79.58	84.92	88.55
AUC	0.573	0.601	0.509

are shown in Tables 7 and 8. This experiment has been done to answer the research questions 4 and 5.

Using PCA as feature selection techniques and with the consideration of high AUC and PD values as well as low PF value, random forest and Naïve Bayes perform well for CM1 dataset compared to the others. Among AIS classifiers, Immunos1 and Immunos99 are the finest. RF and Deci-

Table 8 PD and PF values for different algorithms using PCA in experiment 3

Algorithms	JM1	KC1	CM1
Decision tree, J48			
PD	0.096	0.239	0.041
PF	0.018	0.029	0.004
Random forest			
PD	0.235	0.267	0.041
PF	0.054	0.045	0.027
Naïve Bayes			
PD	0.195	0.337	0.224
PF	0.055	0.080	0.071
NN, Back Propagation			
PD	0.224	0.451	0.000
PF	0.056	0.121	0.007
Decision Table			
PD	0.101	0.166	0.041
PF	0.024	0.019	0.011
AIRS1			
PD	0.366	0.350	0.143
PF	0.257	0.190	0.082
AIRS2			
PD	0.291	0.313	0.122
PF	0.181	0.161	0.094
AIRSParallel			
PD	0.326	0.319	0.163
PF	0.019	0.100	0.065
Immunosl			
PD	0.540	0.663	0.612
PF	0.264	0.252	0.292
Immunos2			
PD	0.000	0.000	0.000
PF	0.000	0.000	0.000
Immunos99			
PD	0.516	0.641	0.571
PF	0.251	0.224	0.272
CLONALG			
PD	0.166	0.067	0.041
PF	0.133	0.057	0.038
CSCA			
PD	0.211	0.242	0.041
PF	0.064	0.040	0.022

Table 9 Accuracy and AUC values for different algorithms using CFS, Best First in experiment 3

Algorithms	JM1	KC1	CM1
Decision tree, J48			
Accuracy	81.01	84.68	89.31
AUC	0.664	0.705	0.542
Random forest			
Accuracy	80.28	84.83	88.15
AUC	**0.710**	**0.786**	0.615
Naïve Bayes			
Accuracy	80.41	82.41	86.55
AUC	0.665	**0.785**	**0.691**
NN, Back Propagation			
Accuracy	80.65	84.54	90.16
AUC	0.500	0.500	0.500
Decision Table			
Accuracy	80.81	84.92	89.16
AUC	**0.701**	**0.781**	0.626
AIRS1			
Accuracy	66.76	76.34	84.54
AUC	0.567	0.602	0.569
AIRS2			
Accuracy	73.36	77.34	82.53
AUC	0.565	0.591	0.530
AIRSParallel			
Accuracy	70.17	79.47	86.14
AUC	0.564	0.588	0.488
Immunos1			
Accuracy	59.99	49.98	69.88
AUC	0.600	0.678	0.697
Immunos2			
Accuracy	80.65	80.23	90.16
AUC	0.500	0.491	0.500
Immunos99			
Accuracy	65.02	62.21	76.51
AUC	0.594	0.705	0.679
CLONALG			
Accuracy	72.92	79.28	87.95
AUC	0.512	0.522	0.497
CSCA			
Accuracy	79.55	83.21	87.75
AUC	0.575	**0.590**	0.505

sion Table are best for both JM1 and KC1 datasets with AUC, PD and PF as a performance evaluation metrics; also Immunos99 performs best among the other AIS algorithms for JM1.

After applying CFS with the *best first* classifier, some of the attributes were eliminated from the 21 of total attributes; seven attributes remain from CM1, eight from KC1 and JM1.

The results are also shown in Tables 9 and 10. The remaining attributes form JM1, KC1 and CM1 after applying CFS, *best first* are listed below:

CM1: loc, iv(g), i, LOComment, LOBlank, uniq_Op, Uniq_Opnd

Table 10 PD and PF values for different algorithms using CFS, Best First in experiment 3

Algorithms	JM1	KC1	CM1
Decision tree, J48			
PD	0.148	0.175	0.000
PF	0.031	0.030	0.009
Random forest			
PD	**0.243**	**0.282**	**0.102**
PF	**0.063**	**0.048**	**0.033**
Naïve Bayes			
PD	**0.223**	**0.365**	**0.306**
PF	**0.056**	**0.092**	**0.073**
NN, Back Propagation			
PD	0.000	0.000	0.000
PF	0.000	0.000	0.000
Decision Table			
PD	0.108	0.178	0.000
PF	0.024	0.028	0.011
AIRS1			
PD	0.402	0.368	0.224
PF	0.269	0.184	0.087
AIRS2			
PD	0.290	0.328	0.163
PF	0.160	0.145	0.102
AIRSParallel			
PD	0.301	0.301	0.041
PF	0.173	0.125	0.065
Immunos1			
PD	0.600	0.936	0.694
PF	0.400	0.058	0.301
Immunos2			
PD	0.000	0.040	0.000
PF	0.000	0.058	0.000
Immunos99			
PD	0.502	0.825	0.571
PF	0.314	0.415	0.214
CLONALG			
PD	0.159	0.129	0.020
PF	0.134	0.086	0.027
CSCA			
PD	**0.217**	**0.239**	0.041
PF	**0.066**	**0.059**	0.031

KC1: v, d, i, LOCode, LOComment, LOBlank, Uniq_Opnd, branchcout

JM1: loc, v(g), ev(g), iv(g), i, LOComment, LOBlank, locCodeAndComment

It should be mentioned here, after applying CFS, *Best First*, there are only slight changes observed in the results, so it means that there is no considerable difference in the results after applying distinct feature selection techniques. The main change would be the execution time reduction. As it is shown in Tables 9 and 10, the best performance for JM1, which is the largest dataset, belongs to decision tree followed by random forest. By checking the AUC, PF and PD values, naïve bayes perform greatly on CM1 dataset as well as the other three. CSCA also performed well among the other AIS classifiers, but the problem with this algorithm is long execution time.

We also applied CFS, *random search* to see whether it has a considerable change in the results or not. It was found that there is no significant difference between selected attributes for KC1 after applying feature selection methods. There were only six attributes selected for CM1, which is less than the *best first* method. The number of selected attributes for JM1 is increased by one compared to the *best first* as well. Since no noticeable differences observed in performance evaluation metrics after building prediction model based on CFS, *random search*, we do not show the results in this section. However, the remaining attributes from JM1, KC1 and CM1 after applying CFS, *random search* are presented as follows:

CM1: loc, iv(g), i, b, LOComment, uniq_Op

KC1: v, d, i, LOCode, LOComment, LOBlank, Uniq_Opnd, branchcout

JM1: loc, v(g), ev(g), iv(g), n, i, LOComment, LOBlank, locCodeAndComment

6.4 Experiment 4

As we noted earlier, each of these datasets has a different rate of defected data; 19 % of the JM1, 10 % of the CM1 and 15 % of KC1 are defected. So in this experiment, the rate of defected data was doubled in CM1 to identify whether any of the classifiers shows any distinctive changes in results compared to the previous trials; this experiment uses 21 method-level metrics to answer the research question 6. We show the results in Table 11.

According to Table 11, the accuracy rate of all algorithms is decreased except for Immunos1 and Immunos99. Therefore, it means that the findings could be a challenging fact because it shows that the performance of each classifier could tightly related to defect rate in the datasets. So previously suggested classifiers may not be the best choices anymore to build a prediction model when the defect rate is changed. Accuracy in almost all the algorithms is fallen down, but if we consider AUC for evaluation, we see that this value grows in two other algorithms that are basically from one category, GLONALG and CSCA [30]. It could be concluded that by increasing the defect rate, the artificial immune classifiers perform better and gives a finest prediction model compared to others.

Table 11 Accuracy and AUC values of different algorithms with different defect rate for experiment 4

Algorithms	CM1 (Old Values)	CM1
Decision tree, J48		
Accuracy	87.95	75.50
AUC	0.558	0.534
Random Forest		
Accuracy	87.95	76.71
AUC	0.723	0.656
Naïve Bayes		
Accuracy	85.34	77.31
AUC	0.658	0.614
NN, Back Propagation		
Accuracy	89.96	80.32
AUC	0.499	0.500
Decision Table		
Accuracy	89.16	79.72
AUC	0.626	0.554
AIRS1		
Accuracy	80.92	66.27
AUC	0.549	0.497
AIRS2		
Accuracy	84.94	68.67
AUC	0.516	0.501
AIRSParallel		
Accuracy	84.74	76.10
AUC	0.543	**0.555**
Immunosl		
Accuracy	32.92	38.35
AUC	0.610	0.574
Immunos2		
Accuracy	89.16	80.32
AUC	0.494	0.500
Immunos99		
Accuracy	36.75	50.00
AUC	0.613	0.600
CLONALG		
Accuracy	87.95	73.69
AUC	0.506	**0.520**
CSCA		
Accuracy	88.15	78.31
AUC	0.489	**0.530**

7 Summary and conclusion

In this paper, we identified fault prediction algorithms based on different machine learning classifiers and distinct feature selection techniques. Since the accuracy rate is not a reliable metrics for performance evaluation, three other metrics were used, AUC, PD and PF which were not used together in other

experiments before. If we consider high AUC and PD values along with low PF value as a well-performed benchmark, random forest performs best on both small and big datasets. According to [4], AIRSParallel performs better than the other AIS, but according to experiment 1 and 3, Immunos99 is the best among the other AIS classifiers. This study shows that applying different feature selection techniques does not have that much effect on the results; they mainly reduce the execution time. Experiment 4 shows that the prediction rate reduced in CM1 dataset when the defected data were doubled manually except for AIRSParallel, CLONALG and mostly CSCA, so it seems that when the rate of defected modules was increased, the mentioned AIS classifiers perform best among the others. We can conclude here that different kinds of feature selection and method-level metrics do not have a considerable effect on the performance of the algorithm, and the most important factor here is the type of algorithm itself; therefore, it is better to improve the algorithms to get better prediction results. In addition, building the model based on large datasets like JM1 or even smaller ones consumes lots of time when CSCA is used compared to the other algorithms but the results are relatively acceptable, especially when we consider AIS classifiers for building models. The results in this study show that AUC, PD and PF could be used as three performance evaluation metrics together for more reliable performance analysis.

Acknowledgments The authors thank to Universiti Teknologi Malaysia (UTM) for some of the facilities and supports during the course of this research under vot 03H02. The Ministry of Science, Technology & Innovation (MOSTI) is also acknowledged for supporting the research under vot 4S062. The authors wish to thank the anonymous reviewers for their comments in improving the manuscript.

Open Access This article is distributed under the terms of the Creative Commons Attribution License which permits any use, distribution, and reproduction in any medium, provided the original author(s) and the source are credited.

References

1. Zheng, J.: Predicting software reliability with neural network ensembles. J. Expert Syst. Appl. **36**, 2116–2122 (2009)
2. Dowd, M., MC Donald, J., Schuh, J.: The Art of Software Security Assessment: Identifying & Preventing Software Vulnerabilities. Addison-Wesley, Boston (2006)
3. Clark, B., Zubrow, D.: How Good is the Software: A Review of Defect Prediction Techniques. In: Software Engineering Symposium, Carreige Mellon University (2001)
4. Catal, C., Diri, B.: Investigating the effect of dataset size, metrics sets, and feature selection techniques on software fault prediction problem. Inf. Sci. **179**(8), 1040–1058 (2009)
5. Xie, X., Ho, J.W.K., Murphy, C., Kaiser, G., Xu, B., Chen, T.Y.: Testing and validating machine learning classifiers by metamorphic testing. J. Syst. Softw. **84**, 544–558 (2011)
6. Koksal, G., Batmaz, I., Testik, M.C.: A review of data mining applications for quality improvement in manufacturing industry. J. Expert Syst. Appl. **38**, 13448–13467 (2011)

7. Hewett, R.: Minig Software defect Data to Support Software testing Management. Springer Science + Business Media, LLC, Berlin (2009)

8. Catal, C., Diri, B.: A systematic review of software fault prediction. J. Expert Syst. Appl. **36**, 7346–7354 (2009)

9. Catal, C.: Software fault prediction: a literature review and current trends. J. Expert Syst. Appl. **38**, 4626–4636 (2011)

10. Evett, M., Khoshgoftaar, T., Chien, P., Allen, E.: GP-based software quality prediction. In: Proceedings of the Third Annual Genetic Programming Conference, San Francisco, CA, pp. 60–65 (1998)

11. Koprinska, I., Poon, J., Clark, J., Chan, J.: Learning to classify e-mail. Inf. Sci. **177**(10), 2167–2187 (2007)

12. Thwin, M.M., Quah, T.: Application of neural networks for software quality prediction using object-oriented metrics. In: Proceedings of the 19th International Conference on Software Maintenance, Amsterdam, The Netherlands, pp. 113–122 (2003)

13. Menzies, T., Greenwald, J., Frank, A.: Data mining static code attributes to learn defect predictors. IEEE Trans. Softw. Eng. **33**(1), 2–13 (2007)

14. El Emam, K., Benlarbi, S., Goel, N., Rai, S.: Comparing case-based reasoning classifiers for predicting high risk software components. J. Syst. Softw. **55**(3), 301–320 (2001)

15. Yuan, X., Khoshgoftaar, T.M., Allen, E.B., Ganesan, K.: An application of fuzzy clustering to software quality prediction. In: Proceedings of the Third IEEE Symposium on Application-Specific Systems and Software Engineering Technology. IEEE Computer Society, Washington, DC (2000)

16. Catal, C., Diri, B.: Software fault prediction with object-oriented metrics based artificial immune recognition system. In: Proceedings of the 8th International Conference on Product Focused Software Process Improvement. Lecture Notes in Computer Science, pp. 300–314. Springer, Riga (2007)

17. Catal, C., Diri, B.: A fault prediction model with limited fault data to improve test process. In: Proceedings of the Ninth International Conference on Product Focused Software Process Improvements. Lecture Notes in Computer Science, pp. 244–257. Springer, Rome (2008)

18. Catal, C., Diri, B.: Software defect prediction using artificial immune recognition system. In: Proceedings of the Fourth IASTED International Conference on Software Engineering, pp. 285–290. IASTED, Innsburk (2007)

19. Zhang, H., Zhang, X.: Comments on data mining static code attributes to learn defect predictors. IEEE Trans. Softw. Eng. (2007)

20. Menzies, T., Dekhtyar, A., Di Stefano, J., Greenwald, J.: Problems with precision: a response to comments on data mining static code attributes to learn defect predictors. IEEE Trans. Softw. Eng. **33**(7), 637–640 (2007)

21. Koru, G., Liu, H.: Building effective defect prediction models in practice. IEEE Softw. **22**(6), 23–29 (2005)

22. Shafi, S, Hassan, S.M., Arshaq, A., Khan, M.J., Shamail, S.: Software quality prediction techniques: a comparative analysis. In: Fourth International Conference on Emerging Technologies, pp. 242–246 (2008)

23. Turhan, B., Bener, A.: Analysis of Naïve Bayes assumption on software fault data: an empirical study. Data Knowl. Eng. **68**(2), 278–290 (2009)

24. Alsmadi, I., Najadat, H.: Evaluating the change of software fault behavior with dataset attributes based on categorical correlation. Adv. Eng. Softw. **42**, 535–546 (2011)

25. Sandhu, P.S., Singh, S., Budhija, N.: Prediction of level of severity of faults in software systems using density based clustering. In: 2011 IEEE International Conference on Software and Computer Applications. IPCSIT, vol. 9 (2011)

26. Turhan, B., Kocak, G., Bener, A.: Data mining source code for locating software bugs; a case study in telecommunication industry. J. Expert Syst. Appl. **36**, 9986–9990 (2009)

27. Brownlee, J.: Artificial immune recognition system: a review and analysis. Technical Report 1–02, Swinburne University of Technology (2005)

28. Watkins, A.: A Resource Limited Artificial Immune Classifier. Master's thesis, Mississippi State University (2001)

29. Watkins, A.: Exploiting immunological metaphors in the development of serial, parallel, and distributed learning algorithms. PhD thesis, Mississippi State University (2005)

30. Brownlee, J.: Clonal selection theory & CLONALG. The clonal selection classification algorithm. Technical Report 2–02, Swinburne University of Technology (2005)

31. Watkins, A., Timmis, J., Boggess, L.: Artificial Immune Recognition System (AIRS): An Immune-Inspired Supervised Learning Algorithm. Genetic Programming and Evolvable Machines, vol. 5, pp. 291–317 (2004)

32. http://users.rcn.com/jkimball.ma.ultranet/BiologyPages/C/ClonalSelection.html. Retrieved 1 Nov 2013

33. Brownlee, J.: Immunos-81—The Misunderstood Artificial Immune System. Technical Report 3–01. Swinburne University of Technology (2005)

34. Langley, P.: Selection of relevant features in machine learning. In: Proceedings of the AAAI Fall Symposium on Relevance. AAAI Press, California (1994)

35. Khoshgoftaar, T.M., Seliya, N., Sundaresh, N.: An empirical study of predicting software faults with case-based reasoning. Softw. Qual. J. **14**(2), 85–111 (2006)

36. Malhi, A.: PCA-Based feature selection scheme for machine defect classification. IEEE Trans. Instrum. Meas. 53(6) (2004)

37. Kohavi, R., John, G.: Wrappers for feature subset selection. Artif. Intell. Special Issue Relev. **97**(1–2), 273–324 (1996)

38. Hall, M.A.: Correlation-based Feature Subset Selection for Machine Learning. PhD dissertation, Department of Computer Science, University of Waikato (1999)

39. http://promise.site.uottawa.ca/SERepository/datasets. Retrieved 01 Dec 2011

40. http://promisedata.org/?cat=5. Retrieved 01 Dec 2011

41. Rakitin, S.: Software Verification and Validation for Practitioners and Managers, 2nd edn. Artech House, London (2001)

42. Shepperd, M., Ince, D.: A critique of three metrics. J. Syst. Softw. **26**(3), 197–210 (1994)

43. Fenton, N.E., Pfleeger, S.: Software Metrics: A Rigorous and Practical Approach. Int'l Thompson Press, New York (1997)

44. http://www.cs.waikato.ac.nz/ml/weka. Retrieved 01 Nov 2011

45. http://promisedata.org/repository/data/pc3/pc3.arff. Retrieved 01 Dec 2011

21

Automatic question generation for supporting argumentation

Nguyen-Thinh Le · Nhu-Phuong Nguyen ·
Kazuhisa Seta · Niels Pinkwart

Abstract Given a discussion topic, students may sometimes not proceed with their argumentation. Can questions which are semantically related to a given discussion topic help students develop further arguments? In this paper, we introduce a technical approach to generating questions upon the request of students during the process of collaborative argumentation. The contribution of this paper lies in combining different NLP technologies and exploiting semantic information to support users develop their arguments in a discussion session via tailored questions of different types.

Keywords Question generation · Argumentation · WordNet

1 Introduction

In a constructivist learning environment, students are usually asked to solve an authentic problem. To solve the problem, students need to find a solution by researching, experimenting, and posing as well as testing hypotheses. Jonassen ([1], p. 226) proposed that a constructivist learning environ-

N.-T. Le (✉) · N. Pinkwart
Humboldt Universität zu Berlin, Berlin, Germany
e-mail: nguyen-thinh.le@hu-berlin.de

N. Pinkwart
e-mail: niels.pinkwart@hu-berlin.de

N.-P. Nguyen
Clausthal University of Technology, Clausthal-Zellerfeld, Germany
e-mail: nhu.p.nguyen@tu-clausthal.de

K. Seta
Osaka Prefecture University, Sakai, Japan
e-mail: seta@mi.s.osakafu-u.ac.jp

ment needs to provide some cognitive tools (also referred to as knowledge construction tools) that are used to "visualize (represent), organize, automate, or supplant thinking skills". One example class of cognitive tools are question generation systems which pose questions related to the problem being solved. The question generation support can potentially be helpful for students during the process of gathering information and building hypotheses: if a student is not able to come up with any idea to investigate the problem to be solved, the learning environment could generate semantics-related questions for the student. Our hypothesis is that automatic question generation may be useful in a constructivist learning environment to support students in solving problems.

LASAD is a constructivist learning environment in which students discuss about a given topic [2]. This web-based collaborative argumentation system provides tools for supporting collaborative argumentation. That is, given a discussion topic, students are required to develop their arguments by creating a diagram. Figure 1 illustrates an argumentation map created by several users collaboratively using the LASAD system. In the system, participants can use typed argument boxes (e.g., claim, fact, explanation) and typed links to represent relationship between the arguments (e.g., support, oppose).

In order to generate questions related to a discussion topic automatically, two question areas need to be addressed:

1. What are the important concepts of discussion topic? How can a question generation system recognize and extract them? Where can the question generation system retrieve information related to the important concepts extracted from discussion topic? The first contribution of this paper is the proposition of an approach to answer

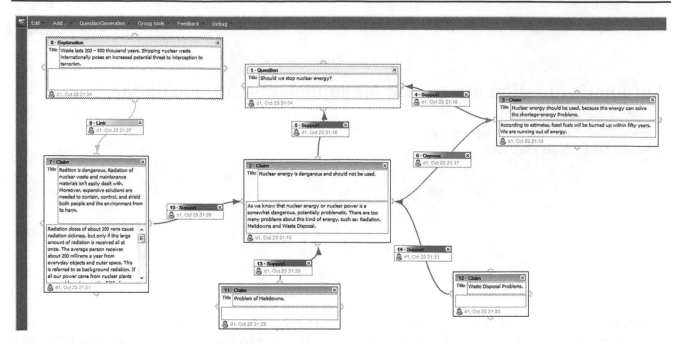

Fig. 1 LASAD: a computer-supported collaborative argumentation system

these questions. The approach consists of the following processes:

- Analyzing grammatical structure of natural language
- Extracting main concepts from documents
- Searching related concepts in a semantic network

2. How can a question generation system use the extracted information to generate questions which have the intention of helping participants of an argumentation session expand their argumentation? The second contribution of this paper is to propose a question generation approach which makes use of semantic information available on WordNet and consists of the following steps:

- Generating questions using question templates
- Generating questions using a syntax-based question generation system

In order to illustrate the semantics-based question generation approach in this paper, we will use the computer-supported collaborative argumentation system LASAD and the natural language English as a study case.

2 Question generation—state of the art

In order to generate questions related to a discussion topic, the topic statement is taken as the basis information. The topic statement is supposed to consist of one or several (grammatically correct) sentences which can serve question generation. Existing question generation approaches can be clas-

sified into three classes: syntax-based[1], template-based, and semantics-based approaches.

Syntax-based question generation systems work through three steps: (1) delete the identified target concept, (2) place a determined question key word on the first position of the question, and (3) convert the verb into a grammatically correct form considering auxiliary and model verbs. For example, the question generation system of Varga and Le [3] uses a set of transformation rules for question formation. For subject–verb–object clauses whose subject has been identified as a target concept, a "Which Verb Object" template is selected and matched against the clause. The question word "Which" then replaces the target concept in the selected clause. For key concepts that are in the object position of a subject–verb–object, the verb phrase is adjusted (i.e., an auxiliary verb is used). Varga and Le reported that generated questions achieved a score of 2.45 (2.85) with respect to relevance and a score of 2.85 (3.1) with respect to syntactic correctness and fluency given a scale between from 1 to 4, with 1 being the best score. Values outside and inside in the brackets indicate ratings of the 1st and 2nd human rater.

The second approach, which is also employed widely in several question generation systems, is template-based [4]. The template-based approach relies on the idea that a question template can capture a class of questions, which are context specific. For example, Chen and colleagues [4] developed the following templates: "What would happen if

---

[1] The syntax-based approach is also referred to as transformation-based in literature because transformation rules are defined and applied on syntax structures of input sentences.

⟨X⟩?" for conditional text, "When would ⟨X⟩?" and "what happens ⟨temporal-expression⟩?" for temporal context, and "Why ⟨auxiliary-verb⟩⟨X⟩?" for linguistic modality, where the place-holder ⟨X⟩ is mapped to semantic roles annotated by a semantic role labeler. These question templates can only be used for these specific entity relationships. For other kinds of entity relationships, new templates must be defined. Hence, the template-based question generation approach is mostly suitable for applications with a special purpose.

In addition to questions that can be generated using phrases in a statement, semantic information related to the issue in a statement can also be exploited to generate semantics-based questions. For example, Jouault and Seta [5,6] proposed to query information to facilitate learners' self-directed learning using Wikipedia. Using this system, students in self-directed learning are asked to build a timeline of events of a history period with causal relationships between these events given an initial document (that can be considered a problem statement). The student develops a concept map containing a chronology by selecting concepts and relationships between concepts from the given initial Wikipedia document to deepen his understanding. While the student creates a concept map, the system also integrates the concept to its map and generates its own concept map by referring to semantic information, i.e., DBpedia [7] and Freebase [8]. The authors used ontological engineering and linked open data (LOD) techniques [9] to generate semantics-based adaptive questions and to recommend documents according to Wikipedia to help students create concept maps for the domain of history. The system's concept map is updated with every modification of the student's one. In addition, the system extracts semantic information from DBpedia and Freebase to select and add related concepts into the existing map. Thus, the system's concept map always contains more concepts than the student's map. Using these related concepts and their relations, the system generates questions for the student to lead to a deeper understanding without forcing to follow a fixed path of learning. One of the great advantages of adopting semantic information rather than natural language resources expected is that the system can give adequate advice based on the machine-understandable domain models without worrying about ambiguity of natural language.

From a technical point of view, automatic question generation can be achieved using a variety of natural language processing techniques which have gained wide acceptance. However, successful deployment of question generation in educational systems is rarely found in literature. Using the semantic information available on the Internet to generate questions to support learning is a relative new research area which is the subject for investigation recently. How can semantic information available on the Internet be processed to generate questions to support students learning in a con-

Table 1 Types and examples of input text

Type	Example
Individual word	Energy/ noun/ go
List of words	Energy, activation energy, and heat energy
Phrase	Problem of meltdowns
Sentence/question	Should we stop nuclear energy?
Paragraph	Nuclear energy is dangerous and should not be used. As we know that nuclear energy or nuclear power is a somewhat dangerous, potentially problematic. There are too many problems about this kind of energy, such as radiation, meltdowns, and waste disposal

structivist environment? The question generation approach proposed in this paper employs all three existing approaches (syntax-based, template-based, and semantics-based) and uses semantic information provided on WordNet to generate questions. The question generation system (QGS) which applies this approach is described in the following section.

3 Question generation

The purpose of generating questions in the context of this paper is to give students ideas related to a discussion topic and guiding them how to expand the topic and continue their argumentation. As an input, the question generation system takes an English text from the discussion topic, which is provided by participants of an argumentation system. The text of a discussion topic can be an individual word, a list of words, a phrase, a sentence/question, or a paragraph. Therefore, recognizing, understanding the content of discussion topic clearly, and taking all types of text that are listed in Table 1 as input is the first step of the QGS system.

Semantics-based question generation approaches use a source of semantic information which is related to the topic being discussed. Since in this paper we focus on using information available on the Internet for generating questions, the source of "semantic information" we look for is on the semantic web. For example, Wikipedia provides definitions of words and descriptions of concepts. While Wikipedia might contain incorrect information due to its contribution mechanism, one of the advantages of Wikipedia is that the definition of many concepts is available in many different languages. If we want to develop a question generation for different languages, Wikipedia might thus be an appropriate source. Beside Wikipedia, WordNet also provides a source of semantic information which can be related to a discussion topic. WordNet [10] is an online lexical reference system for English. Each noun, verb, or adjective represents a lexical concept and has a relation link to hyponyms which represent related concepts. In addition, for most vocabulary WordNet provides example sentences which can be used for generating questions. For example, if we input the word "energy" into WordNet, an example sentence like *"energy can take a wide variety of forms"* for this word is available. If we look for some hyponyms for this word, there are a list of **direct hyponyms** and a list of **full hyponyms**. The list of direct hyponyms provides concepts which are directly related to the word being searched, for example, for "energy", we can find the following direct hyponyms on WordNet: "activation energy", "alternative energy", "atomic energy", "binding energy", "chemical energy", and more. The list of full hyponyms contains a hierarchy of hyponyms which represent direct and indirect related concepts of the word being searched. One of the advantages of WordNet is that it provides accurate information (e.g., hyponyms) and grammatically correct example sentences. For this reason, we use WordNet to generate questions which are relevant and related to a discussion topic.

Concerning the types of questions to be generated, Graesser and Person [11] proposed 16 question categories: verification, disjunctive, concept completion, example, feature specification, quantification, definition, comparison, interpretation, causal antecedent, causal consequence, goal orientation, instrumental/procedural, enablement, expectation, and judgmental. The first 4 categories were classified as simple/shallow, 5–8 as intermediate, and 9–16 as complex/deep questions. This question taxonomy can be used to define appropriate question templates for generating questions.

Questions can also be generated using just main concepts available in a discussion topic (Sect. 3.5). The question generation approach proposed in this paper will use **hyponyms** (Sect. 3.6) and **example sentences** (Sect. 3.7) provided on WordNet for generating semantics-based questions. The question generation approach consists of the following steps.

3.1 Analyzing grammatical structure of natural language

In order to recognize and understand the content of a discussion topic, a natural language parser is used to analyze the grammatical structure of a sentence or a string of words into its constituents, resulting in a parse tree showing their syntactic relation to each other. This parser groups words together (as "phrase") and determines the roles of words in each sentence, for instance, subject, verb, or object.

In order to extract important concepts from a text, a noun or a noun phrase can play a great role. For example, the important word from example (Ex. 3.1) is "nuclear energy"; the important words in example (Ex. 3.2) are "charity" and "energy"; and in example (Ex. 3.3), the main words are "heat

energy" and "type of energy". All of them are nouns or noun phrases.

Ex. 3.1: Should we stop nuclear energy?
Ex. 3.2: We will discuss charity and energy
Ex. 3.3: Heat energy is one of a type of energy
Ex. 3.4: Parents
Ex. 3.5: Go

Although there is only one word "parents" in example (Ex. 3.4), it is a noun and thus, can be the subject of an argumentation. Additionally, it is possible to generate meaningful questions about "parents". In contrast, questions for the word "go", a verb in example (Ex. 3.5), can be almost meaningless. Therefore, a given text first must be analyzed and parsed with a natural language parser to determine which words should be considered important concepts. If there are errors or problems with this analyzing and parsing step, the correctness of generated questions by QGS can be affected.

3.2 Extracting main concepts from documents

After analyzing and parsing the discussion topic with a natural language parser, QGS extracts all important concepts, which are determined as nouns and noun phrases in a discussion topic (Sect. 3.1). In order to retrieve more information, every extracted noun or noun phrase is used as resource to search for its related concepts (hyponyms and example sentences of each hyponym) in the WordNet [12] database.

The concepts retrieved from the WordNet database play important roles for the question generation steps in QGS. Hyponyms give participants of an argumentation session more information related to the extracted nouns and noun phrases. Example sentences for each hyponym add information to that hyponym and might help the participant of an argumentation session understand the use of that hyponym. Therefore, not only the nouns or noun phrases extracted from a discussion topic can be subjects for generating questions, but also hyponyms and example sentences provided on WordNet.

Some noun phrases are less important than individual nouns. For example, the noun phrase in example (Ex. 3.6) cannot be found in the WordNet database. QGS, therefore, only needs to extract the word "sea" as resource for its next steps.

Ex. 3.6: Deep blue sea (Type: Adjective + Adjective + Noun)
Ex. 3.7: Nuclear energy (Type: Noun + Noun)
Ex. 3.8: Energy of activation (Type: Noun + "of" + Noun)

However, some noun phrases like example (Ex. 3.7) and (Ex. 3.8) are common nouns and exist in the WordNet database,

Table 2 Types of extracted noun phrases

Type
Noun + Noun
Noun + "of" + Noun
Adjective + Noun

Table 3 Question templates proposed for QGS

Type	Question
Definition	What is $\langle X \rangle$?
	What do you have in mind when you think about $\langle X \rangle$?
	What does $\langle X \rangle$ remind you of?
Feature/Property	What are the properties of $\langle X \rangle$?
	What are the (opposite)-problems of $\langle X \rangle$?
	What features does $\langle X \rangle$ have?
Example	What is an example of $\langle X \rangle$?
Verification	Is there any problem with the arguments about $\langle X \rangle$?
Judgment	What do you like when you think of or hear about $\langle X \rangle$?
Interpretation	How can $\langle X \rangle$ be used today?
Expectation	How will $\langle X \rangle$ look or be in the future, based on the way it is now?
Quantification	How many sub-topics did your partners talk about?
	Which sub-topics do your partners focus on?
Concept Comparison	What is the difference or relations between these sub-topics?

together with a semantic network and their hyponyms and example sentences. Therefore in this case, "Nuclear energy" is much more important than "nuclear" or "energy" and "Energy of activation" is much more important than "energy" or "activation". However, at least for brainstorming purposes, the more information a question generation system can extract and provide to its users, the more chances there are for stimulating good ideas. That is why after all, not only individual nouns but also noun phrases, whose types are listed in Table 2, are extracted, as these noun phrases might be found in WordNet database. Thus, the result of the concept extraction, for example (Ex. 3.6), is "sea". For example (Ex. 3.7), "nuclear", "energy", and "nuclear energy" are results of the concept extraction. Results, for example (Ex. 3.8), are "energy", "activation", and "energy of activation". Table 2 also contains the noun phrase type "Adjective + Noun", because example (Ex. 3.1) "Should we stop nuclear energy?", as parsed by the Stanford Parser,[2] results in the noun phrase "nuclear energy" of type "Adjective + Noun".

3.3 Searching related concepts in semantic network

As mentioned in Sect. 3.2., WordNet is used as a source of lexical knowledge for searching all concepts related to every noun or noun phrase extracted from a discussion topic. Thus, WordNet provides the QGS more information about the extracted words. However, WordNet does not contain nouns in plural form. For example, consider searching concepts related to "fish" and "children" in example (Ex. 3.9) in WordNet database; the result is unexpected.

(Ex. 3.9) All fish are good for children.

Even though "fish" and "children" are two very common and simple words, WordNet can only recognize "fish", as its singular and plural form are the same. WordNet in this case considers "fish" as a noun in singular form and is able to extract information related to "fish" from its database. However, "children" is totally different from its singular form "child". The word "children" does not exist in the WordNet database, nor there exists any connection between "children" and "child" in the database. Thus, WordNet is not able to

---
[2] http://nlp.stanford.edu:8080/parser/index.jsp.

recognize and cannot provide any concept related to the query "children".

In order to solve the problem caused by WordNet database, a **Plural-to-Singular double-search** method is introduced. First, QGS searches for the concepts related to every extracted noun or noun phrase in the WordNet database normally. If WordNet returns nothing for any extracted noun or noun phrase, this noun or noun phrase is then considered as the word/phrase in plural form. QGS, therefore, tries to turn this plural form into singular form using the stripping common English endings of word method. For example, QGS removes the ending "-en" of "children" and returns "child" as new word. After that, QGS starts searching the concepts related to this new word in the WordNet database one more time (second search).

3.4 Question generation

In order to generate questions, the approach described in this paper proposes using question templates in Table 3, whereas X is the noun or noun phrase extracted from a discussion topic, or each hyponym extracted from WordNet. The question templates are defined according to the question classification proposed in [12].

3.5 Question generation without using WordNet

Using question templates defined in Table 3, we are able to replace the placeholders by nouns and noun phrases extracted

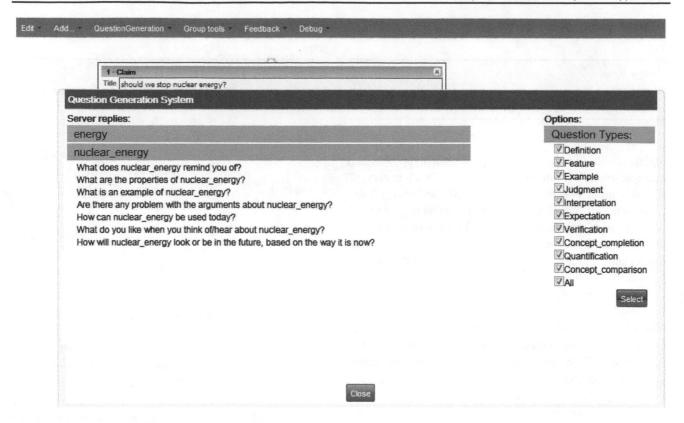

Fig. 2 Questions have been generated without using WordNet

from a discussion topic. For example, the following question templates are filled with the noun phrase "nuclear energy" and result in some questions shown in Fig. 2.

What does ⟨X⟩ remind you of?
What are the properties of ⟨X⟩?
What is an example of ⟨X⟩?

3.6 Question generation using hyponyms

In addition to generating questions without using Word-Net, placeholders in question templates can also be filled with appropriate hyponym values for generating questions. For example, the following question templates can be used to generate questions of the question class "Definition". If the noun "energy" exists in a problem statement, and after inputting this noun into WordNet, we will get several hyponyms, including "activation energy". For example, using the question templates, we are able to generate three possible questions of the class Definition (see Table 4).

Exploiting hyponyms to generate questions, we propose to generate a main question and several supporting questions which help students to think deeper about an issue. The supporting questions can be generated using appropriate question templates. For example, we define Template 1 for the class of "Feature specification" questions. Supporting

Table 4 An example of question template for the question class "Definition"

Type	Question template	Question
Definition	What is ⟨X⟩?	What is **activation energy**?
	What do you have in mind when you think about ⟨X⟩?	What do you have in mind when you think about **activation energy**?
	What does ⟨X⟩ remind you of?	What does **activation energy** remind you of?

questions for this question class are instantiated using question templates 1.1, 1.2, and 1.3 (Table 5). Questions generated using these templates are instances of the question class "Expectation".

Figure 3 illustrates questions which have been generated using hyponyms on WordNet. At first, a list of hyponyms which are related to the noun "nuclear energy" is shown, followed by a list of generated questions. The supporting questions are indented (e.g., "What would you do if they were twice as big (or half as big)?").

3.7 Question generation using examples sentences

As discussed, in addition to hyponyms, WordNet also provides example sentences (for hyponyms) which are grammat-

Table 5 Templates for supporting questions

Type	Question template
Feature specification	Template 1: What are the (opposite)-problems of $\langle X \rangle$?
Expectation	Template 1.1: What would you do if they were twice as big (or half as big)?
Expectation	Template 1.2: How would you think about or deal with them if you were in different time period?
Expectation	Template 1.3: How could (opposite)-problems of $\langle X \rangle$ be stopped?

ically correct. We propose to make use of example sentences to generate questions. For example, for the sentence "Peter has 20 apples", the following questions can be generated (Fig. 4):

There are existing successful question generation tools which are based on input texts. For example, ARK [13] is a syntax-based tool for generating questions from English sentences or phrases. The system operates on syntactic tree structures and defines transformation rules to generate questions. Heilman and Smith [13] reported that the system achieved 43.3 % acceptability for the top 10 ranked questions and produced an average of 6.8 acceptable questions per 250 words on Wikipedia texts. It also introduces a question-ranker system, which scores and ranks every generated question. This score-and-ranking system helps us to know the accuracy rate of questions, which are generated from a given sentence. For the input sentence "Peter has 20 apples", ARK produces

several questions with according accuracy rate and the generated question "How many apples does Peter have?" has the highest accuracy score (2.039) (Fig. 4).

The approach being proposed in this paper exploits the syntax-based question generation tool ARK for generating questions which are semantically related to a given discussion topic. Figure 5 illustrates several questions which have been generated using example sentences available on Word-Net when given a discussion topic "Should we stop nuclear energy?" Using the syntax-based question generation tool ARK, we are able to add one more question type (Concept Completion) to QGS and strengthen questions of the type quantification and verification. With the use of question templates (cf. Sect. 3.4) and a syntax-based question generation tool, QGS can then generate ten question types (Definition, Feature, Example, Judgment, Interpretation, Expectation, Verification, Quantification, Concept comparison, Concept completion).

4 Implementation

The question generation system which is connected with the argumentation system LASAD consists of the following components: the Stanford Parser, a Noun Extractor, a Data Storage, a pool of Question Templates, the ARK syntax-based question generation tool, and WordNet 2.1 as a source of lexical knowledge (Fig. 6).

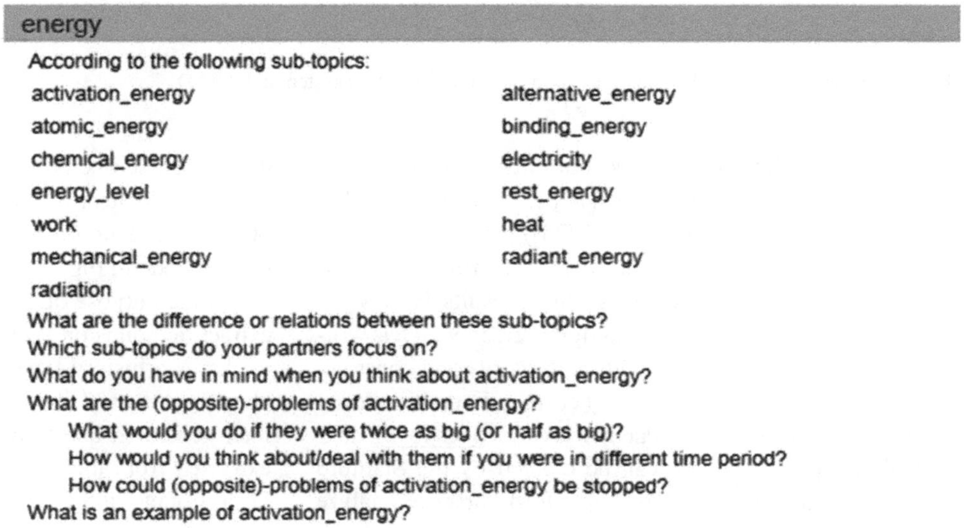

Fig. 3 Questions have been generated using hyponyms on WordNet

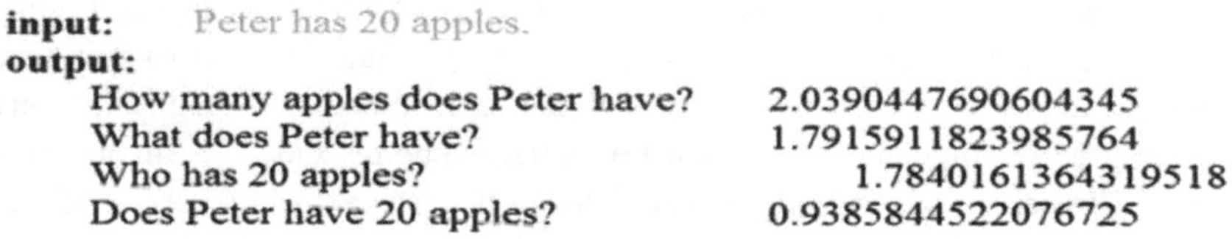

energy

According to the following sub-topics:

activation_energy	alternative_energy
atomic_energy	binding_energy
chemical_energy	electricity
energy_level	rest_energy
work	heat
mechanical_energy	radiant_energy
radiation	

What are the difference or relations between these sub-topics?
Which sub-topics do your partners focus on?
What do you have in mind when you think about activation_energy?
What are the (opposite)-problems of activation_energy?
    What would you do if they were twice as big (or half as big)?
    How would you think about/deal with them if you were in different time period?
    How could (opposite)-problems of activation_energy be stopped?
What is an example of activation_energy?

Fig. 4 An example using the ARK Question Generation and the corresponding accuracy scores

input: Peter has 20 apples.
output:

How many apples does Peter have?	2.0390447690604345
What does Peter have?	1.7915911823985764
Who has 20 apples?	1.7840161364319518
Does Peter have 20 apples?	0.9385844522076725

Fig. 5 Questions have been
generated using example
sentences on WordNet

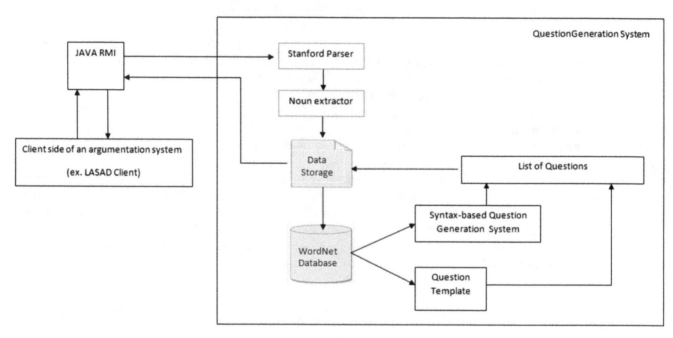

energy

Are catalysts said to reduce the energy of activation during the transition phase of a reaction?
When are catalysts said to reduce the energy of activation?
What are catalysts said to reduce during the transition phase of a reaction?
What are said to reduce the energy of activation during the transition phase of a reaction?
What are catalysts said to reduce the energy of during the transition phase of a reaction?
Did they build a car that runs on electricity?
Who built a car that runs on electricity?
What built a car that runs on electricity?
Are only certain energy levels possible?
What are possible?
Does work equal force times distance?
What equals force times distance?
What does work equal force?

Fig. 6 The architecture of the integration of a question generation system in LASAD

For parsing English phrases, currently Link Grammar Parser [14] and Stanford Parser [15] (a lexicalized Probabilistic Context-Free Grammar (PCFG)) are two of the best semantic parsers. Link Grammar Parser is a rule-based analyzer, which is essential to obtain accurate results. However, a statistical analyzer parser like Stanford Parser, which is written in Java, is more tolerant with both words and constructions, which are not grammatically correct. Even if there are grammatical errors (e.g., "Parents always <u>does loves</u> their childs".), a parse tree still can be created by the Stanford Parser. For this reason, we used Stanford Parser to analyze grammatical structure of input sentences.

The noun extractor has been developed to extract main concepts from a discussion topic (cf. Sect. 3.2). It takes a complex text, which can be a word, a phrase, a sentence, or a paragraph as input and returns a list of extracted nouns and noun phrases (L_{result}) as output. The algorithm starts taking

the best parse tree (which has highest parse score) returned by Stanford Parser. The parse tree will be used to obtain a list of nouns. The algorithm for extracting nouns is illustrated as pseudo-code in Fig. 7.

For the purpose of optimizing the time for searching and extracting nouns on WordNet, the Data Storage component works as a history tracer. It stores all the nouns and noun phrases extracted from the given text of users, along with their generated question-lists in an XML file. If the nouns extracted from the discussion topic statement exists in the Data Storage, the QGS only needs to extract the matching questions-list for each noun and noun phrase from Data Storage and returns these lists to users. In this case, the system does not have to generate questions for each noun phrase. Thus, the performance of the system is optimized.

In order to retrieve semantic information, we use the latest version of the WordNet database 2.1 for Windows. The ARK

Fig. 7 Noun and noun phrase extractor

Algorithm 1 extractNoun(t)

$L_{result} \leftarrow \emptyset$

$T_{parser} \leftarrow$ best parse tree after parsing with Stanford Parser.

$L_{taggedWord} \leftarrow$ extract and store every word, along with its direct POS-tag from tree T_{parser}.

    FOR all word $w_i \in L_{taggedWord}$

        IF (POS tag of w_i is NN | NNS | NNP | NNPS) AND ($w_i \notin L_{result}$) THEN

            $L_{result} \leftarrow$ add w_i

            IF $\exists w_{i-1}$ THEN

                IF (POS tag of w_{i-1} is NN | NNP | NNS | NNPS)

                    AND (noun phrase $w_{i-1}w_i \notin L_{result}$) THEN

                    $L_{result} \leftarrow$ add $w_{i-1}w_i$

                ELSE IF w_{i-1} is the word "of" THEN

                    IF $\exists w_{i-2}$ AND (POS tag of w_{i-2} is NN | NNP | NNS | NNPS) THEN

                        IF noun phrase $w_{i-2}w_{i-1}w_i \notin L_{result}$ THEN

                          $L_{result} \leftarrow$ add $w_{i-2}w_{i-1}w_i$

                    ENDIF

                  ENDIF

                ENDIF

            ENDIF

        ENDIF

    ENDFOR

    RETURN L_{result}

---

question generation tool has been described in Sect. 3.7. The process of question generation consists of five steps:

- Step 1: parse input text and analyze grammatical structure using the Stanford Parser.
- Step 2: extract nouns/noun phrases using the Noun Extractor.
- Step 3: search for the extracted nouns and noun phrases in the Data Storage. If they exist, QGS extracts the matching question lists out of Data Storage and starts Step 5. If the extracted nouns and noun phrases are not stored in Data Storage, QGS starts Step 4.
- Step 4: input extracted nouns and noun phrases into the WordNet database, QGS then extracts all matching hyponyms and example sentences.
- Step 5: Questions are generated based on extracted hyponyms and example sentences provided on WordNet using the pool of Question Templates and the ARK component. Pairs of noun/noun phrase and generated questions are stored in the Data Storage. In addition to generated questions using WordNet, nouns and noun phrases extracted from the discussion topic are also used as input to generate questions.

5 Evaluation

In this section, we report on evaluation about the utility of the algorithm for extracting main concepts from a discussion topic, the quality of generated questions and the efficiency of the Plural-to-Singular transformation method.

5.1 Extracting main concepts

In order to examine if QGS recognizes and extracts the main concepts (the nouns and noun phrases) from the input text (discussion topic) correctly, the following paragraph was used as input:

> "As we know that nuclear energy or nuclear power is somewhat dangerous, potentially problematic. There are too many problems about this kind of energy, such as: Radiation, Meltdowns, and Waste Disposal. Radiation is dangerous. Radiation of nuclear waste and maintenance materials is not easily dealt with. Moreover, expensive solutions are needed to contain, control, and shield both people and the environment from its harm".

Using paragraph as input, QGS could recognize and extract 13 out of 14 expected results that are listed in Table 5. It could not extract the phrase "radiation of nuclear waste", as the structure of this phrase was not declared for QGS. However, QGS extracted nine further extra nouns (from #15 to #23). Eight out of these nine nouns were acceptable, only the noun "many problems" (#17) was almost meaningless, compared to its original "problem" (#3). For brainstorming purposes, the use of extra nouns can actually be very helpful during the next steps of the question generation process. For example, with the extra noun "energy", QGS gave users information about types of energy such as solar energy, wind energy, etc. The users, therefore, could develop their argument, for instance, "if nuclear energy is too dangerous, solar energy or wind energy may be the replacement solution".

5.2 Generating questions

After checking the ability of extracting main concepts from a discussion topic, here, we examine whether QGS generated enough questions.

Eighteen question templates were used to generate questions for not only extracted main concept from a discussion topic, but also for any related concept extracted from Word-Net. Out of eighteen question templates, four templates for the question types Quantification and Concept Comparison were only used for main concepts, for which the system could find at least two related hyponyms on WordNet. In addition, the number of generated questions also depended on the syntax-based question generation tool. For example, generating questions for "nuclear energy" in Table 6, QGS found one hyponym "atom energy" and one example sentence "nuclear energy regarded as a source of electricity for the power grid (for civilian use)" related to "nuclear energy" in WordNet database. Therefore, QGS generated

- Fourteen questions for "nuclear energy" by using question templates, as there was only one hyponym
- Fourteen questions for "atom energy" by using question templates (without four questions of type Quantification and Concept Comparison)
- Four questions by using syntax-based question generation tool ARK (Table 6).

In summary, QGS generated enough question as expected. Note, some generated questions (e.g., the ones generated using the syntax-based question generation tool ARK) are not sound, although they seem to be grammatically correct. Thus, they need to be investigated with respect to their appropriateness (Table 7).

5.3 Efficiency of using plural-to-singular method

The WordNet database was used as the only semantic resource that provided all the important concepts for the question generation process. Since WordNet does not contain any noun in plural form, the plural-to-singular double search method has been introduced in Sect. 3.3. This method pretends that the source noun is in plural form and is implemented for the purpose of searching nouns in the WordNet database. If, after trying all of the cases that the source noun could transform into (e.g. "ladies" could be transformed into "ladie", "ladi", and "lady"), the system still did not find any related concept of any predicted singular form, it would con-

Table 6 List of main concepts extracted from an input paragraph

#	Expected result	Actual result
1.	Nuclear energy	Nuclear energy
2.	Nuclear power	Nuclear power
3.	Problems	Problem
4.	Kind of energy	Kind of energy
5.	Radiation	Radiation
6.	Meltdowns	Meltdowns
7.	Waste disposal	Waste disposal
8.	Radiation of nuclear waste	
9.	Nuclear waste	Nuclear waste
10.	Maintenance materials	Maintenance materials
11.	Expensive Solutions	Expensive Solutions
12.	People	People
13.	Environment	Environment
14.	Harm	Harm
15.		Energy
16.		Power
17.		*Many problems*
18.		Kind
19.		Waste
20.		Disposal
21.		Maintenance
22.		Material
23.		Solution

Table 7 Questions generated by a syntax-based question generation component

Example sentence related to "nuclear energy" on WordNet	Questions generated by ARK
Nuclear energy regarded as a source of electricity for the power grid (for civilian use)	What did nuclear energy regard as for the power grid?
	What regarded as a source of electricity for the power grid?
	What did nuclear energy regard as a source of electricity for?
	Did nuclear energy regard as a source of electricity for the power grid?

sider that the source noun was actually not in plural form and kept the source noun.

In an examination with an irregular plural nouns list[3] that contains 182 plural nouns of all types (special irregular plural nouns (e.g. children, people, men, etc.) and irregular plural nouns ending with -s, -x, -es, -ves, -ies, -ices, -a, -i, -im), the plural-to-singular method recognized and

---

[3] http://de.scribd.com/doc/88260838/Irregular-Nouns-in-English.

worked successfully with the singular forms of 173 out of the 182 irregular plural nouns. It failed to detect the combined plural nouns ("sons-in-law", "runners-up") and the plural nouns that ended with "aux" ("Beaux", "Beraux", "Chateaux", "Plateaux", "Tableaux"). In addition, the system was confused with some plural nouns, including "axes" because the system could detect only *"axe"* as its singular form. It could not detect "axis", either, nor could it completely handle and "busses", because this is plural form of both "bus" and "buss". The system could detect only "buss". In summary, the Plural-to-Singular double search method provided an efficient way to improve the usage of the Word-Net database, as users were not forced to use only nouns in singular forms to receive result from WordNet Database and support from QGS.

6 Discussion, conclusion, and future work

In this paper we have proposed an approach to generating questions to help students during brainstorming activities in which they expand their arguments when participating in a discussion. The approach proposed in this paper combines three question generation approaches: syntax-based, template-based, and semantics-based. This approach generates not only questions based on the main concepts of a given discussion topic, but also questions based on semantic information available on WordNet.

The question generation method proposed in this paper may have drawbacks due to using question templates. That is, the question templates can be very specific for a special domain as discussed in Sect. 3. We were aware of this problem and tried to define question templates which should be general enough for several discussion domains. For example, the question templates in Table 3 can be used to generate questions for the discussion topic "charity" by replacing the placeholder: (1) What is charity? (2) What do you have in mind when you think about charity? (3) What does charity remind you of? These questions are appropriate for helping participants think about the topic when they have to discuss about charity. Whether all question templates are general enough for other discussion topics, this needs to be evaluated and is a part of our future work. Since the goal of our research is to support students during brainstorming argumentation activities, we also intend to conduct an empirical evaluation study for this purpose.

Acknowledgments We would like to thank Jouault Corentin (Osaka Prefecture University) for preparing literature for the state of the art described in this paper.

Open Access This article is distributed under the terms of the Creative Commons Attribution License which permits any use, distribution, and reproduction in any medium, provided the original author(s) and the source are credited.

References

1. Jonassen, D. H.: Designing constructivist learning environments. In: Reigeluth, C. M. (eds.) Instructional Design Theories and Models: A New Paradigm of Instructional Theory, vol. 2, pp. 215–239. Lawrence Erlbaum, Hillsdale (1999)
2. Loll, F., Pinkwart, N., Scheuer, O., McLaren, B. M.: Simplifying the development of argumentation systems using a configurable platform. In: Pinkwart, N., McLaren, B.M. (eds.) Educational Technologies for Teaching Argumentation Skill. Bentham Science Publishers, Sharjah (2012)
3. Varga, A., Le, A. H.: A question generation aystem for the QGSTEC 2010 Task B. In: Proc. of the 3rd WS. on Question Generation, held at the ITS Conf., pp. 80–83 (2010)
4. Chen, W., Aist, G., Mostow, J.: Generating questions automatically from informational text. In: Proceedings of the 2nd Workshop on Question Generation, held at the Conference on AI in, Education, pp. 17–24, (2009)
5. Jouault, C., Seta, K.: Building a semantic open learning space with adaptive question generation support. In: Proceedings of the 21st International Conference on Computers in Education, pp. 41–50 (2013)
6. Jouault C., Seta, K.: Adaptive self-directed learning support by question generation in a semantic open learning space. Int. J. Knowl. Web Intell. (2014)
7. Bizer, C., Lehmann, J., Kobilarov, G., Auer, S., Becker, C., Cyganiak, R., Hellmann, S.: DBpedia-A crystallization point for the Web of Data. Web Sem Sci Serv Agents World Wide Web **7**(3), 154–165 (2009)
8. Bollacker, K., Evans, C., Paritosh, P., Sturge, T., Taylor, J.: Freebase: a collaboratively created graph database for structuring human knowledge. In: Proceedings of the SIGMOD International Conference on Management of Data, pp. 1247–1250, ACM (2008)
9. Heath, T., Bizer, C.: Linked Data: Evolving the Web into a Global Data Space. Morgan & Claypool Publishers, San Rafael (2011)
10. Miller, G.A.: WordNet: a lexical database. Commun ACM **38**(11), 39–41 (1995)
11. Graesser, A.C., Person, N.K.: Question asking during tutoring. Am Educ Res J **31**(1), 104–137 (1994)
12. Heilman, M.: Automatic Factual Question Generation from Text. Ph.D. Dissertation, Carnegie Mellon University. CMU-LTI-11-004 (2011)
13. Heilman, M., Smith, N.A.: Question Generation via Overgenerating Transformations and Ranking. Technical report, Language Technologies Institute, Carnegie Mellon University. CMU-LTI-09-013 (2009)
14. Sleator, D., Temperley, D.: Parsing English with a Link Grammar. In: Proceedings of the 3rd International Workshop on Parsing Technologies (1993)
15. Klein, D., Manning, C. D.: Accurate Unlexicalized Parsing. In: Proceedings of the 41st Meeting of the Association for, Computational Linguistics, pp. 423–430 (2003)

22

Classifying many-class high-dimensional fingerprint datasets using random forest of oblique decision trees

Thanh-Nghi Do · Philippe Lenca · Stéphane Lallich

Abstract Classifying fingerprint images may require an important features extraction step. The scale-invariant feature transform which extracts local descriptors from images is robust to image scale, rotation and also to changes in illumination, noise, etc. It allows to represent an image in term of the comfortable bag-of-visual-words. This representation leads to a very large number of dimensions. In this case, random forest of oblique decision trees is very efficient for a small number of classes. However, in fingerprint classification, there are as many classes as individuals. A multi-class version of random forest of oblique decision trees is thus proposed. The numerical tests on seven real datasets (up to 5,000 dimensions and 389 classes) show that our proposal has very high accuracy and outperforms state-of-the-art algorithms.

Keywords Fingerprint classification · Scale-invariant feature transform · Bag-of-visual-words · Random forest of oblique decision trees

T.-N. Do · P. Lenca
Institut Mines-Telecom; Telecom Bretagne, CNRS UMR 6285
Lab-STICC, Université européenne de Bretagne, Brest, France

P. Lenca
e-mail: philippe.lenca@telecom-bretagne.eu

T.-N. Do (✉)
Can Tho University, Can Tho , Vietnam
e-mail: dtnghi@cit.ctu.edu.vn

S. Lallich
Laboratoire ERIC, Université de Lyon 2, Lyon, France
e-mail: stephane.lallich@univ-lyon2.fr

1 Introduction

Due to their uniqueness and consistency over time [1], fingerprint identification is one of the most well-known technique for person identification. It is successfully used in both government and civilian applications such as suspect and victim identifications, border control, employment background checks, and secure facility access [2]. Fingerprint recognition systems commonly use minutiae (i.e. ridge ending, ridge bifurcation, etc.) as features since a long time. Recently a method based on feature-level fusion of fingerprint and finger-vein has been proposed [3]. Recent advances in technology make each day easier the acquisition of fingerprints features. In addition, there is a growing need for reliable person identification and thus fingerprint technology is more and more popular.

Fingerprint systems mainly focus on two applications: fingerprint matching which computes a match score between two fingerprints, and fingerprint classification which assigns fingerprints into one of the (pre)defined classes. The state-of-the-art methods are based on minutiae points and ridge patterns, including a crossover, core, bifurcation, ridge ending, island, delta and pore [2,4,5]. Useful features and classification algorithms are found in [6,7]. Most of these techniques have no difficulty in matching or classifying good quality fingerprint images. However, dealing with low-quality or partial fingerprint images still remains a challenging pattern recognition problem. Indeed a biometric fingerprint acquisition process is inherently affected by many factors [8]. Fingerprint images are concerned by displacement (the same finger may be captured at different locations or rotated at different angles on the fingerprint reader), partial overlap (part of the fingerprint area fall outside the fingerprint reader), distortion, noise, etc.

An efficient feature extraction technique, called the scale-invariant feature transform (SIFT) was proposed by [9] for detecting and describing local features in images. The local features obtained by the SIFT method are robust to image scale, rotation, changes in illumination, noise and occlusion. Therefore, the SIFT is used for image classification and retrieval. The bag-of-visual-words (BoVW) model based on SIFT extraction is proposed in [10]. Some recent fingerprint techniques [11–13] showed that the SIFT local feature can improve matching tasks.

Unfortunately, when using SIFT and the BoVW models, the number of features could be very large (e.g. thousands dimensions or visual words). We here propose to classify fingerprint images with random forest of oblique decision trees [15, 16] which have shown to have very high accuracy when dealing with very-high-dimensional datasets for few class problems. However, for individual identification each person is considered as a single class. We thus extend this approach to deal with a very large number of classes. Experiments with real datasets and comparison with state-of-the-art algorithms show the efficiency of our proposal.

The paper is organized as follows. Section 2 presents the image representation using the SIFT and the BoVW model. Section 3 briefly introduces random forests of oblique decision trees and then extend this algorithm to multi-classes classification of very-high-dimensional datasets. The experimental results are presented in Sect. 4. We then conclude in Sect. 5.

2 SIFT and bag-of-visual-words model

When dealing with images like fingerprint one has to extract first local descriptors. The SIFT method [9] detects and describes local features in images. SIFT is based on the appearance of the object at particular interest points. It is invariant to image scale, rotation and also robust to changes in illumination, noise, occlusion. It is thus adapted for fingerprint images as pointed out by [11–13].

Step 1 (Fig. 2) detects the interest points in the image. These points are either maximums of Laplace of Gaussian, 3D local extremes of Difference of Gaussian [17], or points detected by a Hessian-affine detector [18]. Figure 1 shows some interest points detected by a Hessian-affine detector for fingerprint images. The local descriptors of interest point are computed on a grey level gradient of the region around the interest point (step 2 in Fig. 2). Each SIFT descriptor is a 128-dimensional vector.

A main stage consists of forming visual words from the local descriptors. Most of approaches perform a k-means [19] on descriptors. Each cluster is considered as a visual word represented by the cluster centre [10] (step 3 in Fig. 2). The set of clusters constitutes a visual vocabulary (step 4 in

Fig. 1 Interest points detected by Hessian-affine detector on a fingerprint

Fig. 2). Each descriptor is then assigned to the nearest cluster (step 5 in Fig. 2). The frequency of a visual word is the number of descriptors attached to the corresponding cluster (step 6 in Fig. 2). An image is then represented by the frequencies of the visual words, i.e. a BoVW.

SIFT method has demonstrated very good qualities to represent images. However, it leads to a very large number of dimensions. Indeed, a large number of descriptors may require a very large number of visual words to be efficient. In addition when dealing with fingerprint classification, the number of classes corresponds to the number of individuals in the dataset. In the next section, we investigate machine learning algorithms for this kind of data.

3 Multi-classes random forest of oblique decision trees

Random forests are one of the most accurate learning algorithms, but their outputs are difficult for humans to interpret [20]. We are here only interested in classification performance.

Reference [21] pointed out that the difficulty of high-dimensional classification is intrinsically caused by the existence of many redundant or noisy features. The comparative studies in [20, 22–25] showed that support vector machines [26], boosting [27] and random forests [28] are appropriate for very high dimensions. However, there are few studies [29, 30] for extremely large number of classes (typically hundreds of classes).

3.1 From random forests to random forests of oblique decision trees

A random forest is an ensemble classifier that consists of (potentially) large collection of decision trees. The algorithm for inducing a random forest was proposed in [28].

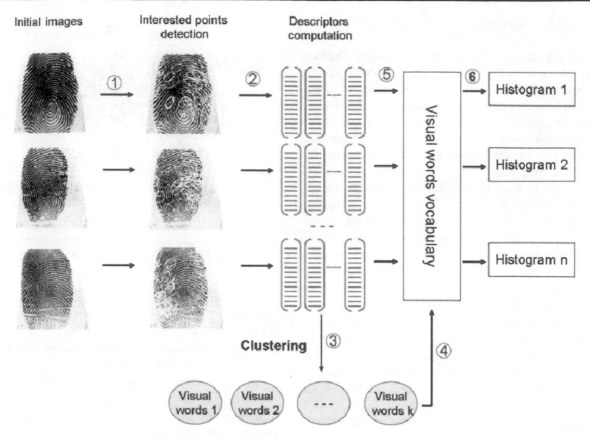

Fig. 2 Bag-of-visual-words model for representing images

The algorithm combines bagging idea [31] and the selection of a random subset of attributes introduced in [32,33] and [34].

Let us consider a training set D of n examples x_i described by p attributes. The bagging approach generates t new training sets B_j, $j = 1 \ldots t$, known as bootstrap sample, each of size n, by sampling n examples from D uniformly and with replacement. The t decision trees in the forest are then fitted using the t bootstrap samples and combined by voting for a classification task or averaging the output for regression task. Each decision tree DT_j ($j = 1, \ldots, t$) in the forest is thus constructed using the bootstrap sample B_j as follows: for each node of the tree, randomly choose p' attributes ($p' << p$) and calculate the best split based on one of these p' attributes; the tree is fully grown and not pruned.

A random forest is thus composed of trees having sufficient diversity (thanks to bagging and random subset of attributes) each of them having low bias (thanks to unpruning). Random forests are known to produce highly accurate classifier and are thus very popular [20].

However, for each tree only a single attribute is used to split each node. Such univariate strategy does not take into account dependencies between attributes. The strength of individual trees could thus be reduced typically when dealing with very-high-dimensional datasets which are likely to contain dependencies among attributes.

One can thus use oblique decision trees (e.g. OC1 [35]) or hybridization in a post-growing phase that uses other classifiers in tree's node (e.g. genetic algorithm [36], neural network [37,38], linear discriminant analysis [39, 40], support vector machines [41]). Recently, ensemble of oblique decision trees has attracted much research interests. For example proximal linear support vector machines [42] (PSVM) are used in [14–16] and ridge regression is proposed in [43] for random forests. The embedded support vector machines (SVM) in a forest of trees have shown very high performance especially for very-high-dimensional datasets [16] and a reasonable number of classes [15].

We thus here extend these approaches to deal with very large number of classes. Indeed, the fingerprint application needs to manage very-high-dimensional points with hundreds of individuals to classify. Furthermore, we provide also the performance analysis of multi-class random oblique decision trees in terms of the error bound and the algorithmic complexity. This theoretical analysis illustrates how our proposed algorithm is efficient in the fingerprint classification with many classes.

3.2 Multi-class random forests of oblique decision trees

We propose to induce a forest of binary oblique decision trees. Our approach will thus build a set of trees that will separate the c classes at each non-terminal node into two subsets of classes of size c_1 and c_2 ($c_1 + c_2 = c$). In such a way, the algorithm will reach terminal nodes (leaves). As proposed in the Random Forest of Oblique Decision Trees algorithm (RF-ODT) [16] these binary splits are done by proximal SVM [42].

The state-of-the-art multi-class SVMs are categorized into two types of approaches. The first one solves an optimization problem for multi-class separation [44,45]. This approach can thus require expensive calculations and parameter tuning.

The second one uses a series of binary SVMs to decompose the multi-class problem (e.g. "One-Versus-All" (OVA) [26]), "One-Versus-One" (OVO [46]) and Decision-Directed Acyclic Graph (DDAG [47]). Decision-Directed Acyclic Graph is rather complex and OVO needs to train $c(c-1)/2$ classifiers, while OVA needs only to build c classifiers.

Hierarchical methods divide the data into two subsets until every subset consists of only one class. The Divide-by-2 (DB2) [48] proposes three strategies (class centroid-based division using k-means [19], class mean distances and balanced subsets) to construct the two subsets of classes. The Dendrogram-based SVM [49] uses ascendant hierarchical clustering method. The Dendrogram clustering algorithms have a complexity that is at least cubic in the number of datapoints compared to the linear complexity of k-means.

Furthermore, the oblique tree construction aims at partitioning the data of the non–terminal node into two subsets. In practice, k-means is the most widely used partitional clustering algorithm because it is simple, easily understandable, and reasonably scalable. The partitional clustering algorithm k-means (setting $k = 2$ due to the data partition at the non-terminal node into two subsets) is the appropriate method.

Our proposal consists of an efficient hybrid method using the previous methods. Multi-Class Oblique Decision Trees (MC-ODT) are build using OVA (for small number of classes, i.e. $c \leq 3$) and a DB2-like method (for, i.e. $c > 3$) to perform the binary multivariate splits with a proximal SVM (denoted OVA-DB2-like approach in the later). These MC-ODT are then used to form a Random Forest of MC-ODT (MCRF-ODT) as illustrated in Fig. 5. Theoretical considerations supporting our approach are presented in Sect. 3.3.

Figure 3 illustrates the OVA-DB2-like approach for $c \leq 3$. On the left-hand side, $c = 3$, the algorithm creates two super classes (a positive part and a negative part). One super class groups together 2 classes and the other one matches the third class. This corresponds to the classical OVA strategy. Therefore, the algorithm only uses the OVA and the biggest

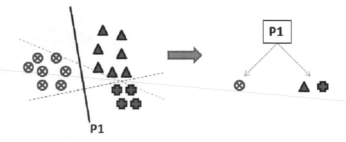

Fig. 3 Oblique splitting for c classes ($c \leq 3$)

margin criteria for performing an oblique binary split PSVM while dealing with $c \leq 3$ (i.e. the plane P_1) as illustrated on the right-hand-side of Fig. 3.

When the number of classes c is greater than 3, a k-means [19] is used on all the datapoints. This improves the quality of the two super classes in comparison with Divide-by-2 which only uses the class centroid (obviously Divide-by-2 is faster, but the quality of the classes is lower).

The most impure cluster is considered as the positive super class, the second cluster as the negative super one. The classes of this cluster (positive part) are then sorted in descending order of class size so that around 15 % of the datapoints of the minority classes are moved to the other cluster (negative part). This is done to reduce the noise in the positive cluster and also to balance the two clusters[1] (in terms of size and number of classes). Finally, the proximal SVM performs the oblique split to separate the two super classes.

These processes (OVA, k-means clustering and PSVM) are repeated to split the datapoints into terminal nodes (w.r.t. two criteria: the first one concerns the minimum size of nodes and the second one concerns the error rate in the node) as illustrated in Fig. 4. The majority class rule is applied to each terminal node.

The pseudocode of the random oblique decision tree algorithm for multi-class (MC-ODT) is presented in Algorithm 1 and the MCRF-ODT algorithm is illustrated in Fig. 5.

3.3 Performance analysis

For a non-terminal node D with c classes, the OVO and DDAG strategies require $\frac{c(c-1)}{2}$ tests (each test corresponds to a binary SVM) to perform a binary oblique split. These strategies thus become intractable when c is large.

The OVA-DB2-like approach used in MC-ODT is designated for separating the data into two balanced super classes. The OVA-DB2-like approach can be considered as the Two-ing rule [50].

---

[1] Our empirical tests, from 2 % up to 30 %, showed that 15 % gives good super classes.

Fig. 4 Oblique splitting for c classes ($c > 3$)

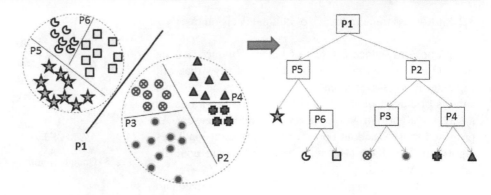

Fig. 5 Multi-class random forest of oblique decision trees

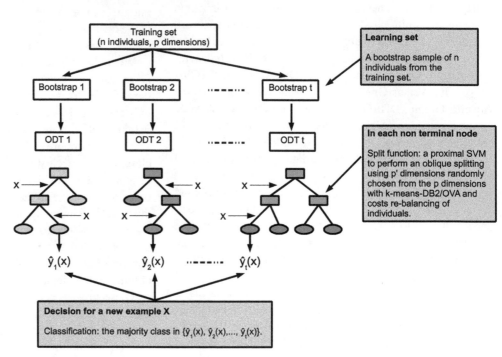

Therefore, the OVA-DB2-like approach tends to produce MC-ODTs with less non-terminal nodes than the OVA method. Thus, it requires less tests and lower computational time.

Error bound

Furthermore, according to [47], if one can classify a random n sample of labelled examples using a perceptron (e.g. a linear SVM) DDAG G (i.e. a DDAG with a perceptron at every node) on c classes containing K decision nodes (e.g. non-terminal nodes) with margins γ_i at node i, then the generalization error bound $\epsilon_j(G)$, with probability greater than $1 - \delta$, is given by:

$$\epsilon_j(G) \leq \frac{130R^2}{n}\left(M'\log(4en)\log(4n) + \log\left(\frac{2(2n)^K}{\delta}\right)\right)$$

(1)

where $M' = \sum_{i=1}^{K}\frac{1}{\gamma_i^2}$ and R is the radius of a hypersphere enclosing all the datapoints.

The error bound thus depends on M' (the margin γ_i's) and K decision nodes (non-terminal nodes). Let, now examine why our proposal has two interesting properties in comparison with the OVA approach:

- as mentioned above a MC-ODT based on the OVA-DB2-like approach has smaller K than the ones using the OVA method.
- the separating boundary (margin size) at a non-terminal node obtained by the OVA-DB2-like approach is larger than the one by the OVA method. As a consequence M' is smaller.

Therefore, the error bound of MC-ODT based on the OVA-DB2-like approach is smaller than the one made by the OVA strategy.

Algorithm 1: Random oblique decision tree for multi-class

> **input** :
>> D bootstrap sample of n datapoints in p dimensions with c classes
>> p' number of random dimensions used to perform oblique splits ($p' < p$)
>> ϵ error_tolerant acceptance at terminal nodes
>> min_obj minimum size of terminal nodes
>
> **output**:
>> **ODT model**
>
> **Learn:**
> **PROC RECURSIVE-ODT**(D, p', ϵ, min_obj)
> **begin**
>> 1- counting the number of datapoints for each class
>> 2- computing the error rate of D upon the majority class as the label of D
>> 3- **if** ($n < min\_obj$) or ($error\_rate < \epsilon$) **then**
>>> {
>>>> - assigning the majority class as the label of D
>>>> - return terminal node D
>>>
>>> }
>>> **else**
>>> {
>>>> - randomly sampling without replacement p' dimensions
>>>> - **if** ($c \leq 3$) **then**
>>>>> {
>>>>>> - PSVM uses One-Versus-All method with the biggest margin strategy to perform a binary oblique split D in p' dimensions into D_{pos} (positive part) and D_{neg} (negative part)
>>>>>
>>>>> }
>>>>> **else**
>>>>> {
>>>>>> - using k-means algorithm to group datapoints in D into two clusters, denoted by $cluster\_1$ and $cluster\_2$
>>>>>> - the most impure cluster is considered as the candidate of the positive class $candidate\_class$
>>>>>> - around 15% of the datapoints of the minority classes in $candidate\_class$ are moved to the other cluster
>>>>>> - PSVM performs a binary oblique split D in p' dimensions (with $candidate\_class$ being the positive class and the rest being the negative class) into D_{pos} (positive part) and D_{neg} (negative part)
>>>>>
>>>>> }
>>>>> - **RECURSIVE-ODT**($D_{pos}, p', \epsilon, min\_obj$)
>>>>> - **RECURSIVE-ODT**($D_{neg}, p', \epsilon, min\_obj$)
>>> }
> **end**

In comparison with the OVO and DDAG approaches, our proposal can reduce the error bound in terms of K. But the margin size at each decision node (two classes separation) obtained by OVO and DDAG is larger than the one obtained by the OVA-DB2-like (two super classes separation). Therefore, it is not easy to compare the error bound in terms M' in this context. However, an optimal split of two classes in D obtained by a binary SVM under OVO or DDAG constraints

can not assure efficient separation of the c classes into two super classes.

Computational costs

According to [47], a binary SVM classification with n training datapoints has an empirical complexity as follows:

$$\Omega(n, 2) \approx \alpha n^{\beta} \qquad (2)$$

where $\beta \approx 2$ for binary SVM algorithms using the decomposition method and some positive constant α.

Let us consider a multi-class classification problem at a non-terminal node D with n training datapoints and c balanced classes (i.e. the number of training datapoints of each class is about n/c). The standard OVA approach needs c tests (binary SVM learning tasks on n training datapoints) to perform a binary oblique split. The algorithmic complexity is:

$$\Omega_{OVA}(n, c) \approx c\alpha n^{\beta} \qquad (3)$$

The OVO or DDAG approaches need $c(c-1)/2$ tests (binary SVM learning tasks on $2n/c$ training datapoints) to perform a binary oblique split at a non-terminal node D. The algorithmic complexity is:

$$\Omega_{OVO,DAG}(n, c) \approx \frac{c(c-1)}{2}\alpha\left(\frac{2n}{c}\right)^{\beta}$$
$$\approx 2^{(\beta-1)}c^{(2-\beta)}\alpha n^{\beta} \qquad (4)$$

The OVA-DB2-like approach requires only one test (binary SVM learning tasks on n training datapoints) to perform a binary oblique split in a non-terminal node D to separate the two super classes (positive and negative parts). The algorithmic complexity is the same as for the binary case (formula 2) which is the smallest complexity. It must be noted that the complexity of the OVA-DB2-like approach in formula (2) does not include the k-means clustering used to create two super classes. But this step requires insignificant time compared with the quadratic programming time.

Let now examine the complexity of building an oblique multi-class classification tree with the OVA-DB2-like approach that tends to maintain, at each node, balanced classes. This strategy can thus build a balanced oblique decision tree (i.e. the tree height is $\lceil \log_2 c \rceil$) and any ith tree level has 2^i nodes having $n/2^i$ training datapoints. Therefore, the complexity of the multi-class oblique tree algorithm based on OVA-DB2-like approaches is:

$$\Omega_{OVA-DB2-like}(n, c) \approx \sum_{i=0}^{\lceil \log_2 c \rceil} \alpha 2^i \left(\frac{n}{2^i}\right)^{\beta}$$
$$= \sum_{i=0}^{\lceil \log_2 c \rceil} \alpha n^{\beta} \left(2^{(1-\beta)}\right)^i \qquad (5)$$

Due to $2^{(1-\beta)} < 1$ $(\beta \approx 2)$, we have:

$$\sum_{i=0}^{\lceil \log_2 c \rceil} \left(2^{(1-\beta)} \right)^i \approx \frac{1}{1 - 2^{(1-\beta)}} \qquad (6)$$

Thus, applying formula (6) to the right side of (5) yields the new algorithmic complexity of the multi-class oblique tree based on the OVA-DB2-like approach as follows.

$$\Omega_{\text{OVA-DB2-like}}(n, c) \approx \frac{\alpha n^\beta}{1 - 2^{(1-\beta)}} = \frac{\alpha n^\beta 2^{(\beta-1)}}{2^{(\beta-1)} - 1} \qquad (7)$$

Formula (7) shows that the training task of a MC-ODT scales $O(n^2)$. Therefore, the complexity of a MCRF-ODT forest is $O(t.n^2)$ for training t models of MC-ODT.

4 Numerical test results

Experiments are conducted with seven real fingerprint datasets (respectively, FPI-57, FPI-78, …, and FPI-389, with 57, 78, …, and 389 colleagues; between 15 and 20 fingerprints were captured for each individual). Fingerprints acquisition was done with Microsoft Fingerprint Reader (optical fingerprint scanner, resolution: 512 DPI, image size: 355×390, colours: 256 levels greyscale). Local descriptors were extracted with the Hessian-affine SIFT detector proposed in [18]. These descriptors were then grouped into 5,000 clusters with k-means algorithm [19] (the number of clusters/visual words was optimized between 500 and over 5,000, 5,000 clusters was the optimum). The BoVW model was thus calculated from these 5,000 visual words. Last, the datasets were splitted into training set and testing set. The datasets are described in Table 1.

The training set was used to tune the parameters of the competitive algorithms including MCRF-ODT (MCRF-ODT is implemented in C++, using the Automatically Tuned Linear Algebra Software [51]), SVM [26] (using the highly efficient standard SVM algorithm LibSVM [52] with OVO for multi-class), kNN [53], C4.5 [54], AdaBoost [27] of C4.5, RF-CART [28]. The Weka library [55] was used for the four last algorithms.

Table 1 Description of seven fingerprint image datasets

Datasets	# Classes	# Dimensions	# Images (train–test)
FPI-57	57	5,000	700–352
FPI-78	78	5,000	950–422
FPI-120	120	5,000	1,438–480
FPI-153	153	5,000	1,700–672
FPI-185	185	5,000	2,000–765
FPI-235	235	5,000	2,485–1,000
FPI-389	389	5,000	4,306–2,000

We tried to use different kernel functions of the SVM algorithm, including a polynomial function of degree d, a RBF (RBF kernel of two datapoints x_i, x_j, $K[i, j] = exp(-\gamma \|x_i - x_j\|^2)$). The optimal parameters for accuracy are the following: RBF kernel (with $\gamma = 0.0001$, $c = 10,000$) for SVM, one neighbour for kNN, at least two example in a leave for C4.5, 200 trees and 1,000 random dimensions for MCRF-ODT, RF-CART, 200 trees for AdaBoost-C4.5. We remark that MCRF-ODT and RF-CART used the out-of-bag samples (the out of the bootstrap samples) during the forest construction for finding the parameters (with $p' = 1,000$, $\epsilon = 0$, min_obj = 2 and $t = 200$), corresponding to the best experimental results.

Given the differences in implementation, including the programming language used (C++ versus Java), a comparison of computational time is not really fair. Table 2, Fig. 6 report average computational times for the faster algorithms to illustrate that MCRF-ODT is very competitive. Obviously, the univariate algorithm RF-CART is faster.

The accuracies of the seven algorithms on the seven datasets are given in Table 3 and Fig. 7.

The experimental results showed that our proposal using SIFT/BoVW and MCRF-ODT has achieved more than 93 % accuracy for fingerprint images classification.

As it was expected, firstly 1-NN, C4.5 and NB methods which are based on an unique classifier are overmatched by LibSVM and ensemble methods, secondly the performance of these methods dramatically decreases with the number of classes. 1-NN, C4.5 and NB are always bottom of the ranking for each of the seven datasets (7th, 6th and 5th position) and they lose a lot of accuracy when the number of classes increases (from 57 to 389), especially 1-NN and C4.5 which, respectively, decrease from 59.9 to 28.75 % and from 75.0 to 45.8 %, while NB decreases only from 85.2 to 74.6 %.

RF-CART and Adaboost-C4.5, which are among the most common ensemble-based methods, occupy an intermediate position, with a slight superiority of RF-CART on Adaboost-C4.5 (mean rank score of, respectively, 3.1 and 3.9). The accuracies of these methods are already somewhat less affected by the increase in the number of classes, decreasing from 93.5 to 86.3 % for RF-CART and from 91.5 to 82 % for Adaboost C4.5.

The best results are always obtained by LibSVM and above all by our multi-class MCRF-ODT, the new proposed method. LibSVM holds the rank 2 on each experimented dataset, with a mean accuracy of 93.4 %, while MCRF-ODT gets the best result on each of the seven datasets with an average accuracy of 95.89 %, which corresponds to an improvement of 2.49 percentage points compared with LibSVM. This superiority of MCRF-ODT on LibSVM is statistically significant, in so far as according to the sign test, the p value of the observed results (7 wins of MCRF-ODT on LibSVM with 7 datasets) is equal to 0.0156. In addition, these two meth-

Table 2 Average time calculation (s/tree, PC-3.4 GHz)

Algorithm	FPI-57	FPI-78	FPI-120	FPI-153	FPI-185	FPI-235	FPI-389
MCRF-ODT	2.5	3.5	6.0	8.5	12.0	15.0	26
AdaBoost-C4.5	4.0	6.0	10.5	14.0	18.5	26.5	90.0
RF-CART	0.7	1.0	2.0	3.0	4.3	6.3	17.0
LibSVM	3.5	6.2	14.3	21.7	30.0	46.0	120.0

Fig. 6 Training time (s/tree)

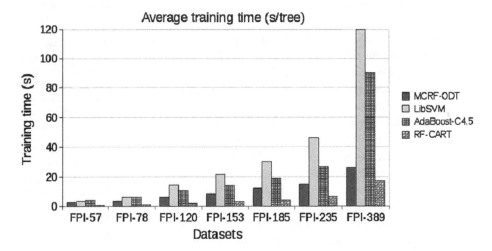

Table 3 Classification results in terms of accuracy (%)

Algorithms	FPI-57	FPI-78	FPI-120	FPI-153	FPI-185	FPI-235	FPI-389
MCRF-ODT	**97.44**	**97.60**	**96.04**	**95.24**	**95.29**	**94.60**	**95.00**
LibSVM	*95.46*	*94.79*	*92.50*	*92.86*	*93.46*	*92.10*	*92.65*
AdaBoost-C4.5	91.48	89.34	89.17	84.52	85.10	84.10	81.95
RF-CART	93.47	92.42	88.33	91.67	89.02	87.50	86.30
C4.5	75.00	69.19	61.67	59.23	55.16	53.60	45.80
NB	85.23	81.52	78.33	75.15	78.30	74.90	74.60
1NN	59.94	51.19	46.88	41.52	36.99	33.20	28.75

Bold values indicate the best algorithm and italic values indicate the second best

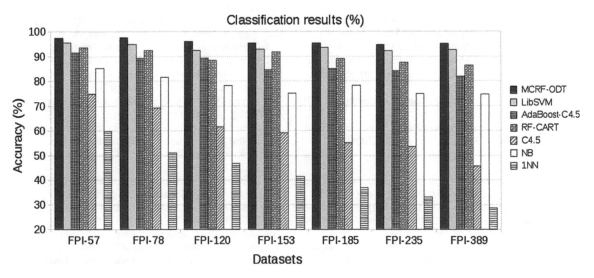

Fig. 7 Classification results in terms of accuracy (%)

ods lose only little efficiency when the number of classes increases, since the corresponding accuracies decrease from 97.60 to 94.60 % for MCRF-ODT and from 95.5 to 92.1 % for LibSVM.

5 Conclusion and future works

We presented a novel approach that achieves high performances for classification tasks of fingerprint images. It associates the BoVW model (induced from the SIFT method which detects and describes local features in images) and an extension of random forest of decision trees to deal with hundreds of classes and thousands of dimensions. The experimental results showed that the Multi-class RF-ODT algorithm is very efficient in comparison with C4.5, random forest RF-CART, AdaBoost of C4.5, support vector machine and k nearest neighbours.

A forthcoming improvement will be to extend this algorithm to deal with extremely large number of classes (e.g. up to thousands of classes). A parallel implementation can greatly speed up learning and classifying tasks of the multiclass RF-ODT algorithm.

Open Access This article is distributed under the terms of the Creative Commons Attribution License which permits any use, distribution, and reproduction in any medium, provided the original author(s) and the source are credited.

References

1. Galton, F.: Finger Prints. Macmillan and Co, London (1892)
2. Maltoni, D., Maio, D., Jain, A., Prabhakar, S.: Handbook of Fingerprint Recognition. Springer, New York (2009)
3. Yang, J., Zhang, X.: Feature-level fusion of fingerprint and fingervein for personal identification. Pattern Recognit. Lett. **33**(5), 623–628 (2012)
4. Jain, A., Feng, J., Nandakumar, K.: Fingerprint matching. IEEE Comput. **43**(2), 36–44 (2010)
5. Yager, N., Amin, A.: Fingerprint verification based on minutiae features: a review. Pattern Anal. Appl. **7**, 94–113 (2004)
6. Yager, N., Amin, A.: Fingerprint classification: a review. Pattern Anal. Appl. **7**, 77–93 (2004)
7. Cappelli, R., Maio, D., Maltoni, D.: A multi-classifier approach to fingerprint classification. Pattern Anal. Appl. **5**, 136–144 (2002)
8. Poh, N., Kittler, J.: A unified framework for biometric expert fusion incorporating quality measures. IEEE Trans. Pattern Anal. Mach. Intell. **34**(1), 3–18 (2012)
9. Lowe, D.: Object recognition from local scale invariant features. In: Proceedings of the 7th International Conference on Computer Vision, pp 1150–1157 (1999)
10. Bosch, A., Zisserman, A., Muñoz, X.: Scene classification via pLSA. In: Proceedings of the European Conference on Computer Vision, pp. 517–530 (2006)
11. Park, U., Pankanti, S., Jain, A.: Fingerprint verification using SIFT features. In: SPIE Defense and Security Symposium (2008)
12. Malathi, S., Meena, C.: Partial fingerprint matching based on SIFT features. Int. J. Comput. Sci. Eng. **2**(4), 1411–1414 (2010)
13. Zhou, R., Sin, S., Li, D., Isshiki, T., Kunieda, H.: Adaptive SIFT-based algorithm for specific fingerprint verification. In: 2011 International Conference on Hand-Based Biometrics (ICHB), pp. 1–6 (2011)
14. Do, T.N., Lallich, S., Pham, N.K., Lenca, P.: Un nouvel algorithme de forêts aléatoires d'arbres obliques particulièrement adapté à la classification de données en grandes dimensions. In: Ganascia, J.G., Gançarski, P. (eds.) Extraction et Gestion des Connaissances 2009, pp. 79–90. Strasbourg, France (2009)
15. Simon, C., Meessen, J., De Vleeschouwer, C.: Embedding proximal support vectors into randomized trees. In: European Symposium on Artificial Neural Networks. Advances in Computational Intelligence and Learning, pp. 373–378 (2009)
16. Do, T.N., Lenca, P., Lallich, S., Pham, N.K.: Classifying very-high-dimensional data with random forests of oblique decision trees. In: Advances in Knowledge Discovery and Management. Studies in Computational Intelligence, vol. 292, pp. 39–55. Springer-Verlag, Berlin (2010)
17. Lowe, D.: Distinctive image features from scale invariant keypoints. Int. J. Comput. Vis., 91–110 (2004)
18. Mikolajczyk, K., Schmid, C.: Scale and affine invariant interest point detectors. Int. J. Comput. Vis. **60**(1), 63–86 (2004)
19. MacQueen, J.: Some methods for classification and analysis of multivariate observations. In: Proceedings of 5th Berkeley Symposium on Mathematical Statistics and Probability, Berkeley, University of California Press, vol. 1, pp. 281–297 (January 1967)
20. Caruana, R., Karampatziakis, N., Yessenalina, A.: An empirical evaluation of supervised learning in high dimensions. In: Proceedings of the 25th International Conference on Machine Learning, pp. 96–103 (2008)
21. Donoho, D.: A high-dimensional data analysis: the curses and blessings of dimensionality (2000).
Accessed 15 Sept 2012
22. Statnikov, A., Aliferis, C., Tsamardinos, I., Hardin, D., Levy, S.: A comprehensive evaluation of multicategory classification methods for microarray gene expression cancer diagnosis. Bioinformatics **21**, 631–643 (2005)
23. Statnikov, A., Wang, L., Aliferis, C.: A comprehensive comparison of random forests and support vector machines for microarray-based cancer classification. BMC Bioinform. **9:319**(1), 10 (2008)
24. Yang, P., Hwa, Y., Zhou, B., Zomaya, A.: A review of ensemble methods in bioinformatics. Curr. Bioinform. **5**(4), 296–308 (2010)
25. Ogutu, J., Piepho, H., Schulz-Streeck, T.: A comparison of random forests, boosting and support vector machines for genomic selection. BMC Proc. **5**, 1–5 (2011)
26. Vapnik, V.: The Nature of Statistical Learning Theory. Springer-Verlag, New York (1995)
27. Freund, Y., Schapire, R.: A decision-theoretic generalization of on-line learning and an application to boosting. In: Computational Learning Theory. Proceedings of the Second European Conference, pp. 23–37 (1995)
28. Breiman, L.: Random forests. Mach. Learn. **45**(1), 5–32 (2001)
29. Liu, T., Yang, Y., Wan, H., Zeng, H., Chen, Z., Ma, W.: Support vector machines classification with a very large-scale taxonomy. SIGKDD Explor. **7**(1), 36–43 (2005)
30. Madani, O., Connor, M.: Large-scale many-class learning. In: SIAM Data Mining, pp. 846–857 (2008)
31. Breiman, L.: Bagging predictors. Mach. Learn. **24**(2), 123–140 (1996)
32. Ho, T.K.: Random decision forest. In: Proceedings of the Third International Conference on Document Analysis and Recognition, pp. 278–282 (1995)
33. Amit, Y., Geman, D.: Shape quantization and recognition with randomized trees. Neural Comput. **9**(7), 1545–1588 (1997)

34. Ho, T.K.: The random subspace method for constructing decision forests. IEEE Trans. Pattern Anal. Mach. Intell. **20**(8), 832–844 (1998)
35. Murthy, S., Kasif, S., Salzberg, S., Beigel, R.: OC1: randomized induction of oblique decision trees. In: Proceedings of the Eleventh National Conference on Artificial Intelligence, pp. 322–327 (1993)
36. Carvalho, D., Freitas, A.: A hybrid decision tree/genetic algorithm method for data mining. Inf. Sci. **163**(1–3), 13–35 (2004)
37. Zhou, Z.H., Chen, Z.Q.: Hybrid decision tree. Knowl. Based Syst. **15**(8), 515–528 (2002)
38. Maji, P.: Efficient design of neural network tree using a new splitting criterion. Neurocomputing **71**(4–6), 787–800 (2008)
39. Loh, W.Y., Vanichsetakul, N.: Tree-structured classification via generalized discriminant analysis (with discussion). J. Am. Stat. Assoc. **83**, 715–728 (1988)
40. Yildiz, O., Alpaydin, E.: Linear discriminant trees. Int. J. Pattern Recognit. Artif. Intell. **19**(3), 323–353 (2005)
41. Wu, W., Bennett, K., Cristianini, N., Shawe-Taylor, J.: Large margin trees for induction and transduction. In: Proceedings of the Sixth International Conference on Machine Learning, pp. 474–483 (1999)
42. Fung, G., Mangasarian, O.: Proximal support vector classifiers. In: Proceedings KDD-2001: Knowledge Discovery and Data Mining, pp. 77–86 (2001)
43. Menze, B.H., Kelm, B.M., Splitthoff, D.N., Koethe, U., Hamprecht, F.A.: On oblique random forests. In: Proceedings of the 2011 European Conference on Machine Learning and Knowledge Discovery in Databases , vol. Part II, ECML PKDD'11, pp. 453–469. Springer-Verlag, New York (2011)
44. Weston, J., Watkins, C.: Support vector machines for multi-class pattern recognition. In: Proceedings of the Seventh European Symposium on Artificial Neural Networks, pp. 219–224 (1999)
45. Guermeur, Y.: SVM multiclasses, théorie et applications. Thèse HDR, Université Nancy I (2007)
46. Kreßel, U.: Pairwise classification and support vector machines. In: Advances in Kernel Methods: Support Vector Learning, pp. 255–268 (1999)
47. Platt, J., Cristianini, N., Shawe-Taylor, J.: Large margin DAGs for multiclass classification. Adv. Neural Inf. Process. Syst. **12**, 547–553 (2000)
48. Vural, V., Dy, J.: A hierarchical method for multi-class support vector machines. In: Proceedings of the Twenty-first International Conference on Machine Learning, pp. 831–838 (2004)
49. Benabdeslem, K., Bennani, Y.: Dendogram-based SVM for multi-class classification. J. Comput. Inf. Technol. **14**(4), 283–289 (2006)
50. Breiman, L., Friedman, J.H., Olshen, R.A., Stone, C.: Classification and Regression Trees. Wadsworth International, Boston (1984)
51. Whaley, R., Dongarra, J.: Automatically tuned linear algebra software. In: CD-ROM Proceedings of the Ninth SIAM Conference on Parallel Processing for Scientific Computing (1999)
52. Chang, C.C., Lin, C.J.: LIBSVM—a library for support vector machines (2001). Accessed 10 Jan 2012
53. Fix, E., Hodges, J.: Discriminatory analysis: small sample performance. In: Technical Report 21–49-004, USAF School of Aviation Medicine, Randolph Field (1952)
54. Quinlan, J.R.: C4.5: Programs for Machine Learning. Morgan Kaufmann, San Mateo (1993)
55. Witten, I., Frank, E.: Data Mining: Practical Machine Learning Tools and Techniques. Morgan Kaufmann, San Mateo (2005)

23

IMSR_PreTree: an improved algorithm for mining sequential rules based on the prefix-tree

Thien-Trang Van · Bay Vo · Bac Le

Abstract Sequential rules generated from sequential patterns express temporal relationships among patterns. Sequential rule mining is an important research problem because it has broad application such as the analyses of customer purchases, web log, DNA sequences, and so on. However, developing an efficient algorithm for mining sequential rules is a difficult problem due to the large size of the sequential pattern set. The larger the sequential pattern set, the longer the mining time. In this paper, we propose a new algorithm called *IMSR_PreTree* which is an improved algorithm of *MSR_PreTree* that mines sequential rules based on prefix-tree. *IMSR_PreTree* also generates rules from frequent sequences stored in a prefix-tree but it prunes the sub trees which give non-significant rules very early in the process of rule generation and avoids tree scanning as much as possible. Thus, *IMSR_PreTree* can significantly reduce the search space during the mining process. Our performance study shows that *IMSR_PreTree* outperforms *MSR_PreTree*, especially on large sequence databases.

Keywords Frequent sequence · Prefix-tree · Sequential rule · Sequence database

T.-T. Van
Faculty of Information Technology, Ho Chi Minh City University
of Technology, Ho Chi Minh, Vietnam
e-mail: vtt.trang@hutech.edu.vn

B. Vo (✉)
Faculty of Information Technology, Ton Duc Thang University,
Ho Chi Minh, Vietnam
e-mail: bayvodinh@gmail.com

B. Le
Faculty of Information Technology, University of Science,
VNU, Ho Chi Minh, Vietnam
e-mail: lhbac@fit.hcmus.edu.vn

1 Introduction

In sequence databases, there are researches on many kinds of rules, such as recurrent rules [13], sequential classification rules [4], sequential rules [14,18,21,22], and so on. In this paper, we focus on usual sequential rule mining. We try to address the problem of effectively generating a full set of sequential rules.

Sequential rule mining is to find the relationships between occurrences of sequential events. A sequential rule is an expression that has form X→Y, i.e., if X occurs in any sequence of the database then Y also occurs in that sequence following X with the high confidence. The mining process is usually decomposed into two phases:

(1) Mining all frequent sequences that have supports above the minimum support threshold (*minSup*)
(2) Generating the desired rules from the frequent sequences if they also satisfy the minimum confidence threshold (*minConf*).

Most of the previous researches with regard to sequential rules require multiples of passes over the full set of frequent sequences. Recently, a sequential rule mining method based on prefix-tree [21] achieves high efficiency. Using prefix-tree, it can immediately determine which sequences contain a given sequence as a prefix. So the rules can be generated directly from those frequent sequences without browsing over the whole set of frequent sequence many times.

The rest of paper is organized as follows: Sect. 2 introduces the basic concepts related to sequence mining and some definitions used throughout the paper. Section 3 presents the related work. The improved algorithm of *MSR_PreTree* is presented in Sect. 4 and an example is given in Sect. 5. Experimental results are conducted in Sect. 6. We summarize our study and discuss the future work in Sect. 7.

2 Preliminary concepts

Let I be a set of distinct items. An itemset is a subset of items (without loss of generality, we assume that items of an itemset are sorted in lexicographic order). A sequence $s = \langle s_1 s_2 \ldots s_n \rangle$ is an ordered list of itemsets. The size of a sequence is the number of itemsets in the sequence. The length of a sequence is the number of items in the sequence. A sequence with length k is called a k-sequence.

A sequence $\beta = \langle b_1 b_2 \ldots b_m \rangle$ is called a subsequence of another sequence $\alpha = \langle a_1 a_2 \ldots a_n \rangle$, denoted as $\beta \subseteq \alpha$, if there exist integers $1 \leq i_1 < i_2 < \cdots < i_m \leq n$ such that $b_1 \subseteq a_{i1}, b_2 \subseteq a_{i2}, \ldots, b_m \subseteq a_{im}$. Given a sequence database, the support of a sequence α is defined as the number of sequences in the sequence database that contains α. Given a $minSup$, we say that a sequence is frequent if its support is greater than or equal to $minSup$. A frequent sequence is also called a sequential pattern.

Definition 1 *(Prefix, incomplete prefix and postfix).* Given a sequence $\alpha = \langle a_1 a_2 \ldots a_n \rangle$ and a sequence $\beta = \langle b_1, b_2, \ldots b_m \rangle$ $(m < n)$, (where each a_i, b_i corresponds to an itemset). β is called prefix of α if and only if $b_i = a_i$ for all $1 \leq i \leq m$. After removing the prefix β of the sequence α, the remaining part of α is a postfix of α. Sequence β is called an incomplete prefix of α if and only if $b_i = a_i$ for $1 \leq i \leq m - 1, b_m \subset a_m$ and all the items in $(a_m - b_m)$ are lexicographically after those in b_m.

Note that from the above definition, a sequence of size k has $(k - 1)$ prefixes. For example, sequence $\langle (A)(BC)(D) \rangle$ have two prefixes: $\langle (A) \rangle$, $\langle (A)(BC) \rangle$. Consequently, $\langle (BC)(D) \rangle$ is the postfix with respect to prefix $\langle (A) \rangle$ and $\langle (D) \rangle$ is the postfix w.r.t prefix $\langle (A)(BC) \rangle$. Neither $\langle (A)(B) \rangle$ nor $\langle (BC) \rangle$ is considered as a prefix of given sequence; however, $\langle (A)(B) \rangle$ is an incomplete prefix of given sequence.

A sequential rule is built by splitting a frequent sequence into two parts: prefix *pre* and postfix *post* (concatenating *pre* with *post*, denoted as *pre* ++ *post*, we have the same pattern as before [14]). We denote a sequential rule as *rule = pre → post (sup, conf)*.

The support of a *rule*: *sup = sup(pre++post)*.

The confidence of a *rule*: *conf = sup(pre++post)/sup(pre)*.

Note that *pre* ++ *post* is a frequent sequence; consequently *pre* is also a frequent sequential pattern (by the Apriori principle [2]). For each frequent sequence f of size k, we can possibly form $(k - 1)$ rules. For example, if we have a frequent sequence $\langle (A)(BC)(D) \rangle$ whose size is 3, then we can generate two rules $\langle (A) \rangle \rightarrow \langle (BC)(D) \rangle$, $\langle (A)(BC) \rangle \rightarrow \langle (D) \rangle$.

Sequential rule mining is to find out all significant rules that satisfy *minSup* and *minConf* from the given database. The support and confidence thresholds are usually predefined by users.

3 Related work

3.1 Mining sequential patterns

Sequential pattern mining is to find all frequent sub sequences as sequential patterns in a sequence database. A sequence database is a large collection of records, where each record is an ordered list of events. Each event can have one or many items. For examples, the customer purchase database is a popular database in which each event is a set of items (itemset) and some other databases such as DNA sequences and Web log data are typically examples of the databases in which all events are single items.

The problem of mining sequential patterns was first introduced by Agrawal and Srikant in [2]. They also presented three algorithms to solve this problem. All these algorithms are variations of the Apriori algorithm [1] proposed by the same authors and used in association rule mining. Many other approaches have been developed since then [2,3,11,12,15,16,19]. The general idea of all methods is outlined as follows: starting with more general (shorter) sequences and extending them towards more specific (longer) ones. However, existing methods uses specified data structures to "represent" the database and have different strategies to traverse and enumerate the search space.

GSP [19] which is also a typical Apriori-like method adopts a multiple pass, candidate generation, and test approach in sequential pattern mining. But it incorporates time constraints, sliding time windows, and taxonomies in sequence patterns. PSP [15] which is another Apriori-based algorithm also builds around GSP, but it uses a different intermediary data structure which is proved more efficient than that used in GSP.

Based on the "divide and conquer" philosophy, FreeSpan [12] is the first algorithm which projects the data sequences into smaller databases for reducing the I/O costs. This strategy has been continually used in PrefixSpan [16]. Starting from the frequent items of the database, PrefixSpan generates projected databases with each frequent item. Thus, the projected databases contain only suffixes of the data-sequences from the original database, grouped by prefixes. The pattern is extended by adding one item in frequent itemsets which are obtained from projected databases. The process is recursively repeated until no frequent item is found in the projected database.

All the above methods utilize the same approach in sequence mining: the horizontal data sequence layout. And the corresponding algorithms make multiples of passes over the data for finding the supports of candidate sequences. Some methods have approached the vertical data layout to overcome this limitation; they are SPADE [22], SPAM [3] and PRISM [10]. Instead of browsing the entire sequence database for each pattern, these algorithms store the information indicating which data sequences contain that pattern so that its support is determined quickly. Moreover, the information of a new pattern is also constructed from old patterns' information.

The SPADE algorithm [22] uses a vertical id-list representation of the database where it stores a list of all input sequence (sequence id) and event identifier (event id) pairs containing the pattern for each level of the search space for each pattern. On the other hand, SPADE uses a lattice-theoretic approach to decompose the search space and uses simple join operations to generate candidate sequences. SPADE discovers all frequent sequences in only three database scans. The SPADE algorithm outperforms GSP by a factor of two at lower support values [22].

SPAM [3] is another method that maintains the information of a pattern. It uses a vertical bitmap representation of the database for both candidate representation and support counting. SPAM outperforms SPADE by about a factor of 2.5 on small datasets and better than an order of magnitude for reasonably large datasets.

PRISM [10] was proposed in 2010. It is one of the most efficient methods for frequent sequence mining [10]. Similar to SPAM, PRISM also utilizes a vertical approach for enumeration and support counting but it is different from the previous algorithms. This algorithm uses the prime block encoding approach to represent candidate sequences and uses join operations over the prime blocks to determine the support of each candidate. Especially, all sequential patterns which are found by this algorithm are organized and stored in a tree structure which is the basis for our proposed algorithm— *MSR_PreTree*.

Besides, there are several sequential pattern mining techniques that are simply applied to web log mining such as WAP-Mine [17] with WAP-tree; and PLWAP [7] with its PLWAP-tree, FS-Miner [6], etc.

3.2 Generating rules from sequential patterns

In this section, we discuss existing contributions in sequential rule mining research. Sequential rules [14, 18, 21, 22] are "if-then rules" with two measures which quantify the support and the confidence of the rule for a given sequence database. For example, if a customer buys a car, then he will also buy a car insurance.

The study in [18] has proposed a method for generating a complete set of sequential rules from frequent sequences and removing redundant rules in the post-mining phase. Based on the description in [18], Lo et al. [14] generalized the *Full* algorithm for mining a full set of sequential rules and it is completely the same algorithm as the RuleGen algorithm proposed by Zaki [22].

Full algorithm: First, the algorithm finds all frequent sequences (*FS*) whose support is no less than *minSup* by using an existing method. For each frequent sequence, the algorithm generates all sequential rules from that frequent sequence. We now describe the process of rule generation in more detail.

For each frequent sequence f of size k, it is possible to generate $(k-1)$ rules. Each rule is expressed as $pre \rightarrow post$, in which pre is a prefix of sequence f and $pre++post = f$. For example, from a sequence $\langle(AB)(B)(C)\rangle$, we can generate two candidate sequential rules: $\langle(AB)\rangle \rightarrow \langle(B)(C)\rangle$ and $\langle(AB)(B)\rangle \rightarrow \langle(C)\rangle$. For each frequent sequence f, *Full* generates and examines every prefixes of f in turn. For each prefix *pre*, it tries to form a rule $pre \rightarrow post$ where *post* is the postfix of f with respect to prefix *pre*. After that, it passes over *FS* to find that the prefix's support and calculates the confidence of that rule. If the confidence is not less than the minimum confidence threshold, we have a significant sequential rule. This process is repeated until all frequent sequences are considered. Let n be the number of sequences in *FS*, and k be the size of the largest sequence in *FS*; the complexity of this algorithm is $O(n*k*n)$ (without including the time of prefix generation). The major cost of *Full* is the database scan. It has to scan the database many times for counting the support of every prefixe of a frequent sequence.

In order to improve the runtime, we proposed two algorithms: *MSR_ImpFull* and *MSR_PreTree* [21].

MSR_ ImpFull algorithm: It is an improved version of *Full*. As mentioned above, to generate rules from a frequent sequence, *Full* has to split it to get the prefix and has to browse *FS* to get the prefix's support. To overcome this, *MSR_ImpFull* sorts *FS* in ascending order of their size before generating rules. After sorting, we have the fact that the sequences which contain sequence X as a prefix must be after X because their size is larger. Therefore, for a frequent sequence f in *FS*, *MSR_ImpFull* does not have to split it; it browses the sequences following f to find which sequences contain f as a prefix. After that, it generates rules from the found sequences and f. The generated rule is $f \rightarrow post$, where post is the postfix of the found sequence with prefix f. The confidence is calculated directly from the found sequence's support and f's support. *MSR_ImpFull* reduces k *FS* scans for each sequence of size k when compared with *Full*. So, if we consider only the number of *FS* scans without the time of prefix checking, then the complexity of *MSR_ImpFull* is $O(n*n)$.

MSR_PreTree algorithm: Although *MSR_ImpFull* algorithm has less number of *FS* scans than *Full*, for each sequence f, it scans all sequences following f to identify which sequence contains f as a prefix. In order to overcome this, *MSR_PreTree* uses a prefix-tree structure presented in Sect. 4. Every node in the prefix-tree is always the prefix of its child nodes (only sequence-extended nodes). Consequently, it is possible to generate rules directly without scanning all frequent sequences for prefix checking.

Besides, Fournier-Viger et al. [8–10] have recently discussed a more general form of sequential rules such that items in the prefix and in the postfix of each rule are unordered. However, our study simply focuses on mining usual sequential rules.

4 An Improved algorithm of MSR_PreTree

4.1 Prefix-Tree

In our approach (*MSR_PreTree*, *IMSR_PreTree*), the set of rules is generated from frequent sequences, which is organized and stored in a prefix-tree structure as illustrated in Fig. 1. In this section, we briefly outline the prefix-tree.

Each node in the prefix-tree stores two pieces of information: label and support, denoted as *label: sup*, in which label is a frequent sequence and support is the support count of that frequent sequence.

The prefix-tree is built recursively as follows: starting from the root of tree at level 0, the root is a virtual node labeled with a null sequence ϕ and the support is 0. At level k, a node is labeled with a k-sequence and its support count. Recursively, we have nodes at the next level $(k + 1)$ by extending the k-sequence with a frequent item. If the support of the new extended sequence satisfies *minSup*, then we store that sequence and continue the extension recursively. There are

two ways to extend a k-sequence: *sequence extension* and *itemset extension* [10]. In *sequence extension*, we add an item to the sequence as a new itemset. Consequently, the size of a sequence-extended sequence always increases.

Remark 1 In sequence extension, a k-sequence α is a prefix of all sequence-extended sequences. Moreover, α is certainly the prefix of all child nodes of the nodes which are sequence-extended of α.

In *itemset extension*, the item is added to the last itemset in the sequence so that the item is greater than all items in the last itemset. So the size of the itemset-extended sequence does not change.

Remark 2 In itemset extension, α is an incomplete prefix of all itemset-extended sequences. Moreover, α is an incomplete prefix of all child nodes of the nodes which are itemset-extended of α.

For example, Fig. 1 shows the prefix-tree of frequent sequences. $\langle (A)(A) \rangle$ and $\langle (A)(B) \rangle$ are sequence-extended sequences of $\langle (A) \rangle$, and $\langle (AB) \rangle$ is an itemset-extended sequence of $\langle (A) \rangle$. Sequence $\langle (A) \rangle$ is a prefix of all sequences in T1 and it is an incomplete prefix of sequences in T2.

4.2 Theorem

In *MSR_PreTree*, for each node r in the prefix-tree, the algorithm browses all the child nodes of r and considers each candidate rule generated by each child node with respect to prefix *r.sequence*, if the candidate rule's confidence satisfies *min-Conf* then that rule is outputted. Thus, the algorithm must still browse the child nodes which produce non-significant rules

Fig. 1 The prefix-tree

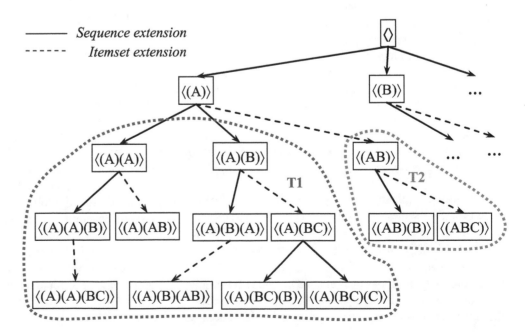

Fig. 2 IMSR_PreTree—an improved algorithm of MSR_PreTree

```
Input: FS - the set of frequent sequences stored in pre-
fix-tree, minConf
Output: All significant rules
Algorithm:
GENERATE_RULES_FROM_PREFIX-TREE()
    1. For each node r at level 1 in prefix-tree
    2.    GENERATE_RULES_FROM_ROOT(r)
GENERATE_RULES_FROM_ROOT(r)
    3. Let pre = r.sequence
    4. For each node nseq ∈ r.Seq_Extended_Set
    5.    For each node l ∈ sub-tree nseq
    6.       Try to form rule = pre→post,
                         pre++post = l.sequence
    7.       If sup(l.sequence)/sup(pre) ≥ minConf
    8.          Output rule
    9.       Else Stop generating rules from l.children
                with prefix pre //according to theorem 1
    10. For each node nseq ∈ r.Seq_Extended_Set
    11.    GENERATE_RULES_FROM_ROOT(nseq)
    12. For each node nseq ∈ r.Items_Extended_Set
    13.    GENERATE_RULES_FROM_ROOT(nseq)
```

with respect to prefix *r.sequence*. For example, if node *r* has 1,000 child nodes, then it has to browse all those nodes, calculates the confidence of all those nodes, and checks the confidence with *minConf* even if there are certainly nodes which produce non-significant rules among those nodes. Considering the recursive characteristic in the implementation, this cost is too high. So, it is necessary to avoid browsing the child nodes which do not produce significant rules. Consequently, the key problem is that how to know which child nodes certainly produce non-significant rules.

To overcome this problem, we improve *MSR_PreTree* to early prune the sub trees which produce non-significant rules. We have the following theorem [5]:

Theorem 1 *Given three nodes n_1, n_2 and n_3 in the prefix-tree, if n_1 is the parent node of n_2, n_2 is the parent node of n_3 and $\frac{sup(n_2)}{sup(n_1)} < minConf$, then $\frac{sup(n_3)}{sup(n_1)} < minConf$.*

Proof Since n_1 is the parent node of n_2 and n_2 is the parent node of n_3, n_1 sequence $\subset n_2.sequence \subset n_3.sequence$. This implies that $n_1.sup \geq n_2.sup \geq n_3.sup$. Thus, $\frac{n_2.sup}{n_1.sup} \geq \frac{n_3.sup}{n_1.sup}$. Since $\frac{n_2.sup}{n_1.sup} < minconf$, it implies $\frac{n_3.sup}{n_1.sup} < minConf$.

According to the above theorem, if a tree node Y is a child node of X in the prefix-tree and *sup(Y)/sup(X) < minConf*, then all the child nodes of Y cannot form rules with X because

the confidence of each generated rule from Y's child nodes is less than *minConf*. For example, consider two nodes $\langle(A)\rangle$ and $\langle(A)(B)\rangle$ in Fig. 4. Assume that *minConf* = 80 %, since $sup(\langle(A)(B)\rangle)/sup(\langle(A)\rangle) = 3/4 < minConf$, the child nodes $\{\langle(A)(B)(B)\rangle, \langle(A)(B)(C)\rangle\}$ of $\langle(A)(B)\rangle$ in prefix-tree cannot generate the rules with prefix $\langle(A)\rangle$.

4.3 IMSR_PreTree algorithm

The improved algorithm of *MSR_PreTree* is shown in Fig. 2. Using PRISM [10] we have a full set of frequent sequences stored in the prefix-tree structure which gathers all sequences with a common prefix into a sub-tree. Thus, we generate rules within each common prefix sub-tree. Starting from the first level, each sub-tree rooted at a node *r* labeled with 1−sequence can be processed independently to generate sequential rules using procedure *GENERATE_RULES_FROM_ROOT(r)*. This procedure is performed using the following steps:

Step 1 Generating rules with the prefix that is a sequence at the root. Let *pre* be the sequence at root node*r (line 3)*. From Remarks 1 and 2, we find that sequence *pre* is the prefix of all the sequences in sequence-extended sub-trees of the root *r*. Hence, we generate only rules from the sequences in these sub-trees in turn. The following are the descriptions of rule generation from each sub-tree with prefix *pre* (lines 3–9).

Fig. 3 Some pruning cases when generating rules with the prefix *R.sequence*

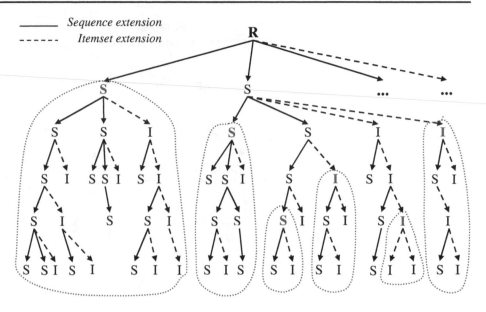

For each *l.sequence* at node *l* in the tree rooted at *nseq* (that is the sub-tree as mentioned above) including the root and sequence-extended children and itemset-extended children, we consider the following rule: pre→post where *post* is a postfix of *l.sequence* with respect to the prefix *pre* (*r.sequence*). We apply the above theorem when we have already determined the confidence of the rule generated from node *l*. If the confidence satisfies *minConf*, we output that rule and repeat recursively on extended children of *l*. Otherwise, we completely prune all the sub-trees of *l*. It means that we do not need to generate rules from all child nodes and descendents of the node *l* with prefix *pre*. After that, we continue considering the other nodes by backtracking up the tree *nseq* if it still has child nodes.

In this process (lines 5–9), we traverse the sub-tree in a depth-first manner so that the pruning technique can be applied. Figure 3 shows some pruning cases when generating rules with the prefix *R.sequence*. The sub-trees rooted at the nodes (highlighted) which generate rules having the confidence less than *minConf* are pruned. These sub-trees are marked by surrounding line.

Step 2: Because all extended nodes of the current root are the prefix of the sub trees at the next level, we call this procedure recursively for every extended-nodes of the root (lines 10–13). This process is recursively repeated until reaching the last level of the tree.

5 An example

In this section, an example is given to illustrate the proposed algorithm for mining sequential rules. Consider the database shown in Table 1. It consists of five data sequences and three different items.

Table 1 An example database

SID	Data sequence
1	⟨(AB)(B)(B)(AB)(B)(AC)⟩
2	⟨(AB)(BC)(BC)⟩
3	⟨(B)(AB)⟩
4	⟨(B)(B)(BC)⟩
5	⟨(AB)(AB)(AB)(A)(BC)⟩

Using PRISM algorithm [10], all found frequent sequences are stored in a prefix-tree. The prefix-tree built from the database in Table 1 with *minSup* = 50 % is shown in Fig. 4. After that, we generate all rules from those frequent sequences. Assume that *minConf* = 80 %.

Table 2 show the result of sequential rule generation from all frequent sequences stored in the prefix-tree. For details, consider the root node ⟨(A)⟩ shown in Fig. 4; the itemset-extended sequence of ⟨(A)⟩ is ⟨(AB)⟩ and the sequence-extended sequences of ⟨(A)⟩ are ⟨(A)(B)⟩ and ⟨(A)(C)⟩. Because ⟨(A)⟩ is an incomplete prefix of ⟨(AB)⟩ and all child nodes of ⟨(AB)⟩ are in T₂, we do not generate rules from those nodes with prefix ⟨(A)⟩. On the contrary, since ⟨(A)⟩ is a prefix of all the sequences in T₁, we generate rules from the sequences in T₁ with prefix ⟨(A)⟩. First, for sequence ⟨(A)(B)⟩ we have a rule: ⟨(A)⟩ → ⟨(B)⟩. However, its confidence is less than *minConf*; we, therefore, eliminate it. Moreover, we completely prune all sub-trees generated from ⟨(A)⟩ → ⟨(B)⟩. It means that we stop generating rules from all child nodes { ⟨(A)(B)(B)⟩, ⟨(A)(B)(C)⟩ } of ⟨(A)(B)⟩ (based on the above theorem). Similarly, for sequence ⟨(A)(C)⟩, we have a candidate rule ⟨(A)⟩ → ⟨(C)⟩ and its confidence does not satisfy *minConf*. Thus, we eliminate it.

Fig. 4 The prefix-tree built from the database in Table 1 with *minSup* = 50 %

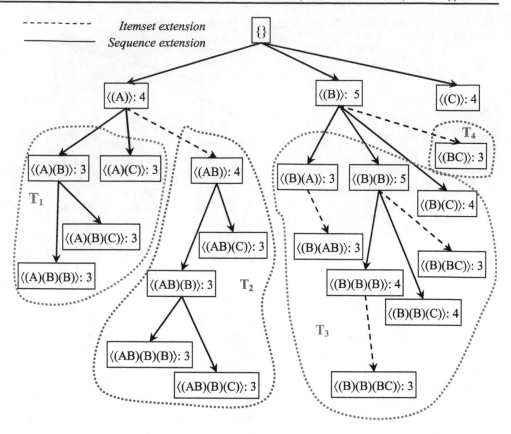

Table 2 The result of sequential rule generation from the frequent sequences stored in prefix-tree, *minConf* = 80 %

Prefix	Sequence	Sequential rule, $conf = sup(X ++ Y)/sup(X) \times 100\%$	$conf \geq minConf$?
⟨(A)⟩: 4	⟨(A)(B)⟩: 3	⟨(A)⟩ → ⟨(B)⟩, 75 %	No
	⟨(A)(B)(B)⟩: 3	Stop generating the rules with prefix ⟨(A)⟩	
	⟨(A)(B)(C)⟩: 3		
	⟨(A)(C)⟩: 3	⟨(A)⟩ → ⟨(C)⟩, 75 %	No
⟨(A)(B)⟩:3	⟨(A)(B)(B)⟩: 3	⟨(A)(B)⟩ → ⟨(B)⟩, 100 %	Yes
	⟨(A)(B)(C)⟩: 3	⟨(A)(B)⟩ → ⟨(C)⟩, 100 %	Yes
⟨(AB)⟩: 4	⟨(AB)(B)⟩: 3	⟨(AB)⟩ → ⟨(B)⟩, 75 %	No
	⟨(AB)(B)(B)⟩: 3	Stop generating the rules with prefix ⟨(AB)⟩	
	⟨(AB)(B)(C)⟩: 3		
	⟨(AB)(C)⟩: 3	⟨(AB)⟩ → ⟨(C)⟩, 75 %	No
⟨(AB)(B)⟩: 3	⟨(AB)(B)(B)⟩: 3	⟨(AB)(B)⟩ → ⟨(B)⟩, 100 %	Yes
	⟨(AB)(B)(C)⟩: 3	⟨(AB)(B)⟩ → ⟨(C)⟩, 100 %	Yes
⟨(B)⟩: 5	⟨(B)(A)⟩: 3	⟨(B)⟩ → ⟨(A)⟩, 60 %	No
	⟨(B)(AB)⟩: 3	Stop generating the rules with prefix ⟨(B)⟩	
	⟨(B)(B)⟩: 5	⟨(B)⟩ → ⟨(B)⟩, 100 %	Yes
	⟨(B)(B)(B)⟩: 4	⟨(B)⟩ → ⟨(B)(B)⟩, 80 %	Yes
	⟨(B)(B)(BC)⟩: 3	⟨(B)⟩ → ⟨(B)(BC)⟩, 60 %	No
	⟨(B)(B)(C)⟩: 4	⟨(B)⟩ → ⟨(B)(C)⟩, 80 %	Yes
	⟨(B)(BC)⟩: 3	⟨(B)⟩ → ⟨(BC)⟩, 60 %	No
	⟨(B)(C)⟩: 4	⟨(B)⟩ → ⟨ (C)⟩, 80 %	Yes
⟨(B)(B)⟩: 5	⟨(B)(B)(B)⟩: 4	⟨(B)(B)⟩ → ⟨(B)⟩, 80 %	Yes
	⟨(B)(B)(BC)⟩: 3	⟨(B)(B)⟩ → ⟨(BC)⟩, 60 %	No
	⟨(B)(B)(C)⟩: 4	⟨(B)(B)⟩ → ⟨(C)⟩, 80 %	Yes

Table 3 Database characteristics (http://www.ics.uci.edu/~mlearn)

Databases	#FS	#Distinct items	Aver. sequence size
Chess	3,196	75	37
Mushroom	8,124	119	23

We repeat the whole above process for all child nodes $\langle(A)(B)\rangle$, $\langle(A)(C)\rangle$ and $\langle(AB)\rangle$. Similar processing is applied to root nodes $\langle(B)\rangle$ and $\langle(C)\rangle$.

6 Experimental results

In this section, we report our experimental results on comparing the performance of *IMSR_PreTree* with *MSR_PreTree*. Results show that *IMSR_PreTree* outperforms *MSR_PreTree* and *IMSR_PreTree* is an efficient and scalable approach for mining sequential patterns in large databases.

Our experiments are performed on a computer with Intel Core 2 Duo CPU T8100 2x2.10GHz, and 2 GB of memory, running Windows XP Professional. All programs are written in C#.

In the past [15], we have already experimented on synthetic databases created from the synthetic data generator provided by IBM and also on real the database Gazelle in which the execution time is less than 1 second. Consequently, to see the difference in time between *MSR_PreTree* and *IMSR_PreTree*, we perform experiments on some databases in which the number of frequent sequences is very large. Relying on that, the number of generated rules is very large too. Chess and Mushroom are the databases used in the problem of mining association rules from frequent itemsets. However, using these databases in the problem of mining sequential rules from frequent sequences, we consider each itemset in these databases is a data sequence. Consequently,

the data sequence's itemset now has only one item. In this manner, Chess and Mushroom are considered as the databases in which a data sequence is a list of 1–itemset, for example, DNA databases, web log, etc. Using these databases, the number of generated sequential rules is up to hundreds of millions of rules.

These databases are downloaded from the UCI Machine Learning Repository [20]. Table 3 shows the characteristics of those databases.

Figure 5 shows the performance comparison of the two algorithms on Chess with *minSup* is 35 and 40 % and *minConf* varying from 50 to 99 %. When the confidence threshold is low, the gap between the numbers of candidate rules and significant rules is small and two algorithms are close in terms of runtime. However, when the confidence threshold is increased, the gaps become clear because there are many more pruned rules. Both algorithms generate the same rules, but *IMSR_PreTree* is more efficient than *MSR_PreTree*. At

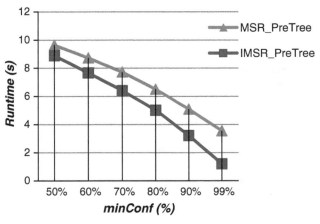

Mushroom with minSup = 5%

Fig. 6 Performance comparison between two algorithms on mushroom

Fig. 5 Performance comparison between two algorithms on chess

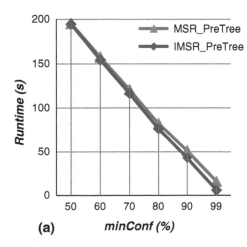

(a)

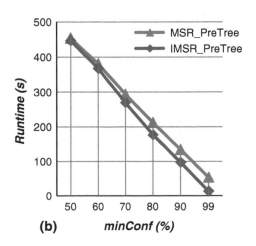

(b)

the highest value of confidence, *IMSR_PreTree* is about 3 and 4 times faster than *MSR_PreTree* with *minSup*=40 and 35 %, respectively. In addition, we see that *IMSR_PreTree* outperforms *MSR_PreTree* by an order of magnitude in most cases. We also test two algorithms on Mushroom and obtain similar results (Fig. 6).

7 Conclusions and future work

In this paper, we have developed an efficient algorithm named *IMSR_PreTree* which is an improved algorithm of *MSR_PreTree* to mine sequential rules from sequence databases. The aim of this improvement is to reduce the cost of sequential rule mining process by pruning the sub trees which give non-significant rules in the early stage of mining. It can greatly reduce the search space during the mining process and it is very effective in mining large databases.

Experimental results show that *IMSR_PreTree* is faster than *MSR_PreTree*. In the future, we will apply this approach to rule generation with many kinds of interestingness measures. Especially, we will use the prefix-tree structure to mine sequential patterns with constraints.

Acknowledgments This work was funded by Vietnam's National Foundation for Science and Technology Development (NAFOSTED) under Grant Number 102.05-2013.20.

Open Access This article is distributed under the terms of the Creative Commons Attribution License which permits any use, distribution, and reproduction in any medium, provided the original author(s) and the source are credited.

References

1. Agrawal, R., Srikant, R.: Fast algorithms for mining association rules. In: Proceedings of the 20th international conference very large data, bases, pp. 487–499 (1994)
2. Agrawal, R., Srikant, R.: Mining sequential patterns. In: Proceedings of the 11th international conference on data engineering, pp. 3–14. IEEE (1995)
3. Ayres, J., Flannick, J., Gehrke, J., Yiu, T.: Sequential pattern mining using a bitmap representation. In: Proceedings of the 8th ACM SIGKDD international conference on knowledge discovery and data mining, pp. 429–435. ACM (2002)
4. Baralis, E., Chiusano, S., Dutto, R.: Applying sequential rules to protein localization prediction. Comput. Math. Appl. **55**(5), 867–878 (2008)
5. Vo, B., Hong, T.P., Le, B.: A lattice-based approach for mining most generalization association rules. Knowl. Based Syst. **45**, 20–30 (2013)
6. El-Sayed, M., Ruiz, C., Rundensteiner, E.A.: FS-Miner: efficient and incremental mining of frequent sequence patterns in web logs. In: Proceedings of the 6th annual ACM international workshop on web information and data management, pp. 128–135 (2004)
7. Ezeife, C.I., Lu, Y., Liu, Y.: PLWAP sequential mining: open source code. In: Proceedings of the 1st international workshop on open source data mining: frequent pattern mining implementations, pp. 26–35 (2005)
8. Fournier-Viger, P., Faghihi, U., Nkambou, R., Nguifo, E.M.: CMRules: mining sequential rules common to several sequences. Knowl. Based Syst. **25**(1), 63–76 (2012)
9. Fournier-Viger, P., Nkambou, R., Tseng, V.S.M.: RuleGrowth: mining sequential rules common to several sequences by pattern-growth. In: Proceedings of the 2011 ACM symposium on applied computing, pp. 956–961 (2011)
10. Fournier-Viger, P., Wu, C.W., Tseng, V.S., Nkambou, R.: Mining sequential rules common to several sequences with the window size constraint. Adv. Artif. Intell. 299–304 (2012)
11. Gouda, K., Hassaan, M., Zaki, M.J.: Prism: an effective approach for frequent sequence mining via prime-block encoding. J. Comput. Syst. Sci. **76**(1), 88–102 (2010)
12. Han, J., Pei, J., Mortazavi-Asl, B., Chen, Q., Dayal, U., Hsu, M.C. FreeSpan: frequent pattern-projected sequential pattern mining. In: Proceedings of the 6th ACM SIGKDD international conference on knowledge discovery and data mining, pp. 355–359 (2000)
13. Lo, D., Khoo, S.-C., Liu, C.: Efficient mining of recurrent rules from a sequence database. In: DASFAA 2008, LNCS vol. 4947, pp. 67–83 (2008)
14. Lo, D., Khoo, S.C., Wong, L.: Non-redundant sequential rules—theory and algorithm. Inf. Syst. **34**(4), 438–453 (2009)
15. Masseglia, F., Cathala, F., Poncelet, P.: The PSP approach for mining sequential patterns. In: PKDD'98, Nantes, France, LNCS vol. 1510, pp. 176–184 (1998)
16. Pei, J., Han, J., Mortazavi-Asl, B., Wang, J., Pinto, H., Chen, Q., Hsu, M.C.: Mining sequential patterns by pattern-growth: the pre-fixspan approach. IEEE Trans. Knowl. Data Eng. **16**(11), 1424–1440 (2004)
17. Pei, J., Han, J., Mortazavi-Asl, B., Zhu, H.: Mining access patterns efficiently from web logs. In: Proceedings of the 4th Pacific-Asia Conference on Knowledge Discovery and Data Mining (PAKDD'00), Kyoto, Japan, pp. 396–407 (2000)
18. Spiliopoulou, M.: Managing interesting rules in sequence mining. In: Proceedings of the Third European Conference on Principles of Data Mining and Knowledge Discovery, Prague, Czech Republic, pp. 554–560 (1999)
19. Srikant, R., Agrawal, R.: Mining sequential patterns: generalizations and performance improvements. In: Proceedings of the 5th International Conference on Extending Database Technology: Advances in Database Technology, Avignon, France, LNCS, pp. 3–17 (1996)
20. UCI Machine Learning Repository.
21. Van, T.T., Vo, B., Le, B.: Mining sequential rules based on prefix-tree. In: Proceedings of the 3rd Asian Conference on Intelligent Information and Database Systems, Daegu, Korea, pp. 147–156 (2011)
22. Zaki, M.J.: SPADE: an efficient algorithm for mining frequent sequences. Mach. Learn. **42**(1–2), 31–60 (2001)

Permissions

All chapters in this book were first published in VJCS, by Springer; hereby published with permission under the Creative Commons Attribution License or equivalent. Every chapter published in this book has been scrutinized by our experts. Their significance has been extensively debated. The topics covered herein carry significant findings which will fuel the growth of the discipline. They may even be implemented as practical applications or may be referred to as a beginning point for another development.

The contributors of this book come from diverse backgrounds, making this book a truly international effort. This book will bring forth new frontiers with its revolutionizing research information and detailed analysis of the nascent developments around the world.

We would like to thank all the contributing authors for lending their expertise to make the book truly unique. They have played a crucial role in the development of this book. Without their invaluable contributions this book wouldn't have been possible. They have made vital efforts to compile up to date information on the varied aspects of this subject to make this book a valuable addition to the collection of many professionals and students.

This book was conceptualized with the vision of imparting up-to-date information and advanced data in this field. To ensure the same, a matchless editorial board was set up. Every individual on the board went through rigorous rounds of assessment to prove their worth. After which they invested a large part of their time researching and compiling the most relevant data for our readers.

The editorial board has been involved in producing this book since its inception. They have spent rigorous hours researching and exploring the diverse topics which have resulted in the successful publishing of this book. They have passed on their knowledge of decades through this book. To expedite this challenging task, the publisher supported the team at every step. A small team of assistant editors was also appointed to further simplify the editing procedure and attain best results for the readers.

Apart from the editorial board, the designing team has also invested a significant amount of their time in understanding the subject and creating the most relevant covers. They scrutinized every image to scout for the most suitable representation of the subject and create an appropriate cover for the book.

The publishing team has been an ardent support to the editorial, designing and production team. Their endless efforts to recruit the best for this project, has resulted in the accomplishment of this book. They are a veteran in the field of academics and their pool of knowledge is as vast as their experience in printing. Their expertise and guidance has proved useful at every step. Their uncompromising quality standards have made this book an exceptional effort. Their encouragement from time to time has been an inspiration for everyone.

The publisher and the editorial board hope that this book will prove to be a valuable piece of knowledge for researchers, students, practitioners and scholars across the globe.

List of Contributors

K. Nakamatsu
School of Human Science and Environment, University of Hyogo, Shinzaike, Himeji 670-0092, Japan

J. M. Abe
ICET-Paulista University, São Paulo, SP, CEP 04026-022, Brazil
Institute of Advanced Studies, University of Sao Paulo, Cidade Universitaria, São Paulo, SP, CEP 05508-970, Brazil

S. T. Cao
Faculty of Information Technology, Vinh University, 182 Le Duan, Vinh, Nghe An, Vietnam

L. A. Nguyen
Institute of Informatics, University of Warsaw, Banacha 2, 02-097 Warsaw, Poland
VNU University of Engineering and Technology, 144 Xuan Thuy, Hanoi, Vietnam

A. Szałas
Institute of Informatics, University of Warsaw, Banacha 2, 02-097 Warsaw, Poland
Department of Computer and Information Science, Linköping University, 581 83 Linköping, Sweden

D. J. Jakóbczak
Department of Electronics and Computer Science, Technical University of Koszalin, Sniadeckich 2, 75-453 Koszalin, Poland

T.-P. Hong
Department of Computer Science and Information Engineering, National University of Kaohsiung, Kaohsiung, Taiwan
Department of Computer Science and Engineering, National Sun Yat-sen University, Kaohsiung, Taiwan

Y.-L. Liou
Department of Electrical Engineering, National University of Kaohsiung, Kaohsiung, Taiwan

S.-L. Wang
Department of Information Management, National University of Kaohsiung, Kaohsiung, Taiwan

B. Vo
Ton Duc Thang University, Ho Chi Minh, Vietnam

Bac Le
Faculty of Information Technology, University of Science, VNU, Ho Chi Minh City, Vietnam

Hung Nguyen
Faculty of Information Technology, University of Science, VNU, Ho Chi Minh City, Vietnam

Dat Tran
Faculty of Information Sciences and Engineering, University of Canberra, Canberra, ACT 2601, Australia

Chi Tran
Faculty of Technical Sciences, WM University, Olsztyn, Poland

Min Su Lee
Computational Omics Lab, School of Informatics and Computing, Indiana University, Bloomington, IN, USA

Sangyoon Oh
Department of Computer Engineering, Ajou University, Suwon, Republic of Korea

Amine Chohra
Images, Signals, and Intelligent Systems Laboratory (LISSI / EA3956), Senart Institute of Technology, Paris East University (UPEC), Avenue Pierre Point, 77127 Lieusaint, France

Nadia Kanaoui
Images, Signals, and Intelligent Systems Laboratory (LISSI / EA3956), Senart Institute of Technology, Paris East University (UPEC), Avenue Pierre Point, 77127 Lieusaint, France

Véronique Amarger
Images, Signals, and Intelligent Systems Laboratory (LISSI / EA3956), Senart Institute of Technology, Paris East University (UPEC), Avenue Pierre Point, 77127 Lieusaint, France

Kurosh Madani
Images, Signals, and Intelligent Systems Laboratory (LISSI / EA3956), Senart Institute of Technology, Paris East University (UPEC), Avenue Pierre Point, 77127 Lieusaint, France

Jair Minoro Abe
Graduate Program in Production Engineering, ICET-Paulista University, R. Dr. Bacelar, 1212, Institute For Advanced Studies, University of São Paulo, São Paulo, Brazil

Helder F. S. Lopes
Institute For Advanced Studies, University of São Paulo, São Paulo, Brazil

Kazumi Nakamatsu
School of Human Science and Environment/H.S.E., University of Hyogo, Kobe, Japan

Yuh-Yih Lu
Minghsin University of Science and Technology, No.1, Xinxing Rd., Xinfeng, Hsinchu 30401, Taiwan, R.O.C

Hsiang-Cheh Huang
National University of Kaohsiung, No. 700 University Road, Kaohsiung 811, Taiwan, R.O.C

Hoai An Le Thi
Laboratory of Theoretical and Applied Computer Science, UFR MIM, University of Lorraine, Ile du Saulcy, 57045 Metz, France

Tao Pham Dinh
Laboratory of Mathematics, LMI, National Institute for Applied Sciences, Rouen, Avenue de l'Université, 76801 Saint-Etienne-du-Rouvray Cedex, France

Hung T. Tran
Budapest University of Technology and Economics, Budapest, Hungary
Viet-Hung Industrial University, Hanoi City, Vietnam

Tien V. Do
Budapest University of Technology and Economics, Budapest, Hungary
Viet-Hung Industrial University, Hanoi City, Vietnam

Laszlo Pap
Budapest University of Technology and Economics, Budapest, Hungary

Zied Yakoubi
LIPN, CNRS UMR 7030, University Paris Nord, Villetaneuse, France

Rushed Kanawati
LIPN, CNRS UMR 7030, University Paris Nord, Villetaneuse, France

Adam Meissner
Institute of Control and Information Engineering, Poznań University of Technology, pl. M. Skłodowskiej-Curie 5, 60-965 Poznan, Poland

Hoang Pham
Department of Industrial and Systems Engineering, Rutgers University, Piscataway, NJ 08854, USA

Khoa Dang Dang
Department of Information Technology, University of Science, 227 Nguyen Van Cu Street, District 5, Ho Chi Minh City, Vietnam

Thai Hoang Le
Department of Information Technology, University of Science, 227 Nguyen Van Cu Street, District 5, Ho Chi Minh City, Vietnam

Thanh-Nghi Do
College of Information Technology, Can Tho University, Can Tho, Vietnam

Bao Rong Chang
Department of Computer Science and Information Engineering, National University of Kaohsiung, Kaohsiung, Taiwan

Hsiu-Fen Tsai
Department of Marketing Management, Shu Te University, Kaohsiung, Taiwan

Yun-Che Tsai
Department of Computer Science and Information Engineering, National University of Kaohsiung, Kaohsiung, Taiwan

Yi-Sheng Chang
Department of Computer Science and Information Engineering, National University of Kaohsiung, Kaohsiung, Taiwan

Van Huy Pham
Department of Mechanical and Automotive Engineering, University of Ulsan, Ulsan, South Korea

Byung Ryong Lee
Department of Mechanical and Automotive Engineering, University of Ulsan, Ulsan, South Korea

Golnoush Abaei
Faculty of Computing, University Technology Malaysia, Johor Baharu, 81310 Johor, Malaysia

Ali Selamat
Faculty of Computing, University Technology Malaysia, Johor Baharu, 81310 Johor, Malaysia

Nguyen-Thinh Le
Humboldt Universität zu Berlin, Berlin, Germany

Nhu-Phuong Nguyen
Clausthal University of Technology, Clausthal-Zellerfeld, Germany

Kazuhisa Seta
Osaka Prefecture University, Sakai, Japan

Niels Pinkwart
Humboldt Universität zu Berlin, Berlin, Germany

T.-N. Do
Institut Mines-Telecom; Telecom Bretagne, CNRS UMR 6285 Lab-STICC, Université européenne de Bretagne, Brest, France
Can Tho University, Can Tho , Vietnam

P. Lenca
Institut Mines-Telecom; Telecom Bretagne, CNRS UMR 6285 Lab-STICC, Université européenne de Bretagne, Brest, France

S. Lallich
Laboratoire ERIC, Université de Lyon 2, Lyon, France

Thien-Trang Van
Faculty of Information Technology, Ho Chi Minh City University of Technology, Ho Chi Minh, Vietnam

Bay Vo
Faculty of Information Technology, Ton Duc Thang University, Ho Chi Minh, Vietnam

Bac Le
Faculty of Information Technology, University of Science, VNU, Ho Chi Minh, Vietnam